Justifying Utopia

Legal History Library

VOLUME 75

Studies in the History of International Law

VOLUME 27

The titles published in this series are listed at *brill.com/shil*

Justifying Utopia

A Legal History of the International Peace Movement (1815–1873)

By

Wouter De Rycke

BRILL | NIJHOFF

LEIDEN | BOSTON

Cover illustration: Daumier, Honoré. 'Les amis de la paix. Résultat du discours Coquerel' (1 September 1849), Boston Public Library, available at: www.digitalcommonwealth.org/search/commonwealth:fq979w274.

This book's research was made possible by funding from the Fonds Wetenschappelijk Onderwijs (FWO).

The Library of Congress Cataloging-in-Publication Data is available online at https://catalog.loc.gov
LC record available at https://lccn.loc.gov/2025012468

Typeface for the Latin, Greek, and Cyrillic scripts: "Brill". See and download: brill.com/brill-typeface.

ISSN 1874-1793
ISBN 978-90-04-73364-0 (hardback)
ISBN 978-90-04-73368-8 (e-book)
DOI 10.1163/9789004733688

'Cet univers désormais sans maître ne lui paraît ni stérile ni futile. Chacun des grains de cette pierre, chaque éclat minéral de cette montagne pleine de nuit, à lui seul, forme un monde. La lutte elle-même vers les sommets suffit à remplir un cœur d'homme. Il faut imaginer Sisyphe heureux.'
ALBERT CAMUS, *Le mythe de Sisyphe* (1942)

Contents

Acknowledgments

I distinctly remember a moment early in the research that eventually led to the book you are now holding. It was one of the many afternoons I spent in the Royal Library in Brussels. I can no longer recall whether it was a Tuesday or a Friday, or even what month it was. All I remember is sitting in front of a file containing what seemed like a random collection of nineteenth-century papers on peace. Much of it dealt with religion or revolved around long-forgotten political controversies. The best resource I had was a massive reference work of more than a thousand pages. It encompassed hundreds of names, each more obscure than the last. I must admit now that, for the most part, it made for rather a dull read. At the same time it was daunting. How on earth was I expected to gain access to all my sources, let alone weave such a complex, intertwined series of events and ideas into a single compelling story? Nonetheless, it had to be done. I had a strong sense that, buried beneath the centuries of dust, there lay not only a fascinating, unjustly forgotten story of past idealism, but also something that should still resonate today. Over the years, my instincts were refined through countless conversations with colleagues and friends, each of whom, in their own ways, encouraged me to keep pushing forward. Without them, this book – and the story it tells – would never have come to fruition.

First and foremost, I am deeply grateful to Randall Lesaffer for including this book in the 'Studies in International Law' series, and to the two anonymous reviewers for their insightful comments and their kind words, which I deeply appreciated. I also owe thanks to my editors at Brill, Petra Stiglmayer and Alessandra Giliberto, whose enthusiasm for the project was truly inspiring.

I am likewise indebted to many colleagues. Many, through their ideas and insights, have contributed in one way or another to shaping the book into what it is today. They include Raphaël Cahen, Stella Ghervas, Stefano Cattelan, Dave De ruysscher, Nel de Mûelenaere, Stefaan Smis, Pieter De Reu, Martti Koskenniemi, Miloš Vec, Daniel Laqua, Randall Lesaffer, Andrea Bianchi, Hendrik Simon, and Luisa Brunori. Thomas Duve should be thanked for hosting me at the Max Planck Institute in Frankfurt. Frederik Dhondt provided input on the practical aspects of the research process. Dirk Heirbaut and Georges Martyn kindled my original interest in legal history through their engaging classes and seminars. In a more general sense, I benefitted greatly from the experience, as well as the friendship, of several junior researchers, including Wout De Cock, Sarah El Amouri and Floris Fonteyn.

Special mention should go to Miroslav Šedivý, who, despite my young age, became an unwavering supporter of my research almost overnight. His writings on nineteenth century politics are required reading for anyone seeking to understand the international relations of that century.

In a book that tells a 'history from below,' it is only fitting that I also acknowledge the great support I received from numerous librarians and archivists, without whose tireless work in rooms with too few windows, no research would be possible.

On a more personal level, I am very grateful to my family. My parents have always been supportive of my studies. Similarly, my brother has helped wherever he could. I have always enjoyed our little weekly online meetings to catch up and relax with a game. After spending most of the day immersed in pacifist texts, I found a certain irony – and satisfaction – in commanding my little colour-coded troops to raid the enemy's town in *Age of Empires*. Contrary to pacifist fears, it did not turn me into a militarist.

My friends too have each played their part in keeping morale high. I will not name them all, except for Joost Depotter. As a lawyer, a historian and a policy coordinator at an N.G.O., he was the perfect sounding board for my ideas on law and society, often offering fresh and unexpected perspectives.

Lastly, I wish to acknowledge Eva for her love and support. Since completing the first draft of the manuscript, we have also been joined by our son Ides. This book is dedicated to them.

Figures

Introduction

> 'All Members shall refrain in their international relations from the threat or use of force against the territorial integrity or political independence of any state, or in any other manner inconsistent with the Purposes of the United Nations.'
>
> Art. 2(4) United Nations Charter

Legal revolutions rarely begin with the passing of a law. They cannot be traced back to any specific book and they are seldom contained to a single person or a small group. To argue in the language of law is to argue in the language of politics, and politics is a process that involves many actors and contextual background factors. When the paradigm in any given legal system slowly begins to shift, it is because its legitimacy has been increasingly successfully challenged in the political arena. Long before political reforms become translated into forms readily discernible to lawyers, they have been passionately contested over time in political society. The civil rights revolution in the United States resulted in no small degree from the country's civil rights movement. Labour laws exist because of strikes and labour unions. Environmental protection regulation is born out of the lobbying efforts of environmentalists. Equal rights for women were not gifted from above, but had to be arduously fought over by generations of activists.

Such has also been the case with the advent of modern public international law. Its most significant difference with the 'classical' law of nations is that it is fundamentally opposed to the use of force. International disputes are to be resolved through diplomacy and law, not violence. For most of its history, the law of nations considered the right to make war a legitimate, if not the supreme, aspect of sovereignty. Today, this paradigm has been replaced with the so-called *ius contra bellum*. Lawyers use this Latin phrase to refer to the general prohibition on the use of force enshrined in the Charter of the United Nations. Leaving aside for now its notable exceptions, it is today almost uncontested that international lawyers have a professional duty to avoid interstate war. Those who do lend their services to aggressor states in an overly blatant way are certain to meet the reprobation of many of their international peers.

 | DOI:10.1163/9789004733688_002

Legal historians have associated this 'moralisation' of international law with numerous historical developments and institutions. Typically, however, those analyses have stayed limited to the circles of professional lawyers, who all moved in institutional environments familiar to practitioners today. Theirs has been a story of courts and international organisations, of lawyers and textbooks. Often, the story only begins in the twentieth century, or in the last five minutes of the nineteenth century. Few if any historians of international law have bothered to pay serious attention to the movement which at one time played a very visible part in the dream of an international order ruled by law. For decades, dozens of little societies popped up, animated by the zeal of thousands of today forgotten men and women, who slowly began to identify themselves as part of an international movement.

This book investigates the prehistory of the modern *ius contra bellum* through the perspective of the international peace movement of the early and mid-nineteenth century. It asks when, how and why the earliest organised pacifists in Western Europe and North America began to turn to international law in their campaigns for peace. Institutions such as the International Court of Justice, the United Nations, or the European Union were politically unthinkable barely a hundred years ago. However, institutions in their broad spiritual vein have been imagined for centuries. Illustrious thinkers like Sully, Saint-Pierre, Rousseau, Bentham, or Kant had all theorised on ways to pacify the international relations of their time. Nonetheless, these plans had remained individual musings, often not taken very seriously even by their own authors. This changed in the beginning of the nineteenth century, around the time when the battle of Waterloo marked the ending of a quarter-century of continuous warfare. A handful of people organised themselves in philanthropical societies. Calling themselves 'friends of peace', they began to proselytise in churches and town halls. They printed hundreds of tracts, ranging from little booklets warning children not to play soldiers, to statistical tables detailing just how expensive the impressive war vessels one could admire in the harbour really were.

As these societies matured, and increasingly dealt with politics, their peace campaign adapted itself to new audiences. As such, the propaganda literature of the international peace movement is replete with proposals for arbitration mechanisms, for international courts, for legal codes, and for various interstate assemblies, ranging from a loose confederation to an actual world state. The peace friends referenced doctrine, observed state practice, and increasingly courted the cooperation of specialist jurists. By 1873, the transformation was complete, when representatives of the peace societies and professional international lawyers worked together to set up one of the first dedicated international law societies. The event symbolically cemented the link between pacifism and legal reform, known as the 'peace through law' movement. This highly influential movement, maybe better understood as a shared pacifist-legalist sensibility, has inspired many of the international legal institutions which symbolise the utopian aspirations of the modern *ius contra bellum.*

This introduction inquires deeper into how the first generations of the peace movement related to public international law's ideological shift towards a *ius contra bellum.* Why has the historiography of international law neglected to give due credit to the early nineteenth century peace movement? To the limited extent that legal historians have paid any attention at all to civil society movements, they have focussed on events from 1873 onwards, when the legalist undertones of pacifism were more readily apparent. In doing so, legal-historical scholarship skipped over a more than half a century of pacifist activity, because of the belief that little of legal substance could be found in the literature of a highly religious and sentimental movement. This is a mistaken view, which cannot be reduced to a mere neglect to engage with the primary sources. Rather, more fundamental assumptions have been at play about what constitutes valid legal argument. These important preliminary concerns are addressed first.

Once these issues are out of the way, our attention will have to move on to the nineteenth century peace movement itself. What constitutes a peace movement? When could one be considered a part of this movement? How do the nineteenth century term 'peace friend' and the modern-day 'pacifist' relate to one another? As we will see, pacifism is a nuanced and sophisticated ideology, that cannot be reduced to any single meaning or set of tenets. It is, and always has been, a pluralist belief system. Contemporary biases have likely influenced the aforementioned neglect of legal historians to detect the pragmatic undertones of the nineteenth century peace campaign. Although certainly utopian in its ultimate aspiration to achieve permanent and universal peace, the people who became attracted to this movement were generally not 'naïve'. Many, if not most, understood perfectly well that their public rhetoric did not match the social and cultural realities in which they lived. They did not need anyone to remind them how substantial the obstacles they faced were, although this never deterred sceptics to constantly remind them anyway. The leadership of the movement was made up of men who professionally held very respectable positions in society. They were professors, judges, lawyers, clergymen, political economists, and eventually even diplomats and members of legislative bodies.

Why would such people 'harm' their reputation by associating themselves with utopian daydreams? It is of course because the caricatures made of the peace movement do not hold up when subjected to closer scrutiny. The international peace movement had from its very beginning been marked by heated internal debates, between those who wanted an immediate and total abolition of *all* war, and those who felt this was unrealistic for the foreseeable future. The movement's search for a legalistic instrument to replace interstate war as the *ultima ratio regum* was likewise characterised by a constant oscillation between utopianism and pragmatism. In that sense, nineteenth century pacifism differed little from the nature of public international law itself.

1 Prehistory of the *ius contra bellum*

While international law has come to span a huge variety of topics, from human rights to investment law, it is seldom disputed that its most important and fundamental rules are the rules governing the use of force. The core of these rules is written in the Charter founding the United Nations in 1945. Article 2(4) stipulates that member states shall refrain from 'the threat or use of force' against other states. It has two exceptions. States are permitted to use their armed forces when authorised by the U.N. Security Council or in self-defence until the Security Council has taken the necessary measures to restore peace and security.[1] These rules constitute the essence of the modern *ius ad bellum* regime – i.e. the right to initiate the use of force. Jurists have elaborated extensively on this core, producing scores of thick textbooks detailing every intricacy, taking into account all acknowledged sources of international law, such as treaty texts, judicial rulings and opinions, and customary law. Even if the phrase *ius contra bellum* is not unanimously adopted by international law scholarship, few mainstream lawyers question the normative significance of the prohibition on the use of force, or the centrality of this prohibition in the international political-legal order established and intended by the Charter.[2]

1 Charter of the United Nations, 24 October 1945, 1 UNTS XVI, arts. 2(4), 24, 25 and 51.

2 Some important authors who use this phrase include Robert Kolb, *Ius Contra Bellum. Le droit international relative au maintien de la paix. Précis* (Basel: Helbing Lichtenhahn 2009), 6; Olivier Corten, *Le droit contre la guerre* (Paris: Pedone 2014), 2, 875–9; Randall Lesaffer, 'Too Much History: From War as Sanction to the Sanctioning of War', in Marc Weller (ed.), *The Oxford Handbook of the Use of Force in International Law*, (Oxford:

1.1 *From the 'Bellicose' Law of Nations to 'Pacific' Public International Law*

The U.N. Charter stands in stark contrast to how the law of nations assessed the use of force before the twentieth century. The European law of nations is traditionally traced back to the early modern writings of the Dutch theologian and jurist Hugo Grotius (1583–1645), whom international lawyers like to endearingly describe as the 'father' of their discipline. Although the importance of the author of *De iure belli ac pacis* can indeed hardly be understated, international law and philosophical musings about it are much older than Grotius. On the theoretical level, individuals have written about when sovereigns are permitted to use deadly force since time immemorial. The Church Father Augustine (354–430) has done much to shape how centuries of Christian scholars conceived of the 'just causes' permitting acts that would otherwise be considered grave sins.[3] On the practical level, the existence of international law is simply a fact of life. In its broadest sense, international law is the constellation of rules between political entities that do not recognise a higher authority. As such, it is of all times and places.[4] It is a 'horizontal' legal order, that kicks into effect whenever neighbouring polities are unable or unwilling to subjugate one another, and must by necessity come to some modus vivendi. As the adage goes: *ubi societas, ibi ius*.[5] A 'universal empire' has never been achieved. That being said, it does not follow that this international law, although practiced everywhere, needs to be 'moral' or 'just', if only because cultural understandings of what is 'moral' or 'just' conduct have historically varied wildly across time and

---

Oxford University Press (hereafter: OUP) 2015), 35–6; Friedrich Rosenfeld, *Die humanitäre Besatzung: Ein Dilemma des ius post bellum* (Nomos: Baden-Baden 2009), 214–5; on the centrality of article 2(4), see for instance the classic book by Louis Henkin, *How Nations behave. Law and Foreign Policy* (London: Pall Mall 1968), 129; this is readily conceded by critics, like Michael Glennon, *Limits of Law, Prerogatives of Power. Interventionism after Kosovo* (Houndmills, Basingstoke Palgrave, 2001), 3.

3 Stephen Neff. *War and the Law of Nations* (Cambridge: Cambridge University Press (hereafter: CUP) 2005), 47–75.

4 This definition is borrowed from Randall Lesaffer. 'International Law and its History: the Story of an Unrequited Love Affair', in Matthew Craven, Malgosia Fitzmaurice, and Maria Vogiatzi (eds.), *Time, History, and International Law* (Den Haag: Martinus Nijhoff 2007), 32.

5 'Wherever there is society, there is law.' A separate opinion in the *North Sea Continental Shelf Case* of the International Court of Justice lamented that lawyers who reject 'the moral, social, and political elements, described as metajuridical, become isolated from international realities (…)'. Aaron Fellmeth and Maurice Horwitz, *Guide to Latin in international law* (Oxford: OUP 2009), 281–2.

place.[6] Applied specifically to the law governing the use of force, the 'old' law of nations, either in early modern Europe or elsewhere, has generally stood rather tolerant to state-sanctioned violence and its juridical consequences. The right of conquest, for instance, has long been seen as a legitimate way to acquire new territory – at least by those who had the necessary power to set the law.[7]

Grotius, despite having been somewhat deified by generations of lawyers, was not a pacifist in any meaningful sense. It is true that, as a devout Protestant inhabiting a deeply religious world, he spent a great deal of effort in trying to reconcile the admonitions of Jesus Christ to 'turn the other cheek' with the justifiability of warfare. In fact, Grotius needed many more pages to do this than to argue for it on the basis of natural law or state practice. However, the Dutchman employed his intellectual prowess to *oppose* the Biblical argument against war. His interpretation of scripture was diametrically opposed to those of Erasmus or the pacifist Christian sects of his day.[8] As is detailed later on, they were also the inverse of the interpretations of the Anglo-American peace societies.[9] Grotius instead relied on the traditional loophole of a *justa causa.*

Without entering into too much detail, a sovereign had to essentially demonstrate that they resorted to force in pursuance of a valid legal claim, normally after every other means had been exhausted.[10] Done this way, a sovereign could in principle sleep soundly, assured that their eternal soul was safe. This was the theory, at least. While just cause doctrine certainly played some part, especially among the more God-fearing princes, its relevance in actual diplomacy and domestic decision-making can be questioned. As one legal historian termed it somewhat provocatively, early modern doctrine was an assembly of 'best practice' rules.[11] One did not simply

6 Jonathan Haidt, *The Righteous Mind. Why Good People are divided by Politics and Religion* (New York, Penguin 2012).

7 Neff, *War* 2005, 59–64, 69–71; see also Sharon Korman, *The Right of Conquest: the Acquisition of Territory by Force in International Law and Practice* (Oxford: Clarendon Press 2003), 7–132.

8 Erasmus wrote an *Anti-Polemus,* against war. He was often cited by peace friends. Matthijs de Blois, 'Blessed [Are] the Peacemakers ... Grotius on the Just War and Christian Pacifism'. *Grotiana* 32 (2011), 20–39.

9 See chapter 1 in particular.

10 Apart from *justa causa,* the criteria were *auctoritas, personae, res,* and *animus.* The latter, often translated as 'rightful intention', essentially meant that one should not feel too good about slaying sinners. Neff, *War* 2005, 49–54.

11 This is borrowed from Jan Lemnitzer. *Power, Law and the End of Privateering* (Basingstoke: Palgrave Macmillan 2014), 2.

walk to someone like, say, Louis XIV, the most powerful man of Europe by many metrics, told from birth that he would be anointed by God to rule over every man, woman and child in his realm, and tell him that he could not do something. It had be broached diplomatically, in the circuitous language of religion or natural law. Apart from the fact that such soft and indeterminate council could be disregarded entirely, human psychology is such that instances of cognitive dissonance tend to resolve themselves quickly. When confronted with personal behaviour that seemingly contradicts accepted social standards, it is relatively easy to rationalise it for oneself or subconsciously seek some sort of confirmation bias. This likely accounts for the fact that in every conflict in which the enemies have decided to offer some legal justification – which has by no means always been done – both parties have, unsurprisingly, declared their cause the only just one. Aware of this, legal doctrine eventually embraced the notion of 'war in due form'. Again summarising the debate, jurists like Emmerich de Vattel (1714–1767) – author of one of the most popular textbooks of the eighteenth and nineteenth centuries – posited that, as long as certain formal considerations were respected, both sides should be seen as in possession of a 'just cause'.[12]

By the late nineteenth century, positivism assumed a much larger role in international legal theory and international lawyers became much more hands-off. Positivism, in its most unadulterated form, holds that natural law simply does not exist. There is no such thing as a universal law, derived either from God's design or human reason, that pre-exists human volition and is 'discovered', rather than created by mutual consent or imposed by a higher secular political authority. International law has to be understood more or less as a true 'science', in the sense that lawyers need to empirically study state practice. According to the legal historian Stephen Neff, who wrote the most accessible general history of international law, this development made international law lose its critical edge, to instead become much more apolitical. Lawyers were taken more seriously in actual policy-making, but not as law-makers. They were 'technicians', subserving law to power rather than the other way around.[13]

In the laws of war, this development translated itself into a shift of focus away from the *ius ad bellum* towards the *ius in bello* – i.e. the laws governing the use of force once it is already employed, typically during a state of war.

---

12 Neff, *War* 2005, 95–130.

13 Stephen Neff, *Justice among Nations. A History of International Law* (Cambridge: Harvard University Press (hereafter: HUP) 2014), 217–9, 226–59.

Someone like the German-British scholar Lassa Oppenheim (1858–1919), the foremost positivist at the turn of the century, did not shy away from framing war as an 'institution' of international law. In the absence of a higher international political authority or a treaty forbidding war, this was the last resort by which to definitively settle a legal dispute.[14] Lawyers did not abandon war entirely to the vicissitudes of politics. They began to work out technical codes of good conduct, to regulate the legal institution of war initiated by those vested with political power. This manifested itself in the Lieber Code of 1863, the Geneva Convention of 1864, the Declaration of St. Petersburg of 1868, the Brussels *projet* of 1874, or the Hague Peace Conferences of 1899 and 1907. If war was to be unavoidable, at least its worst horrors could be somewhat ameliorated, the sentiment went.[15] From this perspective, it took the shock of two world wars for lawyers and politicians to again turn to a stricter regulation of the *ius ad bellum,* eventually culminating in the still-existing U.N.-regime.[16]

1.2 *Narratives of Continuity and Disruption*

This traditional narrative has over the past twenty or so years been challenged in legal scholarship. A number of theses have nuanced the apparent 'exceptionalism' of the twentieth century and have instead underlined the continuity of public international law from the nineteenth into the twentieth century. The most well-known one is often credited with instigating the revival of scholarly interest in the history of international law itself – the so-called 'turn to history' that has blazed through the international legal academy for the past few decades.[17] This is of course the *Gentle Civilizer of Nations* by the Finnish diplomat-turned-professor Martti Koskenniemi. In

14 Oppenheim was not a friend of the peace movement. 'Fanatics of international peace, as well as those innumerable individuals who cannot grasp the idea of a law between sovereign states, frequently consider war and law inconsistent (…) It is not difficult to show the absurdity of this opinion.' Neff, *War* 2005, 161; Lassa Oppenheim. *International Law. A Treatise. Vol II. War and Neutrality* (London: Longmans, Green, and Co. 1906), 55 (§ 53).

15 Oppenheim was again a case in point: 'Although with the outbreak of war all peaceable relations between the belligerents cease, there remain certain mutual legal obligations and duties.' Neff, *War* 2005, 185–90; Oppenheim, *International Law. Vol II* 1906, 55–6 (§ 53).

16 Neff, *War* 2005, 277–398.

17 Thomas Skouteris, 'The Turn to History in International Law', in *Oxford Bibliographies*. 2017, available at 10.1093/obo/9780199796953-0154; see also Ignacio de la Rasilla, *International Law and History* (Cambridge: CUP 2021), 11–40.

this seminal book, Koskenniemi identified a certain liberal 'sensibility' that animated lawyers from the 1870s until roughly the 1960s.

This period is described as a particularly 'heroic' period in the life of international law, during which its proponents shared a certain political faith about society and a peculiar self-confidence about the legal profession. International law was the vehicle that could 'civilise' the chaotic world of politics. This story traces the origins of this reformist sensibility with the professionalisation of international law as autonomous academic discipline in the late 1860s. Up until then, the law of nations was seen by most lawyers as a somewhat exotic branch of the law. Many universities did not teach the subject at all, and those that did, did so only as part of a larger course on natural law or moral philosophy.[18] Independent chairs on international law only began to be set up in earnest from the second half of the century onwards. Concomitantly, the first international law journal, the *Revue de droit international et de législation comparée,* began operations in 1868. Five years later, in 1873, the same people founded in the Belgian city of Ghent the first dedicated scientific society: the *Institut de droit international.* Both the journal and the institute's leading man was the Belgian jurist Gustave Rolin-Jaequemyns (1835–1902). He organised around himself some of the most foremost experts of the age. Together, these 'men of 1873' declared themselves 'the organ of the *conscience juridique* of the civilised world'.[19] Their ambitions were high. The manifesto published by one of its members, the Belgian lawyer and noted political economist Émile de Laveleye (1822–1892), disliked that so many areas of international law were unclear, leaving lawyers unable to determine, for example, the unjust character of aggression.[20]

Other scholars have focussed on the achievements of the 'peace through law' movement after the generation of 1873. The list of milestones begins with the two Hague Peace Conferences. The first conference of 1899 directly led to the Permanent Court of Arbitration. After World War One, the League of Nations was set up to prevent any repetition of this tragedy. Its judicial complement was the Permanent Court of International Justice. The League system did not ban war completely. The Covenant of the League of Nations limited itself to imposing the obligation to exhaust all peaceful means before resorting to war. It was hoped that a mandatory cool-down period

18 Neff, *Justice* 2014, 303–5.

19 Martti Koskenniemi, *The Gentle Civilizer of Nations. The Rise and Fall of International Law 1870–1960* (Cambridge: CUP, 2001), 11–97.

20 *Annuaire de l'institut de droit international. 1877* (Gand: Van Doosselaere 1877), 22–3.

would be enough to prevent war.[21] An actual positive legal prohibition on war only became a reality for the first time in 1928, when fifteen states signed the Pact of Paris, also known as the Kellogg-Briand Pact, or the 'General Treaty for Renunciation of War'. Nearly all of its signatories have been major participants in World War Two or have engaged in bloody colonial wars afterwards, and the Pact has therefore often been dismissed as a joke. Perhaps because similar provisions have been incorporated into the Charter, some scholars have recently tried to rehabilitate the Pact, which is nominally still in effect. They did this in a very dramatic fashion. The Pact of Paris was a supposedly 'transformative treaty', that was almost singlehandedly responsible for heralding in the vaunted steep decline in interstate war since 1945. According to this well-publicised book, there was a clear break between the world before the international legal instruments of the mid-twentieth century, and the world after.[22] This thesis will be called the 'disruption' thesis here, for want of a better word.

This stands in stark contrast to the theses that have emphasised a higher level of continuity between the 'classical' law of nations and modern international law. Koskenniemi's *Gentle Civilizer* has already been mentioned. Other theses have likewise taken a closer look at the nineteenth century. Stephen Neff himself has already observed that just cause doctrine, albeit hollowed out by rising positivism, lived on in a disguised form, in the intricate web of doctrines of 'measures short of war'. These did not deal with all-out interstate war, but with small-scale reprisals and humanitarian interventions.[23] Still other legal historians have emphasised that positivism never won the day entirely. Natural law continued to animate lawyers until deep into the twentieth century. Even to this day, the naturalist imprint on international law is clearly discernible in certain doctrines and implicit sensibilities, such as the concept of *ius cogens* and *erga omnes* obligations – i.e. a

---

21 Lesaffer, 'Sanctioning of War' 2015, 50–2; Covenant of the League of Nations, 28 June 1919, The Avalon Project, Yale Law School, available at avalon.law.yale.edu/20th_century/leagcov.asp, arts. 10–17.

22 Oona Hathaway and Scott Shapiro, *The Internationalists: How a Radical Plan to Outlaw War Remade the World* (New York: Simon & Schuster 2017); this book has gotten a shattering review in Michael Glennon, 'How not to end War'. 18 October 2017, available at: www.lawfaremedia.org/article/how-not-end-war.

23 Already posited by Neff himself. Neff, *War* 2005, 164–5; Randall Lesaffer, 'Peace through Law: The Hague Peace Conferences and the Rise of the Ius Contra Bellum', in Maartje Abbenhuis, Christopher E. Barber and Annalise Higgins (eds.), *War, Peace and International Order? The Legacies of the Hague Peace Conferences of 1899 and 1907* (Abingdon: Routledge 2017), 35–55.

type of 'super law' that is binding to all, regardless of prior consent. One can think, for instance, about the prohibition on aggression.[24]

Like the disruption thesis, the continuity thesis can be taken too far. Two recent authors have made the case that nineteenth century *ius ad bellum* theory never was quite as amoral as conventional legal historiography has claimed it to be. Agatha Verdebout writes of a false twentieth century 'narrative of indifference', whereas Hendrik Simon calls it the 'myth of liberum ius ad bellum'.[25] The argument of both Verdebout and Simon proceeds in a very similar vein. They both primarily rely on doctrinal writings, seeking out those passages in books where the contemporary writer entered into just cause considerations or imposed restrictions on interventions. To a lesser extent, both theses bolster their claims by reference to contemporary state practice. This practice is confined to several instances in which states have publicly justified their resort to force. Specifically, they have taken a look at a few war declarations. Out of the observation that in each instance both sides claimed that its rights had been violated, they have assessed that force was always used as 'a sanction of law'. This combination of doctrine and practice has made both Verdebout and Simon come to the provocative conclusion that already in the nineteenth century there were much stronger longer legal constraints against the use of force than customarily believed. Force was already in the 1800s 'generally prohibited', if not by every

---

24 Michael Glennon, *The Fog of Law. Pragmatism, Security, and International Law* (Stanford: Stanford University Press 2010), 67–76; on the persistence of naturalism in the long 1800s, see Miloš Vec, 'Sources of International Law in the Nineteenth-Century European Tradition. The Myth of Positivism', in Anne Orford and Florian Hoffman (eds.), *The Oxford Handbook on the Sources of International Law* (Oxford: OUP, 2016), 121–45; on article 2(4) as a norm with the character of *ius cogens,* see Nico Schrijver, 'The Ban on the Use of Force in the U.N. Charter', in Marc Weller (ed.), *The Oxford Handbook of the Use of Force in International Law* (Oxford: OUP, 2015), 484–6; 'aggression' as a peremptory norm has been recognised by the International Law Commission in United Nations, International Law Commission, 'Report of the Commission to the General Assembly on the Work of its Fifty-Third Session' (23 April–1 June and 2 July–10 August 2001), UN Doc A/56/10, 85, 112.

25 Agatha Verdebout, *Rewriting Histories of the Use of Force. The Narrative of 'Indifference'* (Cambridge: CUP 2021); Hendrik Simon, 'The Myth of Liberum Ius ad Bellum: Justifying War in 19th-Century Legal Theory and Political Practice'. *European Journal of International Law* 29(1) (2018), 113–36; Agatha Verdebout, 'The Contemporary Discourse on the Use of Force in the Nineteenth Century: a Diachronic and Critical Analysis'. *Journal on the Use of Force and International Law* 1(2) (2014), 223–46; Hendrik Simon, 'Anarchy over Law? Towards a Genealogy of Modern War Justifications (1789–1918)', in Hendrik Simon & Lothar Brock (eds.), *The Justification of War and International Order* (Cambridge: CUP 2021), 147–65

lawyer, at least by a significant part of the contemporary political and legal community.[26]

Although these well-intended studies obviously have merit, especially with regards to their analyses of doctrine, their grander conclusions must be tempered. Experts in modern use of force law have already politely critiqued some of it. Tom Ruys, for instance, has noted that measures short of war were ill-defined concepts that left significant leeway to use force. Similarly, these authors appear to have omitted a not insignificant number of contemporary theorists who all have granted exceptions to their supposed prohibition on intervention, if they prohibited it at all. Lastly, on the level of state practice, Ruys has forwarded the traditional view about war declarations, which holds that any legal language contained in it should not be taken very seriously. Such language was legalistic boilerplate, thinly masking the national interests that actually motivated the – political – decision to go to war.[27]

Both the continuity and the disruption theses on the 'pacification' of use of force law are mistaken, at least in their more exaggerated conclusions. With regards to the latter thesis, as it has highlighted the revolutionary character of either the U.N. or the Paris Pact, it should be clear that international law was more opposed to the *'liberum ius ad bellum'* before the twentieth century than still commonly assumed. On the other hand, the somewhat triumphalist tone underlying the continuity thesis does not sit well either. 'See, the realists were wrong all along!', one might appear invited to read in these hopeful narratives. However, the nineteenth century was by every account a violent period, full of bloodshed we rightfully abhor today. No revisionist account of history will undo even one historical casualty of war. Even if we admitted, *arguendo*, that the continuity thesis accurately portrays the state of international law in that century, why was its history still

26 Verdebout, *Rewriting Histories* 2021, 149; Simon, 'Myth' 2018, 133–6.

27 Tom Ruys, 'From *passé simple* to *futur imparfait?* A Response to Verdebout'. *Journal on the Use of Force and International Law* 2(1) (2015), 3–16; the value of justificatory discourses as sources of law is defended in Hendrik Simon & Lothar Brock, 'The Justification of War and international Order: From Past to Present', in Hendrik Simon & Lothar Brock (eds.), *The Justification of War and International Order* (Cambridge: CUP 2021), 3–25; compare this to the traditional view, which holds that justificatory discourses were propaganda intended for domestic audiences. Frederik Dhondt, 'The Law of Nations and Declarations of War after the Peace of Utrecht'. *History of European Ideas* 42(3) (2016), 329–49; Neff has likewise posited that a declaration of war was by no means always and everywhere an explicit legal requirement; Neff, *War* 2005, 103–11, 175.

marked by massive military expenditure, numerous war scares and inter-state wars? Why did it end in a world war? Finally, and most relevant for the present study, why did there emerge an international peace movement that was centred on the reform of international law in a pacifist sense? Why were the peace societies attacked on every conceivable front, except in their insistence that international law was too permissive about the use of force? The main ones who opposed this were conservatives or militarists, who did not want any utopian laws infringing on this fundamental attribute of sovereignty. There seems to exist a huge gap between several of the conclusions of some modern lawyers and the lived experiences of those who witnessed it first-hand.

2 A Contextualist Approach to Legal History

There does not yet exist a legal history of the peace movement which has put the utopian proposals of its adherents into their proper contexts. As we will see a little bit later in this introduction, peace history has predominantly been the domain of historians and the occasional political scientist. For sure, these scholars have noticed the pacifist debates on arbitration, codification and all manner of international tribunals, but, by and large, the historiography of the international peace movement has not engaged in detail with the legalistic aspects of the peace campaign. However, a great many of the historical actors who raised them had been educated jurists – one of the only degrees granted by nineteenth century universities – and it likewise requires legal training for a modern historian to fully appreciate the intricacies of what was written in this vein.

2.1 *Historians and Lawyers*

Academic history dealing with nineteenth century peace movements has peaked from, roughly, the 1930s to the early 2000s, perhaps influenced by the larger relevance of the peace movement during the Interbellum and the Cold War.[28] As such, most authors have missed the 'turn to history' begun in the 2000s. From then on, the historiography of international law became infinitely more detailed and sophisticated, greatly aiding any study involving nineteenth century international law. Speaking from personal experience,

28 Peter Van den Dungen, 'Peace History: an Introduction'. *Journal of Peace Research* 40(4) (2003), 363–75; see also the first three chapters of Harvey L. Dyck (ed.), *The Pacifist Impulse in Historical Perspective,* (Toronto: University of Toronto Press 1996), 17–72.

it sometimes took considerable detective work to understand what exact event or instrument a source was referencing. Things that matter a great deal at the time are often obscure just a few decades later. In some instances, however, even major concepts have remained stunningly understudied. It was startling to discover, for example, how little recent work has been done about 'arbitration', despite its prominent position in nineteenth century international legal thought.

From the side of lawyers, it is relatively easier to understand why they have neglected to appreciate the legal argumentation produced by the peace movement. As we will likewise see shortly, lawyers have paid scarcely any attention to the early international peace movement. Although the erudition of someone like Martti Koskenniemi stands beyond question, it is indicative of the 'bad' reputation of early organised pacifism that even he dismissed its overt legal dimensions. In the *Gentle Civilizer,* it is told that 'they did not need lawyers to argue what was seen as a political, even a radical task of transformation'. Supposedly, 'the distrust of governments by liberal radicals and, *a fortiori,* socialists was incompatible with an attempt to conceptualize the post-Napoleonic system in terms of legal rules'. The book famously highlights the unique character of the *'conscience juridique'* of the founders of the *Institut de droit international,* the first international law society. The world's second international law society, founded barely a month later by a combination of pacifists and lawyers, is relegated to a mere footnote.[29] Other recent literature on the *Institut de droit international* similarly appears to omit or diminish the legal character of the peace movement at this time.[30]

One cannot help but feel as if modern legal scholarship has unwittingly repeated some of the biases of the more sceptical nineteenth-century lawyers. Rolin-Jaequemyns, the leading man of the *Institut,* was intensely opposed to dilettantes butting in on what he considered a science reserved for expert lawyers. Accordingly, the tensions between some of the 'men of 1873' and the peace societies were palpable. One of the leading peace friends

29 Koskenniemi, *Gentle Civilizer* 2001, 35, 41; Martti Koskenniemi. 'Ruling the World by Law(s): The View from around 1850', in Martti Koskenniemi and Bo Stråth (eds.), *Europe 1815–1914: Creating Community and Ordering the World* (Helsinki: Helsinki University Press 2014), 20.

30 Vincent Genin, *Le laboratoire belge du droit international: Une communauté épistémique et internationale de juristes (1869–1914)* (Bruxelles: Académie Royale 2018), 186; see also Wouter De Rycke, 'Recensie van *Le laboratoire belge du droit international*'. *Pro Memorie. Bijdragen tot de Rechtsgeschiedenis van de Lage Landen* 22(1) (2020), 74–6.

responsible for the Brussels international law conference of 1873 spoke of the 'stolen thunder' by 'the Ghent schemer'. Similarly, some of the above reasons for dismissal of pacifist legal argument are demonstrably incorrect. In reality, both the London and the American peace societies were philanthropical organisations, who wanted little to do with either republicans or socialists. At the international peace congresses, the organisers actively sought ways to court the cooperation of governments. The peace societies were deeply concerned about making their cause come across as 'respectable'. More in general, this study argues that the *conscience juridique* of the 'men of 1873' was not particularly unique in the cultural contexts of the nineteenth century. Something like it existed in many other social strata and had existed for some time long before the first international law societies were established.

Apart from those specifics, every lawyer is trained in a formalist fashion. Whether the course dealt with domestic law or international law, law students are taught the professionally accepted sources of law and the ways in which the legal arguments derived from these sources should be articulated in the appropriate settings, most typically a courtroom. To argue in the language of law is essentially an act of translation. One must select those elements of information in any given incident that can be considered relevant for a legal operation. A man was killed because of murder in the first degree, or because of involuntary manslaughter, etc. Typically, this sort of formalism suits the average legal practitioner just fine. Most jurists only encounter alternative views of looking at the law in specialist courses at university. In public international law too, it can perhaps safely be said that many of its practitioners work in a more or less formalist vein, meaning they tend to draw sharp lines between what is 'legal' and what is 'extra-legal'. Even if some may privately know better, this, at least, is how international law would have been taught to most of them. In this world, the seemingly innocuous remark of a peer that an argument was 'extra-legal' or *de lege ferenda* – i.e. about the law as it should be – might in certain cases amount to a thinly veiled insult.[31]

Although a substantial degree of formalism is a necessity to have an orderly form of legal argument, it is nonetheless untenable from a historical perspective. Categories that are now seen as acceptable legal categories were categories that may very well not have existed a hundred or two

31 This is what Bianchi has labelled as 'traditional approaches'. Andreas Bianchi, *International Law Theories. An Inquiry into Different Ways of Thinking* (Oxford: OUP 2016), 21–43.

hundred years ago. Or, they may have had a name resembling contemporary legal instruments, but their meaning may have been completely different. It is the same with sources. Today, the sources of international law are relatively well-defined, at least in how it is taught in mainstream legal education. In history, these sources were very different. They may have come from sources modern lawyers would regard as sources of national public law or even private law.[32] They may not even be considered a legitimate source at all anymore. Ignoring the odd naturalist lonely toiling away in some hidden, cob-webbed corner of a university hallway, it can be safely said that positivism has overwhelmingly won the day, at least in the ways in which mainstream scholarship prefers to imagine and present itself. Finally, in terms of which entity constitutes the main actor of public international law, it is little questioned that this must first of all be the state. Public international law today is inherently state-centric.[33]

2.2 *Actions Speak Louder than Words*

Critical scholarship has come up with many alternative methodological and intellectual approaches to international law. An important one is to conceive of legal argument as a discourse.[34] The present study agrees that law is a discourse that emerges in political practice, constructed against a backdrop of legal culture and wider cultural knowledge. As such, it is impossible to divorce it from the specific contexts in which it is invoked.[35] Such has already been done by Koskenniemi in the *Gentle Civilizer*, as well as more recently in his monumental *To the Uttermost Parts of the Earth*. The latter history even opens with the claim that its thousand pages do not tell a history of international law at all. Rather, it is 'a history of the legal imagination as it operates in relationship to the use of power in contexts that we would

---

32 This rings especially true for the early modern period and earlier, when the modern concept of the 'state' was not yet the norm. 'International' and 'national' norms were enmeshed in complex interlocking matrices. See e.g. Frederik Dhondt, *Balance of Power and Norm Hierarchy: Franco-British Diplomacy after the Peace of Utrecht* (Leiden: Brill 2015).

33 Influenced by modern sensibilities, many international lawyers and political scientists continue to believe in the 'turning point' that the Peace Westphalia of 1648 represented. However, the 'myth of Westphalia' has been long debunked in specialist scholarship. Stéphane Beaulac, *The Power of Language in the Making of International Law* (Leiden: Martinus Nijhoff 2004) 67–97; Lesaffer, 'Unrequited Love' 2007, 39.

34 Verdebout, *Rewriting Histories* 2021, 6–7; Simon & Brock, 'The Justification of War' 2021, 3–25; see also Beaulac, *Power of Language* 2004, 43–64;

35 Jutta Brunnée and Stephen Toope, *Legitimacy and Legality in International Law. An Interactional Account* (Cambridge: CUP 2010), 15, 20–55.

today call international'. He further specifies that 'it is a history of the ways in which ambitious men, mostly in Europe, used the legal vocabularies available to them in order to react to important events in the surrounding world'.[36] In many ways, this seems to conform also to the way in which nineteenth century pacifists turned to legal argument, as we will extensively find out later.

In contrast to many legal historians, this study additionally holds that there is little reason to exclude any particular kind of actor from the scope of legal discourse thus construed. International lawyers like to speak of themselves as constituting an 'invisible college', or as an epistemic community with a unique *auctoritatis interpositio*.[37] While it would be silly indeed to deny the important role of specialist lawyers in interpreting, applying or making international law, it would be equally ridiculous to claim that they have a monopoly on those acts. Especially the sometimes casually thrown around phrase that lawyers 'make' law is a puzzling one. For one thing, the term 'international lawyer' itself is not a term that has much historical grounding. Most of the men we today view as the great international lawyers of the past would not have described themselves as such. Even Grotius himself used to be as well-known as a theologian than as a lawyer. Furthermore, if the past is anything to go by, these 'international lawyers' have never been the sole 'creators' of international law. 'Interstate' rules have been set down in treaties negotiated by diplomats or politicians, or have crystallised over time into customary law out of the aggregate foreign policies of various governments. These policies have in turn always been influenced by a plethora of ostensibly 'extra-legal' factors. To name just a couple: the relative economic or military power of each state, the expectation of repeat-dealings, a society's cultural beliefs, and the relative clout of various domestic power brokers.[38]

Especially those last two matter a lot in the present study. As we will see, the peace societies tapped into a combination of religious and political-economic assumptions that made a too permissive use of force law appear increasingly odious to significant parts of civil society in a handful of important states. Aided by improvements in communications and broadening

36 Martti Koskenniemi, *To the Uttermost Parts of the Earth. Legal Imagination and International Power, 1300–1870* (Cambridge: CUP 2021), 1.

37 Jean Aspremont, *After Meaning. The Sovereignty of Forms in International Law* (Cheltenham: Elgar 2021), 88–90; Oscar Schachter, 'The Invisible College of International Lawyers'. *Northwestern University Law Review* 72(2) (1977), 217–26.

38 Glennon, *Fog of Law* 2010, 165–9.

ways of political representation, this sentiment eventually found its way into the press and into parliaments. Through these means, the peace movement hoped to influence their state's foreign policy, and, by extension, international law itself. In that sense, it did not matter that much that most peace advocates were not professional international lawyers, setting down their legal views in classical textbook-form.

Adding to this critique of an overly doctrinal legal history, it is a very common observation that the 'law in the books' does not always reflect the law in practice.[39] Legal historians have cautioned not to rely too much on doctrine. Especially before the emergence of positivism, books describing the law of nations were not necessarily influential in policy circles, or representative of state practice. Some of the best-known textbooks, like the one of Vattel, were popular precisely *because* they were filled with internal contradictions, allowing both sides on any given dispute to draw their arguments out of the very same book.[40] In legal theory, Koskenniemi, again, has argued that such tensions are contained in the structure of international legal argument. International law, he famously asserted, is inherently indeterminate. Its discourse oscillates between two poles: apology and utopia. Because international law does not have any central legislator, but is created by the legal subjects themselves in a horizontal legal order, it is paradoxical. It is derived from state will, but it also has to bind states despite their immediate will. Focussing too much on state will reduces law to an apology for power politics, whereas focussing too much on its binding character leads law into the realm of utopia, as it will then lack objective grounding in political reality. Both are sides of the same coin. Ultimately, Koskenniemi advanced, any legal decision is ultimately a political decision.[41] Entire libraries worth of commentary have subsequently been written about this.[42]

Although it is a complete misreading to dismiss this thesis about the 'grammar' of international law as typical postmodern nihilism, the idea of approaching international law as a set of argumentative patterns does not

---

39 Roscoe Pound, 'Law in Books and Law in Action'. *American Law Review* 44(1) (1910), 12–36.

40 Emmanuel Jouannet, 'Les dualismes du Droit des gens', in Vincent Chetail and Peter Haggenmacher (eds.), *Vattel's International Law in a XXIst Century Perspective* (Leiden: Nijhoff 2011), 133–50; Lesaffer, 'Unrequited Love' 2007, 36–7.

41 Martti Koskenniemi, *From Apology to Utopia. The Structure of International Legal Argument* (Cambridge: CUP 2006); see also Martti Koskenniemi, 'The Politics of International Law'. *European Journal of International Law* 1(1) (1990), 4–32.

42 Jean Aspremont, 'Martti Koskenniemi, the Mainstream, and Self-Reflexivity.' *Leiden Journal of International Law* 29(3) (2016), 625–39.

appeal to everyone.[43] Words are just words, they say, but did mother not used to say that actions speak louder than words? Few serious jurists will deny that law is mostly discursive, but it is a discursive *tool*. Law is not an end in itself. Laws are made to achieve certain political goals. The U.N. Charter was according to its preamble designed to 'save succeeding generations from the scourge of war'.[44] In the minds of many, lawyer and non-lawyer alike, reasonable expectation holds that, if its prohibition on the use of force is to be taken seriously as binding law, it must prove that the majority of states have been willing to comply. Significantly, its effectiveness has to be inferred not only from justificatory discourses, but also from 'practice', broadly understandable as the larger political, social and cultural contexts in which law operates.

This is where 'legal realism' comes into play, the intellectual school which has traditionally not been the greatest friend of lawyers specialised in the use of force. No study on the ideal of 'peace through law', even if it is a purely historical one, can ignore that article 2(4) of the Charter has been declared 'dead' almost innumerable times over the decades.[45] One of the most well-known articles, published already way back in 1970, has claimed that the U.N. prohibition was 'imperfect' from the beginning, and has since been 'violated', 'ignored', 'run roughshod over', and 'explained away' so many times that it has functionally ceased to exist as a credible norm.[46] Even sympathetic lawyers will not deny that the Security Council is severely dysfunctional.[47] One particularly caustic, yet prominent 'realist' lawyer concludes: 'the decaying legalist regime has produced a catechism that is overly schematized and scholastic, disconnected from the real world of state behaviour, and unrealistic in its aspirations for state conduct'. He even argues that the prohibition has fallen into 'desuetude', in the sense that it is no longer generally binding.[48] Needless to say, specialists strongly

---

43 See also the new epilogue in Koskenniemi, Martti. *Apology* 2006, 562–617.

44 U.N. Charter, 1945, preamble.

45 Thilo Marauhn, 'How many Deaths can Article 2(4) UN Charter die?', in Hendrik Simon & Lothar Brock (eds.), *The Justification of War and International Order* Cambridge: CUP 2021), 449–69.

46 Thomas Franck, 'Who killed Article 2(4)? Or: changing Norms governing the Use of Force by States'. *The American Journal of International Law* 64(5) (1970), 809–37.

47 Tamsin Philippa Paige, 'Mission Impossible? Reforming the UN Charter to Limit the Veto'. *Journal of International Peacekeeping* 25(2) (2022), 187–94.

48 Glennon, *Limits of Law* 2001, 5; Glennon, *Fog of Law* 2010, 23–7, 77–97.

FIGURE 0.1 A contemporary satire of the Kellogg-Briand pact; or the importance of context when weighing discourse against practice.

disagree.[49] The present study does not concern itself with the intricacies of the extremely heated debate about the efficacy of the U.N.-prohibition. It

49 James Crawford and Rowan Nicholson, 'The Continued Relevance of Established Rules and Institutions relating to the Use of Force', in Marc Weller (ed.), *The Oxford Handbook of the Use of Force in International Law* (Oxford: OUP 2015), 96–113.

only observes that much of the mutual misunderstanding appears to be caused by disagreements over the validity of the formalist categories that use of force law is based on. This is not dissimilar to the aforementioned disagreements that can exist between historians and lawyers. What may be considered radically heterodox in one discipline, is often the very premise of another.

The above is mentioned only because of its relevance for the vernacular legal discourse of the peace movement. We have already alluded earlier to the fact that the 'law in the books' described by some legal historians adhering to the continuity thesis does not align with assessments by contemporaries. Why did the observations of so many laymen, as well as more than one specialist lawyer, contradict the theoretical models exposited in legal doctrine? What are the benefits of 'vernacular' discourses as an epistemological tool to analyse international law as a practical and living political instrument?

2.3 *Vernacular Legal Discourse*

In using the term 'vernacular' legal discourse to describe the legal arguments of the peace societies, this study has been inspired by Lauren Benton. She has explored the juridical concept of 'vernacular constitutionalism'. Benton uses this name to describe the 'powerful vernacular varieties of political theory developed out of the empire's legal politics'. It details how the British imperial constitution came into being in practice across various regional centres by various low-ranking bureaucrats and officials. These were people who often did not have law degrees at all, but were forced to somehow reconcile the realities of their daily duties with the legal traditions of the metropolis and the various local legal systems of the places they were stationed. As Benton put it: 'legal tracts and parliamentary debates scarcely chart the surface of this sprawling constitutionalism'.[50]

Something akin was the case with the nineteenth century peace movement. Although its adherents moved in unofficial circles, they were deeply concerned about how they could translate their ideals into practice. They needed not only to convince politicians and the larger public, but even some of their own fellow society members. In the course of their debates, from 1815 to 1873, the members of the peace societies addressed nearly every fundamental question of international law as it related to the use of force.

---

50 Lauren Benton and Lisa Ford, *Rage for Order. The British Empire and the Origins of International Law. 1800–1850* (Cambridge: HUP 2016), 13–8.

What is law? Where does law come from? Does the law of nations differ from domestic law? Who should be protected by law? Is law limited to just the 'civilised' Christian world, or is it universally valid? Does enforcement matter? How should it be enforced? Does international law need permanent institutions? What is the best suited institution? How would these institutions be set up? What are the necessary conditions for such legal institutions to function? How far should their competences go? Is world government feasible or even desirable? And so on. Most crucially, perhaps, they also asked themselves if law alone was sufficient to make war disappear. By and large, these are questions that have still not been resolved, although the answers of the nineteenth century have thoroughly informed many of the ways in which they are still investigated today.

People in the nineteenth century looked for inspiration in the intellectual cultures they were familiar with. Those with a legal education turned to what they had learned, if anything, about international law in university. Peace friends of every background, with or without law degrees, sought out those textbooks that they could find in local libraries and shops. They turned to diplomatic papers, again to the extent these existed. They read the foreign news sections in popular newspapers and journals. They noticed the examples of diplomatic practice that seemed useful precedents to further emulate and build upon. They were often involved in politics. In the age of constitutionalism, they modified known instruments of national public law into instruments that might also be useful in international relations. If the United States had a Supreme Court, why should independent states not be able to rely on a similar court? More broadly, peace friends turned to the existing 'canon' of peace projects. They read political theorists like Rousseau, Bentham and Kant, and asked themselves if these plans for perpetual peace had any practical merit to them in the political contexts of their 'modern' times. Just like Rousseau answered to Saint-Pierre, who had read Sully's plan, the nineteenth century peace movement read the above, resulting in new additions to that long-running intellectual tradition.[51]

Finally, they turned to religion and larger humanitarian and financial concerns. To label war a sinful activity in the decidedly religious world of the nineteenth century undoubtedly made comparatively greater impact

51 Excellent overviews include Bruno Arcidiacono, *Cinq types de paix. Une histoire des plans de pacification perpétuelle* (*XVII*^e^*–XX*^e^ *siècles*) (Paris: Presses Universitaires de France 2011); Jacob ter Meulen, *Der Gedanke der Internationalen Organisation in seiner Entwicklung, zwei Banden* (The Hague: Martinus Nijhoff 1929); Stella Ghervas, *Conquering Peace from the Enlightenment to the European Union* (Cambridge: HUP, 2021).

than in more secular societies. Of course, not every citizen or politician, either then or today, was particularly religious. Just like an arcane legal argument did not interest most ordinary persons, not everyone cared much about what Jesus had to say if the Christian messiah's teachings conflicted with one's chosen profession or a lucrative business endeavour. Many viewed the Anglo-American peace friends in particular as 'fanatics' with an insufferable holier-than-thou attitude. On the other hand, whether religious or not, or in possession of a law degree or not, the average person tended to take note of how much a naval officer earned even when 'inactive' ashore. The idea that military spending is a bottomless hole is undoubtedly an evergreen resonating well beyond pacifism. Nonetheless, the modern observer should be wary of discounting the sincere religious motivations of historical actors otherwise associated with the political economy of pacifism.

The present study gives relatively little attention to the latter two types of argument. It does so only in order to help understand the more explicitly legal arguments forwarded by peace friends, and to properly contextualise the place of the more overtly legal argument within the larger contemporary peace campaign. It would be regrettable indeed if the effort to recover the legalistic dimensions of the nineteenth century peace societies resulted in giving readers the impression that law was all this movement was concerned about. In fact, the majority of peace friends in this period did not really care much about law. A sympathetic tradesman or clergyman would have attended lectures or given money because they agreed that the 'military spirit' was sinful, or because it cost too much money, or because of both, as well myriad other reasons, such as international insecurity.[52] The motivations of the rank-and-file to support the local peace society in their community have already been treated extensively in the existing literature. However, as one organiser put it, the peace societies had 'many strings to their bow'. The type of language that worked well in a pamphlet or in a Sunday morning church sermon did not necessarily work in the world of official politics. One needed to appropriate the right vocabulary for the right

52 For the larger European context, this study draws from the work of inter alia Miroslav Šedivý, *Crisis among the Great Powers. The Concert of Europe and the Eastern Question* (London: Bloomsbury 2016); Miroslav Šedivý, *The Victory of Realism. The German Quest for International Security 1839–1853* (Paderborn: Brill Schöningh 2024), Mark Jarret, *The Congress of Vienna and its Legacy. War and Great Power Diplomacy after Napoleon* (Tauris: London 2013); Matthias Schulz, *Normen und Praxis. Das Europäische Konzert der Großmächte als Sicherheitsrat, 1815–186* (München: Oldenbourg 2009); Beatrice De Graaf, *Fighting Terror after Napoleon. How Europe became Secure after 1815* (Cambridge: CUP 2020).

setting. During the first arbitration debate in British parliamentary history, the celebrated 'Cobden debate' of 1849, the London Peace Society was satisfied that their M.P. had 'very wisely' decided to take 'lower ground'. The peace society, whose Quaker-dominated leadership condemned *all* war without qualification, praised Richard Cobden's 'consummate tact in suiting his address to his audience'.

This study investigates the characteristics of this vernacular legal discourse along three major axes: co-optation, critique, and ignorance. To begin with the first one: to what extent were peace friends familiar with the classical canon of international law? Which authors did they consult, and to what extent? Did they manage to 'correctly' apply those distinctions between legal concepts, such as they were, in their propaganda? Was there any difference in this legal language according to the intended audience? If they did not respect existing legal categories, why so? The co-optation of legal language directly flows into the second axis: critique. As a pressure group bent on the reform of international law, the peace movement did not necessarily have to accept every established doctrine. Which rules offended them and why? As we will see in the main narrative, much of the pacifists' critique derived from their perception that the law in the books did not match what they thought it to be in practice. This ties in to the critique on formalism mentioned above. This brings us to our last axis: ignorance. Professional lawyers tend to instinctively rebut that laymen simply do not understand the intricacies of international law. To what extent was this critique applicable to the vernacular discourses of the mid-nineteenth century peace friends? Did they really just not know what they were talking about? Which doctrines or concepts were curiously omitted from their analyses? What does this say about the concerns of the peace movement? If the interpretations differed from those of doctrinal writers, to what extent was the incongruence caused by purposeful dissent, or by mere lack of 'professional' knowledge?

Although it is fleshed out in much greater detail in the main narrative, a few more words are needed about terminology. As said before, nineteenth century legal concepts often do not fully correspond anymore to their modern meaning. Sometimes, they were ill-defined even for contemporaries. This is addressed when needed in every chapter. This introduction highlights two in particular, because of their centrality in the study as a whole. The first is the concept of 'arbitration'. As the undisputed legal panacea of much of the nineteenth century peace movement, it consistently returns. This term is generally used here, in the subtitles and in the overall analyses, as an intellectual mediator between past and present. It is a 'catch-all' term to denote any form of non-violent dispute settlement, based on some sort of normative system. In nineteenth century parlance, arbitration could mean anything from purely diplomatic 'mediation' to full-fledged judicial proceedings by a hypothetical 'high court of nations'.[53] The narrative fleshes this out further for every actor discussed. The same goes for the notion of 'federative' peace. Just like arbitration, a 'federation' encompassed many definitions. On one side of the spectrum, a 'federation' might really only designate a loose interstate confederation, but it might equally amount to an actual world state, with only very few competences remaining to its member states. Even today, the difference between the two can in practice be rather semantic.[54] The phrase 'federative peace' too, therefore, is used in the meta-analysis to designate every project that presupposed some sort of institutionalised interstate cooperation, be it a loose congress system or the United States of Europe.

In all, vernacular legal discourses like those of the nineteenth century international peace movement are an underestimated methodological approach to studying the history of public international law. Like all self-respecting professionals, lawyers have set up academic standards that determine an 'in' and an 'out' club. Although the benefits of professionalism are self-evident, these risk to over time obscure the political nature of all law. They risk to exaggerate the extent to which the supposed 'in' club materially impacts the development of international norms, and underplay the degree in which the 'out club' has concerned itself with profound questions of international order. Contrary to what these observations have possibly implied, the relationship between the two clubs does not need to be antagonistic. The history of the peace movement is a case in point. As much as the peace friends may have critiqued international law and its practitioners, they were nearly all ultimately drawn back to law. The conflict of the peace movement was not with international law as a principle, but with the way in which it failed to live up to their grand expectations. As time went on, many professional lawyers agreed, increasingly giving joint institutional

53 Jakob Zollmann, 'Interstate Mediation and Arbitration. Concepts, Cases and Actors of Third Party Dispute Resolution (Seventeenth to Nineteenth Century)', in Karl Härter (ed.), *On Mediation. Historical, Legal, Anthropological and International Perspectives* (New York: Berghahn 2020), 153–80; Neff already noticed in 2014 that nineteenth century arbitration is an understudied subject. Neff, *Justice* 2014, 588.

54 Switzerland is officially still called the Swiss Confederation, despite it being a federal state since 1848. Likewise, the European Union is often described as a *sui generis* legal order.

shape to a shared ideal of 'peace through law'. Much of modern international law, it may be reasonably argued, is ideologically 'pacifist' in nature.

3 The Nineteenth Century Peace Movement

This last part of the introduction enters into pacifism and the peace movement itself. It first details how semantic drift has over the course of the past half-century reduced the variety of meanings of the term 'pacifism'. Modern biases do not do justice to this historical richness. It then applies these ideologies in order to delineate the early and mid-nineteenth century international peace movement. Which actors could be considered part of this international movement? Finally, it studies the extent in which the legal dimensions of early and mid-nineteenth peace activism have already been studied in the literature, and where the present study complements this literature.

3.1 *A 'Pacifist' Movement*

Lawyers who like to oppose the 'pragmatic' nature of law to the 'utopian' idealism of pacifists might be surprised to find out that the word 'pacifism' had originally been devised precisely to distinguish the peace movement as a political movement from other kinds of anti-militarism. Looking back on almost a century of peace campaigns, the French lawyer Émile Arnaud (1864-1921) suggested that the movement needed a new name, a true '-ism' of its own.[55] Up until then, sympathisers had called themselves all sorts of things, such as 'peace friend', 'peace apostle', 'peace crusader', etc. The term *ami de la paix* was the most common one, but it was a generic term. People also described themselves as *ami des paysans, ami des noirs, ami des animaux,* depending on one's particular cause. The phrase *ami de la paix* was additionally not limited exclusively to members of actual peace societies. In the French context of the mid-nineteenth century, for instance, an *ami de la paix* could be anyone who favoured a non-confrontational policy at a specific moment, because they considered it politically expedient, without connecting it to a fundamental resistance to war. Once the political winds had shifted, such 'friends of peace' might potentially again push for a more forceful pursuit of the national interest.

55 Verdiana Grossi, *Le pacifisme européen, 1889–1914* (Bruxelles: Bruylant 1994), 31–2; Sandi Cooper, *Patriotic Pacifism. Waging War on War in Europe, 1815–1914* (Oxford: OUP 1991), 60.

This study only concerns itself with those people who were opposed to war on principle. It studies the long period prior to the breakthrough of the terms 'pacifist' or 'pacifism', although its twentieth century meaning was already prevalent in parts of the nineteenth century peace movement. Arnaud, as the president of the *Ligue internationale de la paix et de liberté,* was the head of an organisation which had from the outset connected international peace with domestic justice. Remarkably, the 'pacifists' of this League had no problem whatsoever with defensive war, and had always openly sympathised with peoples who engaged in armed rebellion against an oppressor. The term 'pacifism' was meant to separate the distinct political-ideological agenda of the international peace movement at the turn of the century of those who opposed war on other grounds, like religion or socialism. That agenda was centred on international law. 'Pacifists' were men and women who politically supported liberal internationalism. The 'pacifist' reform agenda included, among other things, mandatory arbitration, disarmament, international courts, the expansion of neutrality law, and international codification. Many 'pacifists' also advocated for a permanent diplomatic assembly, or for European unification.

Regardless of how its adherents styled themselves, the 'pacific' ideologies of the international peace movement encompassed a couple of broad categories. One of the best and most relevant typologies of the 'thinking about peace and war' throughout history has been provided by Martin Ceadel. This British historian has identified five general categories: 'militarism', 'crusading', 'defencism', 'pacific-ism', and, finally, 'pacifism' proper. The first two are rather self-explanatory. Militarists believe that war is not only unavoidable, but also a positive good. A historical example would be those German generals and ministers who laughed away the peace movement's call for arbitration.[56] Crusaders do not go so far as to think that warfare is inherently praiseworthy, but do believe that even aggressive war is sometimes justified for the greater good. In the nineteenth century, this would include those French republicans who sought to export the values of the French revolutions abroad, for example by intervening in other European insurrections. In a similar vein, the peace societies had to contend around 1848 with the exiled Hungarian revolutionary Lajos Kossuth's appeals for armed support.

More moderate and far more numerous are the adherents of 'defencism'. These are people who do not tolerate aggressive force, but accept that the threat of aggression by others will never disappear entirely. This position

56 Martin Ceadel, *Thinking about Peace and War* (Oxford: OUP, 1989), 21–42.

only partially overlaps with 'realism' in international relations theory, because 'defencism' considers international society only partially anarchic. Sustained periods of stability are certainly possible, but war can never be fully abolished according to this view, because no state will ever consent to any effective limitations to its sovereignty in this regard. 'Defencism' is summarised by *si vis pacem, para bellum.* According to Ceadel, this is probably the most popular theory. It partially explains why peace movements have always been minority movements.[57] Most moderate critics of the nineteenth century movement – i.e. those who sympathised, but did not take it too seriously – probably fell into this category.

The last two categories were the domain of the nineteenth century peace friends, whose creed was *si vis pacem, para pacem.* Most of them were either 'pacificists' or full-blown 'pacifists'. The distinction may be a subtle one, but it was responsible for some of the most heated polemics and even outright schisms within the peace movement. Ceadel's 'pacificist' actually corresponds to the word 'pacifist' as it had been introduced by Arnaud. This type of peace friend feels that society tends to exaggerate the extent in which security depends on military means, as opposed to diplomatic and legal means. Like in any political or social movement, pacificists have had to contend with those fellow-travellers who push the ideology to its outermost extremes. These are the true pacifists as they feature in the popular imagination. Theirs is a simple moral worldview: any and all participation in war is wrong, period. Optimistic pacifists have no problem operating in political life, believing as they do that the march of history is on their side. The religious Anglo-American peace societies had many 'pacifists' proper in their ranks, even in the leadership. They did not always get along well with the 'pacificists' in their societies, or elsewhere. Most continental-European peace friends, as we shall discover, were moderate 'pacificists'. Pessimistic 'pacifism' was a distinctly evangelical affair limited to the Anglo-American world. Convinced that the world was irredeemably sinful, the only way to remain free of sin oneself was to remove oneself from it. Peace societies in this vein, like the New England Non-Resistance Society, were tiny and unabashedly sectarian.

As one might surmise from the above, it is easy to get lost in a forest of tedious terminology. This study will not apply the above categories in any rigorous way because of the very high potential for misunderstandings. The

57 'If you want peace, prepare for war.' Ibid., 72–100. The numerical size of each society is detailed in each chapter.

only opposition maybe worth pursuing is the one between 'pacificists' and 'pacifists'. Indeed, Martin Ceadel himself has consistently used the distinction that he has invented throughout his seminal history of the British peace movement.[58] However, it does not appear as if peace history has adopted Ceadel's nomenclature. In order to respect the multiplicity of meanings of 'pacifism', as well as to convey a sense of temporal distance with the present, the main narrative usually uses the contemporary 'peace friend', although it occasionally uses 'pacifist' to switch things up stylistically. The reader will be able to determine the precise character of any actor's motivations out of the discussion of their ideas. The main use of abstract typologies is to circumscribe the topic. Accordingly, the nineteenth century peace movement should be understood as composed of those people who identified themselves as peace friends, because they believed in 'pacificist' and 'pacifist' ideologies. This working definition needs only a few more touches.

Three other criteria are important to distinguish the peace movement from related actors interested in the peace question. The first is that the pacifist activity had to be part of an organised endeavour, most typically a self-styled 'peace society'. This excludes isolated individuals who conjured up plans for world peace alone in their study. Such individuals are sometimes discussed in the narrative, but only to the extent their plans were picked up by people connected to the organised peace campaign. The second criterium holds that every author or society only endorsed non-violent means towards international reform. This filter is borrowed from Vanessa Lincoln-Lambert's dissertation on early nineteenth century French peace activism. She has dubbed such activism a subspecies of 'reformist internationalism', opposed to conservative and revolutionary forms of internationalism.[59] As much as some continental-European factions of the peace movement flirted with proposals that probably could only be realised through political violence, they must have at least formally abjured it. The last criterium, and perhaps the most debatable one, asks that peace was one of the primary concerns of the organisation. Numerous ideologies

58 Martin Ceadel, *The Origins of War Prevention. The British Peace Movement and International Relations, 1730–1854* (Oxford: Clarendon 1996); Martin Ceadel, *Semi-Detached Idealists. The British Peace Movement and International Relations, 1854–1945* (Oxford: OUP 2000).

59 Vanessa Lincoln, *Organizing International Society: The French Peace Movement and the Origins of Reformist Internationalism, 1821–1853* (Berkeley: unpublished doctoral thesis 2013), 3, 13–28.

believe that their tenets facilitate peace, but most of them do not consider it a primary end in itself. This is partly why most of the Saint-Simonian school and the First International are not treated as part of the peace movement 'proper' here.[60]

It is for the same reason that this study does not include the Red Cross movement. Although there was some substantial overlap with the peace movement, the latter was more ambitious. The peace societies wanted to end war *itself,* and not merely humanise it. Their interest was in the *ius ad bellum,* rather than the *ius in bello.* In fact, they sometimes outright opposed those who sought to ameliorate the suffering during war, because this would only prolong the reign of war itself. War should remain horrible, so that people would continue to feel the need for its abolition. Especially for the religious factions, it was a futile attempt to constrain the behaviour of warriors anyways. In the midst of war, soldiers would not listen to such commands. Conversely, the humanitarian reformers believed that the peace movement was being excessively doctrinarian. As always, this image needs to be nuanced. Numerous members of the peace movement were also involved in the Red Cross movement, and vice versa.[61] Overall, nonetheless, the water was deep enough between the two that the choice for Henri Dunant as the first recipient of the Nobel Peace Prize was controversial. The peace societies demanded that Dunant share the award with a more acceptable peace leader like Frédéric Passy.[62] The overwhelming obsession of modern international lawyers with international humanitarian law is even now occasionally criticised on some of the same grounds as in Dunant's day. Samuel Moyn's book *Humane* partly blames so-called 'ethical' law for the 'forever wars' of the United States.[63]

None of these criteria are fully waterproof, because history is not an exact science. Some individuals were only tangentially related to a peace society, because they may have ever sent in only one prize essay. These 'one-off' contributions could nonetheless have been of major interest for the

60 Other historians have likewise kept socialist anti-militarism out of their definition. E.g. Holger Nehring, 'Peace Movements and Internationalism'. *Moving the Social* 55 (2016), 95.

61 James Crossland, *War, Law and Humanity. The Campaign to control Warfare, 1853–1914* (London: Bloomsbury 2018), 3, 105–110.

62 Cooper, *Patriotic Pacifism* 1991, 81.

63 Samuel Moyn, *Humane. How the United States abandoned Peace and reinvented War* (New York: Farrar, Straus and Giroux 2021), 39–54.

societies, like the 1849 essay of the Belgian lawyer Louis Bara.[64] The views of peace friends were furthermore not set in stone. Some went from 'pacificism' to 'pacifism' or vice versa. Some abandoned pacifism completely. One early officer of the London Peace Society, for instance, managed to trigger a major colonial war in his diplomatic career, the only peace friend to have a war on his conscience.[65] Finally, far from every peace friend supported 'peace-at-any-price'. Peace did not simply mean the absence of war. That alone would not have won many souls. For many members, 'peace' was shorthand for a certain vision on a 'better' future, that could include any number of objectives, from social justice, to political emancipation, to economic liberalisation, etc. Peace signified those political and cultural conditions that ensured long-term international stability.[66] In that sense, modern observers should be careful not to take the sometimes extravagant public rhetoric of the nineteenth century – an era of purple prose if ever there was one – too literally. Many realised well enough that 'permanent and universal' peace was impossible. Even so, some might have actually believed this, especially where religion was a motivator. However this tended to cause frictions with fellow society members who, although also religious themselves, were more circumspect about the timeframe of God's promises.

Nonetheless, all these criteria combined suffice to let the international peace movement come into focus. The historiography of this movement largely deals with the same body of organisations and individuals, who were all part of an intricate social web. Some stood more in the centre, and others more on the periphery, but, generally speaking, they all interacted with each other.

3.2 *An 'International' Movement 'from Below'*

By the very nature of its object, peace activism has always had an internationalist outlook, although its origins and main areas of activity have de facto long been decidedly local. Especially before the advent of intercontinental flight and electronic communication was it extremely difficult to get

---

64 See in detail Wouter De Rycke, 'Legislating Utopia. Louis Bara (1821–1857) and the Liberal-Scientific Restatement of International Law in the Nineteenth Century Peace Movement'. *Journal of the History of International Law* 23(4) (2020), 590–630.

65 John Bowring provoked the Second Opium War as governor of Hong Kong. See chapters 2 and 7.

66 'Peace' in the nineteenth century could mean anything from the status quo to a European civilising mission. For a few important conceptions, see Stella Ghervas, 'Definitions of Peace', in *A Cultural History of Peace in the Age of Empire*, ed. Ingrid Sharp (London: Bloomsbury Academic 2020), 23–41. Each chapter provides further details.

any sort of concerted transnational campaign going. The rise of the 'international' peace movement in the nineteenth century thus partly coincided with the commercial breakthrough of the telegraph, of steamboats, and of the railway. These not only facilitated a properly international campaign, but made more than one peace friend believe that these were technologies and innovations conducive to greater international understanding already by themselves. At the same time, various domestic political developments facilitated the development of a 'Habermasian' public sphere.[67] Reforms in suffrage laws, in press laws, and in laws otherwise regulating the freedom of speech and of assembly coincided with constitutional reforms in many states of the North Atlantic world. Constitutionalists often favoured the legislative branch of government and distrusted the executive branch, that had traditionally had the monopoly, or at least the deciding voice, in matters of peace and war. Peace friends proper were in that regard only part of a much wider call from the middle and upper middle classes in European and North American society for increased representation in spheres that were up until very recently mostly the reserve of the high aristocracy and of royalty.

In those states where these developments were very pronounced, it was maybe to be expected that this clamour for more open and representative deliberations of public policy in the national domain would translate itself into similar clamour for the same in the international domain. To paraphrase the sentiment: ending were the days of monarchs and aristocrats deciding over the lives of millions in secretive backroom shenanigans. In the new 'modern' age of the nineteenth century, many felt, the peoples themselves should have the final word. In their mind, public opinion ruled the world.[68]

As it happened, the first peace societies emerged in Britain and the United States around the same time, largely independent from one another. The societies of both countries responded to the mass experience of warfare after the French Revolution. Some of the American founders had taken part in the Revolutionary War, but most associated war with the War of 1812 and the constant news of terrible battles from Europe. The British founders

67 Geoff Eley, 'Nations, Publics, and Political Cultures: Placing Habermas in the Nineteenth Century', in Craig Calhoun (ed.), *Habermas and the Public Sphere* (Cambridge: MIT 1992), 289–339.

68 Pacifists were not the only pressure group to rely on public opinion. The tiny city-state of Bremen, for instance, mounted a remarkably visible campaign in the 1850s to promote the 'Marcy amendment' to the 1856 Declaration of Paris. Lemnitzer, *Privateering* 2014, 100–10.

originated out of the opposition circles that had opposed British interventionism against Napoleon. The London Peace Society saw the light of day in 1816. A few months earlier, in the winter of 1815, the Massachusetts Peace Society and the New York Peace Society had already been established. The London Peace Society continued to dominate British pacifism until the 1870s, outliving the occasional pretender. In the United States, however, most peace societies were absorbed by the American Peace Society in 1828. Although the American Peace Society purported to be the national society of the country, peace activism remained confined to New England until the 1870s. The British and American peace societies did not cooperate on a very deep level beyond the exchange of each other's propaganda literature until the 1840s. In that decade, the Anglo-Americans set up a first series of international peace congresses in Europe. Such events were held in London, Brussels, Paris and Frankfurt.

Continental-European peace activism was by contrast much more subdued. Organised pacifism in Europe was mostly confined to Switzerland and France. In Switzerland, the Genevan count Jean-Jacques de Sellon set up the *Société de la paix de Genève.* In France, meanwhile, a handful of societies identified themselves with the Anglo-American peace cause, although they did not call themselves 'peace societies'. The first was the *Société de la morale chrétienne,* a philanthropical society dealing with a host of good causes. Another was the *Société d'économie politique.* Many of its leading members were sympathetic to the Anglo-American peace societies, and ensured that the 1849 Paris peace congress was a success. Despite the familiarity of certain elite circles with the Anglo-American peace crusade, every attempt at a domestic peace society proved stillborn. Neither the *Société de la paix de Paris,* nor the *Société de la paix universelle* existed for more than a year. The only European peace society during the 1850s and early 1860s was the *Ligue du bien public,* headed by an exiled Frenchman in Belgium.

An autonomous and viable continental-European peace movement only broke through from 1867 onwards. The war scare caused by the Luxembourg Crisis of that year directly led to three societies: the *Union de la paix,* the *Ligue internationale et permanente de la paix,* and the *Ligue internationale de la paix et de la liberté.* The first two were based in France. The only one to survive and thrive was the second one, that after the Franco-German War changed its name into the *Société française des amis de la paix,* translatable as the French Peace Society. The last one was based in Switzerland, mainly because its French founders were republican *proscrits* opposed to the regime of Napoleon III in France, and by extension every other crowned head in Europe. Although most other peace societies called its first peace congress a war congress in disguise, the Genevan-based League quickly tempered its tone to become a more conventional peace society, even ending up as the one to coin the term 'pacifism'.[69]

Although the peace movement was a mostly American, British, French and Swiss affair in the first half-century of its existence, other nationalities were occasionally also involved. The study includes a handful of Belgians, as well as the odd German, Spanish, or Polish sympathiser. However, it does so only to the extent those actors have had some connection to the aforementioned organisations. They could have been a member, entered into one of their concours, or could have given a lecture or speech at one of their events. Pacific ideologies of course existed also outside of this admittedly narrow circle of states, but before the 1870s this seldom assumed the form of societies that viewed themselves as part of a larger international movement.

It was only after our research period that the peace movement manifested itself elsewhere. The last three decades of the nineteenth century featured the birth of viable peace societies in Belgium, the Netherlands, Italy, Germany, Austria, and a few other countries. At the same time, the number of societies in the original 'core' of the movement also multiplied exponentially, effectively rendering it impossible for a single person to produce a more or less comprehensive overview like this study has tried for the period between 1815 and 1873. The international peace movement never extended much beyond its North Atlantic and European heartland. Self-styled 'peace societies' elsewhere in the world were incredibly rare, and invariably the result of Western influences. In Japan, the *Nihon heiwa-kai,* or the 'Japanese Peace Society', was set up in 1889 upon the impetus of a British pacifist. Again, this says nothing about any other anti-militarist movements that have existed in the world.[70]

In terms of the peace movement's internal composition, the sociological background of the average member was by and large what we might in very broad strokes call 'bourgeois', meaning middle to upper-middle-class. Few if any peace friends were working class, but very few of them belonged to the ranks of the aristocracy either. This general rule of thumb had its exceptions. The leader of the *Société de la morale chrétienne* or the Genevan count de Sellon were both wealthy and had a respectable family lineage. Their influence on the larger peace movement was rather limited. On the

69 See chapter 7.

70 Nehring, 'Peace Movements' 2016, 99.

other side of the spectrum, the American Elihu Burritt grew up in a wooden house with nine siblings. He first worked long hours at the forge until self-education improved his lot in life. Burritt always remained relatively poor. The 'learned blacksmith' grew into one of the most influential peace friends of the nineteenth century. He was not only primarily responsible for the first series of international peace congresses, but also for the 1873 international law conference in Brussels that established the still-existing International Law Association.[71] Most peace friends were in between those two extremes. They were clergymen and merchants of varying stature. Some may have had a large and respectable church to take care of, or owned factories and shipping companies. Many were less well-off. Others were judges, teachers, professors, civil servants, journalists, lawyers and doctors. A few even were diplomats or sat in legislative bodies.

As the above list of professions may have already suggested, mid-nineteenth century peace activism was unfortunately male-dominated. Women were for decades barred from taking any active role in the peace movement. In that sense, it contrasts sharply to its composition in the decades just before 1914, when women took up highly visible and important roles. One of the most well-remembered peace activists of the entire nineteenth century was Bertha von Suttner (1843–1914). Her *Die Waffen nieder!* grew into the *Uncle Tom's Cabin* of the peace movement.[72] However, 'female' peace societies only emerged after 1873. This did not mean that women had up until then not at all been involved, but only that their presence was significantly more obscured from view. The Anglo-American peace societies did not allow women into leadership positions, or even grant them speaking rights during mixed-sex meetings. *A fortiori*, women were unable to contribute much to the official propaganda.[73]

Nonetheless, there were a few exceptions. In spite of the study being centred on the legal discourse of peace activism, in an era when women could

---

71 Burritt is mentioned in every chapter except chapter 4 on Sellon, who predates the start of Burritt's pacifism.

72 Lauren Cohen, 'Representations of Peace. Bertha von Suttner, Activist and Visionary on Dreams, Peace, and Justice', in Ingrid Sharp (ed.), *A Cultural History of Peace in the Age of Empire* (London: Bloomsbury Academic 2020), 93–110.

73 Nicole Bernard-Lubelski, 'Les débuts du pacifisme féminin'. *Les Cahiers du GRIF* 14–15 (1976), 30–3; Sandi Cooper, 'The Work of Women in Nineteenth Century Continental European Peace Movements'. *Peace and Change* 9(4) (1984), 11–28; Sandi Cooper, 'Peace, War, and Gender: the Evolution of Women's Voices', in Ingrid Sharp (ed.), *A Cultural History of Peace in the Age of Empire* (London: Bloomsbury Academic 2020), 57–72.

normally not obtain law degrees, the main narrative attempts to highlight a few hitherto understudied early female voices. In Britain, Mary Roberts was responsible for two important early tracts. In Switzerland, one of the daughters of the Sellon family continued her father's legacy. In France, one of the first peace societies was led by Eugénie Niboyet. In the United States, finally, Julia Ward Howe organised one of the first female peace congresses.

History 'from below' is therefore a relative term. Even otherwise 'progressist' actors such as friends of peace could be exclusionary, as evinced by their often paternalistic attitudes vis-à-vis the working classes, women, or non-Western peoples. Nonetheless, the present author feels the label is justified, considering that the members of the peace movement themselves did not belong to those echelons in government that gave directives to diplomats and determined positions on issues of international law. Foreign policy was – and probably still is – a decidedly elite area of government in which very few individuals had a personally deciding voice. This history of the peace movement features many actors well-known to historians of international law and of international relations who may perhaps have wielded such great power. They were ministers like Metternich, Palmerston and Bismarck, or were honoured with the title of king, czar, emperor and president. However, they all appear here somewhat like they would have appeared to contemporaries; as imposing, distant figures, whom one might have been able to get a written reply from, or even briefly meet in an audience, but who were otherwise far removed from one's daily activities. The same goes for doctrinal authorities. Although scholars such as Wheaton, Lieber, Bluntschli, or Rolin-Jaequemyns usually take centre-stage in legal histories, they feature only intermittently in this one. They were people whose names adorned some of the books consulted by peace friends, but who otherwise remained abstract entities. It was only around 1873, in the last chapter, that the two groups finally met each other in person.

Most nineteenth century peace friends, by contrast, are today decidedly obscure people. This rings doubly true for the many thousands of unknown men and women whose small contributions were barely recorded even at the time. The peace historian Sandi Cooper has given the poignant example of a poor provincial schoolteacher, a 'monsieur Fayette', who took the pains to provide his students with copies of the *Almanach des jeunes amis de la paix* in 1892 to counter the crass nationalism of their history textbooks.[74] In the early peace movement also, one quickly encounters numerous off-hand

74 Cooper, *Patriotic Pacifism* 1991, 9.

references to little stories that suggest hidden worlds. One reads about local ladies who teamed up to provide their pastor with a subscription to the American Peace Society. In 1872, an unknown officer deplored the 'bigots' in his country who cheered the pillaging of Chinese cities. The peace journals constantly featured articles about pastors refusing to bless the local militia, or parents who did not want their children to play with wooden swords or tin soldiers. The names of these persons are, for the most part, gone forever.

To a surprisingly great extent, that obscurity also applies to the leadership and the publicists of the movement. Most are known only to a handful of specialist historians. How many people today will not answer with only 'Henri Dunant', when asked who won the first Nobel Peace Prize?[75] Almost nobody still remembers who William Ladd, William Jay, George Beckwith, Jean-Jacques de Sellon, Henry Richard, Louis Bara and many others have been. This has had its repercussions on how the historiography of international law has handled the early and mid-century peace movement.

3.3 *A 'Forgotten' Movement*

Legal history has largely ignored the legal dimensions of the peace movement between 1815 and 1873. Only a few specialists have written about it, and only briefly so.[76] This stands in stark contrast to how international lawyers once conceived of the peace movement. Whether positive or negative, organised pacifism was very much on the radar of anyone interested in international law in the late nineteenth century and the early twentieth century. The peace movement was a highly prominent movement that campaigned for mandatory arbitration, legal codification, international courts and tribunals, and even European unification. It was very difficult to miss the flood of publications that pleaded for interstate arbitration, or, after the

75 Even in scholarship, surprisingly little has been written about the pacifism of Frédéric Passy. See chapter 7.

76 Cecelia Lynch, 'Peace Movements, Civil Society, and the Development of International Law', in Bardo Fassbender and Anne Peters (ed.), *The Oxford Handbook of the History of International Law* (Oxford: OUP 2012), 203–9; Mark Janis, *The American Tradition of International Law. Great Expectations, 1789–1914* (Oxford: OUP 2004); 95–116; Janis, Mark. *America and the Law of Nations, 1776–1939* (Oxford: OUP 2010), 72–91; Mark Janis, 'North America: American Exceptionalism in International Law', in Bardo Fassbender and Anne Peters (eds.), *The Oxford Handbook of the History of International Law,* (Oxford: OUP 2012), 526–551; Doreen Lustig, 'The Peace Movement and Grassroots International Law'. *Yearbook of International Humanitarian Law* 24 (2021), 165–80.

war, sought to popularise the League of Nations.[77] Of course, many jurists did not share in the enthusiasm, because they remained overall sceptical towards the concept of an international law that could exist 'above' sovereign states.[78] Even at the Hague Peace conferences, many of the lawyers involved were wary of listening to the demands of the peace movement.[79] However, the very fact that sceptical lawyers felt the need to explicitly rebut the pacifists was testament to their relative clout in lawyerly intellectual circles. Although the peace movement was at no point in its existence a mass movement that represented the 'mainstream', such as it was, it was vocal and popular enough to make its voice heard – if not necessarily listened to – in the places that mattered by the last quarter of the century.

Many prominent specialist lawyers stood openly sympathetic to the international peace movement. In Germany, Hans Wehberg (1885–1962) and Walther Schücking (1875–1935) involved themselves in domestic peace societies.[80] In Britain, someone like Thomas Barclay (1853–1941) supported the British peace movement.[81] In France, the lawyers Louis Renault (1843–1918) and Léon Bourgeois (1851–1925) were of a similar vein. The movement also got support in small countries like Belgium. Henri La Fontaine (1854–1943) and Auguste Beernaert (1829–1912) are probably the most famous ones.[82] In the United States, the Secretaries of State Elihu Root (1845–1937) and William Jennings Bryan (1860–1925) openly maintained ties with the peace movement.[83] Several of the above lawyers won the Nobel Peace Prize, in the

77 Zollman, 'Mediation and Arbitration' 2020, 172–173; Grossi, *Pacifisme européen* 1994, 320–7.

78 Jean-Louis Halpérin, *Five Legal Revolutions since the 17th Century. An Analysis of Global Legal History* (Dordrecht: Springer 2014), 157; Zollman, 'Mediation and Arbitration' 2020, 173.

79 Genin, *Laboratoire belge* 2018, 151–87; a more positive appraisal is given by Maartje Abbenhuis, 'Peace, Security, and Deterrence: "The greatest work of civilization". The Hague Peace Conferences of 1899, 1907, and 1915', in Ingrid Sharp (ed.), *A Cultural History of Peace in the Age of Empire* (London: Bloomsbury Academic 2020), 129–42.

80 Mónica García-Salmones, 'Walther Schücking and the Pacifist Traditions of International Law'. *The European Journal of International Law* 22(3) (2011), 755–82; Claudia Denfeld, *Hans Wehberg (1885–1962). Die Organisation der Staatengemeinschaft* (Baden-Baden: Nomos 2007), 158-206.

81 Paul Laity, *The British Peace Movement 1870–1914* (Oxford: OUP, 2001), 169.

82 Nadine Lubelski-Bernard, *Les mouvements et les idéologies pacifistes en belgique 1830–1914* (Bruxelles: unpublished doctoral thesis 1977), 466–98.

83 Zollman, 'Mediation and Arbitration' 2020, 174.

period when this prize was mostly bestowed to members of the international peace movement.[84]

Some of these sympathetic early twentieth-century international lawyers already commented on the early texts produced by the international peace movement. James Brown Scott (1866–1943), one of the first editors-in-chief of the *American Journal of International Law,* said in 1917 that the writings of Ladd and Jay were 'in reality the head and front of the scientific and practicable peace movement'. These texts were written in the 1830s and 1840s, in the period when most modern lawyers dismiss the nineteenth century peace movement as a mostly religious and sentimental affair.[85] Around the same time in Europe, Christian Lange (1869–1938), the secretary-general of the Interparliamentary Union, deplored that the history of the peace movement was so amateurish. He particularly disliked how much of the literature was written by 'jurisconsults', who focussed excessively on the juridical dimensions. Lange eventually published his research into a two-volume *Histoire de l'internationalisme,* one of the seminal early theoretical works on the subject.[86] In 1926, the pacifist lawyer summarised part of it for a *cours* for the Hague Academy of International Law, called *Histoire de la doctrine pacifique et de son influence sur le développement du droit international.* Lange begun already with the pre-Constantine Christians, but devoted much space to the nineteenth century peace societies from 1815 onwards.[87]

Lange's study has of course inevitably become rather dated over the past hundred years and is still in need of a modern update. The works of more modern authors similarly only skim the surface, or focus on relatively narrow subtopics. None of them have dealt in detail with the international peace movement as it existed between 1815 and 1873, the period before the breakthrough of the 'peace through law' movement proper.

As such, the literature suffers from a number of misconceptions and misrepresentations that often recur. The most striking one is the notion that the international peace movement was a more or less exclusively

84 Roger Alford, 'The Nobel Effect: Nobel Peace Prize Laureates as International Norm Entrepreneurs'. *Virginia Journal of International Law* 49(1) (2008), 67–76.

85 James Brown Scott, *Peace through Justice. Three Papers on International Justice and the Means of Attaining It* (Oxford: OUP, 1917), 1–2.

86 Christian Lange, *Histoire de l'internationalisme. Tome I. Jusqu'à la paix de Westphalie (1648)* (La Haye: Martinus Nijhoff 1919), ix–x.

87 Christian Lange, 'Histoire de la doctrine pacifique et de son influence sur le développement du droit international', in *Recueil des cours de l'Académie de droit international de La Haye* (1926, vol. XIII), 364–88.

Anglo-American phenomenon.[88] Although British and American peace bodies were indeed the most important ones until the 1860s, it remains incredibly jarring to imply that organised peace activism elsewhere was therefore negligible, or that similar legalistic notions were not already entertained in other countries too. The present study devotes some considerable effort precisely to actors who may not have written in English, but nonetheless made significant contributions, which were often historically already recognised as such by the Anglo-American peace friends at the time.

One of the main causes of such mistakes is probably the difficulty in going *ad fontes* for this subject, especially for lawyers who may not have the training, time, or resources to delve deep into historical research proper. It is an almost gargantuan undertaking to collect the required materials, let alone read and understand it all . The best general reference work remains the book written by W.H. van der Linden, published in 1987. It is a truly massive tome, with in total 1,099 pages. The bibliography alone is over a hundred pages long. Its back cover sums up the author's intentions: 'No stories, no theories, no pictures, only history'.[89] As reviewers have already noticed, even though it consciously refuses to engage in any analysis, van der Linden's opus remains a monumental achievement.[90] The present author can only agree. In fact, any historian writing about the mid-century peace movement who has not extensively consulted van der Linden is suspect. This Dutch historian has mapped the literature produced by the early international peace movement as exhaustively as a single researcher could hope to be, although it came at the price of ending up with a story about as dry as the Mojave desert.[91] Another major reference work are the bibliographies of the peace movement put together by an old librarian of the Hague Peace Palace Library, Jacob ter Meulen. These lists have the added advantage of

88 Janis, 'American Exceptionalism' 2012, 536; Janis, *America* 2010, 81.

89 Wilhelmus H van der Linden, *The International Peace Movement 1815–1874* (Amsterdam: Tilleul 1987).

90 The book begins and ends abruptly, with neither an introduction nor a conclusion. Cooper has described it as 'a list of ingredients waiting for a chef'. Sandi Cooper, 'Review of *The International Peace Movement*'. *The American Historical Review* 95(3) (1990), 783–4.

91 Occasionally, van der Linden omits something, or offers an interpretation that has been disproven since. On the whole, however, and all jokes aside, this book could not have been written without it.

tracking all the editions and translations of major works, listing their appearance on a yearly basis.[92]

Tracking down the titles of publications or the locations of manuscript archives is one thing, but it is another thing entirely to actually find readable copies. The present author has not a clue how van der Linden did in the 1980s, as it took himself years to do it, using every advantage of the modern age. A quick back-of-the-envelope calculation suggests that fifty percent of the primary sources are still preserved the old fashioned way. They are stored in numerous institutions across Europe and the United States, sometimes only in private archives. The present author has visited many of these old hubs of peace activism in person, some of them several times, which was not easy considering the global pandemic that begun in late 2019 made such travels difficult – to put it mildly.

4 Structure of the Book

In the end, this mass of source material has resulted in the history the reader now sees before them. The next seven chapters recount in detail how the earliest peace societies of the nineteenth century embraced international law in their campaign for a more peaceful world. The narrative proceeds in a chronological and geographical fashion, from 1815 to 1873, with recurring bouts of legal analysis. This is the most readable format, if only in light of the importance of larger contexts when studying international legal discourse, especially that of the vernacular variety. Context is introduced slowly on a 'need-to-know' basis, in order not to overburden the reader too quickly. For this reason, some years are covered in several chapters, each time from different perspectives, adding to the former.[93]

Accordingly, roughly the first half of the book examines in detail the various national origins of the peace movement. Only four states featured pacifist activities in any noteworthy institutional sense in the first half of the 1800s. The first two chapters discuss the birth of peace societies in the

92 Peter van den Dungen (ed.), *From Erasmus to Tolstoy. The Peace Literature of Four Centuries; Jacob ter Meulen's Bibliographies of the Peace Movement before 1899* (New York: Greenwood Press 1990).

93 A thematic approach, similar to a textbook, would perhaps have been more accessible from a more technical-legal perspective, but would have been untenable from a historical and a stylistic perspective.

United States and the United Kingdom respectively. This is only fitting, as it was in these two states where the oldest and most dynamic societies existed. For almost fifty years, no other society in any other country rivalled their popularity. Most peace histories therefore pay only fleeting attention to what was meanwhile happening in the non-English speaking world. This narrative, however, also takes into account two European states that would prove to be important hotbeds of the later movement: Switzerland and France. Small and neutral Switzerland, deeply troubled both from within and without in the 1830s, gave rise to the first short-lived European peace society. Its mighty neighbour France, on the other hand, saw the pacifist aspects of Enlightenment thought carried on into the activities of a number of publicists and societies. The legal dimensions of those efforts have been seldom, if ever, discussed in any detail – even if a quick glance already suffices to belie occasional boasts about Anglo-American 'exceptionalism' in this area.

Each of these first four chapters traces these early efforts from their earliest appearances until their respective early 'climaxes'. For the Americans, this happened when the Mexican War ended in 1848 with an early bilateral arbitration clause. For the British, the Crimean War abruptly ended their first parliamentary arbitration campaign. In Switzerland, the death of the society's founder signalled the end of the society and its attempts to model a European federation after its own nation's example. France, finally, saw its republican hopes brutally dashed when the Second Republic was forced to give way to a Second Empire at the point of the bayonet.

These various national threads interconnect for the first time in the 1840s, when the peace societies managed to organise a succession of international peace congresses. In this widely publicised series of meetings, Anglo-American notions of 'peace through law' were for the first time tried and tested in a European forum. This moment represented the first zenith of the peace societies and, indeed, the point when they actually began to think of themselves as part of a truly international movement. This is recounted in the fifth chapter, with a particular emphasis on European responses to Anglo-American legal proposals.

For the penultimate chapter, the story again redirects its focus to the Anglo-American world. Once the founding generation that had witnessed first-hand the War of 1812 had passed away, war had remained a rather abstract concept for most members of the U.S. peace societies. All this changed dramatically in the 1860s, when their nation became engulfed in a great and terrible Civil War over the long-festering issue of slavery. American peace friends, who had always been very reluctant to support 'just cause' theories – and quick to lecture those who did – were now forced to somehow reconcile their dislike of violence with their loyalty to the Union and their great desire to see slavery ended. Their enthusiastic support for the Northern cause baffled their British colleagues. After the war, however, the Anglo-American peace societies found common ground in their support for the *Alabama claims* arbitration. The London Peace Society, the oldest surviving peace society, achieved the absolute zenith of its success when it managed to get Parliament to pass an arbitration motion in 1873. This achievement quickly inspired numerous attempts to copy it, not least also in Europe, where the peace movement at long last began to take institutional shape.

As such, the last chapter deals with the rise of viable peace societies in Europe. Most of this initially happened in France, where the new societies almost immediately had to deal with the after-effects of the lost Franco-Prussian War. Among their answers were 'legal revanchism' and early calls for the self-determination of peoples as a legal right. Meanwhile in Switzerland, exiled French republicans started a radical branch of the peace movement, firmly centred on the ambition of a 'United States of Europe'. Initially shunned by the rest of the peace movement, this Swiss-based league eventually saw its emphasis on socio-economic justice adopted by the rest of the movement. Nearly all of this culminates in the international meeting held in Brussels in 1873. Delegates of the peace movement, from the United States, Britain and Europe, sat together with some of the era's most distinguished legal scholars to set up one of the world's first international law societies. It was explicitly dedicated to the long-held ideal of 'peace through law'. From that symbolic moment forward, the strands of pacifism and international law became ever more tightly woven together in the minds of a growing number of people.

The story of the legal campaigns of the international peace movement spans many years and crosses many frontiers. It features great wars and bloody revolutions. It involves some of the most famous men of the nineteenth century. It is Victor Hugo openly dreaming of the 'United States of Europe'. It is Garibaldi predicting the downfall of monarchies. It is Lord Palmerston and Richard Cobden sparring in the Commons. It consists of thousands of greater and smaller rallies in as many venues. Above it all looms the dark and brooding shadow of Napoleon and the fear that the 'great war' of the beginning of the century would someday repeat itself. Yet this story, despite its scale, does not begin in the secluded meeting rooms of Vienna, where the plenipotentiaries of powerful European states were redrawing the political map, nor on the island where the emperor was quietly preparing his return. Rather, it begins in a wintry landscape far away on the other side of the freezing waters of the Atlantic, in an unassuming village on the outskirts of Boston. There, on Christmas day 1814, amidst the quiet farming fields of New England, a local pastor issued a pamphlet against war.

CHAPTER 1

United States (1815–1848)

> 'Blessed are the peacemakers: for they shall be called the children of God.'
>
> MATTHEW 5:9

1 Local Beginnings

On Christmas day of 1814, a pamphlet appeared in Massachusetts that would meet with unexpected success. That day, no one was yet aware that the day before, across the Atlantic Ocean, British and American negotiators had finally signed a treaty of peace in Ghent. Likely, it would have mattered little had the author of the *Solemn Review against the Custom of War* known that peace with the British empire was fast approaching.[1] While many in Federalist-dominated New England were opposed to a war that had proven costly to their commercial shipping interests, Noah Worcester (1758–1837), a Unitarian pastor from the outskirts of Boston, had raised his objections from a more fundamental level.[2] He condemned the concept of war itself, based on Christian principles.

Taken by themselves, the arguments of Worcester differed little from what could be read in other contemporary tracts, or even in much older works of Erasmus, or those of pacifist Christian sects like the Quakers. Similarly had his decidedly vague suggestions regarding a 'confederacy of nations' or a 'high court of equity' already been elaborately discussed in the classical works of Saint-Pierre, Kant, Bentham, and others. Arguably, what distinguished Worcester from these preceding authors was his appeal for

1 Noah Worcester, *A Solemn Review of the Custom of War; showing that War is the Effect of a Popular Delusion, and proposing a Remedy* (Stockport: Stanhope Press 1816).

2 Samuel Eliot Morison, 'Dissent in the War of 1812', in Samuel Eliot Morison, Frederik Merk and Frank Freidel (eds.), *Dissent in Three American Wars* (Cambridge: HUP 1970), 3–31; Taylor, Alan. *The Civil War of 1812. American Citizens, British Subjects, Irish Rebels, & Indian Allies* (New York: Random House 2010), 159–182.

 | DOI:10.1163/9789004733688_003

collaborative action in dedicated peace societies: 'Let lawyers, politicians, and divines, men of every class [...] consecrate their talents to the diffusion of light, love, and peace.'[3] True to his avowed purpose, Worcester began a quarterly journal called *The Friend of Peace* in the spring and by next winter the Massachusetts Peace Society was born.[4] By those actions, his *Solemn Review* transformed into an 'epoch-making classic' and 'one the most influential works of the peace movement', reprinted dozens of times over the course of the century, in numerous translations.[5]

To Worcester's great, yet pleasant surprise, he had not been the only one to arrive at this course of action. In Britain, in March 1816, a very short-lived peace society was formed in London, whose exact name has been lost to history. Indicative of the early international impact of the *Solemn Review,* its first tract was to consist of extracts of Worcester's text. This highly obscure early British society, ignored in most historical accounts, should not be confused with the society founded in the British capital a few months later, on 14 June 1816, entitled 'The Society for the Promotion of Permanent and Universal Peace' – soon thereafter better known as the London Peace Society. Likewise, this leading British peace society decided to publish the *Solemn Review* as the first publication of its tract series.[6] The second annual report of the Massachusetts Peace Society wrote that 'a correspondence has commenced' with this new British society, inauguring a century of relatively close trans-Atlantic cooperation in the peace cause. The same report referred to similar newly emerged peace societies in Ohio and Maine, as well as others, 'proposed if not actually established'.[7] More would follow in the next couple of years in other New England states like New Hampshire, Vermont, Rhode Island, Connecticut and Pennsylvania.[8]

However, of the many peace societies formed in the United States around the late 1810s and early 1820s, independently or under the influence of Worcester's propaganda, none was older than the New York Peace Society. In fact, this one had been formed prior even to Worcester's, on 16 August 1815 by David Low Dodge (1774–1852), commonly rendering it the world's 'first'

---

3 Worcester, *Solemn Review* 1816, 7, 17–21, 24.

4 Henry Ware, *Memoirs of the Rev. Noah Worcester, D.D.* (Boston: Munroe 1844), 70–3.

5 Merle Curti, *The American Peace Crusade 1815–1860* (Durham: Duke University Press 1929), 10; Phelps, *Anglo-American Peace Movement* 1930, 44; Valarie Ziegler, *The Advocates of Peace in Antebellum America* (Indianapolis, Indiana University Press 1992), 23.

6 Van der Linden, *Peace Movement* 1987, 2–4, 36. More details in chapter 2.

7 Friend of Peace (hereafter: FP) (1816, n° VII), 33; (1816, n° XI), 16–17.

8 Peter Brock, *Pacifism in the United States. From the Colonial Era to the First World War* (Princeton: Princeton University Press 1968), 474–5.

peace society.[9] Most, if not all, historians of the United States peace movement have focussed exclusively on the Massachusetts Peace Society and the New York Peace Society, since these two peace societies not only included the most prominent activists and publicists, but also represented the two ideological strands of American pacifism.[10] While Worcester sought for a broad base of support for an activism that hinged on the reform of political institutions, Dodge's more elitist and therefore smaller society emphasised individual moral regeneration. Although the ideological differences between Worcester and Dodge should in many instances not be exaggerated, the former's position enabled an overall more flexible approach to Christian just war traditions. The latter one conversely has been regarded as a forerunner to later, more anarchist non-resistance pacifism, abjuring all uses of coercive force.

This chapter turns its gaze to the early beginnings of institutional pacifism in the United States in order to understand how early religious peace advocacy related itself to the various concomitant plans for the reform of the contemporary law of nations. Rather than constituting a relatively minor side-aspect to the theological discourse, law and legal argument was deeply enmeshed in the core of a peace activism that sought to reconcile high religious idealism with the realities of politics and social organisation. Precisely because the leading peace friends were aware of their societal minority position, they attempted to navigate a course between the non-resistant radicalism which animated their most zealous adherents, and a moderation that in their eyes stood the best chance of achieving popular and political success. Law was in these contexts explicitly invoked as an important internal common ground and increasingly put centre stage in the campaign as the movement matured and politicised. The roots of these debates trace back to the very first peace societies.

1.1 *The New York Peace Society*

Radical pacifism in the nineteenth century United States was symbolically born one lonely night in 1805 in a tavern in Providence, Rhode Island. That evening, a young merchant rented a room with two beds and quickly went to rest after ensuring the door was securely locked and his package safe. His caution was understandable, given that the young man not only carried with him his personal money, but also a large sum of his bank, which he

9 Ziegler, *Antebellum* 1992, 21.

10 Others often just spread the propaganda published by the two aforementioned societies.

had reluctantly agreed to transport as well. Deep asleep, he was startled by the noise of the lock bursting of his door, and immediately reached for the two large pistols tucked under his pillow. Only half awake, he but barely made out the dimly lit features of his unsuspecting landlord, just in time to keep his finger from squeezing the trigger and ending the man's life. Both of them having received the fright of their lives, David Low Dodge did not sleep anymore that night.[11]

1.1.1 Divine Law versus Secular Law

The incident rested heavily on Dodge, who, although already a religious man, was at the time still preoccupied with his business ventures and the militia duty he was obliged to perform. Before his departure, his friends had assured him that it was his duty to arm himself for self-defence, though, as he slowly drove his carriage through the countryside the next morning, his mind began to ponder on how his own moral intuitions seemed to conflict with the worldview he had been immersed in since childhood. Why did Christians arm themselves? Over the next couple of years, Dodge started to wonder why 'the Spirit, and the examples of Christ, and the precepts of the gospel [...] appeared against it', but the theologians and moral philosophers 'generally appeared to favour it, except some of the early Christians, and those in the days of the Reformation, as Martin Luther, Erasmus, and a few others, until the times of the Moravians, Quakers, and some other denominations'.[12]

It would take a bout of spotted fever in 1808, which two doctors told him he would probably not survive, for Dodge to finally complete his conversion to radical pacifism and begin work on a first publication, which appeared the next year under the title of *The Mediator's Kingdom not of this World*.[13] As its title indicated, it was a thoroughly religious pamphlet. Not only that, it was truly non-resistant in the sense that it abjured all physical force. The sole paradigm through which peace and war could be examined, was through a decidedly unorthodox reading of the gospel. Essentially, the 'Mosaic dispensation' of the Old Testament, which told of divinely ordained defensive and offensive wars undertaken by the Jewish people, had been

11 Meier-Smith, Matson (ed.), *Memorial of Mr. David Low Dodge, consisting of an Autobiography, prepared at the Request and for the Use of his Children; with a few Selections from his Writings* (Boston: Whipple, 1854), 77–8.

12 Ibid., 75–7, 79.

13 Ibid., 80, 89; David Low Dodge, *The Mediator's Kingdom not of this World; but Spiritual, Heavenly, and Divine ...* (New York: Williams & Whiting 1809).

abrogated by the 'gospel dispensation'. Dodge, along with every other Christian pacifist before and after him, drew attention to Jesus's admonitions at the Sermon on the Mount to refuse the *ius talionis,* but instead to 'resist not evil', and turn the other cheek. The deeper spirit behind these words indicated a clear principle: consequentialist reasoning had to be rejected, so that no true Christian should resist an assassin, but let himself be 'immediately translated to glory', lest he kill his assailant, and condemn himself to 'the abyss of the damned' in eternal hell. Taking for granted that individual morality was indistinguishable from the collective morality of all individual Christians together forming a state, he denied any right to either defensive war or armed intervention. Inspiration was drawn from the example of the earliest Christians.[14]

Being no fool, Dodge knew well enough that his extremely radical theological inferences would be 'looked upon with contempt by the worldly political Christians', especially 'those who are clothed in scarlet'.[15] Heralding the most fanatical subsect of antebellum peace activism, radicals like Dodge consciously positioned themselves outside of mainstream American culture, believing that peace activism was the task of a regenerated minority leading by example.[16] His worldview was a dualistic one that distinguished between the kingdom of heaven, ruled by the law of love, and the 'kingdoms of this world', all of which were 'under the dominion of Satan', and 'must therefore be at war with the Lamb; but the Lamb shall overcome them'. Unsurprisingly, little faith in political institutions was to be expected from such scathing condemnations. To be a political Christian, for Dodge, was to serve two masters, an impossible combination unless one committed 'spiritual whoredom', a sin that had characterised most churches throughout history.[17]

Flying not only directly into the face of more than a thousand years of mainstream theological just war doctrine as first laid out by Saint Augustine, but also against the basic understandings of fellow citizens, a harsh criticism was to meet Dodge almost immediately. In a number of accusatory replies in the polemic that followed publication of the *Mediator's Kingdom,* nearly all of his arguments were attacked. Congruent with received wisdoms, his critics held that the Christian faith and obedience to civil government were naturally compatible with each other, that Dodge was hypocritical by still voting at elections, that the Old Testament had not

14 Dodge, *Mediator's Kingdom* 1809, 23–5, 33–5, 38–40.

15 Ibid., 44.

16 Ziegler, *Antebellum* 1992, 28.

17 Dodge, *Mediator's Kingdom* 1809, 14; 44–6.

been completely annulled, that the 'primitive' Christians had not unanimously rejected 'all' war, and that he had misunderstood the nature of the moral law.[18] The latter argument, essentially based on natural law, held that the moral law contained certain 'appendages', which differed according to time and place. Because this naturalist argument rested on one's personal convictions regarding the relative importance of specific Biblical passages, and on the alleged veracity of historical examples, it remained a profoundly subjective one. Because of its inherent subjectivity, the debate on the precise theological injunctions of scripture would be a nigh-unending one within and without the peace societies, proving the critic's biting end-remarks more than a little premature: 'your pamphlet, and the subject of it, are dismissed forever'.[19]

Undaunted by such criticisms, which he answered to in 1810, Dodge repeated his endeavour again in 1812 in another tract, entitled *War Inconsistent with the Religion of Jesus Christ*.[20] Generally regarded as his most important work, it largely repeated the theological arguments of the previous pamphlet, revolving as it did around an uncompromising non-resistance. A later commentator described the New York merchant as 'a Tolstoy a hundred years before his time'.[21]

Having read the criticisms of his first pamphlet, Dodge, among other issues, this time entered more deeply into the natural law argument raised against him, which held that self-defence was the first law of nature. If all the animals were armed with teeth and claws, why should humans similarly not have a natural right to carry deadly weapons?[22] This objection to Dodge's interpretation of natural law ran parallel to the way self-defence was legitimised in the American common law. There, self-defence was viewed as a law of nature, necessary for the preservation of the individual. Essentially a legal translation of what was really intuitively viewed as common sense, lawyers and philosophers framed their intuitions around an analogy with nature; if the entire physical world was governed by discoverable laws, so was the human world. Because law and religion had not yet

18 *The Duty of a Christian in a Trying Situation: a Letter to the Author of a Pamphlet, entitled "The Mediator's Kingdom …"* (New York: M'Dermut 1810), 9–11, 14, 38; AP (September 1893), 212; Ziegler, *Antebellum* 1992, 69, 109.

19 *Duty of a Christian* 1810, 47.

20 David Low Dodge, *War Inconsistent with the Religion of Jesus Christ, by David Low Dodge. With an Introduction by Edwin D. Mead* (Boston: Ginn 1905).

21 Ibid., ix.

22 Ibid., 82.

been separated, many fundamental legal doctrines, such as self-defence, were seen as based on Christian principles, so even a seemingly purely theological argument potentially entailed powerful legal consequences, should that interpretation be accepted by public opinion.[23] Despite his radicalism, even Dodge did not deny that the laws of nature had to be in agreement with the laws of the gospel, deciding instead to introduce a distinction: the gospel was only in disagreement with the 'laws of corrupt nature'. In a stroke as ingenious as it was without any empirically refutable foundation, Dodge argued that his interpretation of the gospel was instead aligned with the laws of nature prior to the fall of man in the garden of Eden, when even lions were supposedly still harmless and docile creatures.[24]

In spite of this rather tenuous concession, Dodge immediately afterwards reaffirmed his belief that moral – and hence also juridical – obligation could only flow forth from divine will, so that no laws could be enacted through long custom that contravened the divine will – as it was understood by Dodge – without being unlawful. He developed a theology firmly rooted in a harsh and absolutist reading of scripture. Though this doctrine had not yet fully ruled out the possibility of positive law reform, it had explicitly asked true pacifists to personally disobey positive, yet immoral norms from civil government.[25]

Although the average contemporary reader would have believed, as Ziegler undiplomatically put it, that Dodge was 'crazy', he had nonetheless managed to assemble enough of a following that already by early 1812, Dodge and his fellow-minded acquaintances contemplated the formation of a peace society.[26] However, in the heated build-up to the War of 1812, which would finally break out in the summer, the New York peace friends deemed it inopportune to found a society that might be too narrowly associated with the Federalist party, which vehemently opposed the oncoming conflict in New England.[27] While Dodge claimed his society to have already existed de facto for much longer, the New York Peace Society was officially incorporated in August 1815, a couple of months after the close of the war. Counting

23 Stuart Banner, *The Decline of Natural Law. How American Lawyers once used Natural Law and Why they Stopped* (Oxford: OUP, 2021), 31–2, 43, 108.

24 Worcester, his rival from the Massachusetts Peace Society, addressed the same issue, but claimed that nature had to be transcended through Christ's example. Dodge, *War Inconsistent* 1905, 82–3; FP (1823, n° III), 79–80.

25 Dodge, *War Inconsistent* 1905, 83–5; 102–10.

26 Ziegler, *Antebellum* 1992, 32; Meier-Smith, *Memorial* 1854, 95.

27 Morison, 'Dissent' 1970, 4–9; Taylor, *Civil War of 1812* 2010, 125–46.

only about thirty or forty members, it was very much an elite society. Although after two years it had grown to sixty members, and after four years to seventy members, its potential for growth was limited.[28] Every aspiring new member was initially expected to be in 'regular standing' with an evangelical church, and was only admitted after a unanimous vote at the monthly meeting.[29] Those members that did join were also quite well-to-do, belonging to the upper classes of New York society, including businessmen, merchants, clergymen, and various gentlemen who could devote themselves to philanthropy.[30] Many were undoubtedly Federalists.[31] The society's constitution enshrined an absolute condemnation of 'war', without qualification.[32] While these rules were revised several times after the model of the London Peace Society, the society always remained a small club.[33] This was not so much caused by its socio-economic composition – the Massachusetts Peace Society was just as bourgeois – as by its rejection of all war. Of course, that had been Dodge's intent: 'not to form a popular society, but to depend, under God, upon individual personal effort, by conversation and circulating essays'.[34]

In achieving that object, the New York Peace Society was not altogether successful. In spite of the personal wealth of its members – many of whom were involved in a number of benevolent activities – the society itself suffered from a lack of funds.[35] It failed to establish either auxiliary societies or a dedicated journal. In fact, the society had taken up a sizeable subscription to Worcester's *Friend of Peace,* an act of solidarity that Dodge soon came to regret, for it not only involved his own society in some debt, but also because the 'lax doctrines advocated in it (…) decreased the zeal of some of our own members'.[36] Nonetheless, the New York society articulated its radical position in a number of separately published loose tracts.[37]

28 Van der Linden, *Peace Movement* 1987, 31.
29 Meier-Smith, *Memorial* 1854, 99–100.
30 Brock, *Pacifism* 1968, 460.
31 As characterised in the study cited by Ziegler, *Antebellum* 1992, 24.
32 Meier-Smith, *Memorial* 1854, 99; Herald of Peace (hereafter: HP) (May 1819), 153–5.
33 Van der Linden, *Peace Movement* 1987, 30.
34 Meier-Smith, *Memorial* 1854, 95.
35 HP (September 1821), 271, 274.
36 Meier-Smith, *Memorial* 1854, 101.
37 A list of publications is given in the first annual report, published in HP (April 1819), 126–7.

1.1.2 Distrust of Law and Government

All of these publications were strongly rooted in a religious argument similar to that of Dodge, and affirmed the supremacy of divine natural law over human-made positive law. The anonymous third tract of the society, for instance, posited that the authority governments 'claim to annul the law of God, to make murder a virtue, and crime the office of duty [was] impudent and monstrous to the last degree'.[38] Similarly did Dodge's father-in-law, the reverend Aaron Cleveland write in 1815 in a very similar vein: 'Under the gospel dispensation, we may expect no further revelation from Heaven beside the New Testament; no positive laws, nor any alteration or suspension of the letter of the moral law, as contained in the decalogue'.[39] This moral law, ordained by God on mount Sinai, and affirmed by Christ, formed 'a code of *gospel*, as well as *legal* precepts, to be the immutable standard of right and wrong'.[40] From there, it followed that 'if a man may not kill in his individual capacity, then communities of men may not kill'.[41] Virtually every religious peace friend, radical or moderate, equated individual morality with state morality and sought for ways to bring the latter in alignment with the former.

In viewing the world and the normative system that governed it as a monistic whole, the religious nineteenth century peace movement constituted a revisionist movement. After all, it was the same reasoning which had applied to that of the medieval theologians, who also imagined the kings and princes of the *res publica Christiana* to be subservient to a higher body of laws, as much as the lowliest peasant was.[42] Implicitly embedded in their most cherished and fundamental beliefs, was their utter rejection of what Stephen Neff dubbed 'the single greatest conceptual leap that has ever occurred in the history of international law', namely the emancipation of the morality of the state from that of the individual. Notoriously articulated by the Italian political philosopher Niccolo Machiavelli – a deeply reviled name among the moralists of the peace movement – this core doctrine of modern statecraft found its symbolical introduction in international law with Hugo Grotius.[43] His magnum opus *De iure belli ac pacis* emphasised

38 *The Question of War Reviewed* (New York: New York Peace Society 1818), 12.

39 Aaron Cleveland, *Life of Man Inviolable by the Laws of Christ, shown in Two Sermons ...* (Colchester: Skinner 1815), 6.

40 Ibid., 3. Cursive emphasises by the original author, as in any following citations.

41 Ibid., 32.

42 Neff, *Justice* 2014, 51.

43 Neff, *War* 2005, 85–6; The Calumet (July & August 1833), 429.

that it exposited a law that applied only to states.[44] Mainstream doctrine was no different in the early nineteenth century on this foundational tenet, other than that it attached even more importance to state practice than Grotius ever did.[45]

While international legal doctrine was not yet explicitly targeted by the publicists of the New York Peace Society, several of the major correlates to the emancipation of state morality were dismissed as profoundly sinful principles and practices. Adamantly denying states the right to use any physical force whatsoever against another state, radical peace friends held that the legally important concept of 'just cause' was often too difficult to ascertain in practice, and that, at any rate, murder was sinful regardless of whether or not a government had acted with just cause.

The complex legal-moralistic concept of 'just cause' was usually framed in the simplified opposition between defensive and offensive war within the American peace societies. As Cleveland again put it: 'The truth is, that in all wars, both offensive and defensive, operations are continually changing from side to side, as advantages may present; hence the distinction is little thought of, and as little regarded. Invaders and defendants (…) perpetrate the same abominable deeds.'[46] In legal doctrine, however, this distinction between offensive and defensive war, so typical for pacifist debate, was in many ways a misleading oversimplification, considering modern authors, such as Vattel, Klüber or Martens allowed for preventive military actions to be 'defensive', provided some just cause under natural law was given, or after certain formalistic criteria were fulfilled, like a declaration of war.[47] Later on in the nineteenth century, there existed no consensus – especially among positivist authors – whether a distinction should be made between offensive or defensive war, many believing these to be purely moral

44 Neff, *War* 2005, 85; Hugo Grotius (transl. Francis Kelsey; eds. Arthur, E. R. Boak, Henry A. Sanders, Jesse S. Reeves and Herbert F. Right), *De Jure Belli ac Pacis Libri Tres. Volume 2. Book 1* (Oxford: Clarendon Press 1925), 15–7.

45 E.g. Jean-Louis Klüber, *Droit des gens moderne de l'Europe. Tome premier* (Stuttgart: Cotta 1819), 14–5 (§ 2).

46 Cleveland, *Life of Man Inviolable* 1815, 36–7.

47 Neff, *War* 2005, 127; Emer de Vattel, *Le droit des gens ou principes de la loi naturelle, appliqués à la conduite & aux affaires des nations & des souverains. Tome II* (Londres, 1758), 4 (§ 5), 54–7 (§ 66-§ 68); Jean-Louis Klüber, *Droit des gens moderne de l'Europe. Tome second* (Stuttgart: Cotta 1819), 373–5 (§ 235); George Fréderic de Martens, *Précis du droit des gens moderne de l'Europe fondé sur les traités et l'usage. Pour servir d'introduction à un cours politique et diplomatique* (Gottingue: Dieterich 1801), 387–91 (§ 265-§ 266).

concepts devoid of legal significance. Worst of all – and to add insult to injury to radical pacifists – as soon as a 'state of war' came into existence, either through a declaration or through hostile actions, lawyers overwhelmingly agreed that it was from then on legally permissible to take human life, as long as it was justified by military 'necessity', a very vaguely defined concept.[48]

Basing himself on common understandings of the laws of war, the Presbyterian reverend Samuel Whelpley (1766–1817) elaborated more deeply on the political implications of radical pacifism than most other New York Peace Society publicists. He did so in a series of published letters, addressed to the former governor of Massachusetts, Caleb Strong (1745–1819).[49] A firm Federalist, governor Strong had made a name for himself by his controversial opposition to the War of 1812, notoriously refusing to let the state's militia be placed under the command of the federal army, claiming it was intended for the defence of Massachusetts only. Although motivated more by partisan politics than any ideological pacifism, he afterwards joined the Massachusetts Peace Society.[50] Whelpley tailored his message to the governor to flesh out the foreign policy dimensions of non-resistant pacifism.

Most declarations of war, the reverend argued, were barely preceded by negotiations in good faith. Whenever they were entered into, usually 'for the sake of an appearance to the people', negotiations would be 'artfully frustrated' by 'aggrievances greatly exaggerated', 'haughty and insulting attitudes', and 'provoking language and menaces'. Reflecting the age-old scepticism of legal-political realists, Whelpley believed that declarations of war 'often' did not set forth the 'true reasons' of why rulers wished for war. Rather, their 'real motives' were likely 'their own aggrandizement; their security in power; the desire of revenge, of humbling a nation, of gaining

48 Necessity was accompanied by limited attempts to codify the *ius in bello*. Neff, *War* 2005, 186–204.

49 Samuel Whelpley [pseud. Philadelphus], *Letters addressed to Caleb Strong, Esq. Late Governor of Massachusetts, showing that Retaliation, Capital Punishment, and War, are prohibited by the Gospel; justified by no good Principle; not Necessary to the Safety of Individuals or Nations: but Incompatible with their Welfare; Inconsistent with the Christian Character; and Contrary to the Laws of Christ. Third Edition* (Providence: Miller & Hutchens 1818); FP (1816, n° x), 40.

50 David Sterling, 'Caleb, Strong', in *American National Biography Online*. 2000, available at: doi.org/10.1093/anb/9780198606697.article.0300472; Taylor, *Civil War of 1812* 2010, 182; *A Circular Letter from the Massachusetts Peace Society, respectfully addressed to the Various Associations, Presbyteries, Assemblies and Meetings of the Ministers of Religion in the United States* (Cambridge: Hilliard and Metcalf 1816), 15.

merit and favour with another nation, of making some conquest, or of accomplishing some object of ambition'. Not wishing to publicly acknowledge their less than noble actual motivations, rulers 'therefore fasten upon certain acts of their intended adversary, construe them into violations of the law of nations, exaggerate them (…) to provoke new aggressions (…) to render a declaration of war popular'. It was unmistakeable, to the reverend, that 'no nation that wishes to be at war, can long want a pretext'. He disliked that the 'boundaries of defensive war' could be so swelled as to include 'precautionary wars', in a sense that not one war in European history could not this way 'easily be proved to be a defensive war'.[51]

Going further still, Whelpley lamented that many contemporaries no longer made much distinction at all on the origins of a war, so that 'no odium rests on any nation, on the ground of having waged an unjust war'. These people were deeply mistaken, since 'however much men may repose in the legality of such a war, God will judge its authors, and will charge to their account *all* the blood that shall be shed as the blood of murder'. Whelpley, like Dodge and other publicists, opposed to these observations the supremacy of divine law, even invoking the authority of William Blackstone, who held that law contravening the law of God, was 'nugatory, and of no force'.[52]

The reverend Whelpley's criticisms, that will prove to be widely shared across the peace movement, again implicitly targeted core presumptions on the *ius ad bellum* as laid out in popular doctrine. While not every author required the issue of a declaration of war to instigate a state of war, the notion of 'war in due form' had become firmly established by the early nineteenth century. The voluntary or positivist approach, as for instance found in parts of Vattel, regarded the side which respected the required formalities as a legitimate contestant. Even if that party could not prove a substantive just cause, it would not be branded as a violator of the law of nations. Although the traditional natural law requirements founded on *justa causa* lingered on, the trend, especially as the century progressed, veered decidedly towards a recognition of war as an 'institute of international law'. Influenced by a number of factors, the fundamental one was the plain observation, already by Grotius, that, across most wars in history, every opposing party

51 Whelpley, *Letters* 1818, 66–7, 70–1, 95–6.

52 Although Blackstone was more nuanced, his work has often been interpretated like Whelpley did. He also cited Grotius's *De Iure Belli ac Pacis* in reference to the *lex talionis*. Ibid., 69, 75, 77; John Finnis, 'Blackstone's Theoretical Intentions'. *The American Journal of Jurisprudence* 12(1) (1967), 163–183.

had typically claimed just cause.[53] The natural solution was to relegate the subjective question of 'justice' to the innocuous realm of morality, but not law.

That answer was unacceptable to the religious moralists that were the American peace friends. In keeping with their aforementioned revisionist attitudes, they desired a paradigmatic return to the supremacy of religious morality and its deep concerns with the *forum internum* of Christians.[54] Unlike the medieval and early modern theologians, radical religious pacifists like Whelpley, Cleveland, and Dodge fully discarded the concept of *justa causa,* not only because of their idiosyncratic natural law conviction that *all* killing was sinful, which hardly anyone agreed with, but also because of this legal concept's general political inoperability. Unexpectedly enough, in respect to the latter conclusion, radical pacifists and worldly international lawyers were in agreement. Unlike international lawyer's increasing hands-off mentality, however, the strict friends of peace forwarded a fanatically religious solution to this so-called Gordian knot: a foreign policy of absolute non-resistance, that abjured all uses of force, but instead relied, as the Quakers traditionally did, on the divine protection of God.[55]

In that regard, Whelpley's letters stood out from most radical pacifists, including Dodge himself, because they allowed some inroads towards institutional political solutions. Whelpley did not rely exclusively on individual moral conversion like the others, but briefly alluded on the possibility for states to settle their conflicts 'by some grand pacific arbitration'. Perhaps, the reverend wondered, the monarchs of Europe could assemble in one 'grand convention', and during those proceedings 'draw the outlines of a plan for a grand tribunal, before which the differences of nations should be adjusted'. Additionally, politicians and lawyers could perhaps consider 'enlarging and perfecting a code to be adopted as the law of nations'.[56] He could not have suspected that his musings on such possible reforms for international law would be picked up on a grander scale by the later American peace movement. Its antecedents would not, however, be found in the

53 Neff, *War* 2005, 99–100, 167.

54 Tobias Schaffner, 'Francisco Suárez S.J. on the End of Peaceful Order among States and Systematic Doctrinal Scholarship', in *System, Order, and International Law. The Early History of International Legal Thought from Machiavelli to Hegel,* eds. Stefan Kadelbach, Thomas Kleinlein, and David Roth-Isigkeit (Oxford: OUP, 2017), 67, 70, 73, 75.

55 Whelpley, *Letters* 1818, 91, 121; Dodge, *War Inconsistent* 1905, 67–71. The other tracts endorsed the same viewpoints.

56 Whelpley, *Letters* 1818, 82.

rigid dogma's of the New York Peace Society, but in its bigger and more flexible cousin to the north, in Massachusetts. There, a moderate pacifist ideology was being developed, that would ultimately prove the most influential.

1.2 *The Massachusetts Peace Society*

The first real experience of war came to Noah Worcester on the afternoon of 17 June 1775. Amidst the confusion of the rebel retreat from Bunker Hill, a sixteen-year-old fifer almost ran straight into a group of British redcoats. Though having narrowly escaped death or the miseries of captivity, the boy re-enlisted two years later. During that second stint in the militia, he was not so much appalled by the battle he took part in, as he was in 'going over the ground the next day'. While Worcester did not stay in the army, he noticed something had changed, because on the first funeral he attended back home he would reflect: 'I was shocked to find myself (...) so unmoved on such an occasion.'[57]

A self-made man – he claimed to have learned to write on tree-bark – Worcester scratched together a living as a farmer, a cobbler, a schoolteacher and through other odd jobs, while he read what he could and penned short dissertations on religious subjects. Some of these would get published, and Worcester attracted the attention of sympathetic ministers, who encouraged him to become a preacher himself. Though raised a strict Calvinist, Worcester would eventually become a Unitarian minister, albeit one influenced by Quaker principles and increasingly reluctant to lead prayers with the local militia company. The decisive turning point for Worcester came at the outbreak of the War of 1812, which he saw as 'unnecessary, and unjust'. In 1814, a short article originally intended for the religious periodical he edited grew into the *Solemn Review of the Custom of War,* a pamphlet that in turn led to the founding of the Massachusetts Peace Society on 28 December 1815, and of its journal *The Friend of Peace* in 1819.[58] Worcester's life thereafter was mostly dedicated to peace.

Although Worcester, who even as a licensed minister still frequently had to supplement his meagre income through manual labour, could not be more different from the wealthy manufactory-owning merchant Dodge, the Massachusetts Peace Society did not have to feel any inferiority towards its genteel New York counterpart. In both peace societies, the average member

57 It was the battle of Bennington of 16 August 1777, an American victory. Ware, *Memoirs* 1844, 6.

58 Worcester was the sole editor of the *Friend of Peace* during its entire run. Ibid., 62–65, 71–72.

was 'a middle-aged male Protestant with a college education', with Federalist political sympathies and a certain affinity with evangelical reform.[59] In fact, the Massachusetts society could boast both the most numerous and the most esteemed membership. By 1820, the Massachusetts Peace Society counted about 540 members among its ranks, a fifth of them clergymen, as well as thirteen auxiliaries located around and outside the immediate Boston area, totalling some 400 members.[60] Apart from governor Caleb Strong, mentioned earlier, members included also a couple of judges and the president and several professors of Harvard.[61] Indicative of the greater political ambitions of this society, Worcester had even sent out copies of his tracts to such political luminaries as the former presidents John Adams and Thomas Jefferson, as well as John Jay. Adams declined support because he equated the peace society to a non-resistance that would be detrimental to national interests.[62] Jefferson looked at the society with a milder judgment and did not object to an honorary membership, even if he remained sceptical and non-committal, similar to John Jay's reply.[63]

A far broader society than the New York Peace Society, it included a number of other members of note, foremost William Ellery Channing (1780–1842), a famous Unitarian minister, at whose home the founding meeting took place.[64] Still, the success of this new society should not be exaggerated, as enthusiasm – and funding – slowed down after the dissipation of its initial post-war momentum by the mid-1820s. One contemporary recounted that many parts of New England never saw any tract whatsoever, while in Boston whole stacks of *The Friend of Peace* gathered dust on the shelves.[65]

---

59 Worcester's sympathies belonged to the Federalist party, although he disliked excessive partisanship. Ziegler, *Antebellum* 1992, 24; Ware, *Memoirs* 1844, 126.

60 Van der Linden, *Peace Movement* 1987, 32.

61 Brock, *Pacifism* 1968, 472.

62 The elder statesman claimed that 'non-resistance' would lead the 'human flock' to 'soon be fleeced and butchered by one or a few'. He added that the U.S. if anything needed more 'martial spirit', not less. FP (1816, n°4), 25–26.

63 John Jay sympathised, but he firmly believed in the legality of 'just and necessary war'. His son William Jay would be much more involved. FP (1816, n° XI), 28–31; FP (1821, n° VI).

64 Van der Linden, *Peace Movement* 1987, 21; Daniel Howe, 'Channing, William Ellery', in *American National Biography Online*. 2000, available at: doi.org/10.1093/anb/9780198606697.article.0800251

65 Ziegler, *Antebellum* 1992, 24–5.

1.2.1 A Protestant Legal Conscience

In its constitution, the Massachusetts Peace Society subscribed to a diversity-of-opinion approach, meaning that this society did not exclude in advance those who could only condemn offensive war, but not defensive war. The preamble acknowledged that 'a diversity of sentiment has existed among Christians on the question, whether war be not in all cases prohibited by the gospel'. As it stood, however, Worcester and Channing intended their society to be established on 'principles so broad, as to the embrace the friends of peace who differ on this as well as on other subjects'.[66] Toleration was decided upon not only because Channing himself ranked among those in favour of defensive war, but also because of the accommodating and pragmatic personality of Worcester.[67] Perhaps in contrast to what his constitution might suggest, Worcester was actually, like Dodge, convinced that *all* war was 'repugnant to the spirit required by the gospel'. Unlike in New York, the Massachusetts reverend did not want others to completely agree with his own convictions, having formed his own only gradually, believing that 'wholesale censures ever appeared to me antichristian'.[68] Even Dodge, who reluctantly and grudgingly cooperated with Worcester, did not deny that his rival had chosen an intermediate course, 'as a matter of expediency, rather than his own private sentiments'.[69]

Accordingly, much of the religious argument ran parallel between the New York and Massachusetts peace societies. Completely in agreement with the former's propaganda, the *Solemn Review* and the *Friend of Peace* emphasised the pre-eminence of the Sermon on the Mount and the law of love over the bellicose Old Testament. Worcester believed no less in the possibility of a permanent peace as Dodge's radicals, or in a single Christian moral law applicable to individuals as well as states. The similarities stemmed partly from their similar religious affiliations. Both societies generally recruited from evangelical ranks, specifically from Presbyterians, Unitarians, Methodists, Congregationalists and Baptists. Relatively fewer, if any, members joined from the more conservative Episcopalian or Roman Catholic

66 FP (1816, n° 4), 38.

67 William Channing, *A Sermon, preached in Boston, July 23, 1812, the Day of the Publick Fast, appointed by the Executive of the Commonwealth of Massachusetts, in Consequence of the Declaration of War against Great Britain* (Boston: Greenough and Stebbins 1812), 15.

68 Ware, *Memoirs* 1844, 27, 63.

69 Meier-Smith, *Memorial* 1854, 89.

churches.[70] However, official church support remained limited across all Christian denominations.[71] Surprisingly enough, the pacifist Christian sect *par excellence,* the Quakers, was just as uninvolved in the antebellum peace societies. Embroiled in theological infighting, the American Quakers were less politically active than their British counterparts and hesitant to join a movement that appeared ambivalent over the issue of defensive war.

More important than their common composition was the shared object of peace societies to reform society through concerted effort from the bottom up. Both the moderate and the radical factions of the peace movement believed that political success would follow from the gradual conversion of the populace to their pacific ideals.[72] Inspiration was drawn from the then increasingly dominant 'New Light' theology, already on the rise since the late eighteenth century. Jesus Christ, influential evangelical theologians held, had not just prophesised that humanity might be saved in some distant future, but that humanity should work towards its salvation already here on earth. These doctrines, subsequently known as post-Millennialism, characterised the early nineteenth century U.S. 'culture of reform', also known as a 'Protestant Crusade'.

Peace societies formed just part of a vast conglomerate of benevolent Christian societies, dedicated to anti-slavery, temperance, literacy, prison reform, missionary work, the spreading of Bibles and dozens of other such good causes.[73] Applied to peace, the secretary of the New York Peace Society, Eleazar Lord (1788–1871) declared: 'there can be no such thing as a Millennium until the Christian religion actually produces such sentiments and practice as [we] advocate'.[74] Similarly did Worcester admit that 'some may be ready to exclaim, none but God can produce such an effect as the abolition of war; and we must wait for the millennial day', but he also countered that 'God works by human agency and human means'.[75] Worcester saw the hand of God in the success of Wilberforce and his allies in abolishing the

70 Brock, *Pacifism* 1968, 478–9.

71 Ziegler, *Antebellum* 1992, 10, 23–4

72 Gregory Garvey, *Creating the Culture of Reform in Antebellum America* (Athens: University of Georgia Press 2006), 2.

73 Unlike 'Old Light', pre-Millennialist evangelicals, this class of reformers was not necessarily opposed to polities not wholly built on Christian foundations. Garvey, *Culture of Reform* 2006, 10, 24, 95; Richard Carwardine, *Evangelicals and Politics in Antebellum America* (Knoxville: University of Tennessee Press 1997), 15–6.

74 Eleazar Lord, *Thoughts on the Practical Advantages of Those who hold the Doctrines of Peace over Those who vindicate War* (New York: Seymour 1816), 23.

75 Worcester, *Solemn Review* 1816, 4.

slave trade – a precedent repeated hundreds of times in pacifist propaganda.[76]

To modern lawyers and legal historians used to the narrative of the increasing secularisation of law in the nineteenth century, such theological intricacies can quickly strike one as irrelevant, quaint or outdated. However, even in the late nineteenth century, a number of prominent Anglo-American international lawyers were still influenced by similar urges to give the Christian morality of Western society 'political bite', as one scholar has phrased it. Influential authors such as Westlake, Lorimer, Lieber, and others saw in social institutions like international law a vehicle for a religiously inspired perfectioning of international society.[77] The legal-reformist sensibilities of Koskenniemi's 'men of 1873' drew at least in part from the Protestant sensibilities of several of its members, who even in their capacity as lawyers considered state institutions to possess a distinctly Christian character, and approached resorts to natural law in legal discourse as quite valid.[78] In that respect, Gustave Rolin-Jaequemyns's famous 'enlightened opinion of civilized men' has at least once already been explicitly compared to the earlier religious peace campaign's deliberate effort to 'civilize' public opinion.[79]

As the echoes between peace activism and some of the efforts of subsequent activist lawyers already suggest – even though any comparisons should not be taken too far or too literally – the distinction between radical and moderate pacifism could not be drawn so much on its fundamental theological underpinnings, but on its conception of the state and its institutions, such as law. In a clear contrast to Dodge's non-resistant society, the Massachusetts Peace Society introduced a second distinction in order to resolve the problem of the full moral-legal extent of Jesus's Sermon on the Mount. The pessimistic vision of a handful of true Christians isolated within a sinful world was replaced by the more optimistic vision of the state working closely together with the church to help inaugurate the Millennial age. In reality most likely equally based on a disagreement in personal temperaments, the main scriptural foundation to legitimise this choice to a biblically

76 Ibid. E.g. FP (1816, n° VI), 21–25; Adna Heaton, *War and Christianity contrasted; with a Comparative View of their Nature and Effects* ... (New York: Wood & Sons 1816), 57.

77 John Haskell, 'Divine Immanence: the Evangelical Foundations of Modern Anglo-American Approaches to International Law', in *Chinese Journal of International Law* 11(3) (2012), 445.

78 They believed law gave the 'moral sentiment of humanity' material existence. Ibid., 443.

79 Ibid., 446. See also chapter 7 and the general conclusion.

literate audience was found in the thirteenth chapter of Paul's epistle to the Romans.[80] The significant part of it underlined the right of the magistrate to enforce the law: 'be afraid; for he beareth not the sword in vain: for he is the minister of God'.[81] Such words were a far cry from the non-resistant call to ignore positive law that violated divine moral law.

1.2.2 The Domestic Rule of Law

True to their embryonical institutional approach, Worcester and his fellow moderates consistently defined war as but a mere human-made 'custom' that could therefore be changed through positive reform of law and institutions. As the *Solemn Review* asked: 'cannot the state of society and the views of civilized men be so changed as to abolish a barbarous custom, and render wars unnecessary and avoidable?'.[82] 'Evidence' for the viability of this massive reform of international politics was found not only in the recent successes of the anti-slavery and temperance societies, but in a much deeper-rooted faith in the teleological progress of human culture.[83] Of the 'signs of the times' that related to legal reform, Worcester pointed, inter alia, at the British criminal law reforms: 'sanguinary laws, which once were deemed necessary and useful, gradually become abhorrent, lose their force, sink into disrepute [...] Of 200 such laws in Britain, 175 have been cancelled by a public sentiment of reprobation'.[84] Specifically for war, however, Worcester noticed that, while the feudal 'private wars' of the medieval era had disappeared, as well as judicial combats or trials by ordeal, interstate wars had not: 'we have indeed exploded some of the barbarous customs of former ages; but the *worst of all* we have retained, embellished, and idolized'.[85]

Moderate peace friends like Noah Worcester realised that, if the custom of war was to be abolished, education and moral regeneration would not be sufficient, because the ultimate function of war in international law was to substitute a legal trial, in the absence of any higher positive authority other than God. Popular authors such as Vattel defined it as 'that state, in which

80 Ziegler, *Antebellum* 1992, 35–7.

81 Romans 13: 4 (King James Version).

82 Worcester, *Solemn Review* 1816, 4.

83 FP (1816, n° II), 34–7; FP (1816, n° IV), 1–21; David Lawson, *Swords into Plowshares, Spears into Pruninghooks: The Intellectual Foundations of the First American Peace Movement, 1815–1865* (University of New Mexico: unpublished doctoral thesis 1975), 121–3.

84 FP (1821, n° VIII), 17; see also e.g. FP (1827, n° III), 75–7.

85 FP (1816, appendix to vol. 1), 20.

one pursues one's rights by force'.[86] In the minds of friends of peace, such definitions made a mockery of the legal process. Worcester, again in an analogy that would be endlessly repeated in subsequent argument, compared interstate war with a trial by jury governed by common law. Naturally, the comparison did not turn out in favour of war, which was accused of lacking nearly all of the safeguards of procedural justice that individuals could rely on in the domestic legal system.

National juridical models ought to shape international reforms. In a streak of sarcasm, the reverend imagined a fictitious Act of Congress remodelling private conflict resolution after the international example: 'the injured person shall decide for himself what redress is necessary; it shall be lawful for him to maim or destroy the offender [...] it shall be lawful for each party to form alliances with his neighbours', et cetera.[87] Blackstone's commentaries on the advantages of the trial by jury stood as a beacon of legal wisdom, compared to the 'laws and usages of nations'. Worcester deplored that even in the United States – a republic unlike the despotic governments of Europe – Congress could 'by *a bare majority'* of votes, as well as the president's consent, draw the entire nation into war. How could such an 'all-important case' be thus summarily addressed in the Constitution, accounting that the Sixth amendment took such care to enshrine the trial by jury?[88] The ineffectiveness of violence to settle legal disputes was illustrated by tangible political examples. Had the Treaty of Ghent made reparations 'for *all,* or even *one'* of the perceived injuries? Pacifists felt it had only aggravated existing economic hurt.[89] Thus, moderate activists experienced an early latent need to conceptualise legal alternatives. If the modern state was not corrupt, but rather upheld order and individual liberty in the domestic realm, its rationality should be extrapolated to the international sphere.

The *Solemn Review's* most important contribution to the early American peace movement, from the lawyer's point of view, were its early allusions to the necessity of international political organisation. If the eyes of the people could finally be opened on the true nature of war, its 'evils and delusions', Worcester hypothesised, 'would it not be easy to form a confederacy of nations, and organise a high court of equity, to decide national controversies? Why might not such a court be composed of some of the most eminent characters from each nation; and a compliance with the decision of the

86 Vattel, *Droits des gens. Tome second* 1758, 1 (§ 1).
87 FP, (1816, n° X), 14–7.
88 FP, (1816, n° XII), 6–10.
89 FP (1821, n° XII), 34–7.

court be made a point of national honour (…)'. Referring to the quasi-legal function of war in international relations, the reverend felt convinced that no one could reasonably assert that 'right' could not be obtained just as probably through a court of justice, than through any appeal to arms. On the contrary, 'such an appeal is more safe, and more certain, as well as more benevolent, than for the individual to attempt to obtain a redress by his pistol, or his sword'.[90] These passages were still rudimentary asides within a pamphlet otherwise devoted to the religious and moral argument. Compared to many subsequent schemes, Worcester did not yet clarify whether the benches of this court would be filled with specialists of international law, with traditional diplomats or politicians, or, alternatively, with a combination of the two. He described the court as based on 'equity', which was not necessarily the same as a code. Would this 'confederacy of nations' include the 'high court' as well, or did these consist of separate bodies? Few specifics were given.

Of course, the opposite would have been rather more surprising. The main concern of the religious pacifists was to get their peace societies going at all and therefore most propaganda was devoted to the explanation and repetition of the religious or moral argument against war. Hundreds of pages referred to passages of scripture, or to anecdotes intended to strip war of its halo of glory. Extended excerpts from popular accounts of the Napoleonic Wars – sometimes featuring graphic depictions of vast fields of horribly mutilated corpses – intermingled with anecdotes on the realities of military life. Markedly different from the manner in which mainstream American society portrayed military men – then as now – peace propaganda emphasised the harsh discipline of the camp, a place where floggings seemed as common as idling, swearing, gambling, and prostitution.[91] The soldier's typical heroic masculinity made way for the image of a wretch recruited from the lowest echelons of society into a long-term servitude little better than slavery.[92] Attention was also brought to the economical waste of military preparations. Even though the United States maintained a small army and navy compared to the European powers, the costs of these, combined with the militia, were still seen as excessive compared to the costs of civil government, or of pacific alternatives. In yet another case to be repeated hundreds of times by subsequent activists, it was emphasised that

---

90 Worcester, *Solemn Review* 1816,

91 E.g. FP (1816, n° III), 1–27; FP (1823, n° II), 55–7.

92 Unlike the officer class, the common soldier was often seen as 'the very scum and refuse of society'. FP (1816, n° II), 22–25; AP (April 1854), 61.

'the income of all the Bible and Missionary Societies (…) would not more than defray the expense of one ship of the line'.[93] The message of the *Friend of Peace* was tailored to a Christian and tax-paying audience, which would be converted more readily by this common frame of reference, than by legal subtleties far removed from the average reader's daily concerns.

Nevertheless, acknowledging that 'the advocates of peace have many strings to their bow', the legal dimensions of peace were not left wholly undiscussed in the pages of the *Friend of Peace*. Allusions to the pressing need for a 'high tribunal', 'tribunal of honor and equity', 'court of honor', 'court of justice', or even, simply, 'some pacific arrangement' recurrently cropped up.[94] Unfortunately, most of these did not add a whole lot of colour to Worcester's earlier general suggestions. Even the 1816 memorial sent by the Massachusetts Peace Society to the federal Senate spoke only of 'the reference of national controversies to an impartial umpire'.[95] Somewhat more specifically, Worcester praised the successful Russian arbitration in 1822 – over the restitution of slaves evacuated with the British army after the War of 1812 – as an 'example (…) adapted to show the world the proper substitute for war'.[96] Although the arbitration had not been provided for by the Treaty of Ghent, the reverend nonetheless elsewhere referred positively to the three articles within the treaty of Ghent that made provisions for a bilateral British-American commission in case of interpretative boundary disputes, and for the arbitration by a 'friendly sovereign' or 'state', should the British-American commission not come to an agreement.[97] These provisions, Worcester claimed, were 'similar' to the 'high

---

93 FP (1827, n° III), 77–8.

94 FP (1821, n° V), 2; FP (1821, n° IX), 3; *Second Annual Report of the Committee of Inquiry of the Massachusetts Peace Society* (Cambridge: Hilliard and Metcalf), 6; Blakslee, Solomon. *An Address delivered before the Members of the East-Haddam Branch of the Massachusetts Peace Society* (Middletown: Clark & Lyman 1820), 7; FP (1823, n° III), 89; FP (1827, n° IV), 101.

95 FP (1816, n° VIII), 29

96 FP (1821, n° VIII), 37; FP (1827, n° XI), 340; FP (1827, appendix n° 1), 3; Bennett Ostdiek and John Fabian Witt, 'The Czar and the Slaves: Two Puzzles in the History of International Arbitration'. *The American Journal of International Law* 113(3) (2019), 535–67.

97 The commission did not come to an agreement, and the border was only definitively settled by the 1842 Webster-Ashburton Treaty. Treaty of Peace and Amity between his Britannic Majesty and the United States of America, articles 5, 6, and 7, *American State Papers. I. Foreign Relations* (Washington: Gales and Seaton 1833), 745–748; Ostdiek and Witt, 'Czar and the Slaves', 550. David Pletcher, *The Diplomacy of Annexation. Texas, Oregon, and the Mexican War* (Columbia: University of Missouri Press 1973), 24–5.

court' he had proposed in his *Solemn Review* around the same time the diplomats were meeting in Ghent.[98]

1.2.3 Doctrine and Practice

The extent to which Worcester had actually studied arbitration as a substitute still remained limited, because elsewhere he spoke of the Russian czar's 'arbitration' as a 'mediation' between the United States and Britain.[99] However, likely unbeknownst to Worcester, 'arbitration' and 'mediation' were two very different legal concepts. 'Mediation', strictly understood, remained a strictly political affair, while 'arbitration', according to legal doctrine, entailed the examination of a legal question by one or more third parties, at first still typically a head of state.[100] Pacifists and international lawyers alike disagreed in the nineteenth century on the definition of 'arbitration'.[101] Although many subsequent historians would continue to praise, like Worcester had already prematurely done, the early treaties between Britain and the United States as the beginnings of modern arbitration, these 'arbitrations' should be nuanced. None of these commissions managed to settle the boundary, so that following treaties would discard with bilateral commissions, opting instead to resort to a head of state directly, or, later still, to an international college of jurists.[102] Arbitration would continue to be developed in the later U.S. peace movement, by pacifists who had witnessed the fallout of the Treaty of Ghent's failure to definitively settle the Canadian boundary issues. The lonely editor of the *Friend of Peace,* preferring to establish a popular base first, did not examine it all in great detail, and limited himself to promoting whatever forms of pacific dispute resolution he found out about in the press.

A self-educated man interested mostly in theology, Worcester had nonetheless managed to read at least one classic of international legal doctrine: *De iure belli ac pacis.* Grotius's tomes confused him. On the one hand, this 'justly celebrated author' appeared to be an 'advocate of war in certain cases', conceding for instance the right of states to wage war not only in defence, but also to recover debt and property, and to punish offences. Grotius also advocated 'arbitration' as a peaceful substitute, alongside a

98 FP (1816, n° II), 35.

99 FP (1827, appendix n° I), 16.

100 Zollman, 'Mediation and Arbitration' 2020, 163.

101 See chapters 2 and 7 for a more detailed discussion.

102 Zollman, 'Mediation and Arbitration' 2020, 161; Henry King, and James Graham, 'Origins of Modern International Law'. *Dispute Resolution Journal* 51(1) (1995), 48.

congress and more outmoded alternatives. Yet on the other hand, this 'high authority' went into great detail to distinguish between the 'just' and 'unjust' causes of war, and asserted that an individual Christian ought to disobey orders to fight in wars he might have personally deemed unjust. If enough Christians would truly follow their consciences, the reverend reasoned, and acted on Grotius's plea that peace should be chosen if less costly than war, few wars would be waged.[103]

As was to be expected, Worcester latched onto those passages in which Grotius followed Christian morality to the extent it agreed with his own views. However, he sidestepped those passages where Grotius's theological assumptions confirmed classic Augustinian traditions, or where Grotius went even further to describe an entirely human-made 'voluntary' law of nations.[104] The proverbial father of international had in common with Worcester or Dodge that he was a deeply religious man who extensively relied on the Bible as a source not only of moral, but also of legal obligation. Unlike pacifists, however, Grotius remained a lawyer versed in the realities of diplomacy and politics. Thus, Grotius devoted a considerable number of pages of his treatise trying to legitimise war on grounds of so-called 'divine voluntary law' – i.e. Biblical injunctions that could further prohibit what natural or positive law allowed.[105] Many of the relevant scriptural passages Grotius referenced were, in fact, evergreens of the nineteenth century peace movement also. However, this international lawyer used his lawyerly interpretative techniques – alternately reading each passage more restrictively, or more widely, as it suited his purposes – to arrive at the opposite conclusions of peace friends. Contrary to moderate peace friends, Romans 13 did not limit itself to the domestic realm. Isaiah's prophecy of a kingdom where 'they shall beat their swords into ploughshares' could not have any bearing on the justifiability of contemporary wars, let alone on Millennial action. The Sermon on the Mount, likewise, was not addressed to public officials, and furthermore did not apply to serious injustices.[106]

Having cited Grotius only once or twice at any length, even the moderate advocates of peace within the Massachusetts Peace Society held almost as little stock in just cause doctrine as the ones from New York.[107] Drawing on recent and older political events, Worcester and other pacifists could not

103 FP (1827, n°), 161–4.

104 Neff, *War* 2005, 97–98; de Blois, 'Grotius on Pacifism' 2011, 22.

105 de Blois, 'Grotius on Pacifism' 2011, 21–5, 38–9.

106 de Blois, 'Grotius on Pacifism' 2011, 21–5.

107 FP (1821, n° XI), 30; FP (1827, n° V), 137.

think of a single war in which both sides had not solemnly proclaimed to God the justness of their respective causes.[108] The subtle distinction between 'defensive' and 'offensive' war, or – put into Grotian language – between 'just' and 'unjust' war, was regarded as mostly academic. As Worcester reasoned it: 'to speak against offensive wars, or wars of aggression, is to speak against all the wars which are waged. This (…) is a reason why so little has been said in the *Friend of Peace* to distinguish between offensive and defensive war. It would be impossible to make a distinction which each of two rulers at war would not interpret in his own favour.'[109] Even if the Massachusetts Peace Society did not exclude the theoretical possibility of a truly defensive, or 'just', war, this case was seen as so remote that the moderate peace campaign did not therefore rule out the cooperation of those radicals, such as Whelpley, who were interested in pursuing more concrete legal reforms. Neither society seemed to have been aware of the fact that 'defence' as such was a relatively meaningless concept in juridical doctrine, as mentioned above.[110] Largely unaware of the intellectual debates on it, both peace societies agreed that the indeterminate requirements of 'just cause' existed mostly as easily circumventable paper law.

Similar agreement could be found on the existing *ius in bello*. Moderate pacifists could, just as much as radical pacifists, not believe that the 'laws and usages of war' allowed for rulers to conscript and impress citizens into their armies and navies, quarter troops in homes, employ spies, but summarily hang those of the enemy, or even 'burn whole villages, towns and cities'.[111] In short, no worse code could have been devised 'had all the rulers in Christendom sworn allegiance to Satan himself, and applied to him a code of laws after his own heart'.[112]

Of particular interest to Worcester, and many subsequent American peace friends, was the custom of outfitting individual vessels with letters of marque in order to legally raid enemy commerce. No doubt influenced by the role privateers had played in the War of 1812, the *Friend of Peace*

108 E.g. FP (1816, n° XII), 1–3.

109 FP (1823, n° VI), 170.

110 Neff, *War* 2005, 204. See also supra.

111 Atrocities from the Napoleonic Wars were frequently brought up, such as Napoleon's execution of the garrison at Jaffa in 1799, or the British bombardment of Copenhagen in 1807. E.g. FP (1816, n° VIII), 15–24.

112 Ibid., 20.

strongly clamoured for the abolition of this form of legalised piracy.[113] This particular theme would continue to feature prominently in antebellum peace activism right up until the 1856 Declaration of Paris.[114] In keeping with his moderate pacifist views of government, Worcester displayed great interest in a memorial laid down in 1819 before Congress against privateering.[115] He sent a letter promoting the memorial to Thomas Jefferson, and dutifully reported in his journal on its subsequent treatment in the Senate Foreign Relations Committee, and that committee's positive report.[116]

Believing that that such legislative actions could force the United States to unilaterally abandon the practice, the reverend Worcester already prefigured the parliamentary peace campaigns of the next decade.[117] In the late 1820s, a speaker from one of the local peace societies answered the commonly asked question: what good could possibly be expected from a handful of scattered peace societies? 'Do any imagine that these associations (…) will exert any considerable influence on the great ones of the earth?' Aware of their obvious minority position, moderates did not expect that they would immediately be 'heard in the halls of Congress, or in the courts of emperors and kings'; or that, if they were, they would be 'much regarded'. However, pacifist belief in the power of public opinion – reinforced by their earlier mentioned teleological conception of historical progress – ensured that adherents, such as the speaker, were confident in their cause's eventual success. As more and more communities would be converted, the peace voice would find its way into Congress and the House of Commons.[118]

As such, many of the fundamentals required for a political and legal peace campaign had been laid by the earliest peace societies, and especially the Massachusetts Peace Society. Overall in agreement with the religious tenets of the radical pacifists in New York and elsewhere, moderate peace

---

113 Although admitted to be a positive custom, it was rejected on the naturalist ground of being neither 'the law of reason nor conscience'. For instance in FP (1816, n° XI), 22–8; FP (1821, n° II), 12–4; FP (1821, n° V), 29–30; FP (1821, n° IX), 28–33; FP (1821, n° XI), 25–31; FP (1823, n° XI), 342; FP (1827, appendix n° III), 65–7.

114 See chapter 4 for more on pacifism and the Declaration of Paris.

115 John Gallison, *A Proposed Memorial to the Congress of the United States* (Boston: unknown publisher 1819).

116 The former president referred to the 1785 Prussian-American treaty of Amity and Commerce, which Worcester and subsequent peace friends abundantly cited in this context. FP (1821, n° V), 38; FP (1821, n° VI), 31–3; FP (1821, n° VI), 39–40; FP (1821, n° VII), 36–7; FP (1821, n° VII), 38–40; VP (1823, n° VIII), 238–40.

117 FP (1821, n° II), 9–14.

118 FP (1827, appendix n° I), 23–4.

friends distinguished themselves through their greater relative trust in political institutions. Their Millennial aspirations did not necessarily put them out of mainstream legal culture, but corresponded closely to existing modes of legal argument, to the extent natural law was still relied upon in both domestic and international law. However, their uniquely pacifist theological convictions led peace friends to reject most of the concrete normative solutions devised by mainstream international legal doctrine. Although claiming to encompass a broader ideological scope than radicals, moderate peace friends stood just as sceptical as radicals to the accepted legal doctrines of just cause or formal war. Hence, there existed some leeway for a peace organisation that could unite both pacifist factions, and bring about concrete political action, once the popular base had been sufficiently secured.

Politicisation, however, required a more sophisticated and explicitly legalist approach than hitherto contemplated. If war was the international equivalent of a legal trial, it followed that greater thought ought to be given to substitutes. American friends of peace would need to consider in greater detail the means through which arbitration could replace war. They would need to engage more closely with political precedents. They would need to study the classical treatises of international law. Most of all, however, they would need a capable leader, who could coordinate the efforts of the disparate local peace societies, and bring their collective weight to bear on state legislatures and on Congress.

Neither Worcester nor Dodge were fit for that role. Dodge was too radical and exclusionary, while the great moderate, Noah Worcester, felt the burden of his responsibilities to begin to weigh heavily by his seventieth birthday in 1828. Having edited the *Friend of Peace* for years, he wished to dedicate himself more closely to Christ's atonement, a strictly theological issue.[119] His status as a peace leader had by then become entrenched into myth.[120] However, Worcester had reassured himself that the cause was in good hands before he laid down his offices within the Massachusetts Peace Society.

---

119 Ware, *Memoirs* 1844, 77–8.

120 Later admirers pointed out 'the sublime poverty of this bravehearted Apostle – who, to publish his never praised periodical, was content to live on bread and water, make his own shoes, and deny himself most of those comforts, which are to other men necessities'. Holland quoted in Ziegler, *Antebellum* 1992, 25.

In 1828, the *Friend of Peace* announced the founding of the American Peace Society in New York.[121] Most peace societies, including the Massachusetts Peace Society and the New York Peace Society, turned themselves into auxiliaries of the new national organisation. Both Dodge and Worcester retained a membership until the day they died.[122] The helm, however, was from then on in the capable hands of a retired sea captain from Maine, named William Ladd (1778–1841).

2 The American Peace Society

As a young man, William Ladd stared down the barrel of the loaded gun of one of his neighbours. The man had recently lost one of his sons in a duel, and consoled himself by his belief that his son had 'died like a *man*'. Unfortunately, Ladd had immediately replied that the boy had 'died like a *fool*'. Despite his lack of diplomacy, Ladd managed to convince his neighbour to lower his weapon and leave without bloodshed.[123] Unlike with Dodge, the incident did not immediately lead to a pacifist conversion. Still, Ladd had showed himself already in his younger years averse not only to duelling, but also to other immoral elements in U.S. culture, including the ways in which his fellow citizens treated Native Americans and African slaves.[124]

Born in Exeter, New Hampshire, Ladd graduated from Harvard University in 1797, but afterwards chose the life of a merchant captain in the family company. For about fifteen years, he sailed across the world, until the War of 1812 and its accompanying British blockade of American ports caused him to retire from naval life, and take over the family farm in Minot, Maine. A prosperous estate, Ladd became a wealthy man with the leisure time and the financial means needed to devote himself to a good cause. It was only after he spoke with Jesse Appleton (1772–1819), president of Bowdoin College, that Ladd first heard of the existence of peace societies. Sceptical at first, Ladd wrote about it: 'the idea then passed over my mind as the daydream of benevolence; and so everyone views the subject, who does not

121 FP (1827, appendix n° III), 96; FP (1827, appendix n° II), 54–55; FP (1827, n° XII), 384.

122 Lawson, *Swords into Plowshares* 1975, 545–46, 549.

123 John Hemmenway, *The Apostle of Peace. Memoir of William Ladd, with an Introduction by Elihu Burritt* (Boston: American Peace Society 1872), 33–4.

124 See infra in this chapter for more on Native Americans. See chapter 6 for more on slavery.

examine it'. However, a seed had been planted, and soon afterwards Ladd came into the possession of a copy of Worcester's *Solemn Review.* Around the early 1820s, he began to read issues of the *Friend of Peace* and ventured on the road that would lead to his enduring fame.[125]

Ladd's efforts in the peace cause were energetic. Not only publishing the essays of 'Philanthropos', he copy-edited several of the American Peace Society's journals, and provided many of its articles. These journals were the *Harbinger of Peace* until 1831, the *Calumet* until 1835, and the *Advocate of Peace* from 1835 until the 1930s. Unlike Worcester's *Friend of Peace,* with which these formed a continuum as the voice of mainstream American pacifism, these later periodicals contained contributions from a variety of authors, and went through a great many editors, lengths, and publication schedules.[126] Ladd also wrote letters to various European monarchs, as well as a number of tracts and pamphlets on assorted peace issues.[127] The ones which most of all determined his wider legacy were those that related to a congress of nations and the reform of international law. Less handily accessible today, but also of major importance, were the numerous speeches that Ladd gave on countless occasions. Preferring to serve as the society's general agent – he served only one term as president, and another as corresponding secretary – Ladd travelled the lecture circuit for years, constantly trying to recruit new adherents, found new auxiliaries, and convince the American public of a congress of nations.[128]

Despite increasing health issues – including a stroke in 1833 – Ladd persevered in his endeavours, and during his journeys sometimes preached at least three ninety-minute sermons in three different churches on a single Sunday.[129] In the end no longer able to speak standing up, William Ladd passed away in March 1841. Characterised by Peter Brock as 'one of the most attractive figures of the early peace movement', Ladd was praised by those who knew him for many things, but especially for his easygoingness and his

125 Hemmenway, *Memoir Ladd* 1872, 27–38; William Ladd, *The Essays of Philanthropos on Peace & War* (Portland: Shirley & Edwards 1825), 4.

126 David Lawson and Warren Kuehl, 'Journals of the American Peace Society'. *World Affairs* 141(2) (1978), 183–95; Hemmenway, *Memoir Ladd* 1872, 12, 48–50.

127 William Ladd, 'History of the Peace Societies', in Samuel Fish et. al. (eds.), *Scientific Tracts for the Diffusion of Useful Knowledge* (Boston: Light & Stearns 1836), 169–90; William Ladd, *The Hero of Macedon, or History of Alexander the Great viewed in the Light of the Gospel* (Boston: Loring 1832); William Ladd, *On the Duty of Females to promote the Cause of Peace* (Boston: Ford 1836).

128 Lawson, *Swords into Plowshares* 1975, 545.

129 Hemmenway, *Memoir Ladd* 1872, 96–7.

FIGURE 1.1 William Ladd, the amiable founder of the American Peace Society.

sense of humour.[130] Those who have ever had the pleasure of trying to argue with a modern moralist might agree with Ladd's eulogiser: 'the common fault of reformers is, that they are intolerant in their feelings, and denunciatory in their language'. Ladd was not at all disposed to feeling superior, but was always quick to find sympathy through a joke or a story.[131] Revealingly, William Lloyd Garrison (1805–1879), a leader of the radicals, was among the few who took umbrage at Ladd's good-humoured nature. He described him as 'a huge and strange compound of fat, good nature, and

130 Brock, *Pacifism* 1968, 483. One contemporary anecdote had him at a party playing with the children 'as though he were one of them'. Upon being told that an adult should put away childish things, Ladd said: 'Ah, I fear that I shall never be a *man*. I can never be anything more than a *Ladd*'. His friend regretted that Ladd would tell such jokes even from the pulpit. William Ladd, *An Essay on a Congress of Nations for the Adjustment of International Disputes without Resort to Arms, by William Ladd. Reprinted from the Original Edition of 1840 with an Introduction by James Brown Scott. With a New Introduction by Mark Weston Janis* (New Jersey: Lawbook Exchange 2007), ix.

131 Ibid., 268–70.

benevolence'.[132] Arguably, Garrisson had listed the very traits that had allowed his rival to forge the uneasy alliance between radicals and moderates that was the American Peace Society.

In many ways, the American Peace Society was the national successor of the Massachusetts Peace Society. This should not surprise, given that the American Peace Society's original constitution was drafted by none other than Noah Worcester.[133] The document consequently excelled in vagueness regarding the moral distinction between offensive and defensive war, allowing anyone to interpret it as they wished – it spoke only of a society designed to 'diffuse light respecting the evils of war, and the best means of effecting its abolition'.[134] The accompanying first circular, written by Ladd, was written in a similar spirit. The opening issue of the *Harbinger,* containing both documents, indicated that the society, as well as the pages of its periodical, welcomed 'all who seek the abolition of war, whether they hold to the lawfulness of defensive war, or condemn all war in every shape'.[135] That being said, it was as clear to the leadership of the national organisation, as it had been to the peace societies before it, that truly defensive wars were a rare bird indeed. They believed that most every conqueror in human history, from Tamerlane to Napoleon, had tried to justify their wars of naked aggression as 'defensive'. Rather, the American Peace Society would 'not even attempt to define, for to define would be to decide'.[136] Instead, the peace society's official position focussed, like the one in Massachusetts, on turning larger public opinion against 'all wars of aggression', erroneously believing that this would also silence the debate on defensive war. Like Worcester's peace society, the American Peace Society could even outright 'approve' of a real defensive war *'carried on Christian principles',* but in practice not one interstate war ever met with the peace society's official approval.[137]

---

132 Curti, *Crusade* 1929, 83; Aileen Kraditor, *Means and Ends in American Abolitionism. Garrison and his Critics on Strategy and Tactics, 1834–1850* (New York: Random House 1967), ix–x, 27–32.

133 Harbinger of Peace (hereafter: Harbinger) (May 1828), 6.

134 Ibid. 17.

135 Ibid., 7.

136 This continued the mistaken notion among peace friends that 'just cause' equated to defensive war.

137 The U.S. Civil War being the exception, on the grounds that it was not an interstate war. See chapter 6.

The name of the national society was somewhat misleading, because it was more aspirational than descriptive. The more accurate title would have been the 'New England' Peace Society, rather than the 'American' Peace Society. Although a handful of peace societies existed in Southern or Western States, such as Kentucky, Georgia, South Carolina, Ohio and Illinois, these were usually unviable, and did not actively contribute. The New England peace societies wrote with distaste on the habit in the South or in the frontier territories to carry bowie knives and side-arms, and on the duels and gunfights it facilitated.[138] In the South, the peace movement was never popular, associated as it was with Northern abolitionism. Although the American Peace Society went to sometimes great lengths to distinguish its official objective from extraneous ones, most of its individual members did in fact also support other causes, like anti-slavery. Whatever hopes the society entertained of preserving a foothold in the Southern states were carefully destroyed by one of its more radical members, the attorney Thomas Grimké (1786–1834), likely the only person to have possessed both a membership card to a peace society and a slave plantation at the same time. His uncompromising Unionist and non-resistant stances during the South Carolina nullification crisis of the early 1830s made him an outcast in his state, and with him the peace society.[139] More in general, the American Peace Society, though at times remarkably capable to attract attention and make itself heard in Congress and with U.S. presidents, remained the centre of a small movement.[140] The society and its thirtyish auxiliaries never counted more than about 1,500 members prior to the Civil War, within a national

138 AP (November 1838), 133–134; AP (December 1839), 93–94; AP (September & October 1845), 115–6; AP (July 1846), 154–5.

139 Thomas Grimké was for a time a very influential young member of the American Peace Society, but he died young. He claimed that if Charleston were attacked by pirates with him as mayor, he would offer no resistance, but meet the attackers with a procession of Sunday-school children. These factors ensured that the peace movement lost all credibility in the South. The peace society nonetheless paid much attention to his views, which sparked a polemic between opponents and proponents of defensive war. Thomas Grimké, *An Oration on the Absolute Necessity of Union, and the Folly and Madness of Disunion* (Charleston: Riley 1829); Thomas Grimké, *To the People of the State of South-Carolina* (Charleston, 1832); 180–2; Manisha Sinha, *The counterrevolution of Slavery. Politics and Ideology in Antebellum South Carolina* (Chapel Hill: University of North Carolina Press 2000), 95–123; The Calumet (July & August 1832), 225–34; The Calumet (May & June 1833), 403–6; The Calumet (January & February 1834), 524–32.

140 Although many attorneys, judges, professors, merchants and clergymen were involved, the peace movement never found much acceptance in the upper-most layers of politics and business.

population that skyrocketed from about 8,000,000 to 31,000,000 in the same period.[141] Its members were also divided on the society's ideological course.

Uniting both moderates and radicals, the American Peace Society balanced for years on a tightrope between the two factions. William Ladd himself had started off as a moderate, who could not bring himself to deny the theoretical option of a defensive war. Joining him were many of the anonymous members, which included judges, lawyers, and even the occasional military officer. Other notable moderates or 'conservatives' – to the extent that term applied to peace activism – within the society were William Allen (1784–1868), the president of Bowdoin College, judge William Jay (1789–1858), son of supreme court justice John Jay, and George Beckwith (1800–1870), a Harvard graduate and a Congregationalist minister. Especially Beckwith – Ladd's eventual successor as the society's leader – would play a decisive part in the internal power struggle that engulfed the society from the 1830s until the late 1840s.[142]

Opposing the alleged 'conservatives' was the so-called 'reform group'.[143] This small, but vocal and active group included some of the most prominent leaders, beginning with Ladd himself. True to Worcester's ideological development, he had begun to radicalise his pacifism in the 1830s, until he reached the full non-resistant standpoint by 1837. However, even then he did not expect others to agree. Other reformists included Samuel Coues (1797–1867), president of the society in the early 1840s, Joshua Blanchard (1782–1868), a fellow-traveller from the Massachusetts Peace Society up until the post-Civil War Universal Peace Union, Amasa Walker (1799–1875), a representative in the Massachusetts legislature, Thomas Upham (1799–1872), a philosopher from Bowdoin College, and Elihu Burritt (1810–1879), the 'learned blacksmith' and one of the most important peace friends of the nineteenth century. The left-wing included anarchist non-resistants like William Lloyd Garrison or Henry Clarke Wright (1797–1870), considered too extreme even by most reformists.[144]

As was the case for the local peace societies, moderates and reformers did not necessarily disagree on the fundamental theological foundations of pacifism or on the course of action to be pursued. Both agreed that divine

141 Lawson, 'Journals' 1978, 189. These were similar numbers to the British movement. See chapter 2.

142 The Calumet (March & April 1835), 207.

143 Curti, *Crusade* 1929, 88–89.

144 These people are discussed infra.

law trumped positive laws, in the moral realm, and that the panacea against the 'custom' of war was an enlightened public opinion.[145] Similar to the anti-slavery or temperance societies, public opinion had to be moulded through tracts, auxiliary societies, public meetings, and Christian prayer.[146] Known as a man who 'exhibited plain, practical, common sense', Ladd had little patience for sophisticated reasonings on natural law or the deeper nature of man.[147] Humanity was not inherently corrupt, but merely under the delusions of a harmful centuries-old custom.[148] From humanity's axiomatic goodness, it followed that this custom could be unlearnt just as well, through education and political action.

2.1 *The Turn to International Law*

Unlike previous societies, the American Peace Society also paid great attention to the political and legal instruments in which an enlightened public opinion could crystallize itself. Ladd alluded in the first issues of his journals, as well as in later essays, to the need for an increase in arbitration, a congress of nations, and specific issues of international law that needed to be addressed.[149] The *Harbinger* also featured criticisms on the general nature of international law near-identical character to those found among the earlier societies. One author wrote, for instance, that 'the law of nations acknowledges the right of the conqueror'. Unlike ordinary criminals, who were more upfront about the nature of their crimes, the author lamented, monarchs like Frederick the Great hired 'some "laborious civilian"' to draw up a manifesto, but such a document was usually nothing more than a pretext, since it would often be published after the actual invasion had taken place.[150] The *Calumet* was generally of the same tenor, arguing that the law of nations in its current state mostly served as an apology for power politics: 'Selfishness has to a great extent been legalised (…) therefore, the world has been deluged with blood, and the preparations of war regarded as great and necessary works.'[151]

---

145 The New England Non-Resistance Society is likewise discussed infra.

146 Harbinger (May 1828), 11.

147 AP (December 1842), 267.

148 This repeats Worcester and others. Ladd, *Essays of Philanthropos* 1825, 99, 109, 144–5.

149 Ibid., 9–10.

150 'Civilian' meant 'jurist' in this context, as also elsewhere in their propaganda. Harbinger (August 1830), 86.

151 The Calumet (May & June 1832), 194; The Calumet (March & April 1834), 548.

Unlike its predecessors, the American Peace Society was increasingly vocal about actively advancing legal reform. The very first issue of the *Advocate of Peace* dealt with the progress of international law through history. The article was written by one Francis Fellowes (1803–1888), a young Connecticut lawyer, who was the chief editor at the time, and also one of the earliest American peace friends to take a closer look at international law itself.[152] His sources were those to be expected from a young law school graduate, in an era when most curricula did not yet include any courses on the laws of nations.[153] Fellowes did not cite the classical treatises directly, but drew instead from the major law books known to a contemporary American attorney, such as James Kent's *Commentaries on American Law,* and William Blackstone's *Commentaries on the Laws of England.*[154] He also drew from supreme court justice Joseph Story's inaugural address.[155] Maybe because of this, as well Fellowes's intention to legitimise his recourse to the law of nations, the jurist praised the historical progress international law had made since classical antiquity. The Greeks, the Romans, and the people of the middle ages had only known 'barbarous' international laws. The great watershed had taken place with Grotius, who had collected, fashioned and arranged the disparate legal materials into 'a system'. The young jurist's esteem for Grotius was profound. He praised the Dutch scholar as genius akin to Newton, who had done much to bring the 'principles and practices of nations' far closer to the 'precepts of Christianity'. 'Since the time of Grotius', the editor went on, 'the science of international law has been in a state of almost constant progression.' He believed the law of nations had become a 'highly cultivated science. The mutual rights and reciprocal duties of nations are now pretty well defined and understood'. Thus, the young lawyer asked: 'What remains to be done?'[156]

This and other articles by Fellowes during his editorship were illustrative of wider tactical thinking within the peace society, especially because of the legal call to action his pieces contained. Although Fellowes himself was surprisingly optimistic about international law's current state – compared to

152 AP (June 1834), 33–47.

153 Manfred Lachs, *The Teacher in International Law: Teachings and Teaching* (Dordrecht: Martinus Nijhoff 1987), 159–72.

154 AP (June 1834), 41, 44–45; James Kent, *Commentaries on American Law, vol. 1* (New York: Halsted 1826), 1–20.

155 Joseph Story, *A Discourse pronounced upon the Inauguration of the Author as Dane Professor of Law in Harvard University, on the Twenty-Fifth Day of August, 1829* (Boston: Hilliard, Gray, Little, and Wilkins 1829).

156 AP (June 1834), 36–43.

many others – and misread significant parts of Grotius, he was not blind to the deficiencies of the law of nations as pointed out by his peers.[157] Both Blackstone and Kent, to his disliking, still referred to war as 'one of the highest trials of right', even though it almost never settled the underlying legal question that had caused the conflict. Also, according to Fellowes and many others, war lacked the procedural guarantees of penal law: war did not have a disinterested judge, an impartial jury, or a distinction between the legislative and the judicial power of government.[158] Both sides decided their case for themselves, and did not allow the other to defend himself on neutral grounds, so that the whole affair was an *ex parte* proceeding, in flagrant violation of the adage *nemo iudex in causa sua*.[159] Lord Mansfield had always warned of the importance of that fundamental. However, states had to accept that they were accountable to the same Christian morality as individuals.[160] In sum, Fellowes want to transpose the rationality of domestic judicial processes into the law of nations, as inspired by Christianity, a theme repeated throughout the entire later peace through law campaign.

What separated Fellowes and others from most earlier peace friends, was his far more explicit focus on the reform of international law as a focal point of concertation. The feats of Grotius and others had to be built upon by the peace friends. In this important task, Fellowes believed, the competing factions within the peace society could unite in a practical objective that did not ruffle any internal feathers, and would also connect with the larger public. International legal reform, he insisted, did not immediately touch upon the controversial questions of either 'absolute non-resistance', nor on the political feasibility of a 'great international court'.[161] Instead of 'pursuing a shadow', as Fellowes had himself once believed about peace societies, they would finally be seen as seeking realist change. After all, considering what Grotius had achieved by his lonesome, what would the collective efforts of pacifists, radical and moderate, not accomplish with regards to international law? Any criticisms, he imagined, might as well have been directed to Grotius two hundred years ago.[162]

157 This recalls Worcester's dubious readings of Grotius.
158 AP (March 1836), 357–8.
159 Meaning no one can be judge in one's own case.
160 Ibid., 359–361.
161 AP (June 1834), 34–5.
162 Ibid., 42.

2.2 *American Critiques of Law*

Fellowes had reason to suspect that he had hit upon something. In 1836, he reviewed the *Manual of Peace* of professor Thomas Cogswell Upham of Bowdoin College in Maine.[163] The book was one of the most well-known and esteemed publications connected to the American Peace Society.[164] In the year of his death, 1872, Upham was praised in the *Advocate's* obituary for 'this important work', especially the sizeable second and third parts, on the law of nations.[165] Those lengthy passages were, however, preceded by many chapters in which the religious, moral, economical and humanitarian case against war was made.[166] To the fears of moderates like Francis Fellowes, Upham was a moral philosopher who implored the peace societies to adopt 'the principle that, all wars whatever, both offensive and *defensive*, are repugnant to the precepts and spirit of the Gospel, and are sinful'. His reasoning was as simple as it was familiar: 'with scarcely a single exception, all nations which engage in war allege, that they do it in self-defence'. If the peace societies were to rock the boat and attract public attention, Upham felt, they would have to endorse the non-resistant standpoint in public.[167] This, Upham substantiated with religious argumentation familiar since Dodge or the London Peace Society's propaganda.[168] Fellowes could not agree with the notion that the state, 'in the *actual* state of society', could not take human life 'in *certain* cases'.[169] Nonetheless, his positive review took care to emphasise that the improvement of international law could be a shared object for all friends of peace, whatever their motives, be it 'from interest, from reason, from humanity, from justice, from benevolence, from the gospel'.[170] In the lengthy second part of the 'manual', called 'Suggestions on the law of nations', Upham had agreed with his more conservative

163 AP (March 1836), 361–81.

164 Thomas Upham was a Congregationalist minister. His *Manual* received an American Peace Society edition in 1842, regarded by the London Peace Society as one of the best books on peace. Phelps, *Anglo-American Peace Movement* 1930, 71; Alfred Fuchs, 'Upham, Thomas Cogswell', in *American National Biography Online*. 2000, available at: doi.org/10.1093/anb/9780198606697.article.1601684.

165 AP (May 1872), 180–181; Upham, Thomas. *The Manual of Peace; exhibiting the Evils and Remedies of War* (Boston: American Peace Society, 1842), 4.

166 Thomas Upham, *The Manual of Peace* (New York: Leavitt, Lord, & Co., 1836), 7–251.

167 Ibid., 162–163.

168 Upham, *Manual* 1836, 96–145. See also infra and supra in this chapter.

169 Ibid., 371–372.

170 AP (March 1836), 375.

colleagues that international law was 'a vast field', and that 'the time has come for a remodelling of its features'.[171]

Although the American friends of peace always claimed to be working towards universal peace, the specific issues of international law they focussed on resonated strongly with American interests. It should perhaps not surprise that Upham immediately after his reflections on the gospel's uses for international law turned to the subject of neutral rights. As subsequent pacifists would contemplate until well into the twentieth century, a major pacific advance could already be achieved by confining the hostilities to the military forces of the belligerent states.[172] The American Peace Society set itself apart from other pacific voices in the 1830s by its engagement with the laws of maritime neutrality.

That concern could be partly explained by the society's connections to the New England mercantile industry. Major leaders like Coues and Blanchard, for instance, were involved in business ventures that handled several hundred thousand dollars a year.[173] Many members of the society still had first- or second-hand experience with the royal navy's blockades and quasi-blockades of American ports during the Napoleonic wars and the War of 1812. Even if the long-standing policy of the United States had been one of voluntary neutrality in the bloody European wars, this had not sufficiently shielded American merchants from being targeted: either by Napoleon's so-called 'Berlin and Milan decrees' – blockading Britain – or by Britain's orders-in-council – blockading France and its allies.[174] American peace friends like Upham, Ladd, or Jay invoked these precedents by name, denouncing them as violations of the law of nations.[175] Britain's extensive exercise of the rights of search and impressment in the past – which the small American

171 Upham, *Manual* 1836, 262.

172 Ibid., 267–268.

173 Ziegler, *Antebellum* 1992, 92–3.

174 Stephen Neff, *The Rights and Duties of Neutrals. A General History* (Manchester: Manchester University Press 2000), 76–82.

175 Harbinger (July 1830), 53; William Ladd, *Essays on Peace & War. New Series* (Portland: Shirley 1827), 91–2; William Ladd, *An Essay on a Congress of Nations, for the Adjustment of International Disputes without Resort to Arms. Containing the Substance of the Rejected Essays on that Subject with Original Thoughts and a Copious Appendix* (Boston: Whipple and Damrell 1840), 539; *Prize Essays on a Congress of Nations* (Boston: Whipple and Damrell 1840), 141–143; Upham, *Manual* 1836, 271–274; William Jay, *The Life of John Jay: with Selections from the Correspondence and Miscellaneous Papers, vol. I* (New York: Harper 1833), 325–6.

navy was powerless to stop – similarly featured prominently in American pacifist propaganda.[176]

Upham was very comprehensive in his analysis of maritime neutrality law, concluding that the key solution lay in the principle of 'free ships make free goods'.[177] This had been the neutral merchant's rallying cry for a long time. According to old just war theory, neutral trade could only be immoral, and it was therefore customary law to regard *all* enemy property on sea as good prize, regardless of the belligerent or neutral status of the ship's flag.[178] Under the new principle, however, all enemy property on board neutral vessels, except for a limited list of contraband items, was to be protected from capture, even if that meant that neutral property on enemy vessels conversely became fair game.[179]

Without disregarding the political quandaries involved, peace friends like Upham were not content merely with the acceptance of the principle of free ships, free goods. Ideally, private property of *all* individuals, even if citizens of belligerent states, 'ought to be held sacred, not only on board neutral ships, but everywhere'. As long as the trade was not for military purposes, the philosopher argued, all private commerce should be held inviolable.[180] In this, he represented a popular viewpoint within the American Peace Society.[181] This was of course a radical standpoint from a political perspective.

However, much like the peace society itself, Upham was not totally blind to political realities. The advantages of this new norm were not only obvious from the neutral standpoint, he reasoned, but also from those of the belligerent, as they would no longer have to bear the cost to militarily protect their trade, delegating it instead to neutrals.[182] Upham remarked that state practice had increasingly recognised this doctrine in treaties since the mid-seventeenth century, the 1785 U.S:-Prussian treaty being just one example

176 See infra.

177 Related subjects included blockades, contraband, privateering, impressment, and the right of search.

178 Neff, *Neutrals* 2000, 26.

179 Ibid., 29–30; Upham, *Manual* 1836, 285.

180 Upham, *Manual* 1836, 286–7.

181 Among many examples, see Harbinger (January & February 1831), 209; AP (January 1845), 6–8; AP (January 1856), 9–10; Ladd, *Essays* 1827, 87; Ladd, *Essay* 1840, 537; Charles Sumner, *Charles Sumner. His Complete Works. With Introduction by Hon. George Frisbie Hoar. Vol. 8* (Boston: Lee and Shepard, 1900), 60–2.

182 Neff, *Neutrals* 2000, 30.

out of many.[183] Yet, it remained 'uncertain' what the actual legal standard was.[184] Even if the vast majority of commercial trade treaties had included a 'free ships, free goods' provision, the doctrine could not be viable in practice until the greatest naval power had accepted it. Despite several attempts to have it enforced, Upham observed, Britain continued to oppose the doctrine, and searched neutral vessels as it pleased. Not even the 1780 League of Armed Neutrality, instigated by Russia, and joined by a significant number of other states, had dissuaded Britain; unsurprising, considering the royal navy still outnumbered all of their fleets combined.[185] British policy-makers did not wish to voluntarily abandon the massive strategic advantage their immense naval superiority afforded, which they believed had strongly contributed to their victory over Napoleon.[186]

State practice in general was a mess. Official legal justifications were often an affront to 'enlightened reason', according to the American professor. Like other contemporaries, Upham recalled the 1807 British bombardment of Copenhagen, a widespread *cause célèbre* of the arrogance of great powers.[187] He too wondered: 'what value can be attached to a law of nations like this, which can be adduced (…) in support of (…) the burning of cities, and the destruction of fleets, not because they have actually committed acts of transgression against us, but because it is within the range of possibilities (…).' He considered Britain's rivals, like France, to be just as hypocritical. All those justifications contradicted themselves, and were therefore nothing but 'false maxims' and 'alleged rights'. Most principles of 'the existing public law' were 'so broad and indefinite, that ambition and intrigue may deduce from it a colorable pretext for any war whatever'.[188]

Doctrine fared little better. As a professor of philosophy at a seat of learning, he had the possibility of consulting the canon of the law of nations, quoting not only directly from Grotius, but also from Mackintosh, Kent, Ward, Martens, Vattel, Barbeyrac, Burlamaqui, Pufendorf, and Bynkershoek. He found out that all of these writers had shared one very grave 'mistake' with Grotius: they had fatally misunderstood 'the intentions and the spirit

183 Upham, *Manual* 1836, 285.

184 Ibid., 346.

185 Ibid., 285–6; Éric Schnakenbourg, *Entre la guerre et la paix. Neutralité et relations internationales, XVIIe–XVIIIe siècles* (Rennes: Presses Universitaires de Rennes 2013), 201–18.

186 Lemnitzer, *Privateering* 2014, 11.

187 Šedivý, Miroslav. *Si vis Pacem, para Bellum. The Italian Response to International Insecurity, 1830–1848* (Vienna: Austrian Academy of Sciences, 2021), 20, 38–39, 299.

188 Upham, *Manual* 1836, 327–33.

of the New Testament on the subject of war'. Unlike Worcester, Fellowes and others, Upham realised that Grotius had used his scriptural knowledge to delegitimise pacifism. While Grotius had – 'from a preconceived bias on the subject', according to Upham – wilfully misunderstood the gospel's anti-war message, his successors had been too secular in their reasoning, by relying 'upon human authority and human reason alone'.[189] The problem with human authority was that it was typically 'controlled by the pressure of interest, rather than on the dictates of rectitude'. Because of this, 'the law of nations, as it is laid down in professed writers on that law, partially fails, at least, to satisfy the doubts, and to control the conduct of nations'.[190]

If legal textbooks wanted to guide the way, and provide the theoretical outlines for a law of nations that could not be abused at will by politics, then they would have to rely on a rock-solid foundation: 'the gospel ought to be made the standard'.[191] Upham's suggestions laid bare the American religious interpretation of natural law. Peace friends were far from alone in conflating natural law with divine law. It was self-evident for any American jurist in the 1830s that the principles of the common law generally corresponded to God's will, or had to if they were to operate successfully in practice. No one respected a lawyer who simply piled up facts without any sight on the underlying principles of reason and justice that these facts represented. An American judge who invoked natural law around this time would modestly claim that he had only 'discovered' God-given precepts of natural reason, even if he was really setting fully human-made policy. Religion and law were profoundly intertwined in the antebellum United States. One simply could not question God this way – nor the professional self-image of lawyers as the privileged interlocutors of divine will.[192]

Both American attorneys and peace friends like Upham understood that divine natural law needed human agency before it could manifest itself in positive law, and have a material impact. A pacifist like Upham was of course much more radical and idealistic than the average New England attorney. His damning assessments of the many failings of the law of nations led him to reject most sources of international law. Both official diplomats and theorists had proven themselves far too willing to compromise on the tenets of scripture. The only means to bring the wisdom of the New Testament into the positive law of nations, and in doing so give real political

189 Ibid., 254–5, 259, 265, 269, 279–80, 303, 323–4, 388.
190 Upham, *Manual* 1836, 380, 383–5.
191 Ibid., 265–266.
192 Banner, *Natural Law* 2021, 41–2.

teeth to humanity's innate sense of morality, was through 'an international congress'.[193]

2.3 *A Congress of Nations*

The first practical objective of the American Peace Society was to promote the founding of a great international 'congress of nations'. The society envisioned a permanent diplomatic assembly, where the representatives of every 'civilised' state would be able to discuss common issues. This congress had to codify international law through open deliberations on an equal footing. Accompanying this congress was the equally important 'high court of nations', an international judicial court for settling all interstate disputes. These institutions would ensure that states too became subject to the rule of law. Proposals in this vein took American pacifism by storm during the 1830s, and developed into one of the most enduring legal legacies of the early American Peace Society.

Initially, most of the society was in favour of the idea. The greatest pusher of the idea was William Ladd himself. The opening circular in the very first issue of the *Harbinger* already had an appeal for 'amicable discussion and arbitration' by 'a congress of Christian nations'.[194] Ladd had long believed that 'public opinion, as expressed by compact and agreement, among nations' would stop war. His reasoning was the same as Upham's. International law had too long been relying on the 'conflicting opinions of civilians', and on bilateral treaties broken as soon as the parties again came to blows.[195]

Both conservative and reformist members of the society could rally behind this concrete ambition. The reformist member Joshua Blanchard wrote to Ladd from the Massachusetts auxiliary that 'the project of establishing a court of nations' could garner support even from those otherwise uncaring about peace doctrines. According to an anonymous letter, 'one well-directed stroke of policy' could achieve 'splendid' results.[196] Others agreed that such a legal tactic would be more persuasive on the political level than religion alone. The felt that most politicians were 'either warriors themselves, or advocates for the war system'. The clergy of the larger denominations was similarly 'under the same delusions respecting the war policy', or too afraid

193 Ibid., 386–7.

194 The idea had been stirring in his mind for some time, as evident in his essays from the 1820s. Harbinger (May 1828), 10; Ladd, *Essays* 1827, 236.

195 'Civilian' meant 'jurist' in this context. Other authors also used this term. Ladd, *Essays* 1827, 236, 287–8.

196 Harbinger (June 1830), 32–4.

to speak against it.[197] Unsurprisingly, conservative members of the society – always on the lookout for ways to reconcile pacifism with government – were just as intrigued by a 'grand council of nations' or a 'high arbitral tribunal'. These men agreed with their more reformist colleagues that 'what is called the law of nations hardly deserves the name of law'. They complained: 'How can nations be under the governance of public law, when each is a judge in his own cause; when there is no grand court of national justice; (…); no original contract, and solemn, mutual agreement to abide by the decision?'[198] Only the most radical members, many of them budding non-resistants, confessed to having 'little faith' in the plan, because they distrusted government in general as cultural pessimists.[199]

2.3.1 Prize Essays on a Congress of Nations

The growing maturity of the American peace movement manifested itself in its concern for a more intellectually developed plan for a congress of nations. Between 1829 and 1839, the American Peace Society was involved in a long-running essay competition on the subject, a favoured instrument by learned academies and contemporary benevolent societies, including other peace societies. A first premium was offered at the first annual meeting of the society in 1829, which did not achieve much result: even after raising the premium to fifty dollars and postponing it a couple of times until May 1832, only a handful of submissions came in, and none of them were deemed to have much merit.[200] In response, two anonymous gentlemen from New York took matters in hand, raising the premium to a respectable 500 dollars – as well as 100 dollars for the second best – and extending the deadline to the end of 1832.[201] This sizeable financial incentive did the trick, and thirty-seven entries arrived, including one in Latin and one sent in from Rio de Janeiro.[202] Unfortunately, the jury did not succeed in singling out one winner, instead recommending the five best. It eventually took another six years before the American Peace Society simply decided to publish these five texts, as well as a final sixth essay penned by Ladd himself.

197 Harbinger (November 1830), 159.

198 Said by William Allen, a vocal proponent of defensive war. The Calumet (Marx & April 1834), 560–1.

199 The Calumet (July & August 1834), 54.

200 They had to be sent to David Low Dodge in New York. Van der Linden, *Peace Movement* 1987, 133; Harbinger (November 1829), 169.

201 Van der Linden, *Peace Movement* 1987, 134.

202 The Calumet (July & August 1834), 60.

Published in 1840, the *Prize Essays on a Congress of Nations* remained arguably the greatest intellectual achievement of the antebellum American peace movement.[203]

Although the contest was taken extremely seriously by the American Peace Society, the actual prize question was phrased somewhat vague. The original notice merely asked for a dissertation 'on the subject of a congress of nations for the prevention of war' that 'shall specify the particular object of the congress, and the mode by which its stipulations may be enforced'.[204] From 1831 onward, it was further specified that any solution had to be 'without resort to arms', which all eventual winners complied with.[205] No doubt, this was intended to satisfy the pressure of the reformist faction within the society, and made the American plan stand out from most contemporary European schemes.[206]

Although the dogma of non-violence was unassailable, the whole point of the contest was to break out of the narrow evangelical base from which the peace society had up until then been operating. The organisers stressed that contestants could not confine themselves to religious arguments for a congress of nations, but that they would also need to analyse it from the point of view of *international law*. They emphasised that the jury would be recruited from 'among the first jurists and civilians of our country', as well as statesmen and legislators.[207] They outright stated that the society was trying to build up an argument that would appeal to people as 'mental and rational beings' – after all 'a great proportion of national disputes arise where religion has not always been a welcome visitor'.[208]

The jury committee indeed consisted of men living in socio-political spheres the peace society had traditionally not been able to reach. While friends of peace generally did not belong to the working classes, they – save

203 The peace society raised the stakes to 1,000 dollars in 1834. The average income of a common labourer in Massachusetts was about a dollar a day. Some essays had been self-published by their authors in the meantime. Upham, *Manual* 1832; Origen Bacheler, *Dissertation on a Congress of Nations, for the Adjustment of International Disputes without Recourse to Arms* (New York: Collier 1837); John Bolles, *Essay on a Congress of Nations for the Pacific Adjustment of International Disputes* (Boston: Whipple & Damrell 1839); AP (June 1835), 226–27; *Prize Essays* 1840, iii–vi.

204 Harbinger (November 1829), 169.

205 Van der Linden, *Peace Movement* 1987, 139.

206 None of the continental-European prize essays prohibited the violent enforcement of international law.

207 The Calumet (July & August 1831), 64; The Calumet (May & June 1837), 8.

208 The Calumet (July & August 1831), 64.

for a few exceptions – were also far removed from the nation's political elites.[209] However, the two contest organisers had managed to attract for the initial 500 dollar premium the cooperation of none other than Joseph Story (1779–1845), a federal Supreme Court Justice, William Wirt (1772–1834), the former United States Attorney General, and John McLean (1785–1861), also a Justice at the Supreme Court.[210] For the 1,000 dollar premium, this committee was replaced by a no less august follow-up committee: former president John Quincy Adams (1767–1848), the already mentioned 'American Blackstone' James Kent (1763–1847), and the peace society's most celebrated Southern member, the attorney Thomas Grimké, replaced after his death by Daniel Webster (1782–1852), a senator, diplomat and future secretary of state.[211] As much as these lawyers and politicians stood moderately sympathetic to the object of the society, they would have not been convinced by the religious case alone. Even though the society had managed to flex some political clout by attracting such panellists, its influence on Washington elites should not be exaggerated. Apart from Adams, who invariably supported the peace society's petitions in Congress, none of the jurors were otherwise involved in the peace campaign.[212]

The Chief Justice of the Supreme Court, John Marshall (1755–1835), probably represented a much wider consensus in U.S. politics. He wrote back to the American Peace Society – who had sent him a copy of Ladd's 1832 dissertation – that their project for a congress of nations would be immensely

209 Members of state legislatures could be supportive, but most high-profile national politicians remained uninvolved.

210 Edson Whitney, *The American Peace Society. A Centennial History* (Washington: American Peace Society 1928), 51–2. Paul Finkelman, 'Story, Joseph', in *American National Biography Online.* 2000, available at: doi.org/10.1093/anb/9780198606697.article.1100821; Michael Oberg, 'Wirt, William', in *American National Biography Online.* 2000, available at: doi.org/10.1093/anb/9780198606697.article.0300543; Richard Aynes, 'McLean, John', in American National Biography Online. 2000, available at: doi.org/10.1093/anb/9780198606697.article.1100580.

211 *Prize Essays* 1840, iv; Maurice Baxter, 'Webster, Daniel', in *American National Biography Online.* 2000, available at: doi.org/10.1093/anb/9780198606697.article.0300525; Donald Roper, 'Kent, James', in *American National Biography Online.* 2000, available at: doi.org/10.1093/anb/9780198606697.article.1100488; Mary Hargreaves, 'Adams, John Quincy', in *American National Biography Online.* 2000, available at: doi.org/10.1093/anb/9780198606697.article.0300002.

212 Joseph Story was not a pacifist himself, writing in 1845 that he disagreed with the 'doctrine' of Charles Sumner's *True Grandeur of Nations* speech. See also Story's own writings, acknowledging that 'nations must ultimately be left to decide for themselves'. Joseph Story, *The Unsigned Essays of Supreme Court Justice Joseph Story. Early American Views of Law,* ed. Valerie Horowitz (New Jersey: Lawbook Exchange 2015), 251–54.

beneficial to humanity, if only it were 'practicable'. The leading legal mind of the antebellum United States did not even feel bothered to justify why he thought it was not.[213] Samuel J. May, an absolute non-resistant, could not believe that their plan could be so easily dismissed. How could anyone be thus unimpressed with the 'fulfilment of prophecy'?[214] Evidently, their scheme still fell far short of contemporary political realities, even within their own country.

Setbacks like John Marshall's curt dismissal did not prevent the American Peace Society from giving their crowning intellectual achievement a wide circulation. Unlike many of their smaller pamphlets, the thick – and therefore expensive – volume was also explicitly directed to political and intellectual elites. The society's leadership actively sought to deliver free copies 'to the president of the United States, the heads of departments, the governors of every state in the Union, and to every crowned head in Europe, and to the executive of every republic in America'.[215] Additionally, they wanted to furnish the libraries of colleges, academies, law schools, and even public libraries with a copy.[216] It is difficult to gauge the extent to which the society succeeded, but it was nonetheless considerable. A few of the 20,000 copies were presented to queen Victoria, to the duke of Wellington, and king Louis-Philippe. Even today, the volume or the essay by Ladd can be found relatively easily in most historical libraries – which can hardly be said of many other contemporary pacifist publications.[217]

The five preceding essays were written by John Bolles (1809–1878), a prominent legal scholar from Massachusetts, Thomas Upham, who included his essay on a congress of nations in the first edition of his *Manual of Peace*, and three anonymous authors. The real name of 'Hamilton' was never found out by the peace society, and has been forever lost, while 'M.' belonged to one Charles B. Emerson, of whom little is known. The last anonymous author turned out to be one of the contest's sponsors, Origen Bacheler, for a time a very active peace friend from the reborn New York Peace Society.[218]

---

213 The Calumet (November & December 1832), 290.

214 The Calumet (January & February 1834), 517–18.

215 *Prize Essays* 1840, xi; see also the letter from Ladd to the Prussian ambassador, found in [Maine Historical Society, Dorothy M. Gulick collection of papers], coll. 17, box 1, available at: www.mainememory.net/artifact/16151.

216 AP (December 1842), 286.

217 William Butler, 'Congress of Nations: a Nineteenth Century View'. *World Affairs* 128(2) (1965), 103; AP (November 1842), 258; AP (December 1841), 90.

218 *Prize Essays* 1840, VI-IX; AP (June 1841) 19.

2.3.2 'Amphyctionic' Precedents

Anxious to prove that permanent international political organisation was not utopian, every single author drew attention to a common canon of perceived political precedents throughout history. In keeping with the classical education the average intellectual had received in the nineteenth century, just about every early peace friend writing in this vein went back to the Greek Achaean league and Amphyctionic council.[219] These had already been alluded to in the announcement of the Genevan concours, and also in the *Harbinger* and *Calumet,* presumably by Ladd, the editor, who had done the same in his personal publications.[220] This evergreen featured in in a great number of contemporary pacifist publications, not least also outside of the United States.[221] Applied specifically to the United States, however, the ancient Greek example held a particular political resonance, regarded as it was as a forerunner to American democracy.[222] The open-endedness of the argument likely contributed to its popularity, demonstrated by the Southerners who invoked the Achaean league as an example of decentralised government.[223] The peace friends instead focussed on its defensive character.[224] A better example was usually found in the Amphyctionic council. According to Emerson's essay, this interpolity confederacy established a law of nations among its member states, and provided for the pacific adjustment of internal conflicts.[225] It was only an imperfect example, however. Bolles agreed that this Greek 'federal government' made the mistake of including also domestic competences, or allowing for offensive war against third parties. Its failure was inevitable, as 'such was the inevitable fate of a confederacy (…) composed of semi-barbarians, urged on by the fiery impulses of a rude and warlike age, and clothed with power so extensive'.[226]

Peace friends were not alone in the nineteenth century in their reading of the Amphyctionic council of Delphi an 'attempt to embody the notion of

219 *Prize Essays* 1840, 40, 79–81, 160, 181, 306–8, 322, 482, 556–9, 644, 676.

220 Harbinger (January & February 1831), 201; The Calumet (March & April 1834), 561; Ladd, *Essays* 1827, 239–40.

221 See chapters 2, 3, and 4 infra.

222 Richard, Carl. *The Golden Age of the Classics in the United States. Greece, Rome, and the Antebellum United States* (Cambridge: Harvard University Press, 2009), 41–82.

223 Ibid., 49.

224 For instance in *Prize Essays* 1840, 80.

225 Ibid., 306.

226 Ibid., 80.

international justice in an organised institution'.[227] While it did enshrine hints of sovereign equality and a rudimentary arbitration system, it was by no means a 'confederacy' or a 'federal government' in the modern sense. The council remained a loose vehicle of religious fraternisation. Furthermore, the oracle of Delphi was painfully incompetent as an arbitrator, lacking as she did – as seers and prophets tend to do – all of the required clarity and precision, whenever she did not evade the question altogether.[228] Although certain mid-century scholars such as Henry Wheaton already pointed out that it remained a religious, rather than a political institution, many scholars continued to think that Amphyctionic arbitration was done according to 'some kind of international law'.[229]

A more contemporary political 'precedent' worth mentioning in that context, was the Congress of Panama of 1826. This diplomatic assembly of recently independent South-American republics was convened by the influential revolutionary Simón Bolivar to discuss the possibility of Pan-American cooperation, foremost against the Spanish empire.[230] The eventual *Pacto de Union, Liga y Confederacion Perpetual* that emanated from it included an article that urged the ratifying parties to lay down norms applicable among them in peace and war.[231] The invitation had been extended to the United States primarily to involve this non Latin-American state in the proceedings dealing with the codification of international law.[232] Despite the great uncertainty, especially in the United States, about the

227 Paul Vinogradoff's *Historical Types of International Law* as quoted by David Bederman, *International Law in Antiquity* (Cambridge: CUP 2001), 171.

228 Ibid., 60–61, 82–83.

229 Henry Wheaton, *History of the Law of Nations in Europe and America; from the Earliest Times to the Treaty of Washington, 1842* (New York: Gould, Banks 1845), 14–5; Philological Society of London. *Proceedings of the Philological Society for 1852 and 1853. Vol. VI* (London: Bell 1854), 57.

230 Germán De la Reza, 'The Formative Platform of the Congress of Panama (1810–1826): the Pan-American Conjecture revisited'. *Revista Brasileira de Política Internacional* 56(1) (2013), 5–21.

231 United Nations, Secretariat, 'Outline of the Codification of International Law in the Inter-American System with Special Reference to the Methods of Codification' (6 May 1947), UN Doc A/AC.10/8; Tratado de Union, Liga y Confederación perpetua entre las Repúblicas de Colombia, Centro América, Perú y Estados Unidos Mexicanos, 15 de julio de 1826, dipublico.org, available at www.dipublico.org/12355/tratado-de-union-liga-y-confederacion-perpetua-entre-las-republicas-de-colombia-centro-america-peru-y-estados-unidos-mexicanos–15-de-julio-de–1826-congreso-de-panama–1826/, additional article.

232 De la Reza, 'Panama' 2013, 2–3; Dominique Dufour de Pradt, *Congrès de Panama* (Paris: Béchet ainé 1825), 2–3; Ladd, *Essay* 1840, 573–574.

exact purpose and scope of this congress, it was nonetheless grandly entitled the 'Amphyctionic Congress of Panama'.[233] In 1815, Bolivar had imagined a Latin-American version of the *project* of the *abbé* de Saint-Pierre.[234] The widely idealistic, yet vague ambitions of an American 'Areopagus' therefore did not fail to attract the attention of the peace friends of the United States. They did not find it difficult to project their own ambitions on such a nondescript political entity.

While Worcester made only passing mention of it in his journal, Ladd was absolutely fascinated.[235] Already in 1826, Ladd cherished high hopes on its potential to regulate contested issues of maritime law – like privateering and paper blockades – believing that Britain and several smaller European states would follow if the United States was on board.[236] Ladd had drawn inspiration from president John Quincy Adam's favourable message to Congress, who had raised the same issues of maritime neutrality – 'those never-failing fountains of discord and irritation' – and who had been a proponent of the so-called 'Panama mission'.[237] From 1826 until his death in 1840, the leader of the American Peace Society invoked the Congress of Panama as one of the most significant precedents towards a modern, permanent congress of nations. Ladd's canonical synthesis of the scheme devoted some considerable attention to the Congressional debates on the Panama precedent. Ladd had even spent part of the winter of 1838–1839 in Washington researching the state papers on this and other peace-related topics.[238] He emphasised the report of the House Committee on Foreign Relations of March 1826, denying its alleged unconstitutionality, or its incongruency with the foreign policy of avoiding 'entangling alliances', as articulated by Washington's farewell address and the Monroe doctrine. In Ladd's mind, almost every argument in support of the Panama mission was applicable to another, this time truly international congress of nations. As the report had

233 De la Reza, 'Panama' 2013, 5, 12; Andrew Clayton, 'The Debate over the Panama Congress and the Origins of the Second American Party System'. *The Historian* 47(2) (1985), 230.

234 De la Reza, 'Panama' 2013, 9–10.

235 FP (1827, n° v), 159; FP (1827, n° VIII), 249; FP (1827, n° x), 302–303; Ladd, *Essays* 1827, 83–4; Harbinger (January & February 1831), 215; The Calumet (March & April 1832), 172–181; The Calumet (January & February 1833), 239–330; AP (September 1838), 85; AP (February 1839), 195; Ladd, *Essay* 1840, 565–78.

236 Ladd, *Essays* 1827, 87, 259–60.

237 Ladd, *Essay* 1840, 567–9.

238 Ibid., 566.

argued, little was to be feared if the ministers at such a congress could not bind the U.S. government until after a formal ratification.[239]

Of course, the peace societies were aware that the Congress of Panama had been a complete failure. Few Latin-American states actually attended, and of these, only Columbia formally ratified the end-result of the congress. The delegation of the United States famously did not even make it in time, its key member having died from disease en route.[240] Ladd relatively correctly surmised that part of the opposition to the Panama mission had been because of Southern fears that this Congress might threaten slavery, in light of Latin-American desires to drive the Spanish out of slave-filled Cuba.[241] However, Ladd identified the main cause of its failure with its Latin-American setting. To him, the South American republics were at the time still too embroiled in their conflict with Spain. Because they were still at war, they lacked the stability, as well as the required 'understanding' of international law, to host such a congress. Disease-ridden and far-away Panama was furthermore not the ideal choice of location. Had it been organised in, say, Washington, Ladd fancied, European states would have been more disposed to send delegates. The lesson was that governments would be willing to participate in a law-making congress, 'whenever it shall be called *by a respectable state,* well established in its own government'.[242]

Ladd's optimism was partially warranted. On the one hand, he severely underestimated the extent of political hostility in Washington towards a more extensive interpretation of the Monroe doctrine, or the received wisdom to avoid all 'entangling alliances', the latter already a 'foreign-policy dogma' by the 1820s. Congressional opponents feared that even the simple act of sending representatives to Panama already risked the United States of assuming a state of co-belligerency against Spain and its potential European allies, even if solely to discuss issues of a non-belligerent character.[243] There was also wide resistance to president Adams's arguments that political circumstances had changed since Washington's address.[244] The 'Panama mission' did not arrive before its adjournment, because of the heated debates

239 Ibid., 571–2.

240 Jeffrey J. Malanson, 'The Congressional Debate over U.S. Participation in the Congress of Panama, 1825–1826: Washington's Farewell Address, Monroe's Doctrine, and the Fundamental Principles of U.S. Foreign Policy'. *Diplomatic History* 30(5) (2006), 836–7.

241 Ladd, *Essays* 1827, 84–5; Clayton, 'Panama Debate' 1985, 230.

242 Ladd, *Essay* 1840, 576–8.

243 Malanson, 'Panama Debate' 2006, 816–23.

244 Ibid., 825–7.

on it, described by one historian as 'one of the severest parliamentary battles' of the antebellum Congress.[245] Congress's misgivings centred more on Adams's specific intentions for this vaguely defined assembly in Panama, rather than on the fundamental character of the neutral policy of the United States.[246] Ladd overestimated the United States' voluntarism in international reforms. On the other hand, however, a law-making international congress would indeed see the light of day in 1856, producing the Declaration of Paris, proving that a congress of nations could indeed realise credible and major reforms of international law, even if only on a partial and ad hoc basis – and in spite of U.S. resistance.[247]

2.3.3 Christian Universalism

In spite of their universalist aspirations, American peace friends set their congress of nations firmly within the narrow geographical political space of 'civilized and Christian nations'.[248] Nearly every author took it for granted, like, for instance, Upham did, that a 'union of all civilized nations' was needed.[249] If anything, the political discourse of peace friends was even more restrictive than that of many Americans or Europeans, in the sense that the pacifists' standard of 'civilisation' excluded even the better part of European states. Taking Ladd's canonical synthesis as the best example, no doubt informed by the failure of the Congress of Panama, he stated: 'it is not expected, that such a combination of powers would be of a very great geographical extent, as it could only embrace the most civilized, enlightened, and Christian nations'.[250] Defining it more explicitly, Ladd chiefly imagined the United States, Britain, and France to take the lead, because he and the other American peace friends defined civilisation 'pretty much in proportion to the voice which the people have in the government'. Equating civilisation with the degree of political agency afforded to the middle classes, pacifists like Ladd thus sought for an alliance of states viewed as compatible with American democratic traditions. According to Ladd: 'if no more than these three powers are gained, the cause is ours; and the Congress of Nations may go into immediate operation'.[251] Once these three most

245 Ibid., 813–814.
246 Ibid., 837–838.
247 The U.S. never joined the Declaration of Paris.
248 *Prize Essays* 1840, ix, 121, 126, 178, 185–186, 361, 370, 488, 518, 520, 530.
249 Upham, *Manual* 1836, 359, 375.
250 Ladd, *Essay* 1840, 518.
251 Ibid., 629.

'democratic' great powers were converted, Ladd hypothesised, the congress might expand itself to Switzerland – where Sellon had already 'done much' – the South American republics – 'as soon as they have consolidated their governments' – the German states, Belgium, Holland, Denmark, and Sweden. Thereafter, the 'philanthropic and enlightened' Prussian king might then also join, along with the autocratic Russian and Austrian governments, who would not wish to be left out. Even if those powers should decline to join, the congress would still be successful, and the unrestful states of Spain, Portugal, and Italy too would eventually come into the fold.[252]

Evidently, the American pacifists were not immune to the kind of 'parochial universalism' Jennifer Pitts has identified in eighteenth and nineteenth century western discourse, including the perpetual peace projects of Saint-Pierre, Rousseau, or Bentham.[253] Not unlike broader political discourse, the pacifist brand of parochialism had blind spots that could only lead to a further marginalisation of those falling short of the civilisational standard. While constitutionalist criteria factored largely into the equation, these ultimately remained subsidiary means to realise a more fundamental conception of eternal peace as the triumph of Christianity.[254] As Ladd phrased it: 'the storm of war would soon be hushed in Christendom, and that main obstacle being removed, Christianity would soon spread all over the world.'[255] Although they sought to develop a model for a comprehensive and welcoming pacific international order, pacifists like Ladd found it difficult to conceive of a peace based on the political sovereignty of non-Christian polities. Revealingly, this difficult topic barely featured in the prize essays, leaving much ambiguity as to their significance for international order. While someone like Bacheler did speak of extending the invitation 'to Turk, to Persian, to Hindoo and Chinese; to all people, nations, kindred tongues, that dwell on the whole earth', non-Europeans were never the primary locus of concern.[256] Typically, they were mentioned for rhetorical purposes: to show fellow Christians how far they had fallen from their own vaunted standards of conduct, to the point that even 'infidels' often displayed better behaviour.

252 Ibid.

253 Jennifer Pitts, *Boundaries of the International. Law and Empire* (Cambridge: HUP, 2018), 6, 10, 120, 143–4.

254 Ghervas, 'Definitions of Peace' 2020, 29–31.

255 Ladd, *Essay* 1840, 630. See also Elihu Burritt's Anglo-Saxonism, or Hugo's appeal for colonies, rather than revolutions, in his 'United States of Europe' speech in 1849. Van der Linden, *Peace Movement* 1987, 276, 446.

256 *Prize Essays* 1840, 190–191.

Some 'heathens', such as the Chinese, or even 'that prince of infidels', Voltaire, were said to outshine many Christian states in 'moral greatness'.[257]

Similarly, the American peace movement paid fluctuating attention to arguably the most consistent cause of violent conflict in their country: the genocidal expulsion of Native Americans towards the western territories. As Lawson already asserted, the American peace friends of New England were likely not aware of the full magnitude of the repression of the subaltern American peoples.[258] Most peace friends encouraged their cultural assimilation, in the form of their conversion to Christianity, and brought attention to their plight primarily when it became topical due to an escalating conflict, or an ongoing legislative debate. On the other hand, however, the peace friends consistently decried the military campaigns of the United States government as acts of naked and unilateral aggression, dismissed the territorial cession treaties as 'forced on them by the bayonet', and regarded the Native American tribesmen as no more depraved than the average Christian – Worcester felt that although the tribal nations were ferocious in war, they only fought when provoked, unlike 'their more bloody brethren, called Christians'.[259]

Specific episodes that caught the attention of peace societies included the wars against the Florida Seminole tribes from the 1810s until the 1850s, the Black Hawk war of 1832 against the eponymous leader, the Georgian attempts to impose state law on the Cherokee nations around the same period, and the infamous Indian Removal Act of 1830.[260] At various instances, they openly charged their fellow Americans with hypocrisy and selective blindness: 'had these Indians been Greeks or Poles, their heroism would have been extolled to the skies. But alas! They are "guilty of a skin not colored like our own" and but few drop a tear on the grave of a nation of brave men (...) and though we cannot call these tawny warriors Christians, no one can deny that they were heroes'.[261]

Because the American Peace Society regarded the Native American plight foremost as a subspecies of the overarching 'war-system', it did not formulate a specific policy to prevent conflict with subaltern peoples. As it was

257 Ibid., 488–9.

258 Lawson, *Plowshares* 1975, 129.

259 FP (1816, n° II), 31; FP (1821, n° XII), 26–34; FP (1827, n° I), 20; FP (1827, n° XI), 330–332.

260 FP (1821, n° XV), 7–8; FP (1821, n° IV), 12–30; FP (1821, n° V), 14–25; FP (1827, n° I), 18–32; Harbinger (August 1830), 88; The Calumet (March & April 1833), 372–374.

261 Calumet (September & October 1832), 259–263.

doing with the delicate issue of defensive war, the society's leadership firstly hoped that their general condemnation of war would already induce a more benevolent and pacific attitude among the colonisers. The feasibility of a non-militaristic policy vis-à-vis perceived 'savages' – a title many pacifists considered just as applicable to Christians – was heavily promoted through the historical 'precedent' of Pennsylvania. That colony had been founded by an undisputed hero of the American peace movement, the quaker aristocrat William Penn (1644–1718). According to peace friends, Penn had managed to avoid the kind of endemic warfare so typical of colonialism, because his 'paternal tenderness' had made sure that Native Americans were treated with 'kindness', meaning by 'exact and 'impartial justice', not transferring lands except after its sale for a fair price.[262]

While the 'unified voice of historians' might still acknowledge the prolonged peace in Pennsylvania, this case again illustrated the limited historical knowledge of peace friends, fuelling their optimism. Although the more diplomatic and empathic approach of Penn was certainly a contributing factor, pacifists were unaware that Penn's diplomacy was also substantially aided by the fact that the native peoples of the area had already been heavily reduced by epidemics and warfare. Any refugee natives were furthermore settled at the colony's borders, thereby effectively functioning as a security buffer for the war-averse Quakers of the interior, who preferred to let allied tribal warriors take the brunt of frontier conflict.[263]

Looked at from its entirety, the pacifist congress of nations largely excluded subaltern peoples from its concerns, and would have offered little benefits to them. The plan, across all of its iterations, was predicated on the existence of European-style government, and a civilisational standard rooted in Christianity. Across the hundreds of pages of the *Prize Essays,* the contemporary name 'Indian' was scarcely mentioned, and even then only to contrast the law and order ensured by the modern western state to the perceived Hobbesian anarchy of 'the savage tribes of America'.[264] Defining the concept of a 'nation', many understood it as 'a community recognised and treated by the civilized world as a nation', rather than 'a wandering tribe of savages'.[265] Such a linear view of history, which positioned European and

262 Instances of Penn mentioned in this context abounded. E.g. AP (December 1836), 123.

263 Ibid.; Alan Taylor, *American Colonies. The Settling of North America* (New York: Penguin 2002), 268–269; Peter Brock, *The Quaker Peace Testimony 1660 to 1914* (York: Sessions Book Trust 1990), 87–131.

264 *Prize Essays* 1840, 213.

265 Ibid., 463.

North American society as the end-goal of humanity's universal progress, excluded non-Western actors to the extent they did not assimilate to Western standards.[266] As much as pacifists abhorred the violence accompanying imperial and American expansion, their solutions left little agency for the subaltern peoples themselves. Furthermore, their unanimous support for absolute non-intervention in a member state's internal affairs would have left a major discretionary power for the United States within its relations with the Native American peoples, to the extent it increasingly denied them a sovereign status as the nineteenth century progressed.[267]

2.3.4 Reception of Older Peace Plans

While non-Western peoples remained on the periphery for American peace friends, Europe stayed in the centre of attention. Like their European counterparts, Americans were well aware that similar projects for 'permanent and universal peace' had been devised before them. From the early modern age to the very recent past, there existed a rich intellectual tradition in this field.

The one most mentioned in the *Prize Essays* was the 'great scheme' of the French king Henri IV.[268] Unlike many of their contemporaries in Europe, like the Genevan count de Sellon, the Americans did not think highly of the plan. Strongly informed by the religious requests of the contest sponsors, the essayists unanimously agreed that no project should rely on coercion. Bacheler compared Henry IV's total reordering of the European borders to the American plan for a congress of nations: 'the two schemes are radically different'.[269]

The scheme of Henry IV – in reality most likely composed long after the king's death by his former minister, the duke de Sully – had indeed suggested a markedly different pacification scheme.[270] Its outlines were sketched in some detail by Emerson, who correctly assessed that the peace of Henri IV was one based on a restructuring of the European balance of

266 Most peace friends thought this way. See also the next chapters. Pitts, *Boundaries* 2018, 3.

267 After 1871, the U.S. no longer regarded Native American tribes as independent nations with whom it had to negotiate under international law. David Wilkins, *American Indian Sovereignty and the U.S. Supreme Court. The Masking of Justice* (Austin: University of Texas Press 1997), 19–117; 46–54, 145, 160, 185.

268 Bolles, Hamilton, and Upham did not mention any of the classical peace plans.

269 *Prize Essays* 1840, 486.

270 Arcidiacono, *Cinq types de paix* 2011, 218–227.

power, foremost against the house of Austria.[271] Europe was to be divided into a limited number of hereditary and elective monarchies, as well as a few republics, totalling fifteen polities of roughly equal power.[272] These were then to be united in a continuous 'senate' of its member states, supposedly modelled after the 'Amphyctionic Council'. The American friends of peace did not so much question the – historically inaccurate – assertion by Sully that a considerable number of sovereigns, including Elizabeth II of England, had supposedly already assented to the scheme prior to Henri IV's untimely assassination, as they called into doubt the merits of the king's scheme.[273] Whatever the possible benefits of the plan in the time of Henri IV, it was believed that it was 'unquestionably a model which would be impracticable and unsafe to follow at the present day'. Emerson believed that any subdivision of territories by physical force would be self-contradictory: 'our design is peace; and peaceable are all the measures by which we hope to attain it'.[274] Convinced that the 'living, whole and healthful empires of the earth' were the 'result of natural causes', he aimed for a system of international governance that entailed 'no doubtful experiment (…) no political convulsion'.[275] For this reason, the scheme's 'national council' was rejected; its authority was 'too extensive', meddling also in the internal affairs of member states, to the point of armed intervention. American pacifists felt quite unanimously that their congress should never devolve into 'a species of Holy Alliance'.[276]

Not every essay mentioning the 'great scheme', Americans were not always equally well-informed on the rest of the classical pacification canon. Those who did not reflect on Henri IV typically also did not mention other plans.[277] In the pacifist journals too, attention to previous theoretical efforts was fluctuating in the antebellum era.[278] Ladd himself, given his profound interest in the topic, was one of the best informed society members. He gave only passing notice of most of these. William Penn's *Essay on the*

271 Ladd had noticed this anti-Austrian bias as well. Ibid., 75–76, 100–102; *Prize Essays* 1840, 563–564.

272 Arcidiacono, *Cinq types de paix* 2011, 100–101. *Prize Essays* 1840, 321–322.

273 *Prize Essays* 1840, 322–324, 485–486, 563.

274 Ibid., 324–325.

275 Ibid.

276 Ibid., 325–326, 563–565.

277 These were Bolles and Hamilton. Hamilton mistook the idea as novel among jurists and moralists. Ibid., 124.

278 Penn, Kant, and Bentham were seldom mentioned in this context. See infra in this chapter.

Present and Future Peace of Europe was remarkably absent in U.S. peace propaganda; Penn's name cropped up often, but nearly always solely as the example of enlightened governance, or of successful non-resistance.[279] Even Ladd, who had read his peace essay, found it unnecessary to say little more of it than that Penn's essay was 'chiefly remarkable for having been the first thing of the kind in modern times'.[280]

The scheme by Charles-Irénée Castel, dubbed the *abbé* de Saint-Pierre (1658–1743), was among the better known. Worcester never wrote about the old abbot, but under Ladd's leadership occasional summaries were introduced.[281] The plan intrigued Ladd, even if he considered it obscure; Ladd felt it necessary to explain in his essay that this was not the same man as the eighteenth century natural philosopher Bernardin de Saint-Pierre.[282] Drawing from the *Extrait du projet de Saint-Pierre* of 'John James Rousseau [sic]', Ladd also mistakenly believed that no copy of the original had survived. While Saint-Pierre's intentions of setting up 'a system of legislation and arbitration' may have been as admirable as Henri IV's had been, Ladd mused to himself, the plan of Saint-Pierre and Rousseau had nonetheless fallen for the same mistakes: both had relied on the adhesion of every great power, and on the armed enforcement of decrees. Ladd recounted the apocryphal witticism levelled against Saint-Pierre by cardinal Fleury, that the *abbé* only had to convert the heart of every Christian prince for his plan to become a political reality. The leading voice of the American Peace Society countered that sarcasm by retorting that enlightened public opinion would achieve just that in this century.[283]

Other older or contemporary writers were fully absent from the American peace society's writings. Unlike in European schemes, no mention was made of the popular scheme by the French socialist thinker Henri de Saint-Simon (1760–1825). Few if any of the American authors desired the large-scale top-down economic dirigisme as envisioned in European schemes

279 A notable exception that mentioned his peace plan was found in AP (December 1836), 115–132. See also supra.

280 Ladd, *Essay* 1840, 582.

281 Saint-Pierre's only mention was in Adams's dismissive reply. See supra. Mentioned for instance in Harbinger (July 1828), 63–9; Harbinger (January & February 1831), 213; The Calumet (May & June 1832), 210–211; The Calumet (September 1838), 82–3; AP (February 1839), 194.

282 The count de Sellon confused the two as well. Ladd described the schemes of Penn and Saint-Pierre as 'very meagre, crude and undigested'. [Archives d'état de Genève, Famille Revilliod-de Sellon fonds], Archives privées 18.3.8.40; Ladd, *Essay* 1840, 637.

283 Ibid., 583–4.

more influenced by Saint-Simon's ideas.[284] Little better fared the philosopher from Königsberg, Immanuel Kant (1724–1804), who wrote the today highly celebrated essay *Zum Ewigen Frieden.*[285] The first paraphrase of this text was published in a short 1854 article of the *Advocate,* written by Charles Sumner.[286] The essay was virtually unknown up until that point, never mentioned even by Ladd, confirming the assertion of Sumner that Kant's peace philosophy had become largely forgotten.[287] Among the European peace friends also, this famed German philosopher would not be credited as a major source of inspiration until the late 1860s.[288] Even if they had genuinely not read this major early internationalist theorist, American pacifists – along with European pacifists – shared the Kantian notion that the European Enlightenment was a manifestation of humanity's telos, namely the conviction that freedom should be 'realised in public institutions under a constitution'.[289] Kant's proposal for a peace league under the rule of reformed international law corresponded quite closely with the American Peace Society's congress of nations.[290] In that sense, Kant's omission remained far more noteworthy than of many other, equally obscure schemes, such as those composed by Émeric Crucé or George of Poděbrady, seldom if ever mentioned by pacifists in the 1800s.

2.3.5 A 'High Court of Nations'

Apart from Kant, the only other major omission worth mentioning in the context of the American Peace Society's plan for a congress of nations was that of the British philosopher Jeremy Bentham (1748–1832) and his student, James Mill (1773–1836). Ladd claimed that the only true originality of his plan lay with the clear distinction he had drawn between a legislative 'congress of ambassadors', codifying international law, and a judicial 'court of

284 See chapter 4.

285 Simon, 'Myth' 2018, 113–136; Immanuel Kant (ed. Pauline Kleingeld), *'Toward Perpetual Peace' and other Writings on Politics, Peace, and History* (New Haven: Yale University Press 2006), 67–109.

286 He had already alluded to it more succinctly in his 1849 annual address. AP (January 1854), 2–3.

287 Ibid.

288 See chapter 7.

289 Martti Koskenniemi, 'Histories of International Law: Significance and Problems for a Critical View'. *Temple International and Comparative Law Journal* 27(2) (2013), 215–240; De Rycke, 'Legislating Utopia' 2020, 620–621.

290 Kant (ed. Kleingeld), *Writings* 2006, 78–81; AP (January 1854), 2–3.

nations', dependent for its authority exclusively on public opinion.[291] Neither Bentham nor Mill were at all debated in American peace propaganda, Bentham being first mentioned by the scholarly Sumner in 1849, several years after Ladd's death.[292] Bentham's *Plan for an Universal and Perpetual Peace* called for improvements in international law, as well as the establishment of a 'common court of judicature', that was 'not to be armed with coercive powers'.[293] Although written in the 1700s, it was only published after his death in 1843.[294] However, James Mill had based himself on the same notion in his essay for the supplement of the *Encyclopaedia Britannica,* on 'Law of Nations', calling for both a code of international law, and a tribunal to enforce this code, albeit 'never (...) by force of arms'. Unlike Bentham's plan, Mill's essay was published in the 1820s.[295] Stephen Conway has, however, concluded that it seemed 'far from over-fanciful to suggest he might well have been aware of Mill's ideas'.[296] After all, Ladd maintained a rather close correspondence with the London Peace Society and received a great deal of literature from them.[297] Conway's scepticism might furthermore be reinforced by the present observation that Ladd had copied a great deal from the preceding five *Prize Essays.*

Although it was true that Ladd was the only essay author to draw this clear distinction, he had not initially done so. In none of his early inceptions, such as in the *Dissertation on a Congress of Nations* of 1832, or in his articles on the subject in the peace journals, did Ladd distinguish between legislative and judicial competences. In congruency with most antecedent and contemporary peace schemes, either in the United States or in Europe, Ladd had imagined this arbitration to assume the form of some mediation by a third party authority. More particularly, he was influenced, as Worcester had been, by the arbitrations enabled by the Jay Treaty and the Treaty of Ghent. As discussed earlier, these have been somewhat misleadingly called

291 *Prize Essays* 1840, IX-X, 511–512.

292 Charles Sumner, *The War-System of the Commonwealth of Nations: an Address before the American Peace Society* (Boston: Ticknor, Reed, and Fields 1849), 49.

293 Jeremy Bentham (ed. John Bowring), *The Works of Jeremy Bentham, vol. II* (Edinburgh: Simpkin, Marshall & Co., 1843), 552.

294 Stephen Conway, 'Bentham, the Benthamites, and the Nineteenth-Century British Peace Movement'. *Utilitas* 2(2) (1990), 224.

295 James Mill, 'Law of Nations', in *Essays on Government, Jurisprudence, Liberty of the Press, and Law of Nations* (London: Innes 1829), 32.

296 Conway, 'Bentham' 1990, 237–238; contrast this to his omittance in Janis, *American Tradition* 2004, 104–105; Janis, *America* 2010, 80–81.

297 Conway, 'Bentham' 1990, 238.

the 'rebirth' of 'modern' arbitration, seeing how they centred foremost on bilateral commissions, and some third-party awards were rejected.[298] Such was the fate of the 1831 arbitration by the Dutch king William I, on the Maine boundary, whose award Ladd in his 1832 essay still endorsed.[299] Unfortunately, the U.S. Senate rejected it, because Maine – where Ladd was from – and Massachusetts objected to it, and because commentators accused the Dutch monarch of a pro-British bias, and of overstepping his bounds.[300] Perhaps for these reasons, Ladd proposed a mode of arbitration that would not be, 'like an individual, under the influence of any single power', but of a multinational court, 'appointed by all the powers of Christendom'.[301] In this early iteration, Ladd still imagined the 'general congress' of diplomatic ambassadors to function as court of appeal of an otherwise ill-defined 'first court', staying closer to a form political mediation that left open routes of informal diplomatic reconciliation, rather than on a strictly judicial process.

All of the other writers from the 1830s similarly sketched a single international institution, wherein the diplomatic envoys of member states would directly adjudicate all disputes, thereby blurring the fine lines between politics and law.[302] In this, they differed little from other such schemes in Europe, or from the classical peace plans. Some Americans stuck very closely to political practice; Emerson, for example, supposed that 'a single arbitrator, and he the highest executive officer in some neutral state or kingdom, would be the most proper tribunal', though he was not clear elsewhere if a body of state representatives might not be better suited for the 'judicial character' of the congress.[303]

Nonetheless, outside of the U.S., Ladd was not as unique as he assumed. Even apart from Bentham, similar designs for an international judicial court featured in various European peace projects, such as in France, in

298 See supra and the general introduction. Ladd, *Essays* 1827, 236–279; William Ladd, *Dissertation on a Congress of Nations* (Unknown location: Loring 1832), 27; see also every journal article prior to 1839 on a congress of nations mentioned supra.

299 Ladd, *Dissertation* 1832, 27.

300 John Dunbabin, 'The 1831 Dutch Arbitration of the Canadian-American Boundary Dispute: another View'. *The New England Quarterly* 75(4) (2002), 642; Francis Carroll, 'Kings and Crises: Arbitrating the Canadian-American Boundary Dispute and the Belgian Crisis of 1830–1831'. *The New England Quarterly* 73(2) (2000), 179–201.

301 Ladd 1832, *Dissertation* 1832, 27.

302 *Prize Essays* 1840, 64, 135, 158–9, 282, 286–7, 436, 473.

303 Ibid., 282,287-288.

Switzerland, and in Britain. These are discussed in other chapters.[304] Ladd's greatest feat had been not so much his originality, as rather having produced the most popular early account of the workings of an independent international judicial court.

Ladd only mapped out the broad outlines of his scheme, allowing for many details to be addressed later, should his suggestions be taken up in political circles. As a frame of reference, Ladd compared it with both admiralty courts and the U.S. Supreme Court.[305] The inspiration from the latter tribunal was clear from his suggestion that judges should probably hold their office 'during good behaviour', a phrase lifted straight from the Constitution.[306] Echoing the critiques of an author like Upham on admiralty courts, he stressed that a court of nations should be truly independent from government, with an authority recognised across national boundaries.[307] In keeping with the American concerns for non-violence and respect for existing state sovereignty, however, the court would only have an 'advisory' power, and could only accept within its jurisdiction cases 'referred to it, by the free and mutual consent of both parties concerned'. Speaking like a veritable American on the enforcement dilemma, he stressed: 'there is to be no sheriff, or posse'.[308] Its judges would have to be legal experts, appointed by the Congress, protected by the usual diplomatic privileges and immunities, and largely able to regulate its own inner workings, such as its adjournment or its seat of assembly. The exact number of magistrates had to be determined by the Congress, but Ladd desired parity of numbers, suggesting two of every member state. Similar to the Supreme Court, these judges were to reach their verdicts by majority, rather than by unanimity, and have one author the actual verdict.[309] Ladd did not specify whether the entire college of judges would be assigned to every case, whether judges of a state involved in the case would be excluded, or whether dissenting opinions would be allowed.

The Court's primary purpose would be to adjudicate interstate disputes before it, based on the 'true interpretation of existing treaties', and 'the laws enacted by the Congress and ratified by the nations represented'. Whenever positive international law was unclear or absent, the judges would have to

304 See chapter 3.
305 Ladd, *Essay* 1840, 521, 550, 602, 620.
306 Ibid., 522, 551; United States, Constitution, 1789, article III, section 1.
307 Ibid., 620.
308 Ibid., 550.
309 Ibid., 550–1, 603–4.

rely on 'the principles of equity and justice'.[310] Ladd therefore kept open a significant inroad towards natural law argument, in keeping with the peace society's moralism, as well as the accepted methods of contemporary lawyers, such as the essay contest's jury member James Kent, to interpret statute law in accordance with 'natural equity'.[311] Preceding any court rulings, Ladd also hoped that positive international law would already achieve greater conformity to natural justice, than had been hitherto the case. As in the U.S. constitution system, the separation of powers would not be impregnable in this new international system. Since no institution would be better placed than the judicial Court to identify concerns of international law, it would have as its additional 'duty' to periodically suggest unresolved legal issues to the legislative Congress of ambassadors. In this vision, Oscar Schachter's celebrated, albeit elusive 'invisible college of international lawyers', giving voice to the profession's *'conscience juridique',* would be given an official institutional form.[312] Their *opinio iuris* on all matters *de lege ferenda,* for the 'good of mankind and the interests of humanity', Ladd very much hoped, would not be easily discarded by a philanthropically inclined Congress.[313]

Undoubtedly, Ladd was more than a little overoptimistic on the viability of such an unprecedented international court in contemporary politics. Setting aside for now the many counter-arguments to be raised against the plan by contemporaries, even within the peace movement, Ladd miscalculated the role of 'honour' in international politics. Ladd, along with many other peace friends mentioned earlier, noted not without reason that 'honour' was frequently instrumentalised in official discourse, and could contribute to unnecessary escalations.[314] Once invoked, it was difficult for a politician to back down again, for fear of losing face. Ladd hoped that the possibility of turning to an impartial Court, guiding itself foremost by

310 Ibid., 551–2.

311 Kent quoted in Banner, *Natural Law* 2021, 22–3.

312 This bore some resemblance to Bolles's substitute for a state-delegated international codifying commission, as well as the suggestions contained in Louis Bara's prize essay of 1849, as well as the international law societies of the 1870s. Some of these had similar parallels to the International Law Commission. See also the general conclusion. Ibid., 553–4; *Prize Essays* 1840, 56, 91–92; Schachter, 'Invisible College 1977–1978, 217–226.

313 Ibid., 554.

314 Ladd, 552–3; Miroslav Šedivý, 'Honour as a Political-Legal Argument: the French July Monarchy, National Dignity, and Europe, 1830–1840'. *The Czech Historical Review* 116(1) (2018), 86–111.

international law and equity, would offer a way out of a crisis that left everyone's sense of honour intact. In that context, Ladd singled out France as a prime example.

The specific mention of France was interesting. Ladd claimed that French honour would have been better served by turning to a court of nations, than by trying 'to force an unwilling confession' from Mexico, Buenos Aires and the Tahitian queen, in reference to France's recent interventions in those countries.[315] However, Ladd, in his axiomatic optimism, likely underestimated the extent in which honour was deliberately employed to silence criticisms of any illegal actions. In the 1830s, France's aggressive support for non-interventionism essentially constituted a revisionist move to preserve a regional sphere of influence. French politicians recurrently invoked the 'national honour' to excuse actions that could not be legitimated by international law, aware that other states could not openly dismiss such an argument. To say that France exaggerated the value of her 'dignity', was tantamount to a gross insult, one that might even constitute a casus belli.[316] Even though legal textbooks of the era did not explain its applications in political practice, apart from diplomatic protocol, even peace friends were intuitively aware of its political significance. Many propagandists took consistent care to explain that the resort to arbitration was not incompatible with the 'national honour', and that a peaceful compromise reflected better on the national honour than brute force.[317]

More fundamentally, Ladd – maybe fatally – underestimated the political character of international law. In their quest towards an international rule of law, Ladd and other peace friends were unlikely to fully comprehend that neither a Congress nor a Court would escape the politics and partisanship that they so despised both internationally and domestically. Pacifists in favour of these institutions almost unquestioningly assumed that 'philanthropy' would hold sway in this diplomatic assembly.[318] A modern observer – inescapably under the shadow of postmodern doubt – will no doubt dismiss certain nineteenth century assumptions as very naïve and simplistic. Emerson, for instance, asserted with astonishing confidence that 'the exposition of law' was not a 'matter of uncertain conjecture, but of

315 Ladd referred to aggressive French conduct towards the Haitian queen Pōmare IV, as well as the French blockades of Veracruz and the Río de la Plata during the 1830s.

316 Šedivý, 'Honour' 2018, 89, 109.

317 See supra in this chapter for some of the many references to 'honour' by other peace friends. Ibid., 92.

318 *Prize Essays* 1840, 553–554.

almost mathematical calculation', and that any erroneous judicial decisions would 'easily be detected and refuted'.[319] Ladd too presupposed the existence of any 'true interpretation' of treaties, seemingly unaware of the wide range of interpretative techniques developed in common law and civil law legal systems.[320]

2.3.6 An Interstate Parliament

As much as pacifists were overconfident in the eventual possibility of a universally acceptable body of laws, they were in broad agreement that the law of nations as it stood was too indeterminate to serve as an instrument able to transcend politics. Already in 1832 did Ladd sweepingly summarise: 'at present there is no such thing as a law of nations; it is entirely a *beau idéal*, an *ens rationis*.' Under the impression that solely a 'solemn league and covenant' could fixate 'this Proteus', Ladd had stuck to the same views in his canonical 1840 essay.[321] He claimed that textbook writers had managed to elaborate 'a kind of *voluntary* international law (…) which is, for the most part, respected, but which is not confirmed by any compact or agreement, and on which the authors themselves often differ'. The leading man of the American peace movement concluded that 'what is now called the law of nations, is but little better than a nose of wax, which may be twisted either way, to suit the purposes of dominant nations'.[322] The other prize essays were all of the same tenor.[323]

Already in the 1830s, this observation was all but commonplace. Ladd essentially repeated the same exercise as Upham in his *Manual*. It was not unlikely that he had taken inspiration from this earlier work, parts of which had been published in the *Prize Essays*. Whatever had been case, Ladd's essay contained a very interesting list of issues in international law that a congress of nations would need to address. Most of the list dealt with the laws of war. The founder of the American Peace Society focussed heavily on delineating the rights of belligerents against those of neutrals. The other topics were categorised under the general rubric 'measures of utility'. These included slavery, piracy, discovery, colonisation, diplomatic immunities, patents and copyrights, weights and measures, free navigation, disarmament,

319 Ibid., 283.
320 Ibid., 551.
321 Ladd, *Dissertation* 1832, 14.
322 *Prize Essays* 1840, 519.
323 Hamilton writing: 'Of all jurisprudence, that which is international is the most fluctuating and inconsistent.' Ibid., 37, 96, 115, 164, 240–1, 362, 391–5, 435.

and – more idiosyncratically – the restoration or destruction of all military trophies.[324]

An analysis of all of the topics raised by Ladd in all their legal-historical detail would be much too digressing, and would miss Ladd's point that positive codification was needed, because he believed that states had no clear legal guidelines. To read through Ladd's essay was to read through a searing indictment of doctrine similar to the ones by Upham, Bentham, or Kant. The German philosopher had famously derided doctrine as 'tiresome comforters', which possessed 'not the least amount of legal force'.[325] The British philosopher thought equally little of Vattel, a writer he considered 'old-womanish and tautological'.[326] One can only imagine Ladd's perplexing sighs as he too perused the copies of Vattel, Burlamaqui, Pufendorf and Grotius he had turned to for help.[327] Again and again, he had to conclude that these authorities were not in agreement with each other, or that they wrote little of practical use. Ladd marked clear instances where Grotius wrote 'A', but where Burlamaqui argued 'B', or where Grotius made a case for 'A', Burlamaqui for 'B', and Vattel turned out to allow for both 'A' and 'B', depending on the circumstances.[328] Other times, he could not find any answers.

Even though someone like Ladd highly valued the abilities of academic experts, he could not accept that their contradictory legal views were 'sanctioned by no authority', and therefore concluded that international law could only be definitively settled by a law-making diplomatic congress.[329] Working himself through his list of legal questions, he constantly reiterated that consensus would be needed among the official political representatives of states. To decide on a list of contraband items, as for everything else, could 'only be done by a Congress of Nations'.[330] It was clear that Ladd envisioned this Congress as the international equivalent of a national

---

324 Old and tattered captured military standards were a common sight in cathedrals. Ladd hoped that all such trophies – except for works of art – should be thrown on one big heap and burnt. *Prize Essays* 1840, 525–549.

325 Kant (ed. Kleingeld), *Writings* 2006, 79.

326 Bentham continued on Kant's reasoning: 'They come to this: Law is nature – Nature is law. He builds upon a cloud.' John Bowring, *The Works of Jeremey Bentham vol. xx* (Edinburgh: Tait 1842), 584

327 These were the ones cited most often, and which Ladd had presumably read.

328 *Prize Essays* 1840, 526, 541, 543, 546.

329 *Prize Essays* 1840, 603.

330 Ibid., 540.

parliament, that could render 'the law of nations so plain that a court (…) could easily apply those principles to any particular cases'.[331]

Ladd did not offer many details on the exact composition and internal functioning of this Congress, preferring to only provide the essential elements of the plan that ought to be incorporated. Equality of status was one of these, granting one vote to each state, regardless of the size of the delegations. The opening convention would proceed to establish all by-laws as it saw fit. New members would be accepted on the condition they accept the legal *acquis,* duly ratifying it according to their internal political system. No principle of international law could be established, if no unanimous agreement was reached, and ratified by each government afterwards. Once thus accepted by all member states, each principle would represent a multilateral treaty, unable to be annulled except by the consent of all signatories. Ladd admitted that progress would probably be 'very slow', but the Congress 'would be the better for that, and more likely to produce permanent and useful results'. The Court should not wait for codification, deciding cases on 'principles generally known and acknowledged'.[332] The enforcement of the rulings of the Court, or of any acts of the Congress, would depend exclusively on the greatest executive authority one is able to bring to bear on nations: 'the queen of the world', public opinion.[333] Ladd added: 'Not public opinion as it is now, but public opinion when it shall be enlightened by the rays of the gospel of peace.'[334]

American pacifists like Ladd, Upham, and many others, essentially sought to find a mode of global governance that consciously avoided a central political organisation infringing on state sovereignty. Although the American design for a congress of nations has generally been labelled 'utopian', closer analysis ought to nuance that – not always pejorative – framing. Ladd insisted that the principles of non-intervention and absolute non-violence had to be coupled with the absence of an executive, relying totally on the growing strength of public opinion. Anticipating any objections, he relied on the persuasive value of law: 'if it be valid, why have so many wise and able writers taken great pains to compose treatises on the Law of Nations'? Ladd stressed that neither Vattel nor Grotius had 'possessed the physical power to carry their laws into effect; yet their opinion have always had great weight, and they have been considered benefactors to mankind'. If a

331 Ibid., 521.

332 Ibid., 521–4.

333 Ibid., iv, 519

334 Ibid., 587.

great number of such jurists could meet in a peaceful assembly, would they not better than anyone else be able to articulate the 'general will'? The same objections, Ladd felt, might equally be levelled against existing arbitration cases, or any treaty between a stronger and a weaker power.[335]

Even if Ladd probably overestimated the clout of general public opinion in several major states, or its 'enlightened' character, he was not at all wrong in assuming that increasing the solemnity of a codification, by involving major great powers as well as smaller states, would 'raise the political cost of breaking it', as demonstrated by the 1856 Declaration of Paris.[336] If anything, he was perhaps too keen on preserving state sovereignty, in the sense that he still envisioned formal ratification procedures, whereas Jan Lemnitzer identified the waiving of ratification requirements as one of the greatest innovations of the 1856 Declaration, allowing for a legal norm to become internationally accepted in the span of mere months.[337]

The debate on realistic legal instruments did not abate with the death of Ladd in the spring of 1841. That very year, a new alternative was launched by the conservative members of the American Peace Society. Believing that permanent multilateral cooperation was unlikely for the near future, the new leaders of the American peace movement sought for a legal alternative that could be put into effect at short notice, on a limited scale. With Ladd no longer able to bring his charisma and his authority to bear, the fragile alliance between conservative and reformist peace friends came to an end. Over the following years, both factions clashed over the ideological and pragmatical direction of the U.S. peace movement. Like Noah Worcester before him, the good-humoured naval captain from Maine entered into memory as a great 'apostle of peace'. His unassuming tombstone simply read: 'Blessed are the peace-makers, for they shall be called the children of God.'

2.4 *Stipulated Arbitration*

During a special meeting of peace friends in Boston in 1841, the renowned British philanthropist Joseph Sturge (1793–1859), one of the leaders of the London Peace Society, explained an intriguing plan he had been introduced to earlier in his visit to the United States. Would it not be possible, he wondered out loud, to 'prevent war by inserting in every treaty a clause, binding the parties to settle their differences in the last resort by amicable reference

335 *Prize Essays* 1840, 599–601;

336 Lemnitzer, *Privateering* 2014, 193; Neff, *Justice* 2014, 319–320.

337 Ibid., 191.

to an empire mutually chosen'?[338] Sturge's audience was enthusiastic about the proposal, to such an extent that they agreed with Sturge that a 'General Conference' should be held on this and other issues of common interest. These were the first steps towards the first international peace conference, which eventually took place in London, in 1843.[339] The man who had informed Sturge of this novel peace strategy was William Jay, whose prominence in the American Peace Society ensured his ten-year presidency of the society between 1848 and 1858. During those years, he took an active leadership role, unlike most presidents.[340]

The interest of William Jay in arbitration and peace should not surprise. His father, the first Chief Justice of the Federal Supreme Court, John Jay, had in 1794 concluded the eponymous Jay Treaty with Britain, which has already been discussed earlier.[341] Like his father, the younger Jay went into law, eventually becoming a judge in Westchester county, New York. As many other peace friends, the lawyer had a broad interest in the reform movement. A devout Episcopalian – a denomination less represented among peace friends – he championed causes including anti-duelling, temperance, education, and Sabbath observance.[342] In his twenties, Jay had helped organise the American Bible Society.[343] However, of these other interests, he became best known for his vocal abolitionism. Not unusual by itself for a peace friend, he distinguished himself for his early criticism of the American Colonization Society, still favoured by many in the peace society in the mid-1830s.[344] His outspoken and uncompromising stand against slavery, which Jay indicted as 'a heinous sin' that 'ought to be immediately abandoned', ended his legal career in 1843, when the governor caved in to proslavery pressure not to reappoint the troublesome judge.[345]

338 AP (October & November 1842), 21.

339 See chapter 2.

340 Lawson, 'Journals' 1978, 185; Lawson, *Plowshares* 1975, 545.

341 See supra in this chapter.

342 George Cheever, *A Discourse on the Virtues and Public Services of the late Judge Jay* (Boston: American Peace Society 1860), 1–10; Tuckerman, Bayard. *William Jay and the Constitutional Movement for the Abolition of Slavery* (New York: Dodd, Mead & Company 1893), 1–63.

343 Tuckerman, *William Jay* 1983, 11–2.

344 This society sought to transplant African slaves back to Africa. It was seen as deeply problematic even at the time. William Jay, *An Inquiry into the Character and Tendency of the American Colonization, and American Anti-Slavery Societies* (New York: Leavitt, Lord & Co. 1835); Lawson, *Plowshares* 1975, 130.

345 Jay, *Inquiry* 1835, 6; Tuckerman, *William Jay* 1983, 112–125.

From his mid-fifties onwards, 'judge Jay', as he was usually called, devoted himself more exclusively to the peace cause. The roots of his pacifism probably went back far earlier than the 1840s. Proud of his father's accomplishments, the son wrote a two-volume biography on John Jay in the 1830s.[346] The work not only contained a very positive appraisal of the 1794 treaty, but also a couple of letters from the late 1810s on peace. In them, one John Murray Jr. tried to convert the elder Jay to radical pacifism, not unlike the non-resistance of the New York Peace Society.[347] John Jay, a diplomat who had actively supported the Revolutionary war effort, was naturally unconvinced, replying back that the gospel allowed for '*just* and *necessary* war', and that use of force as sanctioned by civil government and the law of nations was not in contravention of the moral law of the gospel.[348] Similar to critiques by Marshall, mentioned earlier, Jay was sceptical about the role of human agency in bringing about the prophesized Millennial age.[349] While the father was unimpressed, the son proved more receptive to the peace message, as indicated by John Jay's off-hand remark that his son William had delivered Murray's letters, along with a number of pamphlets.[350] Although no titles were given, these probably came from the New York or Massachusetts peace societies, judging from their descriptions, as well as their surrounding context. William Jay's latent interest in peace activism manifested itself for the first time in published form in 1842, with a booklet called *War and Peace: the Evils of the First, and a Plan for persevering the Last.*[351] Similar to the inaugural texts of Dodge and Worcester, or the works of Upham and Ladd, it stands as a highly influential classic of nineteenth century pacifist thought.[352]

2.4.1 A *Clause Compromissoire*

Jay recommended that the United States should write into the next treaty with France a clause that any and all disputes on the 'true meaning and

346 Jay, *Life of John Jay* 1833.

347 Ibid., vol I, 322–84; ibid., vol. II, 302–4.

348 Ibid., vol. II, 375–6, 385–98.

349 Ibid., 396–7.

350 Ibid., 404.

351 William Jay, *War and Peace: the Evils of the First, and a Plan for preserving the Last* (London: Ward 1842).

352 Like Ladd's essay, it was republished in 1919 by the Carnegie Foundation. William Jay, *War and Peace: the Evils of the First, and a Plan for preserving the Last. Reprinted from the Original Edition of 1842 with an Introductory Note by James Brown Scott* (New York: OUP, 1919).

intention of any stipulation' of the treaty in question should be submitted to the 'arbitrament of one or more friendly powers', whose decision would be binding.[353] Seeing as how it was to be achieved on a bilateral treaty basis, this instrument soon came to be known as 'stipulated arbitration' in the Anglo-American peace societies. It was also dubbed a *clause compromissoire* in the later nineteenth century, but this was not yet a common name for it for most mid-century peace advocates.

In a sense, Jay's conception of 'stipulated arbitration' was relatively unique, even if he was strongly inspired by a few precedents. Although Jay had been clearly influenced by his father's treaty, it was not identical to the arbitration that John Jay had inscribed in his 1794 treaty, and which had inspired the Treaty of Ghent.[354] Binational commissions were absent from the plan, Jay the younger instead preferring to resort directly to a third power. Perhaps he wanted to avoid the failure of these earlier commissions to come to an agreement.[355] It was also different from later forms of arbitration, most notably the mechanism provided by the Treaty of Washington of 1871, which led to the landmark *Alabama claims* award. William Jay did not yet envision a collegiate body where most commissioners came from third-party states.[356]

Jay defined 'arbitration' as vaguely as Vattel had, whose authority he quoted in support. Specifically, the American judge cited the passage in which the renowned Swiss author asserted that arbitration was 'reasonable' and 'conformable to natural law'.[357] Jay also felt it worthwhile to copy the reference to Switzerland's extensive reliance of arbitration among the various cantons.[358] As will be discussed in the chapter on the Genevan Peace Society, however, internal Swiss 'arbitration' in the 1830s was markedly different from that conceived in international legal doctrine, or that which was practiced among non-Swiss states.[359] Since judge Jay simultaneously defended the impartiality of a third-party state, it must be

353 Jay, *War and Peace* 1842, 40.

354 In the Treaty of Ghent, only the size of the commissions had been reduced to two, to avoid the deadlock that had marked the commissions of the Jay Treaty. King and Graham, 'Origins' 1995, 46.

355 See supra.

356 King and Graham, 'Origins' 1995, 48–49; J. Gillis Wetter, *The International Arbitral Process: Public and Private, vol. 1* (Dobs Ferry: Oceana Publications 1979), 27. See chapter 6 for more on the *Alabama claims*.

357 Jay, *War and Peace* 1842, 40; Vattel, *Droits des gens. Tome second* 1758, 57 (§ 329).

358 Ibid.

359 See chapter 3.

concluded that he still conceived of an 'arbitral award' as the decision of a head of state, aided by political and legal advisors, as had been the case with the Dutch or Russian awards.[360]

However, speaking only of the 'arbitrament of one or more friendly powers', Jay did not offer any specific procedure, other than the broad principle that third-parties should be able to give binding decisions. In that respect, the originality of Jay, usually credited as the sole originator of the scheme by both contemporaries and historians, should be nuanced. Already in 1839, three years before the publication of *War and Peace,* did the New York Peace Society publish a memorial urging Congress to adopt arbitration as the United States' permanent policy. While the document also recommended a congress of nations, this part was interpreted by the national society as requiring the insertion of dedicated arbitration provisions in treaties, following the Swiss example.[361] Jay might very well have taken some inspiration from these precedents. At the very least, he captured the society's desire for a pragmatic legal instrument that could be brought to bear on U.S. political elites.

Any considerations on Jay's originality aside, the indeterminacy of Jay's scheme was in line with its more general lack of conceptualisation in the first half of the nineteenth century. For a considerable time, as had been the case also in the earlier suggestions by Worcester, Ladd, and others, nineteenth century lawyers did not draw any strict line between 'political' mediation, and 'legal' arbitration', in their search for a more 'rational' means of dispute settlement than diplomacy, viewed as emotion-driven and militaristic.[362] While Jay certainly represented a more outspoken turn towards arbitration as a judicial, rather than a political process, his definition of 'arbitration' was still generic enough to accommodate a wide array of specific possibilities, including commissions, single arbitrators, mixed tribunals, or even Benthamite or Ladd-like judicial 'courts'.[363] Arguably, far from proving a liability, it was an advantage. Those sceptical of the political viability of a congress of nations might support a project that relied on a seemingly simple and generally accepted principle, but that could take on any number of concretisations. This partially accounted for the marked speed with which Jay's plan overtook that of Ladd within the Anglo-American peace

---

360 He explicitly referenced these, as well as Prussia's arbitration between the U.S. and Mexico. Ibid., 42–43.

361 AP (March 1839), 222–224.

362 Jay, *War and Peace* 1842, 41; Zollman, 'Mediation and Arbitration' 2020, 156–60.

363 Zollmann, 160.

societies during the 1840s, and eventually the international peace movement as a whole.[364]

A substantial segment of the American Peace Society seemed to agree with Jay that William Ladd's grand dream of a congress of nations was 'utterly chimerical'.[365] This judge was quite adamant about his belief that, 'in the present state of the world', no permanent 'tribunal' could see the light of day. To Jay, reflecting an argument of many, a congress of nations could only be installed *'after'* Christian states had already extensively abandoned 'the military policy'.[366] He did not state that a congress of nations could never become a reality, but rather that it could only be the end result of 'a gradual and progressive work'. In a clear refutation of the radical element of the peace movement, this lawyer strongly believed that 'any attempt to persuade Congress to abandon all military preparations, (…) would only quicken into new vigour the military prejudices of the community'. His father's down-to-earth mentality had not been rejected, considering how Jay's argument could even veer towards a kind of Realpolitik rarely found among radical pacifists. Deviating from the usual moralism, judge Jay asserted that such a treaty with France would rob the British empire of a potential ally in a war with the United States. It would therefore be in the British interest to conclude a similar treaty with the United States, considering the ease with which Jay assumed his country to be able to annex the former's Canadian possessions. Such calculations would not be readily found in Ladd's work. Jay took care to underline that his plan was 'adapted to the existing state of civilized society'.

Crucially, it well looked as if the American Peace Society could have its cake and eat it too: achieve mainstream support, while keeping its radical core content. In the words of the plan's author: 'it is, indeed, perfectly consistent with the precepts of Christianity, but [also] with the selfish dictates of worldly policy. It interferes with no military preparations, and it offends no prejudice of the most ultra advocate of pacific principles.'[367]

---

364 Lynch, 'Peace Movements' 2012, 210–4; Grossi, *Pacifisme européen* 1994, 68, 85, 121, 133–8, 197.

365 Jay, *War and Peace* 1842, 39.

366 Ibid., 38–39, 43. See parallel critiques made in chapters 2 and 5.

367 Jay, *War and Peace* 1842, 38–40, 43–4, 50.

3 Challenges to Early American 'Peace through Law'

As it turned out, Jay had severely underestimated the extent of hostility towards both his and Ladd's legal projects by the so-called 'ultra' factions within the American Peace Society. Bitter factionalism has always divided the American peace movement. Its roots went back already to the movement's two-fold beginnings in the radical New York Peace Society and the moderate Massachusetts Peace Society. William Ladd's skilful diplomacy had managed to keep the American Peace Society united during his lifetime. Unfortunately, the death of the society's charismatic founder in 1841 provoked a prolonged period of internal strife within American organised pacifism.

Three contenders emerged. The first to emerge, and to even outright secede already during Ladd's lifetime, were the self-styled 'non-resistants'. They were by far the most vocal and radical pacifists. They established the New England Non-Resistance Society in 1838, and took the New York Peace Society's distrust of secular law and government to its extreme. The two that remained in the peace society were more restrained. The 'conservatives' or 'moderates' leaned closest to mainstream U.S. opinion, and wanted the peace society to focus exclusively on interstate war. Many of them did not oppose defensive war and 'just cause', although this was a sensitive issue even for them. Opposing the conservatives were the so-called 'reformists'. These peace friends were essentially the optimistic variant of the non-resistants. While reformists too, as true pacifists, condemned defensive war, they were not willing to cut ties with political action. To the contrary, the reformists wanted their society to join hands with other progressist movements, like temperance and abolitionism. What good was peace in a society that kept millions of its inhabitants in slavery?

Between 1840 and the early 1850s, a series of struggles raged throughout the U.S. peace movement. At stake was nothing less than the soul of American pacifism. The three above-mentioned factions all tried to define what it meant to be a 'friend of peace'. What did 'peace' mean? How far could it go? These were key debates, because they strongly informed the legal strategy which the American Peace Society should pursue in its political campaign. Although these battles involved many people, the leading faction members were William Lloyd Garrison for the non-resistants, George Beckwith for the conservatives, and Elihu Burritt for the reformists. Their rivalries profoundly informed the political campaign of the American Peace Society in the antebellum. It also impacted the reactions of the American peace friends when they met their first great trial: the outbreak of war with Mexico.

3.1 *Non-resistance and Law*

The New England Non-Resistance Society was established in 1838 by disgruntled members of the American Peace Society. Although tensions had been simmering under the surface for some while by then, the immediate cause were a number of internal changes within the national peace society. By the mid–1830s, adherents of the society complained of a lack of popular interest, an apathy that most painfully showed itself in chronic funding problems.[368] Up until then, the society had avoided a formal stance against defensive war, rightly believing that the public would never agree with such extremism. At the same time, however, a non-negligible number of the radical members supported the hard-line position of condemning *all* wars, arguing that a clear message would trigger pushback, which could hopefully overcome the prevailing indifference.[369]

Getting messages that several members were considering secession, Ladd made a last-ditch attempt to preserve unity within the society he had founded. At the annual meeting of 1837, its constitution was changed to formally and explicitly condemn 'all war' as contrary to the gospel.[370] Unfortunately, Ladd had miscalculated the impact this sudden change would have on the rest of the society. Many of its more conservative members began pouring in formal letters of protest. One of the most well-respected members, the president of Bowdoin College – where Upham was a professor – promptly gave his resignation. In an angry public letter, he fumed that 'statesmen' would from then on view the peace society as 'a body of visionaries and fanatics, ignorant of the world's affairs'.[371] Resistance continued until the next annual meeting. In the spring of 1838, the opposition succeeded in getting a couple of 'clarifying' resolutions adopted. Although the constitution's letter changed the same, it was now stressed that it did not have any bearing on the right of individual self-defence, that it did not require an individual pledge, and that everyone was welcome, regardless of whether or not they agreed with its principle.[372] This was evidently a very

368 To put things into perspective: the American Bible Society annually received between 15 and 100 times more contributions between 1835 and 1860 than the American Peace Society. Lawson, *Plowshares* 1975, 481–2.

369 Curti, *Crusade* 1929, 72.

370 Ibid., 72–75; AP (June 1837), 19–30.

371 To his credit, Ladd published this damning letter in the *Advocate*. AP (December 1837), 112.

372 AP (March 1838), 192; AP (June 1838), 3–20.

strange compromise. While the reformists and the conservatives continued to vie for control of the society, its most radical members just up and left.[373]

The waters between the two societies were deep from the start. The few members of the American Peace Society present at the new society's founding congress all left within the first thirty minutes, after the assembly had decided to grant full speaking rights to women. It appeared like just another provocation. Only Ladd himself stayed on till the very end. He voted against its constitution, but afterwards continued to attend its annual meetings, allegedly out of a lingering sympathy for those who decided to go 'ultra-high', rather than 'ultra-low' like the rest of the world. Whether Garrison, one of the leaders of the new society, reciprocated those feelings was doubtful. He later confessed to how irritated he had been by his friendly rival's 'broad and irresistible humor', that had disturbed the otherwise 'deep solemnity of the occasion'.[374] Later, in his short-lived journal *The Non-Resistant,* Garrison sneered at the 'disingenuous and equivocal' behaviour of his rival, who claimed sympathy with non-resistance, but in the *Advocate* joined in the American Peace Society's efforts to dissociate itself from his own society.[375]

Ladd was not incorrect in assuming that the New England Non-Resistance Society was a marginal organisation, unable to do 'either much harm or good'.[376] It's 'declaration of sentiments' was signed by only about forty persons, half of which were women.[377] While a modern observer will agree with the society's refusal to accept distinctions of sex, that alone cannot mask the fact that the document was otherwise one of extremes. Its signatories vowed to never defend their person, to neither hold office nor even take part in elections as long as the government had its monopoly on violence, and to voluntarily exclude themselves 'from every legislative and judicial body'. Not stopping there, its members foreswore their allegiance to the United States Constitution.[378] Obviously, such anarchism could impossibly find acceptance in mainstream U.S. society. Counter-cultural by any reasonable standard, non-resistance was rather sectarian. Adin Ballou, for example,

373 *Proceedings of the Peace Convention, held in Boston, in the Marlboro Chapel, September 18, 19, & 20, 1838* (Boston: Knapp 1838); Curti, *Crusade* 1929, 80–81.

374 Ibid., 10; Curti, *Crusade* 1929, 83–84.

375 The Non-Resistant (December 9, 1840), 91; AP (October 1838), 117–20; AP (November 1838), 142–4; AP (December 1838), 161–3; AP (June 1839), 7; AP (August 1839), 31; AP (October 1839), 69–72; AP (December 1840), 232–235; AP (February 1842), 116–9; AP (April 1843), 38–41; Hemmenway, *Memoir Ladd* 1872, 74.

376 Ladd called them 'ultra beyond ultra'. Hemmenway, *Memoir Ladd* 1872, 73, 77.

377 *Proceedings* 1838, 18–20, 28.

378 Ibid., 22–23, 29.

set up the Hopedale Community in 1843, a utopian society.[379] The New England Non-Resistance Society did not have any auxiliaries, and its first journal lasted only two years. Torn apart by internal dissension and lack of funding, it was already defunct well before its last meeting in 1849.[380]

From a legalist perspective, radical non-resistance found comparatively little common ground with the moderates of the American Peace Society. The only source of agreement lay in their assessment of existing international legal doctrine, seen by both as in dire need of reform. A prominent theorist was Henry Clarke Wright (1797–1870), a former agent of the American Peace Society.[381] He wrote that 'the science of public law' ought not to be separated 'from that of ethics'.[382] Like other friends of peace, he considered it fundamentally immoral that a war declaration by a sovereign could drag all individual citizens into a war, as 'the best writers on international law' all agreed upon. He cited from Kent, Story, Marshall, Hall, Grotius, Vattel, Burlamaqui, Pufendorf and Bynkershoek. Similar to Ladd and Upham, Wright did not understand why Bynkershoek did not consider such a 'reversal of natural justice' necessary, while Vattel and Grotius did seem to require a prior declaration. Wright did not know what to make of textbooks contradicting each other on such important issues. In his eyes, a state formally declaring war was as absurd as a pirate formally announcing his intentions of plundering a ship. Both were equally sinful.[383]

Non-resistants such as Wright deviated from moderate pacifists in certain crucial premises. In their theological assumptions, non-resistants laid nearly all emphasis on individual responsibility. Wright defined war not as a traditional interstate conflict, but as the 'right to kill', not only 'men', but also 'the innocent', and the right to turn off one's sense of morality, in order to blindly follow the orders of others who solely acted in terms of expediency.[384] The non-resistant, however, should at all times assume 'personal responsibility', and consider himself above all else 'the subject of the Prince of Peace'. If Kent was correct, that 'every man is a party to the acts of his

379 It lasted about fifteen years before it went bankrupt. Adin Ballou, *Christian Non-Resistance in all its Important Bearings* (Philadelphia: Universal Peace Union 1910), 242.

380 Ziegler, *Antebellum* 1992, 91.

381 AP (June 1837), 19–30; Lewis Perry, 'Wright, Henry Clarke', in *American National Biography Online*. 2000, available at: doi.org/10.1093/anb/9780198606697.article.1500862.

382 He cited Kent. Henry Clarke Wright, *Defensive War proved to be a Denial of Christianity and of the Government of God: with Illustrative Facts and Anecdotes* (London: Gilpin 1846), 107

383 Ibid., 145, 148–9.

384 Ibid., 14–22.

own government', Wright reasoned, that meant that one should refuse to serve in the army or vote on a congressman invested with 'war-making power' by the Constitution.[385]

All existing worldly governments were dismissed as hopelessly corrupt, the U.S. government being no exception. Unlike the American Peace Society, which tried its utmost to tiptoe around the very sensitive topic of the Revolutionary War, venerated as the prime example of a 'just war' by almost everyone, Wright framed Washington as a 'a warrior', who had condoned the 'despotic' repression of loyalists, the pillaging by his troops, and an inhumane military discipline. Worst of all, however, this 'hero' had been a hypocrite. Like many drafters of the Declaration of Independence, George Washington too had been a 'slaveholder' and a 'slave-breeder', leading a government that professed to fight for 'liberty', but had stripped 'one-sixth of the people of all political and personal rights'.[386]

Refusing to see the state as the main vehicle of political action, non-resistants fancied that only the accumulation of individual conversions would in the long run lead to the total overhaul of human government everywhere, the prerequisite for fundamental reform. Garrison did not believe in any scheme that 'supposed the continued existence of those political arrangements [...] we consider as incompatible with the proposed of abiding peace'.[387] An emphasis on individual purity made perfect sense to someone with a deeply religious mindset. If the message of the gospel was straightforward, and God's judgment awaited everyone in the end, there was no reason to be compromising. To die without having earned one's heaven was a fate worse than death.

Accordingly, non-resistants rejected the legal solutions devised within the American Peace Society. Garrison had 'little faith' in a congress or court of nations. It was asserted that no government, 'as now existing', would ever 'honestly and in good faith' accept the congress's authority. Similarly, its acts would be 'but so much empty breath, if unenforced by the military arm'. Its supporters had 'begun at the wrong end', because the conditions required for the success of a congress of nations were the same as those needed to end war. If enough individuals had consented to peaceful dispute settlement, there were ipso facto no more wars to be prevented.[388] They

385 Ibid., 12, 150–1.
386 Ibid., 188–98.
387 The Non-Resistant (February 12, 1840), 9, 11.
388 Ibid., 9, 11.

rejected any system which took the state as its basic building block, but said nothing of violence *within* the state.[389]

A similar fate therefore befell judge Jay's plan for stipulated arbitration. A few years later, Garrison elaborately reviewed the latter's *War and Peace*.[390] As much as the leading man of the Non-Resistance Society professed to respect Jay as a person – a fellow radical abolitionist – he was not able to see its essential difference with 'the favorite project of the late William Ladd, except that it [was] on a smaller scale'.[391] Garrison attacked every argument of Jay by which the latter had tried to argue the political viability of his scheme. Did Jesus himself 'form his scheme "in accordance with the selfish dictates of worldly policy"?', he wondered. Did the apostles 'shock no prejudice', as Jay praised his plan? Garrison did not see benefit in moderation. The precedent of Wilberforce could not convince him, because it had not abolished slavery itself; Garrison was not far off the mark when he declared that in 1842 the foreign slave trade was as alive as it had been in 1783, when Wilberforce first began his campaign.[392] He pressed hard on the weak spot of the American Peace Society: their difficulties in reconciling its condemnation of war with self-defence.[393] A man not known for his sense of tact, Garrison later described it as Jay's 'impotent plan', because it was 'moral imbecility' to try and make a covenant with 'Leviathan'. No longer bothering to be courteous, the non-resistant leader asserted that 'the "treaty-making" remedy has been tried long enough, and found to be utterly worthless'.[394]

3.2 *Reformism and Law*

Outside of the extreme anarchist fringe of antebellum American peace activism, moderate friends of peace likewise could not agree on the course to be pursued. Hegemony over the society changed hands a number of times between 1841 and the early 1850s, the balance of power alternately leaning in favour of the reformists and the conservatives. The reformists' pinnacle of success happened in 1845, when a majority at the annual meeting allowed them to occupy most key positions. It was at this time that Elihu Burritt,

389 The Non-Resistant (December 21, 1839), 3.

390 The Non-Resistant (April 13, 1842), 27; The Non-Resistant (April 27, 1842), 31; The Non-Resistant (May 25, 1842), 38–39.

391 The Non-Resistant (April 13, 1842), 27.

392 There was quite a bit of *imitatio Christi* language in non-resistant literature. The Non-Resistant (May 25, 1842), 38–39; Ziegler, *Antebellum* 1992, 66.

393 The Non-Resistant (May 25, 1842), 39.

394 No biographer has ever described Garrison as an easy-going man. The Non-Resistant (April 27, 1842), 31.

one of the most important nineteenth century peace friends, first made his mark. He assumed editorship of the *Advocate* that year, which he promptly renamed the *Advocate of Peace and Universal Brotherhood.*[395] The new style lasted barely twelve months, until Beckwith – who had reportedly taken the loss of the *Advocate* very hard – rallied enough supporters to regain control over the executive committee at the next annual meeting. Things reached their finale at the annual meeting of 1851, when the meeting degenerated into open yelling and shoving. It only ended when someone called for the police.[396]

In the end, the conservatives led by Beckwith won the day. They represented a majority within the society. Reformists had long been able to punch above their weight mainly due to their greater zeal, and the money they invested as the most dedicated members. Therefore, the eventual compromise granted some concessions to them. They gained supervisory control over the society's finances and its publications, and the constitution stayed intact. The article introduced by Ladd, condemning *all* war, remained in place. However, so did the resolutions that undermined its import. Beckwith also stayed in charge of the society's finances. Most importantly, however, he remained the secretary of the American Peace Society. Beckwith would remain its key officer until his death in 1870, leading the society during the dark days of the Civil War.[397] Many leading reformists, including Burritt, left the society in the wake of Beckwith's conservative victory. The two factions never truly reconciled. Reformist peace activism continued as a strong, albeit minority, force within U.S. pacifism.

As the figurehead of moderation in the American Peace Society, Beckwith sympathised more with the plan of Jay than that of Ladd. Under Beckwith's editorship of the *Advocate,* stipulated arbitration was grandly announced as an 'immediately practical' plan, that could be put to use in petitions sent to the president and Congress.[398] The issue went on to include the relevant extracts from Jay's *War and Peace,* and – interestingly – an article written

395 Articles from this brief interval are also simply abbreviated as 'AP'.

396 Curti, *Crusade* 1929, 89–100

397 In Ziegler's opinion, '[Beckwith] has yet to find a biographer, much less a sympathetic one'. Ziegler was unaware of Lawson's doctoral thesis, who painted Beckwith in a more positive light. Lawson has portrayed him as maybe 'not a charismatic personality', but nonetheless as a 'quiet and forthright man (…) more responsible for the continued existence of the American peace movement than any other person'. Ziegler, *Antebellum* 1992, 79–80, 95–100; Lawson, *Plowshares* 1975, 15.

398 AP (October & November 1842), 241–2.

by the reformist Thomas Upham.[399] Upham's quick conversion to Jay's plan, after having featured in Ladd's *Prize Essays*, was indicative of its potential to transcend the society's pervasive factionalism, as had been originally hoped for by Jay.

The following year, at the British-American peace conference held in London, discussed in the second chapter, the American and London peace societies agreed to prioritise bilateral arbitration clauses over a congress of nations. The latter was not formally rejected, but relegated to an inferior position as a long-term objective.[400] Beckwith made sure that the *Advocate* strongly highlighted this decision. Three years later, in 1846, Beckwith succeeded in having the resolutions of London '43 adopted as the 'proper basis of co-operation in the cause of Peace'.[401] In his *Peace Manual* of 1847, a collection of pacifist tracts not to be confused with Upham's older *Manual of Peace*, Beckwith stressed that the broad principles of London '43, which allowed for a diversity-of-opinion approach in Ladd's vein, had to form the basis of American peace activism.[402] He could barely hide his impatience with radicals, who, according him, wanted to reduce everything to an abstract principle, which invariably tended to lead the discussion astray 'into disputes which have little or no connection with peace'. Rather than trying to argue against war 'only in [their] own favorite way', they should unite on one limited goal, namely the abolition of 'international war'.[403]

The conservatives were not fully successful in their attempts at downplaying the cherished project of their society's popular founder. While as such not opposed to stipulated arbitration, it was clear that many reformists still clung to Ladd's dream for a congress of nations. The increasing focus on stipulated arbitration was at various intervals abruptly interrupted by noticeable upticks in support for a congress of nations.[404] Many were not ready to abandon the scheme in which the society had sunk so much time and effort during the 1830s. Had the *Prize Essays* been written for nothing?

399 Ibid., 243–256.
400 See chapters 2 and 5.
401 AP (June 1846), 137–138.
402 George Beckwith, *The Peace Manual: or, War and its Remedies* (Boston: American Peace Society 1847), 10–1.
403 Ibid., 11–13.
404 E.g. AP (February 1845), 20–4; AP (April 1845), 47–48; AP (November & December 1845), 124–7, 142–4; AP (February 1846), 39–42; AP (October 1846), 227–30; see also AP (May & June 1849), 49–57.

This showed itself in repeated back and forth arguments in the *Advocate* during this troubled time.[405]

The greatest benefit of a congress and court in the eyes of its supporters lay in its potential to codify international law. In the absence of a clear body of positive law, states would pledge themselves to an 'uncertain and unforeseen sacrifice' in light of the 'fluctuating' nature of international law. An international court would be more impartial and consistent in its decisions, and would be less prone to rejections of its decisions 'on the slightest pretence of irregularity', like had been the case in the Dutch arbitral award on the Maine boundary. Crucially important to reformist peace friends, only these institutions could fundamentally address the 'unjust and injurious' facets of the law of nations. No single nation could unilaterally choose to discard these principles, but a congress could form a 'new code of international law', more conformable to the 'spirit of humanity' and 'the light of the age'.[406] Only a congress and court could prevent future wars, because of the permanent bond these formed among its member states. To the extent 'rulers and legislators' were largely disinterested in any closer ties, someone like Blanchard did not believe the same rang true for 'the people at large'.[407]

The most important reformist, stemming from the 'people at large', and worth properly introducing now was Elihu Burritt. Born in 1810 in Connecticut as one of ten children of a small farmer, Burritt had one of the humblest backgrounds imaginable. Despite his relative poverty throughout most of his life, Burritt nonetheless grew into one of the most renowned pacifists of the nineteenth century, ever since Merle Curti rediscovered his legacy.[408] He originally laboured as a blacksmith in his small hometown, wholly unaware of the peace societies. However, he was passionate about learning. His first love was the study of language. Due to his circumstances, Burritt was self-educated. He studied during breaks and until late in the evening. Eventually this polyglot claimed to master nearly fifty languages, earning himself a reputation as 'the learned blacksmith'. Because of this, Burritt became somewhat of a local celebrity. The governor even offered him a

405 AP (December 1842), 276–7; AP (February 1846), 39–42: AP (October 1846), 227–30; AP (November & December 1845), 127.

406 AP (February 1846), 40–41.

407 Ibid., 41–42.

408 Merle Curti (ed), *The Learned Blacksmith. The Letters and Journals of Elihu Burritt* (New York: Wilson-Erickson, 1937), 1–7; his private journals are partially consultable online at newbritain.advantage-preservation.com/.

scholarship for Harvard. However, the autodidact feared that he would feel out of place there. Instead, the turned to the lecture circuit, which paid enough money to get him away from the forge and into a new life of the mind.[409]

During this travels, many of which he did on foot, Burritt came into contact with reformist milieus, such as temperance and abolitionism. It strongly appealed to his deep faith.[410] According to Burritt himself, he was converted to the peace cause by his study of geography. Asked to give a lecture on this subject, he was struck by how the earth's variety of climates ensured a natural interdependence between all the nations of the world. Never having come into contact with any peace society before, Burritt began to independently lecture on peace. Soon enough, the American Peace Society noticed his potential and inducted him into the society.[411]

The newest member of the reformists proved a formidable activist. He set up numerous initiatives. He began a weekly newspaper, *The Christian Citizen,* co-founded the radical Worcester County Peace Society, and began issuing small *'Olive Leaves'*, short articles on peace frequently sent to non-pacifist newspapers. Framing himself as a common-sense 'working man', Burritt above all prized short and inexpensive propaganda aimed at a large audience. In a like vein, Burritt championed 'Ocean Penny Postage', believing that cheap intercontinental mail brought global public opinion together. Unlike most American peace friends, Burritt travelled to Europe, where he achieved his greatest successes. In Britain, he founded the League of Universal Brotherhood, an organisation which, at its height, ended up as the closest thing to a mass peace society in the nineteenth century. Its journal was *The Bond of Brotherhood.*[412] His other achievements included a 'Friendly Address' initiative in the wake of the Oregon boundary crisis of the mid–1840s. In the same decade, Burritt also instigated the first international peace conference of the nineteenth century. Thirty years later, he helped found the Association for the Codification and Reform of the Law of Nations, still known as the International Law Association. In nearly all those activities,

409 Peter Tolis, *Elihu Burritt. Crusader for Brotherhood* (Hamden: Archon Books, 1968), 3–64; Burritt, Elihu. *Walks in the Black Country and its Green Borderland* (London: Sampson, Law, Son, and Marston, 1869).

410 Tolis, *Burritt* 1968, 70–3.

411 Ibid., 115–120, Elihu Burritt, *Ten-Minute Talks on All Sorts of Topics* (Boston: Lee and Shepard, 1874), 17–8

412 Ceadel, *Origins* 1996, 374–5, 389; Tolis, *Burritt* 1968, 126–234; Ziegler, *Antebellum* 1992, 89.

Burritt consistently defended the idea of a congress of nations, and in particular its capacity to codify international law. His views on this are detailed further on, in other chapters. After being removed from the editorship of the *Advocate* by Beckwith in 1846, Burritt left the American Peace Society and his country behind. It was not in America, but in the Old World where he made his mark.

In the United States, meanwhile, Beckwith was increasingly free from 1846 onwards to implement Jay's project into the political campaign. Aware of the continued draw of reformism, Beckwith took care to style himself as the successor of Ladd's centrist policies. He emphasised that the American Peace Society stood for diversity of opinion, and that every motivation stood on an equal footing.[413] As such, the *Advocate* never stopped printing articles that condemned defensive war, or explicated a congress of nations. However, those were mostly paper discussions. Beckwith again revealed his 'Jesuitical manoeuvres' when a congress of nations was increasingly filtered out of the petitions and memorials that the peace society sent to politicians all the way up to the level of the presidency.[414]

3.3 *The Emerging Political Campaign*

The American peace movement's turn to international law in the 1830s coincided with the start of its political campaign. That was no surprise. Although scripture provided the moral legitimisation, pacifism needed to assume a more concrete legal form to have any use in politics. In the beginning years, it was centred on Ladd's notion of a congress of nations.

The first petitions and memorials were not yet sent to Congress, but to the legislature of the state where peace activism had begun, and was particularly strong: the commonwealth of Massachusetts. The first petition had been drafted in 1829 by Thomas Thompson, for a time an active member of the Massachusetts Peace Society.[415] It recommended a 'court of nations'. Because of it lacked other details, and given its date, this 'court' presumably meant a diplomatic assembly, and not an actually judicial court in the vein of Mill. It gathered about 1,200 signatures, but nothing else was done with it because of the limited means of the Massachusetts auxiliary.[416] In 1835,

413 AP (April 1843), 37–8.

414 Curti, *Crusade* 1929, 90, 97–8.

415 He had criticised the peace societies in 1828 for not undertaking political actions, if he was the anonymous author van der Linden suspects. Van der Linden, *Peace Movement* 1987, 134–135.

416 AP (November 1845), 124.

Thompson collaborated with Ladd to present a petition to the legislature of Massachusetts, an effort which was successfully repeated in 1837.[417] In tune with its development in the propaganda, the second petition still spoke of a 'Congress or Court of Nations'. It did not offer much detail, leaving it up to politics to decide whether or not it would be permanent, and which specific form it should take. It merely urged the Massachusetts legislature to request Congress to consider 'some system for the equitable settlement of international disputes'. Religious arguments were almost absent. The document instead stressed the perceived progress of enlightened public opinion and the economic impact of war.[418] The peace societies claimed that their country's constitution and its remoteness from European politics were major reasons why the United States should take the initiative.[419]

The decision to first focus on the state where peace activism enjoyed the strongest relative support proved wise. In both instances, the Massachusetts legislature referred the petitions to a committee that adopted a clearly positive report. Subsequent peace propaganda often referred to these reports to highlight the feasibility of a congress of nations. Both reports agreed with the petitions that 'an umpire' for the settlement of interstate disputes was 'by no means a visionary project'. It similarly cited the Amphyctionic councils or the Swiss diet. It recalled the Quaker origins of the state. The committee members seemed to be well-acquainted with peace literature, mentioning not only Henri IV and Saint-Pierre, but also the London Peace Society and even an oblique reference to the peace society in Geneva.[420] Apparently, Worcester's propaganda had not fallen on deaf ears.

Both reports resulted into motions approving the society's aims. The ones of 1835 were accepted by the state Senate, but did not make it to a vote in the House.[421] The report of 1837 came in early enough, so that its proposals were accepted with great majorities in both houses. This one resolved that Congress or Court of Nations were 'at present the best practical method' to arbitrate disputes, that the president should open negotiations for this purpose with other governments, and that the governor should send copies of

417 A first attempt in 1831 had not gathered enough signatures after a year. Only about 2,500 had been gathered across three states, far below the 10,000 the society had hoped for. Van der Linden, *Peace Movement* 1987, 135.

418 The petitions and reports up until that point were printed in the appendix to the *Prize Essays* 1840, 641–650.

419 The Calumet (July & August 1833), 418–419; The Calumet (March & April 1835), 203–4

420 *Prize Essays* 1840, 643–4, 652–5.

421 Van der Linden, *Peace Movement* 1987, 136.

the report to the other states of the Union. The following year, the Massachusetts legislature resolved, in line with Ladd's two-part plan, that the U.S. president should be informed of a codifying congress of nations, as well as a 'high court of arbitration', as 'a scheme worthy of (...) careful attention'.[422] Even though nothing further came of such resolves, and similar petitions elsewhere had failed, the peace friends were emboldened by these local successes to begin directly addressing the federal Congress.

The New York Peace Society, invigorated by the inspired activism of Bacheler, who had instigated the essay contest on a congress of nations a few years earlier, was the first to bring pacifist concerns before Congress.[423] Though the peace friends of New York had taken the lead, they were supported by petitions from the American Peace Society and some other local societies, totalling about 1,400 signatures, well below expectations.[424] Despite the limited number of signatures, the petition arrived before the House Committee on Foreign Affairs. The committee was asked to consider the viability of an 'international tribunal' to develop an 'international code of law', because the law of nations' ambiguity was identified as a major cause of war. This tribunal did not yet include a separate judicial court, since the petition was drafted a year before Ladd introduced the distinction.[425] Unfortunately, the representatives in Washington proved more sceptical than those in Massachusetts had.

The long report by the South Carolina representative Hugh Legaré (1797–1843) stood sympathetic, but was not convinced of its practicability. Legaré did not believe that 'the unanimous consent of nations' was possible 'in the actual state of the world'. He referred specifically to Britain's pretences in maritime law, 'one of the most important departments of international law'. If the 1780–1783 League of Armed Neutrality had failed, this congressman wondered, what hope would a congress of nations have? Similarly, France, Austria, or Russia were in other respects too influential in the balance of power, so that if even one of these great powers objected, 'it would be fatal to the project of the memorialists'. Legaré turned the example of Henri IV against the peace friends: the French king had at least realised that such revolutionary reform had to be based on 'something solid', such as a real

422 *Prize Essays* 1840, 659–60.

423 This was not the same New York Peace Society as the one founded by Dodge.

424 Van der Linden, *Peace Movement* 1987, 136.

425 *Prize Essays* 1840, 662–663.

balance of power, rather than 'a mere declaration of abstract principles on paper'.[426]

Since he was a conservative lawyer, Legaré could not accept wholesale legal codification. According to him, codifications were only successful to the extent they agreed with the 'opinions, usages, and manners of a people', meaning that it could therefore only go so far. His reasoning was influenced not only by American common law traditions, but also by the German historical school, which was received also in U.S. professional and academic circles.[427] The political conservatism of the founder of this school, the lawyer Friedrich Carl von Savigny, aligned well with Legaré's intuitions, who retorted against Ladd that 'the great bulk and body of the *corpus iuris civilis* is strictly *common law*'. His report stated that 'the Pandects are, from beginning to end, nothing but a repository of the wisdom of the great jurisconsults of a better age'. Legaré argued that the same had applied to the growth of the federal U.S. Constitution: it had developed organically from British and colonial institutions. Any codification ahead of 'the gradual progress of social improvement' was set up to fail.[428]

If Legaré believed that a code would do neither much harm nor good, his hostility to any form of international tribunal was much more profound. He feared that, 'in the actual relations of the great powers', such an institution would be 'perverted to the worst ends', and 'the only republic in the world' should therefore avoid getting entangled. Any such congress would only end up as another Laibach and Verona, or another Holy Alliance. The committee members dismissed the historical examples for these reasons, from the Amphyctionic council to the Holy Roman Empire, believing that all had failed in preventing perennial internal conflict, or being de facto dominated by its most powerful member. Because of these many fundamental misgivings, Legaré could only give a very mild endorsement. The peace societies were advised to continue exerting 'whatever influence they may posses' over public opinion, in order to 'habitually' promote pacific settlements. However, the report concluded that time remained 'the best reformer', and that 'the sword' will for the time being continue to 'prove the surest guarantee of peace'. Prefiguring

426 Ibid., 671–672.

427 Matthias Reimann, 'The Historical School against Codification: Savigny, Carter, and the Defeat of the New York Civil Code'. *The American Journal of Comparative Law* 37(1) (1989), 98; Banner, *Natural Law* 2021, 191.

428 *Prize Essays* 1840, 673–675.

later nineteenth century practice, the committee could only approve of arbitration in limited and ad hoc cases.[429]

Believing that Congress had given them a first thumbs-up, new petitions were sent to Washington, challenging some of Legaré's arguments. Based on Ladd, they stressed that their international court ought to be composed of autonomous judges, that a code would strengthen its impartiality, that there existed precedents, and that specialists as reputable as Vattel supported it. However, Congress became increasingly negative.[430]

More than any arcane discussion on the trustworthiness of historical precedents, the peace friends were pleasantly surprised that their first petition was picked up at all. The specific petition that had led to the Legaré report had after all been signed by just thirty-five people, yet it was supported on the House floor by such eminencies as former president John Quincy Adams and former secretary of state Henry Clay.[431] While John Quincy Adam's sympathy to peace activism was known already from his encouraging letters to Noah Worcester or his jury membership in the *Prize Essays*, Adams likely did not act on the petition merely because it asked for a congress of nations. In its first part, the petitioners of the New York Peace Society had asked Congress to consider a recent decree by the Mexican government to settle the ongoing U.S.-Mexican claims dispute through an arbitrator.

Unwittingly, peace friends had enmeshed themselves in a heated partisan debate through their first petition. The unstable Mexican state, plagued by corruption and misgovernance, had caused a large number of claims by foreign businessmen, from both France and the U.S. The administrations by Andrew Jackson and Martin Van Buren advocated a forceful stance against Mexico, influenced also by debates on the entrance of the former Mexican province of Texas in to the Union. John Quincy Adams was firmly opposed to it, believing that they were looking for a pretext for war with Mexico. Surprisingly, Van Buren agreed to a convention setting up a mixed claims commission in late 1838, in agreement with Congress's formal recommendation of a peaceful settlement.[432] The New York and American

429 'Ibid., 675–678.

430 *Prize Essays* 1840, 679–693; Van der Linden, *Peace Movement* 1987, 136.

431 The American Peace Society advised to send any petitions to these two politicians. AP (November 1838), 142.

432 Pletcher, *Annexation* 1975, 52–57.

peace societies claimed credit for the turn of events, a 'check on the war-spirit' that even they had not anticipated.[433]

Adams informed them in a letter that neither the president nor Congress had previously been aware of any Mexican overtures. It amazed even Adams that the petition's claim had been accurate, when he discovered the Mexicans' official notice. The former president credited the peace societies with preventing war: 'if the petitioners of the peace societies had never rendered to their country any other service, they would have deserved the thanks of the whole nations for this'.[434] This was duly recognised by the other side also: Bacheler soon afterwards received a congratulatory letter from the Mexican minister to the U.S., along with a hundred dollar donation.[435] If this sounded too good to be true for a first foray into politics, it is because it was. In reality, both Adams and the Mexican minister misrepresented the role of Bacheler's petition, since the very next decade judge Jay argued that the administration had wilfully ignored the Mexican proposal, basing himself on congressional documents. The administration had known about it for months, only acting on it when the overture had become public knowledge and citizens' petitions mentioning it became impossible to ignore.[436]

Overall, apart from the accidental political recuperation of their first petition, the influence of the peace movement was not nearly strong enough to influence U.S. foreign policy in any meaningful way. Tensions with Mexico remained high, as well as the latent conflict between the Northern and Southern states. Both were interconnected in the eyes of many Americans, including the politicised peace movement of New England. Events came to a head when, in April 1846, the U.S. Congress formally declared war with Mexico. The first major interstate war of the United States in the peace societies' existence led to the zenith of their popular success.

3.4 *The Mexican War*

The American Peace Society and the New England Non-Resistance Society were quick to condemn the war with Mexico. The non-resistants immediately branded it a 'war for slavery', and did not shy away from openly

433 AP (November 1838), 137–138.

434 Ibid., 138–9.

435 AP (February 1839), 214–215.

436 William Jay, *A Review of the Causes and Consequences of the Mexican War* (Boston: Mussey & Co. 1849), 66–7; Clayton Kohl, *Claims as a Cause of the Mexican War* (New York: Graduate School New York University 1914), 30–44.

wishing for an American military defeat.[437] The American Peace Society did not differ from its radical peers in its damning assessment of the war. There was no ambivalence on it among the members of the society: the war had been one of naked aggression by a powerful state against a weaker neighbour. The 1846 annual report captured the prevailing opinion: 'so clearly are we in the wrong, that no attribute of God, no principle of our religion, no fair construction of international law, no dictate of justice or common sense, can take part with us (...)'.[438] Even worse, this offensive war was believed to have been fought for the expansion of slavery. One of its major causes, apart from a border dispute, had been the annexation of Texas in 1845, a massive new slave state. Many Northern abolitionists suspected that this Southern expansionism was a conspiracy by the slave-holding states to disturb the delicate internal balance of power in the U.S. between North and South.[439] This was the official position of the peace society also, as expressed in its propaganda during and after the war. Since the 1830s, the peace societies had been virtually non-existent in the South. Largely given up for the near future, there was no need to spare the feelings of the planting class of the deep South.

During the war itself, the American Peace Society's public response was quite muted. Beckwith did not consider it wise to hold public meetings, briefly contemplated in the beginning, because of the high 'excitement' in the rest of American society on the war.[440] Intense passion was palpable in the early days, to the extent that even a moderate like judge Jay initially called for the dissolution of the Union.[441] Beckwith claiming that the war 'came upon us so suddenly, that there was no opportunity of protesting against it in advance', the peace society limited itself to petitioning president Polk and Congress. The first one to the president urged for renewed negotiations or reference to an umpire chosen by both sides, explicitly in the Vattelian vein.[442] In their next petition a short while later, the peace society urged the president to accept Britain's offer of mediation, receiving support from the London Peace Society, which sent out similar requests to

437 Ziegler, *Antebellum* 1992, 109–12.

438 AP (June 1846), 140

439 Pletcher, *Annexation* 1975, 113–351; Ziegler, *Antebellum* 1992, 111.

440 Whitney, *Centennial History* 1928, 83.

441 James Brewer Stewart, *Holy Warriors. The Abolitionists and American Slavery* (New York: Hill and Wang 1976), 109–118.

442 AP (January & February 1847), 16–17.

various heads of state.[443] Those petitions sent by the American Peace Society to Congress in turn warned of the 'practical despotism of war', stressing the threat posed to the American republic by presidential overreach and generals invested with too much 'war-power'.[444] The society elsewhere alluded to the ongoing Congressional debate on whether Polk had been acting within constitutional boundaries by his unilateral declaration that a state of war existed between the U.S. and Mexico. The American Peace Society's most elaborate answer to the challenge of the Mexican War addressed these subjects in greater detail: another essay contest, this time on the origins of the Mexican War.

Begun in December 1847, this competition suffered delays like the one from the previous decade, and did not end until two months after the war, in April 1849. The jury consisted of three members, two of which were clergymen. The third juror was, as before, a prominent jurist. Richard Fletcher (1788–1869) had to resign from his duty, because of his appointment to the Massachusetts Supreme Court, but he was replaced by Simon Greenleaf (1783–1853), one of the founders of Harvard Law School.[445] Twelve manuscripts contended for the 500 dollar premium, which was not split this time, but exclusively awarded to the reverend Abiel Livermore (1811–1892), a Unitarian pastor from New Hampshire. His *Review of the Mexican War* was published in 1850.[446] Its closest runner-up was equally published, in 1849, by the peace society's own president, judge Jay.[447] In fact, a number of the other works too eventually saw the light of day, self-published by their authors.[448] The books by Jay and Livermore were sent by the society to the legislatures of the Northern states, as well as both houses of Congress.[449]

---

443 Ibid., 17–18; Van der Linden, *Peace Movement* 1987, 445.

444 Ibid., 18–19. See also AP (August 1848), 236.

445 Whitney, *Centennial History* 1928, 83; AP (April 1849), 46; David Langum, 'Greenleaf, Simon', in *American National Biography Online*. 2000, available at: doi.org/10.1093/anb/9780198606697.article.1100354.

446 AP (April 1849), 45; Abiel Livermore, *The War with Mexico Reviewed* (Boston: Forbes, 1850).

447 Jay, *Review* 1849.

448 Porter, Charles. *Review of the Mexican War, embracing the Causes of the War, the Responsibility of its Commencement, the Purposes of the American Government in its Prosecution, its Benefits and its Evils* (Auburn: Alden & Parsons, 1849); Berry, Philip. *A Review of the Mexican War on Christian Principles: and an Essay on the Means of Preventing War* (Columbia: Johnston, 1849).

449 Whitney, *Centennial History* 1928, 83–84; AP (March & April 1849), 45–48; AP (September & October 1850), 284.

Both Livermore and Jay traced the most immediate roots of the war to Southern slavery. Livermore subscribed to the popular abolitionist theory that saw the war as a Southern plot to expand slavery and undermine the Union. The reverend criticised military expansionism in the United States and took aim at nationalist surges, like the jingoistic Young America movement.[450] Unlike the essays on a congress of nations the decade before, this essay was overtly political. Livermore named names, identifying annexationist Southerners like John C. Calhoun as the chief perpetrators of the Mexican war.[451] Jay was of a similar opinion and laid most of the blame with Southern pro-slavery interests fearful of the 'security and permanency of slave property'.[452] Directed mainly to Northern readers, the American Peace Society – which described Jay's text as 'a masterly performance' – had markedly cast diplomatic niceties aside, no longer expecting sympathy from the South.[453] Despite Beckwith's efforts to steer the peace society away from becoming an anti-slavery society, many of its members drew connections between slavery and the 'war-system'.[454] Revealingly, submissions which did not agree with the link with slavery had been rejected and received but little notice in the *Advocate*.[455]

Although a lot of the argument focussed on religion and the domestic political debates leading up to and during the war, none of the writers omitted international law from their analyses. Livermore pointed at numerous factual instances in which the United States had allegedly violated the laws of war. Drawing from witness accounts and official reports, the reverend charged the U.S. army with the wanton destruction of civilian property, robbery, rape and random killings.[456] The *Advocate* did much the same in its coverage of the war.[457] As a pacifist, Livermore equally condemned the actions that fell within the accepted *ius in bello,* that he labelled the 'legitimate and inevitable horrors' of any military conflict, such as the battle, the camp, the siege, and the hospital.[458] Livermore and the peace society described in great detail the

450 Livermore, *Mexico* 1850, 6–7, 40.
451 Ibid., 23–24; Merk, Frederik. 'Dissent in the Mexican War', in *Dissent* 1970, 39.
452 Jay, *Review* 1849, 12–13, 18, 87–95.
453 AP (May & June 1849), 65.
454 See chapter 6.
455 Porter, *Review* 1849, III-IV; Berry, *Review* 1849, V-VI.
456 Livermore, *Mexico* 1850, 139–156.
457 AP (July 1846), 168–71; AP (November 1846), 255–7; AP (January & February 1847), 6–15; AP (May & June 1847), 54–9; AP (May & June 1848), 211–3.
458 Livermore, *Mexico* 1850, 122–39; AP (May & June 1847), 54–5; AP (January & February 1848), 148–9; AP (March & April 1848), 186–9.

cruelty of Polk's undisciplined volunteers, who had been hastily scrambled to reinforce the regular army and bypass the constitutional restrictions set on traditional militia forces, falling under state jurisdiction.[459] These forces were seen as opportunistic and poorly disciplined adventurers. Historians generally concur that general Zachary Taylor, a reviled character in pacifist circles, often failed to enforce discipline.[460]

Polk and Taylor's alleged violations of the *ius ad bellum* took on both constitutional and international legal aspects. Some of the pacifist charges held little validity. Livermore argued that the Constitution did not allow for offensive war, but such a claim finds no support in its text or in political practice.[461] On other charges, however, the peace society advanced far more convincing arguments. Mirroring the criticism of other opponents of the war, including Whig congressmen, both Jay and Livermore contended that president Polk had abused his constitutional war-powers by sending troops into Monterey and Texas, when these were still disputed territories containing Mexican customhouses. This was also labelled a violation of the law of nations.[462] Within international law, this had some merit, since occupation was a belligerent right, and U.S. forces had entered into the territory prior to a formally established state of war.[463] On the constitutional level, legal historians agree that Polk had attempted to bypass Congress's exclusive war-making power by presenting it with a fait accompli. Presidents before Polk had similarly already used their power as commander-in-chief to send in U.S. forces to a place where they knew these would inevitably get attacked.[464] Once news of the first dead soldiers came in, Polk promptly sent a prewritten war declaration to Congress, where his allies ensured that it passed the vote. Jay, Livermore, along with others, agreed with the motion of censure passed in the House in 1848, that castigated Polk's war as 'unnecessarily and unconstitutionally begun'.[465]

---

459 Matthew Waxman, 'The Mexican-American War and Constitutional War Powers'. 2020, available at www.lawfaremedia.org/article/mexican-american-war-and-constitutional-war-powers.

460 Many soldiers were openly racist towards the Mexicans. Thomas Spahr, *Occupying for Peace, the U.S. Army in Mexico, 1846–1848* (Ohio State University: unpublished doctoral thesis, 2011), 11.

461 Livermore, *Mexico* 1850, 163–164.

462 Ibid., 162–163; Jay, *Review* 1849, 130–131.

463 Neff, *War* 2005, 190.

464 Waxman, 'Constitutional War Powers' 2020.

465 Livermore, *Mexico* 1850, 163.

The international and constitutional scope of the right of belligerent occupation remained heavily contested during the war proper. The war was partly seen in such a negative constitutional light by its many critics because of the president's ambitious territorial war objectives.[466] Rather than merely extending the border to the Rio Grande river, Polk moved to seize the northern Mexican provinces of Alta California and current-day New Mexico. While general Taylor's troops advanced on Mexico City, general Stephen Kearney in the north and west assumed powers normally considered part of civil government. Proclaiming the occupied territories to be U.S. possessions, he appointed judges, officials and even a governor, enacted laws, and executed 'disloyal' inhabitants for treason.[467] These acts did not assuage suspicion, especially in the North, that the republic had embarked on a war of conquest. Livermore and Jay protested that these were 'high-handed violations of the Constitution, and also of the law of nations'.[468]

This was not off the mark. The arguments were certainly plausible from an international legal point of view. Although the right of conquest was widely accepted, doctrine was not agreed on the precise moment of the transfer of sovereignty. Most authors concurred that a formal cession through treaty was the least ambiguous one, even if a conquest in the most strict legal sense entailed effective and total control over the occupied territory, instantly transferring sovereignty already even before any peace treaty.[469] Whether Kearney's forces fulfilled the latter criteria was highly debatable, since he left almost immediately for California with his small army, after he had entered Santa Fe unopposed and declared it U.S. territory.[470] Assuming Kearney at the time still exercised the right of belligerent occupation, he violated the increasingly prevailing opinion that a military occupation ought to have as little impact as possible on civilian life, as

466 Waxman, 'Constitutional War Powers' 2020.

467 Ibid.; Pletcher, *Annexation* 1975, 437–8, 464–9, 499.

468 Livermore, *Mexico* 1850, 165.

469 George Fréderic de Martens, *Précis du droit des gens moderne de l'Europe* (Gottingue: Dieterich 1821), 583 (§ 341); Emer de Vattel, *Droit des gens, ou principes de la loi naturelle, appliquée à la conduite et aux affaires des nations et des souverains. Nouvelle édition. Tome second* (Paris: Aillaud 1830), 234 (§ 197), 250–251 (§ 214–215); Henry Wheaton, *Elements of International Law: with a Sketch of the History of the Science* (Philadelphia: Carey, Lea & Blanchard 1836), 370–1 (§ 1.4); Stephen Neff, *Justice in Blue and Gray. A Legal History of the Civil War* (Cambridge: HUP, 2010), 108–9.

470 Pletcher, *Annexation* 1975, 465.

articulated a few years later by the Lieber code.[471] From the constitutional point of view, quite related to the former, umbrage was taken with 'the dangerous march of executive power'.[472] Although Polk claimed that these 'temporary governments' were set up in accordance with the laws of war, judge Jay rebutted that the president had usurped powers 'belonging only to the legislative branch of government.[473] Whether Polk was correct, depended on whether it was framed as belligerent occupation – in which case the president exercised authority as commander-in-chief – or as a legal conquest already before any peace treaty – in which case only Congress could exercise the legislative powers the president had assumed through his subordinate general.[474] Polk's underhanded resort to international legal argument to circumvent the clear terms of article IV of the Constitution were picked up by Whig congressmen, who, similar to Jay and the peace society, accused the president of wielding 'despotic authority'.[475]

After open hostilities had ended, the American Peace Society showed particular interest in the Treaty of Guadalupe Hidalgo that ended the war. On one level, it was seen as yet another violation of the nation's laws. The chief negotiator on the U.S. side, Nicholas Trist, was a State Department clerk who had actually been recalled by Polk. However, he had ignored the president's direct order and went on to negotiate treaty terms anyway, ironically presenting Polk with a similar kind of fait accompli he had earlier presented to Congress.[476]

On a more fundamental and publicised level, however, the American Peace Society was surprised to find out that article 21 of the treaty arranged for non-compulsory arbitration, in case negotiations failed in the event of any future political or commercial U.S.-Mexican conflict.[477] Livermore praised the article as promoting 'the change from barbarism to law'.[478] One of the rejected essays compared it to the U.S.-Prussian treaty of 1785, wishing the one from 1848 had similarly also included articles on privateering and freedom of trade.[479] Jay was not as impressed. Because arbitration had

471 As eventually codified in the Hague Conventions. Neff, *War* 2005, 190.

472 Livermore, *Mexico* 1850, 165–166.

473 Jay, *Review* 1849, 246–247.

474 This was analogous to reasonings in the Civil War vis-à-vis Northern advances into the Confederacy. Neff, *Blue and Gray* 2010, 109–10.

475 Waxman, 'Constitutional War Powers' 2020; Jay, *Review* 1849, 247.

476 Pletcher, *Annexation* 1975, 528–549; Livermore, *Mexico* 1850, 165–166.

477 Livermore, *Mexico* 1850, 273.

478 Ibid. 272.

479 Berry, *Review* 1849, 30–1.

not been rendered binding to the signatories, he dismissed it as a 'quibbling, shuffling, non-committal article' that would have little practical effect.[480] Although the American Peace Society's leadership did not initially see it as their accomplishment, article 21 was later regularly praised as the first real political achievement of the American peace movement.[481] After all, this had been recommended by them in memorials and petitions, as well as the resolutions of the 1840s peace conferences.[482] However, Merle Curti has already in the 1920s refuted that claim. The first proposal came from the Mexican delegates, and Trist only accepted it after he had ensured that it was non-binding and 'could do no harm'.[483]

Rather than mistakenly taking credit for the arbitration clause, peace friends of the late 1840s used the war as a case study to illustrate the value of pacifism and the practicality of its legal alternatives. Both stipulated arbitration and a congress of nations were repeatedly endorsed. The annual report of 1846 posited that the war would have been avoided if either had been a reality.[484] Beckwith also mentioned both in his letter to Taylor in 1849 after the latter had used his 'war hero' credentials to secure the presidency.[485] The reformist Blanchard, heavily endorsing codification, argued that 'even on the illiberal maxims of international law', the American invasion had been illegal.[486] Livermore's prize essay referred to Jay's plan as articulated at the Brussels peace conference of 1848, but overall esteemed a congress of nations higher, feeling that this solution was more systematic and thorough. The reverend advised his readers to consult Ladd's *Prize Essays*.[487] Conversely, the book by Jay, as heavily subsidized by funds mobilized by Beckwith, did not hide its belief that a congress of nations was only 'excellent (...) in theory'. The peace society's president instead suggested for Congress to vote a joint resolution on mandatory arbitration clauses as a fixed feature of future treaties.[488] If the American Peace Society's propaganda could not completely mask its internal disagreements on the desired

480 Jay, *Review* 1849, 329–30.

481 AP (January 1852), 9; Myers, Denys. 'Law and the Peace Society'. *World Affairs* 127(4), 234.

482 See chapters 5.

483 Merle Curti, 'Pacifist Propaganda and the Treaty of Guadalupe Hidalgo'. *The American Historical Review* 33(3) (1928), 596–598.

484 AP (June 1846), 139

485 AP (January & February) 1849, 5–6.

486 AP (July 1846), 168–169.

487 Livermore, *Mexico* 1850, 272–277.

488 Jay, *Review* 1849, 328–333.

legal course, the peace society had nonetheless managed to project a relatively cohesive and unambiguous anti-war stance to the outside world.

Accordingly, the years of the Mexican War were both the most turbulent, and the most successful years of the American Peace Society's organisational existence.[489] On the one hand, the society was torn by the factional infighting between reformists and conservatives. The outbreak of the Mexican War in 1846 had caused Beckwith's attempted new constitution, which got rid of the condemnation of 'all' war again, to fail, because most feared it would imply an approval of the war.[490] On the other hand, the peace societies for the first time joined in on a much broader anti-war chorus that stood especially strong in the peace movement's heartland of New England.[491] The *Advocate* rejoiced that their own petitions were part of a larger wave. Petitions were sent in from ecclesiastical bodies, like the Unitarians, the Congregationalists, the Methodists, the Presbyterians, and, at long last, even the Quakers. The religious papers also, which had long ignored the peace societies, had begun to reprint the societies' circulars and petition forms.[492] The *Advocate* reported on 'a very encouraging increase of disposition among the people' to attend lectures and to donate.[493] The society's annual meeting of May 1848 attracted such an unprecedented crowd, that nearly all latecomers had to be sent away again – a far cry from the near-empty backrooms where Ladd had once delivered his first lectures.[494] In short, the peace movement had become a small, but nonetheless entrenched fixture in American political life. By that time, the same had happened with the peace societies of Britain.

---

489 Ziegler, *Antebellum* 1992, 113.

490 Curti, *Crusade* 1929, 92, 96.

491 Charles DeBenedetti, *The Peace Reform in American History* (Bloomington: Indiana University Press 1980), 51

492 AP (January & February 1847), 20; AP (November & December 1847), 133–7; AP (March & April 1848), 189–91; AP (July & August 1848), 236.

493 AP (May & June 1848), 215.

494 AP (July & August 1848), 19.

CHAPTER 2

Britain (1815–1856)

> 'They shall beat their swords into ploughshares, and their spears into pruning hooks; nation shall not lift up sword against nation, neither shall they learn war anymore.'
>
> Isaiah 2:4

∴

1 The London Peace Society

On the evening of 19 October 1818, czar Alexander I (1777–1825) received a guest in his chambers at Aix-la-Chapelle. The emperor of Russia, grand duke of Finland, and king of Poland was taking part in the first post-war diplomatic congress after Vienna, convened to discuss the final withdrawal of the armies of occupation from France. Their former adversary was simultaneously admitted into the newly established Quintuple Alliance. Among more subsidiary topics, the plenipotentiaries also discussed means to restrict the slave trade.[1] Thomas Clarkson (1760–1846), one of the founders of the British Anti-Slavery Society, had personally travelled to the German city to lobby with the czar. He also brought various Quaker publications, reflecting Alexander's previous connections with this Protestant sect, peculiar for its principled non-violence.[2] Apart from his own biography of William Penn, Britain's most famous Quaker politician, Clarkson gifted the emperor two exquisitely bound volumes of tracts. They were accompanied by a formal letter from the philanthropical society that had been disseminating these among the British public over the past two years. The founder of the Holy Alliance was pleased to hear that Britain had followed the example of the United States. Not too long ago, he had signed in his own hand a

1 Jarrett, *Vienna and its Legacy* 2013, 180–205; De Graaf, *Fighting Terror* 2020, 390–413.

2 Alexander I had a curious interest in the Society of Friends. When he visited London in 1814, he attended a Quaker service. He also invited British Quakers to Saint-Petersburg. Van der Linden, *Peace Movement* 1987, 43; Ceadel, *Origins* 1996, 512–4; see also Richenda Scott, *Quakers in Russia* (London: MW Books 1964).

 | DOI:10.1163/9789004733688_004

letter to a reverend in Massachusetts giving his praise for a similar initiative. Now, London also possessed a Society for the Promotion of Permanent and Universal Peace.[3] The czar died seven years later, in 1825, and although the peace movement grew disillusioned with his Holy Alliance, the peace society lived on. It quickly took on a simple unofficial name, by which it came to be known for the remainder of the century: the London Peace Society.[4]

Although this organisation was only founded officially in 1816, shortly after the Massachusetts and New York peace societies, it traced its earliest origins back further in time. For the British, the war that had directly led to a surge in peace activism was the prolonged series of armed conflicts Britain had been waging against the French revolutionaries and the Napoleonic empire. Like in the United States, a number of anti-war pamphlets entered into circulation between 1793 and the 1810s, some of them penned by individuals who would eventually take part in attempts at institutionalisation.[5]

The British peace movement knew several false starts. As far as could be ascertained by historians, the idea of a pacific society was first publicly contemplated in 1808, by a clergyman. In the ensuing eight years, anonymous contributors to the *Monthly Magazine,* a miscellaneous journal, intermittently brought it up. In March 1816, they revealed themselves and formed a peace society.[6] Testament to its obscurity, the official name of this association, not recorded in any nineteenth century histories, has been lost in time. The few modern historians who have mentioned it, settled upon the 'Society for Abolishing War'. Likewise, its exact composition and ideology remain largely unknown. From what could be gathered from secondary reports, its object was to 'circulate knowledge' on 'the folly, inutility, and wickedness of war'. This was to be done through 'cheap tracts'. Interestingly, the first tract it published was Noah Worcester's *Solemn Review.* Just as intriguing, the second tract compiled 'apposite and forcible extracts from Grotius on Peace and War'. According to the editors, the main reason why the principles of this legal scholar had 'not had their due effect', was because they were 'locked up in a dead language, and in voluminous

3 Thomas Clarkson, *Thomas Clarkson's Interview with the Emperor Alexander I of Russia, as Aix-la-Chapelle, as told by Himself* (London: Poyser 1930), 17–24; HP (January 1819), 20–1.

4 In 1925, the London Peace society moved out of its offices in New Broad Street, which it had inhabited for more than eighty years. It also changed its name into the 'International Peace Society'. Ceadel, *Idealists* 2000, 193–5.

5 For more details, see Ceadel, *Origins* 1996, 166–221.

6 Van der Linden, *Peace Movement* 1987, 1; Ceadel, *Origins* 1996, 135–6, 202–3, 222.

expensive translations'. The peace society failed in its ambitions. No copies of their second tract appear to have survived. In fact, the society itself vanished soon afterwards, fading from all memory until the 1980s.[7]

This first society was quickly superseded by its contemporary rival. Its foundation happened in fits and starts. In the beginning of June 1814, a peace committee was formed in London. About six or eight gentleman met at the house of William Allen (1770–1843), one of the leading men of the new organisation. A staunch Quaker, he was already well-known for his philanthropical interests, which included the education of poor children and the abolition of slavery.[8] The other early leader worth mentioning for our purposes was Joseph Tregelles Price (1784–1854), a Quaker ironmaster, whose father had already been noted for his charity. Upon his decease, the peace society described him as 'the founder of the society'.[9] No society was formed after that meeting, perhaps because Allen was too busy at the time, or through possible disagreements on whether or not to allow defensive war. At any rate, events caught up with them, for the lull after the victorious entry of the coalition troops into Paris soon ended. In February 1815, news broke that their foe had escaped from Elba and had seized power again. The second preliminary meeting, held on 6 June 1815, was exceptionally poorly timed, taking place twelve days before 140,000 soldiers would clash in the fields near Waterloo. At the pacifist meeting, only three people showed up. It was only after final victory had been secured in Europe that a third attempt succeeded. On 14 June 1816, the constituent assembly agreed on a constitution for 'the Peace Society'.[10]

Unlike the Massachusetts Peace Society or the American Peace Society, the rules of the main British peace society did not tolerate diversity of opinion among its leading members. Rather, they installed a two-tiered membership system. The main business of the society was to be conducted through a small elected Committee. This Committee decided upon the publishing of tracts, the appointment of most officers, and the convocation of meetings. Committee members were obliged to adhere to all of the principles 'on

7 Van der Linden first rediscovered its existence. Monthly Magazine (hereafter: MM) (April 1816), 246–7; MM (September 1816), 159; MM (January 1817), 492; Van der Linden, *Peace Movement* 1987, 2–3; Ceadel, *Origins* 1996, 213–5.

8 Ceadel, *Origins* 1996, 206.

9 Watkin William Price, 'Price, Joseph Tregelles (1784–1854)', in *Dictionary of Welsh Biography*. 1959, available at: biography.wales/article/s-PRIC-TRE-1784; Ceadel, *Origins* 1996, 206; HP (June 1855), 212.

10 HP (January 1819), 24–26; Ceadel, *Origins* 1996, 207–8, 215–6.

which the Society is founded'. Interestingly, these were not articulated very well in the constitution itself. It only specified that that the purpose of the society was to 'print and circulate tracts, and to diffuse information tending to show, that war is inconsistent with the spirit of Christianity and the true interests of mankind'.[11] Similar to the New York Peace Society, a glance on any random pamphlet sufficed to learn that the Committee radically condemned *all* war.

However, the London Peace Society was not completely sectarian. It was telling that Dodge's club, threatened by extinction because of a lack of members, was forced to remodel its statutes after the British example.[12] Ordinary members were merely asked to promote 'peace on earth, and goodwill towards men'.[13] In practice, though, this meant that such members were strongly discouraged from openly voicing critique against the Committee's 'high ground' positions. Still, this small concession allowed a steady trickle of moderate sympathisers to join the society, stimulating just enough influx of new members to keep the society afloat during its tentative early years.[14]

Such ambiguity, similar to the one seen in America, partly stemmed from its religious composition. Despite never being formally a part of the Religious Society of Friends, as the Quakers were known officially, the London Peace Society as an autonomous body was dominated by Quakers. While the peace society welcomed 'persons of every denomination', so-called 'Friends' constituted by far the largest single minority. In the founding years, almost half the Committee was a Friend, while within the organisation as a whole, no less than 53 precent considered themselves a member of this creed.[15] The leadership earnestly attempted to be more ecumenical by keeping the proportion of Quakers in its Committee under half. For this reason, it only very slowly admitted new members during the first two decades, because it proved very difficult to find non-Quakers willing to subscribe to their radically pacifist views. The peace society therefore never really shook its stigma of being a Quaker society, despite only nine percent of British

11 HP (January 1819), 26–7.

12 Because it lacked its own journal, the best place to read the reports of the New York Peace Society was actually the British *Herald*, besides Worcester's *Friend of Peace*. HP (April 1819), 126;

13 HP (January 1819), 26.

14 Ceadel, *Origins* 1996, 226–7.

15 Stephen Conway, 'The Politicization of the Nineteenth-Century Peace Society'. *Historical Research* 66(3) (1993), 273.

Quakers actually joining it. It did not help that Quakers were up until the late 1850s obliged to wear so-called 'plain dress', making them stand out wherever they went.[16] Continental-European observers often remarked on how funny so many of the British peace friends looked.

Organised peace activism in a sense came natural to them. Since their beginning in the seventeenth century, the Quakers had developed a 'peace testimony'. To be understood more as an action guide than a strict theology, their peace testimony entailed strict non-resistance and quietism during times of upheaval. For most nineteenth century Quakers, this was directly applicable also to international relations.[17] Despite persecutions, especially during wartime, many Quakers stayed true to the pacific tendencies of their faith. In 1947, the Quaker religion collectively won the Nobel Peace Prize 'for their pioneering work in the international peace movement'.[18] Within the London Peace Society, they never lost their dominance. Even after it had broadened by the 1850s, Richard Cobden, with whom we will deal extensively later on, remarked that Quakers were 'the main force' of the society with whom he had allied himself.[19] Other members typically belonged to other non-conformist denominations, such as the Unitarians, the Baptists, and the Congregationalists.[20] These dissenting churches were not bound by the hierarchy of the Church of England. As a state church, its doctrine unsurprisingly stipulated that 'it is lawful for Christian men, at the commandment of the Magistrate, to wear weapons, and serve in the wars'.[21] Similar to Catholic priests, it was therefore exceptional for an Anglican clergyman to join a peace society.

This strong non-conformist influence informed the London Peace Society's decision to resolutely choose for the radical pacifist stance.[22] Most of it stemmed from a sincere religious conviction that all forms of war were unchristian. With their American counterparts, religious British peace friends shared an eschatological faith in the Millennium. Millenarianism held that human action in the form of benevolent activities would herald the Second

16 Ceadel, *Origins* 1996, 246–255.

17 Brock, *Peace Testimony* 1990, 24–46.

18 Alford, 'Nobel Effect' 2008, 95.

19 Cobden cited in Ceadel, *Origins* 1996, 247.

20 Conway, 'Politicization' 1993, 273; Ceadel, *Origins* 1996, 252–5.

21 Edward John Bicknell, *A Theological Introduction to the Thirty-Nine Articles of the Church of England* (Eugene: Wipf and Stock, 2007), 440–1.

22 In this chapter, 'radical' without capitalisation refers to its ordinary meaning. Only when 'Radical' is written with a capital letter does it refer to those contemporary political activists strove for parliamentary reform.

Coming of Christ, understood as a thousand year-long golden age of peace and prosperity. David Bogue (1750–1825), an independent religious leader, pushed this post-Millennial argument in a series of sermons and tracts, one of which called for the founding of peace societies, and ended up in the classical tract series of the London Peace Society. In this way, it was disseminated in both Britain and the United States.[23] Just like the Americans, the British were also deeply sceptical about ostensibly 'defensive' wars. In fact, this one was shared by just about every pacifist. From a more pragmatic, but nonetheless relevant perspective, it was also an organisational necessity to support radical non-resistance. Although Quakers did not constitute a decisive majority within the society, all of its most important donors were Friends. Martin Ceadel has reasoned that, faced with the choice between a broader organisation without sufficient funding, or a healthier one led by a small number of highly committed idealists, the founders made a sensible decision.[24]

Moderate pacifism explicitly allowing for defensive war – dubbed 'pacificism' by Ceadel – was not very viable in early nineteenth century Britain. The Society for Abolishing War failed, in spite of its leader's conviction that 'while there are wolves in the world, we much doubt the wisdom of playing the part of lambs, unprepared and unwilling to defend ourselves'.[25] Similar initiatives by other peace societies in the wake of the London society also failed, to the extent that these had adopted a more moderate stance. Provincial anti-war feeling was scattered, the anti-war movement during the fight against Napoleon had lost its original purpose, and none of the other emerging anti-war ideologies had yet attained sufficient popularity. The breakthrough of moderate pacifism in Britain coincided with the rising star of Richard Cobden and the free trade movement.[26] In that sense, it made relative sense that it was the short-lived Society for Abolishing War that devoted its second major pamphlet to Grotius, while the 'father' of international law was only marginally discussed, and often criticised, within the early publications of its more successful rival. As we have seen in the previous chapter, Grotius, however sympathetic he may have stood to peace, was not a pacifist, and typically arrived at the exact opposite scriptural

23 David Bogue, *On Universal Peace; being Extracts from a Discourse delivered in October 1813* (London: Clay 1826); Alexander Tyrrell, 'Making the Millennium: the Mid-Nineteenth Century Peace Movement'. *The Historical Journal* 21(1) (1978), 81.

24 Ceadel, *Origins* 1996, 237, 246.

25 MM (March 1817), 154.

26 Ceadel, *Origins* 1996, 218–219.

interpretations of nineteenth century peace friends. The leadership of the London Peace Society initially felt confident that their far more emotional and absolute case against war offered the most promising course of action. When inevitably asked whether it was not preferable to lax their principles in exchange for wider support and influence, they merely retorted that there was 'no objection to the establishment of other peace societies by those Christians who differ from us' – knowing full well that all such initiatives had ended in failure.[27]

Like the Massachusetts Peace Society in America, the London Peace Society possessed numerous auxiliary peace societies. These played a crucial role in grassroots peace agitation. While the London peace friends set the larger ideological agenda and maintained the closest contacts with any foreign sister organisations, the average Briton living outside of the metropolis typically became acquainted with the existence of a peace movement through local community action. By the early 1820s, there were nineteen 'Corresponding Societies', which was increased to twenty-eight by 1836.[28] These did not have to adopt the absolutist pacifism of the parent organisation, meaning that their Committee members could personally believe in the lawfulness of defensive war. However, this freedom meant little in light of the fact that auxiliaries were prohibited from distributing any publication which had not been previously sanctioned by the London Committee. Rejecting many works, this Committee was evidently attached to its 'high ground' principles, as well as the image it wished to project.[29]

Compared to the 'national' peace society, very little remains known of these local initiatives, even though case studies have nuanced assumptions about their subordinate status.[30] Deeply embedded in highly specific regional contexts, an analysis of all of the auxiliary societies far exceeds the scope of the present story. Since most were less concerned with the international debate involving issues of international law, especially also given the London Committee's censorship, regional initiatives are only brought up in this chapter whenever they become relevant. Specifically, the influence

---

27 HP (October 1821), 289–90; Ceadel, *Origins* 1996, 237.

28 *List of Donors and Subscribers to the Society for the Promotion of Permanent and Universal Peace* (unknown location: unknown publisher 1836), 1–36; *Seventh Annual Report of the Committee of the Society for the Promotion of Permanent and Universal Peace* (London: Bensley 1823), 6.

29 Most auxiliaries simply adopted the rules of the London society. Ceadel, *Origins* 1996, 232–3.

30 E.g. Matthew Scott and Nick Megoran, 'The Newcastle Upon Tyne Peace Society (1815–50)'. *Northern History* XX(XX) (2017), 1–17.

from Manchester and Birmingham was significant, as they contributed to the shift towards arbitration.

Who were the people who decided to campaign in favour of permanent and universal peace? Their religious affiliations have already been detailed. In terms of their social background, most members belonged to what has been described as the 'non-industrial middle classes'.[31] This included humble tailors and small shopkeepers, but also farmers, chemists, bankers, ministers of religion, merchants, and those who simply called themselves 'gentlemen'. The latter two tags could mean anything from small-time retired tradesmen to large land owners, but, generally speaking, the rising manufacturing class of the industrialising north of England did not initially participate. Judging from the locations of auxiliary societies on the map, as well the available membership lists, most British peace friends lived in southern England. This partly countered the immediate intuition that financial interests lay behind their pacifist idealism, while reinforcing the religious explanations.[32] Of course, conspicuous philanthropism probably also played a role for a handful of donors. These 'friends of peace' simply took the opportunity to sponsor a vague, and therefore politically safe, good cause, in order to gain elite social acceptance.[33]

In other class snobberies, the working class was largely excluded from organised peace activism in mid-nineteenth century Britain. Members of the London Peace Society had to pay ten shillings and six pence a year, or make a one-time donation of five pounds and five shillings, putting it far outside the reach of the average labourer.[34] The society's peace propaganda generally did not concern itself with social issues – an important reason why the Parisian pacifist Eugénie Niboyet distanced herself from the British peace movement in the 1840s.[35] After the 1848 February Revolutions, their journal especially detested 'the wild and impracticable theories respecting *labour*, which prevail among the working-classes'.[36] At home, the relationship with Chartism proved complex. Grown out of artisan radicalism in the late 1830s, Chartists campaigned for increased political rights for the non-property

31 Eric Sager, 'The Social Origins of Victorian Pacifism'. *Victorian Studies* 23(2) (1980), 222–5.

32 Conway claims that Joseph Price's ironworks 'almost certainly had much more to gain through war than through its avoidance'. Conway, 'Politicization' 1993, 268–72.

33 Philanthropy and altruism are not synonyms. Sager, 'Social Origins' 1980, 222–5; Conway, "Politicization' 1993, 272.

34 HP (January 1819), 26.

35 See chapter 4.

36 HP (April 1848), 58.

owning working classes, who had been left out of the Great Reform Act of 1832.[37] For the London Peace Society, the surge in violent strikes and riots in British towns necessitated them to turn more attention to domestic issues than previously. In the 1840s, their agents consciously began to lecture to working class audiences and the society itself recruited a handful of converted Chartists. In this period, Elihu Burritt's League of Universal Brotherhood had also crossed the pond, and was raising pledges among common labourers.[38] Overall, however, the society's attitude remained paternalistic. After their relative enfranchisement by the Second Reform Act of 1867, the London Peace Society helped set up the Workmen's Peace Association in 1870, headed by William Randal Cremer (1828–1908), a future Nobel Peace Prize laureate. Financially entirely dependent on the London society, it was de facto treated as an auxiliary, expected to be deferential and uncontroversial.[39]

A similar lot befell women. Numerically, about one in ten subscribing members were female, which was roughly the same as in other contemporary philanthropical organisations.[40] As progressive and dissident as the society was on war, as conventional it was on the role of women in their association. Conformable to contemporary cultural expectations, women were forbidden to speak in assemblies where men were also present, and were likewise barred from sitting in any committees. These rules were scrupulously observed for decades. At the European peace conferences, no woman was given delegate status. Only in 1889 did the society invite a female Quaker to its Committee, who turned it down. Apart from William Lloyd Garrison, only Elihu Burritt specifically reached out to women, through his network of so-called Olive Leaf Circles. These were local, all-female clubs, which raised funds for Burritt's pacifist 'Olive Leave' messages in newspapers, through the sale of arts and crafts at charity fairs.[41]

Although highly exclusionary on the formal level, the British society did not altogether reject female peace activism. Their views largely coincided with those of William Ladd and the American Peace Society.[42] Essentially,

37 Edward Royle and Roger Lockyer, *Chartism* (London: Routledge 2014), 17–26.

38 Van der Linden, *Peace Movement* 1987, 200–2, 287–315; Ceadel, *Origins* 1996, 325–35.

39 Cremer won it in 1903. Alford, 'Nobel Effect' 2008, 267–79; Ceadel, *Idealists* 2000, 86–92.

40 By contrast, the Bible Society already boasted 23 percent women in 1817. Conway, 'Politicization' 1993, 267–8.

41 Ceadel, *Origins* 1996, 260–1; Ceadel, *Idealists* 2000, 29–30.

42 Ladd believed women should focus their efforts on the home and their local parish, although he was not opposed to tract-writing. Ladd, *Duty of Females* 1836.

female peace friends were encouraged to advocate pacific principles 'in their domestic and social circles', as mothers and teachers. Publicly, a handful of 'ladies' auxiliaries' were established, but these mainly spread the tracts endorsed by the London Committee.[43] Only in 1874 did the Committee set up a so-called Ladies' Peace Association, but it was treated in much the same patronising way as its working class equivalent. The significant rise of women in the international peace movement, through societies created by their own agency, occurred mostly after the 1870s.[44]

Because of this, only a few female peace friends have been able to publicly voice their own opinions within the early institutional peace movement. This made it all the more remarkable that two tracts of the London Peace Society were penned by 'A Lady'. Rendered anonymous by the conventions of polite society at the time, her identity was Mary Roberts (1788–1864), a Quaker lady, who wrote a number of popular literary works on the natural surroundings of her country village. The journal of the London Peace Society described the author of two of their canonical texts as 'a superior and cultivated mind'.[45]

All in all, the peace societies of the United Kingdom remained part of a small movement for most of the nineteenth century. The London Peace Society never transformed into the vehicle of a mass movement in the Victorian era, reaching its plateau of 1,500 members already by the mid-1820s, a figure comparable to the membership totals of the American Peace Society for most of the century. By the turn of the twentieth century, this had only risen to 1,600 members.[46] To put these numbers into perspective: the British anti-slavery movement could count on several hundreds of thousands of adherents.[47] While not every abolitionist was a pacifist, most pacifists were

43 By the 1850s, all of these auxiliaries had gone defunct. HP (October, November & December 1823), 195.

44 Ceadel, *Idealists* 2000, 99–100. See also the introduction.

45 Again first uncovered by Van der Linden. Mary Roberts [pseud. A Lady], *An Examination of the Principles which are considered to support the Practice of War* (London: Clay 1840); Mary Roberts [pseud. A Lady], *Historical Illustrations of the Origin and Consequences of War* (London: Clay, 1840). First published in 1823 and 1831 respectively. Van der Linden, *Peace Movement* 1987, 12–13; Peter Osborne, 'Roberts, Mary (1788–1864)', in *Oxford Dictionary of National Biography*. 2004, available at: doi.org/10.1093/ref:odnb/23767; HP (January, February & March 1834), 273.

46 The addition of new recruits was offset by the loss of existing members. Ceadel, *Origins* 1996, 19, 222–3, 286.

47 Petitions against aspects of slavery or the slave trade in the 1830s regularly got well over one million signatures. Seymour Drescher, *Capitalism and Antislavery. British Mobilisation in Comparative Perspective* (London: Macmillan 1986), 91–2.

also abolitionists, just like in the United States.[48] British pacifism only grew into a more or less mainstream political force in the inter-war period of the twentieth century.[49]

Lack of numbers of course did not necessarily entail lack of influence. As the society put it in 1852, at the height of its popularity, if 'it seems to be the fashion to laugh at the Peace Society (...) if they are only a set of amiable lunatics', why did they have the support of parliamentarians like Cobden, or foreign celebrities like Humboldt and Girardin? 'Would their congress in Exeter Hall be crowded as it was last year with the wealthiest and most educated classes?'[50] In the late 1840s and early 1850s, the London Peace Society had been particularly productive. The society had co-organised the peace conferences alternately held in Brussels, Paris and Frankfurt. In the domestic political scene, their prolonged parliamentary petition campaign had culminated in an arbitration motion, proposed and argued by Cobden in 1849. They had also mounted some visible campaigns against the militia bills, in the wake of French invasion panics. If the attacks launched in *The Times* and *Punch* were anything to go by, the average citizen of the British empire, from Edinburgh to Calcutta, able to follow the news, had by then heard of the existence of a peace movement.[51]

2 The Turn to International Law

The London Peace Society underwent a dramatic transformation between these events and its early years. At its inception, in 1816, the society viewed itself as a strictly religious association. Its position was one of quietism, in agreement with the Quaker faith of its main founders and nearly half of its members. They admitted only small exceptions to this policy. Whenever the opportunity presented itself, such as with Clarkson's mission to the czar,

48 Joseph Sturge, for instance, was heavily involved in both movements. The *Herald* reported extensively on the anti-slavery movement.

49 The immediate aftermath of the Great War provided a very hostile climate to those seen as not having done their duty, but the crises of the 1920s and 1930s shifted public opinion more in their favour. Ceadel, *Idealists* 2000, 239–81.

50 HP (December 1852), 134–135. The phrase 'Exeter Hall meeting' was a Victorian byword for philanthropism.

51 The relationship between the peace societies and the press could charitably be described as 'turbulent'. Journalists of *The Times* and the satirical *Punch Magazine* typically had a field day when assigned a piece on the peace movement. The latter was well-aware of this. See for instance HP (July 1853), 234–7.

they sent letters to important men of state. They also provided a running commentary on foreign current events in the pages of their long-running journal, the *Herald of Peace*. In general, however, the society was content to focus on the decidedly indirect, long-term goal of preaching an anti-war interpretation of Christianity to the middle classes, through small tracts and lectures. When this policy got increasingly questioned by the organisation's grassroots in the 1830s, the Committee repeated its mantra that peace was 'altogether unconnected with political discussion'. To remain focussed on the conversion of individuals, rather than political action, was to be safeguarded against 'any reasonable imputation of disloyalty' and 'party feelings'.[52]

Eventually, the Committee was forced to cave in to the combined pressure from inside and outside the society. Inside, auxiliary societies had slowly begun to independently petition Parliament, taking inspiration not only from the successes of the British anti-slavery campaign, but also by the example coming from the United States peace movement. Outside, Ladd was anxious to get his congress of nations essays out before the British public, and his more conservative successor Beckwith was just as keen on getting a concerted trans-Atlantic political campaign going. Once involved in politics, the political leanings of the average British peace friend could no longer be pretended away. While during the quietist years a number of Conservatives found their way into the society, most members had privately always favoured Whig and Radical candidates in elections. Upon the formation of the Liberal Party, it was the Radical wing of the new political party that provided the most sympathetic M.P.'s. The most important among them, apart from Cobden – 'the international man' – was John Bright (1811–1889), a Quaker and free trader.[53]

This gradual process of politicisation increasingly forced British peace advocates to reconceptualise their religious and moralist pacifism into more secular legal models. Like their American colleagues, they came to understand that effective political action necessitated the development of a new type of argument. They needed a language able to transcend the ideological divide between the society's absolutist core and wider political society. As

52 In 1851, the society still complained that it had more difficulty attracting large crowds to its meetings, compared to other societies, because they were not identified as strongly 'with any religious sect or political party'.

HP (April, May & June 1833), 113–114; HP (February 1851), 89.

53 Conway, 'Politicization' 1993, 276, 281; Ceadel, *Origins* 1996, 272.

the institutional arena changed in which pacifists were to operate, from the pulpits to Parliament, they needed to adapt to their new audience and political allies. While scriptural arguments were certainly not maladapted to a culture where Christianity still held almost universal sway in private life, they would never convince a critical mass of electors, and by extension the elected political elites. Norms, both cultural and juridical, invariably operate inside a hierarchy.[54] Mainstream society, as embodied by the Church of England and diplomatic practice, largely agreed with the peace societies that peace was preferable to war. Unfortunately, the vaunted tenets of the Gospel were invariably subordinated to political expediency whenever it mattered.

By no means extremist revolutionaries bent on the overthrow of most governments, the publicists of the London Peace Society were faced with the unenviable task of translating their 'high ground' principles into concrete legal solutions operable in both domestic and international politics. If these strayed too far from the religious utopia dreamed of by the society's base, support might have dried up. On the other hand, if their proposed juridical reforms stayed too rigid, the peace friends would have failed the test of political pragmatism, accomplishing nothing.

2.1 *Critiques of Law*

The London Peace Society explicated its ideological programme in a variety of publications. Their main press organ was the aforementioned *Herald of Peace,* begun as a monthly in 1819, turning into a quarterly between 1822 and 1845, until popularity made it into another monthly. Continued until the 1930s, when the society became defunct, the journal functioned as the best information channel on the nineteenth century international peace movement. Its columns meticulously reported on all main controversies of the movement, not only in Britain and the United States, but also in Europe. Whenever it downplayed or omitted internal infights, like in the American journals, the manuscript records provide further insight.[55] Although every annual report was reprinted in full in this journal, they were often also printed separately, and sent to the other peace societies and allied associations, at home and abroad. The society also disseminated small public

54 Koskenniemi, *Uttermost Parts* 2021, 7.

55 The records were at the time of writing held privately, which refused access. Fortunately, Martin Ceadel's studies are based on these records, although it also took him years before he was granted access. Ceadel, *Origins* 1996, 3, 266.

letters and booklets, whose target audience ranged from queen Victoria or the prime minister all the way down to school children.[56]

Apart from the *Herald* and these miscellaneous publications, contemporaries could read more about pacifism in a series of thirteen tracts, that detailed all of the doctrines of the peace society. Published between 1817 and 1840, and spanning sixteen to forty-four pages, they were written by a variety of authors. Their first tract was Worcester's *Solemn Review*, which had reached the British isles before the society was founded.[57] They swiftly added several ones of their own, many written by Quakers. Apart from the two tracts by Roberts, one came from Clarkson, and the others were composed by Joseph Gurney (1788–1847), a theologian, Jonathan Dymond (1796–1828), a moral philosopher, and Thomas Hancock (1783–1849), a doctor.[58] The six others were a mixed bag. John Scott (1757–1832), an evangelical banker, composed the most religious non-Quaker pamphlet, along with David Bogue.[59] In a more secular vein, the society published extracts from Erasmus's (1466–1536) works, and from Eugène Labaume's (1783–1849) first-hand account of the 1812 French campaign against Russia.[60] The least

56 Gustave de Molinari was relieved in the 1870s that the peace movement had at last stopped waging war on 'little tin soldiers', but had shifted its focus more on serious issues like international law. See chapter 7.

57 Noah Worcester, *The Substance of a Pamphlet, entitled a Solemn Review of the Custom of War: Showing, that War is the Effect of Popular Delusion, and Proposing a Remedy* (London: Lomax 1816).

58 Thomas Clarkson, *An Essay on the Doctrines and Practice of the Early Christians as they Relate to War. Addressed to those who Profess to have Regard for the Christian Name* (London: Bensley 1840); Joseph Gurney, *An Essay on War, and on its Lawfulness under the Christian Dispensation* (London: Clay 1840); Jonathan Dymond, *Observations on the Applicability of the Pacific Principles of the New Testament to the Conduct of States; and on the Limitations which those Principles Impose on the Rights of Self-Defence* (London: Clay 1840); Thomas Hancock, *The Principles of Peace exemplified in the Conduct of the Society of Friends in Ireland, during the Rebellion of the Year 1798 with some Preliminary and Concluding observations. In Three Parts* (London: Clay 1840). Van der Linden, *Peace Movement* 1987, 12–13; Edward Milligan, 'Gurney, Joseph John (1788–1847)', in *Oxford Dictionary of National Biography*. 2004, available at: doi.org/10.1093/ref:odnb/11771; Hugh Brogan, 'Clarkson, Thomas (1760–1846)', in *Oxford Dictionary of National Biography*. 2004, available at: doi.org/10.1093/ref:odnb/5545; Magee, Karl. 'Hancock, Thomas (1783–1849)', in *Oxford Dictionary of National Biography*. 2004, available at: doi.org/10.1093/ref:odnb/12187; Dymond is introduced infra.

59 John Scott, *War Inconsistent with the Doctrine and Example of Jesus Christ. In a Letter to a Friend* (London: Clay 1840); Ceadel, *Origins* 1996, 171–2; Van der Linden, *Peace Movement* 1987, 12.

60 Desiderius Erasmus (ed. Evan Rees), *Extracts from the Writings of Erasmus, on the Subject of War* (London: Clay 1840). Van der Linden, *Peace Movement* 1987, 12; Ross Dealy,

religious one of the series consisted of two chapters from a book by the French minister of finance under Louis XVI, Jacques Necker (1732–1804). In them, Necker asserted that war led to exorbitant financial damage.[61] Coming in at number thirteen, Ladd's rebuttal of common *Obstacles and Objections to the Cause of Peace* ended the series with another American text.[62]

Through extensive reprints over the century, these thirteen tracts reached canonical status. As the society matured, circulation increased. The first edition of Clarkson's text in 1817 consisted of only 3,000 copies, but its 1819 and 1820 editions ran up to 10,000 copies each. By 1823, almost 270,000 total publications had been printed, which had risen to little over 640,000 by 1833[63] By 1840, when the final tract of the series was first published in Britain, members of the society boasted that over one and a half million propaganda pieces had been spread, with 365,000 released that year alone.[64] They were also compiled into a single volume that same year, under the unambiguous title *All War Antichristian*. Both the compilation and the separate tracts were reprinted up until the late nineteenth century, in various editions. Used also for proselytising in Europe, the majority of these tracts were translated into French, though a few were also translated into German, Dutch, Spanish and Italian. However, the most extensive international exchange was undoubtedly with the United States. Two texts of the British series were originally published across the pond. Conversely, many of the British tracts received an American edition. Especially Dymond was popular in the entire Anglo-American peace movement, particularly among the more orthodox religious pacifists. In the end, every British tract was reproduced, partially or fully, in the pages of the American pacifist press – and vice versa.[65]

'The Dynamics of Erasmus' Thought on War'. *Erasmus Studies* 4(1) (1984), 53–67; Rees, Evan. *Sketches of the Horrors of War, chiefly selected from Labaume's Narrative of the Campaign in Russia, in 1812. Translated from the French, with some Observations* (London: Clay 1840).

61 Jacques Necker (ed. John Bevans), *Reflections on the Calamities of War, and the Superior Policy of Peace: translated from the French* (London: Clay 1840). Van der Linden, *Peace Movement* 1987, 13.

62 William Ladd, *Obstacles and Objections to the Cause of Permanent and Universal Peace, considered* (London: Thomas Ward 1840).

63 Van der Linden, *Peace Movement* 1987, 11–2.

64 Henry MacNamara, *Peace, Permanent and Universal: its Practicability, Value, and Consistency with Divine Revelation. A Prize Essay* (London: Saunders and Otley 1841), 296.

65 Dymond's tract was still regularly printed by the late nineteenth century. The last edition appeared in 1896. See the overview in ter Meulen, *Peace Literature* 1990, 79–104;

Tonally, early British propaganda was virtually identical to that produced by Worcester, Dodge, or Ladd. It was overwhelmingly religious and moralising. The British peace advocates emphasised the sinful nature of *all* violence, be it done under a just cause or not. Gurney illustrated the typical case. Bringing up the battle of Waterloo, he argued that 'the *visible* effects (…) were sufficiently appalling', but 'did Christians fully know the *invisible* consequences of such a contest (…) could they trace the flight of thousands of immortal souls (…) into the world of eternal retribution'?[66] The more direct, human, effects of war were also lavishly detailed. The society was especially keen on stripping war and military life of its theatrical aspects. To counteract popular imagery of colourful parades, with banners and music, pacifist propaganda conjured up a decidedly more sober and realistic image. In a series of lithographs, modelled after William Hogarth's *A Rake's Progress,* the society portrayed a naïve youth, drunk on either mistaken notions of glory or – more likely – the recruiting sergeant's ale, who enlists into the army. The boy very soon discovers that he has, de facto, become a prisoner. Forced into a harsh discipline, filled with temptations into vice, he eventually marches into a battle. Grievously wounded, he gets abandoned by his comrades and has to fend off corpse looters during the night. The man, now with one arm, returns home destitute and alone.[67] Such drawings conveyed the gist of the numerous anecdotes and poems which abundantly featured in the *Herald*.[68] Typically, they were accompanied by preaching that warned of eternal hell and damnation for those who had sinned.[69] Although a couple of strictly economic arguments made their way into the *Herald,* its main message was that only Christianity 'lays the axe to the root of every corrupt tree'.[70]

The theological argumentation of the London Peace Society was likewise similar to that developed in American pacifist circles. Both largely drew from the same scriptural passages and made similar inferences and interpretations. All publicists admitted that the Old Testament described

this chapter mostly cites from *All War Anti-Christian; or the Principles of Peace, as contained in the Holy Scriptures, explained and proved by the Tracts of the Society for the Promotion of Permanent and Universal Peace* (London: Thomas Ward 1840).

66 Gurney, *Essay* 1840, 21.

67 As found in the collection of Auguste Visschers. [Brussels, Royal Library of Belgium, General Catalogue, II 70.245 A Vol. 1].

68 Many featured a little while later in the American *Advocate.*

69 'Therefore they fear not him that can kill the body only, but Him who can destroy both body and soul in Hell.' HP (January, February & March 1822), 10–11.

70 HP (December 1820), 378.

numerous divinely ordained holy wars fought by the Jewish people, but they countered that this dispensation had been wholly superseded by the New Testament. Under 'the Gospel dispensation', Jesus Christ had taught his disciples that they had to forego the *ius talionis* – an eye for an eye – but had to turn the other cheek. They engaged in dense discussions on the 'actual' meaning of Isaiah 2:4 or Romans 13, arriving at the same conclusions as the Americans. Much the same debate happened on whether or not the pre-Constantine Church fathers admitted the possibility of military service for Christians; the British, like the Americans, deducing that they must have been against it.[71]

As we have seen in the previous chapter, Grotius had typically reached the opposite conclusions.[72] Gurney, one of the most respected contemporary Quaker theologians – he even provoked a schism among American Quakers – was aware that his learned predecessor had justified war. In his manual for young Quakers, this man observed that Grotius, in his *De iure belli ac pacis,* recounted that Mosaic law urged the total extermination of certain enemies of the ancient Hebrews.[73] Admitting that this reading of Deuteronomy was 'indisputably' correct, Gurney was nonetheless surprised that Grotius 'did not notice the argument which it so obviously affords, in favour of the doctrine that under the Christian dispensation, war is unlawful'.[74] In his tract for the peace society, the Quaker elaborated on whether or not the Gospel had annulled this injunction. In his legal treatise, Grotius had selected several passages from the New Testament, which in his eyes proved that 'the right to war was not completely annulled by the law of Christ'. One detailed how John the Baptist had advised soldiers that they 'should do violence to no man'. For Grotius, this suggested a narrow obligation to abstain from any deceit and violence in their personal dealings. If God had wanted men to refuse military service altogether, his prophet surely would have been more explicit. Gurney disagreed, and argued that John the Baptist's utterances could at best be construed as neutral, and that, furthermore, as a prophet, he had merely heralded the coming of the kingdom of heaven – also contrary to Grotius. The Friends drew their pacifism

71 Many of these arguments recurred. E.g. Clarkson, *Essay* 1840, 4, 11; Hancock, *Principles* 1840, 12–9, 37–9: Roberts, *Principles* 1840, 7–10; Gurney, *Essay* 1840, 17–20.

72 See chapter 1.

73 Grotius, *Belli ac Pacis. Book 1* 1925, 62 (Ch. II, title VI).

74 Gurney, Joseph. *Observations on the Religious Peculiarities of the Society of Friends* (London: Arch, 1824), 283.

from 'that more perfect revelation of the moral law of God, which distinguishes the dispensation of the gospel of Christ'.[75]

The implications of the peace society's religious doctrines on contemporary international law were not overlooked. Like the Americans, and many continental-Europeans discussed in other chapters, the British peace friends held it in incredibly low esteem. Observing that war was legitimised within mainstream doctrine, an editor from the *Herald* reported in 1821 that 'that what is called the law of nations, is to a dreadful extent the law of barbarity and injustice'. Speaking of Christians, the author went on: 'is it not a shame for them to attempt to justify by the law of nations, a course of conduct which is positively forbidden by God? (…) If such are the principles and maxims of war, is it not the time that they should be discarded and abolished by every Christian people?' The article's title was 'The Cloak for Crimes'.[76] Earlier that year, the journal had entered into the reasons why rulers had thus distorted Christ's teachings: 'the laws of war were originally the laws of barbarians – made according to their own hearts. These laws, with some modifications and improvements, are now the laws of war among nations called civilized, but they are still a barbarous code'. Only few of the descendants of the original barbarian leaders 'who acquired crowns' had been 'worthy of the name of Christians'.[77] Speaking of war declarations, the British likewise agreed with Americans that rulers were all sorely mistaken 'that a declaration of war can authorize the most flagrant violations of the moral law'.[78] In such war declarations, 'the laboured reasonings of those who have most ingeniously discussed the legal question on War, will be sifted for proofs and decisions to vindicate the appeal to the sword; nor will it be difficult to discover some plausible colour in the shape of precedent or analogy, to satisfy the scruples of those who have already suffered their minds to be impressed with the persuasion that such an appeal may be lawfully made'.[79] In other articles, international law was similarly derided as being, for the most part, little more than a cynical apology for power politics.[80]

---

75 Grotius, *Belli ac Pacis. Book 1* 1925, 63–70 (Ch. II, title VII); Gurney, *Essay* 1840, 6–7.

76 HP (November 1821), 351.

77 HP (July 1821), 204–5.

78 HP (April 1820), 127.

79 HP ((July, August & September 1822), 152.

80 E.g. HP (December 1819), 357; HP (June 1821), 178–88; HP (July 1821), 204–5; HP (January, February & March 1826), 25–6; HP (October, November & December 1835), 222; HP (January 1838), 8–9; HP (January 1842), 90; HP (July 1843), 328.

2.2 *Quaker views*

Intellectually, the Quaker philosopher Jonathan Dymond developed the most sophisticated critique of existing legal doctrine within the early peace society. Dymond ranked among the peace society's most respected provincial supporters. Running a draper's shop in Exeter, in Southwestern England, he articulated his earliest thoughts on war in 1819. The resulting essay was published in 1823. Soon after the book's publication, Dymond became a member of the London Peace Society. In 1824, he first met the British peace friends in person, when he travelled to London to attend the annual May meeting of the Society of Friends. The Committee of the peace society then and there decided to make the promising young intellectual a member of its body. They also voted to turn his book into a tract of the society, which appeared in 1825, under the lengthy title *Observations on the Applicability of the Pacific Principles of the New Testament to the Conduct of States: and on the Limitations which those Principles Impose on the Rights of Self-Defence.* Dymond also established an auxiliary society in his hometown that same year, which he led as secretary. Despite only ever having attended two Committee meetings, this Quaker shopkeeper was tremendously influential among radical pacifists. His premature death in 1828 because of a throat illness did not diminish his status. The posthumously published *Essays on the Principles of Morality* completed his religious and philosophical examinations of what it meant to be a pacifist.[81] Widely read also in the United States, Dymond's tract became one of nineteenth century Britain's most famous pacifist texts. Ceadel's history of the London Peace Society described its early decades as 'the Jonathan Dymond era'.[82]

Already on the first page of his peace society tract, Dymond's dim view of the defenders of the just war tradition shone through. Unlike the pacifist tracts that preceded his, he assumed it as a premise 'that Christianity is a system of peace' and that 'no one can question the obligation of those duties without questioning Christianity itself'. Rather, what intrigued Dymond was why, 'in the application of these precepts to our conduct in life, we find endless excuses for disobeying them, and endless casuistry to justify our disobedience'. Why did so many learned jurists find exceptions to the general norms of Christianity, which ought to apply both to the sovereign and the subject of the state alike? The Quaker identified two main reasons. The first

81 Jonathan Dymond, *Essays on the Principles of Morality, and on the Private and Political Rights and Obligations of Mankind* (London: Hamilton, Adams & Co. 1836).

82 Ceadel, *Origins* 1996, 222–224; Brock, *Peace Testimony* 1990, 257–264; Lange, 'Histoire de la doctrine pacifique' 1927, 367–369; Beales, *History* 1931, 54.

argument held that there existed no international law, 'of general authority amongst nations', which protected states from the violence of another.[83]

In one of his posthumously published essays, Dymond elaborated on the deficiencies of the law of nations. Like everyone else, he was aware that international legal obligations derived from positive law and natural law. An orthodox Quaker, Dymond naturally set more stock in the latter, advising sovereigns to follow positive legal norms whenever they were in accordance with Christianity. Even if they did not go even nearly far enough, such laws should be obeyed. 'Incoherent and inconsistent as the law of nations is, when it is examined by the moral law, it is pleasant to contemplate the good tendency of some of its requisitions.' Dymond referred to cases in admiralty courts in which judges had ruled against their own government, and modest cases where the laws of war had been somewhat humanised since antiquity.[84]

Nonetheless, it was equally clear that an exclusive reliance on the positive maxims of international law had limitations. Theoretically, these were supposed to only bind those states that had explicitly or tacitly consented to them. Had this been the case in actual state practice? Anticipating the peace society's later critiques of colonialism, the Quaker referred to the customary law that allowed a state to claim *terra nullius* for its own. If uninhabited land, and neighboured only by European states, fair enough, reasoned Dymond. But what about those states which had never heard of this norm? What if South Pacific states hypothetically possessed a law of nations that obliged states to equally divide newly-discovered lands? 'How happens it that the Englishman possesses a sounder right to exclude all other nations?' Even then, 'unhappily our law of nations goes much further'. That same doctrine applied even to inhabited countries: 'the law of nations has talked, with perfect coolness, of setting up a standard', permitting Europeans to claim legal rights, 'as if the previous inhabitants possessed no other claim or right than the bears and wolves'. Revealing the absurdity of this argument, which was widely accepted in contemporary legal doctrine, Dymond asked 'what we should say to a canoe-full of Indians who should *discover* England, and take possession of it in the name of their chief?'[85] Because the non-Western world had been excluded from the positive laws of nations, it should not surprise that 'the history of European settlements has been, so

83 Dymond, *Observations* 1840, 3–5.

84 Dymond, *Essays* 1836, 92–3.

85 Ibid., 93–4.

far as the aborigines were concerned, too much a history of outrage, and treachery, and blood'.[86]

It was evident that only divine moral law, as understood by Quakerism, offered norms guaranteeing stable and pacific international relations. The moral law was similar, but not synonymous to natural law for Dymond. By natural law, the philosopher understood a collection of natural rights, such as the right to life and personal liberty, as well as a series of natural impulses. The reason why Dymond subordinated these to the moral law, was because the instinct of self-preservation was typically used as a key reason to legitimise personal self-defence in the Anglo-American common law. Reasoning like Worcester in the United States, Dymond rejected the normative character of natural examples, drawing from his belief that Jesus had taught absolute personal non-resistance.[87] 'A law possesses no authority; the authority rests only in the legislator: and as nature makes no laws, a law of nature involves no obligation but that which is imposed by the Divine Will'. Furthermore, as international law was 'not wont to tighten the bonds of morality' in itself, the Christian moral law was presumably still responsible for those instances where international law was duly observed.[88]

The absence of a universally binding and just system of positive international law caused apologists of power politics to invoke 'utility and expediency' as exceptions to the Christian prohibition of all war. This was the second major explanation identified by Dymond as to the, in his eyes, illegitimate separation between private and state morality. Like others, he was dismayed that Grotius appeared to acknowledge that a treaty in violation of Christian morality still contained, as far as the voluntary law of nations was concerned, binding norms for those states that agreed to it.[89]

While Grotius was mentioned only briefly once, in one of the posthumous essays, Dymond across his entire oeuvre intensely attacked a more modern author, whose philosophical standpoints largely overlapped with

86 Ibid., 94; Antony Anghie, *Imperialism, Sovereignty and the Making of International Law* (Cambridge: CUP, 2004), 40–65; on of *terra nullius*, see Emmanuelle Tourme-Jouannet, *Le droit international, le capitalisme et la terre* (Bruxelles: Bruylant, 2021), 121–48, 174–215; Andrew Fitzmaurice, 'The Genealogy of *Terra Nullius*'. *Australian Historical Studies* 38(129) (2007), 1–15.

87 Dymond, *Essays* 1836, 81–3; this was analogous to U.S. common law. Banner, *Natural Law* 2021, 43.

88 Dymond, *Essays* 1836, 86, 92; Dymond, *Observations* 1840, 14–5.

89 Dymond, *Essays* 1836, 93; Dymond, *Observations* 1840, 5; according to Grotius, voluntary law in violation of natural law did not make an act in accordance with the latter lawful. It could only withhold punishment. Neff, *Justice* 2014, 161–2.

those assumed in legal doctrine: William Paley (1743–1805). Paley was well-known in early nineteenth century Britain, and also in the United States, for his *Principles of Moral and Political Philosophy*. Published in 1785, it was an enormously popular textbook at institutes of higher learning, being adopted as mandatory reading at universities like Cambridge, until the book's influence began to wane in the 1830s.[90] An important aspect of what both contributed to its success and its eventual decline, was its author's experimentation with 'theological utilitarianism'. A complex set of ideas, it was captured in Paley's own epigram: 'Whatever is expedient, is right'. This motto meant to convey that what seemed self-interested or immoral on the surface level, often contributed to greater good when interpreted from a larger perspective. For example, a Christian might live a pious life for the utterly selfish reason of avoiding hell and attaining heaven, but this unquestionably also contributed to the collective well-being of society.[91] His influence was immense, since politicians and journalists liked to throw his name around as a byword for political wisdom. Predictably, it was conflated with Machiavellianism by critics of the mainstream, such as Romantics or evangelical Christians.[92]

Belonging to the latter camp, Dymond detested the legitimation this sort of moral philosophy could provide for just cause doctrines. He disapprovingly cited a passage from the famous treatise, which stated that, while no advantage could be had from private persons breaking the law, 'in the case of empires, this may sometimes be doubted'. The Quaker was grossly offended by the suggestion that philosophers could not 'pronounce that any rule of morality is so rigid as to bend to no exception'. Paley himself alluded to the possibility of a state violating a manifestly unjust treaty – like one that hypothetically blocked a river passage, causing grave food shortages.[93]

90 William Paley, *The Principles of Moral and Political Philosophy* (London: Baldwyn 1821); Graham Cole, 'William Paley's Natural Theology: An Anglican Classic?'. *Journal of Anglican Studies* 5(2) (2007), 209–25; Niall O'Flaherty, *Utilitarianism in the Age of Enlightenment. The Moral and Political Thought of William Paley* (Cambridge: CUP, 2019), 102; Dan Lloyd Le Mahieu, *The Mind of William Paley: A Philosopher and His Age* (Lincoln: University of Nebraska Press 1976), 158–62; Ziegler, *Antebellum* 1992, 82–3.

91 Paley, *Principles* 1821, 33–5, 46.

92 Machiavelli himself, it must be said, was not the amoral cynic of his reputation. Dymond, *Observations* 1840, 8; O'Flaherty, *Paley* 2019, 5; David Roth-Isigkeit, 'Niccolò Machiavelli's International Legal Thought: Culture, Contingency, and Construction' in Stefan Kadelbach, Thomas Kleinlein, and David Roth-Isigkeit (eds.), *System, Order, and International Law. The Early History of International Legal Thought from Machiavelli to Hegel* (Oxford: OUP, 2017), 19–37.

93 Paley, *Principles* 1821, 497–498.

Paley's philosophy was more nuanced than Dymond let on. Paley immediately counterbalanced his own argument by cautioning of the precedent the unilateral annulment of a treaty potentially posed to the international order as a whole: 'one and almost the only method of averting or closing the calamities of war (…) is lost to the world forever'.[94] Nonetheless, it was apparent why his reasoning offended the Quaker. Like Dymond, Paley pointed out the absurdities of the doctrine of *terra nullius*. Unlike Dymond, however, he defended it, by his assertion that 'the rule already proposed, however arbitrary, possesses one principle quality of a rule – determination and certainty'. If such norms did not exist at all, the European powers would engage in endless colonial wars. Adding further insult to injury, he interpreted John the Baptist's advice to the soldiers in the same way as Grotius. Paley did not pretend to offer a single, all-encompassing, panacea to these conundrums. The philosopher merely posited them to explain 'the hesitation that we sometimes feel, in applying rules of personal probity to the conduct of nations'.[95]

To Dymond, Paley's concessions sounded less like philosophical doubt, and more like blasphemy. By premising the indeterminateness of the laws contained in the Gospel, Paley 'indirectly [admitted] the insufficiency of Christian principles on occasions which most materially affect the happiness and welfare of mankind!' That could not do. The Quaker proceeded to charge his opponent with the same indeterminateness. How could mortals select the relevant criteria for setting aside the laws of God? Paley's adages led to a slippery slope: 'If (…) we may dispense with his laws in one instance, why may we not dispense with them in ten? Why may we not abrogate them altogether?' For Paley, the methods to reconcile interstate war with scripture were the traditional just causes as explicated by legal scholarship. He listed 'precaution, defence, or reparation'. Paley reiterated mainstream legal thought by stating that 'in a larger sense, every just war is a *defensive* war, inasmuch as every just war supposes an injury perpetrated, attempted, or feared'. Dymond rejected every single one. To him, they 'flippantly dispense with the principles of Christian obligation'. Most were also 'so lamentably vague and indeterminate', 'technical', 'inapplicable to the circumstances of society', and 'incapable of being practically applied'. A norm that could mean anything, ultimately meant nothing at all. As he put this: 'a morality that will not be practiced, (…) that cannot be practiced, is a useless

94 Dymond, *Observations* 1840, 7–8; Paley, *Principles* 1821, 498.

95 Paley, *Principles* 1821, 496–498, 500–501. See supra for Grotius's interpretation of these verses.

morality. It is a *theory* of morals.' Just cause doctrine provided too much subjective latitude, whereas 'we want clearer and more exclusive rules; we want more obvious and immediate sanctions'.[96]

For a convinced Quaker like Dymond, a straightforward and practical normative panacea did exist: Christian forbearance. States, like individuals, were expected to adopt absolute non-resistance. He did not mince words. Christianity expected people to suppress their natural instincts: 'all of them are to be regulated and restrained'. This standard applied equally to self-preservation. The entity of the state was not exempt: 'the pacific laws of our religion are binding upon all men; upon the King, and upon every individual who advises him; upon every member of a legislature; upon every officer and agent; and upon every private citizen'. If an individual was not permitted to attack the burglar who has his arm lifted to murder them, the state was likewise prohibited from mounting an armed defence of its territory. Allowing only individual self-defence, but not collective defence, would be inconsistent, and open the door to an exception that would swallow up most of the norm: 'if one man may kill one, two may kill two, and ten may kill ten; and an army may kill an army: and this is defensive war'. Even if such laxities did not de facto void the rule, they would tolerate 'a very wide range of justifiable warfare'.[97] Dymond's argument differed little from that of religious pacifists in the United States.

The leadership of the London Peace Society, who fully supported this 'high ground' rationale, gave only mild assurances to those who – understandably – felt a bit queasy about the potential prospect of allowing themselves to be killed. From the religious perspective, Dymond asserted in one of his writings that 'what is most expedient with respect to another world, is most expedient with respect to the present'. The laws of God had to be obeyed for their own sake, and not for whatever benefit might be reaped from them here on earth. Nonetheless, God only seldom demanded true sacrifice. In 'perhaps nineteen cases out of twenty', obeying the moral law also benefitted present life.[98] Like the Americans, the British peace friends argued that non-resistance also offered more tangible and pragmatic security benefits than armies. Many of them being Quakers, they again and again referred to historical instances of their own sect, which had 'proven' that God protected those who abjured violence. The perceived absence of Native

96 Dymond, *Observations* 1840, 11–2 Paley, *Principles* 1821, 496–8, 501–2.

97 War of actual self-defence were 'perhaps the fewest'. Dymond, *Essays* 1836, 9; Dymond, *Observations* 1840, 14–17.

98 Dymond, *Essays* 1836, 89.

American warfare in Pennsylvania, a colony founded by Quakers, was constantly cited as evidence that non-resistance also functioned on 'national' levels.[99] Clarkson's biography of William Penn heavily emphasised this aspect.[100] Hancock's three-part tract was even entirely devoted to the 'miraculous' safeguarding of Quaker communities during the Irish Rebellion of 1798.[101] Like with Pennsylvania, the story was exaggerated and neglected many factors. In reality, Irish Quakers did not escape unscathed, suffering considerable property losses by looters. As a minority sect, one largely withdrawn from mainstream society, they also did not pose a threat to either side. That being said, only one Friend was recorded killed during the entire uprising, which caused over 10,000 deaths overall.[102]

This early and long-lasting preoccupation with individual responsibility precluded the development of more substantive institutional solutions. By utterly rejecting most of the principles on which the law of nations was premised, the peace society found it difficult to salvage anything. Dymond was yet again a case in point: 'if principles of justice are to decide what the law of nations shall authorize, it will be needful to establish a new code tomorrow'. However, a great portion of international law was devoted to regulating 'the conduct of war' – the *ius in bello.* Since 'the practices of war' were 'so foreign to principles of justice and morality', it was without purpose to 'attempt to found the code upon them'.[103] Dymond's aversion of the laws of war never truly disappeared among radical peace friends, and constituted an important reason for why the international peace movement could not be equated with more humanitarian movements, like the Red Cross, that sprang up from the 1860s onwards. Although there were ideological overlaps, and a degree of mutual sympathy, true pacifists like Dymond and his successors in the Committee wanted to abolish war altogether, and not merely soften it.[104] In legal terms, most of the focus of the peace movement, in Britain and elsewhere, laid on issues of *ius ad bellum,* rather than *ius in bello,* especially among religious peace friends, who were the most prevalent for a long time. In 1856, the peace society still described the laws of war as

99 Dymond, *Essays* 1836, 23–5; examples abounded, e.g. HP (December 1819), 363.

100 Thomas Clarkson, *Memoirs of the Private and Public Life of William Penn. Volume I* (London: Taylor 1813), 339–45, 357; Clarkson, *Memoirs of William Penn. Volume II* 1813, 436–63.

101 Hancock, *Principles, part III* 1840, 34–9.

102 Brock, *Peace Testimony* 1990, 215–21.

103 Dymond, *Essays* 1836, 93.

104 Crossland, *Campaign to control Warfare* 2018, 27–8, 105–7.

'an impossible attempt to effect a compromise between the ferocity of human passion and the benign spirit of Christianity'.[105]

Consequently, to the limited extent that the London Peace Society in its early decades paid attention to political or legal alternatives to war, it looked at means to avoid it: mediation or arbitration. Like friends of peace elsewhere, they first turned to what they were familiar with in private legal disputes. As one of the leading Quaker theoreticians, Dymond again pointed the way. This time presumably speaking for large swathes of society, he examined it in light of 'the morality of legal practice'. 'If it should be asked why, in a book of general morality, the writer selects for observation, the practice of a particular profession, the answer is simply (…) this particular profession peculiarly needs it'.[106]

His reasons were largely the same as would, arguably, also be given today. Court proceedings were expensive, stressful, and slow. Many lawyers were furthermore amoral, in the sense that they sought out every technicality in the law that served the interests of their client, regardless of larger morality; 'Lawyers familiarize to their minds the notion, that whatever is legally right is right'. Delving deeper into their own depravity, lawyers went from insisting upon legal technicalities, 'to an endeavour to *pervert* the law, then to the giving a false colouring to facts, and then onward and still onward until witnesses are abashed and confounded, until juries are misled (…) deliberate untruths are solemnly averred, until, in a word, all the pitiable and degrading spectacles are exhibited, which are now exhibited in legal practice.'[107]

Instead, Dymond preferred less formalistic dispute settlement mechanisms, more accommodating to his own Quaker sensibilities. The contemporary court system was separated into two opposed jurisdictions. Most courts relied on the common law, composed of a mixture of statutory law and precedent. The second system consisted of so-called courts of equity. Until the reorganisation of the British court system in 1873 by the Judicature Acts, which abolished the distinction, the Court of Chancery possessed the power to mitigate aspects of positive law, as administered in ordinary courts. In the seventeenth century, equity served to 'correct men's consciences (…) and to soften and mollify the extremity of the law'.[108] Unlike the

105 HP (December 1856), 135.
106 Dymond, *Essays* 1836, 155
107 Ibid., 156–7.
108 As it was put in the 1615 *Earl of Oxford Case,* cited by John Hamilton Baker, *An Introduction to Legal History* (Oxford: OUP, 2019), 104, 110–5, 122–4.

common law courts, the chancellor and his legal aides were, in theory, much more flexible in assessing equity. Procedure offered more options. The absence of a jury entailed that the judge assessed the facts. An equitable remedy could also do more than award damages. Although equity very often simply affirmed positive law, equity courts were immensely popular. Even by the nineteenth century, the Chancery was still popularly known as 'a court of conscience'.[109]

Dymond championed a highly idealised version of arbitral procedures based on equity. The practice of the Court of Chancery belied conventional illusions surrounding equity. Its myriad defects were caught most famously in the 1850s novel *Bleak House*. In it, Charles Dickens satirised the extremely slow and inefficient procedures within the Chancery, bringing no end to despair for all involved.[110] Substantively, equity had by then furthermore long lost all relationship with natural law. Nineteenth century jurists recurrently lamented that the popular mind still thought of equity as synonymous to conscience.[111] In reality, a flood of cases and the need for internal clarity and consistency had turned 'equity' into a clearly defined legal concept, with its own body of case law, and byzantine procedural regulations. Ironically, the jurisdiction that had grown out of a need to alleviate the worst tendencies of the common law, had itself fallen prey to that which it was originally intended to combat.[112]

The Quaker was not blind to these deficiencies. He knew the Chancery was a court of equity 'rather in name than in fact', and that modern equity jurisprudence relied far more on precedent than on the merits of the individual case. In fact, Dymond gave in to nuance when he conceded that every judicial system stayed 'imperfect and alloyed; a mixture of evil and good'. Nonetheless, his priorities were: 'Private adjustment is the best mode; arbitration is good; law is good only when it is the sole alternative.'[113] Overall, this moralist underestimated the degree to which every sophisticated society, especially an industrialising empire like Britain, required detailed positive legislation.[114]

---

109 Baker, *Introduction* 2019, 114.

110 Simon Petch, 'Law, Equity, and Conscience in Victorian England'. *Victorian Literature and Culture* 25(1) (1997), 126.

111 Selden and Bentham already derided the concept as 'arbitrary'. Ibid., 125–130. See also chapter 5.

112 Baker, *Introduction* 2019, 120–4.

113 Dymond, *Essays* 1836, 150, 403, 405, 410–1.

114 For Dymond, even property disputes could be settle by equity, rather than law. Ibid., 414.

Distrust of legal trials and positive law partly explained why international arbitration was eventually accepted by the London Peace Society, while it stayed lukewarm to proposals for an international court, or the codification of international law. Dymond did not cry in the desert when he espoused that, although Holy Writ did not condemn every recourse to a judicial court, excessive litigiousness was sinful.[115] This reflected ancient Quaker practice. Until the late nineteenth century, many Friends were accustomed to settle disputes within their congregation, even on strictly legal matters, through arbitration governed by local community standards. Maintaining group cohesion was seen as more important than protecting individual legal rights. Done outside of the regular court system, awards had to be executed within the community, and enforced through peer pressure. To the extent this was feasible, Quakers likewise tried to avoid lawsuits with outsiders.[116]

2.3 *Benthamite views*

Only one adherent of the London Peace Society explicitly suggested an international judicial court, that was supposed to rely as much as possible on a positive code of law. Testament to his character, Jeremy Bentham began paying a double annual subscription to the peace society in the early 1820s. In doing so, Bentham joined a religious association which condemned defensive war and abhorred utilitarianism – despite himself being a leading utilitarian philosopher who never doubted the right to resist aggression, as well as being a closet non-believer.[117] As observed in the first chapter, neither Bentham nor his disciple Mill featured much in peace propaganda on either side of the Atlantic. In a rare early mention in the *Herald,* in 1853, the editor dismissed the plan for a 'European Code and a Court of Nations' as too ambitious.[118] To be fair, the philosopher did not make much of an effort to promote his peace plan within the society. A reputedly shy man, he

115 Ibid., 151–3.

116 Peter Philips, 'Ancient and Comely Order: The Use and Disuse of Arbitration by New York Quakers'. *Journal of Dispute Resolution* 2016 (1), 81–114; Alfred Searle, 'Friends (Quakers) and Arbitration'. *Arbitration: The International Journal of Arbitration, Mediation, and Dispute Management* 16(3) (1950), 53–90.

117 His suggestion in 1789 for a 'Pacific or Philharmonic Society' might have been the first recorded call for a peace society. Stephen Conway, 'Benthamites' 1990, 223–224; Conway, Stephen. 'Bentham on Peace and War'. *Utilitas* 1(1) (1989), 93–4; Ceadel, *Origins* 1996, 67–8.

118 HP (June 1853), 228

remained a passive member and never attended any meetings. Bentham's influence was exclusively indirect, through his writings and his followers.[119]

There were relatively few public Benthamites in the peace society, but the most significant one was John Bowring (1792–1872). Like his celebrated friend, Bowring was an odd duck within the society. After all, of all the peace friends of the entire nineteenth century, he alone had the dubious honour of having almost single-handedly begun a major international war. As the British governor of Hong Kong in 1856, Bowring severe handling of the 'Arrow incident' instigated the outbreak of hostilities that led to the Second Opium War (1856–1860), which was also known as the 'Arrow War' at the time.[120] A war widely condemned by the peace society, Bowring had by then abandoned pacifism.[121] Later in life, this lapsed pacifist nonetheless still maintained that the peace campaign for arbitration clauses contributed to the erection of 'an international tribunal – that great desideratum'. This court had to 'propound and administer a code of international law, for, whatever may be the power of a *lex non scripta,* authoritative international law there is none'. Like his mentor, Bowring had little love for both equity and natural law – in stark contrast to someone like Dymond.[122]

Through Bowring, these Benthamite notions might have influenced the American peace societies, who were not as sectarian as the main British peace society. Bowring edited the posthumous *Works of Jeremy Bentham,* in which the peace plan was first published.[123] He was also acquainted with Mill's articles on international law.[124] Within the London Peace Society, he

---

119 Conway, 'Bentham' 1990, 223–4.

120 War was probably inevitable, given the clash between European trade interests and Chinese protectionism. Nonetheless, Bowring's decision to use force in response to a minor incident involving a British-flagged trade vessel, the Arrow, set off a chain of events that directly led to open hostilities. Philip Bowring, 'Sir John Bowring: the Imperial Role of a Lifelong Liberal'. *Asian Affairs* 42(3) (2011), 423–424; Andrew Phillips, 'Saving Civilization from Empire: Belligerency, Pacifism and the Two Faces of Civilization during the Second Opium War'. *European Journal of International Relations* 18(1) (2011), 14–15.

121 In his autobiography, he defended himself that 'no man was ever a more ardent lover of peace than I (…) but with barbarous – ay, and sometimes with civilized nations, the words of peace are uttered in vain'. John Bowring, *Autobiographical Recollections of Sir John Bowring. With a brief Memoir by Lewin B. Bowring* (London: Henry S. King 1877), 217–8; Stephen Conway, 'John Bowring and the Nineteenth-Century Peace Movement'. *Historical Research* 64(155) (1991), 344–58.

122 Bowring, *Recollections* 1877, 268.

123 Bentham (ed. Bowring), *Works. vol. II* 1843, 552. See also chapter 1.

124 Conway, 'Bentham' 1990, 242.

had acted as foreign secretary in the 1820s, an important post that put him in charge of correspondence with the American peace societies.[125] As discussed in the previous chapter, a plausible case could be made that William Ladd's congress of nations project had been directly influenced by Bentham or Mill. In light of the pivotal role played by the American Peace Society in the politicisation of the British peace movement, the London Peace Society's most unlikely member might therefore have, unwittingly, ended up among its more influential ones in the long term.

3 The Emerging Political Campaign

In the thirty years before the British arbitration campaign began in earnest, the London Committee was as vague on the specifics of what they wanted achieved politically as the Americans. A possible permanent congress of nations was never theoretically discussed until Ladd's efforts reached them from overseas. True enough, Noah Worcester had already superficially contemplated international political cooperation, but the British remained just as vague as their American colleague. The purely religious message took precedent. Nonetheless, even in the early years, they intuitively realised that something more concrete should be attached to their sermons, when addressing high men of state. In the address that Clarkson handed over to the czar at Aix-la-Chapelle, their Committee implored the plenipotentiaries to 'take an example from the administration of justice in small communities'. If private disputes were settled by law, why should interstate disputes not similarly be judged before a 'high general tribunal of arbiters', whom the sovereigns would appoint?[126] From the United States, the *Herald* that same year copied a call from the Massachusetts Congregationalist Church that called for a 'new law of nations' and a 'grand tribunal of empires'.[127] Likewise in 1819, the *Herald* devoted its first major article to arbitration. The anonymous writer referred not only to the classic schemes of Henri IV and Sully, Saint-Pierre and William Penn, but also to the Aix-la-Chapelle congress and the arbitration provision provided for under the Treaty of Ghent.[128] Like the Americans, the British consistently reported on the

125 This made his part in the war with China all the more disappointing for his former colleagues. Ceadel, *Origins* 1996, 342, 348, 520, 353.

126 HP (January 1819), 12.

127 Ibid., 88.

128 HP (August 1819), 225–7. See also chapter 1.

international arbitrations they read about in the newspapers, including not only the 1822 Russian arbitration between the United States and Britain, but also various forms of 'mediation' or 'arbitration' by a third party, in Europe and the Americas.[129]

However, the reader of peace propaganda was, up until the 1840s, largely left in the dark as to what should be properly understood by 'arbitration'. In 1833, a letter to the editor of the *Herald* supposed that 'few of your readers have heard of the suggestion of Mr. Penn to establish a great diet on the continent for the preservation of the peace of Europe'.[130] From sporadic articles like this, however, comparatively little could be definitively assumed. Mentions of 'arbitration' in the *Herald* tended to be lapidary, and not a single tract was specifically devoted to the subject. In an annual report of the Hibernian Peace Society, it could be discovered that the Irish pacifists supported arbitration in the Vattelian sense, meaning as one voluntarily entrusted to 'a third uninterested Monarch'.[131] Whether the London Peace Society shared their preference for this sort of arbitration could not be verified. Most probably, they understood it in the same convoluted way as contemporary American, French, and Genevan peace advocates – i.e. as an umbrella term for all forms of political mediation, binding or non-binding, bilateral or multilateral, and not necessarily strictly dependent on legal norms.

Hints of the popular reception of the purely religious tract campaign undertaken by the Committee could be gleaned from the way it defended itself. In an exceptionally long article from January 1834, titled 'A vindication of the peace society and its publications', the Committee responded to a review of its tract series in a broadsheet paper. The review had been scathing. Among other issues, it held that the peace society could never hope to achieve 'its extraordinary object'. Scanning the various publications, the reviewer concluded that 'very few of these tracts appear to be adapted for the perusal of sceptics, or persons who have not yet turned their attention to the enquiry. They are only fit for readers whose minds are already made

129 HP (September 1819), 286; HP (January, February & March 1822), 56–58; HP (January, February & March 1825), 55–7; HP (April, May & June 1826), 68, 94; HP (October, November & December 1826), 201; HP (January, February & March 1828), 319; HP (April, May & June 1829), 82; HP (October, November & December 1831), 209; HP (July 1840), 130.

130 HP (April, May & June 1833), 105–6.

131 HP (October, November & December 1826), 201. Little is known about this Irish peace society.

up'.[132] The society replied by going over every single one of their tracts, to show that they were not just preaching to the choir. Near the end, they emphasised that the society 'does not fanatically overlook the means by which it may attain its end'. Interestingly, the article referred to the efforts in the United States and Geneva towards an 'arbitral tribunal', rather than the activities of their own society. From their own tracts, they mostly brought up the usual religious arguments.[133]

Those would have impossibly convinced any sceptic to change their mind. Absolute non-resistance, demanded even when attacked by an aggressor, was simply not a platform that could hope to garner mainstream support in Britain, or anywhere else in the world. If the London Peace Society wanted to shake its doctrinarian reputation, it would have to adopt, refine, and further develop the political tactics and legal instruments that were becoming popular among its peers elsewhere. Although the religious 'high ground' always remained the most important argument against war, this would now be complemented with a more secular campaign in favour of international arbitration.

3.1 *Petitions for a Congress of Nations*

Ten years later, in 1843, readers of *The Times,* the most widely read newspaper of the British empire – and therefore the world – could read the following: 'We have often commented on the fanaticism of association, as a distinguishing characteristic of the social eccentricities of modern times; but of all the developments of this disease which it has ever been our lot to handle, there is not one which can bear an instant's comparison with the vagaries and delusions of those unhappy individuals who have just been figuring before the world (in our columns) under the title of "The Universal Peace Convention"'.[134] The British peace societies, being brought under international public attention by articles like this, were undeterred. Six years later, in the run-up to Cobden's arbitration motion, the *Herald* assessed that 'all the symptoms are favourable, and not the least so is the fact, that the *Times* has been again vehemently sneering, and indulging as is its wont, in misrepresentation and abuse'.[135]

---

132 HP (January, February & March 1834), 263–88.

133 It was prompted by an earlier article in this paper that had mistakenly claimed that Britain did not have any peace societies, indicative of the obscurity of the peace movement at this time. Ibid., 265–85.

134 As copied in HP (October 1843), 453.

135 HP (January 1849), 225; *The Proceedings of the First General Peace Convention: held in London, June 22, 1843, and the Two Following Days: with the Papers laid before the*

Indeed, the 1840s proved to be remarkably successful for the London Peace Society. In its issue of June 1850, the *Herald* announced that it would double in size, since it had become too small 'as the organ of a movement of such magnitude and importance as ours has now become'. The same issue announced that work on the peace society's new and enlarged offices would soon be completed.[136] The shift had also been mental. The London Committee now recommended members to publicly support electoral candidates who supported 'some legalized system of arbitration'.[137] In a bafflingly unexpected move to anyone acquainted with the society's history, the *Herald* unabashedly wrote in 1849, on one such electoral speech, that the speaker 'does not hold the preposterous opinion, that the question of peace ought in no way to be connected with politics'.[138]

The pressure to petition Parliament first sprang from bottom-up. In the early 1830s, the auxiliaries began to notice that both in the United States and in Geneva, peace friends were apparently taking more concrete political action in favour of arbitration and some form of tribunal, congress, or court of nations. The found out about this through extensive lines of communication, in the first place through the *Herald's* substantial 'foreign correspondence' columns.[139] Initially, these auxiliaries still respected the decision of the London Committee to 'extend correct opinion' to the British public, that would indirectly remove 'the impediments which exist to the introduction of a more complete system of international law, and of an authorized tribunal for appealing to public justice against any breach of such law'.[140]

It were provincial sympathisers who fumed that the London Committee's insistence on the 'high ground' was suffocating. By 1842, in an unusually frank article, dissenters accused the metropolitan leadership of existing only to pay its own officers and of issuing a journal read only by a small inner circle.[141] It was at this time that two future leaders of the movement first became involved in peace activism. In Manchester, Richard Cobden joined the Committee of a new Manchester auxiliary. In Birmingham, Joseph Sturge (1793–1859) emerged as a central figure. Both will be introduced

Convention, the Letters read, &c. &c. (London: Peace Society's Office 1843), 2; Ceadel, *Origins* 1996, 342.

136 HP (June 1850), 499–500, 509.

137 HP (July 1857), 320.

138 HP (February 1849), 246.

139 E.g. HP (October, November & December) 1831), 212; HP (January, February & March 1832), 275, 283–4; HP (April, May & June 1832), 353–4.

140 July, August, and September 1831), 153.

141 As paraphrased from Ceadel, *Origins* 1996, 307.

more properly later. Suffice it to say for now that there existed a very real risk in the late 1830s and early 1840s of a rupture. The Manchester society, composed of free traders, acted quite independently, despite their 'auxiliary' status. Birmingham outright boasted a rival society, that unsuccessfully tried to become the new 'national' peace society.[142] In Newcastle, the auxiliary even declared itself wholly independent, before it went back into the fold in 1850.[143] This revolt by 'the country' stemmed not so much from ideological disagreement with the London Committee's 'high ground' pacifism, but rather its dogged unwillingness to engage with mainstream British society. In the end, the London Committee was set before a fait accompli. In 1836, the peace movement presented its first petition to the Commons, asking it to aid the peaceful settlement of international disputes involving Britain. It had been sent not by the metropolitan pacifists, but by the Southampton auxiliary. They had not asked permission from London.[144]

Adding to this mounting pressure front, both the American peace societies and the Genevan count de Sellon frequently asked their British colleagues to join in their efforts to introduce legal solutions into the peace campaign. Until his death in 1839, the president of the Genevan Peace Society kept the British peace friends extensively abreast of his actions. The British frequently indulged the well-meaning Genevan aristocrat by publishing whatever material he sent them, so that the average issue of the *Herald* in the 1830s, more likely than not, featured some letter or report from Switzerland. As detailed in the next chapter, count de Sellon was a firm believer in peace through law. Talking about his interest in a congress of nations, he hoped the British might pick up the idea as well.[145]

Likewise, the Americans clearly politicised following the formation of the American Peace Society by Ladd, who immediately opened an essay contest on a congress of nations and international law. Both the national society and several of its auxiliaries called on the British societies to follow their example. In 1831, the Connecticut Peace Society – the one that originally founded the *Advocate of Peace* – explicitly asked the London society to start sending memorials to the British government in favour of a congress of nations that would prepare 'the final establishment of the laws of nations

142 Ibid., 308–310.

143 Scott and Megoran, 'Newcastle Upon Tyne Peace Society' 2017, 1–17.

144 Conway, 'Politicization' 1993, 276; *Journals of the House of Common. Vol. 91* (London: Stationery Office 1836), 804.

145 HP (July, August & September 1831), 159

upon the basis of the gospel principle'. Occasionally, similar American calls appeared in the British pacifist press.[146]

The Committee eventually caved. At the society's annual meeting of 1834, the editor of the *Herald* stated that he 'saw no impropriety in presenting such petitions to Parliament'. During this meeting, the British peace friends adopted a resolution recommending arbitration to 'the powers of Europe and America'.[147] However, no concrete action was taken for five more years. In 1839, this changed. That year, the Committee received an exceptionally reprimanding letter from Beckwith, the second-in-command of Ladd in the American Peace Society. The closest allies of the British had lost their patience.[148] Combined with the internal pressure from the auxiliaries, the peace society sent its first petition to the Commons. It was presented by Edward Baines (1800–1890), a non-conformist M.P. who had earlier supported the Reform Act. The American influence was obvious. Just like Ladd's congress of nations proposals, the petition asked the formation of 'a great council, for the purpose of settling international the principles of international law, and of organizing a high court of appeal, in which all national disputes may be adjusted'. Their first attempt was not a success. Like Bouvet's congress of nations proposal before the French National Assembly in 1849, several representatives burst into laughter upon hearing it. The petition was ordered to lie on the table, i.e. shelved without further consequence.[149]

Nonetheless, a significant precedent had been set. In the words of Stephen Conway: 'It was as if a drain had been unblocked.' A trickle became a flood, until, by 1845, petition signing had developed into a fixture at the end of every public meeting or lecture, and thousands of people attached their names to lists that would be sent to Parliament. The increased press attention that these petitions and other activities brought to the London Peace Society bolstered its self-confidence.[150]

146 E.g. HP (October, November & December 1831), 212; HP (September 1836), 38.

147 HP (April, May & June 1834), 334–6.

148 Conway, 'Politicization' 1993, 276.

149 HP (July 1839), 319–320; *Journals of the House of Common. Vol. 94* (London: Stationery Office, 1839), 177; HP (July 1839), 320. See chapter 4 for information on Francisque Bouvet.

150 It became a tradition to invite an M.P. to chair the peace society's annual meeting. Conway, 'Politicization' 1993, 276; Ceadel, *Origins* 1996, 294–5; from 1845 on, the *Herald* mentioned new petitions under the heading 'Peace Proceedings in England'. E.g. HP (October 1845), 362; in 1846, the society reported that over 200 petitions had been delivered during the last parliamentary session; HP (October 1846), 151–2.

3.2 *Responses to Imperialism and Colonialism*

An important factor that contributed to both the politicisation of the British peace movement and its increasing relative popular success was rising geopolitical insecurity. This insecurity grew out of a series of international incidents both within Europe and outside Europe. The society's pessimism about the near future was aptly captured in the opening pages of the *Herald* of January 1841, called: 'Thoughts on the present disturbed state of the nations'. Its tone was sombre: 'The political horizon is everywhere covered with dark portentous clouds, which are charged with all the elements of war, and are only waiting to be agitated a little more (...)'.[151] The 1840s began with the Syria Crisis, that directly bled into the Rhine Crisis, when France and the German states nearly went to all-out war.[152] These events coincided with ongoing boundary disputes with the United States, which periodically alarmed citizens in both states. The Maine boundary was only settled in 1842, and the Oregon one in 1846. Although Britain itself was never in any real danger, Anglo-French tensions and internal unrest in France provoked irrational 'invasion panics' among portions of the British public: in 1847–1848, instigated by a naval arms race and the February Revolution, and again in 1851, following the coup d'état of Louis-Napoléon Bonaparte and the emergence of the Second French Empire.[153] In general, the European revolutions of 1848 caused also Britons, like other Europeans, to fear that a major European war was at hand. In both 1846 and 1848, the government failed in its attempts to revive the militia, although the scares at the end of the decade instigated another militia bill, this time successful. In all three instances, however, the London Peace Society attacked the bills through a series of campaigns that hugely benefitted its public profile.[154]

151 HP (January 1841), 205.

152 Miroslav Šedivý, T*he Decline of the Congress System. Metternich, Italy and European Diplomacy* (London: Tauris 2018), 125–43; the Rhine Crisis is further mentioned infra, and again in chapter 4 from the French perspective.

153 Charles Iain Hamilton, *Anglo-French Naval Rivalry, 1840–1870* (Cambridge: Clarendon Press 1993), 15–29; David Morgan-Owen, 'Scares, Panics, and Strategy: the Politics of Security and British Invasion Scares before 1914'. *Diplomacy and Statecraft* 33(3) (2022), 444–5; Laurence Guymer, 'The Wedding Planners: Lord Aberdeen, Henry Bulwer, and the Spanish Marriages, 1841–1846'. *Diplomacy and Statecraft* 21(4) (2010), 549–73; see also Richard Cobden, *The Three Panics. An Historical Episode* (London: Ward & Co. 1862).

154 Ceadel, *Origins* 1996, 357–367, 470; Morgan-Owen, 'Scares' 2022, 445.

The *Herald* extensively commented on all of these domestic and international crises.[155]

If not all of these events culminated into armed conflict, in spite of such fears, colonial wars directly affected or interested many Britons. As citizens of the largest and most powerful European empire of the nineteenth century, there was no shortage of such conflicts. In its aforementioned article of January 1840, the *Herald* took especial umbrage at the fact that 'the cause of the threatened wars lie in nations many thousand miles from Europe'. It seemed apparent to the society that the 'old plea of self-defence' was a complete sham, if 'the armies and fleets employed must leave all that is dear to them, before they can reach the scene of contest'. Was the public really supposed to believe that the Chinese should be punished 'for daring to execute their laws against smuggling', and that Syrian towns had to be bombarded for the national benefit? 'Let those who can, believe these pretences.'[156] Flipping through the pages of the *Herald* over its entire nineteenth century run is to read through the colonial history of the British empire. For the 1840s, the major incidents were the Opium War (1839–1842), the First Afghan War (1839–1842), the conflicts with the Sikhs in northern India, the Xhosa peoples in South Africa, the Māori in New-Zealand, as well as several interventions in South-America and the Middle East.[157]

Of the various national peace movements, the British had the distinction of having been the most unequivocally against colonialism. While peace friends in the United States or France were equally against colonial violence, they were more diffident on the issue. The American peace societies were more concerned with the lot of their own Native American tribes, whereas the French peace friends typically rejected colonial warfare, but not the larger principle that Christians had a duty to 'civilise' the non-Western world. Initially, the British felt the same. As committed Christians, they

155 See e.g. HP (July 1840), 106–10; HP (January 1841), 225; HP (July 1842), 129; HP (July 1844), 99; HP (June 1845), 287; HP (January 1846), 8–10, 15–6; HP (April 1846), 49–51, 59–61; HP (May 1846), 65–7; HP (August 1846), 113–7; HP (November 1846), 166–9; HP (January 1847), 193–5; HP (August 1847), 330–4; HP (November 1847), 370, 377; HP (December 1847), 387–9; HP (January 1848), 1–5; HP (February 1848), 28–9; HP (April 1848), 52, 56–9; HP (May 1848), 65–70; HP (July 1848), 97–9; HP (August 1848), 113–6; HP (May 1849), 293–6; HP (June 1849), 308, 312–4; HP (July 1849), 325; HP (August 1849), 346–7.

156 HP (January 1840), 205–6.

157 See the overview in Andrew Porter (ed.). *The Oxford History of the British Empire. Volume III. The Nineteenth Century* (Oxford: OUP, 1999).

praised the efforts of missionaries, although already in 1820 the society felt that 'the influence of the Holy Spirit' alone sufficed. Indigenous peoples would adopt Western customs in due time, as 'civilization is one of the blessings always attendant upon its progress'.[158]

However, as time progressed and the incidents of violence in distant lands stacked up, the London Peace Society radicalised its tone. A powerful influence on the society's attitude, apart from its own moral radicalisation, was the Aborigines Protection Society, established in 1837. Like had been the case with the London Peace Society, Quakers and abolitionists played a big part in its founding. In fact, the leadership of the two societies overlapped, as both included Allen, Sturge and Clarkson.[159] Another direct influence was the book by the Quaker William Howitt (1792–1879), who published in 1838 a controversial work entitled *Colonization and Christianity*.[160] The journal of the society copied copious extracts from the book whose perusal seemed 'enough to make one blush that he is a man'. In it, Howitt condemned every aspect of Western colonialism. According to him, its history meant only 'contempt of all faith in treaties – the basest policy – the most scandalous profligacy of public morals – the most abominable international laws!' The society fully agreed with the author that 'the real object' of the colonisation of India had been 'wealth and power', while the ostensible objectives of spreading Christianity and 'seeking the good of the natives' were nothing but 'pretence'. If it was up to Howitt, Britain had to 'stamp the whole system of usage towards the natives with that general and indignant odium which must demolish it at once and forever'.[161] In keeping with this message, the first petitions of the peace society in the 1840s did not promote arbitration, but protested the wars in China and Afghanistan.[162] The first peace conference of 1843 similarly adopted a resolution

158 HP (January 1820), 5.

159 Charles Swaisland, 'The Aborigines Protection Society, 1837-1909'. *Slavery & Abolition: a Journal of Slave and Post-Slave Studies* 21(2) (2000), 265–80.

160 William Howitt, *Colonization and Christianity. A Popular History of the Treatment of the Natives by the Europeans in All their Colonies* (London: Longman, Orme, Brown, Green & Longman 1838); Mandler, Peter. 'Howitt, William (1792–1879)', in *Oxford Dictionary of National Biography*. 2004, available at: doi.org/10.1093/ref:odnb/13998.

161 HP (April 1840), 57–73.

162 Conway, 'Politicization' 1993, 276; *Journals of the House of Common. Vol. 95* (London: Stationery Office 1840), 109; *Journals of the House of Common. Vol. 97* (London: Stationery Office 1840), 383.

condemning these conflicts.[163] The reports on colonial affairs in the *Herald* were of a similar tone.[164]

In a speech given in connection to the London Peace Society in 1852, Louis Alexis Chamerovzow (1816–1875) dissected the justifications given to colonialism under international law. The report in the *Herald* admitted that 'the subject of the law of nations (...), although of much importance, had not hitherto met with the attention it deserved.[165] As the new assistant secretary of the Aborigines Protection Society, Chamerovzow reiterated the main points of a book he had published four years earlier, on the legal rights of the Māori of New Zealand.[166] His essential points of contention largely overlapped with those which Dymond had already formulated in the 1820s, but he entered into a more technical legal analysis, despite not being professionally trained as a lawyer. Like the Quaker moralist, he explicitly rejected a law of nations based exclusively on state practice, because, 'unless they were originally good in themselves, they only laid the foundation of permanent injustice and inequity'. Positive international law 'was not found on the laws of equity, but on expediency'. Like other moralists, he asserted that 'the actual law of nations was founded on the laws of nature'.[167]

His book provided greater detail. Drawing extensively from Vattel, the seminal introduction to any dilettante interested in the subject, Chamerovzow emphasised the passages in the Swiss classic that relied on *ius naturalis* reasoning to define sovereignty and argue the legal equality of states, whatever the form of government. If all men were equal, and their natural rights were universal, it logically followed that all other rights derived from this foundation applied equally to indigenous peoples as they

---

163 *Proceedings London* 1843, 13, 23.

164 E.g. HP (July 1842), 137; HP (January 1843), 256–7, 259–61; HP (April 1844), 93–5; HP (April 1846), 49–51; HP (May 1846), 65–72; HP (November 1846), 166–9; HP (March 1848), 37; HP (January 1850), 430–2; HP (February 1850), 435–9; HP (March 1850), 451–66; HP (April 1850), 467–9; HP (May 1850), 483–91.

165 HP (January 1852), 8.

166 He also co-organised the 1848 Brussels peace conference, was involved in the short-lived Stop-the-War League during the Crimean War, and accompanied Richard and Sturge during their effort to lobby for an arbitration clause in the Paris peace treaty. Chamerovzow. Louis-Alexis. *The New Zealand Question and the Rights of Aborigines* (London: Newby 1848); Richard Huzzy, 'Chamerovzow, Louis Alexis (1816–1875), in *Oxford Dictionary of National Biography*. 2010, available at: doi.org/10.1093/ref:odnb/101107; Ceadel, *Origins* 1996, 407, 466, 536; Ceadel, *Idealists* 2000, 52–3.

167 HP (January 1852), 8. See supra for Dymond's similar conviction.

did to Europeans.[168] He then proceeded to the right of discovery. Still relying on Vattel, he claimed that discovery only conferred sovereign rights, opposable to a third state, to the extent that such land was uninhabited, as well as occupied and used by the discovering state. Furthermore, no discovering state could claim more than it could reasonably populate and cultivate. The European discoverers had themselves ignored any markings a rival had previously placed, or the papal treaty that had divided the world between Spain and Portugal.[169] However, virtually all European colonies had been founded in already inhabited lands. Therefore, the right of discovery, 'if sovereignty and independence mean anything', had to privilege the indigenous peoples, rather than the European latecomers.[170]

Chamerovzow dismissed or refuted popular contemporary counter-arguments. Apologists pointed out that Vattel had added that the indigenous peoples themselves had a duty to cultivate their lands. The Swiss writer presumed that the New World had been only sparsely populated, whereas Europe was overpopulated.[171] Chamerovzow disagreed, both in its common legal interpretation, as well as in its factual applications. Legally, an unqualified interpretation of such a principle would open the door to all warfare: 'the invading nation, holding the *Jus Gentium* in one hand, and the sword in the other, might legitimately use the latter to despoil the natural occupant, and next proceed to justify the act by an appeal to the former'.[172] Factually, though Chamerovzow was not aware of the modern insight that the non-Western world was far more densely populated than early modern Europeans ever realised, he asserted that the Māori were 'an agricultural people', who fulfilled their obligations under international law.[173] As if to drive his point home, he added – like a few contemporary French peace friends – that the European states were themselves still replete with

168 Chamerovzow, *Rights of Aborigines* 1848, 25–9; he referred to Emer de Vattel, *Droit des gens, ou principes de la loi naturelle, appliquée à la conduite et aux affaires des nations et des souverains. Nouvelle édition. Tome premier* (Paris: Aillaud 1830), 38 (§ 4), 42–8 (§ 11–§ 19).

169 Chamerovzow, *Rights of Aborigines* 1848, 33–6; Vattel, *Droits des gens. Tome I* 1830, 221–2 (§ 207–§ 208); on the 1494 Treaty of Tordesillas, see also Jouannet, *La terre* 2021, 33–6, 121–48.

170 Chamerovzow, *Rights of Aborigines* 1848, 52–3.

171 Ibid., 38: Vattel, *Droits des gens. Tome I* 1830, 223–4 (§ 209).

172 Chamerovzow, *Rights of Aborigines* 1848, 39–41.

173 He did not accept the common legal notion that indigenous peoples had to be agricultural to exercise sovereign rights over the land. Ibid., 40, 184.

stretches of uncultivated land.[174] The amateur jurist likewise did not accept the vaunted standard of civilisation as a loophole. Unlike the vast majority of jurists involved in colonial projects, he refused to acknowledge that the ignorance of indigenous peoples of European international law annulled their rights under this law. The fact that their customs were alien to those of Europeans was irrelevant. If they were excluded from the European legal system this way, 'there is opened a wide field for oppression, injustice and inhumanity. (…) there would exist no safety for any people; for it would suffice to set up a standard of civilisation, and to declare war against all who did not attain it'.[175] An absolutist pacifist himself, Chamerovzow a fortiori did not even entertain the thought that right of conquest – 'might against right' – could confer legal title.[176]

Therefore, to the extent that the law of nations still accommodated justifications for aggression, or even preparations for self-defence – 'the first step towards (…) aggression' – it had to be reformed. Principle should have the force of law, 'as it was superior to law'. Chamerovzow had no doubt that 'by little and little the present system (…) would be modified and altered, so at last to become one founded only on the great principles of Christianity'. This reformed international juridical code was 'a requirement of the nineteenth century' demanded by 'the voice of the people'. He therefore fully endorsed the peace movement's campaign for arbitration.[177]

3.3 *Reception of U.S. Legal Proposals*

What did 'arbitration' mean? Like their sister society in the United States, the London Peace Society would have to decide what they should specifically propose. The first petitions had been very vague, perhaps too vague. The debate among British peace friends mirrored simultaneous debates within the American Peace Society, which had become politicised nearly a decade earlier. Because the U.S. peace movement had already formulated several plans, the British naturally studied the plans which reached them from their closest allies overseas.

174 HP (January 1852), 8; see chapter 4 for similar remarks by French critics of the conquest of Algeria.

175 Chamerovzow, *Rights of Aborigines* 1848, 47–52, 77–82.

176 Ibid., 32–33. This and the abovementioned legal arguments refuted by Chamerovzow are also identified in Jouannet, *La terre* 2021, 151–271; on the 'standard of civilisation', see Pitts, *Boundaries* 2018, 12–37.

177 HP (January 1852), 8–9.

In 1839, the London Committee agreed to hold an essay contest. They had been pressed for years by William Ladd to do this, as well as eventually also by the grassroots, who felt such an initiative might raise public awareness. One subscriber had complained their movement was 'scarcely known in some quarters, and especially in the high places of earth'.[178] Unlike the American *Prize Essays*, but similar to the contest the British sponsored in France in 1840, contestants were not specifically asked to theoretically develop a congress of nations. Rather, they only needed to demonstrate that 'war, under all circumstances, is inconsistent with precepts of the Gospel' and substantiate 'the best means of settling all disputes between nations without recourse to arms'. The three clergymen of the jury settled the affair already in January 1841. Second prize – twenty guineas – was awarded to one A.G., whose real identity was never found out by the jury or by modern historians. The society published his essay in 1847.[179]

The grand laurate, on the other hand, soon took up a visible role in the society: Henry MacNamara (1820–1873). Having written the essay while finishing law school, thereby earning him a respectable hundred guineas in pocket money, MacNamara later became a barrister and a county court judge.[180] In the 1840s, this young man played some part in the legal translation of the society's 'high ground' pacifism, presenting a paper on international law at the London peace conference of 1843.[181] As he grew older, he loosened his radicalism. In 1847, Macnamara appeared on a membership list of the Peace of Nations Society, another very obscure and short-lived rival to the London Peace Society. Like the Society for Abolishing War of 1816, it could not reject defensive war.[182] At the time of his essay, however, he still supported hard-line pacifism – per the requirements of the concours.

Religious radicalism prevented neither of the British prize essays from engaging with possible legal solutions. Like the essays written around the same period in the United States, Geneva and France, their juridical investigation only came after a lengthy general condemnation of war, which interested the average reader the most. Nothing in these preliminary chapters would have particularly amazed anyone with even a passing acquaintance

---

178 HP (January 1839), 227–8.

179 HP (April 1841), 308; A.G, *Peace (Permanent and Universal). The Law of Christ* (London: Ward & Co. 1847).

180 Ceadel, *Origins* 1996, 292.

181 See infra.

182 This likely explains why the *Herald* ignored it. Van der Linden, *Peace Movement* 1987, 203.

with pacifist literature. MacNamara extensively cited from the tracts produced by the Anglo-American peace societies, including Channing, Gurney, Clarkson and Dymond.[183] The prize laurate quoted the latter author almost verbatim. Like Dymond's classic, he could not accept just cause doctrine as a legitimate exception to the Gospel prohibition on war. Defensive war, 'synonymous in common language with justifiable war, as having a just cause', had to be condemned also. MacNamara pointed to all the arguments formulated by the Quaker theorist against the idea that some forms of war could be justified, without inevitably voiding the norm. 'If an army may fight in defence of their own lives, they may (…) fight in defence of the lives of others: if they may fight in the defence of the lives of others, they will fight in defence of their property; if in defence of their property, they will fight in defence of political rights; if in defence of rights, they will fight in promotion of interests (…)'. He concluded, like most religious pacifists, that 'the truth is, that the distinction can only exist in theory; in *practice* it is useless'.[184]

A.G.'s essay was of a similar tenor. He called 'necessity', another common shorthand for just cause arguments, 'the tyrant's plea'. To invoke an exception to the divine prohibition on all uses of force, whether private or public, was 'a monstrous libel upon the benevolence, the power, the wisdom of God – that the same plea has been urged in the defence of all crimes in all ages'. Like MacNamara, he agreed that force should never be countered with force. Christians had to choose non-resistance. After all: 'the blood of its martyrs is the seed of the church'.[185] Nonetheless, both essayists explored institutionalised normative solutions that could prevent crises from escalating to the point that such martyrdom would be required. MacNamara considered himself neither a utopian nor a satirist, who could content themselves with critique. No, he would 'endeavour to propose some feasible plan'.[186]

In the case of the grand laureate, this plan had already come readymade from overseas. In a review of his book in *The Spectator,* it was pointed out that the writer had 'apparently read to write a book, not written a book because he has thought and read'. In 'the most important part' of the book, the author had merely copied the plan suggested earlier 'by an American

183 E.g. MacNamara, *Peace* 1841, 11, 12, 22, 33, 62, 96, 119, 125, 133, 157, 166.
184 Ibid., 94–96.
185 A.G., *Peace* 1847, 98–9, 106.
186 MacNamara, *Peace* 1841, 165.

writer'.[187] Indeed, Macnamara had extensively studied the American *Prize Essays on a Congress of Nations,* published two years earlier by the American Peace Society. His most important influence was Ladd, although he also referred to Bolles and Upham – uncoincidentally the three most legalistic essays of the seven-hundred page tome.[188] Although the law student duly acknowledged his influences, he would not have passed the test of modern plagiarism, for he added almost nothing original. Like the introductory parts of his book, MacNamara seemed to have contented himself with simply paraphrasing or outright quoting others. His critique of the law of nations was identical to that of Upham and Ladd, using the exact same doctrinal sources and legal cases.[189] If it was not for the occasional reference to a British tract, or count de Sellon, his book might just as well have been written by an American.[190] MacNamara's congress of nations was likewise composed of a legislative congress of ambassadors, and a judicial court of nations.[191] To him, this system was preferable to both Vattelian arbitration and a temporary diplomatic congress, convened ad hoc to discuss a specific event. Ladd's plan seemed better suited to codify the law of nations. Institutionally enshrined multilateralism would raise the political costs of violating positive international law, or ignoring the jurisdiction of an international court.[192]

By contrast, the runner-up essay by A.G. took a more independent course. Like the grand winner, he had carefully studied the American examples. Unlike MacNamara, he thought the peace societies of the United States were too ambitious. Ladd's congress of ambassadors would not only concern itself with the international laws of war, but would also regulate a wide variety of other subjects of international interest, like the abolition of the slave trade, the improvement of communication, and aspects of private international law.[193] While not disagreeing that these were all laudable objectives, a law-making congress should restrain itself to its core business of maintaining international peace: 'Nothing could be more disastrous than the assumption of general legislative power. It would create a general authority to which no state would care to appeal.' Such a congress would still be necessary,

187 The Spectator (6 November 1841), 20.

188 MacNamara, *Peace* 1841, 223, 227, 231, 236–7, 274.

189 For instance the list of issues of international law that needed to be reformed. Ibid., 230–9.

190 Ibid., 281, 291–2, 297.

191 Ibid., 223–41.

192 Ibid., 240, 289.

193 See chapter 1.

however, since the 'omission of first principles' had been the cause of failure of previous attempts at interstate cooperation. A.G. did not offer many specifics, other than that the congress should be composed of both 'a body of eminent lawyers', and statesmen from the various states involved.[194]

This British essayist likewise thought Ladd too radical in his vision of an international judicial court. He preferred disputes to be settled through a court of arbitration. The anonymous writer took care to distinguish his arbitral tribunal not only from the American conception of an international court, but also from domestic arbitration procedures. Unlike Ladd and MacNamara, he did not appear to have envisioned a permanent institution, but an ad hoc tribunal, composed of two types of arbiters. Each party would be able to appoint at least one 'president', who decided on the applicable norms and procedural regulations. These had to respect the general principles enacted by the law-making congress. However, the facts would have to be judged by a separate jury, who could also determine the amount of any damages. These jury members would not decide through majority vote, like the judges in Ladd's proposal: 'Their unanimity is essential: without it, there would be every temptation to the use of unjust influence.'[195]

Its proceedings would not be analogous to British mercantile arbitration either. Drawing from Blackstone's *Commentaries,* the essayist pointed at several key differences. Domestic arbitration could under certain circumstances be commanded, whereas international arbitration should always originate from previous mutual agreement. It likewise did not work with a jury, but exclusively with arbitrators, who decided on both law and fact. Lastly, awards thus given in accordance with relevant statute law could be executed like any other court order.[196] An international arbitral award, however, could not be enforced through violent means, but had to rely exclusively on the 'the honour of the appellants', as well as the 'universal suspicion and resentment' with which any violation of an award would regarded by the international community. Although the author did not entirely conform to the Vattelian template, he stayed quite close to it, in his concern to avoid a politically impracticable dispute settlement mechanism.

---

194 A.G., *Peace* 1847, 112–3.

195 Ibid., 114.

196 Ibid., 111–2; William Blackstone, *Commentaries on the Laws of England. Volume II* (New York: William E. Dean 1853), 16–18; G. Ellenbogen, 'English Arbitration Practice'. *Law and Contemporary Problems* 17(4) (1952), 656–78.

Unlike a congress, he only needed 'the voluntary union (...) of two or more states'.[197]

As such, the London Peace Society's essay competition did not settle on any definitive legal course. The jury had awarded both the more far-reaching American solution, as well as the more restrained ambition that did not rely on a vast international organisation, but which could already function on the bilateral level. That both essays proscribed defensive war confirmed what Francis Fellowes, the editor of the American *Advocate,* had already articulated in 1836: a peace through law campaign had the potential to broaden the peace movement's popular appeal, without necessarily compromising the religious sensibilities of its most zealous members.[198] Not a word was said about the possibility of the armed enforcement of international law. Their solutions were likewise not very technical or specific, but that was not absolutely necessary either. Even state practice and legal doctrine did not define 'arbitration' in a detailed manner in the 1840s. It was more important that the peace societies began to hammer the point home that there existed a third option, between the abandonment of one's rights, and the 'final arbitrament of the sword'. According to the runner-up, there needed to be 'some appeal without compromise of equality; some law without degradation; some just decision without war; and if so, the cause is lost, the question decided, and whose then, is the responsibility and the guilt?'[199] The Committee had only to decide what general 'arbitration' plan to support in its burgeoning petition campaign.

By the summer of next year, this question was largely resolved. A couple of months after the contest was decided in London, a minor event across the Atlantic Ocean set the stage for the future British arbitration movement. On 22 May 1841, Joseph Sturge visited the Connecticut home of judge Jay. He was visiting the United States to consult with the American abolitionist movement, and William Jay was a prominent abolitionist, at whose house run-away slaves sometimes called. As it happened, the American judge also read extracts of a manuscript on international peace he had been working on. His guest was immediately convinced of the potential of his host's proposal to include a binding arbitration clause in every future international treaty. Sturge described it as 'beautifully simple, and of easy application'. He then and there asked for a manuscript copy of the relevant passages, which he attached in the appendix to this travel account, published the

197 A.G., *Peace* 1847, 112, 114–5.

198 See chapter 1.

199 A.G., *Peace* 1847, 110–111.

next year.[200] Back home, he became the first lobbyist on behalf of stipulated arbitration.

Sturge was a force to be reckoned with in the British peace movement. A devout Quaker, like many others, he had joined the London Peace Society at the age of twenty-five. The son of a freeholder, his Birmingham corn business had prospered to the extent that it abundantly afforded him the two key elements needed for a philanthropist to succeed: time and money. Sturge was initially attracted to temperance and anti-slavery. He became especially involved in the latter movement; in the famed group painting of the 1840 World Anti-Slavery Convention, he was depicted right next to the main speaker.[201] Those who personally knew Sturge, described him as an optimist, with an uncomplicated sense of righteousness that ensured that the man went straight for the high ground in every cause.[202] In the temperance movement, he was a teetotaller. In the anti-slavery movement, he helped found the British and Foreign Anti-Slavery Society, which pursued the worldwide abolition of slavery. In the Anti-Corn Law League, he wanted all tariffs abolished. During the dreary years of the Crimean War, when most peace friends kept silent, Sturge took the typical slur describing pacifism as 'peace-at-any-price' as a great compliment.[203] During the 1840s, events conspired to complicate his black-and-white worldview.[204] Combined with his repeated failures to get into official politics – he failed to get elected to Parliament in 1842, 1844, and 1847 – Ceadel has claimed that peace activism might have provided 'a more rewarding outlet for his energies'. Although this energetic character declined to join the London Committee, his personal wealth and support among the provincial base ensured he came to be recognised as the British peace movement's 'animating spirit', as Henry Richard later put it – himself the 'animating spirit' of the second half of the century.[205]

---

200 Joseph Sturge, *A Visit to the United States in 1841* (London: Hamilton, Adams, and Co. 1842), 55–7, liii–lxi.

201 Douglas Maynard, 'The World's Anti-Slavery Convention of 1840'. *The Mississippi Valley Historical Review* 47(3) (1960), 452.

202 Henry Richard wrote 'it was no more use trying to move him than to move the Alps'. Ceadel, *Origins* 1996, 302–305; Henry Richard, *Memoirs of Joseph Sturge* (London: Partridge 1865), 598–9.

203 Ceadel, *Idealists* 2000, 41.

204 Ceadel pointed out that Garrisonian anti-slavery and Chartism put him in the unaccustomed role of being the moderate in the room. Ceadel, *Origins* 1996, 304–5.

205 Ibid., 305; Richard, *Memoirs of Sturge* 1865, 428. Henry Richard is introduced infra in this chapter.

The rest of the London Peace Society soon shared Sturge's enthusiasm for Jay's plan for stipulated arbitration. The first American edition of Jay's book in 1842 was accompanied that same year by 'a large edition' printed by the Committee of the London Peace Society. In the foreword of the British edition, the London leadership admitted that the work did not fully espouse all of the principles of their own body.[206] Nonetheless, Jay had treated the subject 'in a somewhat novel, and certainly very powerful and convincing manner'. Therefore, they 'fully believe its wide circulation just now, must materially aid the good cause of peace'.[207] At the peace society's annual meeting that year, the plan was brought up in glowing terms. Those present were well aware that their meetings were popularly seen as 'an assembly of well-meaning, philanthropic enthusiasts' with 'no clear views of the practical difficulty which stands in the way'. Addressing the M.P.'s present, the speaker called for Parliament to send an address to the government, 'to secure a general agreement among [states] to declare that arbitration ought to be had recourse to'. He suggested arbitration by friendly powers appointed ad hoc, rather than any permanent 'court of review and settlement', because a permanent court might not be able to guarantee its neutrality.[208] Around the same time, a remarkable letter appeared in the *Herald*. In it, MacNamara publicly distanced himself from the scheme which he had the year before still defended in his prize essay. Referencing Sturge's *A Visit to the United States*, the jurist confessed that he had been converted to Jay's plan for stipulated arbitration.[209]

Why did the London Peace Society drop the project for a permanent court and congress of nations, as adopted by their own prize essay, so quickly? They hinted at their own reasons in various places. MacNamara already provided an important one in his letter. Speaking of precedent, he wrote that, 'to us lawyers', it meant everything.[210] The Committee tended to agree. Roberts had herself alluded to a congress of nations as a possible alternative to war. However, the Committee had added a footnote, referring to the Anglo-American arbitrations awarded under the provisions of the Treaty of Ghent. It queried whether this was not preferable to Roberts's congress; 'The principle is the same, but the mode is less complex, and less

206 Jay had argued that arbitration was in Britain's interest, as the U.S. could easily attack Canada.

207 Jay, *War and Peace* 1842, iii–iv.

208 HP (July 1842), 134–6.

209 Ibid., 155–6.

210 Ibid., 156.

liable to objection; it has also the advantage of having been tried, and proved successful'.[211] This model was furthermore more similar to the arbitral procedures known to Quakers, or the mercantile arbitrations that evangelical philanthropists, many of them business owners, were already well familiar with. Both of these options were also explicitly forwarded in pacifist circles, by Dymond and the anonymous prize essayist.[212]

Instruments already experimented with in diplomacy furthermore seemed less politically sensitive. The peace society was emerging only slowly and carefully from a long quietist phase. Despite their idealism, its members were acutely aware of the fact that they formed a tiny minority within society. They knew perfectly well that many dismissed them as naïve dreamers. Their long-standing political pessimism went hand in hand with their religiously inspired distaste of the sinful positive legislation produced by politicians. A congress of nations that had to codify international law offered no strict guarantees for a new law of nations in accordance with divine natural law, while such an ambitious project did expose them to more charges of utopianism – as evinced by the reception of their first petition.[213] Stipulated arbitration, on the other hand, offered more possibilities for some third party to find recourse in equity, as actually done by the king of the Netherlands in his award of 1831.

Lastly, the peace movement's small size made it disproportionally dependent on the preferences of a handful of key people. The loss of even one major sponsor or motivating leader regularly put the entire organisation at risk. In the American Peace Society, the loss of Ladd in 1839 caused not only much personal grief, but also a severe financial blow. Their founder had been keeping their society out of debt by regular donations from his own fortune. Ladd's successor Beckwith had a very hard time keeping the American Peace Society financially afloat for years afterwards.[214] Ladd's death had larger ideological repercussions also. With him, the greatest champion of a congress of nations had passed away. Sturge visited the United States mere days after his passing, and only met with Jay. As seen in the previous chapter, Jay and Beckwith eventually came out the victors of the long-running power struggle between moderates and radical reformists in the American

211 They specifically referred to the 1831 award of the Dutch King, also brought up by the Americans and Richard Cobden. Roberts, *Principles* 1840, 25–26; Carroll, 'Canadian-American Boundary Dispute' 2000, 179–201.

212 HP (July 1842), 136.

213 HP (March 1845), 239; HP (May 1845), 277.

214 Ziegler, *Antebellum* 1992, 92; Whitney, *Centennial History* 1928, 63; AP (May 1864, 56–7.

Peace Society. Sturge, being a man who preferred simple solutions to complex problems, personally favoured the juridical plan that seemed the least complicated. Given his substantial influence in British peace circles, the London Peace Society naturally listened to whatever this man proposed.

3.4 *Entrenchment of Stipulated Arbitration*

Sturge's vision culminated in 1843 in the first international peace conference. The project had been first contemplated at the end of his visit to the United States, two years before. At a meeting of the American Peace Society in Boston, the British philanthropist suggested an international conference 'to deliberate upon the best method of adjusting international disputes'. Specifically, Sturge wanted this conference to adopt judge Jay's plan for stipulated arbitration. The Americans were enthusiastic about it, and adopted resolutions agreeing with both proposals.[215] Back in Britain, the Birmingham Quaker likewise successfully persuaded the London Committee and the other leading peace friends to join in this transatlantic effort. The peace conference was directly inspired by the success of the 1840 World Anti-slavery Convention, that Sturge had co-organised. It was even deliberately timed to coincide with the end of the Second General Anti-Slavery Convention, organised from 13 to 20 June 1843 in London.[216] The organisers of the peace conference hoped that this would induce many participants to attend the pacifist meeting also. After all, many members of their own society were themselves abolitionists who would attend the anti-slavery conference. At a preliminary meeting, held in May, the London Peace Society again explicitly forwarded the plan of judge Jay as a concrete point on the agenda of the upcoming conference. In preparation, they had printed 4,000 copies of Jay's essay. No mention was made of Ladd's congress.[217]

All things considered, the peace conference held in London from 22 to 24 June was a success. Over 300 delegates registered, although the exact number of actual participants was never totally verified. The proceedings claimed that there were about 150 delegates.[218] According to Ceadel's estimations, there were some 120 delegates on the first day, and just over thirty on the second and third days. No exact numbers ever were given with regards to the audience, but the conference's official report itself admitted that it was 'not very numerous'. This was confirmed by the press. It

215 Sturge, *Visit* 1842, 139–40; see also AP (October 1841), 66–7.

216 *Proceedings London* 1843, 5.

217 HP (July 1842), 113–9, 155–6; HP (January 1843), 231–4. Ceadel, *Origins* 1996, 311.

218 *Proceedings London* 1843, 2.

appeared that most abolitionist had stayed home. Likewise, the label 'international' proved to be more aspirational than descriptive, for the vast majority of the delegates were British, and members of a peace society. Only some twenty Americans had undertaken the very long and expensive journey to London. Few continental-Europeans were present. They likely did not number more than ten at best. The most important among them was the Marquis de la Rochefoucauld-Liancourt, the president of the *Société de la morale chrétienne,* who gave two very long – and according to Ceadel 'tedious' – speeches, which largely ignored the topic at hand.[219] The organisers were evidently also wary of a meeting that stood theoretically open to people uninvolved in organised peace activism, for the whole conference was tightly regulated. Delegates were not allowed to question that war – in general, without qualification – was in 'opposition to the spirit of Christianity, the prosperity of nations, and the true interests of mankind'. They could only discuss the best means to attain peace. All spontaneity was further killed by the requirement that every new proposal had to be communicated beforehand in writing. Most of the conference therefore consisted of readings of preprepared papers, without a lot of debate.[220]

Nonetheless, the British peace friends had crossed a significant bridge. While the conference itself had ultimately ended up a modest affair, the London Peace Society was afterwards impressed with the amount of attention it had given to their small movement. The *Herald* devoted no less than ten pages to press coverage, from the religious press to such bastions like the *Times*.[221] On the Continent too, it was the London conference of 1843 that first put the Anglo-American peace movement on the radar of the *Société d'économie politique,* many of whose members would six years later co-organise the celebrated Paris peace conference. It also inspired the founders of the *Société de la paix de Paris*.[222]

The first London peace conference set the course for the legal agenda promoted by the later peace conferences held in Europe. The most significant resolution reflected a compromise between Ladd and Jay, albeit strongly in favour of the latter. MacNamara read the introductory paper. The lawyer first introduced judge Jay's plan for arbitration clauses. According to him, the proposal was specific, simple, tangible and well-

219 Ibid., 6, 11; 16–20, 36–37; Ceadel, *Origins* 1996, 338–40.

220 Academics might recognise the difficulty of staying awake when the speaker just monotonously reads of a piece of paper. *Proceedings London* 1843, 7–8.

221 HP (October 1843), 451–62.

222 See chapter 4.

circumscribed. In short, it offered the peace movement something which it had arguably been lacking thus far: purpose. The progress of the peace movement could be easily checked by the extent to which states began to adopt arbitration clauses in treaties. Pacifism could henceforth be crystalised into a well-defined political campaign. 'How different does it appear from the complicated treaties entered into between nations, made but to be broken (…)?' Its practicality was proven by both state practice and doctrine. He referred to several of the precedents discussed earlier. All in all, his argumentation differed little from Jay's, citing the same passages from Vattel.[223]

The addition of Martens as a doctrinal authority, however, was novel, albeit somewhat misleading. MacNamara had highlighted the passage in the German scholar's treatise that called war an ultima ratio. The lawyer conveniently forgot to add that Martens had, in the parts dealing specifically with arbitration, claimed that this method had 'become increasingly rare', as it was found to be 'generally inadequate, especially because of the absence of an executive power'.[224]

By comparison, MacNamara devoted only a few lines to the essay he had adopted wholesale in his prize essay a mere two or three years earlier. He did not disavow it entirely. Rather, he side-tracked Ladd's great ambition. The young lawyer called it an obvious 'work of ages', whereas the 'temporary substitute for war' of judge Jay could be 'adopted at once by all the nations of Christendom'. Their 'main ultimate object' would remain a congress and court of nations, but they should 'suspend for a time' their direct efforts towards it. The official resolutions agreed with MacNamara, and stated that 'while recommending the plan of judge Jay, (…) [they] still regard, as peace societies have from their origin regarded, and as especially set forth by the late W. Ladd, Esq. a Congress of nations, to settle and perfect the code of international law, and a High Court of nations, to interpret and apply that law for the settlement of international disputes, should be kept in view (…) as one of the best practical modes of settling peacefully and satisfactorily such international disputes'.[225]

223 See chapter 1. *Proceedings London* 1843, 58–69.

224 This description stayed constant. George Fréderic de Martens, *Précis du droit des gens moderne de l'Europe. Tome second* (Paris: Guillaumin 1856), 19–20 (§ 176); *Proceedings London* 1843, 60–5; Koskenniemi, Martti. 'Into Positivism: Georg Friedrich von Martens (1756–1821) and Modern International Law'. *Constellations. An International Journal of Critical and Democratic Theory* 15(2) (2008), 189–207.

225 *Proceedings London* 1843, 33–4, 65–6.

Obviously, this awkward phrasing was meant to mask the fact that the delegates had not been able to unanimously agree to drop the project into which the American Peace Society had sunk so much time and resources. Unfortunately, neither the official proceedings nor the peace society's archives have recorded the private discussions on this contentious issue. A few hints could be gleaned from the proceedings. After MacNamara had finished reading his paper, it was moved that no discussion should be held on the floor, but that a closed committee would frame the resolutions to be distilled from it. One of this committee's members, the American George Gibbes, made a comment out of turn that made it into the official record. Gibbes protested that he 'did not believe that the United States would ever be brought to submit their differences with another power to arbitration, before they knew *the laws* by which these differences were to be judged'. He was immediately shushed that such matters should be reserved for the committee. Presumably, the American repeated his qualms about Jay's conception of arbitration in this committee. At least one other American delegate, who also sat in the *petit comité,* supported the codification of international law, as ascertained by remarks made at home and at later peace conferences.[226] This objection proved to be a powerful one, for it caused two incidents of dissent at the peace conferences of '48 and '49. More than one continental-European had just as little faith in equity-based arbitrations.[227]

Unlike the peace friends of the United States or the European mainland, the London Peace Society quickly embraced the new course. That same year, MacNamara made the United Law Society agree on a resolution urging a *clause compromissoire* in treaties.[228] Making good on their promise to campaign in high politics, a deputation of the conference presented a memorial, recommending the insertion of arbitration clauses in every future treaty, to 'the governments of the civilised world'. The pacifists were granted audiences with prime minister Robert Peel, and the kings of Belgium and France. In all three cases, the society claimed they were listened to with interest. All three made vague promises to take the proposal into consideration.[229] The London Peace Society delivered other memorials to the rest of London's diplomatic corps, in the hope they would forward it to their governments. By 1844, 54 governments had been contacted this way, including

226 This was Amasa Walker (1799–1875). He briefly returns in chapter 5. *Proceedings London* 1843, 22–3.

227 See chapters 4 and 5.

228 HP (October 1843), 467.

229 Ibid., 462–4.

the czar's and the sultan's.[230] Similar addresses were later sent to other places where political crises erupted, like Haiti and Switzerland.[231]

From 1846 onwards, against the background of increasing Anglo-French tensions and the Oregon Crisis, the London Peace Society and its auxiliaries renewed their parliamentary petition campaign. Over the next three years, many dozens of petitions in favour of arbitration reached the Commons. Judging from reports in the *Herald*, two hundred petitions were sent to Parliament in 1846, a figure that had climbed to three hundred by 1848.[232] They did not fare much better than the first one had; every single one was ordered to lie on the table. The peace society was undaunted. If its petitions frequently elicited 'laughter and oh! oh!', one member grumbled at the annual meeting, they should pay them back in kind, and mock the next M.P. who tried to increase the military budget by claiming that French armies were on the verge of landing at the cliffs of Dover.[233] There were already signs, however, that the campaign was growing more ambitious. Between 1847 and 1848, the phrasing of the petitions was beginning to slightly deviate from Jay's template. Rather than advocating a specific clause in a treaty, implying that arbitration was only mandatory in disputes related to provisions of that treaty, many petitions now demanded a general treaty of arbitration, ensuring that *all* disputes, on whatever issue, between the signatories had to be settled via arbitration.[234] This change reflected the personal preferences of a new ally of the peace societies, one whose political prestige was such that he, like Ladd, Jay, or Sturge, could materially impact the course of the larger peace movement.

230 They even got a reply from Venezuela. HP (July 1844), 99; HP (October 1844), 168.

231 HP (October 1844), 190–192; HP (May 1845), 278–280.

232 The average petition garnered between fifty and a hundred signatures. HP (November 1845), 375–6; HP (October 1846), 151–3; HP (June 1847), 276–77; HP (June 1848), 86.

233 HP (June 1848), 93–5.

234 Petitions for a clause included in *Journals of the House of Common. Vol. 101* (London: Stationery Office 1846), 24, 172, 257, 347, 400, 467, 723, 838, 962. This changed into petitions for a treaty starting from *Journals of the House of Common. Vol. 101* (London: Stationery Office 1846), 1256. From 1846 onwards, the majority of petitions from the London Peace Society or its auxiliaries asked for a treaty. *Journals of the House of Common. Vol. 102* (London: Stationery Office 1847), 235, 245, 319, 348, 371, 382, 500; *Journals of the House of Common. Vol. 103* (London: Stationery Office 1848), 67, 106, 124, 136, 235, 243, 196–197, 222, 224, 230, 256, 278, 289, 294, 403, 693. In 1849, in the run-up to Cobden's motion, almost every petition asked for a treaty. *Journals of the House of Common. Vol. 104* (London: Stationery Office 1849), 60, 78, 104, 113, 115, 127, 141, 146, 150, 155, 165, 169, 189, 194, 198, 202, 206, 209, 213, 217, 220, 239, 244, 253, 261, 270, 278, 282, 292, 295, 299, 307, 323, 334, 358, 368, 376, 380, 383, 388, 400, 408.

3.5 *Cobden and the Arbitration Debate*

That man was Richard Cobden (1804–1865), whose position in British Radicalism had become nigh unassailable after the Anti-Corn Law League, of which he had been the figurehead, had culminated in the repeal of the 'corn laws' in 1846. Their repeal has canonically been regarded in British history as the first breakthrough of free trade policies.[235] Ideologically, Cobden belonged to the Manchester school of British liberalism. Its adepts stemmed from the entrepreneurial class of the industrialising north of England, centred around the textile town of Manchester.[236] Their main adversaries were the aristocratic landowners, whose political power people like Cobden sought to end. In their eyes, the traditional gentry and the peers clung onto outmoded mercantilist views that unnecessarily limited Britain's commercial expansion. High tariffs on most imported grains, benefitting their own estates, kept food prices artificially high, causing poverty. Dropping trade restrictions would drop the costs of bread, while simultaneously stimulating British manufactory exports.[237] Like the French political economists with whom the leader of the Anti-Corn Law movement maintained extensive personal connections, Manchester liberalism was influenced by classical liberal political-economic theory, as theorised by Adam Smith and Jean-Baptiste Say.[238] French and British economic peace friends both maintained that their domestic policy proposals had implications for international relations. British adherents opposed the imperialistic and self-serving foreign policy of the nobility with the pacifying potential of free trade. Why pursue endless colonial wars, mostly to provide sons of the aristocracy with military commissions, whereas this money could be saved to lower taxes? Increasing economic interdependence, they felt, would disincentivize

235 Douglas Irwin and Maksym Chepeliev, 'The Economic Consequences of Sir Robert Peel: a Quantitative Assessment of the Repeal of the Corn Laws'. *The Economic Journal* 161(640) (2020), 3322–37.

236 John Morley, *The Life of Richard Cobden. Volume 1* (Cambridge: CUP, 2010), 18–29; see also Simon Morgan, 'From Warehouse Clerk to Corn Law Celebrity', in *Rethinking Nineteenth Century Liberalism. Richard Cobden Bicentenary Essays* (London: Routledge 2017), 39–55.

237 F. M. L. Thompson, 'Cobden, Free Trade in Land and the Road to the Abbey National', in *Rethinking Nineteenth Century Liberalism. Richard Cobden Bicentenary Essays* (London: Routledge 2017), 68–79; Koskenniemi, *Uttermost Parts* 2021, 674–6.

238 See chapter 4 for Cobden's French connection.

international war.[239] As Cobden himself summarised it: 'Free trade is the international law of the Almighty.'[240]

This aphorism encapsulated all the essentials of Cobden's pacifism. In a sense, it would be mistaken to contrast the more materialistic views of the Manchester free traders with the religious sensibilities of the London Peace Society and its auxiliaries. The Manchester and Salford auxiliary consisted of numerous Quakers, just like any other peace society.[241] Cobden, himself a devout Anglican, joined its Committee sometime in the 1840s. However, he had been interested in pacifism already since his late twenties. Those who knew Cobden in those early days commented on his sympathy for the Quakers, as well as his rejection of defensive war. From his private correspondence with Sturge, it seemed that Cobden never completely abandoned his absolutist pacifist beliefs, although he always denied being a true non-resistant in his public career.[242] In 1840, Cobden brought up his intellectual influences: 'Think you that Jonathan Dymond penned his principles of morality for the bookshelf? No, they are wholly practical'. Referring specifically to the chapter on war, he argued that Dymond's remarks were 'entirely applicable to Palmerston and his colleagues'.[243] In December 1849, Cobden confessed: 'I go as far as any "Friend" in my confidence in the peace principle. I am convinced that if a community were formed upon the non-aggression and non-defensive principle, *to begin with,* it would be stronger against the attacks of other nations under the shield of that principle than behind fortifications or ships of war.'[244] Conversely, many religious peace friends connected the principle of free trade with providence. Even Dymond's peace society already claimed that 'these commercial maxims tend powerfully to the promotion of peace'.[245] Likeminded musings could be found in the *Herald* or in the tracts for decades.[246]

---

239 Ceadel, Martin. 189–202.

240 Richard Cobden (ed. F.W. Chesson), *The Political Writings of Richard Cobden* (London: Cassel 1886), 460.

241 Ceadel, *Origins* 1996, 491.

242 Ibid., 296–297, 348–349.

243 Cobden referred to chapter 19, on war. Richard Cobden (ed. Anthony Howe), *The Letters of Richard Cobden. Volume 1. 1815–1847* (Oxford: OUP 2007), 207–208.

244 Richard Cobden (ed. Anthony Howe), *The Letters of Richard Cobden. Volume 2. 1848–1853* (Oxford: OUP, 2010), 173–4.

245 HP (January, February & March 1827), 5; as quoted in Ceadel *Origins* 1996, 276.

246 It was already a minor theme in the tract of Mary Roberts. Roberts, *Principles* 1840, 17–8.

Nonetheless, the Manchester peace friends led by Cobden approached the peace issue from a more instrumentalist perspective than the London Peace Society. That was evident from the way Cobden himself got only belatedly involved in organised peace activism, despite his long-standing interests in pacifism. He was present as a delegate of the Manchester auxiliary at the preliminary meeting to put the finishing touches to the programme of the upcoming general peace convention in London. In his intervention, the Manchester manufacturer tried to convince the organisers to put free trade on the agenda.[247] Still consumed by the Anti-Corn Law campaign, Cobden tried to recruit the peace movement into the free trade movement, rather than the other way around. As no resolution about free trade was eventually adopted, he had evidently been unsuccessful. Afterwards, the Mancunian peace society lost most of its interest in the London Peace Society, as it was more interested in the economic case against war than the national society, despite both sharing similar religious beliefs.[248]

FIGURE 2.1 The French cartoonist Honoré Daumier knew of a new job for French generals should Cobden get his way.

247 HP (July 1842), 118.

248 Ceadel, *Origins* 1996, 491.

Cobden only joined the peace movement in earnest after the 1848 Brussels peace conference. After this conference, the first truly pluralist and international peace meeting of the century, the London Peace Society set up a Peace Congress Committee. This autonomous sister organisation was put in charge of overseeing the organisation of all future European conferences. An important reason for its existence, as opposed to simply letting the London Peace Society organise the whole affair, was to accommodate a certain degree of ideological pluralism.[249] After all the, most British peace friends were radical non-resistants, convinced of the superiority of the 'high ground'. The constitutions of most peace societies connected to the London Peace Society required as much. However, this had to be laxed if they wanted to get outsiders on board. British free traders and European peace friends were both less interested in such moralism. As the Quakers found out in Paris, French sympathisers were completely immune to any religious argument against defensive war, however well-crafted.[250] By contrast, arbitration did pique their interest, although it would still be many decades before the continental-European peace movement adopted the same platform as the Anglo-American peace societies.[251] Cobden joined the organising committee of these conferences as he was coming of the high of the Anti-Corn Law campaign, and his interest turned to financial reform. He saw arbitration as a natural corollary to reducing military expenditure.[252] The prestige that this man, known in every corner of the British empire, and in Europe and the United States, brought to the peace movement could hardly be exaggerated. At every conference he attended in person, he was invariably the star attraction.[253]

Substantially, Cobden pressed his personal preferences into the legal campaign. The resolutions of the Brussels conference, in whose organisation and proceedings he had been uninvolved, were still in the vein of London '43. However, in a letter of adhesion that he had written for this conference, Cobden agreed with the arbitration resolution, but suggested whether it would not be more feasible to advocate for separate treaties, 'entered into *for the express purpose'* of arbitration. The gradual shift in the phrasing of the domestic British arbitration petitions, as observed earlier, was therefore likely due to the influence of Cobden. No other prominent peace friend had

249 Ibid., 416.

250 See chapter 5.

251 See chapter 7.

252 Cobden (ed. Howe), *Letters* 2010, XXV–XXVII.

253 Ibid., XXI–XXII. He was personally present at Paris, Frankfurt, and London.

raised this nuance.[254] Perhaps it was also no coincidence that the resolutions of the next conferences no longer made any mention to arbitration clauses, but only vaguely to 'arbitration' in general.[255] With regards to Ladd's congress of nations, Cobden followed the tendency of Sturge and MacNamara to reject it. In several letters, the Radical M.P. expressed his doubts. In his Brussels letter, he claimed that he 'shall be in doubt', until he had heard the arguments of its defenders.[256] In a letter to Sturge, he added: 'I doubt whether your idea of establishing a High Court of Nations is quite the thing'. He had fears 'there would be danger of intrigue and corruption if you had a permanent Court'.[257] Eventually, Cobden even tried to get the resolutions on a congress of nations scrapped entirely in the Peace Congress Committee, much to Elihu Burritt's grief.[258]

Cobden's revulsion from the whole idea of a permanent diplomatic assembly likely stemmed from his larger contempt for traditional diplomacy. In nearly all of his public utterances, the Manchester free trader seemed to use the word 'diplomatist' more as an insult than as a compliment. According to him, these men represented the interests of the landed classes, rather than 'all orders of society'. The economy needed geopolitical stability and predictability, but diplomats were in Cobden's mind constantly creating artificial crises, using 'schoolboy rhetoric upon the balance of power'.[259] During the Frankfurt peace conference, he was as explicit as he could possibly be: 'It is not necessary that we should have a tribunal erected to act in all cases of arbitration (…): for when you come to that point (I am now speaking to diplomatists), that you cannot settle a dispute, we hold you responsible for referring that dispute to arbitration'. He proceeded: 'if you cannot find means of adjusting such matter without calling upon us (…), I say, make way, gentlemen, for some other diplomatists who will do the work of the nations of the world, for which you are so well paid, in a more workmanlike manner.' Disliking gunboat diplomacy, Cobden exclaimed: 'let us offer justice instead of war'.[260]

---

254 *The Peace Congress at Brussels, on the 20th, 21st, and 22nd of September 1848* (London: Thomas Ward 1848), 19

255 See chapter 5.

256 *Congress Brussels* 1848, 19.

257 Cobden (ed. Howe), *Letters* 2010, 60.

258 Van der Linden, *Peace Movement* 1987, 371–2. See again chapter 5.

259 Cobden (ed. Chesson), *Writings* 1886, 253–4.

260 *Report of the Proceedings of the Third General Peace Congress, held in Frankfort, on the 22nd, 23rd, and 24th August, 1850* (London: Gilpin 1851), 19–21. See infra in this chapter for more on non-interventionism.

With Richard Cobden's support, the London Peace Society's first arbitration campaign culminated in the first parliamentary debate on whether or not to recommend a general treaty of arbitration to the British government.[261] Around January 1849, Cobden decided to introduce a private member's motion to the Commons. Unlike the petitions of the peace societies, a motion of a member of the House could not be as easily ignored, especially not one coming from an M.P. of Cobden's stature. The motion was organised in close concert with the British peace movement. For more than half a year, while Cobden was struggling to get a timeslot reserved, both the London Peace Society and the Peace Congress Committee engaged in a protracted 'out-of-doors' campaign to raise support for what would be their greatest political effort thus far.[262] Numerous rallies and lectures were held, during which members of the peace societies gathered signatures and letters to M.P.'s. At Cobden's request, the leaders of the British peace movement even held an impressive last rally in London's Exeter Hall at the eve of the debate, where thousands gathered to give their hero one last big cheer before he would walk into the arena the next day.[263]

Unfortunately for the peace societies, their out-of-doors assistance, however valuable, also put their political champion into somewhat of a predicament. As Ceadel has also observed, although Cobden might have been a closet radical pacifist himself, he was politically savvy enough to realise that any overt identification with people whom most M.P.'s regarded as religious fanatics would likely doom his effort. The more pluralist Peace Congress Committee, the vehicle used to lure free traders into the peace movement, certainly felt that they had best tone down the religious references. Very few people believed, like the Quakers, that God would magically swoop in to protect the meek. In fact, this had been the reason why Cobden had changed the objective of his motion from disarmament, which had been his first plan, to arbitration. The Peace Congress Committee had thought that non-pacifists would dislike any unilateral weakening of the national defences, whereas absolute pacifists only accepted total abolition, as a mere reduction might imply that they still supported the principle of self-defence.[264] In stark contrast to traditional pacifist propaganda, flyers of the

261 *Journals 104* 1849, 381.

262 HP (January 1849), 225–8; HP (February 1849), 241–5; HP (March 1849), 257–64; HP (April 1849), 273–7; 297–8, HP (May 1849), 303.

263 HP (July 1849), 332; Ceadel, *Origins* 1996, 429–30.

264 Ibid., 427, 430.

Peace Congress Committee defended arbitration because it was 'more rational', 'more humane', and 'incomparably cheaper than war'.[265]

In his opening statements, Cobden consequently took great care to emphasise that he did not only represent the peace societies, but also 'that numerous portion of the middle classes of this country' who simply wanted greater geopolitical stability. Whether Cobden succeeded in distancing himself from the radical core of his backing, was debateable. One opponent quickly observed that 'the hon. Member would seem to disown his friends', waving with his hand a press report of the Exeter Hall meeting of the night before.[266] At any rate, the London Peace Society did not seem to mind. They reported that Cobden had 'very wisely' decided to take 'lower ground'. Cobden had communicated his tactical intentions beforehand, and afterwards the society praised that his speech 'abounds with proof of his consummate tact in suiting his address to his audience'.[267]

This 'lower ground' coincided with arguments previously developed by British and American peace friends. True to Jay or MacNamara, the peace friend from Manchester spent a large amount of his time highlighting precedents in state practice. The arbitration cases Cobden brought up were well-known in Anglo-American pacifist propaganda, and included the awards given under the Jay Treaty of 1794 and the Treaty of Ghent of 1814.[268] He did not want to limit himself to monarchs, however. Perhaps it was better to select individuals, 'whether designated commissioners or plenipotentiaries', or arbitrators appointed by all states involved, themselves able to call in an umpire, like in domestic arbitrations. Insisting that his proposal was 'practical', Cobden maintained that an arbitration treaty would be scrupulously observed, since no state would want to risk a war 'with a country so powerful as England'. In an unusual bout of optimism, he furthermore believed that most wars did not arise out of treaty violations, because 'as a rule [treaties] are fulfilled and observed'. Rather, most disputes originated out of 'accidental collisions', which diplomats had escalated into armed conflict,

265 HP (January 1849), 228–30.

266 *Hansard's Parliamentary Debates: Third Series. Vol. CVI.* (London: Woodfall 1849), 54, 69.

267 *The Question of Arbitration in the House of Commons. Being the Substance of the Debate on Mr. Cobden's Motion in Favour of Arbitration Treaties instead of War, for the Settlement of International Disputes. With an Appendix.* (London: Gilpin 1849), 20; HP (July 1849), 333.

268 *Hansard's CVI* 1849, 55–6.

usually by involving 'the old cry of honour'.[269] If one diplomat could be vested with the authority to legally bind the entire nation, like Lord Castlereagh at the Congress of Vienna, why could commissioners or arbitrators not be granted similar powers?[270]

Near the end of his speech, Cobden again distanced himself from the more drastic positions of the peace societies. Anticipating what he apparently saw as an inevitable attack, Cobden denied that he had 'a grand project for putting the whole world under some court of justice'. His motion was not about some 'congress of nations with a code of laws – a supreme court of appeal, with an army to support its decisions'. Cobden was adamant: 'I have no such plan in view at all'. Although war was not a legitimate means to enforce the law of nations in his eyes, he nonetheless even conceded the traditional just cause argument that any violation of an arbitration treaty could be enforced like the breach of any other treaty. Cobden concluded that Britain might begin with the United States or France. If enough of the larger and more powerful states would sign arbitration treaties, he mused, perhaps the accumulated precedents would solidify, in the course of time, into 'a kind of common law amongst nations'.[271]

Upon finishing his defence, Cobden saw himself assailed by the nation's political elite, among them none other than the foreign secretary, Lord Palmerston (1784–1865), and the prime minister, John Russell (1792–1878). Although both were Whigs, they ranked far too high in the government of an empire whose immense power and influence was still yearly expanding, to be receptive to pacifism. They were not about to let their hands become tied by such idealistic treaties. Palmerston especially was already known for his manhandling of any minor league player in European politics who forgot his place. In 1840, it had been Palmerston who had sent the Mediterranean fleet to Sicily after king Ferdinand II (1810–1859) had dared to sign a contract with a couple of French exporters of sulphur, to the detriment of British merchants. Contemporary diplomats and lawyers virtually all agreed that the seizing of every ship sailing under the Neapolitan flag was manifestly illegal under international law. Ferdinand II was effectively bullied into a accepting a French mediation, which, in the eyes of historians, was

269 One M.P. immediately answered Cobden's rhetorical question on whether the national honour justified war by booming out 'certainly'. Ibid., 64.

270 Palmerston would rebut that diplomats worked under strict instructions from their government, unlike arbitrators or judges. Ibid., 58–9, 85.

271 Ibid., 66–68.

decided beforehand, and merely a cover for assessing how much the Italians would have to pay to both the British and the French.[272]

Palmerston's predilection for gunboat diplomacy did not end there. The year following the debate on the arbitration motion, the Royal Navy appeared off the coast of Athens, blockading the Greek mainland. The Greek government had refused to pay compensation to a dubious British merchant, whose house had been ransacked by a mob. Palmerston famously justified his decisions in the 'Don Pacifico affair' by appealing to an update of *civis Romanus sum:* 'so also a British subject, in whatever land he may be, shall feel confident that the watchful eye and the strong arm of England will protect him from injustice and wrong'.[273] In short, Cobden was dealing with a man hardly to be found at a silent prayer meeting. In fact, the Don Pacifico affair of the next year turned Palmerston's already dim views of the peace society into unadulterated hatred. The affair had led to a vote of confidence in Parliament, during which the peace society supported Cobden's public attacks. Having survived the vote, the politician served his revenge cold. In the early 1850s, when the popularity of the peace movement was declining, numerous members were being charged with seditious libel for opposing the Militia Act. The replies of Palmerston, who had become home secretary, to the peace society's pleas for amnesty were reportedly 'very curt and sulky'.[274] No love was lost between Britain's most popular politician of the 1840s and the peace society. Upon Palmerston's death in 1865, the *Herald* listed his track record and assessed that his policies had been 'blustering, arrogant, and dictatorial'. When hearing of the peace movement, he had in their eyes 'laughed it to scorn'. In sum, the society was relieved when the noble Lord Henry John Temple, 3rd Viscount Palmerston, was finally dead.[275]

In 1849, Palmerston engaged in detail with the arguments advanced by Cobden. Having had first-hand experience of several of the precedents of arbitration and mediation mentioned, the foreign secretary decided to, rather pedantically, school his adversary on doctrine and state practice.

---

272 Šedivý, *Decline* 2018, 107–23; John Davis, 'Palmerston and the Sicilian Sulphur Crisis of 1840: an Episode in the Imperialism of Free Trade'. *Risorgimento* 1(2) (1982), 19.

273 The *Herald* condemned it as a 'menacing display of an immense naval force against the feeblest kingdom of Europe'. Dolphus Jr. Whitten, 'The Don Pacifico Affair'. *The Historian* 48(2) (1986), 261–2; HP (June 1850), 503; HP (March 1854), 31; *Hansard's Parliamentary Debates: Third Series. Vol. CXII.* (London: Woodfall 1850), 380–444.

274 Henry Richard's diary as cited in Ceadel, *Origins* 1996, 446–7.

275 HP (November 1865), 265–6.

In line with the textbook definitions of Vattel or Martens, Palmerston explained that 'hon. members ought not to lose sight of the distinction which is frequently forgotten between arbitration and mediation', the latter merely being a third party offering good offices. That being said, he pointedly observed that most of the precedents of 'arbitration' listed by Cobden had in reality been cases of mediation. Palmerston ruthlessly exploited the informational gap between himself and the peace movement. Although the architect of the sulphur 'mediation' had not read it, he would for instance have been amused by MacNamara's positive appraisal of the handling of that dispute. The lawyer had cited it as an example of a sovereign mediating 'with calmness and impartiality'.[276]

Palmerston did deconstruct the arbitrations over the U.S.-Canadian border. He conceded that these cases leaned closest to textbook definitions. However, to the extent these instances could be viewed as proper 'arbitrations', they only provided examples of failure. According to the Treaty of Ghent, commissioners from both states would first attempt to settle any boundary disputes. The secretary had not been impressed by the work of these experts. Their only task had been to apply the latitudes and longitudes, as described in the treaty, to the map. According to his layman's reckoning: 'nothing could be more easy than that'. In practice, however, 'one maintained that the parallel was to depend upon calculations commencing at the centre of the earth, and the other that the computations were to be made from the centre of the sun; they were therefore as far apart as the earth from the sun'. For Palmerston, that proved that scientific experts were no real substitute for traditional diplomats. The commissioners having failed, the treaty then arranged for arbitration by a third party sovereign. That road had fared little better: 'My hon. friend can hardly imagine how much time elapsed before we could come to any agreement as to the choice of sovereign (…).' Furthermore, when the Dutch king had, 'after a very long period of time', finally offered his award, the United States government had refused to accept it. The Maine boundary was only definitively circumscribed by the Webster-Ashburton treaty of 1842. Palmerston claimed that 'the Oregon question was settled in pretty nearly the same way'.[277] Factually, in this instance, Palmerston had indeed offered the better analysis than the peace advocates, who, in spite of their general political scepticism,

276 MacNamara, *Peace* 1841, 248. At the time, some within the peace society even blamed the victim, claiming that Ferdinand II had been the unreasonable and needlessly aggressive one. HP (July 1840), 130–1.

277 *Hansard's CVI* 1849, 82–6.

could still be rather ignorant or outright naïve about recent political history. They of course did not have the benefit of insider's knowledge or historical hindsight.

More in general, the foreign secretary disliked the idea of third-party arbitration being imposed by treaty law. According to his sober realist view of international politics, such an obligation only made sense in the context of 'a higher and superior authority – the authority of some legal tribunal, which enforces concurrence'. Supported by roars of 'hear, hear' from the backbenches, Palmerston denied the feasibility of any permanent 'European tribunal' in the near future. Even in the longer term, he could not see its uses. Even if all European governments suddenly became 'perfectly just, perfectly impartial, perfectly disinterested', a tribunal would ipso facto 'supersede itself', because its members would already be willing to settle their disputes peacefully, with or without it. That was furthermore a very big 'if'. Like most other opponents of the peace movement, Palmerston had a fundamentally different worldview. Unlike the average pacifist, who believed people could be educated into better morals, Palmerston stayed firmly within 'the present, imperfect condition of human nature'. As he said it: 'Governments, like individuals, are actuated by unfounded and suspicious jealousies of each other (…) by interested motives of various kinds, interests conflicting with each other.' This British politician did not believe that a state as powerful and entangled in international politics like Britain could find sufficiently impartial arbitrators. He feared that any overture in this direction would also threaten national security, lest rival states would start to believe 'that the manly spirit of Englishmen is dead'.[278]

Cobden had made a judicious call in distancing himself from William Ladd's scheme for a congress of nations. It appeared that he had caught his opponents off-guard. As Palmerston's above remarks already indicated, the foreign secretary had anticipated that Cobden would propose governmental arbitration within some sort of larger institutional framework. According to him, Cobden 'has been obliged not to propose what many persons, including myself, imagined his plan to be'. Elsewhere, the Lord asked himself what the reasons were 'why my hon. friend abstained from the proposal which was generally expected to come from him (…)?'[279] Palmerston had, after all, been somewhat aware of the political programme of the peace movement, since he had a few years before received Ladd's essay on a

278 Ibid., 79–82, 87–8.
279 Ibid., 81.

congress of nations.[280] Palmerston's scepticism, also shared by Russell in his own speech, confirmed the suspicions of pragmatists like Cobden, Jay and Beckwith that the strategic choice for a permanent diplomatic assembly and an international court was a dead end for the time being.[281] In Cobden's assessment: 'I know that many Members came down to the House to oppose me – upon the assumption that I was going to advocate for a Congress of Nations, who went away without voting when they found out that my plan merely meant a voluntary pledge of arbitration.'[282]

Despite this intense criticism by Palmerston, Russell and a handful of other hostile M.P.'s, Cobden handled himself well. In his concluding comments, he claimed that the foreign secretary had partly attacked a strawman. The Manchester pacifist did not engage with Palmerston's legalistic nuances, but played to his own strengths. He claimed his larger point had been that these disputes may have been settled peacefully, but that their outcome had always been uncertain, and accompanied by too much scaremongering and permanent increases in the military budget. Was there actual peace when more than 2,000,000 men lived under arms in Europe, at enormous costs? 'To say that Europe was living in a state of peace was a misnomer; it was an armed truce and nothing else.'[283] In spite of the secretary's blustering, Cobden thought he had put 'the noble lord' on the spot. Palmerston had not been able to bring himself to shoot down the arbitration motion altogether, but had instead opted for a procedural device through which the motion could be dismissed, without a substantive vote.[284] It appeared that even such a hard-headed lover of gunboats like Palmerston was hesitant to be seen voting against a measure intended solely to promote international peace. Furthermore, seven M.P.'s had publicly spoken in support of the motion.[285] The result of Cobden's efforts soon became clear: 176 M.P.'s were in favour of dismissal of the motion, opposed to 79 M.P.'s against.[286]

---

280 See chapter 1.

281 Russell said he fully agreed with 'that old maxim', *si vis pacem, para bellum*. Ibid., 109–17.

282 HP (July 1849), 333.

283 *Question of Arbitration* 1849, 19.

284 Palmerston asked to 'move the previous question'. This allowed Palmerston to dismiss Cobden's motion while keeping up a semblance of sympathy for it. *Hansard's CVI* 1849, 90.

285 One even was a Conservative. Ceadel, *Origins* 1996, 431.

286 *Hansard's CVI* 1849, 119–121.

Although the arbitration motion had not been carried, the London Peace Society was satisfied with the outcome. Their analysis of the vote learned them that parliamentary support had been strongest among M.P.'s representing constituencies where the peace societies had canvassed most intensely. Even better, according to their calculations, these constituencies ranked among the most populous of the country. When counting the actual total of people represented by each M.P. who had voted, the London Committee estimated that a majority of the British populace had been in favour of the motion. Cobden himself was visibly relieved that the parliamentary minority had been large enough to spare him public humiliation. He recalled how the first petitions in favour of arbitration treaties had been met with 'jeers and laughter'.[287]

The London Peace Society's optimism was in a sense premature. Even at the 1899 and 1907 Hague Peace Conferences, which both considered introducing compulsory international arbitration, most plenipotentiaries were firmly against the idea. These objections did not only come from diplomats who represented unapologetically militarist great powers like Prussia or Austria, but also from small states like Belgium, or from bastions of the peace movement like the United States, where lawyers and politicians up to the level of secretary of state supported arbitration and the peace societies.[288] The simple truth was that Palmerston's instinctive resistance against arbitration was broadly shared among political and academic elites throughout the nineteenth century and well beyond. Several of the fundamental arguments first raised by Palmerston in his verbal sparring with Cobden would be reiterated in some form or another by others. Whether any given dispute was considered arbitrable depended on a host of extra-legal factors, such as the parties' relative power balance, the strategic significance of the specific issue at stake, the influence of public opinion, or even simply the parties' estimated chances of success. As criticised by peace friends, emotions and the passions of 'national honour' likewise entered into this equation.[289] Anxious of safeguarding state sovereignty, the typical exception

287 With the caveat that a significant amount of M.P.'s did not vote at all, leaving their opinion uncertain. HP (July 1849), 332–3; *Question of Arbitration* 1849, 24.

288 Zollman, 'Mediation and Arbitration' 2020, 174; Genin, *Laboratoire belge* 2018, 151–178; contrast Genin's caution with the more optimistic readings of Abbenhuis, Maartje. *The Hague Conferences and International Politics, 1898–1915* (London: Bloomsbury, 2019), 114–6. 161–2.

289 Zollman, 'Mediation and Arbitration' 2020, 321; on the role of honour as a political-legal argument, see Šedivý, 'Honour' 2018, 86–111.

invariably attached to an arbitration clause excluded disputes touching on 'vital interests', a term usually – and unsurprisingly – left undefined.[290]

More fundamentally, the London Peace Society's views, like other nineteenth century peace friends, imposed a false dichotomy between diplomacy and instruments of international law. Like Cobden, the British society associated the former with the subjectivity and irrationality of politics, while the latter promised objectivity and impartiality. In doing so, they seemed to have forgotten part of their own critiques, as espoused by Dymond and others, that most of positive international law consisted of 'immoral' rules originating from political expediency. They underestimated the extent of legalist argumentation in diplomacy, and overestimated the extent to which legalised types of international dispute settlement, such as also arbitration, were supposedly apolitical.[291] This was the longer-term price paid by the British for abandoning Ladd's grander dream of a congress of nations, in exchange for relative parliamentary success. Although unquestionably completely utopian in the era's cultural contexts, a truly international political authority – constituting a higher locus of sovereignty – would theoretically solve the paradox inherent to a horizontal legal order – i.e. international laws that were supposed to be derived from the consent of states, were also supposed to bind these states, despite their immediate will.[292] In a more vertical legal order, an individual state would not as easily be able to hide behind the trusted shield of sovereignty, inevitably raised in practice whenever an arbitration clause became too inconvenient.

Unaware of these future difficulties, but emboldened by the noted success of their 1849 campaign, the London Peace Society and its auxiliaries continued to deliver arbitration petitions to Parliament the following years. In the *Herald* and at public meetings, the British peace friends hardened in their support for a legally binding arbitration mechanism. At the request of the American Peace Society, a delegation of the London Peace Society met with the foreign secretary, Lord Clarendon (1800–1870), in 1853 to lobby for an arbitration clause in an upcoming fisheries treaty, in which they

290 Its subjectivity was lamented by Belgian lawyers around the time of the 1899 Hague Peace Conference. Already in 1849, Palmerston thought it unwise to entrust 'matters of vital interest' to a third party, not controlled by any government. Genin, *Laboratoire belge* 2018, 160; Neff, *Justice* 2014, 330; *Question of Arbitration* 1849, 9.

291 Legal argumentation in early modern diplomacy has been analysed in Dhondt, *Balance of Power* 2015.

292 Koskenniemi, *Apology* 1989, 474, 482–4.

may have succeeded.[293] That year, the British also held two large peace conferences, in Manchester and Edinburgh, which reaffirmed the quest for a treaty of arbitration.[294] Around this time, Cobden also entertained the prospect of proposing a new arbitration motion.[295] Unfortunately, the British peace movement was forced to fully and immediately suspend the entire arbitration campaign when news reached the popular press that the latest Russo-Ottoman crisis was escalating into war. Faced with waves of jingoism and the first great power war in half a century, British pacifists found themselves an embattled minority after the British government decided to intervene.

4 Challenges to Early British 'Peace through Law'

Less than a decade after Cobden had brought the politicised British peace movement to the zenith of its existence, the political tide was shifting against them. Their last conference, held in Edinburgh a mere week after the Ottoman Empire had declared war on Russia, proved to be the movement's swan song before it was plunged into another dark age. The press heaped abuse onto the organisers. The *Herald* wrote of 'sarcasm', 'contempt', 'banter', 'clumsy ridicule', 'gross misrepresentation' and 'angry invective'.[296] As if to symbolise the end of an era, Joseph Price, one of the last living founders of the London Peace Society, died the following year. In politics too, the peace society was fighting a losing battle against public opinion. One of their most prominent parliamentary supporters, John Bright, was burned in effigy by an angry mob in his very own constituency after publishing a public letter against the war. Bystanders could read the following inscription on the puppet's chest: 'Bright, the friend of Nicholas.' Bright's antiwar opposition cost him his seat at the next general election.[297] Evidently, outspoken loyalty to peace to the detriment of queen and country came with a price.

293 See chapter 6.
294 HP (February 1853), 161; HP (November 1853), 288.
295 HP (May 1853), 221–2.
296 HP (November 1853), 290–1; HP (December 1853), 302.
297 See also infra. Van der Linden, *Peace Movement* 1987, 463; Le Constitutionnel (25 November 1854), 3.

4.1 *Non-interventionism*

In the three years preceding the Crimean War, the British peace movement had further radicalised its position on foreign policy. To some degree, the London Peace Society had likely always been in favour of British non-interventionism, given its own longstanding policy of 'non-interference with the party politics of the day', as informed by the Quaker peace testimony.[298] However, only by 1850 did they integrate it into their official platform. At the peace conference of Frankfurt that summer, the Peace Congress Committee set a resolution 'that this Congress, acknowledging the principle of non-intervention, recognizes it to be the sole right of every state to regulate its own affairs'.[299] This had been a novelty. However, the position was affirmed by similar resolutions at the 1851 London conference – the last more or less international one – as well as the two purely British conferences held in Manchester and Edinburgh in 1853.[300] In that last conference, the resolution specified that armed intervention 'by threatened or actual violence (…) is a frequent cause of bitter and desolating wars (…) and that this country ought to abstain from entering into any treaties or alliances binding the government to intervene by force of arms in the domestic concerns of any other people'.[301] In 1855, as British troops were in the final months of the dreary siege of Sebastopol, the *Herald* pointed out the legal consequences of British hegemony: 'One of the greatest evils to which we are exposed at this moment arises from the obligations we have incurred by treaty to guarantee the existence, and to meddle in the affairs, domestic and foreign, of the smaller states of Europe. At present we have on our hands Belgium and Greece, and Spain, and Portugal (…).' Additionally, their imperial state had 'forty colonies of her own to manage in all parts of the globe'.[302]

That same article pointed to an immediate cause of the peace society's attack on British imperialism, in its title: 'The oppressed nationalities'. The series of democratic or nationalist uprisings across the Continent in 1848 had caused a surge in support for interventionism. While British peace advocates may have stood overall sympathetic to the plight of the European ethnicities who wanted national independence, British pacifists only

298 HP (April, May & June 1833) 114.

299 *Proceedings Frankfurt* 1851, 42.

300 *Report of the Proceedings of the Fourth General Peace Congress, held in Exeter Hall, London, on the 22nd, 23rd, and 24th July, 1851* (London: Gilpin 1851), 52; HP (February 1853), 169; HP (November 1853), 289.

301 HP (November 1853), 289.

302 HP (August 1855), 236–237.

endorsed moral support. In particular, the arrival of the exiled Hungarian nationalist leader Lajos Kossuth (1802–1894) made more than one British heart stir with sympathy.[303] Touring England in the autumn of 1851, Kossuth was warmly received everywhere he went. The firebrand passionately pleaded for not only moral, but also armed intervention by the British empire against Russia, which had itself intervened to repress the uprising that the Austrian emperor did not seem able to contain. He did so not unsuccessfully, for a vocal segment of British Radicalism was willing to support the use of force to curtail Russia. In legal terms, Kossuth argued for the right of counter-intervention to uphold the overarching principle of non-intervention. Even the philosopher John Stuart Mill seemed to agree with this line of reasoning.[304] When Kossuth next travelled to the United States, the American Peace Society produced a detailed rebuttal, in the form of a public letter by judge Jay.[305]

In the *Herald,* the British elaborately protested this 'vague sentiment of sympathy for the oppressed nationalities of Europe.' They maintained that Kossuth's idea of forceful intervention was absurd. 'In the first place, then, it involves a complete and immediate rupture with nearly all the established governments of Europe'. Secondly, these new governments, once established in Hungary, Italy, or Poland, would presumably not want Britain dictate their form of government for them, and would thus likely 'fall into internal anarchy', considering these nationalists were themselves divided on the topic. Thirdly, the peace society asked itself, why should Britain be exempt from this revolutionary tidal wave, and not fall itself prey to civil war between monarchists and republicans?[306] Though the argument was this time not framed in legal language, unlike that of the Americans, it corresponded well with the general direction mainstream legal doctrine was heading toward. Increasing positivism attached greater importance and more profound implications to sovereignty and non-intervention than had been the case in previous centuries.[307] For the British peace movement, non-intervention likewise aligned well with its own campaign for stipulated arbitration, an

303 Zsuzsanna Lada, 'The Invention of a Hero: Lajos Kossuth in England (1851)'. *European History Quarterly* 43(1) (2013), 8–9, 13–20.

304 Cobden (ed. Howe), *Letters* 2010, XXXIV; Gregory Claeys, 'Mazzini, Kossuth and British Radicalism, 1848–1854'. *Journal of British Studies* 28(3) (1989), 244–55; Ceadel, *Origins* 1996, 472.

305 See chapter 6.

306 HP (August 1855), 237.

307 Neff, *Justice* 2014, 244–5.

instrument preferred over a congress of nations not least because it was perceived to leave state sovereignty more intact.

4.2 *The Crimean War*

Theoretical debates notwithstanding, the major crisis of the 1850s associated with interventionism was of course the Crimean War against Russia. Many speakers at the ill-fated Edinburgh conference of October 1853, being held as a fleet was steaming towards the Turkish capital, identified Britain's many political or legal commitments to third states as a key reason for the threatened escalation. A popular contemporary argument held that Britain had treaty obligations to guarantee the territorial integrity of the Ottoman Empire. The opponents of this view pointed out that Britain had signed no such treaty. Perhaps these war-hawks referred to the 1841 London Straits Convention, that had blocked the Bosporus and the Dardanelles to all non-Ottoman warships, or the Kuchuk Kainardzhi Treaty of 1774, which gave the czar rights to protect Orthodox Christians in the Ottoman Empire, whose alleged violation had provided the Russians with their main pretext for the war declaration.[308] However, Britain was not even a party to the latter agreement. One speaker at Edinburgh therefore deplored that, even in the absence of a positive legal commitment, 'there was at least an understood obligation that we are bound under existing circumstances to fight for Turkey'.[309]

When the British entry into the war seemed inevitable by March 1854, the society printed an article in the *Herald* dissecting other common justifications. It pointed out that Britain was being extremely hypocritical when it claimed to be standing up to bullies, when, as recently as 1850, they themselves had sent gunboats to Greece. Nine years earlier, the government did not have any qualms either to 'force the will of the Porte', on the weak basis of 'some old treaty' that was found.[310] Another, and more fundamental, legitimisation held that the European balance of power would be

308 These were treaties identified by the peace society. HP (January 1855), 147; HP (June 1855), 209; Orlando Figes, *Crimea* (London: Penguin, 2010), 64, 98, 109–110.

309 HP (November 1853), 291; *Report of the Proceedings of the Peace Conference at Edinburgh, October 12th and 13th, 1853* (Edinburgh: Thomas Nelson 1853), 13.

310 This referred to an incident in 1841 in which Palmerston had pressured the sultan into granting permission for the construction of a Protestant Church in Jerusalem. Although only France had a treaty right to do so, the foreign secretary asserted that any right granted to France should belong equally to Britain. Refusal to recognise this would be considered an insult to the British Crown. The Porte yielded. HP (March 1854), 30–31; also brought up in John Bright, *The Letter of John Bright, Esq., M.P., on the*

threatened in the case of a Russian victory. Politically speaking, this was the major reason why the British cabinet decided to intervene in support of the Ottomans.[311] However, to what extent was this motive legally justifiable? Predictably, the peace society thought it could not be done. 'Why, the principles of what is called international law, to which our statesmen are so fond of referring, peremptorily disallow such a pretence for hostilities.' In support, they cited a passage from Grotius upholding that 'it is a thing contrary to all the rules of justice, to maintain (...) a right to attack anyone, for the sole reason that he *may* have it in his power to annoy us'.[312]

As with just about everything in international legal doctrine, the peace society had cherrypicked the argument that suited its case best. In reality, doctrine was divided. Vattel seemingly concurred with Grotius, but he added an important exception: if a state's legitimate growth was accompanied by a menacing attitude, others could resort to force.[313] Martens was even more radical, and asserted that the assessment of whether or not the balance was endangered was a completely political decision.[314] Among modern British scholars, Robert Phillimore's *Commentaries on International Law,* published in 1854, the same year as the society's article, extensively argued the case that armed intervention was legally justified when the aggrandisement of a particular state threatened 'the liberties of the rest of the world'.[315] At the turn of the century, Lassa Oppenheim's standard textbook though it 'obvious' that interventions for the sake of the balance of power were legally excusable, given the absence of any higher authority capable of keeping powerful states in check.[316] Nonetheless, other legal authors agreed with Cobden and the peace movement's opinion that this doctrine was far

War, Verified and Illustrated by Extracts from the Parliamentary Documents, &c. (London: Cash 1854), 14.

311 As Palmerston admitted in 1855: 'We went to war not so much to keep the sultan and the Muslims in Turkey as to keep the Russians out of it.' Cited in Figes, *Crimea* 2010, 195

312 HP (March 1854), 32–33; Grotius, *Belli ac Pacis* 1925, 184 (book II, Ch. I, title XVII).

313 Alfred Vagts and Detlev Vagts, 'The Balance of Power in International Law: a History of an Idea'. *The American Journal of International Law* 73(4) (1979), 562; Vattel, *Droits des gens. Tome second* 1758, 32–34 (§ 43).

314 Vagts and Vagts, 'Balance of Power' 1979, 563; George Fréderic de Martens, *Précis du droit des gens moderne de l'Europe. Tome premier* (Paris: Guillaumin 1856), 320–1 (§ 124)

315 Vagts and Vagts, 'Balance of Power' 1979, 569; Robert Phillimore, *Commentaries on International Law. Volume 1* (Philadelphia: Johnson 1854), 315, 333–45.

316 Vagts and Vagts, 'Balance of Power' 1979, 570; Oppenheim, Lassa. *International Law. A Treatise* (London: Longmans, Green and Co. 1912), 193–4 (§ 136).

too subjective to be considered a legal norm. Already in one of Cobden's earliest publications on foreign policy, the then still anonymous 'Manchester manufacturer' listed some popular definitions of the concept by Vattel, Gentz, and Lord Brougham. He concluded that not only were their definitions 'so vague as to impart no knowledge even of the writer's meaning', but these authors also provided no evidence whatsoever that the European states had ever, 'by written, verbal, or implied agreement', indicated that the power balance constituted a binding legal principle. Therefore, the theory was nothing else but 'a creation of the politician's brain'.[317] Legal scholars who agreed with this assessment included Klüber and Kaltenborn, as well as, later on, the Nobel Peace Prize runner-up Friedrich Martens.[318]

Generally speaking, the doctrine that regarded the balance of power as a binding legal norm, whose violation warranted armed intervention, was most supported by more conservative lawyers writing in the interests of great powers, which had the most to lose in the case of any upset of this balance by a competitor or an upstart state. Other lawyers who supported balance of power reasonings did so out of their disbelief that both a congress of nations or institutionalised arbitration, like proposed by the peace movement, would be practical. A balance of power, to this school of authors, provided the most realistic means through which the legal right to war could be limited. If states realised that any conquest would be offset by a realignment of the political positions of other states, many wars would be rendered futile in advance.[319]

During the Crimean War itself, the British peace movement kept a relatively low profile. Patriotism mingled with Russophobia proved a powerful toxic in British society. Not unlike the lot that would befall the American Peace Society during the American Civil War five years later, the London Peace Society got torn apart internally at the same time as it was besieged externally. Internally, many free traders and other more moderate adherents abandoned their pacifism, or diluted it by claiming that Britain was fighting under a just cause in this specific war. Externally, all sympathetic M.P.'s likewise dropped their public support for the peace societies, lest they would suffer the same fate as Bright. Cobden, who had long disbelieved that there would be an actual war, similarly advised his friends in the peace societies to lay low.[320] The annual report of 1855 was drenched in gloom. 'The

---

317 Cobden (ed. Chesson), *Writings* 1886, 198–202.

318 Vagts and Vagts, 'Balance of Power' 1979, 567, 574.

319 Ibid., 565–7, 574, 578–9.

320 Ceadel, *Idealists* 2000, 40–5.

position of the Committee during the past year has been one of extreme difficulty (…)'. The London Peace Society had been forced 'to steer between the opposite extremes of timidity and rashness'. On the one hand, if peace friends had done nothing, it would have been 'a cowardly desertion of their post in the hour of peril'. On the other hand, public support for the war was so high that 'there was real danger, by unwise and untimely activity, of greatly exasperating the evil they were anxious to allay'.

Therefore, the Committee decided against organising controversial public meetings, but to instead restrict themselves to distributing tracts and pamphlets. Most of these had been written before the war. This included everything from the usual religious material to peace conference reports. Of the tracts released since the conflict began in earnest, the society gave most attention to a peace society edition of the controversial public letter from

FIGURE 2.2 Another Daumier cartoon, this time depicting the effectuality of peace propaganda in wartime.

Bright. Although it got this M.P.'s effigy burned, the Committee believed it was 'founded on impregnable truth'.[321]

John Bright (1811–1889) shared many traits with Richard Cobden, his long-time friend and political ally. Like his fellow townsman from Manchester, Bright first made his name in the Anti-Corn Law League. In 1843, he was elected to Parliament. Bright's political career reflected his individualistic-liberal values. A firm abolitionist, he supported the Northern cause during the American Civil War. Both Charles Sumner and Abraham Lincoln held him in high esteem. In India, Bright was likewise in favour of more lenient British rule. Arguably, his greatest feat of arms occurred in the mid-1860s. The inventor of the phrase 'England is the mother of all parliaments', he was likewise instrumental in the passing of the Second Reform Act, that extended the franchise to skilled artisans. However, it left out unskilled workers, such as the kind who laboured in Bright's Manchester textile factories, and were living in some of the worst slums in town. Human morality being endless shades of grey, Bright's resistance to social reform reflected a darker side of his belief in individual independence.[322] In the peace movement also, Bright was more complicated than many of his biographers made him out to be. Like many other peace friends, the new Radical M.P. was a Quaker, but he was too much of a politician to publicly reveal himself as a radical pacifist. In fact, Like Cobden, historians have been somewhat uncertain about whether Bright even was one privately. Most probably, he was not, given that he at one point informed Sturge: 'I have never advocated the extreme peace principle in public, or in private.'[323]

Although this man might never have argued against defensive war, he stood extremely critical about the justness of the war then being fought in the Crimea. Bright's public letter had been occasioned by a former fellow traveller in the Anti-Corn Law League, who had invited him to a meeting of the Manchester Patriotic Fund. The fundraiser was held for war widows and orphans. The Committee of the London Peace Society, consisting of radical pacifists, acknowledged that it was undoubtedly a good cause, but

321 The society distributed some 400,000 tracts and pamphlets this way. HP (June 1855), 209–11.

322 Miles Taylor, 'Bright, John (1811–1889)', in *Oxford Dictionary of National Biography*. 2004, available at: doi.org/10.1093/ref:odnb/3421; Donald Read, 'John Bright', in *Encyclopaedia Britannica*. 2022, available at: www.britannica.com/biography/John-Bright.

323 Sandra Holton, 'John Bright, Radical Politics, and the Ethos of Quakerism'. *Albion: a Quarterly Journal concerned with British Studies* 34(4) (2002), 584–605; Bright quoted in Ceadel, *Origins* 1996, 350.

discouraged participance on the grounds that even indirect support still amounted to support for the larger war system.[324] Bright did not go that far, but attacked his former colleague for allegedly using the event to also argue in favour of the justness of the war. He believed that was highly inappropriate, as it was of course the war that had created those widows and orphans in the first place. He suggested that those who had championed it, and 'have made themselves responsible for it', should also contribute the most to its victims.[325]

Like many other peace friends, the Manchester Radical was totally unimpressed by his opponent's references to Vattel. In ordinary diplomatic practice, this Swiss classic had been so popular because of its normative ambivalence, allowing opposing sides to both use Vattel.[326] For Bright, that meant that any attempt to justify the war through international legal doctrine was farcical from the outset. Already in the opening paragraphs of his public letter, the famous orator displayed the sort of blunt honesty for which he was widely known: 'I am not surprised at the difference between your opinion of mine, if you decide a question of this nature, by an appeal to *Vattel*. The "law of nations" is not my law, and at best it is a code full of confusion and contradictions'. For Bright, it was founded on custom, rather than 'higher morality', and legal custom had 'always been determined by the will of the strongest'. For Bright, whatever the author of some legal textbook did or did not condone was for the most part academic. Whether a war was legally justifiable or not was 'totally different' from the far more important question of whether or not it was also correct policy. The First Crusade or the wars against the American and French revolutionaries might have been fought with a just cause according to legal authorities, but 'no man in his senses in this country will now say that the policy of George III towards the American colonies was a wise policy, or that war a righteous war'. Bright concluded: 'you must excuse me if I refuse altogether to pin my faith upon *Vattel*'.[327]

An underlying belief in positivism likely accounted as to why Bright could not write down the name of Vattel without putting it in condescending italics. Like many adherents of the international peace movement, he was at heart a moralist. He did not deny the existence of a higher morality, that *ought* to regulate interstate affairs. However, also

324 Van der Linden, *Peace Movement* 1987, 463.

325 Bright, *Letter on the War* 1854, 2.

326 Jouannet, 'Dualismes' 2011, 149–50.

327 Bright, *Letter on the War* 1854, 2–3.

like other contemporaries – pacifist or not – Bright was too sober to believe that actual diplomacy was conducted according to grand moral principles. He read Vattel, and legal scholarship in general, through distinctly nineteenth century glasses. Bright's world order was one of sovereign states and their colonial dependencies. The only norms that could conceivably apply in practice were those which states had agreed among themselves. Near the turn of the century, the Swiss classic would finally fall from its pedestal, to be replaced by positivists like Oppenheim.[328] Legal historians have observed that nineteenth century audiences only read 'half' of Vattel's books, in an anachronistic and reductionist way. They had little understanding or patience for the multi-layered approach of this early modern work, which combined a core of rules affirmed by actual state practice with a broader 'code of good conduct'. The latter was more ethical in nature, and was concerned with such subjects like the Christian soul's *forum internum* and the Enlightenment belief in moral perfectionism. In the nineteenth century, these connotations were fading. Especially for men like Bright, who did not see the utility of Vattel's indeterminateness like diplomats did, the many internal contradictions and unclarities of the Swiss author just sounded too wishy-washy to be of any value in policy-making. Even more, it all just seemed like a cynical disguise for imperialism – recall Dymond's exasperated call for 'clearer rules' or Cobden's revulsion of 'diplomatists'.[329]

Bright's and the London Peace Society's relatively positivistic concern for state practice was evident from the rest of his letter. It had almost doubled in size in the peace society's edition, largely because of the addition of numerous and lengthy footnotes. Each note added positive evidence for Bright's claims that the government had deliberately led the country into a perfectly avoidable war. The so-called diplomatic 'blue books' formed the society's main primary source. In doing so, their original intent was reversed, since these coloured volumes containing official selections of diplomatic letters and other documents were published for propagandistic purposes.[330] According to the letter, there had been just such an occasion to avoid war in 1853, when a great power conference had produced

328 Amanda Perreau-Saussine, 'Lauterpacht and Vattel on the Sources of International Law: the Place of Private Law Analogies and General Principles', in Vincent Chetail and Peter Haggenmacher (eds.), *Vattel's International Law in a XXIst Century Perspective* (Leiden: Nijhoff 2011), 179; Neff, *Justice* 2014, 218–9, 228.

329 Jouannet, 'Dualismes' 2011, 134, 149. See also supra in this chapter.

330 Matthias Hartwig, 'Colour Books', in *Encyclopedia of Public International Law. Vol. 9, ed. Rudolf Bernhardt* (Amsterdam: North Holland 1986), 26–7

a political compromise called the 'Vienna note'. This document of 'mediation' was accepted by the czar, but rejected by the sultan, who had been led to believe by the British ambassador that Britain would intervene in his support in the case of armed conflict. Bright detected a glaring inconsistency in the fact that Britain had first supported the 'award' of this 'court of arbitration', but had quickly afterwards claimed that it had been 'totally inadmissible'.[331]

In reality, the British entry into the Russian war had been caused by a number of factors. One was miscommunication between London and the embassy. Another reason was that the great powers assembled at the Vienna conference had been unable or unwilling to force the sultan to accept their 'mediation' or 'arbitration'. In contrast, during the 1839 Syria Crisis, they had sent actual forces to enforce the decision. The British cabinet's indecisiveness, Russo-Turkish clashes and pressure from the more hawkish segments of public opinion eventually led to war with Russia.[332] Although neither Bright nor the peace societies knew all of these details, they agreed that Britain should have chosen non-intervention.[333]

While Bright's public attack against Britain's participance was widely spread – even reaching Russia – the rest of the London Peace Society's propaganda was more modest.[334] The *Herald's* news articles were still mostly religious and humanitarian in tone. The Crimean War was one of the first modern wars extensively reported on by newspaper correspondents, illustrators and photographers. These reporters travelled with the army itself, allowing for a relatively accurate and up-to-date insight into the campaigns as they were progressing. Thanks to technologies like the telegraph, such news could be transmitted in a matter of hours, rather than days or weeks.[335] Horrific press reports on sanitary conditions in British field hospitals led to the mission of Florence Nightingale. They also stimulated a degree of anti-war feeling. Sensing this, the *Herald* abounded in these years with articles graphically describing massacres against civilians, the aftermaths of battles, or the mundane brutalities of daily camp life, filled with vice and disease.

331 Bright, *Letter on the War* 1854, 12–3.

332 David Goldfrank, *The Origins of the Crimean War* (London: Routledge 1994); 219–65: Candan Badem, *The Ottoman Crimean War (1853–1856)* (Leiden: Brill 2010), 177–80; Figes, *Crimea* 2010, 122–9

333 Bright, *Letter on the War* 1854, 14–5.

334 Van der Linden, *Peace Movement* 1987, 463.

335 Stefanie Markovits, 'Rushing into Print: "Participatory Journalism" during the Crimean War'. *Victorian Studies* 50(4) (2008), 559–586.

For the average reader, such reports would undoubtedly have made a far bigger impression than theoretical debates on arbitration. The society wondered aloud whether orphans would agree that their father had 'perished gloriously "for the revision of the treaty of 1841, in the interest of the balance of power"'.[336]

Near the end of the war, the British peace movement grew more ambitious. War-weariness caused by the incompetent British military leadership was increasingly turning public opinion in favour of peace talks. Palmerston had in early 1855 become prime minister and wanted to continue the war to permanently cripple Russia. However, he was forced by a combination of domestic pressure and overtures from France and Austria to accept the beginning of negotiations. In February 1856, Paris became the scene of a multilateral congress between the parties involved.[337] The Peace Conference Committee, which had been the least restrained peace organisation during the war, sensed a unique opportunity.[338] The 'congress of nations' in the French capital should be persuaded to incorporate a binding arbitration clause into the expected peace treaty. A circular recruited potential allies. They first sent a delegation to the prime minister. It was a sizeable group, including eighteen M.P.'s and many stalwarts of the peace movement, like Sturge, Cobden, Chamerovzow and Henry Richard.[339]

Henry Richard had been secretary of the London Peace Society since 1848, a post he had retained until 1855, although he remained one of the central leaders of the peace society until the 1880s, as their 'honorary Secretary'. Welsh-born, Richard was a Calvinistic minister, who only married at the ripe age of fifty-four, until then being de facto wedded to the peace society. He was himself a radical pacifist, per the requirements of the peace society, but he was diplomatic enough to cultivate close relationships with more moderate adherents. Like Beckwith in the United States, or Cobden in his own country, he grasped that only moderate solutions had any chance of political success.[340] After becoming a Liberal M.P. in 1868, it was Richard

336 HP (January 1855), 3.

337 Most contentious issues had already been resolved before the congress met. Figes, *Crimea* 2010, 400–18.

338 Apart from the short-lived Stop-the-War League, which was made up of London-based journalists and activists with little prior connections with the peace movement. Ceadel, *Idealists* 2000, 48–53.

339 More than fifty men walked through Palmerston's front door. HP (April 1856), 38–9.

340 Throughout the Crimean War, he had supported arbitration in the *Herald*. Stephen Frick, 'Henry Richard and the Treaty of Paris of 1856'. *National Library of Wales Journal* XVII (1972), 300.

who brought the British peace movement its long-awaited prize: in 1873, the House of Commons passed his arbitration motion, triggering a wave of similar motions in other European parliaments.[341] Near the end of his life, in the late Victorian era, Henry Richard had come to personify the voice of British pacifism. His statue in Wales, which still stands today, described him as 'the Apostle of Peace'. Having devoted much of his life to the British peace movement, Richard had been the glue that kept the London Peace Society united in the face of many challenges over the span of nearly four decades.[342]

Richard also read the memorial to the prime minister in his private residence that midday in March of 1856. The argument was broadly similar to that of Cobden seven years earlier during the debate on his arbitration motion. Like others before him, Richard especially stressed that arbitration would be extremely useful for the mandatory cooldown it interposed during crises. He believed that many wars did not become inevitable because a peaceful solution was impossible, but because events got 'inflamed by angry recriminations and the clamorous outcries of popular passion'. Perhaps Richard had the vitriolic backlash of the 1853 Edinburgh conference in mind. More in general, international arbitration could 'bring the great interests of nations within the cognisance of certain fixed rules of justice and right'. Unfortunately for the memorialists, the prime minister standing before them was Palmerston. He was seemingly welcoming, even offering the same qualified support to the principle as he did in 1849. However, he repeated his critique that binding arbitration was not practicable in the current political climate. Cobden rebutted that the 1854 Reciprocity Treaty between the United States and Britain had included an arbitration clause.[343] In a reply that would be repeated again and again by future politicians, the prime minister held that arbitration could only be resorted to in case of 'minor matters which did not involve great questions of national right'. Palmerston assessed that peace societies 'must yet have great influence on the general opinion of mankind'. Given his earlier dealings with the peace movement, this was likely his polite way of saying he could impossibly care less. Still, it spoke to the relative popularity of the peace movement that such a ruthless 'realist' like the prime minister, the biggest war-hawk of the allies, nonetheless condescended to receive them.

341 See chapter 6.

342 Ceadel, *Origins* 1996, 395.

343 See chapter 6 for more on this treaty. HP (April 1856), 39–40.

Suspecting that Palmerston privately probably disliked them, Richard and Sturge afterwards set out to Paris itself to personally convince the French emperor and all of the plenipotentiaries they could meet. The memorial they took with them was somewhat modified to better suit foreigners, but the concluding proposal for some binding arbitration clause in the peace treaty had remained the same. In their report in the *Herald,* the two men claimed that they had indirectly forwarded the document to the diplomatic representatives of France, Russia, Austria, Prussia, Piedmont-Sardinia, and even the Ottomans.[344] More sobering details could be gleaned from their private travel journals. Richard complained that all of the diplomatic delegations in the city were brushing them off. He was hoping that Michel Chevalier, who had shown his support for the European peace conferences, would be able to arrange an audience with Napoleon III, but the French political economist was out of town. Sturge and Richard were therefore forced to spend most of their time playing the tourist with their friend Chamerovzow, who was also there on unrelated business. As Richard drily noted down: 'this waiting upon the great is not an occupation particularly gratifying to one's self-respect'.[345] Similarly, Sturge wrote to Cobden that even if some delegation was contemplating an arbitration clause, 'none of them will like to have it known that they have any suggestions from us of the peace party'.[346]

Unbeknownst to them at the time, their trip had not been in vain. As they were fruitlessly soliciting a meeting with the French emperor, they did notedly meet with the British foreign secretary, Lord Clarendon. Unlike Palmerston, Clarendon stood more sympathetic to the peace friends. Before the war, in 1854, he might have acted on their suggestion to add an arbitration clause to the Reciprocity Treaty.[347] Richard, Sturge and Clarendon had a frank conversation, even sharing a laugh when the need to protect Britain's national honour came up. The foreign secretary said 'it would be difficult' to convince any government to commit themselves in advance to binding arbitration, but he added: 'I will do what I can'.[348]

344 HP (May 1856), 57.

345 They also dined with the *Société d'économie politique.* According to Richard, the topic of the evening's debate was 'sufficiently dry'. Frick, 'Henry Richard and the Treaty of Paris' 1972, 301–8.

346 Ibid., 309.

347 See chapter 6.

348 Ibid., 303.

As it happened, Clarendon kept his word. Protocol 23 of the Paris Peace Treaty recommended that the signatories first seek recourse to the 'good offices of a Friendly Power' before turning to arms.[349] However, as criticised also by French friends of peace like the journalist Émile de Girardin, only a true optimist could read a real political – let alone legal – commitment in the use of the word 'wish' or 'as far as circumstances permit'.[350] The protocol was deliberately left vague and non-binding. As evident from the official report, the plenipotentiaries only accepted it after repeated assurances that it would not 'in any case oppose limits to the liberty of judgment' of a state, or constitute 'a right' or 'an engagement'.[351] Clarendon had asked permission beforehand from Palmerston, who had not objected. Neither politician regarded the Protocol as an arbitration clause, but as an encouragement to non-binding 'mediation'. In another memo, the foreign secretary acknowledged that 'the peace folks in England may not think it goes far enough as they want binding arbitration, but reasonable people will be satisfied with the first step made in a right direction'.[352]

In fact, the London Peace Society was eager to trumpet any sort of political victory after three years of invective and abuse. The *Herald* reproduced the state papers on the Protocol at length.[353] In their report, the Committee called it 'the greatest encouragement to the friends of peace to persevere in the advocacy of their principles'. Although they would have indeed preferred 'a positive and mutual obligation', the leadership was pleased that 'measures that were but a short time ago were branded as utopian and visionary' were beginning to be seen as 'practical statesmanship'. In short, the treaty of 1856 was 'an immense gain'. Even William Ewart Gladstone (1809–1898), who would be prime minister when Richard succeeded in his arbitration motion in 1873, praised the 23rd Protocol in the Commons as containing 'at least a qualified disapproval of a resort to war'.[354]

Later that year, another unexpected gain came from Paris. The Declaration of Paris, as agreed upon by the principal European great powers, had

349 'Whereupon the Plenipotentiaries do not hesitate to express, in the name of their Governments, the wish that States between which any serious misunderstanding may arise, should, before appealing to arms, have recourse, as far as circumstances might allow, to the good offices of a friendly Power.' Phillimore, *Commentaries* 1871, 609–11.

350 See chapter 4.

351 Phillimore, *Commentaries* 1871, 610–1.

352 Quoted in Frick, 'Henry Richard and the Treaty of Paris' 1972, 310.

353 HP (June 1856), 61–2.

354 Ibid., 64–5.

abolished privateering and expanded maritime neutral rights.[355] In this instance, the international peace movement had nothing to do with it. Nonetheless, the British peace friends called attention to it as 'a subject of great importance' for the 'future peace of the world'. Specifically, they wondered aloud why the United States had refrained from acceding to the Declaration. The argument in the *Herald* was broadly similar to Jan Lemnitzer's recent thesis, holding that the United States would not give up its main means of naval defence without securing the protection of *all* private property on sea. This was the gist of the so-called Marcy Amendment, which Britain, as the century's premier naval power, refused to accept.[356] The London Peace Society of course did not represent the interests of the British government. Therefore, they fully supported the adoption of the Marcy Amendment. Like the 23rd Protocol of the Paris Peace Treaty, this would again be 'an incalculable gain'. In this case, they were clearly asking too much. Lord Clarendon did not even send back a reply, other than a formal acknowledgement of its receipt.[357]

Overall, the London Peace Society had weathered the storm of war. In their own assessment, they had 'no regrets'. Leaving aside a number of defections from moderate adherents, the more absolute core of the peace society had indeed stayed true to their principles, despite 'great unpopularity and odium'.[358] In a larger sense, the Crimean War had affirmed the potential of stipulated arbitration in the political peace campaign. Its potential to unite both moderate and radical adherents had already been proven in the 1840s. However, the parliamentary debate of 1849 had been inconclusive about its operability in wider political circles. The fact that such a clause had seemingly been adopted into state practice at a multilateral diplomatic congress provided explicit encouragement that the strategy could also function internationally. It helped that the indeterminateness of the instrument persisted into the 23rd Protocol of the Paris Peace Treaty. For Palmerston and Clarendon, it was just another instance of political mediation, which was in no way intended to limit the sovereignty of each state. For the British peace friends, on the other hand, it was the vehicle on which to project their utopian vision of the future. Insider pragmatism and outsider idealism had briefly interconnected with each other. For the rest of the century,

355 Declaration respecting Maritime Law between Austria, France, Great Britain, Prussia, Russia, Sardinia, and Turkey, 16 April 1856, 15 CTS 1.

356 See chapter 6. HP (October 1856), 109; Lemnitzer, *Privateering* 2014, 80, 204–6.

357 HP (March 1870, 26.

358 HP (June 1856), 66.

stipulated arbitration would remain the British peace movement's premier political objective. In Europe, however, the dream of a centralised international institution lived on. One of its most ardent early defenders in the international peace movement did not come from a wet island in the North Sea, but from the mountainous heart of the Continent: Switzerland.

CHAPTER 3

Switzerland (1830–1839)

> 'Rendez la guerre impossible par vos institutions, législateurs chrétiens! Voilà mon refrain, mon delenda est Cartago!'
>
> Count Jean-Jacques de Sellon (1829)

1 The Genevan Peace Society

Attentive readers of the *Advocate of Peace* discovered a curious letter in the issue of September 1836, sent to the journal by Henry Barnard (1811–1900), a young gentleman recently graduated from Yale Law School in the midst of a grand tour through Europe. It described a strange monument facing the otherwise tranquil shore of Lake Geneva, dedicated to the same cause as that espoused by the American peace friends, yet hundreds of miles away on the other side of the Atlantic, in the alpine heart of the European continent. The sculpture assumed the shape of an obelisk, carved out of one solid block of marble, each side adorned with dedications. Some dedications referred to monarchs and statesmen, like Henri IV (1553–1610) and the duke de Sully (1559–1641), 'who had proposed a congress of nations as the arbiter of international disputes'; duke Leopold of Tuscany (1747–1792), known for abolishing the death penalty; and even the French writer François Fénelon (1651–1715), whose *Télémaque* had provided the *dauphins* a mirror for the ideal pacific monarch.[1] Others belonged to influential intellectuals, like Cesare Beccaria (1738–1794), praised for his 'eloquent treatise' which had 'contributed to the reformation of the criminal law in Europe'; or Saint-Pierre (1658–1743) and his peace plan. Yet other inscriptions referred to still living or only recently deceased people, whose inclusion at first glance seemed to have been random: the very young French lawyer Charles Lucas (1803–1889),

1 AP (September 1836), 81–2.

 | DOI:10.1163/9789004733688_005

the Belgian penitentiary expert Édouard Ducpétiaux (1804–1868), the American jurist Edward Livingston (1764–1836) and even the Orléanist cabinet leader Casimir Périer (1877–1832), among others, were all deemed worthy of commemoration.[2]

What united this eclectic assembly was each personage's perceived contribution to the development of the core principle symbolised by the edifice: the inviolability of the life of man. The monument was intended to serve as a lasting memorial to the lifelong obsession of the American visitor's host, a middle-aged and somewhat sickly Genevan aristocrat of substantial wealth, multi-lingual and well-connected, permeated by Calvinist Christianity, who to this purpose had set up the *Société de la paix de Genève*.[3] This chapter analyses the essentials of count Jean-Jacques de Sellon's idiosyncratic nine-year campaign for 'peace through law'. It is somewhat unique, in the sense that it is the only chapter to focus one just one person. This is because the peace society in continental Europe was primarily the work of this one man.[4]

The first part sketches count de Sellon's career, with special attention to his interests in peace. The second section scrutinises his explicitly legalist approach to peace activism. As the largest and most important section, it is subdivided according to Sellon's religious convictions, his interactions with legal doctrine and lawyers, the specifics of his arbitral tribunal, its connections with ongoing Swiss constitutional developments, and finally the influence of greater European affairs. The third section highlights Sellon's networks, and reflects on the legacy of the first peace society in the heartland of Europe. The story of this little society offers insight into the dynamics of early European pacifism.[5]

---

2 Casimir Périer was likely selected because of his comparatively peaceful foreign policy, though he did gain notoriety for instigating the controversial French military occupation of the Italian municipality of Ancona in February 1832. William Ladd too mourned 'Perrier' [sic] as 'the most influential friend of peace in the world'. Ibid., 82–83; Jean-Jacques de Sellon, *Cahier de lithographies relatives à la Société de la Paix de Genève* (Genève: Bonnant 1833), 3–5; AP (December 1839), 90; Šedivý, *Decline* 2018, 61–79.

3 AP (September 1836), 82. Jean-Jacques de Sellon, *Notice historique sur la Société de la paix, fondé à Genève en 1830, par M. le comte de Sellon* (Genève, Bonnant, 1833), 5–6.

4 Sellon, *Notice historique* 1833, 3–6.

5 This chapter has already appeared in a slightly abbreviated form in Wouter De Rycke, 'Peace through Law in Early Nineteenth Century Switzerland. Jean-Jacques de Sellon (1782–1839) and the Société de la paix de Genève (1830–1839)', in R. Cahen, S. L. Kimble, P. Allorant, W. Badier et S. Morris (eds.), *Relations internationales et droit(s). Acteurs, institutions et législations comparées (1815–1914)* (Paris, Pedone 2024), 203–44.

1.1 *Life of Jean-Jacques de Sellon*

Any account of the first continental-European peace society stands synonymous to the account of the life of its principal founder, president, sponsor and publicist: the Genevan count Jean-Jacques de Sellon. Born on 21 January 1782 as the heir of a wealthy family, the scion was destined to inherit the family castle of Allaman in neighbouring Vaud, a stately townhouse in Geneva, a noble title, as well as a substantial fortune.[6] Later on, he would add to his properties the estate near Geneva where the obelisk would be erected. This comfortable position in afforded the aristocrat with the required leisure time to commit himself to philanthropy. Several episodes of his life warrant mentioning.

Fitting to his station, he was raised at home by a private tutor, the Alsatian pastor Pierre Witz, son-in-law of the well-known pastor Johann Friedrich Oberlin. Sellon's strong admiration for Oberlin's socially concerned form of Christianity defined his very religious worldview.[7] Apart from scriptural instruction, he also acquired knowledge of political and philosophical subjects, even if there are no indications he ever enrolled as a university student.[8] Drawing from an inclination towards religious philanthropism inculcated from an early age, it became ingrained in the count's mind that

6 Henry Deonna, 'SELLON, de SELLON', in *Dictionnaire historique et biographique de la Suisse,* vol. VI (Neuchâtel: Administration du dictionnaire historique et biographique de la Suisse 1932), 153–4; Lucien Boussonas, 'Sellon, Jean-Jacques de', in *Dictionnaire historique de la Suisse.* 2010, available at: hls-dhs-dss.ch/fr/articles/026552/2010-05-03/; Gabriël Mützenberg, 'Jean-Jacques de Sellon. Une société de la paix en 1830'. *Librarium. Revue de la société suisse des bibliophiles* 35(2) (1992), 108; Ivo Rens and Klaus-Gerd Giesen, 'Jean-Jacques de Sellon, pacifiste et précurseur de 'l'esprit de Genève'. *Revue suisse d'histoire* 35(3) (1985), 262.

7 He kept a portrait of Oberlin in his mansion. Jean-Jacques Gardes, *Notice sur le comte de Sellon, suivie d'une élégie chrétienne à sa famille* (Nismes: Durand-Belle, 1839), 5–6; Rens and Klaus-Gerd, 'Précurseur' 1985, 262; Jean-Jacques de Sellon, *Fragmens de l'Émile de Rousseau, et des lettres de Lord Chesterfield sur l'éducation, publiés par M. de Sellon, président de la Société de la Paix de Genève; avec ses notes et ses réflexions. Dédiés par lui à ses neveux et petits-neveux de Cavour* (Genève: Gruaz, 1833), 26; Sellon, Jean-Jacques de. *Lettre de l'auteur du concours ouvert à Genève en 1816, en faveur de l'abolition de la peine de mort, à l'un de ses honorables collègues du Conseil souverain* (Genève: Lador 1827), 57; Jean-Jacques de Sellon, *Nouveaux mélanges politiques, moraux et littéraires n° 3* (Genève: Gruaz, 1838), 342–51.

8 Beatrice Luginbühl, *Im Kampf gegen die Todesstrafe: Jean-Jacques Comte de Sellon (1782–1839). Ein Plädoyer für die Unantastbarkeit des menschlichen Lebens* (Zürich: Schulthess Juristische Medien 2000), 42, 139.

FIGURE 3.1 Jean-Jacques de Sellon in full regalia. A proud man, he listed the two essay concours he instigated as specific accomplishments.

the same Christian principles taught from childhood also governed political society.[9]

9 Jean-Jacques de Sellon, *Fragmens de l'ouvrage intitule: de l'influences des mœurs sur les lois, et de l'influence des lois sur les mœurs, auquel l'Académie française a décerné un prix extraordinaire de 10,000 francs; par M. Matter ...* (Genève: Vignier 1833), 48–9.

According to Sellon's own narrative, his first experience with this doctrine manifested itself during an Italian journey with his parents in the 1790s. Contrasting his prolonged stays in Naples, Rome, and Florence, it struck the – apparently precocious – eleven or twelve year old that while the former two cities ran rampant with crime, the latter seemed curiously exempt from this. Yet Tuscany was the only state that had abolished the death penalty, beginning with grand-duke Leopold in 1763. At a time when the newspapers were daily 'plastered with the names of victims of the revolutionary axe', it led him to conclude that the death penalty was as unjust and unethical in politics as murder was in private affairs. This conviction co-existed with an equal abhorrence of war, imprinted upon him by the images of trains of sick and malnourished prisoners of war in southern Germany in the same trip . Back home as an adolescent, he was shocked by the sight of foreign troops in Geneva's familiar streets.[10] Simultaneously, however, the count joined the Genevan militia from an early age and remained a proud captain there until his deteriorating health forced him to step down.[11]

In political life, the count held a long-time seat on the *Conseil souverain et représentatif.* This institution represented for years the most democratic element of the cantonal government of Geneva, despite its steep age and property requirements for office, and its total lack of legislative initiative.[12] Besides an insistence that this assembly should be given the right of legislative initiative, the young Sellon made a name for himself by pleading twice, in 1816 and again ten years later, for a cantonal abolition of capital punishment. Both times, he was disappointed by a lack of support, because the executive *Conseil d'état* – the real power in Genevan politics – brushed him off with the excuse that this should wait until the next revision of the criminal code.[13]

10 He had a bit of a temper. In 1819, he was sentenced to four days in prison for engaging in a fistfight with a corporal. Sellon, *Nouveaux mélanges n° 3* 1838, 74–5; Christiane Genequand, 'Un philanthrope de choc: J.-J. de Sellon en prison pour injures et coups'. *Revue du vieux Genève* 15 (1985), 40–5; Sellon, *Notice historique 1833*, 3–4; Luginbühl, *Plädoyer* 2000, 7.

11 Gabriel Mützenberg, 'Une société' 1992, 110.

12 Geneva, Constitution pour la ville et république de Genève, 24 August 1814, title 2, art. 5, § 1; see also infra.

13 Jean-Jacques de Sellon, *Un mot sur la proposition de M. J.-J. de Sellon, pour la suppression de la peine de mort, suivi des point principaux qui doivent être traités dans le concours, et de quelques fragmens sur ce sujet* (Genève: Le Double 1826), 3–4; Jean-Jacques de Sellon, *Appendice des fragmens de M. de Sellon, publiés en 1834* (Genève: Gruaz

Realising that a parliamentary approach would be unfeasible for the foreseeable future, the count instead turned more directly to public opinion . His first brochure was published the year his second motion failed, and detailed his intent to hold a contest on the means to abolish capital punishment. This precedent opened up for the next thirteen years a great floodgate of books, brochures, and pamphlets. There was little doubt that the Swiss count ranked among the peace movement's most prolific publicists. As a rich philanthropist, Sellon had many of these published at his own expense, and sent out freely. Frustratingly – for a modern researcher at least – he never gathered his thoughts in a single treatise, instead choosing to 'jot down thoughts as they appear on the end of my pen'.[14] As his impressive recipient list already suggested, this aristocrat shied away from popular activism, preferring to influence but select elites: the principal Genevan social clubs, mayors of major towns, academic societies, the other peace societies, and assorted high-standing individuals across Europe, including no one less than the pope. Famously, Sellon got back an approving reply from Frederick-William III of Prussia, although its significance should not be exaggerated, despite his boasting.[15]

Count de Sellon had been induced to shift his focus from the death penalty to war and peace due to the international events of 1830. While already his first brochure cited the preface of Rousseau's edition to Saint-Pierre's plan, Sellon published a *Lettre sur la guerre* in the summer of 1830 in

1835), 204–6; Jean-Jacques de Sellon, *Traduction littérale du préambule du code de Léopold, grand-duc de Toscane, en Vertu duquel il a aboli la peine de mort dans ses états, accompagnée de quelques notes de M. de Sellon* (Genève: Gruaz 1831), 3.

14 The first and to date probably still only truly comprehensive account was published in the German pacifist journal *Die Friedens-Warte.* Die Friedens-Warte (October 1931), 309–13; Sellon, *Un mot* 1826, 5; Jean-Jacques de Sellon, *Qu'est-ce que la société de la paix* (Genève: Fick 1835), 8–9; Jean-Jacques de Sellon, *Nouveaux fragmens de M. de Sellon, président de la Société de la paix de Genève, commencés au mois de juin 1833, et faisant suite à ceux publiés par lui au mois de janvier de la même année, dédiés aux mères de famille, présentes et à venir* (Genève: Gruaz 1834), 204.

15 The Holy See never replied. Jean-Jacques de Sellon, *Lettre de M. de Sellon, président de la société de la paix de Genève, à l'éditeur des Archives de cette société* (Genève: Schmiedt 1832), 5–34; Jean-Jacques de Sellon, *Résumé des efforts tentés par le comte de Sellon, fondateur de la société de la paix de Genève, pour introduire dans les codes nationaux et dans les lois internationales le principe de l'inviolabilité de la vie de l'homme; suivi de deux programmes destinés à servir cette cause (en lui procurant des défenseurs habiles parmi les concurrents qui aspirant aux prix promis par ces deux programmes) et de quelques réflexions sur le progrès journaliers qu'elle fait dans le monde civilisé* (Genève: Gruaz 1836), 30–31; Archives de la société de la paix de Genève (hereafter: ASPG) (August 1831), 58–60.

response to the French invasion of Algiers. The indignant Count denounced the attack as without just cause, instead proposing to solve the question of the Barbary corsairs through missionary and trade efforts with the cooperation of Muhammad Ali of Egypt. Shortly afterwards, the July Revolution in France deposed the last Bourbon king Charles X, triggering in turn an armed rebellion in Belgium against king William I of the United Kingdom of the Netherlands. In the autumn of that same year, Polish rebels called upon themselves the wrath of the czar, who suppressed their uprising with great force. Meanwhile in the West, many liberals were clamouring for the new Orléanist king Louis-Phillippe to intervene against Austrian rule in Italy.[16] In such a volatile climate, the disturbed Genevan Count published two more booklets: the first called for a permanent international tribunal, and the second announced a new prize concours elaborating the former idea. On 1 December 1830, finally, having by then grown aware of peace societies in Britain and America, and deciding to copy their example, Count de Sellon presided over the inaugural meeting of the *Société de la paix de Genève*.[17]

The Genevan Peace Society's primary objective entailed the 'enlightenment of opinion on the evils of war and the best means of achieving permanent and universal peace'.[18] Because of the far more politically sensitive character of this object, membership of the peace society was not as prestigious as that which had earlier joined his campaign against capital punishment. Most of its thirty members belonged to the local clergy, along with a handful of members of the *Conseil représentatif.* Revealingly, one former jury member of the capital punishment contest refused to give his support this time.[19] The 'society' effectively functioned as a one-man-show, with the other members merely acting like an 'entourage' for their president, as put by one historian.[20] Nearly all of its publications, including the four issues

---

16 Sellon mistakenly thought a European congress would be convened in Rome, though one did start in London in December. Sellon, *Un mot* 1826, 161–1652; Jean-Jacques Rousseau, *Collection complète des œuvres de J.J. Rousseau. Tome vingt-troisième* (Genève: unknown publisher 1782), 3–52; Jean-Jacques de Sellon, *Lettre sur la guerre, adressée à M. de ***, suivi de la 2e édition d'un article sur l'Afrique, publié en 1829* (Genève: Vignier 1830), 11, 17; Šedivý, *Decline* 2018, 41–52; Jean-Jacques de Sellon, *Vœux adressés au futur congrès* (Genève: Vignier 1830); ASPG (August 1831); Mützenberg, 'Une société' 1992, 127; Sellon, *Lettre de l'auteur* 1827, 55–6; ASPG (August 1831), 1–6.

17 Sellon, *Lettre de l'auteur* 1827, 55–6 ; ASPG (August 1831), 1–6.

18 Ibid., 33.

19 Rens and Klaus-Gerd, 'Précurseur' 1985, 282.

20 Van der Linden, *Peace Movement* 1987, 122.

of the Archives, the society's infrequently appearing journal, were penned by Sellon himself.[21] The exception was the eventual 'winner' of the much-delayed essay concours, the *Organon des Vollkommenen Friedens,* written by a professor in *Staatsrecht* from Zürich, Johann Baptist Sartorius (1798–1884).[22]

Having reluctantly withdrawn from the *Conseil* as well as the militia in 1834 due to his deteriorating health, Count de Sellon spent the rest of his life penning new works, invariably signed with 'founder and president of the Genevan Peace Society'.[23] Aside from a few other pet projects – among them getting a public statue for Calvin erected – Sellon's life was dominated by concerns for peace until 7 June 1839, when, at the age of fifty-seven and plagued by arthritis, this Swiss *ami de la paix* reached the end of his crusade.[24]

2 Early Swiss 'Peace through Law'

Because Count de Sellon was not a lawyer, the founder of what might be considered the first peace society in mainland Europe has never been studied by legal historians. Most scholars have touched only superficially on the legalist governance system Sellon developed for Europe starting from the late 1820s.[25] As a consequence, some of the count's views have been quite misrepresented.[26] The best studies on Sellon have focussed on his proposals for domestic criminal law reform. However, any modern attempt to artificially separate his campaign against capital punishment from

---

21 The four issues appeared in August 1831, March 1832, February 1834, and August 1837.

22 See infra. Johann Baptist Sartorius, *Organon des Vollkommenen Friedens. Gekrönte Preisschrift* (Zürich, Höhr 1837).

23 Rens and Klaus-Gerd, 'Précurseur' 1985, 266.

24 Ibid.; Gardes, *Notice* 1839, 13.

25 Van der Linden, *Peace Movement* 1987, 121–6; David Cortright, *Peace. A history of Movements and Ideas* (Cambridge: CUP, 2008), 28; Ceadel, *Origins* 1996, 274, 352; Cooper, *Patriotic Pacifism* 1991, 16–9; Lynch, 'Peace Movements' 2012, 204.

26 Sandi Cooper's *Patriotic pacifism,* to many readers the go-to English-language history of the nineteenth century peace movement, wrote that 'for Sellon, the heart of an organized peace was a permanent tribunal staffed with trained jurists'. A close reading of the source texts reveals, however, that his vision most likely leaned closer to a diplomatic representation within a congress of nations, rather than on a separate tribunal. Cooper, *Patriotic Pacifism* 1991, 19.

his anti-war campaign will fatally misunderstand Sellon's motivations for both.[27]

As his obelisk already illustrated, the two dimensions of his public life represented two sides of the same coin; both flowed naturally from the inviolability of the life of fellow man.[28] As written above, already in his inaugural brochure on capital punishment did Sellon touch upon peace and war, later explicitly calling it 'the first milestone on the path that would lead me to founding a peace society'.[29] Other early texts on capital punishment were similarly punctuated with seemingly off-topic asides into motifs that Sellon would develop further in his later pacifist booklets. These in turn continued to include references to his earlier philanthropical activities against the death penalty. To the Swiss count, both issues dealt with *'des maux irréparables'* and innocents being dragged to their deaths. He added that the legality of capital punishment was often deduced from that of war.[30] A government-sanctioned execution was little more than a 'war to the death' of society against the individual, just like war amounted to 'a vast death sentence'.[31] Unsurprisingly, Sellon correspondingly also adopted the common contemporary analogy between wars and duels, concluding that all attacks on human life should be made illegal.[32] Christianity applied to all communities, and also to every form of law.

2.1 *Religion*

As already implied by his efforts to get Calvin memorialised, count de Sellon was a deeply religious man. This did not distinguish him much from his peers in Britain and the United States, convinced that it lay in their religious duty to oppose war. Unlike the Anglo-American peace friends, however, the

27 Only two pages of Luginbühl's monograph allude to the peace society, even though Sellon referred to it on the title page of every single one of his publications in the 1830s. Luginbühl, *Plädoyer* 2000, 32–3.

28 Sellon, Jean-Jacques de. *Mes Réflexions. Tome II* (Genève: Lador, 1829), 227–8.

29 Sellon, *Un mot* 1826, 162; Jean-Jacques de Sellon, *Fragmens des ouvrages de Jérémie Bentham, accompagnés de réflexions de M. de Sellon, membre du conseil souverain de Genève. Dédiées aux amis du gouvernements représentatif* (Genève: Vignier 1831), 8.

30 Many Anglo-Americans argued similarly. ASPG (March 1832), 137–8.

31 Sellon, *Nouveaux mélanges n° 3* 1838, 352.

32 Jean-Jacques de Sellon, *Extraits tirés d'un journal allemand, destiné à rendre compte de la législation et du droit dans toutes les contrées civilises. Dirigés par MM. Zacharie et Mittermaier, accompagnés d'annotations et de réflexions de M. J. J. de Sellon* (Genève: Barbezat 1829), 52; Sellon, Jean-Jacques de. *Adresse du fondateur de la société de la paix de Genève, aux chrétiens de toutes les communions et de tous les pays* (Genève: Gruaz 1834), 33–5.

count lived in the heart of Europe, in a religious landscape holding distinct political resonances.

The Confederation's twenty-two cantons were divided across those with Catholic and those with Protestant majorities. At the same time, the 1820s onwards resound in Swiss political history as the era of *Régéneration,* when liberal and radical pressure caused cantons to revise their old constitutions, abolishing privileges, or sometimes even introducing a separation of powers and the beginnings of direct democracy.[33] By the 1830s, these two trends coalesced as Swiss conservatism identified itself with Swiss Catholicism, feeling threatened not only by Protestant attempts at state control over the Church's prerogatives, but also by rifts with aggrieved rural Ultramontanist minorities.[34] Civil strife led to armed skirmishes in several cantons throughout the 1830s and 1840s, causing the confederal Diet to intervene militarily at multiple occasions. In 1847, it culminated in a national civil war after seven Catholic cantons had formed a *Sonderbund.*[35]

Supported by the teachings of contemporary Genevan theologians, broadly similar to simultaneous trends toward more humanistic and progressist readings of the Bible among Anglo-American peace friends, Sellon asserted his personal right to interpret scripture as his own conscience and intellect dictated. To assist him, he turned to the examples of the 'primitive' Christians, whose practices he considered pure expressions of the 'spirit of the Gospel'.[36] This too was not very original, because most religious peace advocates did as much. Like those others, the Genevan count concluded that the New Testament had begun a 'revolution' tantamount to a divine condemnation of war.[37] Sellon further proved this by summarising the most explicit scriptural passages.[38]

---

33 Clive Church and Randolph Head, *A Concise History of Switzerland* (Cambridge: CUP, 2013), 150; Alfred Kölz, *Histoire constitutionnelle de la Suisse moderne. Ses fondements idéologiques et son évolution institutionnelle dans le contexte européen, de la fin de l'Ancien Régime à 1848* (Berne: Stämpfli 2006), 239–409.

34 Ultramontanists favoured absolute papal supremacy. Kölz, *Histoire constitutionnelle* 2006, 367–71.

35 Church and Head, *Concise History* 2013, 158–159; Kölz, *Histoire constitutionnelle* 2006, 597–601.

36 There was an ongoing Protestant *Réveil.* Jean-Jacques de Sellon, *Recueil des lettres adressées aux archives de la société de la paix par son président* (Genève: Gruaz 1832), 103; Olivier Fatio, 'L'enseignement de la théologie à l'Académie de Genève en 1831', in Olivier Fatio (ed.), *Genève protestante* (Genève: Labor et Fides 1983), 145–7.

37 Jean-Jacques de Sellon, *La guerre est-elle une œuvre chrétienne?* (Genève: Jarrys 1833), 1–4; Sellon, *Résumé des efforts* 1836, 24.

38 Sellon, *La guerre chrétienne?* 1833, 1–4.

Like the Anglo-American peace friends around the same time, count de Sellon realised that religion was not enough. Similar to someone like William Ladd, the founder of the American Peace Society, Sellon did not doubt that political action was required for tangible progress. Whatever his religious idealism, the count was also a firm believer in the rule of law.[39] Underlining that the first Christians had tried to escape military duty by all 'legal means', the task ahead was set: *'rendez la guerre impossible par vos institutions, législateurs chrétiens! Voilà mon refrain, mon delenda est Cartago!'* It necessitated 'the most intimate connection between the spirit of the Gospel and the politics of the nineteenth century'.[40] Peace activism had to be supported by the authority of 'the most capable jurisconsults'. Aware of the charge of impracticality levelled against pacifists, Sellon had faith that juridical experts, applying their constitutional theories in parliaments, would never tolerate their work to be dismissed as mere utopias. The Gospel contained many fine principles, the count's editor admitted, but nothing had 'the character of a positive law' that definitively circumscribed the legal from the illegal.[41]

Nonetheless, Sellon's sense of religion was also distinct from that of the Anglo-American societies at this time. Like just about every continental-European peace friend to come, he took it for granted that defensive war was justifiable within Christianity.[42] A fortiori, he was totally immune to the kind of anarchistic non-resistance that was giving Ladd a headache in the 1830s.[43] The count must have been aware of the debates on defensive war and non-resistance within the other peace societies, as he received copies of both the *Herald* and the *Advocate*.[44] However, he never mentioned it in any of his letters or booklets. Those distinctly evangelical concerns were so alien in European politics that even the Anglo-American peace societies' greatest ally in Europe preferred to pretend they did not exist. Rather, Sellon preferred to work with lawyers to devise legal methods to address Switzerland's very real internal and external security concerns.

39 Jean-Jacques de Sellon, *Mes Réflexions. Tome II* (Genève: Lador 1829), 70–1.
40 Ibid., 143; loose letter attached to Sellon, *Fragmens Bentham* 1831.
41 Ibid.; ASPG (August 1831), 21.
42 See infra.
43 See chapter 1.
44 See infra.

2.2 *Legal Doctrine*

Not a lawyer himself, but instead a well-connected local notable, Sellon compensated by attracting the cooperation of prominent lawyers in his public campaigns. The count had picked up the habit in his campaign against capital punishment. The 1826 concours emphasised legal concerns such as the need for comparative legal studies and a new criminal code.[45] Further reflective of his deference to gentlemen of the law, the majority of his jury consisted of well-respected Genevan jurists.[46] They awarded first prize to Charles Lucas, explaining his mention on the obelisk.[47] Afterwards, the count kept this course, as exemplified by his correspondence with someone like the Heidelberg professor Carl Joseph Anton Mittermaier (1787–1867), a German abolitionist.[48] Besides personal contacts, he also undertook an extensive, albeit dilettante, lecture of relevant literature, apparent from numerous references to legal periodicals and related texts in his works on capital punishment.[49]

When the president of the Genevan Peace Society tried to copy this model into his peace activism, it met with mixed success. As he believed Swiss and European security depended on the existence of an international institution that would introduce the principle of representative government into international law, he attached particular value to expert opinion on constitutional and international law.[50] However, this time around it proved more difficult to involve lawyers. Specialists of the law of nations did not appear in Sellon's long list of correspondents. Even Pellegrino Rossi (1787–1848) did not write to him in that capacity.[51] A perhaps strange lacuna, it should be kept in mind that that the 1830s predated the professionalisation of public international law. Many universities either not taught this subject at all, or only as a subfield of natural law.[52] Specifically, the *Conseil d'état* distrusted the study of public law by the upcoming Genevan elite, which

---

45 Sellon, *Lettre de l'auteur* 1827, 3–6.

46 ASPG (August 1831), 42.

47 Charles Lucas, *Du système pénal et du système répressif en général, de la peine de mort en particulier* (Paris: Béchet 1827).

48 Luginbühl, *Plädoyer* 2000, 140–9.

49 E.g. Sellon, *Journal allemand* 1829.

50 Loose letter attached to Sellon, *Fragmens Bentham* 1831.

51 Rossi, who was a professor at the *Académie* at the time, had sat on his jury against capital punishment, but did not appear in the peace campaign.. Sellon, *Lettre à l'éditeur* 1832, 50; Jean-Jacques de Sellon, *Recueil des lettres à l'éditeur* (Genève: Gruaz 1832), 211.

52 Lachs, *Teacher* 1987, 159–172.

is why the *Académie* discussed neither *lois constitutionelles*, nor the law of nations in the curriculum of the 1830s, despite some attempts to have it taught.[53]

As an educated nobleman with a membership to the local literary societies, Sellon had managed to acquire for himself a scattershot grasp of doctrine. Only a handful of scholars was ever mentioned by name in his texts, and often just in a rhetorical way, or to guide the interested reader further – the count himself admitted there was little methodology to it, merely highlighting some ideas to be developed further by someone 'more capable than me'.[54]

One of the authors Sellon did mention frequently was the most celebrated one of all: Hugo Grotius. Interestingly, the Calvinist count referred to the 'founding father' of international law in his today rather lesser-known capacity as a theologian, incessantly citing the passage in *De iure belli ac pacis* in which Grotius wrote that 'a Christian could do nothing more agreeable to God than to abjure war'. Combined with those parts of Grotius's magnum opus that focussed on the – more or less – pacific means of dispute settlement, such as single combat, a mediating congress, or third-party arbitration, Sellon deduced that Grotius had stood sympathetic to peace already in the seventeenth century.[55]

Overall, however, just like the Anglo-American religious peace friends, the count remained largely unimpressed by international legal doctrine.

53 Charles Borgeaud, *Histoire de l'université de Genève. L'Académie et l'université de au XIXe siècle, 1814–1900* (Genève: Georg 1934), 109; Alessandro Campanelli, 'Le Règlement du 2 octobre 1820 et la création de la faculté de droit de Genève. *Commentationes Historiae Iuris Helveticae* 17 (2020), 106.

54 *Mes Réflexions t. II* 1829, 76–77.

55 '(…) *aussi le célèbre Grotius tombe-t-il lui-même dans des contradictions continuelles quand il cherche à concilier le droit avec le force'.* Strangely, he also pointed at chapter XXV of the second book of *De Jure Belli ac Pacis,* which details when war can be waged on behalf of others. Sellon, *Recueil des lettres* 1832, 22, 269; Sellon. *Lettre sur la guerre et un article sur l'Afrique* 1830, 13; Sellon, *Adresse aux chrétiens* 1834, 11; Sellon, *Résumé des efforts* 1836, 17–24; Sellon, Jean-Jacques de. *Lettre écrite par le comte de Sellon à M. ***, étudiant en droit à l'Académie de Genève, en réponse à celle qu'il lui avait adressée, le 13 janvier 1838 en son nom et au nom de ses collègues, pour le remercier de l'envoi d'un opuscule intitule Quelques questions* … (Genève: Gruaz 1838), 9; David Bogue (eds. Jean-Jacques de Sellon and Susanne Guers). *Paix universelle Durant le millénium. Discours prononcé à Gosport par David Bogue, accompagné de notes, et suivi du traité de la Sainte Alliance* (Genève: Guers, 1829), 25; Grotius, *Belli ac Pacis. Volume 2, Book 2* 1925, 578–586 (Ch. XXV), 587 (Ch. XXVI, title III).

Even Grotius himself could not truly be called a friend of peace.[56] In the eyes of Sellon, 'Grotius as a Christian' was constantly contradicted by 'Grotius as a statesman' when he tried to reconcile law with force. Every attempt to cut the 'Gordian knot' by 'the sword' would render the study of law 'useless' and make it look 'ridiculous', he warned the law students.[57] On the whole, Sellon felt that the publicists of the law of nations had proven themselves far too eager to serve as the handmaid to 'human passions', rather than to stand 'like a dam' against them. Whenever anyone of them had experienced a brief breakthrough of conscience, it had been 'quickly extinguished in favour of special interests'.[58] The count's criticisms of doctrine rang similar to that of many contemporary and subsequent peace friends, both in North America and Europe.

Such critiques were not limited to the circles of peace societies either, as indicated in the work that had served as the count's key gateway into doctrine. The *Annales Diplomatiques* by the French lawyer François-André Isambert (1792–1857) analysed in its lengthy *prolegomenon* the progress of European and North American public law.[59] Sellon agreed with a lot of it in his summary of it. Among other questions, he proved to be intrigued by Grotius and his translator Barbeyrac's notion of a Christian league, suspecting some of it might be useful to a nineteenth century league of nations.[60] He shared Isambert's dislike of Hobbes's pessimistic worldview or his support for royal absolutism.[61] From Pufendorf and Wolff, Sellon understood that treaty obligations were to be annulled if an ally waged an unjust war.[62] Basing himself on Wolff, Vattel had written the most widely quoted work on the *'droit des gens naturel',* but it had huge flaws. The count agreed with Isambert that its acknowledgment of the right of conquest was deplorable.[63] Curiously, Sellon's summary ended abruptly on the terse mention that the modern treatises by Martens and Klüber were 'esteemed', without any of his usual commentary.[64] Why did Sellon decline to comment on such relevant writers, who detailed relatively up-to-date positive law?

56 See the general introduction, as well as chapters 1 and 2.

57 Sellon, *Résumé des efforts* 1836, 42; Sellon, *Lettre à un étudiant en droit* 1838, 9.

58 Bogue, *Paix universelle* 1829, 25.

59 François-André Isambert, *Annales politiques et diplomatiques, ou manuel du publiciste et de l'homme d'état* (Paris: Constantin 1823), xiii-xiv.

60 Sellon, *Mes Réflexions t. II* 1829, 87, 89–90; Isambert, *Annales* 1823, cxcviii–cxcic.

61 Sellon, *Mes Réflexions t. II* 1829, 87, 94.

62 Ibid., 96–98; Isambert, *Annales* 1823, clxv.

63 Sellon, *Mes Réflexions t. II* 1829, 100; Isambert, *Annales* 1823, cxcviii–cxcic.

64 Sellon, *Mes Réflexions t. II* 1829, 101–3.

It was likely because the count attached an ambiguous importance to international legal scholarship for his campaign. Sellon was not an exception to the prevailing sentiment that natural law remained very real as a foundation of legal reform. To someone as religious as him, it was evident that human laws formed only an imperfect reflection of natural law, as inspired by divine reason.[65] There could be no doubt that the inviolability of human life was a heavenly principle, with only God enjoying the right of life and death.[66] Human laws and customs were fleeting. Already many of the 'maxims of Grotius and Pufendorf' had become dated.[67] It must have been extremely difficult for the count to draw extensively on positivist-leaning authors such as Klüber or Martens, since so many of their precepts violated the laws of God.[68] He only invoked state practice sporadically in his activism, and only when thought to be in support. Doctrine was largely absent in the count's writings from 1830 onwards.

At the same time, however, the count was a practical man, just like his counterpart in the American Peace Society. What good were the laws of nature if these were not followed or enforced in actual politics? Academically, Sellon certainly respected those like Wolff who wrote long and complicated tracts on natural law, but he did not consider himself a theorist. Claiming his convictions had been 'cemented' since Tuscany, he expected others to work out the finer points, as manifest in his essay concours and his public appeals. Drawing on a more extreme interpretation of natural law than any mainstream author, the whole purpose of his campaign for peace was to align the *'droit commun'* and the *'droit des gens'* with the 'morals of the nineteenth century'.[69] Rather than entertaining antiquarian notions on the supremacy of natural law, the Swiss Count sought to reconcile natural law with state practice through an international institution capable of generating positive law conformable to the principle of the inviolability of human life, which he called an arbitral tribunal of nations.

65 Sellon, *Fragmens Matter* 1833, 24–5.

66 Jean-Jacques de Sellon, *Seconde lettre du fondateur de la société de la paix de Genève, aux journaux de tous les pays, sur les effets du discours du président des États-Unis contre la France* (Genève: unknown publisher 1833), 18–9.

67 Sellon, *Mes Réflexions t. II* 1829, 97.

68 All of these authors were mentioned in Isambert, Annales 1823, cclxciv–cclxv, ccxcvii–ccxcviii.

69 Sellon, *Journal allemand* 1829, 77–8; Sellon, *Mes Réflexions t. II* 1829, 77.

2.3 *An Arbitral Tribunal of Nations*

A permanent international political-legal institution was the central objective of the Genevan Peace Society. The grand dream of count de Sellon was a world state that united humanity under a single government and a single God. Acknowledging that this was of course unrealistic, he 'reduced' it to the intermediate step of a great federation with a permanent Diet, where representatives of member states could discuss all topics of common interest, streamlining diplomacy.[70]

The count had already sketched the outlines of this tribunal in a pamphlet from 1830. He heavily stressed that this congress of nations *'constitué en tribunal arbitral'* would never interfere in the internal affairs of member states. In tribute to the inviolability of human life, the congress would also invite member states to abolish capital punishment, like the Congress of Vienna's declaration against the slave trade. Its primary purpose would be the arbitration of all interstate conflicts, its verdicts to be enforced by military force upon majority decision. Ideally, the police force would consist of militia, rather than professional soldiers.[71] Over the years, the tribunal's competences would only increase in Sellon's imagination, evolving into a general forum to debate and plan human progress, including fiscal and commercial policy, infrastructural works, and the coordination of an idealised European colonisation – 'civilisation' – of Africa.[72]

Its composition remained rather vague, though other remarks throughout his oeuvre indicated the count imagined it would consist in the first place of states from the 'civilised world', meaning states from Europe and its colonial offshoot, the United States.[73] While the admission of so-called liberal states like Britain and France was not original, appearing in most such schemes, Sellon also wished for conservative powers to be involved, such Austria or Russia. Where public opinion would suffice to convince states with a representative government, the count believed that security might do the trick for the more authoritarian governments. Had Russia not suffered from Napoleon's invasion? Would the czar not rather put his serfs to use in fields and factories, rather than in barracks? Large standing armies only

---

70 Sellon, *Nouveaux mélanges n° 3* 1838, 451–2; Sellon, *Traduction littérale* 1831, 33.

71 Sellon even contemplated inviting U.S. militia forces to Europe to enforce international law. Needless to say, this was an absurd idea. In 1847, the militias of the *Sonderbund* already balked at the prospect of having to fight outside of their own canton. Sellon, *Vœux* 1830, 3–6, 10.

72 Sellon, *Recueil des lettres* 1832, 282–284.

73 Sellon, *Vœux* 1830, 8.

served to incite wars of aggression. Sellon considered every state eligible that respected the law of nations.[74]

Whatever the tribunal's composition, Sellon claimed its underlying notion was no personal fantasy, but mirrored that of the *Grand Dessein* of the French king Henri IV, as written down in the thirtieth book of the memoirs of his loyal minister, the duke de Sully. This was a familiar phrase to anyone who had read even just one pamphlet of the count, as he mentioned at least once in literally every single publication of his in the 1830s. Sellon instrumentalised the reference to one of France's most beloved kings to legitimise his controversial campaign to the larger public. Instead of mere armchair philosophy, the tribunal was framed as the one-time ambition of one of France's greatest monarchs, who had proven his merit both on the battlefield and in politics. Such a man was no utopian.

In reality, of course, the *Grand Dessein* had been just that. For one thing, neither Henri IV nor Sully had been particularly peace-loving men when they were alive. They had been as pragmatic in politics and coldblooded in war as any other early modern statesman. During the French wars of religion, Henri IV converted several times from Catholicism to Protestantism and back – he is reported to have said *'Paris vaut bien une messe'*.[75] Secondly, no account of the peace plan was written by the king himself. Most of it, and perhaps all of it, had been the brainchild of Sully, who was too well-versed in war and politics to think of it as little more than some thought experiment.[76] Apart from personal idiosyncrasies, the obsession of the count with the *Grand Dessein* was thus probably partially caused by the contemporary cult of *le bon roi Henri*, actively promoted by the French state to legitimise the Bourbon Restoration.[77] In Geneva, straddling the French border, those specifically French political connotations were less apparent, but the onetime Calvinist king's reputation as the one who ended the French wars of religion must have endeared him to an elitist and religious aristocrat like Sellon, who described the author of the Edict of Nantes as a 'supporter of Protestantism'.[78]

---

74 Ibid., 6–9.

75 Ronald Love, 'The Symbiosis of Religion and Politics: Reassessing the Final Conversion of Henri IV'. *Historical Reflections* 21(1) (1995), 28–32.

76 Arcidiacono, *Cinq types de paix* 2011, 100–2.

77 This practice was continued by the Orléanist monarchy after 1830. Emmanuel de Waresquiel, *Penser la Restauration, 1814–1830* (Paris: Tallandier 2020), 319–342.

78 Ibid., 319, 328, 341–2.

Despite his idolatry of Henri IV, the president of the Genevan Peace Society realised the plan had been drafted in an earlier era, and needed to be modernised. He was interested in what was practical 'today', in terms of its concrete execution, since the European balance of power, due to the rise of Russia and Prussia, had changed dramatically since the 1600s.[79] The count was also aware that the original plan had been written with French geopolitical ambitions in mind, targeting the Habsburgs in Austria in particular. It had also assumed a *res publica Christiana* against the Ottoman Turks, viewed as 'irreconcilable enemies of the Cross'.[80] Finally, it had envisioned a new arrangement for Europe, with only six remaining hereditary monarchies, and three federative republics, all of approximately equal power, though maintaining some power discrepancies.[81]

More than any territorial changes or a specific league was Sellon fascinated by Sully's idea of a *'diète permanente'*, an assembly serving as the final arbiter between states.[82] Also dubbed by him as a *'conseil général'*, or a kind of senatorial body 'modelled after the Greek Amphyctionic Council', its concrete form and procedures would in the *Grand Dessein* be determined by the representatives during their first meetings. Sellon thought of this as another wise decision of the old king: better to first lay the groundwork, than to immediately lose oneself in technical details.[83]

Sellon knew that Henri IV and Sully had not been the only authors of peace plans, acknowledging that Saint-Pierre and Jean-Jacques Rousseau had published similar projects, even if these did not possess the same 'authority' as the one by the king.[84] Both had built on the original plan by

---

79 Jean-Jacques de Sellon, *Fragmens extraits des mémoires de Commines et de l'histoire des ducs de Bourgogne, suivis des scènes dramatiques* (Genève: Barbezat 1829), 107–113.

80 The count stood much more sympathetic to the Ottomans. He felt that Christian states had violated the law of nations more than the Ottomans. At one point, he even cited verses from the Koran to prove that Islam was just as receptive to pacifism. Although Sellon, like his contemporaries, was convinced of the superiority of Christianity, he was relatively openminded. ASPG (August 1831), 20, 49; Sellon, *Recueil des lettres* 1832, 29; Mützenberg, 'Une société' 1992, 118; Gallavresi, Giuseppe. 'Le *centenaire d'un précurseur: Jean*-Jacques de Sellon'. In *Revue internationale de la croix rouge* 149 (1931), 356; Sellon, *Adresse aux chrétiens* 1834, 19; Sellon, *Adresse aux chrétiens* 1834, 33–5; Sellon, *Mes Réflexions t. II* 1829, 223; Sellon, *Nouveaux mélanges n° 3* 1838, 233, 529.

81 Dominique Gaurier, 'Cosmopolis and Utopia', in Bardo Fassbender and Anne Peters (eds.,), *The Oxford Handbook of the History of International Law* (Oxford: OUP 2012), 255–6.

82 ASPG (August 1831), 51.

83 Sellon, *Fragmens des mémoires* 1829, 114–5.

84 Sellon, *Un mot* 1826, 162.

Henri IV, according to the Swiss friend of peace. Saint-Pierre had indeed suggested that the *Grand Dessein* could be resurrected in the eighteenth century.[85] Sellon had drawn from Rousseau's *Extrait du projet de Saint-Pierre*, copying its five articles of perpetual peace, which the eighteenth century Genevan philosopher had restated from Saint-Pierre.[86] Like he had done with Henri IV's project, he pointed out that the balance of power had again shifted, but that the underlying principles of this plan were 'eternal and invariable', since the inviolability of life constituted 'a natural law, a social law, and a positive law' that suffered 'no modification'.[87] Most articles aligned well with his readings of Henri IV, as they emphasised mandatory arbitration in a permanent 'alliance', non-interference, collective enforcement, as well as the settlement of territorial claims, based on possession, and – interestingly – treaty stipulations, which in Sellon's context of the 1830s would have meant those of Vienna.[88]

Much of what had remained uncommented was revealing for the Genevan aristocrat's blind spots. For example, despite his purported support for Europe's oppressed nationalities, he did not appear to have realised that the fixation of borders based on possession and existing treaties – two possibly contradictory criteria – would have been infuriating to huge masses of nationalist dissidents across Europe, especially in Germany and Italy. Many of these were enjoying Swiss asylum, and sought to destroy the Vienna settlement.[89] The count's social ambitions for the tribunal would likewise have drawn protests of unwanted interference by governments, and would have remained unsatisfactory for the working classes, as Sellon remained, true to his noble class, overall conservative in his social views – his adage was everything for the people, nothing by the people', despising *'niveleurs'*.[90] More generally, Sellon's readings of history and politics could be highly unsophisticated. Not only did he put too much stock in Sully as an eyewitness, he defended rather absurd claims that, had Henri IV not been assassinated, the

85 Gaurier, 'Cosmopolis' 2012, 258; Charles Irénée Castel de Saint-Pierre, *Projet pour rendre la paix perpétuelle en Europe. Tome premier* (unknown publisher 1712), 8–10, 128–49.

86 Sellon, *Mes Réflexions t. II* 1829, 54–65.

87 Ibid., 54.

88 Ibid., 55–8, 62.

89 Šedivý, *Si vis Pacem* 2021, 16.

90 Sellon, *Fragmens Bentham* 1831. 5; Jean-Jacques de Sellon, *Considérations sur l'initiative* (Genève: Lador 1831), 13; Sellon, *Recueil des lettres* 1832, 125.

Thirty Years' War or the War of the Spanish Succession could have been avoided by the tribunal.[91] Many more such doubts could be raised.

Personal fixations likely accounted for other notable gaps in the count's knowledge. Conspicuously absent in his otherwise impressive oeuvre, for instance, was Rousseau's *Jugement sur la paix perpétuelle,* in which the Swiss philosopher was more critical about the prospects of Saint-Pierre's vision – and by extension that of Henri IV – being realised.[92] Likewise, another omission related to the famous philosopher from Königsberg, Immanuel Kant *Zum Ewigen Frieden* was never mentioned in detail, although the count had undoubtedly read some of Kant's work, as he listed this thinker as another step in the long chain of plans that began – as always – with Henri IV.[93] Similarly did Sellon know that William Penn had worked 'on the same œuvre' as Henri IV, but he did not mention the *Essay towards the Present and Future Peace of Europe* by name.[94] No mention at all was made of more obscure schemes by Éméric Crucé or George of Poděbrady.[95]

More modern peace schemes also remained absent, despite certain parallels. The arbitral tribunal's top-down coordination of major public works by an elite class of international representatives bore a Saint-Simonian flavour, but this theorist's name, or his peace plan, were hardly mentioned. Sellon, as a Calvinist aristocrat, did not have any sympathy for an ideology that wished to abolish the right of inheritance, or had started a crypto-religious secular cult.[96] Similarly, it was impossible to find a trace of the peace plan of Jeremy Bentham. That should likewise not come as a surprise. As noticed in the chapter on the British, Bentham's peace plan was unknown within the London Peace Society during the 1830s.[97] Even should count de Sellon have somehow stumbled across this old project, some of it also palpably

---

91 Sellon, *Mes Réflexions t. II* 1829, 149–53.

92 Rousseau, *Œuvres complètes t. 23* 1782, 70–71.

93 Sellon, *Recueil des lettres* 1832, 68.

94 Jean-Jacques de Sellon, *Dialogue sur la peine de mort, sur le système pénitentiaire et sur la guerre* (Genève: Jarrys 1834), 14.

95 Géraldine Cazals, 'Le grand dessein d'Emeric Crucé: une paix générale et la liberté de commerce par tout le monde', in Philippe Sturmel (ed.), *Les échanges maritimes et commerciaux de l'Antiquité à nos jours, vol. 1* (Paris, L'Harmattan, 2014), 113–90.

96 Rouchdi Fakkar, *L'influence internationale de Saint-Simon et ses disciples* (Genève: Chevalier 1967); 30–1, 44–5, 55; Sellon dismissed the need for Saint-Simonianism in Jean-Jacques de Sellon, *Nouveaux mélanges politiques, moraux et littéraires n°1* (Genève: Gruaz 1837), ix; Krause's plan was equally absent. Raphaël Cahen, 'Le projet européen de Krause', in Oscar Ferreira (ed.), *Krausisme juridique et politique en Europe* (Paris: Classiques Garnier 2021), 267–8.

97 See chapter 2.

contradicted Sellon's own vision. The utilitarian philosopher had endorsed a separate international judicature, similar to the *Prize Essays* of the American Peace Society.[98] The count only republished Bentham's aphorisms on parliamentary government, reflective of his ideal of seeing representative government incorporated into international law.[99]

Curiously enough, count de Sellon paid equally little heed to the results of his prize essay concours on peace. He spent most attention to it in the last issue of the *Archives,* published two years before this death. Like the American *Prize Essays,* whose competition ran in the same decade, it took more than one round. In the end, it took many years before the affair could be wrapped up. At fault were both the quality of the contributions and unspecified problems within the jury. When the original deadline lapsed in 1832, only seven *mémoires* had reached Geneva, and only one of these possessed the required length. Four years and numerous extensions later, the frustrated count finally decided to call it quits by May 1836. He was obviously somewhat disgruntled, because not one author won the gold medal worth 400 francs. Three received an honourable mention, but only one of them got the silver medal. This was the *Organon des Vollkommenen Friedens* by the aforementioned Sartorius.[100]

Of all the peace projects that reached the international peace movement in the nineteenth century, the one written by Sartorius was relatively unique. Unlike the others, this one had been thought up by a German scholar. As mentioned in the general introduction, Germans were barely involved in early organised peace activism.[101] Although Sartorius was a *Privatdozent* in Zürich, he was originally from Bavaria, and had studied in Heidelberg. Later in his career, the professor returned to his *alma mater* to teach ecclesiastical law, civil law, and criminal procedure. Like so many other law scholars of the mid-century, there are no indications that he ever specialised in the law of nations, although he was well-versed in German

---

98 See chapter 1.

99 There were several Benthamites in Genevan intellectual elites at the time, who also moved in Sellon's social circle. Sellon, *Fragmens Bentham* 1831, 32–43; Cyprian Blamires, *The French Revolution and the Creation of Benthamism* (Basingstoke: Palgrave Macmillan 2008), 305–6.

100 ASPG (March 1832), 125–6; ASPG (February 1834), 5–8; Sellon, *Résumé des efforts* 1836, 58–9; ASPG (August 1837), 1–84.

101 For other minor instances of German involvement, see chapters 5 and 7.

public law, to which public international law owes a great intellectual debt.[102]

Even so, the professor's legal background clearly showed itself throughout his long and dense text. Unlike many other prize essayists, Sartorius proceeded in an exceptionally rigorous intellectual way, drawing on a wide range of sources. He clearly knew what he was doing. Whereas peace advocates in the United States and Britain were mostly erudite on scripture, but very vague on the distinction between defensive and offensive war, Sartorius was incredibly fine-grained. He accurately mapped out every condition by which just cause doctrine sought to legitimise war.[103] As a specialist of public law, he cited every major handbook. International law textbooks appeared not as often, Wolff being the exception.[104] Because he believed war to be just under certain conditions, as the 'lesser' violation of the legal order, Sartorius was equally exceptional for devoting much space to the *ius in bello*.[105] In his eyes, war could be justified only to the extent it served to restore the legal rights of the offended party and restore the state of peace between them, which was the natural legal order. The *Faustrecht* was a contradiction in terms, because that violated the natural rule of peace. As might be surmised from this, and his reliance on Wolff, Sartorius was a naturalist who never doubted that natural law was the supreme source of law. Like other peace friends, he felt that 'historical or positive law' was 'a product of human whim', and thus subjected to human 'instincts and errors'.[106] Not being a fool, he understood perfectly well that, because of this, just cause doctrine was ineffective in preventing war. The only way to get rid of war as a '*Nothmittel*' was through 'a complete repair of the practical law of nations'.[107]

For Sartorius, the solution lay in an '*allgemeinen republikanischen Völkerstaat*'.[108] The entire second part of his essay was dedicated to fleshing out

---

102 On the importance of German public law, see Koskenniemi, *Uttermost Parts* 2021, 797–951; Andreas Volkmer, *Kriegsverhütung und Friedenssicherung durch Internationale Organisation: Deutsche Ideen und Pläne 1815–1871* (Marburg: unpublished doctoral thesis 2012), 219–220.

103 Sartorius, *Organon* 1837, 32–35; see also Neff, *War* 2005, 49–54.

104 He cited Behr, Bauer, Rotheck, and Luden, among others. Sartorius, *Organon* 1837, 37–9.

105 He did add that the purpose of his essay was not to repeat what could already be read in handbooks of public law. Ibid., 92–4, 103–8.

106 Ibid., 75–6.

107 Ibid., 90.

108 Ibid., 228.

how this would work institutionally. The *Völkerstaat* was not a world state, nor any mere interstate confederation like Sellon, Ladd, and other contemporaries had envisioned it. Rather, it was somewhere in between. The key distinction with other peace plans was that Sartorius wanted the representatives to not represent member states, but the nationalities directly. In turn, once elected, these representatives would not represent the interests of their own peoples, but the interests of the entire community. In order to avoid an abuse of power, Sartorius conjured up a complex system of institutional checks and balances. The most important one was a separation of power between the legislative and the executive power. There would be a Senate and a single Regent, assisted by a Council of State and various other officials. Significantly, this political entity was also supposed to have some kind of *'Gerichtshof'* and a *'Tribunat'*, which Sartorius ranked with the executive power, although its function was more or less that of an independent judiciary. The German professor admitted that his detailed blueprint could be modified. The important thing was that it had to be 'Kantian in spirit'; meaning the polity had to be representative, non-secretive, and subject to the rule of law. Like Kant, and also his disciple Fichte, whom he quoted much more than Kant, Sartorius had a deep teleological faith in human progress. Peace would only be realistic when there was an international *'Rechtszustand'*. The rule of law – *'Rechtsherrschaft'* – should no longer be open to question.[109]

This only partly agreed with count de Sellon's sensibilities. He most strongly agreed with Sartorius's insistence that states, like individuals, had to be able to settle their disputes in a 'legal way'. However, on many other issues, he felt the need to add some corrections. For one, his laureate had 'perhaps pushed his concessions to partisans of war a bit too far'. Although the count agreed that defensive war was justifiable, he would have liked for Sartorius to not dwell on the *ius in bello* as much. Citizens should be able to defend their countries without being bothered by the need for uniforms, whereas *'la raison d'état'* would surely make officers ignore such idealistic regulations. While these might have been details, Sellon took much more umbrage at Sartorius's idea of a *Völkerstaat*. He did not object to the notion as such, but he stressed that only part of it was useful. Like Ladd in the United States, the Genevan nobleman did not want international cooperation to be conditioned on drastic internal reform within states. Neither

---

109 Ibid., 244–50, 296; ter Meulen, *Gedanke* 1929, 245–252. See chapter 7 for the Kantian influences on the peace movement.

Sartorius nor Sellon were democrats. Only the 'elite' of society should have a say in these matters.[110] Evidently, this must have been reason enough for Sellon to withhold first prize to Sartorius and his curious book.

As for the *Organon* itself, it faded into obscurity over the course of the nineteenth century. Its author published the work himself in 1837. Sellon at one point hinted that a French translation would see the light of day, but this never materialised. Like other peace propaganda, Sellon delivered a handful of copies to a few literary societies.[111] The *Advocate* duly announced the laureate of their colleague's concours. The American journal even reported that it 'circulated among the cabinets and courts of Europe', but this was based on nothing more than wishful thinking. Sartorius's inaccessible book, which was wholly in German, printed in Fraktur, and filled with arcane references to *Staatslehre* and Idealist philosophy, was never discussed for its contents, neither in the *Advocate* nor in the *Herald*.[112] While it was barely picked up by the international peace movement of the mid-nineteenth century, it was never completely forgotten. The most apt description was given by a pacifist of the twentieth-century interbellum, who saw it as 'the first comprehensive work on the peace question and a league of nations in the German language'.[113] As a quite early German 'pacifist' work, the *Organon* remains a very obscure text. Count de Sellon's publications are comparatively better known, if only because of his involvement in constitutional developments in Switzerland during the 1830s.

2.4 *Swiss Constitutionalism*

Congruent with the international peace movement's usual optimism about human progress, Sellon noted with satisfaction that constitutions enshrining parliamentary government were on the rise.[114] All of his published propaganda was premised on the notion that constitutional and representative government ensured the highest levels of stability and prosperity. This type of government installed a 'legal order' that replaced arbitrariness.

110 ASPG (August 1837), 34–84.

111 Sellon, *Nouveaux mélanges n° 3* 1838, 166; Jean-Jacques de Sellon, *Kurzer Inbegriff der Arbeiten des Grafen von Sellon. Stifter und Präsident der Friedensgesellschaft zu Genf* (Genf: Gruaz 1836), 16.

112 AP (December 1834), 147, 158; AP (February 1839), 195.

113 Hans Wehberg, 'Graf Sellon, ein Vorkämpfer des Völkerbundes (Zum 100jährigen Jubiläum der ersten Friedensgesellschafts des Kontinents)'. *Die Friedens-Warte* 30(12) (1930), 356.

114 Sellon, *Nouveaux mélanges n°1* 1837, XIII–XVII.

with predictability, based on laws that had been articulated by the 'general will'.[115]

Pointing at political precedents, Sellon advanced a position that closely mirrored Kant's definition of a republican state in his first definitive article of perpetual peace.[116] Britain too had a government respecting 'the national wish', instead of 'the King's inclinations'.[117] Likewise, in French history, the count recounted the debate in the *Assemblée nationale* of 14 May 1790. That day, a naval armaments bill proposed by the king's minister took on a very constitutional dimension, when *'la gauche patriote'* reframed it into the fundamental question of whether or not *'la nation'* had to accept the executive's monopoly on foreign policy.[118] In the same vein did he refer approvingly to article 50 of the French constitution of 1799, stipulating that declarations of war should be discussed by the legislative like any ordinary law.[119] Disregarding possible historical caveats to his interpretations, Count de Sellon was convinced that 'the nation's elite' was far better placed than diplomats, who resembled 'military surgeons grown calloused by their daily horrors', to decide on peace and war.[120] In Genevan politics too, Sellon advocated a shift in power away from the *conseil d'état* toward his own *conseil représentatif*.[121]

The count advocated for similarly drastic constitutional reforms on the confederal level in his own Switzerland. During Sellon's lifetime, the Swiss cantons were tied only loosely together by a juridical charter agreed upon by traditional cantonal elites in 1815. The *Pacte Fédéral* contained fifteen vaguely drafted articles that underlined the sovereignty of each Swiss canton, with only limited competences relinquished to the central

115 Sellon, *Journal allemand* 1829, 10; Sellon, *Mes Réflexions t. II* 1829, 70–1.

116 Sellon never mentioned Kant explicitly in this context. Kant (ed. Kleingeld), *Writings* 2006, 74–8.

117 *Fragmens Bentham* 1831, 43. The count was probably influenced by Montesquieu and de Lolme, whom he referred to in other texts. Jean-Jacques de Sellon, *Quelques questions de droit pénal, constitutionnel et international, soumises à messieurs les étudiants de la faculté de droit de l'académie de Genève, pour leurs exercices* (Genève: Pelletier 1838), 19, 24.

118 Sellon, *Mes Réflexions t. II* 1829, 111–112.

119 Jean-Jacques de Sellon, *Lettre du fondateur de la société de la paix de Genève, à l'un de ses honorables collègues, sur la séance anniversaire du premier décembre 1833* (Genève: Vignier 1833), 20.

120 Sellon, *Mes Réflexions t. II* 1829, 114–5.

121 Jean-Jacques de Sellon, *À qui appartiennent le titre et les droits de la souveraineté dans la République et Canton de Genève?* (Genève: unknown publisher 1831), 4–5, 10.

government.[122] Individual political rights were absent, although the Pact did install an arbitration procedure, as well as a collective security mechanism.[123] The main element that hinted that this document, despite its name, might be a constitution, rather than a mere treaty, was its rejection of unanimity in the central Swiss Diet, even if representatives remained dependent on the official instructions of their cantonal government, similar to traditional diplomats.[124]

While manifold reasons existed why ever more liberals, radicals, and nationalists sought to alter the Federal Pact, an important factor related to wide demand for a more effective central government, able to preserve the peace within and without the borders of Switzerland. Those security concerns most strongly animated the president of the peace society, who felt unsettled by a series of domestic upheavals insufficiently addressed, if not caused, by the Federal Pact. A rural revolt in Basel in the early 1830s instigated several military attempts by cantonal authorities to bring the separatists back in line, only to leave dozens dead. The Diet had to intervene with 4,000 troops. Similar troubles in Schwyz brought 8,000 troops into that canton.[125] Pressuring the Genevan delegation at the Diet to enforce article 8 of the Pact, that empowered the Diet to take 'all necessary measures' to guarantee 'internal security', the count had no objections to the use of armed force for the prevention of any dissolution. While Sellon saw 'civil war desolate the cantons of Neuchâtel and Basel', he considered the Pact's primary weakness to be its incertitude on whether the central government or the cantonal government held supreme authority.[126]

In doing so, the count enmeshed himself into a wider contemporary debate on the reform of the Swiss confederacy. Continued clamour for it led in 1832 to a committee on the revision of the Pact, ending in a compromise report by the already briefly mentioned Pellegrino Rossi, who proposed a *projet d'Acte Fédéral*. Severely toned down compared to the radical proposals that had occasioned it, the *pacte Rossi* still did not survive the cantonal votes on it.[127] Sellon's own proposal covered a middle ground. Not quite aligning himself with radical Swiss federalism, which also wanted a bill of rights, the Genevan Count focussed more on means to improve

122 Kölz, *Histoire constitutionnelle* 2006, 200–1.

123 Ibid.; Pacte Fédéral, 9 September 1814, articles 2, 3 and 5.

124 Kölz, *Histoire constitutionnelle* 2006, 202.

125 Church and Head, *Concise History* 2013, 150–2.

126 Sellon, *Recueil des lettres* 1832, 161–3.

127 Kölz, *Histoire constitutionnelle* 2006, 424.

the central government's arbitration and enforcement competences. For instance, he briefly contemplated housing a federal 'commissar' in each canton, who would ensure strict compliance with the Pact, able to call in 'federal contingents' if even 'one faction' displayed 'illegal wishes'. Such action would be unlikely if the Diet allowed for legislative initiative – analogous to what Sellon wished for Geneva. Cantonal representatives should have a direct line with the executive.[128] Ultimately, the best means to settle 'family disputes' was by an internal Swiss arbitral tribunal.[129]

Conceptually, the count was not very clear on what he understood by 'arbitration'. In this, he was hardly different from the Anglo-American peace societies. Like other contemporary peace friends, Sellon could have meant it in a more judicial sense, or in a more overtly political sense. The second one was the older approach.[130] Drawing on both Sellon's suggestions for the reform of the Pact, and his interpretations of its existing mechanisms, it became obvious that he understood arbitration in a more traditional way. From the Pact's articles 1 and 8 – describing its purpose to ensure internal and external security – combined with article 4 – detailing that any canton could ask its neighbours or the Diet for assistance – he deduced a catch-all norm that granted the Diet the right to intervene both 'with persuasion' as well as 'with force' to quell unrest.[131] Some years later, the count similarly emphasised its article 5 on the arbitration procedure, which stipulated that any dispute should be submitted to 'confederal law', even if others stated, rather confusingly, that the arbiters would settle disputes *'à l'amiable et par la voie de conciliation'*.[132] Although the Pact lacked immensely in legal clarity – left deliberately vague by its drafters to protect cantonal sovereignty – Sellon consistently sought to maximise the confederal competences of the Diet, that he idealised as a representative institution that should exercise both legislative and quasi-judicial functions. It was congruent with his readings of old peace plans or his admiration for parliamentary democracy. The 'general will' of enlightened elites could be expressed through a majority

---

128 Jean-Jacques de Sellon, *Lettre de M. de Sellon, président de la société de la paix de Genève, à M. ***, sur le Pacte Fédéral et sur les travaux des sociétés de la paix de l'Amérique septentrionale, de l'Angleterre et celle de Genève* (Genève: Gruaz 1832), 5–7.

129 Jean-Jacques de Sellon, *Réflexions sur la révision du pacte fédéral de 1815* (Genève: Vignier 1833), 3–4.

130 See the general introduction, as well as chapters 1 and 2.

131 Sellon, *Recueil des lettres* 1832, 60–1.

132 Sellon, *Résumé des efforts* 1836, 36.

vote, not only on legislative matters, but also in those instances where a dispute needed settling.[133]

It did not demand much of a mental leap for count de Sellon to see in Switzerland's patchwork of unevenly balanced, ostensibly cooperating, yet competing cantonal polities, each of them jealously guarding their cantonal sovereignty because of their own linguistic, religious, political, and cultural peculiarities, a miniature version of the European continent itself, akin to how 'an architect's model represented the larger edifice'.[134] Why should the Swiss Federal Pact, as Sellon understood it, maybe 'with a few [...] modifications', not serve as an example for the international arbitral tribunal?[135] It inscribed the Swiss aristocrat inscribed into a grander tradition, as both the classical peace schemes, as well as most contemporary schemes, drew inspiration from domestic 'precedents'. It also aligned with his monistic and elitist worldview, which held that the religious conscience of the enlightened upper classes was expressed best through representative government, that gave expression to God-ordained natural laws that functioned just as well on the individual, the cantonal, the national, and the international level. Nonetheless, European politics did retain certain distinct dynamics that had to be taken into account.

2.5 *European Politics*

Revealingly, the president of the peace society in Geneva assured his readers that the 'Swiss doctor' to discover the cure to war would not only have served humanity writ large, but he would also have contributed to 'the preservation of his Swiss fatherland'.[136] Contemporary Swiss readers would have immediately grasped the connotations. Externally, Switzerland's chief bulwark against great power encroachment was its neutrality, as enshrined at the Congress of Vienna. Sellon underlined that his country's neutrality was 'one of the bases of public law in Europe', recognised by 'all the powers'.[137] With this, Sellon differed little from most compatriots – Geneva's official position during the crisis of 1830 held that international respect for the legal

133 This 'legislative' conception of arbitration also lived powerfully in French peace circles. See chapter 4.

134 Sellon, *Recueil des lettres* 1832, 301

135 Ibid., 59; Sellon, *Résumé des efforts* 1836, 35–40.

136 Sellon, *Résumé des efforts* 1836, 5.

137 Sellon, *Considérations* 1831, 24.

guarantees of 1815 needed to be insisted on by the Diet.[138] Although it had been a great diplomatic victory in Vienna, subsequent European politics intermittently discomforted many Swiss citizens, including the count. Not only remembering past violations of their sovereignty by both the French and the Allied troops, he and others felt that the crisis of 1830 had only been narrowly averted from escalating into a big European war between so-called 'liberal' Britain and France and 'absolutist' Austria and Russia. If the scare had turned hot, it would have been a war which would have caught the neutral Swiss in the middle.[139] In general, the spectre of interference by foreign powers factored strongly into Swiss nationalism and its clamour for a more unified state.[140]

This was because neutrality ever remained a precarious statute. In order to strengthen it, Sellon not only entertained rather whimsical notions, like the replacement of professional soldiers everywhere by militiamen, but also the generalisation of neutral statuses in Europe.[141] He urged 'every Christian prince' to write a clause of permanent neutrality into the 'fundamental articles' of his realm's public law. Despite this militia captain's posturing on the abilities of the Swiss militias to command respect for Switzerland's neutrality 'by force' if need be, he evidently was not fully convinced of this, since he still thought it advantageous if more of the 'Christian' community adopted neutral policies, and offered substantial guarantees through it by embedding that neutrality into the framework of an international tribunal.[142] Unsurprisingly, the count observed the Belgian Revolution with profound interest. He supported the London Conference's decision to permanently neutralise the new state, and added that this status should be extended to other geopolitical hazard areas, such as Piedmont, parts of Germany, and the entirety of Poland.[143] He conceded that some conservative critics 'spoke with a profound disdain of the neutrality of states of the second or third order' – reflecting the idea that neutrality was seen as a constraint, if imposed rather than chosen, as had indeed been the case for

138 Irène Hermann, *Genève entre république et canton. Les vicissitudes d'une intégration nationale (1814–1846)* (Genève: Passé Présent 2003), 204–205.

139 Modern historians prefers to describe the latter as 'conservative', rather than 'absolutist'. Sellon, *Considérations* 1831, 5–6.

140 Thomas Christian Müller, 'Switzerland 1847/49. A Provisional, Successful End of a 'Democratic Revolution'?', in Dieter Dowe et al. (eds.), *Europe in 1848: Revolution and Reform* (New York: Berghahn 2001), 231–5.

141 Sellon, *Résumé des efforts* 1836, 48.

142 Sellon, *Considérations* 1831, 24.

143 Sellon, *Recueil des lettres* 1832, 120–123.

Belgium. Nonetheless, regardless of whether their status was chosen or imposed, neutrals could form 'a truly holy league', influential enough to separate any belligerents 'both in fact and law'.[144]

A league arguably less 'holy', despite its name, was of course the Holy Alliance, held by the Genevan peace friend in ambivalent regard. At least twice did he reproduce its treaty text in entirety, believing that its three short and vague articles – which had been derided by Lord Castlereagh as 'a piece of sublime mysticism' – 'seemed to have invited all Christian monarchs to found a new international law, based on respect for the life of man'.[145] The treaty of this Alliance needed in Sellon's eyes only a few modifications to serve as the basis for 'the international law of Europe'.[146] Indeed, it was not difficult to see how a religious peace friend like the count would have been intrigued by it, speaking as the treaty did of uniting an Orthodox czar, a Catholic emperor, and a Protestant king through 'fraternity', each sovereign swearing to defend 'religion, peace, and justice' in 'the same family', and inviting others to likewise contribute to the 'fortune of long-agitated nations'.[147]

However, simultaneously, Sellon was not blind to the manifest discrepancy between the purported objectives of this treaty and its actual implementation in political practice. Although he considered it to be an important milestone towards an international tribunal, Sellon acknowledged the alliance's imperfections.[148] Overt analogies between the Federal Pact and the Holy Alliance appeared suspect: even viewed from *La Fenêtre,* the count saw that the Holy Alliance clearly proscribed representative government in Madrid, Turin and Naples, and did so without a consensual

144 A more developed version of this idea would later feature in Édouard Descamps's *pacigérat* in the early twentieth century. The Genevan League also flirted with similar proposals after 1867. See chapter 7. Jean-Jacques de Sellon, *Quelques observations de M. de Sellon sur l'ouvrage intitulé 'Nécessité du maintien de la peine de mort, tant pour les crimes politiques que pour les crimes privés'* (Genève: Gruaz 1831), 132; Frederik Dhondt, 'Permanent Neutrality or Permanent Insecurity? Obligation and Self-Interest in the Defence of Belgian Neutrality, 1830–1870', in Inge Van Hulle & Randall Lesaffer (eds.), *International Law in the Long Nineteenth Century (1776–1914). From the Public Law of Europe to Global International Law?* (Leiden: Brill 2019), 159–185; Dhondt, Frederik, 'Descamps' 2021, 56–179.

145 Bogue, *Paix universelle* 1829, 64.

146 Sellon, *Mes Réflexions t. II* 1829, 233–43.

147 Holy Alliance between Austria, Prussia and Russia, 8 February 1815, 65 CTS 199, art. 1.; Sellon, *Mes Réflexions t. II* 1829, 238; Bogue, *Paix universelle* 1829, 66–7.

148 Sellon, *Vœux* 1830, 12–3.

basis, unlike the Pact.[149] The powers of the Holy Alliance had fought constitutional government since the fall of Napoleon's empire, and not all of its members had joined willingly, unlike how Sellon envisioned states would join the tribunal.[150] He confessed that contemporaries held 'mixed opinions' on the subject.[151]

While many would regard the count's relatively positive interpretation of the Holy Alliance already during his lifetime as deeply naïve, he was not fully off the mark. Though the Diet had been forced into an unenthusiastic adhesion in 1817, like other small powers, peace friends had initially similarly welcomed the czar's initiative, interpreting it rather prima facie like the count had done.[152] It briefly made Alexander I somewhat of a hero of the peace movement, not unlike the lot that would befall his distant successor Nicholas II for convening the 1899 Hague Peace Conference.[153] Unknown to contemporaries, recent research has actually proven that Alexander's handwritten original draft had used a bit more radical language – exposing it to subversive potential – which did not make it past the ever-vigilant Austrian chancellor Metternich. Whatever czar Alexander I's original intentions, the congresses of Troppau, Laibach and Verona, the deeds of Nicholas I – *le gendarme de l'Europe* – and the brutal repression of the 1848 revolutions cemented the 'black legend' of the Holy Alliance to posterity.[154] Already during the 1820s, peace friends had been growing disillusioned with it, only increasing in numbers over the years.[155] By 1833, the American Peace Society already lamented that its principal states had not acted 'upon their avowed principles'.[156]

Swiss elites were especially sensitive to cases of great power misconduct, because the confederation – despite some army reforms and attempts at

149 Sellon, *Recueil des lettres* 1832, 210–1.

150 Sellon, *Considérations* 1831, 24–5.

151 Sellon, *Nouveaux mélanges n° 3* 1838, xiii, 162–3.

152 William Martin, *Histoire de la Suisse* (Lausanne: Payot, 1963), 249.

153 Beales, *History of Peace* 1931, 41; Fyodor Martens, *Traité de droit international. Tome 1* (Paris, Chevalier Maresq. 1883), 169, 173.

154 Stella Ghervas, 'La Sainte-Alliance: un pacte pacifique européen comme antidote à l'Empire', in Sylvie Aprile, Christina Cassina, Philippe Darriulat and René Leboutte (eds.), *Europe de papier. Projets européens au XIXe siècle* (Villeneuve d'Ascq: Presses universitaires du Septentrion 2015), 50–1, 63–6.

155 Van der Linden, *Peace Movement* 1987, 42–6.

156 The Calumet (January & February 1833), 324; the *Prize Essays* and the Legaré report also dismissed the Holy Alliance as a positive example. Similar critiques would be raised during the peace congresses. See chapters 1 and 5.

federalisation – remained subject to external pressure throughout the 1820s and 1830s.[157] Progressives in 'regenerated' cantons stood sympathetic to the liberal and radical causes elsewhere on the continent, and welcomed dissidents fleeing persecution. This fell perfectly within their sovereign prerogatives, as ensured by the Pact.[158] Ignoring such legal subtleties, the three leading powers of the Holy Alliance – Austria, Russia, and Prussia – forced the Diet to enact a highly controversial *Conclusum sur la presse et les étrangers* in 1823, after Metternich had threatened to revoke the country's neutral status. To be applied by the cantons directly, this initially led to a few expulsions and a tightening of censorship laws, but in the long run it stimulated Swiss nationalism, and the Diet quietly repealed it in 1829, even if it would enact similar *conclusa* in 1834 and 1836 through French pressure.[159] Count de Sellon commented on at least three of the multiple diplomatic incidents caused by asylum in the 1830s.

The first such incident was connected to larger European nationalism. In early February 1834, the exiled leader of the 'Young Italy' movement, Giuseppe Mazzini (1805–1872), who had been staying in Geneva despite Piedmontese, French and Austrian pressure to expel him, had tried to launch a revolutionary expedition on Savoy from his Swiss base.[160] The attempt was a total failure: only two hundred showed up, and they all ran into a trap at the border laid by an overwhelming Piedmontese force, who had been warned months in advance by Austrian spies.[161] A humiliating affront to Swiss neutrality, it led to a barrage of vindictive diplomatic notes by other governments.[162] Sellon was just as incensed. He argued that both cantonal and confederal public law were very clear that neutrality obligated both the government and each individual citizen to act as guarantor, and that they should hinder any acts hostile to other states. This conformed to the accepted legal obligation for a neutral to disallow a single

157 Church and Head, *Concise History* 2013, 154.

158 As this was not included in the Pact, it remained a discretionary cantonal power.

159 Hermann, *Genève* 2003, 205–7; Martin, *Suisse* 1963, 250–1; François Genoud, 'Conclusum sur la presse et les étrangers', in *Dictionnaire historique de la Suisse*. 2005, available at: hls-dhs-dss.ch/fr/articles/017228/2005-08-10/; Müller, 'Switzerland' 2001, 232.

160 Müller, 'Switzerland' 2001, 231.

161 Jean Charles Biaudet, *La Suisse et la monarchie de juillet, 1830–1838* (Lausanne: Roth 1941), 146–54.

162 Amédée Gabourd, *Histoire contemporaine comprenant les principaux événements qui se sont accomplis depuis la révolution de 1830 jusqu'à nos jours et résumant, durant la même période, le mouvement social, artistique et littéraire. Tome deuxième* (Paris: Didot 1864), 448.

side – assuming non-state revolutionaries could be equated to belligerents – to undertake hostile acts on its territory. On the other hand, no state could be forced to extradite any asylum seeker against its own will under international law.[163]

Two years later, a similar such incident made Sellon to investigate the legal ambiguities on neutrality further. It had begun in Paris, around midday of 28 July 1835, when the French king Louis-Philippe was ambushed in the street by a torrent of 400 projectiles, launched from an improvised volley gun by the Corsican conspirator Giuseppe Fieschi (1790–1836). While the king was only grazed on the forehead – unlike many innocent bystanders – the king's popularity soared, and many republicans fled to Switzerland in the ensuing crackdown. It caused the cabinet of Adolphe Thiers (1797–1877) to pursue a far less lenient policy to the country, more in line with that of Metternich.[164]

According to the count's take on the events, the diplomatic corps 'never ceased to complain' about the lack of extraditions.[165] The most vocal among them was of course the French ambassador, the duke de Montebello (1801–1874), who bluntly demanded that requests were to be executed, or the powers would come down and arrest them themselves. Both to Sellon and later historians, such an 'imperative note' escalated things, because the Diet had already been complying, so that it was now faced with the delicate issue of how to proceed without appearing to give in to intimidation.[166] This dilemma became more complicated, when the Swiss arrested a man called Auguste Conseil on the specific request of Montebello. Upon interrogation, this man confessed to being an *agent provocateur* sent by the French minister of the interior, equipped with forged passports to that purpose. Caught red-handed, the French government did not back down, but instead denied every involvement, and accused the Swiss Diet of lying. France imposed a blockade and sent troops to the Swiss – and thus Genevan – frontier, only cooling down after

163 Jean-Jacques de Sellon, *Courtes réflexions de M. de Sellon sur l'événement du 1er février 1834* (Genève: unknown publisher 1834), 3–4; Klüber, Jean-Louis. *Droit des gens moderne de l'Europe. Tome premier* (Paris: Aillaud 1831), 133–4 (§ 80); Jean-Louis Klüber, *Droit des gens moderne de l'Europe. Tome second* (Paris: Aillaud 1831), 86–7 (§ 284).

164 Philippe Gern, 'France. Les relations politiques', in *Dictionnaire historique de la Suisse.* 2018, available at: hls-dhs-dss.ch/fr/articles/003354/2018-01-22; Biaudet, *Suisse* 1941, 329–36.

165 Jean-Jacques de Sellon, *Lettre du fondateur de la société de la paix de Genève aux sociétés de la paix de l'Angleterre et des États-Unis d'Amérique, sur le différend qui s'est élevé entre la France et la Suisse* (Genève: Oursel 1836), 11.

166 Biaudet, *Suisse* 1941, 380–8.

British mediation, which led the Diet to issue a clearly insincere 'apology' dismissing the affair as 'a misunderstanding', despite resistance of a few cantons, including Geneva. These refused to sully the 'national honour', feeling backed by Britain, the Pact, and international law.[167]

Apart from the war scare itself, the count engaged with several of the legal dimensions of the so-called 'Conseil affair'. Unquestionably, France had interfered in Swiss internal affairs, violating the country's sovereignty. A wholly internal report on the incident by the Diet 'could have been legal, but became political' due to the French ambassador's infuriating meddling. Montebello had called for the aforementioned blockade because of the report's release.[168] Sellon naturally complained that accredited diplomats could not complain in any official capacity on any acts taking place within the representative institutions of their host state, and which were not directed to a foreign government. Similarly, Montebello had insinuated that the 'federal' character of Switzerland had partially caused these tensions, again violating international law: 'legal propagandists' condemned such criticism of a European state's system of government in official diplomatic missives. One of the most essential aspects of sovereignty was the liberty to choose one's own system of government.[169]

More generally, Sellon emphasised his reliance on international law by formulating eight 'questions of international law' that had arisen out of the incident, and deemed 'vital' to preserve world peace and the independence of nations.[170] The questions were evidently tailored to the concrete situation of Switzerland, and would, if unambiguously resolved in legal doctrine, have indeed given the Swiss confederation a number of additional legal arguments to shore up its case vis-à-vis the neighbouring great powers. As the confederation was but a minor power, its external security rested on its ability to convince its guarantors that they had legal obligations to protect Swiss independence, which did not escape Sellon. On some of his legal 'questions', doctrine was already unambiguous: sovereignty evidently implied that foreign diplomats had no business interfering with the internal

167 Ibid., 364–75, 402–211; Sellon, *Lettre sur le différend* 1836, 15.

168 Sellon, *Lettre sur le différend* 1836, 11–2.

169 Ibid., iv–vii.

170 Ibid., 13. Although he claimed to have sent out these questions to various learned academies, he never published any responses. None could be found in his preserved correspondence.

justice system of another state, or critiquing its mode of government.[171] Others were unlikely to yield any positive results: despite Sellon's wishes for the tribunal, mediation and arbitration could not be forced unto an unwilling state – at least in legal theory.[172] Sellon must have been aware of those facts, and may have sought simple affirmation *de lege lata,* or, alternatively, wanted specialists to develop arguments de lege ferenda, should positive law or mainstream assumptions on natural law prove unhelpful.

On other questions, however, doctrine was genuinely not at all clear. How did traditional neutrality law relate itself to the actions of non-state actors? How could asylum seekers be distinguished from common criminals and political dissidents? Someone like Vattel had written briefly and vaguely of 'foreigners' deserving protection, but existing legal doctrine was overall an unwieldy instrument to settle interstate disputes on such a sensitive political issue. Its novelty was reflected in the normative and terminological ambiguity found in embryonical domestic refugee laws, that alternately labelled them *'exilés', 'refugiés', 'proscrits',* or *'émigrants'*.[173]

Despite the best efforts of the president of the peace society in Geneva, the critical asylum question continued to fester, until it brought Switzerland on the brink of war in the summer of 1838. By far the most serious war scare with France, the half-paralysed count once more took to his pen, as the nation was in uproar and the militias of several cantons were mobilising, ready to meet the French troops which had taken up position all across the frontier. The immediate cause this time had been French demands to extradite Louis-Napoléon Bonaparte (1808–1873), who had returned from the United States after a failed coup two years earlier. France's claims again rested on a weak legal basis, as the prince had been naturalized into a citizen of Thurgau, and this topic still fell under cantonal sovereignty, according to the Pact.[174] However, just like before, French ire was directed to the entire confederation, causing Sellon to fume that the Parisian *Journal des*

171 Ibid., all of the questions were listed in an unnumbered and folded attachment to this document. Vattel, *Droit des gens. Tome premier* 1830, 68–9 (§ 26 – § 28), 338 (§ 93); Klüber, *Droit des gens. Tome premier*, 33–4 (§ 21).

172 In practice, this could very much be done. Klüber, *Droit des gens. Tome second* 1831, 149–52 (§ 318 – § 319).

173 Vattel, *Droit des gens. Tome premier* 1830, 343–45 (§ 101 – § 104§ 101 – § 104); Sylvie Aprile, 'L'accueil des réfugiés en Europe au XIXe siècle. Des lois pour assister ou pour renvoyer'. *Monde(s)* 1 (2019), 15, 31.

174 Hermann, *Genève* 2003, 207–8; Martin, *Suisse* 1963, 256.

débats confused a sovereign canton with a French *département*.[175] As previously, Sellon used the incident to push for a European arbitral tribunal that could decide on such issues, though he pressed for the king of Prussia's mediation in the meantime.[176] Calling defensive war a God-given natural right, he endorsed the Diet's refusal to yield, although he was much relieved that loyalty to the 'national honour' did not require bloodshed in the end, because the nephew of the old emperor had decided to quit the country voluntarily.[177]

3 Reception

Sellon's inability to disavow defensive force to defend Switzerland's sovereignty set him apart from the contemporary Anglo-American peace movement, but it did not prevent him from maintaining excellent ties with the two big peace societies of his time. From the very beginning, he had initiated a correspondence with them lasting until his decease. Apart from some letters and assorted Anglo-American publications preserved in his archive, this showed itself in the pages of the periodicals of the Anglophone peace societies.[178] The British *Herald of Peace* regularly published the count's letters or delivered updates of his activities in the 'Foreign Intelligence' section.[179] Although more difficult because of the great geographical distance, the U.S. *Advocate of Peace* likewise thought very highly of its distant ally.

175 Jean-Jacques de Sellon, *À MM. les journalistes de tous les pays* (Genève: unknown publisher 1838), 1.

176 Jean-Jacques de Sellon, *Nouveaux mélanges politiques, moraux et littéraires n° 4* (Genève: Gruaz 1838), cxiii–cxiv.

177 It is worth mentioning in this context that Sellon had overt Bonapartists sympathies. Of course, critics did not fail to notice the absurdity of a 'friend of peace' admiring Napoleon. The count was little bothered by this. See also chapter 4. *Lettre du comte de Sellon*, in [Archives d'état de Genève, Famille Revilliod-de Sellon fonds], Archives privées 18.4.1.44; Hermann, *Genève* 2003, 206–8 ; Sellon, *Lettre du fondateur* 1833, 14–5; Sellon, *Fragmens Matter* 1833, 57; Rens and Klaus-Gerd, 'Précurseur' 1985, 263; Paul-Émile Schazmann, 'Le comte Jean-Jacques de Sellon, philanthrope suisse'. *Larousse mensuel* 365 (1937), 748.

178 Sellon, *Lettre à l'éditeur* 1832, 5; see also the documents in [Archives d'état de Genève, Famille Revilliod-de Sellon fonds], Archives privées 18.3.5.34, 18.3.5.35, 18.3.5.36, 18.3.5.37, and 18.3.6].

179 E.g. HP (October 1839), 368–72. Sellon was mentioned in almost every issue. See other references in chapter 2.

The Americans even believed Sellon had personally helped prevent civil war, rather overestimating their new honorary member's political clout.[180]

In spite of these ties, it was remarkable that there appeared to be little intellectual exchange between Sellon and the Anglo-American societies. This observation does not refer to the material exchange of physical documents, which seemed to have been copious. The British and Americans sent plenty of copies of their journals, pamphlets, and books, some of which Sellon kept for himself, but much of which he sought to spread further, even if most of it still ended up in local libraries such as the *Société de lecture de Genève*.[181] Likewise, the count sent much of his output abroad, some of which was reprinted in full in their journals, though far from all of it.[182]

It does, however, remain uncertain to what extent the count had actually read and absorbed these sometimes sizeable English-language works, as they did not seem to have been quoted in any way, despite containing relevant suggestions on a congress of nations and legal reform, like for example Thomas Upham's *Manual of Peace* or Ladd's *Dissertation on a Congress of Nations*. The scheme by Ladd especially advocated for a 'court of nations' distinct from the 'congress of nations' itself, similar to the domestic function of the United States Supreme Court.[183] Sellon, by contrast, did not mention any international judicial court, because he passed away before his American counterpart adopted this distinction himself. Only around 1839 did Ladd begin to talk about a 'high court of nations'. Ladd's thought was influenced by political, cultural, and legal factors that were much more alien to the Swiss aristocrat. While the latter worshiped Henri IV, Americans contrasted their own congress to the old *Grand Dessein*, which they portrayed as too reliant on physical compulsion. U.S. pacifism was opposed to the use of force to enforce international law, out of religious reasons. They turned toward the U.S. constitution and its clear separation of judicial and legislative powers.[184]

The domestical analogies between Switzerland and the United States were fundamentally different. Neither the American veneration of the U.S.

180 The Calumet (July & August 1834), 59; AP (June 1840), 148.

181 Jean-Jacques de Sellon, *Programme d'un concours ouvert par le fondateur de la société de la paix de Genève, et faisant suite à celui qui indiquait: les meilleurs moyens de procurer une paix générale et permanente* (Genève: unknown publisher 1836), 6; Sellon, *Qu'est-ce que?* 1835, 8–9.

182 The Calumet (March & April 1834), 570–3; The Calumet (July & August 1833), 440–1; HP (July, August & September 1833), 426–7.

183 Receipt of these works was confirmed in Sellon, *Programme* 1835, 6–7.

184 See chapter 1.

constitution, nor non-resistance featured much in the mind of this Swiss nobleman. His experience with public law was with the amalgam of emphatically sovereign Swiss cantonal polities, many of which did not yet possess a separation of powers, further destabilised by imminent internal and external threats. Together with his elitism, his idealisation of the militia, or his deference to older plans, Sellon sketched a plan for peace he considered viable in Swiss and European politics, where rivalrous aristocratic elites still held most sway in foreign policy.

Unfortunately for the count, his society suffered from the same scepticism and snide remarks that befell virtually all peace friends of the nineteenth century. It could be gleaned from his own offhand complaints that peace activism was not just reserved for 'wealthy men'.[185] The press campaign was similarly not completely successful, as some of his pieces were rejected due to repetitiveness.[186] The nobleman complained that well-meaning philanthropists like himself often met with 'a disdainful silence' or 'some sarcastic epigram'.[187] Although his last will and testament stipulated for the *Archives* to be published for another ten years upon his decease, this was not meant to be.[188] Having spent little effort building anything even resembling a broad base of support – unlike the Anglo-American peace societies – his society fell apart immediately upon his death in 1839. Sellon's successor, Henri Boissier (1762–1845), neglected his responsibilities, never convening another meeting of the peace society, despite pressure from Sellon's widow Cécile de Sellon (1792–1863). The *Advocate* continued to refer to the Genevan Peace Society for a while, until the American Peace Society's annual report of 1841 concluded they had heard little from their Swiss friends since the passing of the 'great and good' Genevan count. The little 'flame' in the heart of Europe seemed to be extinguished.[189]

Unknown to the Americans, it remained smouldering. Interestingly, this small light was carried on by the women of the Sellon family. Though it could not be fully substantiated earlier, it has already been suggested that his widow had used some of her husband's money to finance *La paix des*

---

185 Sellon, *Résumé des efforts* 1836, 9; Sellon, *Lettre sur le Pacte Fédéral et sur les travaux des sociétés de la paix* 1832, 39.

186 The present author, having read nearly all of them, can attest to this. Luginbühl, *Plädoyer* 2000, 34.

187 Sellon, *Lettre sur le différend* 1836, 14.

188 Sellon's testaments and codicils are preserved in [Archives d'état de Genève, Famille Revilliod-de Sellon fonds], Archives privées 18.1.1.

189 Rens and Klaus-Gerd, 'Précurseur' 1985, 284–285; Sellon, *Programme* 1835, 5; AP (June 1840), 148; AP (June 1841), 19.

deux mondes in 1844, the periodical of one France's first peace societies, the *Société de la paix de Paris*, that was co-founded by Eugénie Niboyet (1796–1883), a rare early female peace friend.[190] The discovery of issues of this paper, as well as other post–1839 peace writings, in Sellon's archive reinforces this hypothesis.[191] Indeed, decades later, his youngest daughter Valentine de Sellon (1823–1904) had not forgotten her father's idealism, appearing at the 1878 congress of Frédéric *Passy's Société des amis de la paix*, which she interpreted as a vindication of her father's vision.[192] A poet, countess Valentine agitated against capital punishment and war in her writings. She appeared to have been reasonably well-informed about the peace activism of her generation. She interpreted the movement's growth and the conversion of many specialists of international law to pacifist ideas as indications that the dream of Henri IV and Saint-Pierre, as was reinterpreted by her old father, and now by the *Alabama claims* or the *Institut de droit international*, was slowly becoming a reality.[193]

The count himself, however, was fading into obscurity. By the early twentieth century, not all peace friends had forgotten the Genevan society, but when they cared to mention it, they did so only for antiquarian purposes, or to emphasise the long history of the movement. Often, they merely noted with fascination that the 'now barely remembered' society had received a letter from the Prussian king.[194] Few if any of its tactics had been explicitly adopted, apart from the notion that law should restrain the use of force. This was understandable. Its historical Swiss context had disappeared, the war of the *Sonderbund* having ended in a resounding victory of the federalists. Inside the larger peace movement, pacifism had largely abandoned old hierarchical visions of imposed arbitration, having turned to voluntary arbitration on a bilateral basis, guided by a reformed legal code. This had been the course adopted by the Anglo-American societies from the 1840s

---

190 Van der Linden, *Peace Movement* 1987, 213.

191 Her papers also included letters from Frédéric Passy and Hodgson Pratt. [Archives d'état de Genève, Famille Revilliod-de Sellon fonds], Archives privées 18.1.2.8.

192 Valentine de Sellon, *Discours prononcé par la comtesse Valentine de Sellon au banquet d'honneur du congrès international de la paix offert par le comité français au comité étrangers le 4 octobre 1878* (Paris: Hennuyer 1878), 3.

193 Both are discussed in chapters 6 and 7. Valentine de Sellon, *La peine de mort au vingtième siècle* (Paris: Guillaumin 1877), 37–38; Valentine de Sellon, *Feuilles éparses* (Paris: Guillaumin 1878), 70–71; Valentine de Sellon, *Comptes-rendus de la presse sur les écrits de Valentine de Sellon. Lettres tirées de sa correspondance* (Paris: Dentu 1882), 8.

194 L'Indépendance belge (2 January 1898) 2–3; Alfred Fried, *Handbuch der Friedensbewegung* (Berlin: Verlag der Friedens-Warte 1911), 60.

onwards, and later stimulated by the milestone *Alabama claims* arbitration. While some pacifists still supported federative forms of peace, this was by the late nineteenth century connected to domestic justice in in a more radical way than ever conceived by the count. When a new peace society was born in Geneva in 1867, the new League was set on abolishing monarchy everywhere. They were firm republicans, uninterested in the writings of a dead aristocrat obsessed with a king who had been dead even longer.[195]

Sellon's concern for international organisation reappeared in international law and the international peace movement with the outbreak of the Great War, which all the world's arbitration clauses had failed to prevent. Collective security regulated by a permanent institution was born with the League of Nations. Though most unlikely that the old count had been actively in the minds of its creators, some pacifist jurists in the interbellum were involved in remembrance activities of this 'precursor', including Henri La Fontaine (1854–1943), Christian Lange (1869–1938), and Hans Wehberg (1885–1962).[196] The Genevan Count had been an embodiment of the 'spirit of Geneva', that had also seen the rise of the Red Cross, the Alabama arbitration and the League of Nations.[197] Even later, Sandi Cooper has labelled Sellon's pacifist campaign 'an uncanny collection of ideas that prefigured most of the thinking of continental peace activists for decades to come'. While this was not untrue, she has also claimed that to him, 'he heart of an organized peace was a permanent tribunal staffed with trained jurists'.[198]

This chapter has contextualised and corrected this. Despite its overlaps with Anglo-American peace activism, or European peace activism as it began to gradually emerge in the decades after his death, Sellon's early legalist 'war on war' remained in many important respects distinct. Shaped by specific cultural-historical contexts, the risk has been real that certain key

---

195 See chapter 7. ASPG (August 1837), 16–7.

196 Lange, 'Histoire de la doctrine pacifique' 1923, 37; Die Friedens-Warte (n° 12, 1930/30), 354–6; Die Friedens-Warte (n° 2, 1931/31), 42;

197 Claims that Henri Dunant had been influenced by Sellon have always been unsubstantiated. Henri Dunant's philanthropism was very different from that of Sellon. The count called the idea that war could be regulated 'a dangerous illusion'. ASPG (August 1837), 49; Robert de Traz, *L'esprit de Genève. Préface d'Alfred Dufour* (Lausanne: Éditions l'Age d'Homme 1995), 11, 31–2; Mützenberg, 'Une société' 1992, 286; Rens and Klaus-Gerd, 'Précurseur' 1985, 286; Die Friedens-Warte (n° 7/8, 1930/30), 221; Gabriel Mützenberg, 'David Dunant, oncle et précurseur du fondateur de la Croix-Rouge'. *Revue suisse d'histoire* 30(3) (1980), 381–3; David Dunant, *Aux mânes de Jean-Jacques comte de Sellon, citoyen de Genève, philanthrope par excellence* (Genève: Gruaz 1839).

198 Cooper, *Patriotic Pacifism* 1991, 19–20.

FIGURE 3.2 One of several lithographs of the obelisk that the count sent abroad and gave to visitors.

terminology within its propaganda could be misread. Though he had not accomplished any of his impossibly grand goals, the story of count Jean-Jacques de Sellon illustrated the peculiar conditions under which a peace society could emerge on the European mainland already in the 1830s, the normative arguments it could imagine, and the pitfalls it would inevitably encounter. Like other European examples to follow, Sellon was proof that a pacifist legal 'sensibility' already existed earlier in the century, decades before the birth of academic institutes of international law and the professionalisation of the discipline.

Testament to that legacy, a few whispers of Sellon's zeal linger to this day. One is the obelisk, which today still stands in the *Cimetière des rois,* reserved for Geneva's most accomplished citizens. Another can be found among the trees and peacocks of the Ariana park surrounding the seat of the United Nations in Geneva. Likely few if any of the diplomats, lawyers, and employees of N.G.O.s realise that their offices overlook the house where once walked a man dreaming of great kings of the past, wishing for a better future, a house that he called *La Fenêtre.*

CHAPTER 4

France (1815–1867)

'Association européenne… Code européen… Institut européen… Famille européenne!…'

FRANCISQUE BOUVET (1853)

1 Pacifism and French Society

On 15 December 1840, the people of Paris crowded together on the streets of their proud capital. Passers-by had to shuffle through a flurry of high hats, umbrellas and shoulders if they wanted to catch a glimpse of the cortège that solemnly crawled its way towards the imposing *Hôtel des Invalides*. Completing the scenery were the banners, military trophies and incense burners that lined the road on both sides of the procession. Clearly, the city's officials had spared no expense to emphasise the pomp and circumstance of the occasion. Most British subjects residing in the French capital had understood its covert political implications and had wisely quit the city beforehand. Anglo-French tensions had risen considerably since the Syrian Crisis of that same year had diplomatically isolated France from the other great powers.[1] Escalating into a war-scare with the German Confederation over the left bank of the Rhine, Paris was at the same time being enveloped by a string of impressive fortifications.[2] One of the rare British witnesses to the return of Napoleon I, legendary emperor of the French, to his homeland therefore likened it more to 'the car of a mighty conqueror returning in triumph to the capital', than to any ordinary funeral.[3]

The man in question was Stephen Rigaud (1777–1861), an English painter from Huguenot descent. Acting as the London Peace Society's principal European travelling agent, he intermittently toured the Continent between 1840 and 1847, until financial and other difficulties forced the British peace

1 Šedivý, *Crisis* 2017, 49–113.
2 Šedivý, *Decline* 2018, 125–43.
3 HP (April 1841), 282.

 | DOI:10.1163/9789004733688_006

friends to no longer renew the expensive contract.[4] During his extensive travels, Rigaud succeeded in founding a number of small peace societies in Europe, usually fairly short-lived. In Belgium, for instance, he launched societies in Brussels and Mons, sowing seeds from which Elihu Burritt would benefit when he began his peace conference campaign a while later, in 1848.[5] Although this British agent also proselytized in places like Holland, Switzerland, and several of the German states, his first stop was typically France – gateway to the Continent and seat to its most prestigious lingua franca.[6]

The British and American pacifist publicists considered this large and powerful European country, maybe somewhat paradoxically, as both the most progressive and the most war-like Western state, and therefore as the logical focal point of their European effort. As mentioned in previous chapters, many of the Anglo-American proposals of the 1830s and 1840s in favour of a congress of nations or stipulated arbitration consciously included France as the chief state to be incorporated into the envisioned legal system, right after, or along with, Britain and the United States themselves. They placed the July Monarchy among 'the three constitutional nations of the world'.[7] After all, the reign of Louis-Philippe d'Orléans as *roi des français* – as opposed to *roi de France* – was marked by relatively greater political freedoms than under the Restoration. His governments had also repeatedly showed their desire to maintain peace in Europe, as expressed in the *entente cordiale* with the British empire. This gave the Anglo-American peace societies reason to assume that the French intelligentsia might be receptive to their campaign.[8]

At the same time, domestic unrest in France repeatedly disturbed many outside of France's borders. The opposition against Louis-Philippe ranged from legitimists seeking to restore the Bourbons, to Bonapartists rallying around Louis-Napoléon, to myriad republican and socialist factions, favouring moderate to radical reforms in such delicate issues as suffrage or

4 Most attention and funding between 1848 and 1851 went to the European peace conferences. HP (April 1841), 281; Ceadel, *Origins* 1996, 288–9, 393; Van der Linden, *Peace Movement* 1987, 206.

5 Lubelski-Bernard, *Mouvements pacifistes en Belgique* 1977, 325–334.

6 Most of the tracts of the London Peace Society were translated into French. An overview can be found in ter Meulen, *Bibliographies* 1990, 78–103.

7 A phrase used by George Gibbes, *A Letter to the American Peace Society* (Paris: Brière 1842), 27. Gibbes was first mentioned in chapter 2. He took part in the 1843 Anglo-American peace conference in London.

8 Guy Antonetti, *Louis-Philippe* (Paris: Fayard 1994), 461–7, 645–60.

property laws.[9] France's inability to stabilise these societal fault lines provoked two revolutions and a coup d'état, while the political system veered from constitutional monarchy, to republican experiment, to authoritarian rule under another Bonaparte. Although declining birth rates hindered France's historic ability to regenerate large military forces, many French also still prided themselves on the great military victories of the Revolutionary and Napoleonic eras.[10] Coupled with recurring war-scares, or the colonial adventure in Algeria, many British feared that the spectre of revolution and conquest was still alive. Napoleonic trauma continued to haunt the popular imagination of the British world to the extent that even the American Peace Society – affected by wider Anglophone bias – described France as 'a warlike and most powerful nation' to king Louis-Philippe himself.[11] In 1822, the London Peace Society repeated their countrymen's distaste for their old adversary by calling it 'a nation where the spirit of war and military triumph were objects of almost universal devotion, where scepticism and unbelief in Christianity had obtained almost universal sway'. Those old prejudices would die hard.[12]

Despite its reputation among contemporary British and Americans, France was not as inhospitable to organised peace activism as might be expected. On the one hand, a popular military culture was very much alive in nearly all social strata, just as it was in any other major European state. Stephen Rigaud recounted that, at the height of the Rhine Crisis, a Sunday school boy came strutting up to his teacher and confidently asserted *"Il nous faut la guerre"* "Why so?", said the teacher. *"Notre honneur est blessé"*.[13] On the other hand, debates on the topic of war and peace intermittently flared up. Until the breakthrough of homegrown peace associations in 1867, however, these exchanges remained confined almost exclusively to a few

9 Gabriel de Broglie, *La monarchie de Juillet 1830–1848* (Paris: Fayard 2011), 57–88; Pierre Rosanvallon, *La démocratie inachevée* (Paris: Gallimard 2000), 141–167.

10 Christophe Charle (transl. Miriam Kochan). *A Social History of France in the Nineteenth Century* (Oxford: Berg 1994), 8–26.

11 In a letter presented by Rigaud to the king himself. *Journal de la Société de la Morale Chrétienne* (hereafter: JSMC) (III° série, tome II, n° 1), 3; see also Gibbes, *Letter* 1842, 4.

12 In 1841, the Society of Christian Morals was annoyed that so many seemed surprised by the fact that Frenchmen were holding an essay competition on peace: 'One seems to believe everywhere that we are always a turbulent and effervescent people, incapable of wisdom, and incompatible, so to speak, with public peace.' JSMC (série II, tome XIX, n° 5), 266. Van der Linden, *Peace Movement* 1987, 67; HP (November 1819), 324–5; HP (April-May-June 1822), 67–8.

13 AP (August 1843), 89.

inner circles of intellectuals.[14] It was in these intellectual circles that the London Peace Society wished to ingratiate itself with Rigaud's missions. While the English agent may have been met only with 'bitter invectives against England' in the Parisian *cafés* that cold December, he found a far warmer welcome in the secluded meeting rooms of the *Société de la morale chrétienne*.[15] A philanthropical society that had styled itself from its inception as also a peace society, it only installed a dedicated peace committee in early 1841, upon the concrete request of Rigaud.

This chapter explores the chief varieties of organised peace activism, such as they existed, in France prior to the 1867 Luxembourg Crisis, which traditionally heralds the beginning of French pacifism in historiography.[16] Hardly any legal histories thus far seem to exist on the myriad French publicists who wrote in the early and mid-century.[17] General histories of pacifism similarly pay only limited, or hardly any, attention to the French case, due to the predominance of the Anglo-American peace societies.[18] Specialised histories of continental-European pacifism include the well-known ones by van der Linden and Cooper, although another study of some note was penned by Vanessa Lincoln-Lambert.[19] In her excellent, yet sadly unpublished doctoral dissertation, she focuses exclusively on the intricacies of the French peace movement up until 1853. Though the monograph eschews legal analysis in favour of social and intellectual history, it does provide a useful analytical framework to define and select the relevant actors for any narrative about a political space that did not contain a straightforward set of 'peace societies', unlike the Anglo-American world or Switzerland.[20]

In keeping with a functional definition of organised peace work, set out in the general introduction, the early French peace movement can be subdivided into a number of distinct categories. The first one relates to the religious foundations of its activism. This one chiefly includes authors connected to the aforementioned Society of Christian Morals. A second category turns to so-called economic friends of peace, and incorporates French varieties of free trade and laisser-faire economic policies. These

14 Nadine-Josette Chaline, *Empêcher la guerre. Le pacifisme du début du XIXe siècle à la veille de la Seconde Guerre mondiale* (Amiens: Encrage 2015), 16.

15 AP (August 1843, 89); HP (April 1841), 282.

16 See chapter 7.

17 A relative exception are the articles of Carol Bergami, cited infra.

18 The American authors Janis and Lynch, cited previously, barely discuss non-English speaking contemporaries.

19 Lincoln, *French Peace Movement* 2013.

20 Ibid., 9–10.

authors mostly came into the fold around the time of the 1849 Paris peace conference. The third category of Lincoln-Lambert, that of the so-called 'political' publicists, is not maintained here. As our story centres on legal analysis, all publicists from every category could be seen as 'political'. Rather, our third category consists of the earliest French attempts to establish peace societies, again inspired by the Anglo-American example. Interestingly, one of the seminal figures here was female: the indomitable Eugénie Niboyet, who escaped traditional discriminations against women in the early peace movement. Finally, for the 1850s and 1860s, there are those publicists who wrote under the restrictions of the Second Empire. As always, the categories are made for the sake of narrative cohesion, and remain somewhat artificial, since most French peace friends, like anywhere else, were animated by intersecting motivations. Their views also did not always remain static over the years.

One school of authors that might seem to be notably missing from this chapter are the early French 'utopian' socialists. In the mid-century, these mostly included the disciples of Henri de Saint-Simon (1760–1825), author of a plan for perpetual peace in 1814, and Charles Fourier (1772–1837), known for his vision of a society consisting of self-governing *phalanstères*. Though fluctuating across time, the schools of thought they instigated were generally far more divided on the peace question than most 'proper' peace friends. As argued by both van der Linden and Lincoln-Lambert, a significant number of Saint-Simonians still fancied the notion that 'one last war' could remodel international society, setting an agenda greatly beyond the pale for the moderate reformists involved in the peace movement. Organisationally, few convinced Saint-Simonians took part in the events or intellectual exchanges of the international peace movement. The only two Saint-Simonians who attended the peace conferences were jeered when they praised the Concert of Europe, or advocated for military intervention in support of foreign revolutions.[21] Fourier likewise flirted with violent revolt, rejected Saint-Pierre's peace plan, and was overall more interested in domestic social reform.[22]

Among later socialist intellectuals, the anarchical Pierre-Joseph Proudhon (1809–1865) was openly critical of the peace movement, disbelieving that peace could flow from the actions of Quakers and lawyers. The economists sympathetic to the peace movement in turn scorned Proudhon as *'roi des*

21 See chapter 5.

22 Lincoln, *French Peace Movement* 2013, 24–27.

utopistes'.[23] The attitudes of the First International were also ambivalent, but predominantly critical, especially those of Karl Marx (1818–1883).[24] Nonetheless, even if these socialist schools could not be considered part of the peace movement, several of the individuals discussed in this chapter were influenced by socialist ideas and concerns.

For the same reasons, the republicans who seized power in 1848 could on the whole not be equated with the international peace movement. Like the socialists – with whom there were many overlaps – republicans believed that the mainstream breakthrough of their ideology would stimulate general pacification. However, many rejected strictly non-violent means towards this end, or did not engage with the peace societies of Britain and America. The most significant French republican connected to the larger peace movement was Francisque Bouvet. The international peace movement came to face ardent French republicanism most intensely – and controversially – in 1867.[25]

French peace advocates therefore arguably met with a more hostile political climate than their peers in Britain or the United States. The conservative ruling elites, radical republicans, and revolutionary socialists all endorsed or tolerated the legitimacy of force, domestically and internationally. Joseph de Maistre (1753–1821) philosophically articulated a popular view that glorified war as part of divine natural law.[26] Non-violent Christian sects were all but non-existent, Quakers being seen as quaint curiosities.[27] For extended periods of time, public meetings and the liberty of the press were subject to severe restrictions. To campaign for non-violent international reform meant to expose oneself on multiple fronts. Yet, in spite of these adverse conditions, French peace advocates still managed to develop

23 Francisque Bouvet, who did attend the peace conferences, likewise rebutted Proudhon. Francisque Bouvet, *Lettre adressée à citoyen Proudhon* (Bourg: Milliet-Bottier 1849); Journal des économistes (hereafter: JE) (1849, tome 24), 173; JE (1850, tome 26), 84; Pierre-Joseph Proudhon, *La guerre et la paix. Recherches sur le principe et la constitution du droit des gens* (Paris: Lévy Frères 1861), 381–2; Pierre-Joseph Proudhon, *Du principe fédératif et de la nécessité de reconstituer le parti de la révolution* (Paris: Dentu 1863), 88.

24 See chapter 7.

25 See again chapter 7.

26 Stephan Nitz, *Theorien des Friedens und des Krieges. Kommentierte Bibliographie zur Theoriegeschichte. Band I: Altertum bis 1830* (Baden-Baden: Nomos 2010), 464–70.

27 Even Garnier could not help himself from commenting on the dress of the British Quakers, especially their hats. See for instance JE (1851, tome 29), 324.

their own distinctive set of normative solutions, as they navigated between the prevailing forces of monarchy, republic and empire.

2 Imagining Peace after Napoleon

Any educated Frenchman would have been either amused or insulted by the suggestion that British or American evangelicals were uniquely prescient or enlightened on the peace question. Had France after all not been at the forefront of civilisation in the past century? Had their nation not produced the *philosophes* and the Revolution that had swept across the continent, destroying ancient privileges and empires? One of the most common motifs in French peace literature in the nineteenth century was the leading role reserved for the French nation in the reform of international law and politics. Carol Bergami has underlined the centrality of the domestic political model in the argument of the mid-century French peace friends. Peace was presumed to emerge from the export of the French political-legal model to the rest of Europe and the wider world.[28] This rather striking characteristic of French peace publications was dubbed by van der Linden – a Dutch author – as 'typically French idealistic or revolutionary chauvinism'.[29]

Whatever one's personal appreciation, it can hardly be denied that French *amis de la paix* had a rich intellectual prehistory to draw from. In the eighteenth century, a clearly discernible anti-war stance had emerged, which was visible, among other places, in Diderot's and d'Alemberts *Encyclopédie.* Its entry on peace was among the first to define peace as the 'normal' state of humanity, and war as a blight upon the international body politic.[30] By then, Saint-Pierre had long published his ideas for perpetual peace. When the Revolution broke out, a fundamental debate broke out among its leading politicians and intellectuals. Summarising the study of Marc Bélissa, two broad factions emerged in this period. Both were agreed that citizens had to universally 'reconquer' their rights from the *ancien*

28 Carol Bergami, 'Européisme et cosmopolitisme. D'une spécificité européenne dans le pacifisme français des années 1840'. *La Contemporaine* 2012/4(108) (2012), 7–12; Carol Bergami, 'Quelle démocratie pour quelle organisation internationale? Le pacifisme français et la naissance d'un constitutionnalisme républicain, 1840–1889'. *Les cahiers Irice* 2(12) (2014), 17–30.

29 In defence of the French: it is difficult not to read similar chauvinism in British or U.S. texts. Van der Linden, *Peace Movement* 1987, 111; see for example the very title of Janis, 'American Exceptionalism' 2012, 525.

30 Ghervas, *Conquering Peace* 2021, 61–65.

régime. A 'public' political space had to be carved out, to replace the private international sphere of the hated monarchical dynasties. This separated into two familiar creeds.

The first, more idealistic, line of thought held that universal brotherhood reigned supreme, giving credence to the notion of a 'cosmopolitan law of nations'. This type of reasoning relied heavily on natural law. An illustration of this in actual political debate was the unsuccessful 1790 *Déclaration du droit des gens* by the abbé Grégoire.[31] The other, rather more pragmatic, branch did not seek a drastic rupture with the past, but sought to reinforce the power of the 'nation'. Sceptical of unenforceable natural law claims, these thinkers maintained that the international order should be composed of sovereign nation-states, linked together by positive law.[32] Their conceptions of popular sovereignty left a deep mark on the nationalism of the nineteenth century.[33] They also influenced later pacifism.

The Napoleonic wars and their immediate aftermath again stimulated intellectual debates on peace and war in France. Numerous greater and smaller pamphlets and essays appeared around the time of the Congress of Vienna, written by a wide variety of individuals. Because many of these received only a limited circulation, were penned before the year 1815, or were not picked up by subsequent peace friends, these will not be discussed in detail here.[34]

One such plan, for instance, came from the lawyer J.J.B. Gondon, who published a three-volume commentary on public law and the law of nations in 1808. Gondon rejected one single federation, instead favouring an intergovernmental organisation for the pacific settlement of disputes. Among its salient features, the organisation was to include a tribunal, distinct from the legislative congress of princely ambassadors. This juridical tribunal ought to be composed of expert jurists, and had to apply the laws of nations as

31 Marc Bélissa, 'La déclaration du droit des gens de l'abbé Grégoire (juin 1793, 4 floréal an III)'. 2010, available at: revolution-francaise.net/2010/10/06/399-declaration-droit-des-gens-abbe-gregoire-juin–1793.

32 Marc Bélissa, *Fraternité universelle et intérêt national (1713–1795). Les cosmopolitiques du droit des gens* (Paris: Kimé 1998), 437–40.

33 Edward James Kolla, *Sovereignty, International Law, and the French Revolution* (Cambridge: CUP 2017), 270–98.

34 See the overviews in ter Meulen, *Gedanke 1929*, 93–153; Christian Lange and August Schou, *Histoire de l'internationalisme. Tome II. De la paix de Westphalie jusqu'au congrès de Vienne (1815)* (Oslo: Aschehoug 1954), 142–4.

codified by the congress.[35] Gondon's scheme thus, incidentally, nuances bold claims about the 'exceptional' character of the American Peace Society's congress of nations.[36]

An equally interesting aspect of Gondon's plan, however, was that it proposed emperor Napoleon taking the initiative.[37] While Anglo-American peace propaganda consistently portrayed the emperor as a monstrous mass murderer, French peace advocates maintained a far more complex relationship with their national hero. Although many Bonapartists were decidedly authoritarian, the emperor's legacy was equivocal enough to permit many on the French republican left to still identify with the progressist Jacobin aspects of his policies. This liberal connotation persisted into the reign of Louis-Napoléon Bonaparte, who insisted that the 'Napoleonic ideas' were essentially peaceful in nature.[38]

The agonies of revolution, terror and war did not engender dedicated peace societies in France the same way they did in Britain and the United States. In the archives, at least one reference was found to a self-styled *Société d'amis de la paix*, before which Nicolas de Condorcet (1743–1794) gave a lecture in 1789.[39] However, none of the histories of the French peace movement, both by contemporaries and by historians, mention it. Considering Condorcet's speech limited itself exclusively to domestic political issues, this society and any other possible 'peace societies' presumably had little to nothing in common with their nineteenth century namesakes. Only in 1821 did the first experiment emerge.

2.1 *Christian Pacifism*

That year, both the British *Herald of Peace* and the American *Friend of Peace* reported on the founding of a new peace association in France. Citing a letter from the London Peace Society, the American Noah Worcester rejoiced that 'the leaven of peace and good will is at work on the

35 J.J.B. Gondon, *Du droit public et du droit des gens, ou principes d'association civile et politique; suivis d'un projet de paix générale et perpétuelle. Tome III* (Paris: Brasseur 1807), 85–313; ter Meulen, *Gedanke 1929*, 100–9.

36 Just like Sartorius in Switzerland. See chapters 1 and 3.

37 Lange and Schou, *Histoire de l'internationalisme* 1954, 428–430.

38 'Jacobinism' in this context should be understood as policies ostensibly amenable to popular sovereignty. Frédéric Bluche, *Le bonapartisme* (Paris: Presses Universitaires de France 1981), 27–30; Sudhir Hazareesingh, *La légende de Napoléon* (Paris: Tallandier 2005), 195–229.

39 Nicolas de Condorcet, *Réflexions sur ce qui a été fait et sur ce qui reste à faire, lues dans une Société d'Amis de la paix* (Paris: imprimerie de l'Assemblée Nationale 1789).

continent'.[40] He wrote that the new society might well be regarded 'as one of the most important institutions of the present age'.[41] The humble founder of the Massachusetts Peace Society was particularly impressed by its august membership and the promise that held: 'a few men near the throne, who are imbued with pacific sentiments, may cause a great change in the policy of a nation, celebrated for its exploits in war.'[42] The London Peace Society was just as enthusiastic, later asserting that its existence should 'silence those who view as utopian' the aims of the peace movement, 'and should dispose them to at least listen to the proposal for the establishment of a Court of Nations'.[43]

The founders of the *Société de la morale chrétienne* were indeed men to be reckoned with. Their initial president, duke François-Alexandre-Frédéric de la Rochefoucauld-Liancourt (1747–1827), was the patriarch to one of France's eldest and wealthiest noble families. Upon his death, he was succeeded by his third son, marquis Frédéric Gaëtan (1779–1863).[44] Other early members belonged to similarly aristocratic circles. They included Victor de Broglie (1785–1870), member of the Chamber of Peers, Alexandre de Laborde (1773–1842), an archaeologist, and François Guizot (1787–1874), who would come to dominate French politics in the July Monarchy. They were joined by duke Louis-Philippe d'Orléans, the future king, as well as Benjamin Constant (1767–1830), Alexis de Tocqueville (1805–1859) and Alphonse de Lamartine (1790–1869).[45] All in all, the society counted about 400 members by 1829.[46] Virtually all were liberals, many also wielding considerable influence. In effect, the society constituted 'a veritable Who's Who of the leaders of the liberal opposition in the 1820s and of the future governing elite of the July Monarchy that was to follow'. Its limited size was due to the high annual membership cost of 25 francs – when the average daily wage for a worker was 2 francs – as well as the prohibition on public gatherings up until the Second Republic. Its elite composition was further reinforced by the fact that nearly a third

40 FP (1823, n° II), 68.
41 FP (1823, n° VI), 192.
42 FP (1823, n° VII), 212–213.
43 HP (January-February-March 1833), 83.
44 Van der Linden, *Peace Movement* 1987, 71–7.
45 Lincoln, *French Peace Movement* 2013, 29–30.
46 Van der Linden, *Peace Movement* 1987, 73–4.

were Protestants, vastly out of proportion to their number in the rest of the country, which was 98 percent Catholic.[47]

Even if this philanthropical club was no 'peace society' in the strict Anglo-American sense, it shared many connections with the international peace movement. The Society of Christian Morals enjoyed a close relationship with the London Peace Society from its very incipience. A British peace society member had been present at its foundational meetings, and later on, the society regularly reported on the activities of the Anglo-American peace societies in its long-running journal.[48] It maintained a polite and continuous correspondence with the British, and, to a lesser extent, the Americans and Sellon. They also published several British tracts in full in its journal, though only ever translations made by the British themselves.[49] Although this organisation had not officially titled itself a 'peace society', it afterwards repeatedly described itself as the 'true peace society of France', ranking itself, in French fashion, just below the London Peace Society, but above those of America and Geneva.[50]

Despite the Parisian society's own sense of identification with the peace societies, its personal track record in the international peace movement in its first twenty years was modest at best. In reality, the Anglo-Americans soon became relatively disillusioned with the Society of Christian Morals. Its founders had rejected the British proposal to explicitly name their society a 'peace society', because they feared it would undermine their credibility. Consequently, the British never lent it any financial support and preferred to view it as a kind of 'auxiliary', rather than a peace society.[51] Indeed, until Rigaud's visit, the society was far more concerned with issues such as orphans, urban poverty, and anti-slavery, all of which had separate committees. The eventual peace committee also never hosted any independent activities, apart from its initial essay competition, funded entirely by the British.

Ideologically, the concern of the French society with peace was nonetheless more or less authentic, manifest from its frequently recurring discussions of the topic, and their consistent refusal to simply co-opt the positions

47 Lawrence Charles Jennings, *French Anti-Slavery. The Movement for the Abolition of Slavery in France, 1802–1848* (Cambridge, CUP 2000), 9–54; Lincoln, *French Peace Movement* 2013, 31–2.

48 Van der Linden, *Peace Movement* 1987, 71–3.

49 For instance the tract by the 'Lady'. JSMC (I° série, tome VIII, n° 44), 81–112.

50 JSMC (II° série, tome XIV, n° 2), 145–146.

51 Van der Linden, *Peace Movement* 1987, 75.

of the Anglo-American peace societies. Non-resistance did not exist in France, just like it did not in the rest of Europe. Upon the death of Mathieu-Guillaume-Thérèse Villenave (1762–1846), the lawyer who had served as the first president of the peace committee, the society applauded that he had never seen pacifism as 'rigorous and absolute, like a mathematical principle applicable everywhere and always, without distinction'.[52] When non-resistance was advocated in a translated British tract, the society added a footnote that it did not share this British conviction.[53]

Contrary to what its name might suggest, the society relied far more on secular argumentation than its 'sister' organisations in Britain or America. This did not entail that religion was wholly absent in its propaganda – Niboyet won second prize in the society's essay contest to prove the existence of God – but rather that they approached the subject from a different theological standpoint. Whereas many of the leading Anglo-American publicists could be highly doctrinarian in their interpretation of scripture, the Society of Christian Morals was generally more concerned with a more immediate, 'practical', Christianity. Instead of sin and damnation, they paid more attention to the consequences of war for those still living. As their journal put it: 'for us, the love of peace is more a humanitarian than a religious thought, whereas in London, Manchester, Boston and Philadelphia, religion is more powerful than the humanitarian thought'.[54] Consequently, pacification arguments considered to be 'lower ground' from the Anglo-American point of view, abounded more and earlier in French texts than in contemporary English-language ones.

Nonetheless, the society devoted only limited attention to international law prior to 1841. Although the opening issue of its journal already mentioned the pacification plans of Henri IV, William Penn and Saint-Pierre, it never entered into any greater detail other than that all three had proposed some form of *'congrès général'* that would arbiter among states, to prevent war. While praising the objective of these authors, the journal's contributors usually also recognised that these schemes were seen as impracticable

---

52 JSMC (III° série, tome VII, n° 3), 132; Jean-Marie Quérard, *La France littéraire, ou dictionnaire bibliographique. Tome dixième* (Paris: Didot frères 1839), 183–8.

53 JSMC (I° série, tome VIII, n° 48), 365.

54 In a telling anecdote, Villenave once came into conflict with a British peace friend for holding the annual meeting on a Sunday. JSMC (III° série, tome VII, n° 3), 136; Société de la morale chrétienne, *XXIVe séance générale annuelle* (Paris: Bureau de la société de la morale chrétienne 1845), 34–35; Lincoln, *French Peace Movement* 2013, 39.

utopias by most commentators.[55] In legal doctrine, the society similarly did not seek to dramatically overturn existing custom. The French sympathisers contented themselves with the observation that Christianity had already historically softened the laws of war. Intellectuals like the bishop Bossuet (1627–1704) were credited with moral improvements that had led to legal changes: 'he gave birth to a certain law of nations; war will have its laws; the fury of combat, its limits; and victory, its magnanimity'.[56] Some of the clergymen connected to the society occasionally preached on peace, but only through a religious lens. The well-known Protestant pastor Athanase Coquerel *père* (1795–1868), the translator during the Paris peace congress, preached that Christendom could only know peace through faith.[57]

2.1.1 Prize Essays of the Peace Committee

This changed after Rigaud's visit in early 1841. At its inception, the peace committee's primary task was to oversee the concours suggested by the London Peace Society, in response to the dangerous war-scare produced by the Rhine Crisis.[58] To encourage French participation, the London society had set aside the sizeable sum of 1,250 francs. A thousand francs were to be awarded to the winner, a hundred to the runner-up, the remainder covering organisational expenses. Under such generous conditions, the organisation readily agreed. The marquis himself initially led his newest committee, although its day-to-day leader quickly became the already mentioned Villenave. Its fifteen members also included Rigaud, representing the London Peace Society, as well as politicians like Alphonse de Lamartine, author of the *Marseillaise de la paix,* and Hyppolite Carnot (1801–1888), another soon-to-be leading man in the Second Republic. Among the others sat three clergymen and five *avocats*.[59] Unfortunately, this Committee soon became mostly inactive. Its original members would erect an independent, yet equally short-lived, Parisian Peace Society in 1844.[60]

The organisers of this essay contest were aided by the fact that a similar contest was, in fact, already underway. Henri Grégoire (1750–1831), one of the leading clerical figures of the French Revolution, had left a thousand

55 JSMC (1° série, tome I, n° 1), 44–5.

56 JSMC (1° série, tome VII, n° 40), 218, 226, 244.

57 Athanase Coquerel, *Sermons de A.L.C. Coquerel* (Amsterdam: Delachaux 1819), 195; Athanase Coquerel, *Sermons par Athanase Coquerel* (Paris: Cherbuliez, 1843), 212–213.

58 Société de la morale chrétienne, *XXIV*^{e} *séance générale annuelle* 1845, 11–12.

59 JSMC (série II, tome 19, n° 1), 5–9; *Proceedings Paris* 1849, 2.

60 See infra in this chapter.

francs in his will for the best essay on the civic duties of the military.[61] Hyppolite Carnot, the executor of the old *abbé's* testament, had entrusted it to the Society of Christian Morals. As had been the case with similar contests elsewhere, the affair dragged on for years, because a lack of suitable entries caused the deadline to be pushed back again and again, so that it was still running in 1841, despite having originally started in 1837. Only three essays were ever sent in for Grégoire's concours. Because of this, as well as their similar subject matters, the society decided to award both prizes to the same essays at the annual meeting of 1842.[62]

Villenave wrote an elaborate jury report on the main contest, the one backed by the London Peace Society. In contrast to the long-running contest of the American Peace Society of the 1830s, but similar to the British contest, this one had not specifically asked contenders to reason in favour of a congress of nations. Instead, it generally asked them to expound 'the means to achieve universal and permanent peace'. Perhaps inspired by Anglo-American examples, the society further specified that authors had to address this large question in three parts. Mirroring the structure of the English-language prize essays, authors first had to show that war was both hostile to the Christian religion, as well as to 'feelings of humanity' and the 'prosperity of nations'. As the jury report admitted, these first two were not difficult to argue. However, it was the third part, on the best means to pacifically settle disputes among states, which was clearly 'the least easy one, but also the most important one'. Villenave thought that on this issue, 'still for a long time, perhaps, chimeras of idealism and utopias of virtue will reveal themselves'. He showed himself a good deal more sceptical than the Americans: 'all that can reasonably be expected, is the work, which most satisfyingly establishes not the next reality of success, but its possibility in the more or less distant future.' The mere act of introducing a pacific alternative to the civilised world, Villenave mused, *'c'est déjà un progrès'*.[63]

Out of twenty-four submissions, two received a money prize. The most important one was written by Constantin Pecqueur (1801–1887), a socialist journalist. In 1839, he had earned some intellectual respectability when he took home the annual prize of the *Académie des sciences morales et*

61 Another such posthumous contest was on the best means to 'cure' artists of their tendency towards obsequiousness. Van der Linden, *Peace Movement* 1987, 208.

62 JSMC (série II, tome XIX, n° II), 65–7; JSMC (série II, tome XXII, n° 3), 121–30.

63 Jury report included in Patrice Bazan, *D'une paix universelle et permanente* (Paris: Baudouin 1842), xi–xv; JSMC (série II, tome XIX, n° 1), 3–4.

politiques, for a treatise on political economy.[64] Born into a bourgeois family in the north of France, he moved to Paris in this early twenties. There, the writer flirted with both Saint-Simonianism and Fourierism. Eventually, he drifted away from both traditions to become an independent socialist. By the 1840s, he was part of the republican circles around Louis Blanc (1811–1882), but he refused political office when his friend rose to power following the Revolution of 1848. After the Bonapartist coup d'état, he withdrew from public life, although he remained a journalist until the 1870s.[65] Pecqueur received 600 francs for his essay, *De la paix, de son principe et de sa réalisation,* published that same year.[66]

In contrast to Pecqueur, little is known about the other contestants. His fellow prize-winner, Patrice Bazan, from the department of the Manche, won 400 francs for his *D'une paix universelle et permanente,* similarly appearing in 1842. Bazan's book is of lesser interest, as it focussed more intensely on the prize question by Grégoire. Two of the rejected essays equally saw the light of day in book-form around this time. One was unabashedly chauvinistic, written by a Saint-Simonian army captain, one Ferdinand Durand.[67] The jury deemed it too 'political'. This was putting it mildly. Durand portrayed France as the centre of Enlightenment, threatened on land by Russia, and at sea by the commercial avarice of Britain. He also called the king of Naples an 'imbecile'.[68] The other rejected essay came from the pen of Philippe-René Marchand, a doctor. His *Nouveau projet de traité de paix perpétuelle* was written in explicit response to the Rhine Crisis and included a full draft treaty.[69]

---

64 Constantin Pecqueur, *Économie sociale des intérêts du commerce de l'industrie et de l'agriculture, et de la civilisation en général* (Paris: Desessart 1839).

65 Vanessa Lincoln Lambert, 'Between Global Governance and European Union: the Writings of Constantin Pecqueur', in *Europe de papier* 2015, 114–5; Clément Coste, Ludovic Frobert and Marie Lauricella (eds.). *De la république de Constantin Pecqueur (1801–1887)* (Besançon: Presses universitaires de Franche-Comté 2017), 9–19.

66 Constantin Pecqueur, *De la paix. De son principe et de sa réalisation* (Paris: Capelle 1842).

67 Ferdinand Durand, *Des tendances pacifiques de la société européenne, et du rôle des armées dans l'avenir. Deuxième édition* (Paris: Dumaine 1844).

68 Ibid., 17–55, 394–7; Van der Linden, *Peace Movement* 1987, 116; ter Meulen, *Gedanke 1929*, 230–1.

69 Philippe-René Marchand, *Nouveau projet de traité de paix perpétuelle* (Paris: Renouard 1842), 339–87; Van der Linden, *Peace Movement* 1987, 124; ter Meulen, *Gedanke 1929*, 219–30.

2.1.2 A Congress and Court of Nations

While each plan possessed its own idiosyncrasies, a consequence of the open-ended essay question, all four nonetheless identified some form of congress of nations as the optimal political pacification mechanism. Villenave noticed this too, to his relative dislike. Just like his late American counterpart, William Ladd, the president of the peace committee recounted cardinal Fleury's classic criticism of Saint-Pierre, namely that the *projet* depended only on a dramatic change of heart of just about every European prince for it to work. Unlike the characteristically overoptimistic Ladd, Villenave dug up the anecdote to underline his belief that the day where states subjected their sovereignty to a higher political authority was still very far removed. Instead of regarding the essays as the basis for a public campaign in the American vein, Villenave viewed them as made for a handful of 'enlightened men', rather than the ignorant masses. The notion of a congress of nations would have to 'mature under the rays of civilisation' before it could possibly become a political reality.[70] True enough, the essays only ever reached a limited circle of intellectuals. In fact, their contents remained mostly unknown even to the peace societies, similar to the fate of the earlier Genevan prize essay.[71]

While their obscurity likely stimulated occasional claims that only the Americans produced 'specific plans', the essays proved themselves aware of the intellectual genealogy of the notion of federative peace.[72] Saint-Pierre was well-known.[73] Most were also more optimistic than Villenave. Displaying the sort of optimism often seen in English-language texts, Bazan asserted that his century was more amenable to the establishment of a permanent diplomatic congress than the eighteenth century had been: 'is it almost no longer possible to doubt the realisation of the grand idea of the *abbé* de Saint-Pierre.'[74] Like other essay writers, he listed a host of familiar examples of civilisational progress and earlier political precedents, such as the German and Swiss Confederations.[75] Similarly did everyone know of Henri IV and Sully's *grand dessein*.[76] Nobody seemed as obsessed with *le*

70 Bazan, *Paix* 1842, xvi–xvii.

71 Bazan's book was sent to the American Peace Society, but it was never discussed. AP (March 1843), 34.

72 Janis, *America* 2010, 80.

73 Bazan, *Paix* 1842, 1; Marchand, *Projet* 1842, 1; Pecqueur, *Paix* 1842, 294, 313, 331, 398, 405.

74 Bazan, *Paix* 1842, 55.

75 Bazan, *Paix* 1842, 67; Marchand, *Projet* 1842, 3; Pecqueur, *Paix* 1842, 312, 319–20, 450.

76 Bazan, *Paix* 1842, 33; Marchand, *Projet* 1842, 1; Pecqueur, *Paix* 1842, 405; Durand, *Tendances* 1844, 48.

bon roi as count de Sellon had been, though, even if Marchand acted in a similar spirit by dramatically reimagining the European borders.[77] Other pacification plans were cited haphazardly. Marchand, for instance, had also read one of the early pamphlets of Francisque Bouvet, whom we will meet later on.[78] However, only Pecqueur showed himself exceptionally erudite on this front.

The winning author was clearly well-read. Unlike most other mid-century peace friends, Pecqueur explicitly referred to Immanuel Kant's *Zum Ewigen Frieden*. He agreed with the German philosopher that peace was not the natural condition of humanity, but had to be won through reciprocal security guarantees. Such guarantees were only credible in a legal world order, where international law would be duly enforced.[79] Citing Rousseau, the journalist argued that only law – in the more abstract and idealistic sense of *la loi* – could ensure freedom and security, without degrading into tyranny. These accomplishments of civil law, Pecqueur hypothesised, were 'daily and insensibly' gaining ground in international law also, as long as one maintained a little 'faith' in the law of nations.[80]

In somewhat Saint-Simonian vein, and unlike the Americans, Pecqueur's congress also coordinated international public works, such as canals and railroads, financing these with international tax laws. The erstwhile Saint-Simonian confessed that Saint-Simon himself believed that such a far-reaching international organisation could only become politically realisable after revolutions and wars. That is why Pecqueur emphasised that, in order to avoid this bleak future, all necessary concessions had to be implemented gradually by the ruling classes.[81] He claimed that he had only read Saint-Simon's *De la réorganisation de la société européenne* after he had finished his own essay, calling it *'très-rare'* to find in bookshops. True or not, Pecqueur's social sensibilities surfaced when he reproached Saint-Simon for putting too much emphasis on material wealth. To him, representative government meant that the poor should also get a vote. Pecqueur rejected Saint-Simon's proposals for both a wealth-based European Chamber of Peers, as well as a hereditary European king.[82]

77 Marchand, *Projet* 1842, 27–93.
78 Ibid., 337.
79 Pecqueur, *Paix* 1842, 264, 366.
80 Ibid., 310–1.
81 Ibid., 327, 396.
82 Ibid., 410–4; Lincoln Lambert, 'Writings' 2015, 121–2.

Near the end of this long book, Pecqueur made mention of two other notable peace plans that he had allegedly discovered only after he had originally submitted his own essay. He was not uncritical. Pecqueur blamed Gondon, just like Saint-Simon, for his disregard of representative government. The legislative congress could never be composed solely of princes ruling by divine right. Allowing these men to proclaim international laws and appoint magistrates to the international court was to uphold 'exorbitant privileges'.[83] Gondon's aristocratic worldview could not stand further from the other plan that had caught Pecqueur's attention. A certain William Ladd had published an *Essay on a Congress of Nations* that envisioned international institutions remarkably similar to his own. Ladd's international legal order, too, consisted of a legislative congress and an international court, the same in all but name as Pecqueur's own *'congrès européen ou cosmopolite'* and *'tribunal des nations'*. He added a summary of the American text, with special attention to information on the Congress of Panama.[84]

This naturally begs the question: who was first? Chronologically speaking, Ladd had published first, suggesting that his French counterpart had plagiarised him. On the other hand, however, Ladd was not the first either to propose an international court. In the Anglophone world, Bentham and Mill had preceded him, quite alike to Gondon in the Francophone and Sartorius in the Germanophone spheres. In fact, even within the same competition, Marchand had also recommended a functional division of powers for the international congress, delegating the judiciary to a separate international court. Like Ladd, he referred to the Constitution of the United States.[85] Therefore, Pecqueur must have either arrived at the notion of an international judiciary independently from Ladd and anyone else, or, alternatively, borrowed from others without giving credit, like Ladd might have done also. The first hypothesis seems the most plausible one, considering Pecqueur's deviations from Ladd.[86]

Still, it remained striking that at least two *mémoires* vested the power of arbitration into the hands of a judicial court. In doing so, they seemed to break with deep-seated French constitutional mistrust for a *gouvernement des juges*. Especially because they indicated to be inspired by the American Supreme Court, an institution with the power of judicial review that did not even try to hide its overt political affiliations. Nineteenth century French

83 Pecqueur, *Paix* 1842, 410.

84 Ibid., 414–30. See chapter 1 for Ladd's interpretation of the Congress of Panama.

85 Marchand, *Projet* 1842, 163–7.

86 Pecqueur, *Paix* 1842, 387.

juridical thought, on the other hand, was extremely wary of any possible repetition of the venal excesses of judicial overreach under the *ancien régime*. French jurisprudence was characterised by *légicentrisme*.[87] Judges should but exegetically apply the law as set by the law-maker, but never make it themselves. Rousseau's *volonté générale* could not be discovered by any individual magistrate, but was set by the nation through its representative institutions. In its theoretical premises, if not necessarily as much in practice, this doctrine thus diverged sharply from the common law tradition.

How and why then did they advocate an international court? First, both Pecqueur, Marchand, and even Gondon, did not draw inspiration exclusively from the model of the United States. Just across the border, they took a deep interest in the institutions of the Holy Roman Empire and the German Confederation. Pecqueur praised the latter's recent reintroduction of *Austrägalgerichtsbarkeit,* a type of intra-confederal arbitral system. For the same reason, he also referred to the Swiss *Pacte Fédéral*.[88] Second, inspiration did not mean copy. As with anything, the general principle was more important than fine print. States were to follow a judicial procedure, but most publicists seldom offered much in the way of practical detail. No one mentioned equity as a source of law, or spoke of the possibility of judicial review and *stare decisis*.

The most detailed author, Pecqueur, envisioned two courts. The first one, meant for the European confederation, was likened to the French *Cour de Cassation* and the *Conseil de prud'hommes*.[89] Similar to the latter institution – meant to settle labour disputes, on which sat the *patrons* themselves – the European *assemblée de prud'hommes* consisted not only of jurisconsults, but also included intellectuals, industrialists, and even artists. The second high court, for the world state, he called the *cour suprême de justice internationale*.[90] That was actually a misnomer. As much as these names resembled modern-day institutions like the I.C.J., they were meant for a different world order. Both the *assemblée* and the *cour suprême* were appendages to a greater authority of international public law. In both instances, its competences outstripped those of the United Nations. Member states were

87 Bergami, 'Quelle démocratie' 2014, 21, 29; Mona Ozouf, 'Le légicentrisme républicain', in Mona Ozouf and François Furet (eds.), *Le siècle de l'avènement républicain* (Paris: Gallimard 1993), 441–7.

88 Pecqueur, *Paix* 1842, 232, 384–37.

89 Pecqueur, *Paix* 1842, 385–7.

90 Ibid., 395.

subordinated to this political authority, and were thereby taken out of the horizontal world of sovereign states, and into a vertical order, akin to the position of individuals within the domestic legal system. This *cour suprême* had by every standard ceased to be an 'international' – or, more properly speaking, an 'interstate' – court, since states had lost all attributions of sovereignty. None of this violated French *légicentrisme,* because, in both instances, judges remained bound by humanity's *volonté générale* as expressed in the supranational representative assembly.[91]

2.1.3 Cosmopolitanism and Europeanism

Most authors struggled with how to conceptualise the geographical space in which these legal-political institutions were to operate. Generally speaking, French *amis de la paix* focussed, like everyone else in the international peace movement, foremost on the so-called 'civilised' world. Analysing this further, however, early French peace ideologies engaged with both the larger intellectual history of Europeanism and with contemporary domestic politics. As remarked by Carol Bergami, they faced the task of reconciling their high ideals of universalism with the sober realities of having to actually create a political space in which enforceable positive laws could function. The congress of nations, installing a higher authority of public law above the state, looked like the answer to this conundrum. Yet, how could this authority establish its legitimacy in the existing world of sovereign states? How could *la grande nation* ever accept a loss of its sovereignty? If pacifist ideals clashed with patriotism, it stood no chance at all in public opinion. Universalism had to be compatible with particularism.[92]

Accordingly, most publicists privileged France in one way or another in their vision of international governance. French revolutionary republicanism, as it had developed between 1789 and the 1840s, had often imagined peace as the territorial extension of the enlightened values of *la patrie.*[93] Military expansionism was, of course, not an option for friends of peace. The Revolutionary era nonetheless provided another solution. Had the *Déclaration du droit de l'homme et du citoyen* of 1789 not articulated a universal array of natural rights, albeit in the bosom of French law? Many republicans, from Jules Bastide (1800–1879) to Victor Hugo, subscribed to the notion that positive law, when representing *la volonté générale,* had universalist potential. As it went without saying that *la France* led the progress of civilisation,

91 Ibid., 303, 373.

92 Bergami, 'Européisme' 2012, 7–12.

93 Ibid., 8.

its domestic example should lead the way. To the extent other states shared or copied French cultural values, they could become part of this shared international legal space.[94] Although such chauvinism was pervasive in contemporary French texts, it would be unfair to single out only the French. Like we have seen in previous chapters, American, British and Swiss publicists likewise singled out their respective states as the leading example for the rest of the world.[95] National pride appeared to induce parochial universalisms everywhere.[96]

Of the four publicists, Marchand decidedly belonged to the branch of post-Revolutionary thought which set more stock in a system of clearly delineated states, than in an encompassing cosmopolitan law. As he cautioned: 'we should not push the idea of unity too far'.[97] Only a permanent diplomatic congress could realistically devise an international legal code, and enforce it afterwards. As a result, 'here, the law of nations will become part of public law.' This logically entailed that, for the polities remaining on the peripheries, the state of nature continued, so that their respect for the legal code still depended on their voluntary adhesion, or – more ominously – the pressure exerted by 'such a powerful confederation'.[98] The power bloc stayed firmly within Europe, largely because Marchand considered it a long overdue correction of the hated Congress of Vienna. Mirroring popular dislike of the treaty that had humiliated France, Europe's borders were to be redrafted from a blank slate. Unsurprisingly, France gained the left bank of the Rhine, as well as all of Belgium. The Netherlands and Denmark were to be annexed by Germany. Citing from the conservative philosopher Louis de Bonald (1754–1840), Marchand felt that small states only existed by the grace of the great powers.[99]

The prizewinning essay by Bazan similarly desired a fixation of the European map, but was slightly more generous in its conception. While a powerful state like France was of course to take the lead, Bazan did not require the disappearance of Europe's minor states, but opted for a tiered approach. In a first step, the general assembly would be composed of the British, the Belgians, the Dutch, the Scandinavians and the rest of Europe. Interestingly, Bazan also included the 'Muscovites' and even the Ottomans, 'currently on

94 Ibid., 8–10.

95 See their respective chapters supra.

96 Pitts, *Boundaries* 2018.

97 Marchand, *Projet* 1842, 54.

98 Ibid., 183–4.

99 Ibid., 68.

the road to civilisation'. Only in a second step would come the United States, followed in the next step by the South-American states, once their 'wobbly institutions' were stabilised. Last to come into the fold were the 'numerous populations' of Asia and Africa. Although he interpreted their 'retrograde' state of civilisation as the 'logical consequence' of their pagan ways, Bazan imagined that one day, these peoples, too, could join the 'grand union'. At present, however, only Europe and America were in a position to confederate.[100]

French peace advocates overall maintained an ambiguous relationship with colonialism. As was the case with many Anglo-Americans, most mid-century peace friends in this country did not have any principled objection to the 'civilising' mission as such. Durand was crudely racist, dividing humanity in an idiosyncratic succession of divinely created races, with black Africans at the bottom and white Europeans at the top.[101] Bazan, on the other hand, who did receive recognition from the *société*, also an important anti-slavery society, was occasionally more indulgent. He praised the Chinese for their 'pacific' foreign policy, preferring to build a Great Wall than to engage in endless wars of conquest, like the Europeans.[102] Such orientalist stereotypes aside, however, Bazan also underlined Christian superiority. The Turks were barbarous 'half-Europeans', the Koran was said to consecrate slavery, and the Asians were depicted as 'idolaters [...] even more hostile to peace and civilisation than the Arabs'.[103] Marchand, meanwhile, imagined the age of peace to be also the age of *'le grand mouvement de colonisation'*.[104] In his great speech before the 1849 Paris peace conference, Victor Hugo expressed a similar hope: *'Au lieu de faire des révolutions, on ferait des colonies!'*.[105]

Compared to the peace societies, French *amis de la paix* were rather more equivocal on the legitimacy of armed force for this 'civilising' mission. Among the rejected essays, Marchand was clearest about his double standards. His positivist mindset and his cultural biases led him to distinguish between member states of the confederation, governed by its internal public

100 Bazan, *Paix* 1842, 63–4.

101 Durand, *Tendances* 1844, 22–3.

102 Bazan, *Paix* 1842, 111–2. Bazan's image of China was typically Orientalist, in the sense that he regarded this non-Western polity as static and one-dimensional.

103 Bazan, *Paix* 1842, 49–52

104 Marchand, *Projet* 1842, 228.

105 *Congrès des amis de la paix universelle réuni à Paris en 1849* (Paris: Guillaumin 1850), 3–5.

law, and polities outside of its jurisdiction. Inside – within Europe – war had ceased to be *'civilisatrice',* meaning that its evils were no longer balanced by any upside. Therefore, the acceptable just causes within the *ius ad bellum* had to be severely circumscribed. Outside, however, the congress would, 'in spite of all its moderation and patience', have to spread civilisation through conquest. Because it was folly to believe that any of the great powers would voluntarily abandon their empires, they could keep their existing prerogatives. Natural law stipulated that no one could infringe on *'un droit acquis'.* Predictably, this 'moral law' did not apply to those falling short of the standard of civilisation, since 'the earth does not belong by right to the first occupant, but the one who knows how to use it'. As far as Marchand was concerned, the 'titles of Europeans to the New World' were 'incontestable'. Because conquests against European states were forbidden, all proposed border changes in Europe had to be paid for with indemnities. That was not necessary in the 'uncivilised' world, where natural law gave Christian states a just cause for wars for 'colonial works'.[106] In all, Marchand's justifications did not differ significantly from those espoused by contemporary European jurists.[107]

While none of the other essayists were such blunt apologists for imperialism, it must be recognised that very few showed any particular concern for the plight of subaltern peoples. Bazan, for instance, set it as a *conditio sine qua non* that the existing territorial status quo had to be frozen. Perhaps later on, the peoples of Poland and Italy could regain their independence in a peaceful manner, but this was an 'entirely secondary' question, that did not 'intimately relate to the peace of the world'.[108] In light of the many bloody revolutions and wars that were to come and had occurred already, such dismissals were more than a little myopic. Furthermore, outside of Europe, Bazan's critique of wars of conquest collided hard with his unwavering support for the war in Algeria. Bazan depicted the cause of France as just, since it was not only a war against piracy, but also one against 'Islamism'.[109]

The decades-long armed conflict in Algeria did not produce an organised domestic opposition like the Mexican War caused in the United States. The *Société de la morale Chrétienne,* connected with the ruling establishment after 1830, seldom challenged the *ius ad bellum* grounds of the war that annually extracted such a costly human toll. Although their journal did report

106 Marchand, *Paix* 1842, 192–207, 306.

107 Koskenniemi, *Gentle Civilizer* 2001, 98–178; Anghie, *Imperialism* 2004, 32–114.

108 Bazan, *Paix* 1842, 64–5.

109 Ibid., 56–7, 60.

negatively on the conflict in North Africa, articles typically dealt with administrative mismanagement, considered the root cause of the Algerian resistance. The society professed to believe more in the soft power of missionaries, than in the hard power of soldiers. One article praised the alleged British model: '[the missionaries] have established an administration that is without doubt a little despotic, but above all moral and religious. They provide education to the indigenous people. They have founded manufactories and make good workers of the adults, while offering elementary instruction to their children.'[110] The issue of colonial warfare was not explicitly linked to the colonial project as such. Few of these men, having never set foot in Algeria themselves, realised the structural violence inherent to colonialism. They also did not touch upon the fact that colonies played an essential part in the need for resources in the context of imperial competition.[111] Perhaps they realised this, but this could not be admitted.

Only slowly did doubt creep in. An article of 1845 wondered aloud whether the Algerians had not remained better off under the Turks, than under the French.[112] Later in 1845, fifteen years after the initial invasion, the society's peace committee explicitly denounced the war for the first time: 'there has never been a war more sacred than theirs, and never was an attack as unjust as the one they are repulsing'. The argument was not so much based on religion, as it was on the inordinate financial and human cost.[113] The society also agreed with the thrust of Francisque Bouvet's repeated 'violent' attacks against the war.[114] However, it never conducted any public anti-war campaign beyond a few scattered articles. The economic and institutional peace friends were generally of the same tenor.[115]

Arguably, no publicist connected to the Society of Christian Morals condemned colonial conquests as much as Constantin Pecqueur. His internationalism had arisen out of a blend of Christian ethics, Europeanism, and veritable cosmopolitanism. Like any other child of the age, he was fundamentally inspired by Christianity: 'the final consequence of a truly *Catholic* Christianity is the institution of universal justice, charged with settling the

110 JSMC (série II, tome V), 62–3.
111 Christopher Bayly, *The Birth of the Modern World 1780–1914* (Oxford: Blackwell 2004), 134–8.
112 JSMC (série III, tome IV, n° 3), 136.
113 JSMC (série III, tome IV, n° 3), 219–24.
114 JSMC (série III, tome V, n° 1), 44–9.
115 E.g. La paix des deux mondes (hereafter: PDM) (19 August 1844), 1; JE (série I, tome VIX, 1851), 18–33.

disputes of nations'.[116] However, the man was remarkably nondogmatic about his religiosity to contemporary standards – a not uncommon trait for an *ami de la paix*.[117] For Pecqueur, non-European polities did not need to convert to Christianity to join in the international political-legal system. Reasoning almost as a Protestant, Pecqueur posited that the Gospel's general message abhorred war and contained eternal truths, regardless of whether or not one believed in them. Individuals and states could only be forced to respect 'universal moral law', meaning laws meant to protect life and property. Because Christ had condemned violence as a legal remedy, the individual had to respect the civil justice system of the state. In turn, the state – as the collective of individuals – had to respect the international justice system of a supranational power.[118]

For its initial stages, Pecqueur agreed with some of the other essayists that this supranational power had to emerge in Europe first. In his historical reading, Europe had once before already been united under a single superior authority: the medieval popes. Pecqueur said of the lost *res publica Christiana:* 'the supreme tribunal imagined by Saint-Pierre, and which he thought to be without precedent, was [...] nothing but an incomplete rehash of this institution, whose power was fully moral, but real'.[119] The Reformation had shattered this unity, but, over the subsequent centuries, a common European political and intellectual culture had developed. Increasing commerce, technological improvements, intellectual exchanges, and international law had decreased the significance of borders. Europe had but to look at the United States for a modern example. The states of Europe could do the same.[120]

For this to succeed, Europeans would have to abandon nationalism. Pecqueur did not mean pacific patriotism. He himself contrasted Russian authoritarianism with the liberal traditions of France: '*la France* has incarnated all saintly virtues of Christianity'. What Pecqueur did reject, was the ideology that glorified the nation-state as the *telos* of a society's historical development, causing isolationism and aggressive war. Nationalists confounded means with ends: 'political independence and national existence are not the primary goal of peoples; these are subordinate to the higher

116 Pecqueur, *Paix* 1842, 164.

117 William Ladd and count de Sellon had also been relatively tolerant for their time. See chapters 1 and 3.

118 Pecqueur, *Paix* 1842, 27–8.

119 Ibid., 313.

120 Ibid., 314–6, 389–96.

questions of justice and universal brotherhood'. Pecqueur harked back to the ideals of '89: 'Brothers! Associate! Correspond together! No more frontiers, or customs! We are all children of God!'. Few friends of peace in the 1840s used the word 'cosmopolitan' as much as Constantin Pecqueur.[121]

What was true for nationalism, was true for Europeanism also. Pecqueur considered the European confederation as but another intermediate step towards a truly universal world state. He recognised that the non-European world did not share the same religious and political institutions as the West. Therefore, he argued that: 'the principle of universal religious and political tolerance is an absolute condition for universal peace'. Pecqueur used 'tolerance' in the more restricted sense, meaning that no armed force was permissible in the civilisational project, 'otherwise the causes of wars would be infinite'. Indigenous peoples should still be 'elevated' into the Christian standard of civilisation, but only through 'moral and pacific propaganda'.[122] Although Pecqueur's stance on colonialism was as idealised as those of his contemporaries, he viewed it in a grander scheme. Colonisations had to be an organised European enterprise, not only to prevent imperialist competition, but also – and rather shockingly for many contemporaries – to 'amiably prepare the marriage of the races, the fusion of nationalities, [and] the unity of Europe and the world'.[123] Not every land had to become a European dependency. To those well-established, but still alien, polities of Asia, the European powers should send ambassadors. Integration into European diplomacy would acquaint the 'Oriental' world with Christianity, political economy, and the precepts of international law. Almost uniquely to Pecqueur, he saw little reason to exclude such 'lagging nations' from the cosmopolitan pact, even before they had fully embraced European cultural and legal standards.[124]

2.1.4 Conceptualising the 'New Public Law'

Cosmopolitanism did not prevent Pecqueur, like most other French peace friends, from otherwise subscribing to a very sober and positivist view of international law. On the most fundamental level, Pecqueur did not renounce natural law. To him, all international law was nothing but the 'morality of nations', which was valid everywhere and knew no *'étrangers'.*

121 Ibid., 65, 165, 276–7.

122 Ibid., 355.

123 Marchand also wished the congress to organise colonisation communally. Ibid., 229–30; Marchand, *Paix* 1842, 161, 292–8.

124 Pecqueur, *Paix* 1842, 240, 355.

However, international law meant little in practice if it could not be enforced by 'positive justice' or an 'international coercive force'. World peace required 'a power that by law could oppose a superior force' to transgressor states.[125] Confirming this, Pecqueur believed, similar to the Anglo-American societies, that the law of nations was already a fact of political life. Even if no supranational institutions yet existed, public opinion ensured that the law of nations had progressed in tune with the progress of morality. He marvelled that 'most maxims of modern international law were unknown by the ancients'. States could already not simply violate these maxims with impunity, as doing so would expose them to sanctions. That 'law of humanity', equivalent to the 'normal state of humanity', was perfecting itself in unison with the realisation of 'universal association'.[126]

Pecqueur briefly contemplated the positions of the peace societies. He hoped that an international court vested with only moral authority could already produce the same effect as one backed by an armed force. In numerous passages, however, he backed the old natural law notion that regarded war as a police action, albeit now regulated under positive cosmopolitan law.[127] Pecqueur's purpose was not to promote *'la paix à tout prix'*. This was an unpopular phrase in contemporary political life, hurled around as an insult to depict adversaries as unpatriotic.[128] Less concerned with French pride than contemporaries, however, Pecqueur despised it, because the sentiment behind it hurt his most basic ethical intuitions: 'it would mean impunity for the wicked and decree the triumph of evil over good; it would be to deprive justice of its rights'.[129]

This stood in sharp contrast to ongoing debates within the American Peace Society. There, a radical like Thomas Grimké could still ignite a full-blown polemic with his provocative claim that he would meet attacking pirates with a procession of Sunday school children. Had he suggested this in French peace circles, Grimké would have immediately lost all credibility.[130] Bazan considered defensive war the ultimate example of a just war, 'saintly

125 De la paix, 261–3.

126 Ibid., 250, 261–3, 305–7.

127 Ibid., 32–3, 262, 306.

128 Pecqueur, Niboyet, Girardin, and Bouvet all explicitly denounced *'la paix à a tout prix'*. PDM (4 April 1844), 1; Francisque Bouvet, *Introduction à l'établissement d'un droit public européen* (Paris: Dentu 1856), 265–6.

129 Pecqueur, *Paix* 1842, 261.

130 See chapter 1. In fact, it made Grimké lose all credibility in the eyes of most Americans too.

even'.[131] Many went much further than recognising the natural right of self-defence. For Marchand, the necessity of a 'federal army' for this institution was evident: 'What would it be, if deprived of this principle of force? [...] Barely anything more than all of these congresses that we have seen come and go since 1815'.[132]

The new world order imagined by the peace committee and the essayists did not seek to abolish all war, but sought to incorporate it within a larger framework of codified international law. Villenave's report noted that most of the essays wished for the law of nations to be fixated by treaty, which he dubbed the *'Charte de la Paix'*.[133] Of the published essays, only Durand did not specifically address this issue. Bazan did not offer much in the way of details, other than that the congress should settle the norms by which arbitrations should be conducted.[134] Marchand, on the other hand, recurrently discussed the *'nouveau droit public'*. He distinguished four cases where the 'right of conquest' was still warranted: commerce, science, colonial works, and those done 'exclusively in the interest of foreign peoples'. The causes themselves were less important than the procedural requirement that they had to be clearly defined in a 'formal law'. The law had to be guaranteed by the aggregate forces of all member states, guided by the collective opinion of 'all reasonable publicists'. Marchand professed to be inspired by Montesquieu.[135]

Pecqueur broadly agreed. Although he did not endorse wars of conquest of any kind, including any against non-Europeans, Pecqueur shared the underlying conviction that armed intervention should only be resorted to within a structural framework of positive law. His cosmopolitan *'armée de la paix'* was by no means an army of conscientious objectors. Its task was to uphold the norms enacted by the international congress, which controlled it directly.[136] In keeping with his distaste for absolute conceptions of sovereignty – impossible given the natural sociability of nations – Pecqueur allowed these peacekeeping forces to operate with extraterritorial jurisdiction, beyond the sovereign borders of the congress. Of course, he knew that unwanted intervention, in the absence of a cosmopolitan authority, amounted to a pretty clear-cut violation of international law. Pecqueur

131 Bazan, *Paix* 1842, 6.
132 Marchand, *Paix* 1842, 159.
133 Bazan, *Paix* 1842, xvii.
134 Ibid., 61, 65.
135 Marchand, *Paix* 1842, 193.
136 Pecqueur, *Paix* 1842, 221–36.

solved it through procedural and substantive safeguards. Procedurally, he cited Vattel that only a legitimate authority could claim such a right. Furthermore, the decision could only be taken multilaterally. Substantively, the intervening force was limited to stopping the bloodshed. By setting itself between both parties, the intervention thus only served to pave the way to a pacific dispute settlement, based on the legal merits of the case. In general, Pecqueur's rule of thumb was that each and every use of force under an 'efficient law of nations' had to be done 'impartially', 'in the name of justice', and 'in the general interest of nations'. Unwittingly, much corresponded to medieval just war theory, when theologians demanded that just war had to be done with *'recta intentio'*, meaning only for 'good'. Less concerned with a soul's salvation than the old scholastics, Pecqueur used it as a stopgap until the establishment of a true world government with compulsory jurisdiction by a global supreme court of justice.[137]

Until that time, Pecqueur advocated increasing the resort to arbitrations by a third power. He drew upon arguments familiar to the larger peace movement. These included the Swiss precedent – based on Vattel – as well as more recent 'arbitration' cases, such as those following the Belgian Revolution or the Anglo-Neapolitan sulphur dispute. As this second example revealed, Pecqueur did not have a watertight definition of 'arbitration'. The 'mediation' of France in the so-called Sulphur War was blatantly biased in favour of the British, for political reasons.[138] Had Pecqueur known all the details, it would have only strengthened his conviction that the means of pacific dispute settlement had to be further improved. As many times as the Concert of Europe prevented wars, 'this alliance is still exclusive, incomplete, and coarse; the great powers still have afterthoughts of conquest'. Still, he hoped that some of the precedents, at least, had proven that arbitrators could be impartial and just. As much as 'opinion of the peoples' was still strongly against 'all legal intervention', he hoped that, one day, *'toute querelle, tout différend, toute guerre entre nations'* would transform into a 'procedure' before an international judicial power.[139]

The substantive norms which would come under scrutiny under the proceedings of this future legal world order were similar to those wished for by the peace societies. Similar to Ladd, both Marchand and Pecqueur turned their attention to reforms in the *ius in bello*. Some of these precepts were

137 Pecqueur, *Paix* 1842, 216–25.

138 Also mentioned as a useful precedent by Bazan, *Paix* 1842, 62–3; Šedivý, *Decline* 2018, 107–23.

139 Pecqueur, *Paix* 1842, 294, 340, 344–5, 351–2.

basic reiterations of existing proscriptions in doctrine and customary law. Pecqueur occasionally turned to Vattel for support in favour of his prohibitions on pillaging, sacking, the mistreatment of women and children, or the wanton destruction of monuments, artworks, temples, and farms without clear military necessity.[140] The essayists still wished these to be included in a treaty, because, in the words of Marchand: 'I know that the law of nations forbids it. Unfortunately, the facts are not always, not even today, in accord with law [...] No nation speaks up against [the right of pillage], because it is tacitly allowed everywhere'.[141] Similar positive legal prohibitions were also needed against the rights of privateering and the slave trade.[142]

Pecqueur was the most elaborate essayist in terms of *de lege ferenda*. Interestingly, Pecqueur put some emphasis on the laws of maritime neutrality. Like the American Peace Society, he brought up the 1785 Prussian-American treaty of Amity and Commerce, and advocated in favour of the principle that *'la pavillon couvre la marchandise'* and the right of effective blockade.[143] Considering the suspicious similarities to the American project elsewhere, it is not unreasonable to assume that Pecqueur might have taken these examples from American propaganda. He was certainly aware of the existence of the peace societies, even if he thought them too scant in number to exert any real influence.[144]

Whether he arrived at his positions independently or not, Pecqueur deviated from existing models when these clashed with his own beliefs. It could also reveal the author's relative naïveté. Pecqueur denied the 'natural' right to restrict access to its territory and trade. That clearly contradicted Vattel, who alleged that trade an 'imperfect' right, meaning it could be prohibited by a sovereign authority. The Swiss scholar had explicitly pointed to China for his example.[145] For a cosmopolitan visionary like Pecqueur, this could not be. Instead, he approved of the recent British success in getting China to open its ports, an act that had brought Kant's ideal of 'cosmopolitan law' closer to reality. It was 'above all praise', and should be repeated by the full European Concert through 'patient, but active diplomacy'. Pecqueur did not

140 Marchand argued against broadly the same things. Ibid., 360–2, 364–5. Marchand, *Paix* 1842, 187–92.

141 Ibid., 189–90.

142 Ibid., 184–5; Bazan, *Paix* 1842, 104–6.

143 Pecqueur, *Paix* 1842, 358–60, 363–4

144 Ibid., 168–9.

145 Vattel, *Droit des gens. Tome premier* 1830, 121–122 (§ 94).

enter much into the fact that the 'unequal' Treaty of Nanking of 1842 was signed at gunpoint at the conclusion of the First Opium War.[146]

As hard-headed and unsentimental as the world of actual politics could be, this was the only domain that could produce tangible results. Although none of the French publicists refuted that one could damn one's soul through great sin – an overriding concern for British Quakers – this mattered little for the here and now. As we have seen by now, natural law arguments cropped up again and again, but none were deemed sufficient by themselves. Similar to mainstream lawyers of the era, everyone presupposed the existence of timeless and universal principles. The trick was to convince statesmen of these principles, so they would modify positive international law accordingly. For Marchand, the congress of nations had to 'bring international law into line with the eternal principles of justice'.[147]

Pecqueur, as usual, engaged in the most sophisticated argument. Having read more than the others, he made sure to build his future world-state firmly on the solid bedrock of immutable natural law. Predictably, Pecqueur was enamoured by Wolff's notion of a *'civitas maxima'*, or the implied global republic shimmering underneath the surface of everyday politics. The *civitas maxima* being Wolff's translation of the Aristotelean concept of natural sociability among individuals, it was compatible with Pecqueur's own teleological belief in a natural law of universal association.[148] There should be little surprise that Wolff's more state-centred vulgariser, Vattel, could not hope for the same praise from Pecqueur. Like most other careful readers of Vattel's tomes, he soon discovered numerous internal contradictions. States were said to be sovereign, yet simultaneously also bound by natural law, with any violations enforceable by others. 'With a little bit of logic', Pecqueur deduced, 'one can prove that nations have to submit themselves to a universal power'. Vattel argued that a state could believe that it was right, while acting illegally, with no one able to accuse it for violating the laws of society. *Singulier argument!'* Imagine this for the individual! 'How many people are not deeply convinced that they are right, while being wrong in the eyes of the tribunals!' The 'great sophism' of Vattel with regards to sovereignty was never adopted by Grotius. This scholar had championed the sovereign's right to make war upon a state which made itself guilty of 'grave

146 Kant had identified travel restrictions as a cause of war. Count de Sellon also referred to this. Pecqueur, *Paix* 1842, 362–3; Kant (ed. Kleingeld), *Writings* 2006, 82–5; on the First Opium War, see chapter 2.

147 Marchand, *Paix* 1842, 192.

148 See supra. Neff, *Justice* 2014, 185–7; Pecqueur, *Paix* 1842, 291.

faults against the laws of nature'.[149] Even the conservative Prussian statesman Ancillon had identified the latent war-threat over Europe with the lack of 'external guarantees' for the law of nations.[150] A monarch could easily begin a war.

More than anyone else in the competition, or even within the aristocratic *Société de la morale chrétienne,* Pecqueur advocated democratic constitutionalism as the necessary condition for any confederation or future world state. Similar to Kant's republicanism, he posited that, within a dynastic constitution the power to declare war was best divested from the executive, and given to the legislative authority. Unlike Kant, Pecqueur wished this representative legislative body to be elected by the 'entire social body', rich and poor. He dismissed the *Pax Romana,* because the vast majority of the populace lived in squalid circumstances. The more diplomacy represented the genuine interests of the people, the more war would become less and less thinkable. While a temporary anti-war alliance did not a priori exclude authoritarian powers like Austria and Russia, a European 'federal congress' would have to be internally homogenous. Every member state had to be a constitutional one, with a sufficiently democratic representative government.[151] Other than this, he did not discuss the inner workings of the congress in detail. Like everywhere, Pecqueur and the others preferred to outline only the broad contours, confident that the details would be worked out once the general principle was accepted. They all limited themselves to broad suggestions for majority voting procedures, public discussions, and the legal equality of the 'civilised' states.

All written under the direct impact of the Syria and Rhine Crises, the essays attempted to artificially create an international order where the ethereal promises of natural law where backed by a positive authority. Natural law informed visions of a political sphere beyond the state, yet this politicisation of natural law had to be done through instruments of public law, i.e. some form of confederation. The pacification plans produced by the tension between universalism and particularism echoed the preceding *projets* by

---

149 Ibid., 292–293.

150 Johann Peter Friedrich Ancillon (1767–1837), was a well-known historian. Bouvet and Molinari likewise cited his observation that natural law, without an enforcement mechanism, was purely moral and thus unable to prevent war. Friedrich Ancillon, *Tableau des révolutions du système politique de l'Europe depuis la fin du quinzième siècle. Première partie. Tome premier* (Berlin: Quien 1803), iv–v; Gustave de Molinari, *La question d'Orient envisagée au point de vue de l'économie politique et du droit public* (Paris: Hennuyer 1854), 6, 29–30; Bouvet, *Droit public* 1856, 174.

151 Pecqueur, *Paix* 1842, 89–92, 337–8, 352, 414; Kant (ed. Kleingeld), *Writings* 2006, 76–7.

Henri IV or Saint-Pierre. Far from mere epigones, however this new generation of pacific publicists addressed many of the political, economic, and social questions that had arisen out of the French Revolution. Elsewhere within the French peace movement, however, these same questions were answered differently. Hesitant about the prospect of supranational government, the so-called 'economic' peace friends generally put more trust in the natural laws of political economy.

2.2 *Economic Pacifism*

Picture an empty meadow in the middle of the countryside. Apart from a few scattered farmhouses on the horizon, not a living soul can be seen or heard. The place seems, for all intents and purposes, completely abandoned. Suddenly, two men emerge from opposite sides of the green. They take up positions across each other in the centre. Declaring war on each other, they draw weapons and two shots ring out into the air. A few birds fly out of the trees, but otherwise the rustling of the branches continues uninterrupted, while blood seeps into the earth below.

Now consider the *rue de la Madeleine,* Brussels's premier shopping avenue. The energy of commerce radiates from the luxurious window displays, shouting newspaper boys and elegant ladies browsing the latest Parisian fashions. The same two men step out into the middle of the street. Again, they declare war on each other. Again, they draw their guns. Only this time, total bedlam ensues. People run away screaming, ducking for cover as stray bullets shatter glass and bone. If allowed to persist, the street would soon be devoid of all life. Sure enough, the police soon arrives on the scene, or, if none comes, a handful of bystanders gather their courage and step into the fray. As the combatants are forcefully dragged away, they invoke their natural right to avenge wrongs. 'That may be', mutter the disgruntled citizens, 'but not at our expense. We have rights too!'

Thus went the parable repeatedly told by Gustave de Molinari (1819–1912) to illustrate the interests political economy had in pacification and international law.[152] Whether war damned the soul or not could be debated endlessly by theologians, but it was plain for all to see that war, above everything else, was bad for business. Like their influential British peers, they

152 As paraphrased from Gustave de Molinari, *Questions d'économie politique et de droit public. Tome II* (Paris: Guillaumin 1861), 330–331; Gustave de Molinari, *Le droit de la paix et le droit de la guerre* (Paris: Guillaumin 1887), 10–11; for most of the nineteenth century, at least in Belgium, courses on international law were part of chairs of political economy in law faculties. Genin, *laboratoire belge* 2018, 78.

stood resolutely in favour of free exchange in the widest possible sense. Free trade would increase welfare, lessen national prejudices, and provide the most solid possible foundation for a stable peace. In full agreement with the British free traders, many political economists campaigned for reductions in military spending. A standing army was seen as an anachronism, responsible for continuous geopolitical tensions and high taxes, which combined to provoke interstate war and revolution. As with the Christian variety of pacifism, the French free traders could not be fully equated with their overseas counterparts. Unlike Cobden, who favoured absolute non-interference, the 'economic' *amis de la paix* of France endorsed foreign policies that could be surprisingly assertive.

Similar to the publicists of the *Société de la morale chrétienne,* the political economists were only loosely organised institutionally. Most were involved in the *Société d'économie politique,* founded in 1842, along with the highly influential *Journal des économistes.* Its founders included Joseph Garnier (1813–1881), a republican journalist, Hippolyte Passy (1793–1880), uncle and inspirer of none other than Frédéric Passy, Pellegrino Rossi, whom we have encountered already in our discussion of Sellon, and Gilbert Guillaumin (1801–1864), the famous liberal publisher. Other characters of note connected to these circles were Frédéric Bastiat (1801–1850), translator and friend of Cobden, Michel Chevalier (1806–1879), known for the Cobden-Chevalier free trade agreement, and the aforementioned Gustave de Molinari, strictly speaking a Belgian, but a longtime expatriate with many ties to Parisian intellectual life. Last worth mentioning was Émile de Girardin (1802–1881), a journalistic pioneer. As with the aristocratic philanthropists united by Rochefoucauld-Liancourt, none were exclusively dedicated to peace issues, but each played a significant part in the contemporary peace debate.[153]

Their debate was not divorced from that within the international peace movement. Many took part in the Paris Peace Conference of 1849 and remained interested afterwards. Especially Garnier was an active adherent, acting as secretary to the conferences of 1849 and 1850 and editing the former's official French proceedings. They were printed at Guillaumin's press.[154] For many years afterwards, Garnier made sure as editor-in-chief that the *Journal des économistes* regularly reported on the activities of the peace societies. This was attested to in its own columns, where some

153 Chevalier is discussed under 'Bonapartist pacifism' in this chapter. Lincoln, *French Peace Movement* 2013, 47–9.

154 *Congrès Paris* 1850, VIII, 1.

criticised this editorial policy: 'our journal poses itself as the organ of this pacific movement, or at least shows itself to be an unquestionable supporter'. Garnier was not at all deterred.[155] Other economists participating in the peace conferences included Bastiat, Chevalier, Girardin and Molinari.[156] Their interest in peace was not limited to the conferences. Molinari, for instance, wrote articles on peace for the *Dictionnaire de l'économie politique,* and made it a prominent theme in the *Économiste belge,* whose articles were often reproduced in the *Journal des économistes.*[157] Likewise, Girardin popularised economic arguments for peace in the pages of his iconic newspaper *La Presse,* one of France's first inexpensive newspapers, sold *en masse* in the streets, rather than by subscription only.[158]

According to the historian Cooper, such initiatives were 'much more influential than a proliferation of peace committees could have been'.[159] After all, the reach of those titles far exceeded that of the small *Journal de la Société de la morale chrétienne.*[160] What must have shocked contemporaries, was that this 'chimera of international arbitration, essentially old hat renewed by Saint-Pierre and Kant' – as one critical economist put it – was being openly advocated by such respectable gentlemen.[161]

2.2.1 'Scientific' Natural Law

Such critique was only half-founded. Many economists were disinclined to support a supranational political-legal institution, because their creed was less government, not more. Similar to the British free traders, they believed in a number of natural laws, dressed up in the scientific-materialistic garb of political economy. The century's 'classical' liberalism revolved around a selection of axioms, held to have universal validity. The fundamental assumption was that society was naturally harmonious, if the individual was given maximal freedom of action. Adam Smith's 'invisible hand' would ensure the optimal division of labour and production within and between states. Although they promoted fierce competition to achieve this equilibrium, liberal economists did not allow this to escalate into violence.

155 JE (série I, tome XXX, 1851), 145–53.

156 Either physically, or through a letter of adhesion. *Congrès Paris* 1850, 7, 25–6, 37, 40, 43, 49, 50, 59; *Proceedings Frankfurt* 1851, VIII, 8–10, 27–30, 37, 72–3.

157 Molinari is discussed infra.

158 Pellissier, Pierre. *Émile de Girardin. Prince de la presse* (Paris: Denoël, 1985), 97–102.

159 Cooper, *Patriotic Pacifism* 1991, 21.

160 The JSMC was printed on only a couple of hundred copies. JSMC (série II, tome XIX, n° 3), 139–140.

161 JE (série I, tome XXX, 1851), 147; Lincoln, *French Peace Movement* 2013, 58.

Government's principal – or even only – mission was to protect life, liberty and property. Of course, the liberal economic programme, despite its mainstream breakthrough over the course of the nineteenth century, did not emancipate everyone. Labourers, women and the colonised were legally and de facto excluded. In its theoretical premises, however, liberal political-economic theory was ostensibly peaceful.[162] If government had to legally guarantee peace domestically, states had to provide similar legal guarantees internationally.

Garnier was the most outspoken economist in this vein about the legal programme of the peace movement. Defending the ongoing peace conference movement, Joseph Garnier posited that the modern-day peace friends framed the problem 'more practical' than Saint-Pierre or Kant. Although Garnier did not enter into detail, he likely had the same objections against a congress of nations in mind as Jay and Cobden.[163] The editor of the *Journal des économistes* pointed out that that stipulated arbitration would be conducted by *'véritables prud'hommes',* appointed ad hoc, guided by 'wisdom and foresight', and backed by 'universal public opinion'. For Garnier, this novel type of arbitration appeared much more desirable than arbitrations conducted by state officials, implied to be under the sway of special interests. The introduction and generalisation of this type of judicial procedure interested him much more than the intractable debate on the legitimacy of defensive war. War should cease to be viewed as the ultimate sanction of international law. Even if the measures of the conference were 'derisory', and might not do any good, at the very least they 'could not do any harm' either.[164]

Garnier reported on each peace conference following Paris, each of which supported the Anglo-American arbitration model.[165] In the next decade, the journal set high hopes on the Treaty of Paris of 1856. The editors were exhilarated that important notions of political economy, especially the 'solidarity of interests', were for the first time discussed in high political circles. Even if a system of European arbitration had not seen the light of day, it was 'destined to be realised sooner or later'.[166] Evidently, the peace

---

162 Neff, *Justice* 2014, 269–79.

163 See chapters 1 and 2.

164 JE (série I, tome XXX, 1851), 151–2.

165 JE (série I, tome XIV, 1849), 152–73; JE (série I, tome XXVII, 1850), 187–195; JE (série I, tome XXIX, 1851), 323–339; JEE (série I, tome XXXIV, 1853), 318; JE (série I, tome XXX VII, 1853), 289–94.

166 JE (série II, tome X, 1856), 310.

movement had overcome the political economists' initial prejudices. In 1843, when the London peace conference first put the peace societies on its radar, the *journal des économistes* had feared that these Christian friends of peace might potentially lose themselves in *'un rigorisme qui dépasse le but'*.[167]

Otherwise, the *Société d'économie politique* did not propose important institutional remedies, unlike the Anglo-American peace societies. Typically, the publicists connected to the society spoke out against or in favour of specific government policies. When dealing autonomously with peace, they focussed on tariffs and tax issues. International law in itself mostly appeared in the context of international trade law and the rights of neutrals. In the latter areas, the journal showed itself impressed with the legal accomplishments of the Congress of Paris.[168]

By the 1860s, the *journal des économistes* had ceased most of its overt peace propaganda. Reviews of the latest editions of Martens and Vattel did not betray any pacifist sentiment. On the contrary, the appraisal of Hautefeuille's *Droits et devoirs des neutres* reiterated de Maistre's conviction that war was morally and politically 'inevitable'.[169] Similarly, the review of Paul Pradier-Fodéré's edition of Vattel legitimised the Algerian quagmire. Basing himself on the standard of civilisation and self-defence, the reviewer concluded that France had stayed within the limits of international law.[170] Even at the height of the momentum generated by the peace conferences, the paper's editors did not object to colonialism as such. They understood it as a connection of overseas trade and missionary outposts, enabling commerce and Christianity to spread across the globe. Economic peace friends were often opposed to colonial empires, not necessarily out of humanitarian considerations, but because they rejected the system of state subsidies and monopolies these entailed.[171] Apart from that, they shared the colonial idealism of their contemporaries, like the *Société de la morale chrétienne*. Only a handful of French economic peace friends outright opposed colonialism as such, foremost Frédéric Passy.[172]

---

167 JE (série I, tome VIII, 1844), 87.

168 JE (série II, tome X, 1856), 310–4.

169 Charles Vergé (1810–1890) was one of the founding members of the *Institut de droit international*. JE (série II, tome XXV, 1860), 228–9.

170 JE (série II, tome XXXXI, 1864), 243–5.

171 Lincoln, *French Peace Movement* 2013, 63–8.

172 See chapter 7. Armand Mattelart, *Histoire de l'utopie planétaire. De la cité prophétique à la société globale* (Paris: La Découverte, 2009), 201–202.

2.2.2 A Congress of Nations

A few economic peace friends leaned closer towards the more institutionalised solutions. One of the most influential ones was Émile de Girardin, the newspaper man. Although not an academic, the fundamentals of his pacifism rested not so much on humanitarianism, as it did on the economic costs of the fiscal-military state. In fact, historians have cast doubt on the sincerity of his activism, because Girardin tended not to practice what he preached. In 1851, he cried for armed resistance against president Louis-Napoleon's coup d'état. Twenty years later, in the lead-up to the Franco-Prussian War, he abandoned all pretence of believing in universal peace through his virulently anti-Prussian calls for war. By then, he was still notorious for having shot and killed a noted competitor in a duel in 1836 – a particularly egregious act for a self-declared 'friend of peace'.[173] These dubious convictions returned throughout his public life. As a public author, Girardin seldom sailed against the political wind, switching from Orléanism, to republicanism, to Bonapartism, and republicanism again.[174] Despite his opportunistic instincts, this flamboyant man addressed the peace conferences of Paris and Frankfurt.[175] His active involvement testified to the relative popularity of the peace conference programme in French intellectual society, because someone like Girardin would never otherwise have wanted to associate himself with it. In turn, the peace societies were glad to get the public support of the owner of a much-talked-about paper with a print run of over 60,000 copies.[176]

Girardin's expressed his potpourri of fluctuating pacifist ideas not only in his speeches at the peace conferences, but across his prodigious oeuvre, from the Paris peace conference up until the Franco-Prussian War. The main thrust of his activism was broadly similar to that of most other economic pacifists of France. Essentially, both European diplomacy and the peace movement had to become more 'scientific', meaning that both had to respect certain discoverable natural laws with a universal validity. As Girardin opened his *La politique universelle* of 1852: *'la science n'a pas de patrie'*.

---

173 One of his biographers wondered if people managed to keep a straight face when the murderer of Armand Carrel proposed to ban duels. Lincoln, *French Peace Movement* 2013, 52–3; Pellissier, *Girardin* 1985, 274–275.

174 Ibid., 397–9.

175 *Congrès Paris* 1850, 40–1; *Proceedings Frankfurt* 1850, 3, 8–10.

176 *La Presse* was one of the few French newspapers that reported positively on the Paris conference. La Presse (23 August 1849), 1–2; La Presse (25 August 1849), 1–2; 'La Presse'. Unknown date, available at: www.retronews.fr/titre-de-presse/presse.

The preface accompanied this sentiment with an appropriate quote from Burlamaqui's *Principes du droit naturel*.[177]

Around the time of the Paris conference, Girardin posited that the *'politique de la paix'* demanded the overhaul of international law. The law of nations of the 1840s was not suited for this progressive era. He thus wrote: 'war and the past have had their law of nations, peace and the future impatiently await theirs.' Instead of wasting time with 'sterile' and 'ridiculous' objections, it would be better to get on with laying out the foundations for a *'code des nations'*, ensuring the legal equality of states and dispute settlement mechanisms. France needed diplomats who were educated in the law of nations and possessed the will to introduce reforms.[178]

A concrete area of reform, Girardin suggested, could be the introduction of the principle of non-intervention as a general principle of international law. He specifically singled out Adolphe Thiers for his ardent support for an intervention against Mazzini's Roman Republic. Girardin denounced chessboard games over spheres of influence: 'this word: *'influence'*, costs France more than a million a day; what does it offer us? What has it given us since 1815? What has our 1823 expedition in Spain given us? What has our 1831 expedition in Ancona given us? What has our 1832 expedition in Antwerp given us? What have our armaments given us in 1840?'. The treaties of Vienna could not be an obstacle. Austria's illegal annexation of Cracow in 1846, a city-state that had been ensured permanent neutral status, had effectively meant that the Vienna settlement had been torn apart by the signatories' own hands – 'from then on, they could never again invoke it'.[179]

From the Crimean War onwards, Girardin shifted his focus more explicitly to European diplomatic alternatives to the conservative Vienna settlement. He dismissed the Treaty of Paris's 23rd Protocol on arbitration as a half-measure. Rather than accepting the consequences of adopting this principle, the treaty had hesitated *'à mi-chemin'*. Girardin was referring to the fact that arbitration had been left fully optional and non-binding. This appeared in stark contrast to article 8 of the treaty itself, which stipulated that any dispute threatening the peace between the Ottomans and the

177 Girardin, Émile de. *La politique universelle. Décrets de l'avenir* (Paris: Librairie Nouvelle, 1855), 7.

178 Girardin, Émile de. *Les 52. VII–VIII. La politique de la paix* (Paris: Lévy Frères, 1849), 192–6.

179 Ibid., 263, 279–80, 287–8; Émile de Girardin, *L'Empereur Napoléon III et l'Europe* (Bruxelles: Librairie de l'Office de Publicité 1859), 31–32.

signatory powers was subject to obligatory mediation.[180] For Girardin, the Protocol had to establish an unambiguous obligation to produce the desired pacification. He composed a redacted version, modelled on article 8, that dropped the expressions 'wish' and 'as circumstances permit' from its text.[181] This, and only this, Girardin declared, would lead to European disarmament. Unfortunately, the protocol's writers had, 'instead of doing the logical thing, conducted diplomacy'. They had openly assured that state sovereignty would not be harmed.[182] Clearly, Europe was in need of a more encompassing solution.

According to his later reflections, emperor Napoleon III had missed a great opportunity in 1856 to call together a permanent congress of nations. Girardin had grown disillusioned with Europe's repeated failed attempts to inaugurate a '*politique nouvelle*' between 1789 and the 1850s. The Oriental Question, the Polish Question, and the others remained as unresolved as ever. Revolution and war had both failed. As he put it: 'there is no European law anymore (…) divine right is the negation of popular right (…) the right of conquest is the negation of the right of nationality'. France and England supported the right of nationality against Russia and Austria over Poland and Italy, but invoked the right of conquest over Algeria or Hindustan.[183] How could the European states resolve these contradictions without violence?

Inspired by so-called 'Napoleonic ideas' of European unity, Girardin proposed a great diplomatic congress, composed of all European states, great and small, to settle all ongoing disputes, including the Oriental question. France could play a crucial role as the congress's central negotiator, playing out claims against one another, drawing concessions from all participants.[184] Every sea strait should furthermore be permanently neutralised. These reforms were to be codified in a single treaty, called 'the Treaty of 1860'. Once accepted by all of Europe, it would, in the long run, lead to the unity of currency, weights and measures, and taxes.[185] Girardin added few specifics

180 General Treaty for the Re-Establishment of Peace between Austria, France, Great Britain, Prussia, Sardinia and Turkey, and Russia, 30 March 1856, 114 CTS 409, art. 8; Émile de Girardin, *L'équilibre européen* (Paris: Lévy Frères 1859), 44.

181 The revised article went thusly: '*S'il survenait entre les puissances signataires un dissentiment qui menaçât le maintien de leurs relations, chacune de ces puissances, avant de recourir à l'emploi de la force, mettra les autres Parties contractantes en mesure de prévenir cette extrémité par leur action médiatrice.*' Ibid., 45.

182 Ibid. 42–48.

183 Girardin, *L'empereur* 1859, 6–14.

184 Girardin, *L'empereur* 1859, 32–8.

185 Ibid., 5–8; 42–6.

beyond this. Elsewhere, he spoke of a 'pacific confederation' with a 'federal army', inspired by the German Confederation or Switzerland.[186] His overall intent was to provide a positive legal framework in which the interests of each state were safeguarded. As he felt commerce to be in everyone's interest, Girardin otherwise let the hidden laws of political economy play out naturally. Still, the question remains how serious a man with such keen political instincts as Girardin truly meant it all.[187]

2.2.3 Reconciling Science with Politics

A man far less enamoured with the legacy of the great emperor or the vanities of great powers was Gustave de Molinari. As a Belgian, he represented the voice of Europe's small and neutral states in the mid-century continental peace movement. Despite coming from a country that many in France more or less openly desired to see annexed by *la patrie* – not least of whom emperor Napoleon III himself – Molinari was well-respected in French peace circles. After all, he spent much of his career and life in France. He was a member of the *Société d'économie politique* and the *Association pour la liberté des échanges*.[188] Politically, Molinari advocated a near-absolute *laisser-faire*. He stood extremely hostile to socialism, earning him more than one hostile reference in Marx's *Das Kapital*. Within the peace movement, Molinari took part in the Paris peace conference, even attending the rallies in Britain.[189] The coup d'état forced him back to Belgium, where he set up *L'économiste belge*. Around the same time, he also published a compilation of Saint-Pierre's works.[190] In 1868, he returned to Paris to join the editorial board of the *Journal des économistes*. A few years later, he became the editor-in-chief of the *Journal des débats*. He died in 1912.[191]

---

186 Émile de Girardin, *Questions de mon temps, 1836 à 1856. Questions politiques. Tome neuvième* (Paris: Serriere 1858), 794; Émile de Girardin, *La paix* (Paris: Libraire Nouvelle 1855), 30; Girardin, *Politique de la paix* 1849, 194–5, 263, 287–8.

187 Perhaps he wrote them to get into the emperor's good graces, considering the fawning over Napoleon I's 'genius' across most of Girardin's 1850s peace writings. The annex to his *La paix* contained copious passages from the *Idées napoléoniennes* and the *Mémorial de Sainte-Hélène*. Girardin, *La paix* 1855, 35–48.

188 Van der Linden, *Peace Movement* 1987, 491.

189 Lincoln, *French Peace Movement* 2013, 50; Van der Linden, *Peace Movement* 1987, 491; *Congrès Paris* 1850, 59.

190 Gustave de Molinari, *L'abbé de Saint-Pierre. Membre exclu de l'académie française. Sa vie et ses œuvres* (Paris: Guillaumin 1857).

191 Nadine Lubelski-Bernard, 'de MOLINARI, Gustave', in *Nouvelle biographie nationale*, vol. 6 (Bruxelles: Académie royale des sciences, des lettres, et des beaux-arts de Belgique 2001), 135–43.

Like Cobden, Garnier, Girardin and the other economic pacifists, Molinari wanted peace activism to be 'scientific'. In 1873, Molinari looked with satisfaction at how friends of peace sat shoulder to shoulder with lawyers and economists to discuss important issues of international law. He recalled how the peace movement long appeared content to 'declare war on the little tin soldiers that parents carelessly put in the hands of their children'. At last, sentimentality had given way for more practical considerations.[192] Although Molinari's statement was a major simplification, in light of our story so far, it could not be denied he was totally unimpressed with any pacifist measure that did not strictly rely on positive legislation conformable to immutable social laws. He agreed with most of the peace movement that, in the grand scheme of things, a 'universal concert' would inevitably establish itself through the natural development of civilisation. This process could be accelerated or slowed down. If peace propaganda wanted to be effective, it had to precisely show the economic cost of war, and offer the available legal remedies to avoid wars. For him, the primary task of the peace movement was to 'vulgarise the principles of political economy and the law of nations'.[193] In van der Linden's summary of Molinari: 'the philanthropic phase of the peace movement was drawing to a close; the phase of the lawyers was nearing'.[194]

Despite that, Molinari stood extremely sceptical towards an arbitral tribunal. In his entry on 'Peace' in the *Dictionnaire de l'économie politique* of 1853, Molinari critiqued the *projets* by Henri IV and Saint-Pierre.[195] Their great mistake was that they, 'like most schools of socialism', put far too much faith in 'artificial organisation'. If even the most bellicose states were convinced they had more interest in maintaining peace, they could always find ways to settle their dispute, regardless of any 'organised tribunal'. Conversely, if a state reasoned that it had more to gain by war, would a 'fragile institution' like a tribunal deter it? Of course, an executive authority could be put at its service, but that would only add to the problem. Refusals to submit to the tribunal's authority would inevitably lead to war, precisely that which it was meant to avoid. Additionally, any states willing to enforce

---

192 Journal des débats (31 October 1873), 1–2.

193 Molinari, *Saint-Pierre* 1857, 59–60.

194 Van der Linden, *Peace Movement* 1987, 609.

195 Saint-Pierre belonged to that class of architects who 'build a floor and forget to add the staircase'. Molinari, *Saint-Pierre* 1857, 34–5; Gustave de Molinari, 'Paix – Guerre', in Charles Coquelin and Gilbert Guillaumin (eds.) *Dictionnaire de l'économie politique. Tome second* (Paris: Guillaumin, 1853), 311.

verdicts would be de facto put on a permanent war footing – *'beau moyen d'assurer la paix universelle!'*[196]

The only way forward to permanent peace was the gradual and natural reduction of the risk of war. Specifically, Molinari took umbrage at those belligerent rights that hurt neutral trade. Drawing from Wheaton's history of international law, he detailed the harmful effects of blockades, privateers and excessively open-ended contraband lists on the global economy. Molinari hailed the breakthrough of 'free ships make free goods' in the Crimean War.[197] Overall, however, he could not conceive of 'a more backwards science' than the one studying the laws of nations. It had failed to recognise all of the immensely consequential economic and technological innovations of the nineteenth century. In his words: 'the law of nations has stayed in the same form it was modelled in by the Grotiuses, the Pufendorfs, the Seldens, the Bynkershoeks, and the other jurisconsults before the age of Watt and Adam Smith'. The future *'droit de la paix'* had to respect the 'new phenomenon of international solidarity', which demanded that no one could wage war at the financial expense of third parties.[198]

It was hardly a coincidence that both Sellon and Molinari personally hailed from small and neutral states threatened by powerful neighbours. Yet in contrast to the Swiss aristocrat, who favoured the neutralisation of large swaths of Europe, this Belgian economist wanted nothing less than a *'Sainte Alliance de la paix'* of the smaller powers. Molinari did not mean to outright exclude the great powers, but instead preferred to enlarge the existing Concert of Europe. As a Belgian, he could easily agree with Wheaton's critique on Bentham's perpetual peace league. According to Wheaton, the English philosopher had neglected all means to prevent the peace league from ending up dominated by 'its most powerful members'.[199] For Molinari, however, the threat of annexation seemed all too real. The *Économiste belge* extensively reported on the many territorial claims within Europe.[200] It appeared to him that Europe' smaller states were all 'destined, in the more or less distant future, to become absorbed by *les grands*'.[201] Even discounting this fear, Molinari disliked the tendency of great powers to unite in concert and

196 Ibid.

197 Molinari, Gustave de. *Questions. Tome II* 1861, 287–323.

198 Ibid., 326–31.

199 Molinari, *Saint-Pierre* 1857, 114–5.

200 E.g. *Économiste belge* (hereafter: EB) (5 April 1855), 5–6; EB (20 November 1856), 8; EB (29 October 1859), 453; EB (25 August 1860), 1.

201 EB (7 October 1865), 216.

dictate their terms. Furthermore, whenever one of those powers threatened the peace, the system inevitably broke down, as proven by the Crimean and Italian Wars.[202]

The regularity of international or revolutionary conflicts over the past couple of decades warranted the creation of a 'special tribunal with regular sessions'. Cases could be brought before it by directly involved parties, or by neutrals harmed in their interests. If accepted, the tribunal would allow the parties to settle their differences amiably, but if this failed, the tribunal would judge. Its members should preferably be appointed proportionate to the productive power of each state. There were few specifics beyond this, like whether these men had to be jurists or whether they were to strictly follow juridical guidelines only. Judging from Molinari's scepticism elsewhere about both a purely judicial international court and an international legal code, he likely meant the tribunal to be partially a political forum, like most contemporaries.[203]

The most important for Molinari was that each member state of the international community could resort to *'une justice supérieure'* and *'une force publique'*. In spite of his modern-day libertarian reputation, Molinari agreed that *'une industrie dangereuse et insalubre'* could be forcibly held accountable to a higher normative standard, constraining individual agency.[204] He rejected the idea that states would never renounce, not even partially, their right to use armed force – 'if this theory was true, no treaty would ever be possible'.[205] This emphasis on enforcing international law was his main bone of contention with the rest of the peace movement. By the 1880s, he was not surprised that most still dismissed pacifists as *'simples utopistes'* with 'little influence in in the world'. In his opinion, 'the friends of peace imagine too much, in the innocence of their heart, that judges can do without gendarmes'.[206]

Molinari's peculiar brand of pacifism revealed the surprisingly wide range of legal positions possible within the economic faction of the peace

202 Like many, Molinari conflated the Concert of Europe with the Holy Alliance. Gustave de Molinari, *Questions. Tome II* 1861, 333–6; Gustave de Molinari, *Le congrès européen* (Bruxelles: Lacroix, Verboeckhoven, et Compagnie 1864), 39–40, 49–50.

203 Ibid., 39–50; Gustave de Molinari, *Questions. Tome II* 1861, 335–6; EB (14 July 1866), 157–60.

204 Molinari, *Congrès* 1864, 34–36; Gustave de Molinari, *Les soirées de la rue de Saint-Lazare. Entretiens sur les lois économiques et défense de la propriété* (Paris: Guillaumin 1849), 330–1.

205 Molinari, *Congrès* 1864, 25–38.

206 Molinari, *Évolution politique* 1884, 190; Molinari, *Droit de la paix* 1887, 14–5.

movement. Deference for individual liberties did not stop the economic French peace friends from turning to international law to limit the liberty of the state to wage war. An array of 'scientific' natural laws determined the scope of the legal reforms deemed feasible, or even possible, in the political world. It seemed pointless to try and introduce a principle that went against human nature, defined in terms of the universal desire to increase one's individual wealth and security. This scientism, which effectively sought to find an 'objective' ground for peace, reflected broader attempts by international lawyers in the mid-century to turn the confusing mess of state practice into a coherent and universally applicable normative system.

A deep aversion of statism ensured that leading peace friends, like Joseph Garnier, agreed with the international programme of stipulated arbitration, the plan that depended the least on a centralised locus of international government. This conformed to the wishes of 'conservatives' or 'moderates' in the Anglo-American peace movement, including Jay and Cobden. The economic French peace friends who did advocate closer international co-operation, like Girardin or Molinari, also eschewed a global state. They supported a confederative solution, because it seemed more suited to guarantee 'life, liberty, and property'. Any multilateral congress or confederation in this vein was to limit itself to ensuring the stable functioning of the markets, similar to domestic government. An international court and a legal code were seen as consequences of the realisation of the natural laws of free trade, rather than as necessary preconditions for peace, like they were for Ladd or Burritt in the American Peace Society. Economic interdependence would naturally lead states to adopt common normative standards and institutions, under the increasing pressure of public opinion.

True enough, around the time of the entry of the *Société d'économie politique* into the peace movement, the first autonomous peace societies sprang up in France. Although small and short-lived attempts, they remained notable for their ambition to introduce pacifist ideals directly into the political arena. In stark contrast to the sensibilities of most of the economists, however, the first initiative occupied itself with the lot of the working classes. Even more remarkable for contemporaries, it was led by a woman.

2.3 *Organised Pacifism*

In February 1844, a new Parisian newspaper saw the light of day. Titled *La paix des deux mondes*, its title explicitly referred to the periodical's intent to serve as a mediator between the Anglo-American peace societies and the

French public. Its initial subtitle was: '*écho des sociétés de la paix*'.[207] Its opening page revealed a deep admiration for the Anglo-American London peace conference the year before. Philanthropical societies had managed to assemble 2,000 people to discuss the best means towards peace. They had ultimately agreed on Jay's proposal for stipulated arbitration. As the paper opined: 'what these two great states have realised, France would not dare to undertake? (…) Its heart fights for all that is great, generous, useful, and peace, which it sees as a blessing, will become from now on a need'. The article informed that a peace committee had been formed a few years earlier, along with a concours, but that this 'partial' attempt would soon be completed by a peace society.[208] That society was the *Société de la paix de Paris,* headed by Eugénie Niboyet (1796–1883).

2.3.1 The *Société de la paix de Paris*

Niboyet carved out a remarkable career as a writer and social activist, in spite of the many prejudices against women in nineteenth century French society. She was born in Lyon into a liberal-bourgeois milieu. In her twenties, she dutifully married a lawyer, although the marriage was not a happy one. In 1829, in mutual agreement with her husband, she moved to Paris, where she made a living with her pen.[209] In the capital, she became enmeshed in Saint-Simonian and Fourierist circles. Likewise, she won prizes from the *Société de la morale chrétienne* in 1836 and 1842. Her talents were recognised further when she got accepted into the society proper in 1839. She quickly chaired the Committee of Charity and Beneficence, which under her leadership dealt with care for imprisoned women and their children. Niboyet was also elected to the editorial board of the society's journal.[210] Although she was no radical revolutionary, she did tend to seek out the edges of acceptable political discourse. In particular, Niboyet was not prepared to compromise on women's rights, an issue for which she received an enormous amount of pushback. She passed away in 1883, having lived a hard life. Her cause did not die with her. She lived just long enough to see

207 It had no connection to the *Revue des deux mondes,* although its name might have been inspired by this well-known periodical. Eugénie Niboyet, *Letter of 27 July 1844* [Bibliothèque Marguerite Durand, Niboyet, Eugénie fonds], 091 NIB Res.

208 PDM (15 February 1844), 1.

209 Alice Primi, *Femmes de progrès. Françaises et allemandes engagées dans leur siècle, 1844–1870* (Rennes: Presses universitaires de Rennes, 2010), 143; Michèle Riot-Sarcy, *Histoire du féminisme* (Paris: La Découverte 2015), 35–48.

210 JSMC (série II, tome XIX, n° 1), 9–13; JSMC (série III, tome I, n° 1), 2.

her being honoured by the international feminist movement that was beginning to take shape.[211]

Similar to the New-England Non-Resistance Society in the United States, the Parisian Peace Society resulted from a rupture within a larger organisation. Once again, the English agent Stephen Rigaud was involved. For his fourth continental trip on behalf of the London Peace Society, in early 1844, he returned to Paris. He brought with him a letter of the British society, politely yet firmly insisting that the Peace Committee of the Society of Christian Morals should finally undertake some action of its own accord. They suggested the dissemination of 'small tracts', similar to the British example. However, Rigaud was rebuffed by the French society. Instead, he accepted a third-party invitation to discuss the topic of a genuine peace society in Paris. The meetings took place at Niboyet's house, where the British agent discovered she had assembled many original members of the former Peace Committee. Apparently, they too had all been disenchanted by the society's lacklustre support, and preferred 'a real and active peace society'. By May 1844, this new society had become a reality.[212]

The first 'proper' peace society of France was a modest affair. It peaked at approximately fifty-two members.[213] A notable collaborator to the *Paix des deux mondes,* though not necessarily also the peace society, was Patrice Bazan, one of the laureates of the Peace Committee's essay contest.[214] Pecqueur was likewise asked to contribute, but he never appeared in the newspaper's columns, suggesting he had declined.[215] Another adherent of note was countess Cécile de Sellon. It should be recalled here that the late count had bequeathed some money in his will for a peace periodical. This had likely been used to fund the *Paix des deux mondes,* since the paper identified the Sellon family as its original sponsor.[216] His widow and his daughters had stayed in touch with the larger peace movement. They hosted Rigaud in Geneva, who was happy that the Sellon ladies were 'still devoted to the cause of peace', even if they were unsuccessful in their attempts to revive

211 Michèle Riot-Sarcey, 'Histoire et autobiographie. "Le vrai livre des femmes" d'Eugénie Niboyet'. *Romantisme* 56(1) (1987), 59–68.

212 HP (October 1844), 173–5; Van der Linden, *Peace Movement* 1987, 213–4.

213 Ibid.; PDM (14 June 1844), 1–2.

214 PDM (15 February 1844), 1.

215 Constantin Pecqueur, *Letter from Eugénie Niboyet* [International Institute for Social History, Constantin Pecqueur papers], ARCH01044, nr. 55, available online at: hdl.handle.net/10622/ARCH01044.55; HP (January 1847), 218; Van der Linden, *Peace Movement* 1987, 213; HP (October 1844), 174–5.

216 PDM (30 May 1844), 2.

the Genevan Peace Society.[217] As a whole, female peace friends played a relatively visible role in the new society. Nearly a fifth of the newspaper's collaborators were women, which was unheard of in other societies.[218] Only the radical New England Non-Resistance Society was even more welcoming to women, but nobody in France had heard of it. The American honorary members of the Parisian Peace Society all belonged to the American Peace Society.[219]

To give substance to their ideology, the society installed an essay contest on 'the means to realise a permanent and universal peace'. The grand laureate was to receive a gold medal worth 300 francs.[220] However, nothing ever came of it. In the brief timespan wherein the *Paix des deux mondes* exclusively concerned itself with peace, the Parisian Peace Society explicitly alluded to Jay's plan for stipulated arbitration. In an otherwise approving review, it criticised Bazan's idea to just redraw the European map. The Anglo-American plan seemed much more realistic.[221] Whether this reviewer represented the society's official position was difficult to say. Later, another contributor opined that 'a universal federation', similar to an Amphyctionic council, offered the best guarantee for peace.[222]

Be that as it may, there was never much doubt that the Anglo-American peace societies were based on *'un christianisme mal entendu'*. Though Rigaud did not enter into it in his reports, the French society did not condemn 'all' war, like the London Peace Society. Rather, in keeping with the general thrust of French and European pacifism, the society explicitly rejected the principle of *'paix à tout prix'* – 'unworthy of self-respecting nations' – but advocated 'a strong peace, based on justice, maintained by right'.[223] Defensive war was doubtlessly agreeable with natural law. Was every attack supposed to be a divine ordeal? Did humans not already defend themselves against the forces of nature, by wearing clothes? The Parisian pacifists were uninterested in 'pursuing a useless perfectionism'.[224]

Disagreement with the London Peace Society did not end there. A year after the first issue, Niboyet explained why she had retitled her newspaper

217 HP (October 1844), 176.
218 PDM (15 February 1844), 1.
219 Van der Linden, *Peace Movement* 1987, 214.
220 Ibid.; PDM (20 June 1844), 6.
221 PDM (2 March 1844), 4–5.
222 PDM (5 September 1844), 1.
223 PDM (14 June 1844), 1.
224 PDM (2 October 1844), 1–2.

FIGURE 4.1 The satirical journal Charivari was one of many outlets to relentlessly mock feminist initiatives like Niboyet's *La voix des femmes* in the spring of 1848.

L'Avenir. Journal des intérêts sociaux. This name reflected more accurately the concerns of the editorial board. Only a few months into the newspaper, peace had already given way to social issues as the dominant theme. By the autumn, the peace movement was barely mentioned anymore. Although this partially reflected Niboyet's own intellectual journey, she also took explicit umbrage with the London Peace Society's social conservatism. Like Beckwith in the United States, the British leadership consisted of upper-middle class men unwilling to admit the unequal distribution of wealth. In a scathing article, Niboyet charged that peace could only have a solid foundation when everyone benefitted from it – 'and we know not what the poor people of England stand to win with the present peace'. The British could preach 'peace at any price' as much as they wanted, but 'when the rich and powerful do nothing for the poor, a conflict sooner or later becomes inevitable'.[225] The Parisian Peace Society did not need to worry about losing its journal by that move, because it had by then ceased to exist. When Rigaud returned the following year, he did not even mention it in his report. *L'Avenir* in turn did not survive the year.[226]

2.3.2 The *Société de la paix universelle*

Much more is known about the last institutional initiative to emerge out of the tumultuous 1840s. As with the Parisian Peace Society, it traced its origins to the dissident papers. Far away from Paris, in the department of the Ain, bordering Geneva, a medical doctor called Francisque Bouvet (1799–1871) had risen to national prominence. He was one of those friends of peace who led an eccentric and therefore interesting life. The son of an officer in the republican army during the Revolutionary Wars, Bouvet was fiercely republican from a young age. Unable to keep his opinions to himself, he was detained twice in his youth for speaking out against the Restoration. The second time, he was bailed out by none other than Benjamin Constant. Romantic and idealist, the young man took part in the Greek War of Independence. Upon his return home after several years in the Near East, his anti-monarchism led him to write a book that earned him another three-month stint in jail. Bouvet had invited Louis-Philippe to abdicate in favour of a new republic. He described the constitutional July Monarchy as a 'bastard system', nothing but 'a kind of Jesuitical half-measure between tyranny and liberty'.[227] He eventually returned to the village he grew up in, where he authored several books on his political and religious ideas. In those years, Bouvet also set up a regional paper, the *Réveil de l'Ain*, a weekly

225 PDM (28 November 1844), 1–2.

226 Van der Linden, *Peace Movement* 1987, 215.

227 The spirit of the July Revolution had been 'betrayed' by Louis-Philippe's government. Francisque Bouvet (ed. C.M. Lesaulnier) *République ou monarchie, ou principes d'ordre social* (Paris: Mie 1832), xv.

whose notoriety far exceeded its readership. The newspaper's critical and political articles again brought Bouvet before a judge, this time twice in the same year. On both occasions, the jury acquitted him. When news of the February Revolution reached the department, Bouvet's reputation as a republican firebrand brought him not into a royalist courtroom, as had up until then been the case, but into the hallowed halls of the National Assembly of the Second Republic. *Citoyen* Bouvet served from 1848 to 1849, taking a seat on the left.[228]

As a politician, Bouvet was chiefly remarkable for having brought the ideals of the peace movement into the parliamentary deliberations of the Republic. In the most noteworthy episode, he proposed an amendment to article 5 of the new republican constitution. The article in question captured the aversion of the French republicans to the past conservative interventions of the European Concert. France was constitutionally rendered unable to wage wars of conquest, or use its forces 'against the liberty of any people'.[229] Caught in the larger optimism of the Constituent Assembly, Bouvet gave a long speech in which he argued that France had a duty to internationalise its revolutionary ideals, because *liberté, égalité, fraternité* were universal truths. Humanity needed an 'international jurisdiction, a grand jury, or universal assembly of peoples, that would replace war, guarantee treaties, adjudicate all disputes between governments, and redistribute the costs of grand works of general interest'.[230] This certainly caught the attention of his fellow representatives, but hardly in the way Bouvet would have liked. When the amendment was read aloud on voting day, the president of the assembly was twice interrupted by general 'hilarity'. Feeling humiliated, Bouvet refused to offer more explanation, and the issue was dropped without a discussion or a vote.[231]

228 *Biographie des neuf cents députés à l'assemblée nationale,* ed. (Paris: unknown publisher 1848), 1–5; Roman d'Amat, 'BOUVET (François-Joseph-Francisque)', in M. Prevost and Roman d'Amat (eds.), *Dictionnaire de biographie française. Tome septième* (Paris: Letouzey 1956), 73–4; M.T. Laurin, 'Un précurseur de la Société des Nations. Francisque Bouvet, représentant de l'Ain en 1848'. *La révolution de 1848 et les révolutions du XIXe siècle* 21(105) (1924), 129–31.

229 The Constituent Assembly clarified that, notwithstanding this article, the conquest of Algeria remained legitimate. France, Constitution de 1848, IIe République, 4 November 1848, art. V; *Le moniteur universel. Journal officiel de la république française* (hereafter: Moniteur) (8 September 1848), 2351.

230 Moniteur (6 September 1848), 2318–2319.

231 The passage in the *Moniteur* deserves to be cited in full: '"*Elle désire qu'un jury international, un congrès universel et perpétuel des peuples* (*On rit*), *puisse, un jour, remplacer la guerre, juger les différents élevés entres les États, garantir les traités, et régulariser*

Bouvet's other legislative attempt equally failed. In March 1849, the Committee on Foreign Affairs presented a negative report on his bill recommending a universal congress. The rapporteur did not deny that an international jurisdiction would be 'the greatest conquest of the modern era'. However, the committee saw the proposed law as unrealistic. Would the great powers, 'of which the military element is still the essential element of their activities', collaborate on the 'juridical peace' proposed by France? It seemed a less-than-ideal time to propose a grand plan for perpetual peace, when most of Europe was in the grip of revolution. The report was again not debated. Those interested could read the manifesto of the peace society led by the bill's author.[232]

This society was the *Société de la paix universelle.* Its first name was the *Union des peuples,* but it changed its name to fit better alongside the Anglo-American peace societies. Almost nothing is known about it, apart from its manifesto and the fact that Bouvet was its president. This peace society only lasted a couple of months, similar to the Parisian Peace Society.[233] It likely had few members. Bouvet was nonetheless eager to acquaint himself with the larger peace movement. His immediate contact was Elihu Burritt, who had been staying in Paris to set up the first European peace conference. Through Burritt, Bouvet became an active organiser or participant in all of the peace conferences, including the one in London of 1850. In doing so, he grew into a known quantity to the leading peace friends, to the point that even Jay referred to him.[234] Despite sharing many similar ideas with the Americans, Bouvet had developed his core notions years before his first acquaintance with the peace societies. The Syrian crisis of 1840 had first spurred him to think about a new international legal order.[235] In later

l'activité humaine, en vue du progrès pacifique des sociétés dans la moralité et le bien-être.' (Nouvelle hilarité.)" Moniteur (8 September 1848), 2351.

232 Moniteur (5 April 1849), 1248.

233 Lincoln mistakenly writes that this was the 'first' real peace society of France, forgetting about Niboyet. Lincoln, *French Peace Movement* 2013, 76.

234 Jay, *Review* 1849, 327–8; Van der Linden, *Peace Movement* 1987, 330–331; *Congrès Bruxelles* 1849, 10–7, 21–4, 55–6; *Congrès Paris* 1850, iv–v, viii, 1, 20–1; *Proceedings London* 1851, 69–70.

235 Francisque Bouvet, *Du rôle de la France dans la question d'Orient. Congrès universel et perpétuel à Constantinople* (Nantua: Arène 1840); Journal de l'Ain (22 January 1841), 1; La Phalange (12 February 1844), 316–8; La Phalange (24 February 1844), 404–7.

writings, he further developed his argument, albeit without ever straying from his first ideas.[236]

Many of Bouvet's suggestions corresponded to the ambitions of the international peace movement, albeit modified by typically French concerns and ambitions. Like the Americans, Sellon, Pecqueur, and some of the other French peace friends, Bouvet favoured a 'permanent and universal congress'. This institution was to function as the 'supreme tribunal', a *'gouvernement des gouvernements',* ruling by 'moral force'.[237] Like all other French peace friends, this did not mean that defensive war was to be outlawed, or that the confederated states would be unable to militarily enforce decisions as an *ultima ratio*. Although sympathetic to the peace societies, he deplored that these were 'compromised' by two classes of men. The first were people who imagined themselves 'apostles of the Gospel charged with the special task of conserving its principle, and elevating it above all human transaction'. By contrast, the second were people 'whose vision did not reach past the borders of their check books'. Both were absolutists who wanted 'peace at any price', no matter the cost. If the peace movement 'persisted in its sentimentalism', they would do more harm than good. After all, *'la morale est rarement ignorée, mais elle est encore plus rarement suivie'*. The *abbé* Grégoire's principles of the law of nations were well-intended, but added nothing to what was already known from the Gospel. Bouvet wanted the peace movement to become more 'strategic' and 'scientific', meaning that it had to focus on politics and law.[238] Like Pecqueur, Girardin, and Molinari, he equated pragmatism with juridical solutions.

As had been explicitly argued within the American Peace Society, more narrow-scoped debates on law could provide points of agreement across ideological boundaries. As a left-leaning republican, Bouvet's pacifism was more secular than the Society of Christian morals, and not *laisser-faire* enough for many within the Society of Political Economy.[239] Still, he concurred with both that international law had to disincentive or limit the sovereign right to wage war. Bouvet wished to undo the mistakes of the Treaty of Vienna, 'dictated by the right of the strongest'. It had failed to prevent the 'armed peace' between the European monarchies, saddling their states with

236 Francisque Bouvet, *La guerre et la civilisation* (Paris: Dentu 1855); the second edition was entitled *Introduction à l'établissement d'un droit public européen.*

237 Bouvet, *Congrès universel* 1840, 14.

238 Bouvet, *Droit public* 1856, 264–9.

239 Ibid., 229–31.

massive debts.[240] Disarmament could only be done through multilateral cooperation. To avoid military expenditure from spiralling out of control again, all states would have to agree on a code of international law. Basically repeating the same observation as someone like Worcester – a religious peace friend if ever there was one – Bouvet underlined that war never fundamentally solved any question. 'After all forces and physical resources are exhausted, are we not always brought back to the authority of arguments and law?'[241]

Despite his positivist sensibilities, Bouvet too based the destiny of world order on natural law. God had planted the roots of the 'constitution of societies', and while humans could mutilate or nourish this 'tree', they could never stop it from growing its branches. Bouvet connected the history of the law of nations, with pacification plans and greater political events. From Grotius onwards, obstacles had been gradually put in the way of the laws of war. As these laws became more delineated, people equally began to grow aware of the need for a jurisdiction to enforce these laws. Grotius, Pufendorf and Wolff had not yet envisioned European unity. Vattel had dismissed it as a utopian 'dream'. By the nineteenth century, however, Ancillon had observed that the lack of positive international laws was the cause of most wars, joined by Martens, who had allegedly said that it was 'easy' to draw up a law-making treaty. Burlamaqui and Sylvestro Pinheiro-Ferreira had both written in a similar spirit by illustrating the necessity of putting states 'in harmony'.[242]

To this long list of jurists, Bouvet added the famous writers who had envisioned a federative peace, including Penn, Saint-Pierre, Bentham, Kant, Fichte, Gondon, Saint-Simon, Fourier and even the recent publications by Girardin and Pecqueur. Interestingly, he did not refer to Ladd, though it was improbable that someone as well-connected as Bouvet would not have heard of him. Whatever the case may be, Bouvet did not enter into detail on any single author.[243]

They were only confirming what Bouvet had also noticed in high politics. From Westphalia to the Congress of Vienna, the natural law of sociability that led society towards ever greater unity was visibly gaining ground. Even

240 Bouvet, *Congrès universel* 1840, 19; Bouvet, Francisque. *La Turquie et les cabinets de l'Europe depuis le XVe siècle. La question de l'Orient* (Paris: Giraud 1853), 249–50.

241 Bouvet, *Congrès universel* 1840, 19–20.

242 Bouvet, *Droit public* 1856, 1–168, 175, 205–10.

243 Ibid., 206–219; largely repeated in Francisque Bouvet, *Le problème européen* (Paris: Renou et Maulde 1866), 27–8.

in the reactionary atmosphere of Vienna, people had 'seriously spoken about the possibility of realising a European Amphyctionic council, and a repressive system against infractions of the public peace'. The Holy Alliance likewise had been intended to make the peoples live in brotherhood under the precepts of the Gospel. 'Only the ignorant' could believe that 'the question of permanent and universal peace' was only the dream of *'un honnête abbé du siècle dernier'*.[244]

Bouvet's congress of nations at first glance seemed broadly similar to Pecqueur and Ladd. Lincoln-Lambert already described his positions as 'closer to the American peace advocates', as Bouvet did not propose a world state, like Pecqueur.[245] States were to act as sovereign members of an interstate confederation, similar to Ladd. However, Bouvet had not adopted the distinguishing feature of this American plan. Despite having read Pecqueur and Gondon, Bouvet did not suggest an independent international court, as a judicial body distinct from the legislative congress. Like most confederative peace plans, Bouvet attributed to his own institution both legislative, judicial, and executive powers. There was no division of powers to speak of, in contrast to Ladd. As Bouvet wrote it: 'The congress of nations would possess a juridical and purely international character. It would edit an international code (…) revise treaties, and assure the execution (…)'.[246]

Despite substantive overlaps with American notions of a confederative peace, Bouvet stayed within the French republican tradition. This potentially explained his differences with Ladd and Pecqueur, who were both more inspired by the United States constitution. As mentioned earlier, republicans in France mistrusted a *gouvernement des juges*. Or put more positively, they deeply venerated the *volonté générale* as expressed by the people. Like Bergami also wrote, the international project of the deputy of the Ain could not be seen separately from the post–1848 electoral reform campaign. Republican ideology held that representatives did not have a mere imperative mandate, in which they were only delegated power by every individual voter. Instead, representatives continued to independently use their reason to reach the most rational consensus. The more the *nation* had taken part in the election, the more reasonable and rational the outcome of the deliberation would be. In sum, *la volonté générale* and *la raison*

244 Bouvet, *Droit public* 1856, 205–21, 266–7.

245 Lincoln, *French Peace Movement* 2013, 71.

246 Bouvet, *Droit public* 1856, 229.

générale became synonymous. After the February Revolution, therefore, France became the first country to install universal male suffrage.[247]

For Bouvet, the same applied to the community of states: '[this theory] is understood exactly as the legal institutions that have shaped civil society'. He championed *'l'unité dans la diversité'.* The congress of nations of *citoyen* Bouvet could be composed of states of grossly unequal power, or with radically opposed constitutions. Representatives of republics could sit alongside those of great monarchical empires. True, their interests would clash hard and often, but was the same not true also in national parliaments? Arguments in favour of a confederation of republics, or a holy alliance of monarchies, were 'the very negation of the social principle'.[248] Bouvet's republicanism, in all its idealism, could not be further removed from the solutions of someone like Molinari. As we know, this Belgian had decidedly less confidence in the reasonableness of great powers, especially when united in congress.

Bouvet's Bonapartism would have appalled Molinari even more, had he read any of his books. In fact, it would have mystified just about every peace friend outside of France. Parts of the republican left emphasised the progressist aspects of Napoleon I's record, like the *Code Civil* or his plebiscites. The late emperor was a concrete precedent for France's unique mission to civilise the world. French peace friends, like many socialists, sought to get rid of the martial connotations attached to national glory. The 'conquests of peace' proved that peace was compatible with patriotism. Bouvet's project and its relentless chauvinism was no different from other French pacification plans. He believed in 'the dream of Henri IV and Napoleon I (…) We believe in a providential mission for our France'.[249]

This likely contributed to Bouvet's remarkable shift of allegiance after the coup d'état. After some hesitation, this erstwhile republican became a loyal subject of the emperor. His publications of the 1850s and 1860s fully supported the ostensibly pacific politics of Napoleon III. He faithfully served him in the Ministry of Foreign Affairs, even being awarded the position of

247 Bouvet, *République* 1832, 114–21; Bergami, 'Quelle démocratie' 2014, 19–21; Rosanvallon, *Démocratie* 2000, 171–95.

248 Bouvet, *Droit public* 1856, 197–202.

249 Bouvet, *Droit public* 1856, 203–4; Carol Bergami, 'Entre tradition de 1848 et souvenir napoléonien. Un européisme politique rallié au Second Empire', in Sylvie Aprile, Christina Cassina, Philippe Darriulat and René Leboutte (eds.), *Europe de papier. Projets européens au XIXe siècle* (Villeneuve d'Ascq: Presses universitaires du Septentrion 2015), 146–148.

consul in Mosul.[250] The 1850s and 1860s were a gloomy affair overall for the peace movement, and Bouvet lost touch with it. By the time of the Franco-Prussian War, Bouvet had abandoned his interest in pacifism. He died shortly afterwards, but not before seeing another republic rise up in his beloved France.[251]

3 Imagining Peace in the Second Empire

'L'empire, c'est la paix!' So went the most iconic passage in what was arguably one of the most famous speeches of Napoleon III (1808–1873), emperor of the French. He gave it in Bordeaux in October 1852, near the end of his tour through the so-called *hexagone* of mainland France, meant to reinforce his grip on power. A year earlier, in the night of 1 on 2 December 1851, the president had sent out his troops to occupy key positions in Paris, disband the National Assembly and force a revision of the constitution. At the cost of thousands of dead, imprisoned, deported and exiled dissidents, the coup d'état had become a political fact. A plebiscite later that month endorsed the dictatorship. On 2 December 1852, Napoleon III would complete his lifelong ambition and proclaim the empire.[252]

In the Bordeaux speech anticipating this, the emperor set out the broad contours of his domestic and international policy. Among his intended audiences he surely calculated the other governments of Europe, who needed to be reassured that the reborn French empire had no ambition to repeat the military expansionism of its predecessor. Rather, the new emperor would 'conquer' the political divide, spread Christianity and bring economic prosperity to France.[253] Intended even more so for Napoleon III's domestic audience, however, the speech revealed why this authoritarian regime still managed to seduce some of the republican *quarante-huitards,* like Bouvet, to support the new regime. Bonapartist theorists legitimised the massive expansion of the executive power by claiming that the plebiscites confirming the regime had ensured that the *volonté générale* of the French nation remained respected. Napoleon III had after all not abolished universal

250 Francisque Bouvet, *Letter dated 25 February 1856* [Archives diplomatiques du ministère des affaires étrangères, dossier Bouvet, Francisque], 393QO/595.

251 Bergami, 'Entre tradition' 2015, 150–1; Laurin, 'Précurseur' 1924, 131.

252 Louis-Napoléon Bonaparte, *Œuvres de Napoléon III. Tome troisième* (Paris: Plon, Amyot 1869), 343; Jacques Bainville, *Les dictateurs* (Paris: Perrin 2019), 123–129.

253 Bonaparte, *Œuvres. Tome III* 1869, 342–4.

suffrage. As one supporter synthesised it: *'L'Empereur n'est pas un homme, c'est un peuple'*.[254]

Of course, the Bonapartist regime was full of internal contradictions. Despite claiming to stand for peace, Napoleon III pursued an active foreign policy, getting France embroiled in three major wars: in the Crimea from 1853 to 1856, in Italy in 1859, and in Mexico from 1862 to 1867. The emperor ultimately even fell from power following the disastrous war he had undertaken against Bismarck's Prussia. Domestically, although the empire somewhat 'liberalised' in the 1860s, from the Cobden-Chevalier free trade agreement onwards, it remained overall very much characterised by Caesarism. Remarkable industrial and commercial growth in the 1850s was coupled with blatant cronyism and the introduction of a workers' booklet restricting freedom of movement. The 'democratic' practice of occasional plebiscites and a relatively large suffrage was undermined by the existence of 'official candidates' to elections, and the disappearance of the freedom of expression. Tight censorship laws had ensured that many newspapers were shut down. The right of assembly was severely limited. It caused many opposition figures, from legitimists to republicans, to seek refuge abroad. Those who stayed were left with very little room for manoeuvre.[255]

Unsurprisingly, the 1850s and early 1860s produced fewer pacifist initiatives than the 1840s. There were no known attempts to erect a peace society up until the 1867 Luxembourg Crisis, in the latter years of the empire, when a certain liberalisation had already set in. Accordingly, the peace friends of these years mostly consisted of individual publicists.[256] Most, like Bouvet and Girardin, wrote in response to foreign policy actions of Napoleon III. One former adherent of the peace conferences, Michel Chevalier, even joined the government itself. As the emperor's chief economic advisor, he publicly defended the former's foreign policy, aligning it with his own peace ideas. With his English friend Richard Cobden, Chevalier brought the economic peace friends a great victory, when France and Britain signed the 'Cobden-Chevalier' free trade agreement in 1860. This success stood in sharp contrast to the condition of those who preferred exile over silence. Biding their time in Switzerland, Belgium, Britain and elsewhere, many

254 Rosanvallon, *Démocratie* 2000, 209–11.

255 Jean-Claude Caron and Michel Vernus, *L'Europe au 19e siècle. Des nations aux nationalismes (1815–1914)* (Malakoff: Armand Colin 2019), 191–214.

256 Most authors were unconnected to the international peace movement, and not attached to non-violent means of reform. Many simply redrew the European borders. They are not further discussed for this reason. See ter Meulen, *Gedanke 1929*, 331–6.

FIGURE 4.2 Bonapartist propaganda heavily emphasised the regime's ostensibly peaceful politics, foreign and domestic.

FIGURE 4.3 As usual, Daumier proved more skeptical of grandiose claims of peace.

republican *proscrits* would join the post–1867 societies. Until then, the most significant French peace advocate linking the 1840s with the upcoming generations was Edmond Potonié, founder of the *Ligue du bien public.*

3.1 *Bonapartist Views on Peace*

Before his rise to power, prince Louis-Napoléon had already presented the gist of his international ambitions in his *Idées Napoléoniennes* from 1839.

He drew heavily from Napoleon's *Mémorial de Sainte-Hélène,* an apologetic work in which the deposed emperor had tried to reframe his achievements.[257] Essentially, France needed a strong, central executive power to consolidate the gains of the French Revolution, protect national self-determination and revise the Vienna settlement. All of this would restore France to its rightful position as the foremost great power of Europe.[258] While many outside of France could agree with several of these principles, for various reasons, the books were generally meant for domestic consumption. Molinari, looking at it from the Belgian perspective, found most of this Bonapartist revisionism beyond absurd. Napoleon I had complained that that the idea of a Holy Alliance had been 'stolen' from him. Napoleon III claimed that the Corsican general had, in fact, all along had some master-plan to introduce a European code and a European *cour de cassation.*[259] Molinari, however, recalled an anecdote purportedly set at the height of Napoleon's dominion over Europe. When asked where the emperor believed all of his great political upheavals would lead to, he answered that he had 'no idea' – 'and it appears that, this time, he told the truth'.[260] For Molinari, Napoleon III likewise had no larger objective as emperor other than maintaining his hold on power and ensuring the continuity of his dynasty.[261]

Inside France, however, these 'Napoleonic ideas' exerted some considerable influence on advocates of peace who had not rejected the new regime, the only ones able to express their ideas within the country itself. We have already noted Girardin's ambiguous sympathies with imperial policies.[262] In Bouvet's works too, we can find ample citations from the works of Napoleon III, beginning in his 1853 *La Turquie et les cabinets de l'Europe,* the work in which he first publicly revealed his support for the imperial regime. 'European association ... European code ... European institution ... European

257 The *Mémorial* played a crucial part in the construction of the *légende napoléonienne.* It was authored by Emmanuel de Las Cases, *Mémorial de Sainte-Hélène. 8 volumes* (Bruxelles: Remy 1822–1823); Louis-Napoléon Bonaparte, *Des idées napoléoniennes* (Paris: Paulin 1839), 173–186; Robert Morrissey, *Napoléon et l'héritage de la gloire* (Paris: Presses universitaires de France 2010), 170–209.

258 Bonaparte, *Idées* 1839, 173–86, 195–201.

259 Ibid., 176–77.

260 Molinari, *Congrès* 1864, 10–1.

261 Gustave de Molinari, *Napoléon III, publiciste* (Bruxelles: Lacroix, Van Meenen & Compagnie 1861), V-VI.

262 See supra in this chapter.

family! This policy (…) is the one of Napoleon III, like it has been that of Louis-Napoléon (…)'.[263]

In 1856, Bouvet repeated his call for a new European public law. He argued that the mistakes made in Vienna and subsequent congresses had directly led to the Crimean War. Only French ideas could herald a stable peace. The man who had said that the empire meant peace, could find glory for his country in 'this association of peoples that was the sublime vision of the captive of Saint-Helena'.[264] He continued this line in all of his publications on peace. Until as late as 1866, a year before Passy launched the new wave of institutional pacifism, Bouvet regarded the harmonisation of the interests and law of the European states as 'the mission of the Bonaparte dynasty'.[265]

The precedent of the 1856 Paris Congress inspired both the emperor and French peace friends to suggest even more ambitious proposals to reform international politics and law through multilateral diplomacy. The politically most significant attempt came from the emperor himself. Claiming that the January Uprising in Poland needed an international solution, he addressed the *Corps législatif* on 5 November 1863 announcing his intent to convene another European congress. The day before, he had sent a letter in this sense to most European cabinets. The call itself was vague. The delegates of every European power were to devise an order reconciling the interests of sovereigns with those of the peoples, 'without any preconceived system' in mind. His inspirations were the congresses of Westphalia and Vienna in the past. Whether Napoleon III had any concrete suggestions or not, the move certainly fitted in his quest to destroy the Vienna settlement. According to him, it was already 'falling apart on all sides'.[266] The proposal quickly proved still-born. Like with Metternich's initiative in 1840, Britain rejected it.[267] The international peace movement was likewise sceptical. Burritt was the most enthusiastic, claiming that the French emperor had adopted the same programme as that of the 1849 Paris peace conference. However, Cobden, Girardin, Molinari and others needed more concrete

263 Bouvet, *La Turquie* 1853, 259.

264 Bouvet, *Droit public* 1856, 176–91, 188–9, 239–52.

265 Bouvet, *Problème* 1866, 10.

266 Louis-Napoléon Bonaparte, *Œuvres de Napoléon III. Tome cinquième* (Paris: Plon, Amyot 1869), 200–13.

267 Van der Linden, *Peace Movement* 1987, 512–3.

results before they would believe the man who had been waging war in Italy and Mexico.[268]

Someone who did believe in the emperor was Michel Chevalier. Chevalier theorised on pacification from the centre of the imperial universe. His interest in the topic went back all the way to his days as a Saint-Simonian, when he was the editor-in-chief of the Saint-Simonian journal *Le Globe* in the early 1830s. In a series of articles, afterwards compiled into a short brochure called *Le système de la Méditerranée,* he articulated his first major theory. Chevalier sought for a means to reconcile the East with the West, since he believed their 'civilisational' conflict had been a perennial cause of war over the centuries. Chevalier set about achieving this through 'universal association', that he regarded as more than a mere 'confederation of peoples or a commercial treaty between cabinets'. Memorably, he proposed a vast railroad network connecting Europe with the Near East. This network would stimulate economic exchange and intercultural communication.[269] Importantly, this 'Mediterranean system', that could be expanded to encompass the entire world, still needed a legal complement to enable its operation. Like the peace friends, Saint-Simonians favoured some Amphyctionic council and an accompanying European public law to replace the monarchical Vienna settlement, although not necessarily through peaceful means.[270]

Chevalier's famous conversion to political and economic liberalism by the 1840s did not diminish his pacifism. While certainly dramatic, and counter to the career of other Saint-Simonians, who got enamoured with Fourierist socialism, Chevalier's ideological leap was not as abrupt as it had usually been described. While he shared the free trade idealism of Garnier and the *Société d'économie politique,* the erstwhile Saint-Simonian generally allowed for more state intervention in the economy than his peers.[271] It did

268 Ibid.

269 Michel Chevalier, *Politique européenne* (Paris: Bureau du Globe 1832), 97–105; Michel Chevalier, *Politique industrielle et système de la méditerranée* (Paris: unknown publisher 1832), 129–50; Jérôme Debrune, 'Le système de la méditerranée de Michel Chevalier'. *Confluences Méditerranée* 36(1) (2001), 187; Nere Basabe, 'L'Europe au-delà de ses frontières: l'élargissement de l'espace européen dans les projets de 1830–1848', in Sylvie Aprile, Christina Cassina, Philippe Darriulat and René Leboutte (eds.), *Europe de papier. Projets européens au XIXe siècle* (Villeneuve d'Ascq: Presses universitaires du Septentrion 2015), 255.

270 *Revue des deux mondes* (série IV, tome XXIII, 1840), 248–9; Basabe, 'L'Europe' 2015, 258.

271 Michael Drolet, 'Industry, Class and Society: A Historiographic Reinterpretation of Michel Chevalier'. *English Historical Review* CXXIII(504) (2008), 1271.

not diminish his rising star. Chevalier accepted various prestigious positions in both the July Monarchy, the Second Republic and the Second Empire. In intellectual life, he joined the academic establishment as holder of the chair of political economy at the *Collège de France.* Chevalier was also an *académicien* of the *Académie des sciences morales et politiques.* In the Second Empire, Napoleon III appointed him into his *Conseil d'état,* in which Chevalier was active from 1852 to 1860. In 1860, the emperor promoted his longtime advisor to the imperial senate, a prestigious position. In that august body, Chevalier revealed that his loyalty was not unconditional. In 1870, amid hundreds of war cries in the papers – not least also in Girardin's – he voted against the war declaration, the only senator to do so.[272]

Chevalier's marked career had likewise not prevented him from keeping abreast of the international peace movement. He was away on business during the Paris peace conference, but he sent a letter of adhesion. In it, the professor criticised the 'armed peace' and protectionist policies.[273] Unable to accompany the French delegation to Britain for the post-conference rallies, he nonetheless again wrote positively to the London Peace Society.[274] The Frankfurt peace congress committee therefore counted Chevalier among its most respected French sympathisers.[275] He was uninvolved in the two attempts to found a French peace society in the 1840s. However, Chevalier did join Passy's league, which emerged out of his own economic pacifist circles.[276] According to Potonié, he also supported the *Ligue du bien public.*[277]

Did international law exist for someone like Chevalier? *'Oui et non.'* International norms undeniably existed, but most were vague, arbitrary and barely enforced. He used Wheaton's definition, which revealed an rationalist interest in perfectibility. Wheaton had asserted that law was ultimately based on reason.[278] Chevalier also quoted a British judge that international law was the 'formal expression of the public opinion of the civilised world'.[279] *'C'est très bien pensé',* concluded Chevalier with a sense of irony.

272 Ibid., 1231–2.

273 *Proceedings Paris* 1849, 109–11; *Congrès Paris* 1850, 7, 50, 59

274 JE (série I, tome XXIV, 1849), 434–6.

275 *Proceedings Frankfurt* 1851, VIII.

276 Drolet, 'Chevalier' 2008, 1233.

277 Edmond Potonié-Pierre, *Historique du mouvement pacifique* (Berne: Steiger & Cie 1899), 101–2.

278 Revue des deux mondes (15 May 1872), 396–14; Wheaton, *Elements* 1836, 46 (§ 11).

279 This was Hugh Cairns (1819–1885), Lord Chancellor at the time.

What better law than one based on reason and justice? However, how could any minority be brought to accept the wishes of a majority, however enlightened? Was public opinion not itself vacillating and easily misled?[280] In contrast to the sensibilities of Ferrer, Bara and the jurists of the soon-to-be-founded International Law Institute, Chevalier continued to put his faith in a federative international institution, the sole authority capable of imposing a hierarchy and enforcing the rules.

Chevalier saw such an institution as logically developing out of the breakthrough of free trade. Like Cobden in Britain, linked the liberalisation of trade with pacification. On many occasions, Chevalier criticised the armed peace.[281] In debates on free trade, he invariably talked about the impact it would have on international relations: 'The moment a stranger becomes a man that I have ceased to hate (…) the prism that international hatreds have held before my eyes falls off, and I see everything in other colours, in its true colours.'[282] Like Cobden, he hailed the Anglo-French free trade agreement of 1860 as a triumph of the peace movement.[283]

Unlike his British counterpart Cobden, Chevalier advocated a more politically far-reaching juridical complement than stipulated arbitration. Like Napoleon III, he wanted a 'new treaty of Westphalia'. The Viennese treaties of 1815 had been violated so often that it had become 'impossible to demand further respect for them'. He repeated the complaint of many within France, not least the emperor himself, that they had been 'dictated by a blind hatred towards France'. The result was that Europe lacked a generally recognised treaty which guaranteed the balance of power. No one knew security, but all paid for *'la paix armée'*. Europe needed a system of positive international law, like it already had a Christian morality from Madrid to Saint-Petersburg. The 'system of isolation' and the absence of any control had as a direct consequence the 'demoralisation of international law'.[284] The means to preserve the sovereignty of smaller states was to establish a permanent European congress. This congress was to take the form of an interstate confederation, or a loose federation. Besides familiar models like the Amphyctionic Council or a less reactionary version of the Holy Alliance, Chevalier pointed to the United States. Risen victorious out

280 Revue des deux mondes (15 May 1872), 400.

281 E.g. Michel Chevalier, *Du progrès. Discours à l'ouverture de son cours au collége de France* (Paris: Guillaumin 1852), 6; Revue des deux mondes (1 June 1866), 758–85.

282 Chevalier, *Du progrès* 1852, 21.

283 Drolet, 'Chevalier' 2008, 1.

284 Revue des deux mondes (1 June 1866), 766–77.

of its great Civil War, the Union had proven that two species of sovereignty, one general, one local, based on subsidiarity, could co-exist and prosper. Europe needed to form a similar union. The mistakes of the first half of the century would probably not be repeated. Representative government was breaking through across Europe. Even the czar had emancipated the Russian serfs. Under such conditions, a collective authority would presumably not 'open the gate for tyranny' again.[285]

3.2 *Dissident Views on Peace*

Edmond Potonié (1829–1902) was not quite so sure about this. From the 1850s to the early 1860s, Potonié led the only discernible peace society in France: the *Ligue du bien public*. His league was well-integrated in the larger peace movement. It had among its adherents leading pacifists like Molinari, Chevalier, Passy and Henry Richard. Members of the London Peace Society had partially financed the initiative. To escape imperial censorship, the league was officially based in Antwerp.[286] Potonié was well-connected. His father, a successful businessman, had in the 1840s co-organised the Paris peace conference. Potonié at the time was only twenty years old. In his history of the international peace movement of 1899, one of the first of its kind, he reminisced how Victor Hugo used to take him out on walks. The next year, Potonié was one of only seven French delegates in Frankfurt. Both instances left a deep impression on the young man. In old age, he still cherished his journey to the Frankfurt conference as among the best days of his life. He met many adherents of the peace conferences in person, including Bouvet, Bastiat, Garnier, Girardin, Richard and Cobden.[287] From Cobden in particular, Potonié absorbed a penchant for free trade.[288]

Later in life, during the 1850s and 1860s, Potonié shifted towards moderate socialism. His network came to include intellectuals of the labour movement, leading to some of his work getting reprinted in the circles of the First International.[289] Like Niboyet before him, Potonié tried to bridge the gap between the bourgeois peace societies and the socialists. Unfortunately, most of the sources on his networks have disappeared. Potonié lost his

285 Ibid., 784.

286 Cooper, *Patriotic pacifism* 1991, 31.

287 He was deeply charmed by their cosmopolitanism and open-mindedness. He lovingly recalled Garnier as prone to pedantry, and Guillaumin as a little fellow proud to be the editor of '*Messieurs les Économistes*'. Potonié-Pierre, *Historique* 1899, 76–81.

288 Ibid., 9, 15, 37, 107; Le Rameau d'Olivier (May 1877), 3.

289 Van der Linden, *Peace Movement* 1987, 588–93.

papers in the Paris Commune. The communard police prefect had them all seized and they ended up in flames, along with the rest of the police building.[290]

The programme of his league has been preserved in various publications.[291] In stark contrast to the peace societies of Britain and America, but similar to the short-lived Parisian Peace Society, Potonié found it impossible to disconnect peace from social justice. The *Ligue du bien public* campaigned for the separation of church and state, freedom of assembly, freedom of the press, abolition of capital punishment, state-sponsored elementary education, co-operative self-help societies for the working classes, and the legal equality of the sexes.[292]

The latter was a controversial topic within the peace societies, which were slow to integrate women in leadership positions, but it held a personal significance for Potonié. In fact, he preferred to call himself Potonié-Pierre in later life, in reflection of his relationship with the feminist Eugénie Pierre (1844–1898). They refused to legally marry, but took on each other's names to reflect their equality. Most of Eugénie's publications dealt with the emancipation of women – she claimed to have coined the term 'feminism' – but she shared her partner's pacifism. In 1895, Eugénie established the *Union internationale des femmes pour la paix.* The radical agenda promoted by Edmond proved too sweeping for the more socially conservative peace societies of Richard and Passy, who preferred to persuade existing governments and were reluctant to tarnish their reputation with social radicalism.[293]

Legally, Potonié-Pierre seemed to moderately support a federative solution. It was discussed in the first issue of the league's short-lived periodical, the *Correspondance cosmopolite.* The project in question was written by John Noble, a member of the London Peace Society. Its outline was broadly similar to previous ones. The inhabitant of Brighton called for an international institution to revise the law of nations. Though uncertain on whether he wanted to call it an international tribunal or a supreme court of nations, Noble stuck fairly close to existing diplomatic precedent. It did not feature a self-standing judicial court, but was composed of a single assembly that periodically convened in a city of its choosing. Each member state

290 Potonié-Pierre, *Historique* 1899, 94–5.

291 Foremost in his short-lived journal *Correspondance cosmopolite.* It was also reprinted in the British *Herald of Peace.*

292 Correspondance cosmopolite (1866, n°1) 5–16; Potonié-Pierre, *Historique* 1899, 82–7, 116–7; Cooper, *Patriotic Pacifism* 1991, 31-2.

293 Potonié-Pierre, *Historique* 1899, 97–8; Cooper, *Patriotic Pacifism* 1991, 32.

appointed two delegates, who were vested by their home state with the power to declare war and peace, but who did not have to be lawyers. This assembly could also arbitrate interstate disputes, settling matters through majority vote after a public discussion. It did not concern itself with the internal affairs of its members. In the usual Anglo-American fashion, the ultimate sanction for infractions was not armed force, but economic 'non-intercourse'.[294]

Like other socialists, however, Potonié-Pierre was less concerned with the superstructure of politics and law and more with provoking dramatic underlying social change. He did not spend any specific attention to it in the league's periodical. In fact, another issue featured two short letters disbelieving that European federation could be realised anytime soon.[295] Potonié-Pierre might have printed the plan out of courtesy, considering Noble had been an important donator.[296] In his peace history, the topic, which returned so often across so many publicists, did not feature much. He considered this part of the peace conferences as 'less interesting' than other ones. The republican *ancien* reproduced most of Burritt's speech on international law, but concluded that little had changed in fifty years.[297]

Potonié-Pierre reflected ruefully that the new wave of peace activism had stolen his thunder. Both the *Ligue internationale et permanente de la paix* and the *Ligue de la paix et de la liberté* surpassed Potonié-Pierre's own league in number and in fame, despite being founded later. It stung him that the league of Passy was more successful, despite being narrowly legalist in focus. The message was too watered down to be really effective, for how could peace be established in such an unjust world? Potonié-Pierre thought it telling that Napoleon III let Passy be, whereas his own propaganda was frequently confiscated at the border. He preferred the radical Swiss-based league, which shared the 'same goal, the same programme, the same adherents'. There was no mistaking that the *Ligue du bien public* had directly inspired it. It was unfortunate that this league's leaders were 'ungrateful', and never publicly credited their spiritual predecessor organisation. In Potonié-Pierre's eyes, the *Ligue du bien public* had bridged the era of the peace congresses and the later nineteenth century peace movement.[298]

294 Correspondance cosmopolite (1866, n° 1), 2–5; Potonié-Pierre, *Historique* 1899, 99–101.

295 Correspondance cosmopolite (unknown year, unknown issue), 219–21.

296 Van der Linden, *Peace Movement* 1987, 590.

297 Potonié-Pierre, *Historique* 1899, 55–65.

298 Ibid., 87–93.

Although the *Ligue du bien public* was indeed about the only active European peace society between the early 1850s and the late 1860s, Potonié-Pierre's history must be taken with a grain of salt. Both Passy and the republican *proscrits* had numerous connections with the peace movement. Composed of younger men than the generation which had organised and taken part in the peace conferences, the peace societies founded in 1867 consciously engaged with the agenda set by their predecessors, while in some instances also introducing new concerns and ambitions. Before that, the main event in European pacifism had been the series of international peace congresses organised in the 1840s.

CHAPTER 5

Internationalising the movement (1848–1851)

> 'Créer la justice internationale, c'est le vrai moyen d'abolir la guerre.'
>
> LOUIS BARA (1849)

1 The Mid-Century Peace Congresses

In the middle of the summer of 1849, Paris hosted a most unusual spectacle. Around eleven o'clock in the morning, an eclectic crowd began filing into the spacious *salle Saint-Cécile.* Black-clad Quakers mingled with the fashionably dressed Parisian bourgeoisie. By noon, close to two thousand people had taken their seat. As they waited, they could gaze at the room's decoration. All around the walls, the *tricolore* was bundled together with the flags of the United Kingdom, the United States, Belgium, the Netherlands and various other states. Suddenly, the audience's murmur got interrupted by loud cheers and applause. The organising committee had entered the great room and mounted the stage. Informed spectators could detect among them the faces of foreign celebrities like Richard Cobden, as well as local notables like *abbé* Deguerry, the popular curate of the *église de la Madeleine,* one of the city's most prestigious churches. Since the archbishop of the capital had declined the presidency of the meeting due to health reasons, the honour of opening the proceedings descended to the noted novelist and political agitator Victor Hugo.[1]

Hugo held his speech as Europe was still in the aftermath of a revolutionary shockwave. Just a year before, Paris had been the scene of bloody skirmishes between insurrectionist citizens and royalist troops. Just weeks before, a French expeditionary force had chased a fellow republican government out of Rome and reinstated the pope. The city's labourers had rioted in protest, so that martial law was in effect. Simultaneously, news was just

1 *Proceedings Paris* 1849, 9–10, 15, 36.

 DOI:10.1163/9789004733688_007

coming in about how Kossuth's Hungarian nationalists had laid down their arms, overwhelmed after the czar had intervened to the rescue of the Austrian emperor. Everyone present must have felt that international tensions in Europe were at an all-time high.[2] Would another major war again scourge the continent, like had happened after 1789?

Under these foreboding circumstances, Hugo conjured up a radically opposed vision for the future. He compared the contemporary state of Europe to the way France had once been. If someone had four centuries ago predicted to Lorraine, Picardy, Normandy, Brittany, Auvergne, Provence, or any of the other regions, that they would all someday be part of one country, ruled by a single assembly, they would have been relentlessly mocked. Everyone who took themselves seriously, Hugo mused, would have cried out: 'What a dreamer! What a fantastic dream! (…) What an absurd chimera!' Yet, he told his audience, the dream had been realised. France had been unified.[3]

Victor Hugo knew that many of those listening had likewise been subjected to every kind of scorn under the sun. Who in their right mind could seriously believe in a permanent and universal peace, especially at a time like this? The president of the congress then turned to Europe. The European states of 1849 were in the same position as the provinces of France had been in the past. To those who would mock the ideals of those gathered that day in Paris, he answered: 'A day will come when war will appear as absurd, and be as impossible, between Paris and London, between St. Petersburg and Berlin, between Vienna and Turin, as it would be now been Rouen and Amiens, between Boston and Philadelphia. (…) A day will come when bullets and shells will be replaced by votes, by the universal suffrage of nations, by the venerable arbitration of a great sovereign Senate, which will be to Europe what the Parliament is to England, what the Diet is to Germany, or what the Legislative Assembly is to France. A day will come when a cannon will be exhibited in museums, just as an instrument of torture is now, and people will be astonished how such a thing could have been.' They would be united into the 'United States of Europe'! This vision he contrasted with the deplorable political condition of Europe during the 1840s, where the latent fear of war had led to disproportionate armaments and expenditure. Nonetheless, he did not doubt the ultimate triumph of 'the cause of civilisation by means of peace'.

2 Van der Linden, *Peace Movement* 1987, 332.

3 *Congrès Paris* 1850, 3–4 ; *Proceedings Paris* 1849, 10–1.

Upon the president's impassioned final exclamation 'You are all brothers!', the entire room, which had been intermittently interrupting him with cheers and applause, was caught up in a feverish clamour. The British and Americans jumped to their feet, and waving their hats and handkerchiefs, burst into three 'English cheers': 'Hip, hip, hurra!'[4]

In several respects, the 1849 Paris peace congress signified the most important event of the entire nineteenth century peace movement. Among the larger public, the main cultural artifact of the early international peace movement remains the speech of Victor Hugo. Although he did not invent the 'United States of Europe' as a slogan, he has come to be the historical person most closely identified with it. Such has been the wider historical significance of his speech, that its most famous passages, as reproduced above, are still often cited today. Testament to the lasting rhetorical value of Hugo's stirring address, comparatively less attention has been given to the actual peace congress for which he had written it.[5]

Nonetheless, the international peace congresses themselves had significant contemporary relevance also. While Anglo-American agents and the peace propaganda they carried had crossed the Channel already numerous times before, the congresses situated themselves one a whole other level. These meetings brought the Anglo-American peace friends in direct contact with sympathetic continental elites. While, due to processes of self-selection, these encounters for the most part passed cordially, ideological dissent could not be avoided entirely. Internally, the carefully constructed *entente cordiale* between the Americans and the British was challenged by Elihu Burritt and his League of Universal Brotherhood. Unlike Beckwith, Richard and Cobden, who wielded the most clout in the American and London peace societies, the idealistic American expat in Britain vied for more sweeping reform. Burritt consistently pushed for a political congress of nations, in Ladd's spirit, which would directly concern itself with the codification of international law. Burritt's position was steadily marginalised, in tune with the deterioration of the League, his main source of influence in the peace movement.

4 *Congrès Paris* 1850, 4–5 ; *Proceedings Paris* 1849, 11–4.

5 Thomas Hippler, 'From nationalist Peace to democratic War. The Peace Congresses in Paris (1849) and Geneva (1867)', in Thomas Hippler and Miloš Vec (eds.), *Paradoxes of Peace in Nineteenth Century Europe* (Oxford: OUP 2015), 174; Verdiana Grossi, 'Victor Hugo et sa perception des États-Unis d'Europe', in Marta Petricioli, Donatella Cherubini, and Alessandra Anteghini (eds.), *Les États-Unis d'Europe. Un projet pacifiste* (Bern: Peter Lang 2004), 49–73.

Externally, the Anglo-American societies were only moderately successful in converting European sympathisers to their political-legal programme. Different ideological and educational backgrounds caused much misunderstanding. Specifically, few Europeans conceptualised 'arbitration' in the way that the English-language peace friends did. The project of Jay was largely unknown, whereas older peace schemes, mostly born in the early modern era, remained the first point of reference for most European intellectuals interested in the peace question. As we have seen in previous chapters, these plans were of a more federative nature than most Anglo-Americans were comfortable with. As the speech of Victor Hugo already hinted, early continental-European peace thought still overlapped with grander and older visions of European unity. Continental participants embedded 'arbitration' in a larger multilateral framework that built on existing congress diplomacy. At the same time, they were not as religiously doctrinarian as the Protestant peace societies. Overall, Europeans were more sympathetic to liberal interventionism than Anglo-American pacifists. Accordingly, they tended to

FIGURE 5.1 Yet another caricature of Daumier, this time making fun of Victor Hugo's speech at the 1849 Paris peace congress.

FIGURE 5.2 The friends of peace engage in universal brotherhood – a far cry from the many political fissures that divided the movement.

preserve just cause doctrines. More influenced by the civil law than the common law tradition, they were also more uncomfortable with settlement mechanisms that did not rely on a pre-existing code.

All these factors combined to produce an undercurrent of dissent against the Anglo-American legal reform programme. At the congresses themselves, the peace societies met with unexpected protests and repeated blatant violations of the rules of debate. The Brussels congress in particular produced one of the most enduring and influential critiques of the Anglo-American peace movement. Louis Bara, a young Belgian lawyer, anticipated the crucial divide that would occur in the 1870s. Bara did not want to rely on arbitration without an accompanying code. Significantly, this international legal code had to be prepared by professional jurists in a non-official capacity. Only to be realised by the international law societies of 1873, nearly every major legalist peace idea of the subsequent decades had thus already been articulated during these mid-century international gatherings.

Before entering into the intricacies of this legal debate, we must understand the larger background against which it was held. Just as legal argument can never be separated from its underlying politics, it would be senseless to try and appreciate the political debates of a social movement separate from the milieu in which it operates. Who took part in the peace congresses, and what did the rest of the world think of it?

1.1 *International Ideological Diversity*

In 1849, the Anglo-American peace societies were absolutely thrilled with the success of the peace congress in Paris. Every issue of the British *Herald,* from September to December, was devoted to coverage of the event and all subsequent propaganda meetings in Britain. Combined with Cobden's arbitration motion, debated earlier that same summer, their movement had won for itself a hitherto unimaginable amount of attention. Almost the entire Parisian press corps felt obliged to write about it. Since Paris was one of the communication centres of Europe, French press reports were copied by the wider European press. As to be expected, reactions were mixed. A number of papers wrote about the event in glowing terms, foremost Girardin's *La Presse.*[6] More liberal-leaning newspapers, like *L'indépendance belge,* similarly reported moderately positively.[7]

Other outlets showed themselves less enamoured. The *Revue des deux-mondes,* one of France's most influential periodical journals, was every bit as scathing as *The Times* had been back home in Britain. The journal sarcastically wrote that it could only admire those 'modestly dressed Quakers who had so bravely crossed the Atlantic Ocean, and in their humble attire applauded speeches that they did not understand'. 'England was fortunate with its eccentrics', but a Frenchman should know better. Hugo might be content 'contemplating all the colours of the rainbow', but serious people should pay more attention to the 'sombre horizon' and the 'horrible war that is approaching' – 'Europe is in arms, and France waits!'[8] The cultural world was not indifferent to the event either. Never ones to lose a golden opportunity for comedy, the theatres set up parodies of the proceedings. Similarly, Honoré Daumier drew up a full series of mocking caricatures. In Britain, The *Nonconformist* assessed that the peace movement had become 'the best abused movement in Europe'. Nonetheless, overall, the peace societies could hardly disguise their delight of standing in the centre of so much

6 HP (October 1849), 378–82; HP (November 1849), 387–90.

7 L'Indépendance belge (24 August 1849), 2; L'Indépendance belge (26 August 1849), 2, 5.

8 This showed how uninformed many critics were, since none of the Americans were Quakers. *Revue des deux mondes* (1 September 1849), 873–5.

attention. Cobden wrote to his wife: 'All of our good Quaker friends are in capital spirits.'[9]

Their satisfaction with the European proceedings drew attention away from the fact that the peace societies had originally been reluctant to cooperate with such a risky endeavour. The first congress, held in Brussels in 1848, had been the brainchild of Elihu Burritt. It should be recalled that Burritt had in 1845 briefly been the 'reformist' editor of the American *Advocate of Peace.* He grew somewhat disillusioned with the American Peace Society in the spring of 1846, when the conservative factions again took power within the organisation. Along with the outbreak of the Mexican War, the 'learned blacksmith' decided to leave his homeland and expatriate himself to Britain. He had been drawn to the evangelical traditions of that country, which were just as strong as in the United States. Burritt firmly believed in Anglo-Saxonism. According to his publications and correspondence, the 'Anglo-Saxon race' had a divine mission to spread the light of Christianity and civilisation in the world.[10]

Upon reaching British shores, he set about founding a so-called 'League of Universal Brotherhood'. This new peace society raised individual pledges to never serve in the military or support any armed conflict whatsoever. Not stopping there, this organisation aspired to be what Burritt had failed to change the American Peace Society into. It was dedicated to vast social reforms, including not only strict pacifism, but also anti-slavery, suffrage and the lot of the working classes.[11]

The London Peace Society's relationship with Burritt's League was relatively cordial, if mistrustful. They frequently cooperated with their American colleague, inviting him to speak at public meetings. For a time, he was in fact considered one of the country's best-known pacifists. On all other fronts, however, Burritt's League was too radical. Like Beckwith in the U.S., British leaders frowned on Burritt's political ideals. Richard Cobden was never a fan. The name of Burritt's organisation alone already repelled him. In 1850, the factory owner wrote that 'brotherhood' was similar to *'fraternité'*, a word that had been dragged through the mud by 'red republicans and socialists'.[12]

---

9 HP (November 1849), 394; *Non-Conformist* cited in Ceadel, *Origins* 1996, 436; Cobden cited in Van der Linden, *Peace Movement* 1987, 339.

10 Van der Linden, *Peace Movement* 1987, 276–7.

11 Tolis, *Burritt* 1968, 146.

12 Van der Linden, *Peace Movement* 1987, 277; Cobden (ed. Howe), *Letters* 2010, 261–2.

Burritt's success was largely built on sand. The League's pledge did not amount to a very significant commitment. It was never equivalent to a paid membership, and Leaguers had to essentially trust on everyone's good faith to uphold it until long after the meeting during which they had signed it. Like other societies, the League also relied too much on its founder. Unfortunately, the autodidact drove himself hard, and became increasingly prone to what we might today qualify as 'burn-outs'. He kept travelling between Britain and America, leaving the League leaderless for extended periods of time. By the 1850s, the League has lost most of its membership and did not survive the ordeals of the Crimean War. In 1857, Henry Richard absorbed what was left of it into the London Peace Society. The League also had a journal, called the *Bond of Brotherhood,* founded in 1846. This journal continued as a stand-alone peace publication for ten more years, until 1867.[13]

Still, the first peace congress, held in the summer of 1848, would never have come about if not for the leader of the League of Universal Brotherhood. According to his own account, he first got the idea during a train ride in February of 1848, just before a new revolution erupted in France. Burritt travelled to Paris two months later to recruit potential local collaborators. The undaunted ambition revealed by this project could hardly be exaggerated. Burritt's avowed linguistic skills – he claimed to be able to speak dozens of language – turned out to be mostly theoretical. Having learnt French exclusively from books, the American discovered that he could only communicate very poorly with the French in person. His connections also did not carry over as well into France. Burritt did meet with a number of people, but they were all men whom the historian van der Linden has categorised as rather fringe 'communists'. Paris itself was also deemed unsuitable as a location. The inhabitants of the city rioted in June 1848 against the government's decision not to intervene militarily in Italy, meaning that a peace congress could be construed as a pro-government political demonstration. In response, the police shut down all 'political clubs'. Burritt had bitten of more than he could chew.[14]

At the end of July, very close to the intended date, he finally began to include the London Peace Society. Its Committee agreed, but on their conditions. They wanted a fully apolitical meeting with governmental permission, that did not conflict with their own Christian anti-war ideology. Rather last-minute, the affair was moved to nearby Brussels. Belgium's

13 This journal is occasionally cited. Ceadel, *Origins* 1996, 58–9, 395; Ceadel, *Idealists* 2000, 44, 57–8.

14 Van der Linden, *Peace Movement* 1987, 322–5.

liberal government was much more be sympathetic. The London Peace Society was already relatively well-connected there, as the city at the time possessed a peace society, founded by their agent. The congress eventually proceeded relatively well, leading to a desire to renew the experiment in other cities.[15]

From that point on, the peace congress movement grew out of Burritt's hands, and developed into a general initiative of the Anglo-American peace societies. Its leading actors were the London Peace Society, as led by Richard and Sturge, with the added support of Richard Cobden and an increasing number of local European collaborators. Several of the latter are introduced later. Though Burritt remained one of the animating spirits of the congresses, these were henceforward organised by the 'Peace Congress Committee'. As mentioned earlier, one of the major reasons for its existence was to allow an outwardly moderate peace advocate like Cobden to become involved, without identifying himself too much with the more absolutist London Peace Society, whom many of Cobden's other supporters dismissed as hopeless utopians.[16] Vis-à-vis the friendly competition of Burritt's League, the new organisation also helped to efface the distinct identity of the League. Burritt was aware of this attempt. He privately complained that at meetings of the Peace Congress Committee the Peace Society's representatives grossly outnumbered the odd three or four of his own League. His despair grew even greater when he received word from Joseph Sturge, his closest friend within the London Peace Society, that the other leaders had been questioning his competency to lead the movement.[17]

Four such peace congresses were held in total. The third congress, following the ones from Brussels in 1848 and Paris in 1849, was held in Frankfurt in 1850. Like the congresses of Paris and Brussels, it was held under gloomy geopolitical circumstances. It was held in the rotunda of the *Paulskirche,* which had just two years before hosted the *Frankfurter Nationalversammlung,* the first and short-lived elected 'national' parliament of Germany. The body had been forcefully dissolved after the Prussian king Frederick William had rejected its provisional constitution. At the time of the congress, the city was filled with troops from Austria, Prussia and Bavaria, and it had been placed under a military government. To the north, Prussia and several allies were fighting Denmark over the provinces of

15 Van der Linden, *Peace Movement* 1987, 324–5; Lubelski-Bernard. *Mouvements pacifistes en Belgique* 1977, 325–34.

16 See chapter 2. Ceadel, *Idealists* 2000, 28–9.

17 Van der Linden, *Peace Movement* 1987, 328–9.

Schleswig-Holstein.[18] According to the proceedings, the gathered 'friends of peace' drew more than one amazed gaze from the city's burghers. In turn, Cobden was more than a little surprised to find the Austrian general von Haynau sitting in his audience. Haynau had been in command of Austrian troops repressing uprisings in Hungary and Italy, and had in that capacity earned himself nicknames like 'the hyena of Brescia' and 'the hangman of Arad'. Cobden joked that Haynau was 'about the last man I thought we should have converted'.[19] The last peace congress was occasioned by a more hopeful event. The opening of the Great Exhibition in May 1851 in London was received by the peace societies as a 'peace congress' in its own right. Like the 1843 London convention, the London congress of 1851 hoped it could redirect some of the international attention towards itself.[20]

Given these circumstances, the organisers knew that the potential for political strife was great. The European congresses attracted sympathisers with divergent ideological, religious and professional backgrounds. They already had some first-hand experience with the mutual misunderstandings this could cause. British free traders could be mystified by the dogmatism of Quakers, who themselves were sometimes appalled by the materialism apparently animating the former. In the United States, Beckwith had difficulties coming to grasp with the endless call of reformists for the society to also speak out against issues like slavery. He believed this would render their society too diffuse for the public. The reformists in turn thought it absurd that the single biggest cause of human suffering in their country was left unaddressed, if only for the perennial danger of political violence it presented. Prior to the Brussels peace conference, Burritt himself was already exasperated by the insistence of some of his contacts to include socialist principles on the agenda.[21] How could the Peace Congress Committee ensure that these congresses did not devolve into a chaotic mess, exposing the disunity of the international peace movement for all to see? The congresses were intended to be propaganda meetings, projecting a coherent and practical reform agenda to the outside world.[22] Essentially, they were all intended to attract the 'right' kind of people. Politically speaking, they

18 Vanessa Lambert, 'The Dynamics of Transnational Activism: the International Peace Congresses, 1843–51'. *The International History Review* 38(1) (2016), 127; Van der Linden, *Peace Movement* 1987, 342.

19 *Proceedings Frankfurt* 1851, 21.

20 *Proceedings London* 1851, x–xi, 21, 37.

21 See the chapters supra. Van der Linden, *Peace Movement* 1987, 323.

22 Lambert, 'Dynamics' 2015, 126–44.

could be classified as belonging to what passed as the 'centre', or perhaps the 'centre-left', in contemporary Western-European politics.

How many Europeans actually participated in these peace congresses, largely organised by foreign peace societies? In Brussels, some 170 Belgians were reported present. Only a small number spoke at the congress, enabling their names to be recorded. They constituted the largest foreign element, as there were only a handful of Frenchmen. Other European nationalities were absent, or were too small to be considered as a group. In Paris, there were only a hundred Frenchmen, joined by thirty Germans and nineteen Belgians. In Frankfurt, German attendance was downright disappointing. Some fifty people registered, but the number of actual attendants was always lower than the number of registrations. This time, the proceedings did not provide an exact number, probably because the London Peace Society was embarrassed by the glaring lack of German interest. At the last congress, held in London in 1851, 1,000 delegates took part, but only a smattering came from the mainland.[23]

At every congress, the British delegation, each time numbering in the hundreds, far outnumbered everyone else. While the British peace societies would have preferred more foreign delegates, it did not turn the meetings themselves into failures. The audience was always larger than the number of delegates. In Paris and London, the organisers had to turn down people without tickets, for rooms that could contain 2,000 and 3,500 spectators respectively. Like at other such conventions, women were denied official delegate status. However, they each time made up significant portions of the audience. Press coverage ensured that the peace congresses won disproportionate public attention. Finally, those foreign delegates who did participate typically belonged to the more influential social classes. Most were upper-middle-class, including lawyers, professors, pastors and journalists. Many simply described themselves as 'gentlemen', which said enough.[24]

One such man was the Belgian magistrate and civil servant Auguste Visschers (1804–1874). Cabinet leader Rogier recommended him in 1848 to the Anglo-American organisers as the man who could arrange all of the practicalities on such a short notice. Visschers had studied law in the 1820s, which had led to stints as a judge and a successful career within the Belgian civil service. In the late 1840s, he oversaw the burgeoning Belgian mining industry, an important economic domain. Not only was

23 Van der Linden, *Peace Movement* 1987, 326–7, 335–6, 344–5, 353.

24 Lambert, 'Dynamics' 2015, 129–30.

Visschers a competent administrator, he shared a keen interest in social reform. He had campaigned for stricter legislation on duels, and stood in favour of the abolition of capital punishment and the improvement of penitentiary conditions. Later on, he experimented with savings banks for miners. Like many within the peace movement, his concern with the working classes was paternalistic, and he distrusted socialism. The lower classes had to work themselves up, provided they were given an education or a proper vocational training. In 1848, Visschers was one of the few Belgians already familiar with the peace movement. As a young man, he had toured Europe, during which the lawyer had encountered the *Société de la morale chrétienne* and the London Peace Society. In Geneva, he had spoken with count de Sellon.[25]

Of the various European collaborators, Visschers warranted special mention, because he remained a pillar of the peace movement in Europe his entire life. In 1848, he was president of the congress. Unlike other European adherents, Visschers faithfully attended every other congress, including the strictly Anglo-American ones of Manchester and Edinburgh of 1853, where he ended up as virtually the only non-English speaking member.[26] In 1864, he headed the Belgian committee of the recently founded Red Cross. A decade later, Burritt, the American Peace Society, and a number of lawyers sought to set up an international conference on the reform of international law. Settling on Brussels as a location, they did not need to think long about who to again contact.[27] Apart from his speeches at these international meetings, Visschers mainly contributed to the international peace movement as a facilitator. He did not publish anything, but was clearly well-informed. His library and personal notes contained many key texts, including issues of the *Herald* and Sumner's *True Grandeur* speech.[28] Visschers also supported Potonié's *Ligue du bien public* and Passy's *Ligue internationale et permanente de la paix*.[29] Throughout his long career, this jurist endorsed the legal reform agenda promoted by the humanitarians of his day.

25 Nadine Lubelski-Bernard, 'VISSCHERS (Auguste)', in *Biographie nationale de Belgique*, vol. XLIV (Bruxelles: Bruylant 1985), 746–68; Thomas D'Haeninck, *Sociale hervormers op zoek naar een moreel reveil. Een sociaal-historische en transnationale studie naar de aanwezigheid van Belgen op internationale hervormingscongressen, 1850–1914* (Ghent: unpublished doctoral thesis 2018), 4, 110, 115, 161–2.

26 *Proceedings London* 1851, 10.

27 Lubelski-Bernard, 'VISSCHERS' 1985, 765.

28 [KBR, Auguste Visschers papers], *Abolition de la guerre* II. 1793.

29 Lubelski-Bernard, 'VISSCHERS' 1985, 767.

In the 1840s, the big debate was between proponents of arbitration and those of codification. Like in the internal debates in Britain and the United States, the underlying question at the international congresses was about the practical limitations of the peace campaign. How could international law be instrumentalised to achieve the desired goal? In other words: who was the pragmatic realist, and who was unwittingly playing the part of the misguided utopian? Both sides of course accused each other of this sin.

1.2 *Anglo-American Support for Arbitration*

The speeches Visschers made at the successive peace congresses between 1848 and 1851 reflected the ideal impact Cobden, Sturge, and Richard hoped to exert on continental elites. In his inaugural address of 1848, Visschers had still called the 'federation of the great human family' the great end-goal of the evolution of human society. Like other educated Europeans interested in peace thought, the congress president invoked the ancient Greek Amphyctionic Council and the Swiss or German examples. He also drew attention to the unrealised projects of Henri IV, Saint-Pierre, Rousseau, or *abbé* Grégoire's *Déclaration des droits des gens.*[30] However, sometime during the run-up to the following congress, Visschers was persuaded to the Anglo-American point of view that disregarded federative solutions.

From Paris onwards, the Belgian co-organiser publicly defended more limited forms of arbitration. At Frankfurt, for instance, Visschers underlined that he did not believe that there would ever be 'one code', 'one high court', or 'one supreme diet' with a universal jurisdiction. Unity would emerge from a pluralist system of co-existing 'federal institutions', limited by treaties and international law Comparing the laws governing political society with Humboldt's 'law of universal attraction' in the physical world, he concluded that the doctrines of the congress were not just 'hollow reveries', but had already 'become a science'. Although all this was probably still somewhat too ethereal for the likes of Cobden, who never framed it quite like that, it was nonetheless a step-up from the 'utopian' ambition that sought some grand permanent diplomatic assembly. Although Visschers never truly abandoned the ultimate dream of a 'European confederation', as he styled it in London '51, he also did not believe in sweeping reforms through a single institution. The 'public law' of Europe had to be improved gradually through an increased resort to international arbitration.[31]

30 *Congress Brussels* 1848, 5.

31 *Proceedings London* 1851, 27–9.

The most important resolution of each congress was invariably the one recommending arbitration to governments. Its importance was evident from the way it was invariably the first of the 'practical' measures discussed.[32] Arbitration was followed by a resolution calling for disarmament.[33] Only once these fundamental topics were discussed, did the resolution based on William Ladd's scheme enter the picture. It should be recalled that the founder of the American Peace Society had proposed an international system based on a permanent congress of nations, a high court of nations, and a code of international law. It was also a personal favourite of Burritt. However, the resolution endorsing this trio markedly dropped in importance and scope at each successive congress. In Brussels, it still came immediately after the resolution on arbitration, and regarded it as of the 'highest importance' that such a system would be installed. In Paris, on the other hand, the congress only recommended 'to prepare public opinion' for this ambition. In Frankfurt, the resolution made no more mention of a permanent international judicial court. It had also given way in the agenda to resolutions against war loans and armed interventions. Finally, by London in 1851, it had dropped almost entirely to the bottom. Watered down even more, the resolution also did not speak about a congress of nations any longer. It only recommended 'to prepare public opinion' in their countries 'with a view for the formation of an authoritative code of international law'.[34] Meanwhile, the resolution on arbitration never budged from its pre-eminent position in the most visible place at the beginning. Its phrasing had also not changed as drastically as the one on a congress of nations. In Brussels, arbitration was still linked to a possible 'supreme international court'. However, the ensuing congresses remained more vague, and merely called for governments to rely on 'competent and impartial arbitrators'.[35]

The programme of the peace congresses reflected the predominance of the London Peace Society in the Peace Congress Committee. Both Cobden and Sturge were firmly in favour of arbitration as it had been first proposed

32 In Brussels and Frankfurt, it was preceded by a formulaic and vague resolution condemning war. *Congress Brussels* 1848, 15; *Proceedings Frankfurt* 1851, 5.

33 *Congress Brussels* 1848, 15, 24, 31; *Proceedings Paris* 1849, 19, 65; *Proceedings Frankfurt* 1851, 5, 10, 51; *Proceedings London* 1851), 29, 69.

34 *Congress Brussels* 1848, 31; *Proceedings Paris* 1849, 65; *Proceedings Frankfurt* 1851, 51; *Proceedings London* 1851), 69.

35 *Congress Brussels* 1848, 24; *Proceedings Paris* 1849, 19; *Proceedings Frankfurt* 1851, 10; *Proceedings London* 1851), 10.

by judge Jay in the United States. In 1848, Cobden had openly questioned the viability of a congress of nations in his letter of adhesion to the Brussels congress. During the Commons debate of 1849, the free trader had again distanced himself from it, throwing Palmerston off guard that way. Henry Richard was on the same page as his two friends. From the minutes of the Congress Committee, as well as Burritt's diary entries, it was revealed that the other organisers, including Visschers, had wanted to scrap the resolution altogether before the Paris congress, when Burritt was temporarily absent. Burritt had a 'grim' talk with Cobden and Richard afterwards, which put the resolution back on the agenda, albeit on the last day. Before the Frankfurt congress, Cobden tried it again, only for the leader of the League of Universal Brotherhood to yet again become so upset that the resolution was kept, albeit in a reduced form. Just before London '51, Cobden made another attempt to get rid of it, but again only succeeded in shrinking the resolution even further.[36]

For this reason, the debate on the respective merits of stipulated arbitration or a congress of nations during the congresses themselves was largely a rehash of older debates within the Anglo-American peace societies. The British displayed their feelings about Burritt's pet resolution best by completely silencing it. Delegates from the London Peace Society or its auxiliaries simply did not talk about it. They either spoke for different resolutions, or ignored the topic at hand. Although the latter was a bad habit overall during these meetings, it could not be denied that the British peace societies stayed lukewarm at best to what eventually came to be known, even for Burritt, as 'the American plan'.[37]

The only known instance of British support occurred during the reading of the introductory paper of the arbitration resolution in Brussels, the one congress for which Burritt had still been the lead organiser. It was written by William Stokes, a paid agent of the London Peace Society. Stokes still adhered to the conciliary line of London '43. The man endorsed arbitration mainly on the grounds that this 'embryo state of arbitration', which relied on appeals to 'simple justice', would eventually ripen high-profile minds to accept the 'greater and more complete work' that was a congress of nations. This congress could identify the leading principles which had guided the ad hoc arbitrations up until then, and remodel them into a multilaterally acceptable code of international law. This in turn would allow the formation

36 Van der Linden, *Peace Movement* 1987, 371–2.

37 'I deeply regret that the task has devolved upon me to present to this assembly a proposition which has been denominated *American* (…)'. *Proceedings Frankfurt* 1851, 51.

of a 'court of nations', that would itself foster international goodwill even more, and in the long run render standing armies obsolete.[38] The American influence of Ladd was obvious. Stokes never changed his mind. As late as the 1860s, this Briton published a booklet in favour of a congress of nations. His position was not the official one of the London society.[39]

Burritt's relative isolation was painfully evident from the fact that at each congress, it fell upon him to introduce the resolution recommending the 'American' plan. Each time, he read some variation of a short paper he had written shortly before the Brussels congress. As far as could be ascertained, it first appeared in the *Bond of Brotherhood,* although it was later also printed in the *Herald,* which had copied it from a British Quaker journal.[40] The paper's main thrust never substantially changed. Like Stokes in 1848 or MacNamara in 1843, Burritt promoted essentially the same project as Ladd. The chief concern of Ladd's spiritual successor lay with the unsettled and immoral nature of the law of nations. None of his critique was particularly original. Like others before and after him, the learned blacksmith complained that international law as a body of truly binding norms did not really exist: 'We have, in truth, no such law; and what passes under the name, is of recent origin, and insufficient authority.' He conceded that 'Grotius and his commentators' had exerted 'a benign influence', but theirs was a work of scholars, rather than legislators. States could adhere to such treatises, but could equally decide to ignore whatever lone jurists had written in their study. 'It is not law, but argument; not decrees, but rules; not a code, but a treatise (…)'.[41]

Like Ladd, Burritt did not suggest a wholesale redrafting of international law, but rather that 'the system of maxims, opinion, and precedents' as described in legal doctrine should be bestowed with added political legitimacy. The analogy with domestic legal systems informed Burritt's definition of legitimacy. He believed that 'in this constitutional age' legitimate political authority could only be derived from 'the suffrage of nations' in the form of an 'international legislature'. Burritt suggested that the diplomatic congress should appoint a 'Committee on international law', composed of 'the most profound statesmen and jurists' from each member state. This body would

38 *Congress Brussels* 1848, 16–9.

39 Van der Linden, *Peace Movement* 1987, 510; William Stokes, *A Permanent Congress of Nations as a Substitute for War in the Settlement of International Disputes* (Manchester: Brimner 1860).

40 BB (May 1848), 37–39; HP (September 1848), 129–31.

41 *Congress Brussels* 1848, 24.

piecemeal release proposals *de lege ferenda,* ensuring each clause to be discussed separately by the congress of nations, national parliaments, and the press. This way, Burritt reckoned, a 'well-digested' code might see the light of day in the span of perhaps only six months. Once this was completed, he agreed with Ladd that a 'permanent high court of nations' needed to be established, which would adjudicate interstate disputes according to the legal code. This, and only this, he concluded, would eventually lead all of humanity into 'the chain of universal order'.[42]

Much more noteworthy than the originality of Burritt's legal proposals was the sheer stubbornness with which he defended them. This was of course the same man who had worked himself up from decidedly humble origins, declined a Harvard scholarship, set up a peace organisation which briefly rivalled the London Peace Society in Britain, and organised a congress in Europe amidst revolution and war, without speaking decent French or possessing any meaningful local connections. This was not a man to be deterred by adversity. Still, he did not always hide his frustrations well. In Frankfurt, he let it slip that he would have preferred someone else presenting the codification resolution for a change. Burritt also lamented that the measure was seen as '*American*', whereas, according to him, it was 'as old as the idea of international law'. He referred to the Amphyctionic council and authors like Saint-Pierre.[43] By the final meeting in London, he exasperatedly remarked at the very beginning of his speech that it was the third consecutive time the task had fallen on his shoulders.[44] Although Burritt appeared to be preaching in the desert during the era of the first peace congresses, he would ultimately find success near the end of his life. Six years before his death, in 1873, Burritt succeeded in convincing the new leadership of the American Peace Society to host an international conference in Brussels. He interpreted the organisation born at this meeting, today known as the International Law Association, as a spiritual successor to the project first proposed by himself twenty years earlier in the same city.[45]

A handful of non-British delegates responded positively to Burritt's ambitious project. Some of the most understanding supporters naturally came from the United States. The most vocal among them was Amasa Walker, part of the reformist faction in the American Peace Society, and also a member of the Massachusetts legislature, the state where the movement found

42 *Congress Brussels* 1848, 24–7.
43 *Proceedings Frankfurt* 1851, 51.
44 *Proceedings London* 1851, 69–70.
45 See chapter 7.

its strongest base of support. At Paris, the politician gave a long speech in favour of a congress of nations as conceived by Ladd, whom he explicitly named. Also like Burritt, he believed in a cooperative effort between jurists and politicians to codify international law. Without this code, Walker felt, any 'high court of arbitration' would never function.[46] Walker was the only American in Europe to publicly support Burritt.

A number of Europeans supported federative plans somewhat similar to Burritt's. One of the most notable proponents of some form of international legislative congress was the republican member of the French National Assembly Francisque Bouvet, whose efforts have already been discussed.[47] Bouvet attended the meetings of Brussels, Paris and London. Like others, he put the development of a 'universal jurisdiction' into an evolutionary historical narrative. Delegates like Bouvet illustrated why the prohibition on discussions of contemporary political events was impossible to uphold. In Paris, he roused the entire room into great fervour by singing the praises of the 'heroic' Hungarian resistance and the ill-fated Roman republic.[48] In London, Bouvet similarly again identified the pope, in true French republican fashion, as the main culprit responsible for preventing human progress.[49] As evident from the above, there was never exact agreement on the legal concepts these congresses were supposed to promote. While Anglo-Americans referred to the ideas of Jay or Cobden, most Europeans were still unfamiliar with those project. Rather, delegates were only expected to endorse arbitration, in whatever form or shape.

Considering the vastly different educational and ideological backgrounds of many participants, they were often just talking past each other. Many simply kept themselves to truisms on war and peace, even when the topic at hand was arbitration or a legal code. The Chartist delegate Henry Vincent (1813–1878) stressed that a large public meeting was the time nor the place for technical intricacies. The speaker just before him, an American, had added a caveat that arbitrations had to be performed by an independent and permanent tribunal, rather than ad hoc by another executive power, as had up until then typically been the case. The Englishman berated the American for it, since he believed that 'details' were 'the business of a smaller meeting'.[50] Vincent's position was not illogical. Though the peace

46 *Proceedings Paris* 1849, 67–72.

47 See chapter 4.

48 *Proceedings Paris* 184914, 37–40; *Congrès Paris* 1850, 20–1.

49 *Proceedings London* 1851, 70–2.

50 Ibid., 29–32.

societies had by the late 1840s already invested considerable energy elaborating specifics, an overly detailed set of proposals ran the risk of provoking needless discussions at more pluralist meetings like the European congresses, potentially alienating supporters. For a propaganda meeting recommending a few general anti-war principles, vagueness was not a weakness if it ensured unity.

1.3 *Continental-European Support for Codification*

Unfortunately, as always, the devil was in the details. Not every delegate accepted this lack of clarity. Despite all of their precautions, the organisers were unable to prevent every act of dissidence. The official proceedings published by the London Peace Society usually shared an unfortunate tendency to gloss over such incidents. In their Paris report, for instance, the British simply wrote of a speech they did not agree with, given by a zealous Fourierist, that it was 'so rambling' that it was not worthy of reproduction. The French proceedings also had not copied it, but they added that it had shocked the British part of the audience, although the French had appeared more entertained than anything else.[51] In Frankfurt, similar mishaps occurred. Some of the few Germans present had defended the right to defensive war, or had wanted the congress to discuss the Danish war. Oftentimes, the full-text of their speech was missing or only briefly paraphrased in the English-language proceedings.[52]

In the realm of legal discussion, the Brussels congress proved the most turbulent one. All meetings attracted their contrarians and in 1848 this honour had fallen to the Spanish delegate, Ramon de la Sagra (1798–1871). Like the Italian delegate Bertinatti, he just happened to be in town at the time. In the 1840s, de la Sagra had a seat in the Spanish national Parliament for the liberal party. He was also a Proudhonist, to whose ideology he had been converted in the 1830s.[53] He had not intended to take an active part, but was pressured to participate. The organisers soon came to regret that. In his diary, Burritt wrote that while most of the room jumped to its feet when the opening resolution condemning war was read, there was 'one solitary

51 He had supposedly compared himself to Christ. *Proceedings Paris* 1849, 30–1; *Congrès Paris* 1849, 13.

52 E.g. *Proceedings Frankfurt* 1851, 43.

53 Van der Linden, *Peace Movement* 1987, 327; George Woodcock, *Anarchism: a History of Libertarian Ideas and Movements* (Toronto: Broadview Encore Editions 2004), 299.

exception'.[54] Ramon de la Sagra had clearly been unimpressed. When he rose to address the audience on the arbitration resolution, he did not mince words. 'Peace', he said, 'is not a principle, but the consequences of the state of social order.' If there existed no 'harmony' within society, armed force was needed to enforce the law. The Spaniard was one of the few congress delegates who voiced his belief that public opinion alone would not suffice to enforce arbitral awards. To do away with standing armies, he asserted, was to 'establish anarchy'. Although de la Sagra's views were undoubtedly much more widespread in society than those of the peace movement, especially in governmental circles, these were obviously unacceptable within the context of a pacifist congress. The others all jumped on him, which of course only made de la Sagra double down even more. In the end, much of the discussion on both arbitration and a congress of nations was derailed this way.[55] Afterwards, he sparked a small polemic through a booklet, sharply titled *Utopie de la paix.*[56]

De la Sagra had not been the only delegate to controversially vote against the arbitration resolution in Brussels. There had been another one. This was Willem Hendrik Suringar (1790–1872), who had accepted to represent the Netherlands at the congresses of Brussels and Paris. Suringar was another of those itinerant gentleman philanthropists who was enmeshed in Europe's general social reform circles. He was interested in such various subjects as penitentiary reform, sewage systems and poor relief institutions.[57] Like de la Sagra, he was nearby at the time and only visited the congress out of curiosity, taking a seat at the back, but he was also called into a more active role. Unlike his Spanish peer, Suringar was more diplomatic and better in tune with the sensibilities of the peace movement. His speeches were abbreviated in the English-language proceedings. Conveniently, these neglected to include the important proviso that the Dutchman had attached to his support for arbitration. In his opinion, arbitration could only function with a

---

54 Elihu Burritt (ed. Chas. Northend), *Elihu Burritt; a Memorial Volume containing a Sketch of his Life and Labors, with Selections from his Writings and Lectures, and Extracts from his Private Journals in Europe and America* (New York: Appleton 1879), 57.

55 *Congress Brussels* 1848, 30–1, 43.

56 Ramon De la Sagra, *Utopie de la paix. Extraits des doctrines émises au congrès de la paix réuni à Bruxelles au mois de septembre 1848* (Paris: Capelle 1849); Ferdinand E. A. Gasc., *Lettres à M. Ramon de la Sagra sur l'utopie de la paix* (Paris: Ledoyen 1851).

57 Chris Leonards and Nico Randeraad, 'Building a Transnational Network of Social Reform in the Nineteenth Century', in Davide Rodogno, Bernhard Struck and Jakob Vogel (eds.), *Shaping the Transnational Sphere Experts, Networks and Issues from the 1840s to the 1930s* (New York: Berghahn 2015), 117.

pre-existing international legal code. Otherwise, the process would be too subjective. He afterwards privately confided that certain 'arbitrations' had in the past not always been just. Like the Belgian Visschers, the Dutchman singled out the London conference of 1830. For these reasons, Suringar was also opposed to the disarmament resolutions. Without either a code and a permanent court of arbitration, disarmament was premature. The army was needed not only to occasionally enforce arbitral awards *manu militari,* but also to keep domestic law and order. Suringar had been disquieted by a few recent riots in Paris and Amsterdam. Similar to Cobden and the French political economists, Suringar despised the 'hotheads' and 'communists' who were always challenging 'legal authority'. The events of 1848 had proven their latent threat.[58]

While these two delegates inserted false notes into the congresses, neither was awarded 1,000 francs to methodically tear down the legal programme of the peace movement, as it had been painstakingly developed by the Anglo-American peace societies over the course of many years. Yet this had been the exact achievement of Louis Bara (1821–1857).[59] Bara was a twenty-eight year old Belgian jurist, who won first place with a prize essay in 1849. He had written it in response to a concours organised by the Peace Congress Committee in the aftermath of the 1848 Brussels congress. Perhaps in a bid to attract more publicity, the Committee had asked to write an 'exposition of rational and practical means for attaining the abolition of war'. All entries had to be written in French.[60] As an incentive, the Anglo-American peace societies had set aside 2,000 Belgian francs – a very considerable sum.[61] The Belgian Royal Academy had agreed to provide the jury.[62] Like had already occurred in Brussels, the effort horribly misfired from the point of view of the Congress Committee. When announcing the results in Paris the following year, Auguste Visschers felt it necessary to stress that the laureate's opinions did not necessarily reflect those of the Committee. Visscher's diplomatic precautions were necessary, considering his essay had unashamedly declared war a legal and moral 'right', which had 'saved more

58 Van der Linden, *Peace Movement* 1987, 327, 366, 404; Willem Hendrik Suringar, *Discours prononcé par M. Suringar, d'Amsterdam, vice-président au congrès de la paix, dans la deuxième séance, tenue à Paris le 23 aout 1849* (Paris: Ducloux 1849), 3, 7–8.

59 The following passages on Louis Bara are an abbreviated version of De Rycke, 'Legislating Utopia' 2020, 590–630.

60 *Congress Brussels* 1849, 45.

61 *Congrès Paris* 1849, 8–9; Van der Linden, *Peace Movement* 1987, 337.

62 De Rycke, 'Legislating Utopia' 2020, 599.

FIGURE 5.3 Peace advocates showing the way to resolve differences with harmony and respect.

than once the liberty of the world'. In fact, their winning author had wondered aloud whether 'total war might not be the real need of this era'.[63]

2 Law Caught between Science and Morality

With the meeting of the minds of the international peace movement came the hour of truth. Which plan should prevail? The Anglo-American organisers of the congresses wanted to focus exclusively on arbitration as it had been conceptualised by Jay in the early 1840s. The peace societies had made this choice already at the conference of 1843, and because only they had the organisational capacity to undertake any kind of sustained political campaign, this was the strategy that would be pursued.

However, already at the very hour of its general adoption, dissidents formulated powerful critiques against it. These debates were not just about practicalities and pragmatism. Underneath the surface, there lingered a philosophical question about the nature of law. Where did law derive its legitimacy from? For the Americans and British peace friends, there could be no doubt that the first and most important source of law was holy scripture. When they came to Europe, however, they encountered men who could write more than two hundred pages on peace, without citing the Bible once. These people sought to introduce an objectivity into international law that did not depend on whether or not one believed in Christianity. The laws of 'science' applied whether one believed in them or not.

2.1 *International Law as the 'Science of Peace'*

For Louis Bara, a young graduate from the anticlerical *Université libre de Bruxelles,* the instrument for preserving international peace was the 'science' of international law.[64] In his views, the programme of the peace congress held in Brussels was misguided at best, and counter-productive at worst. The great mistake of the Anglo-American peace societies was that they were overly concerned with the administration of law, while there did not yet exist any international law worthy of the name to be applied. The proponents of arbitration had to remember that 'arbitration' and 'arbitrariness' had a common etymology. What tangible, *actual,* progress had really been

63 Louis Bara (ed. Charles Potvin), *La science de la paix. Programme. Mémoire couronné, à Paris, en 1849, par le congrès des sociétés anglo-américaines des amis de la paix* (Bruxelles: Muquardt 1872), 55, 199, 201.

64 De Rycke, 'Legislating Utopia' 2020, 596–602.

made since the peace societies began operations around 1816? None. They were proposing ideas manifestly ahead of their time. They should not be surprised that their motions invariably failed before parliaments. What needed to be established first, was not *'la jurisdiction internationale'*, but *'la justice internationale'*.[65]

Bara cited Rossi's review from Henry Wheaton's *Elements of International Law* at length: 'the erudition of Grotius, the geometric forms of Wolff, the superficial simplicity of Vattel and the practical guide of Martens' had not been enough. Far too often, one had be content with *'de l'à peu près'*: too many unclear principles which could not support all of its logical consequences, too many rules hollowed out by numerous exceptions, no doctrine not forced to compromise itself unconvincingly with an opposing doctrine. International law seemed like little more than a servile translation of diplomacy, in particular that of states hegemonic enough to impose their rules.[66]

Like others before him, Bara tried to overcome the indeterminateness of international law through an analogy with domestic legal systems. International justice entailed three steps: a code regulating in the abstract, a court system capable of settling disputes according to said code, and an executive authority tasked with enforcing judgments. Disarmament could only follow the establishment of an international rule of law. The opposite order was absurd, as that would only leave states without means of defence. So far, none of Bara's analysis clashed with the sentiments underlying the Anglo-American legal programme. However, the Belgian author distinguished himself through his unique focus on methodology. As Bara wrote in his essay's epigraph: *'C'est de la manière dont on s'y prend pour faire une chose qui dérive le succès de l'entreprise.'*[67]

Bara felt that neither a body of arbitral awards nor positive legislation by a congress of nations were credible means towards an international legal code. A congress of nations would not materialise in the near future. Conversely, arbitrations were not conducted systematically enough. Bara dismissed most of the sources of international law. Equity stood synonymous to vagueness. Natural law was little better. The need for positive law proved that the theoretical labours of the likes of Pufendorf were impracticable in actual diplomacy. Customary law was slightly more tangible, but this positive source of law remained highly ambiguous. It also risked bestowing a

65 Bara, *Paix* 1872, 13–4, 18, 155.

66 Ibid., 41–2, 44; the original review by Rossi was published in *Archives de droit et de législation* (Bruxelles: Société belge de librairie 1837), 553–75.

67 Bara, *Paix* 1872, 6, 204.

veneer of justice on what were obvious wrongs. How many customs, the lawyer wondered, actually benefitted humanity? None of these sources were acceptable foundations for a just legal system. Only written law was suitable for science.[68]

Therefore, Bara suggested that the peace societies abandon all actions for arbitration and a congress of nations, and redirect their focus to the theoretical elaboration of a code of international law. The peace societies should engage in wide preliminary historical and comparative studies. He suggested that they use their financial means to attract a body of qualified legal experts, who could cooperate on the basis of a shared scientific methodology. Bara compared it to how Tribonian had succeeded in preparing the basis for the code of Justinian. This way, the records of the peace societies would become rich repositories of knowledge on international and constitutional law. Eventually, all that work should crystallise into two milestone scientific restatements of international law. The first one was a declaration of rational principles that *ought* to govern interstate relations, to be announced at an international specialist conference. Evidently, this list would be a list entirely *de lege ferenda,* but it would hold great moral authority, and serve as the campaign guide for future political efforts. The second restatement should limit itself exclusively to norms that had already been accepted by state practice, to the extent comparative research had proven. The peace movement should lobby states to confirm this more moderate list by means of a multilateral law-making treaty. Even if the material scope of this 'first charter of universal justice' was extremely restricted, its acceptance would already hugely benefit international relations. It would habituate states to legal reasoning in diplomacy, and form the steppingstone from which to launch more ambitious reforms. Over the decades, the treaty would slowly expand, until it would have transformed into a universal code of international law.[69]

Bara took the analogy with private law rather far and literally. His comparisons with the Napoleonic civil code and the 'centuries of wisdom' it allegedly contained were not just rhetorical. International law had to copy directly from national law. An improved 'logical' division of 'international civil law' had to include such topics as personal status law, property law, commercial law, administrative law, and criminal law.[70] To a modern

68 Ibid., 154–5, 206.

69 Ibid., 20–1, 41–9, 135, 158–60, 213, 228, 248.

70 Ibid, 94, 115–6, 157, 215.

observer, this may seem charmingly idiosyncratic, but it coincided with a contemporary trend in jurisprudence, particularly in Germany, that like Bara recognised the inoperability of natural law. It sought to develop a new autonomous 'scientific' legal science, based on intrinsically rational principles derived from Roman law, embodied in the various national codes inspired by it. This naturalist-tinged 'classical' legal thought, dominated by Savigny and Pandectist jurisprudence, understood private law to express logical and universal principles. International law was not yet customarily taught in European law schools in the 1840s – Bara himself wrote that the curriculum in his law school had barely mentioned it – but he was extensively instructed in Pandect law.[71]

Although methodology was its primary concern, the prize essay nonetheless touched upon several of the material changes it would like to see in international law thus corrected. Bara did not minutely list draft articles the same way as the draft codes of Pasquale Fiore, or David Dudley Field later on in the century. However, like any *de lege ferenda* writer, Bara could not resist the temptation entirely. If the Belgian civil code precluded any obligations in violation of public order and good morals, he mused, perhaps international law should have a similar doctrine. He of course did not explain how this 'morality' should be construed, but his other suggestions elsewhere overall corresponded with the sensibilities of the contemporary progressist upper classes in Belgium. Most of it was textbook liberalism. Dreams of universal monarchy were immoral. The abolition of slavery and serfdom was a debt to humanity requiring financial contributions also of non-slaveholding states. Free trade was a necessity. All waterways should be opened under the motto of *aqua libera*. Public works benefitting humanity as a whole, like a canal in Panama, might even justify international taxes.[72]

In doing so, Bara again ruffled the feathers of the Anglo-American peace movement. Unlike many British or American evangelicals, this Belgian liberal agreed with other Europeans, like Bouvet, that Europe's oppressed nationalities had a right to revolt. The principle of national self-determination could under certain conditions overrule the more conservative principle of legitimacy, as had been enshrined in the Vienna settlement. It echoed

71 Ibid., 192. Koskenniemi, 'View from around 1850' 2014, 19–73, 21, 25–37; Léon Vanderkindere, *L'Université de Bruxelles, 1834–1884. Notice historique faite à la demande du Conseil d'Administration* (Bruxelles: Weissenbruch 1884), LXVII.

72 Ibid., 42–3, 80, 104, 109–10, 112–3, 116, 120–1, 142, 190–1.

contemporary theories by Italian jurists like Mancini or Pierantoni.[73] For Bara, a nation was not a *res in commercio* that could be broken apart and attached back together on monarchical whim, for the sake of the balance of power. While other states might temporarily exercise authority over 'infant peoples', the 'tutor' should justify the privileges over its 'pupil' through its assistance to the latter's path to democratic self-governance. If the former proved corrupt or unwilling to do so, the colonised people had a right revolt. The argument betrayed Bara's bourgeois paternalism, his fascination with the private law analogy, as well as his nationalism.[74]

Nationalism equally informed Bara's views on the laws of war. In another act of blasphemy against the pacifist creed, Bara concluded that war at the moment remained perfectly legitimate. How else would the people assert their just rights in the face of tyranny? A realistic prohibition of war would evolve naturally in tune with gradual slow expansion of democracy and the international legal code. In the realm of the *ius ad bellum,* Bara kept the old distinctions between just and unjust wars. If war remained permissible for the foreseeable future, this meant that only the way it was to be conducted could be reformed. This idealistic lawyer therefore recommended reforms in the *ius in bello.* Unlike British Quakers, who felt uneasy about what they interpreted as moral laxities, Bara recommended a series of context-free principles applicable to every party to the conflict, like a prohibition against the intentional targeting of civilians. In doing so, he anticipated the many initiatives of lawyers later in the century to develop technical codes of military good conduct.[75]

Predictably, the work was initially silenced to death by the Anglo-American peace societies. Barely a word could be read about it in the *Herald* or the *Advocate.* It was naturally also not included in any tract series. The prize essay had violated just about every taboo imaginable for British or American friends of peace. It would take thirty years for the controversial essay to resurface as a stand-alone book. In 1871, *Les Amis Philanthropes,* the most well-connected masonic lodge of Brussels, decided to investigate the peace question. Its principal supporter, Charles Potvin (1818–1902), wished for a 'scientific' approach, similar to Quetelet's critique

73 Eloisa Mura, 'The Construction of the International Law Discipline in Italy between the Mancinian and Positive Schools', in Giulio Bartolini (ed.), *A History of International Law in Italy* (Oxford: OUP 2020), 109–225.

74 Bara, *Paix* 1872, 42, 96, 99–104, 105–6, 201–2.

75 Ibid., 14, 55–6, 58–63, 124–30, 182–4; Neff, *War* 2005, 161–6, 186–7.

of international law.[76] However, he soon became more intrigued by a lesser-known author. It remains unclear how exactly Potvin discovered the by then almost completely forgotten prize essay. Perhaps some lodge members still remembered Bara. The author himself had died at a rather young age in 1857, from the consequences of tuberculosis. For years, he had unsuccessfully tried to get his ten-volume manuscript on scientific methodology reviewed by the Royal Academy, to no avail.[77] However it happened, Auguste Visschers eventually managed to find the long-lost prize essay in his old congress papers. Potvin arranged three meetings to discuss the work within the lodge, which afterward consented to finance its publication. In 1872, Bara's essay finally appeared for the wider public. It was accompanied by an introduction of Potvin, who had also given it a more ambitious new title: *La science de la paix*.[78]

Its appearance triggered the first and only mention of Bara's work in the *Herald*. The journal noted that this book was a different beast from most prize essays. The journal outright admitted that such works were typically barely read by the larger public, because of their tendency 'to be characterised by a too obsequious adherence to all the views and ideas presumed by their writers to be acceptable to the parties initiating the competition'. If nothing else, Bara's book could not be accused of that. Even so, the review concluded that still it could not fully agree with Bara's plan, because it 'almost entirely ignores the strongest of all sources – the gospel of Christ'.[79]

European interest in the book was much higher, leading to a remarkable second life for Bara's old essay. Although the book itself did not sell in great numbers in the aftermath of the Franco-German War, it was read and discussed by influential publicists and lawyers. Potvin himself worked tirelessly to promote Bara's legacy, to whose ideas he had evidently grown attached. He brought it up several times in the *Revue de Belgique*, claiming the work had lost none of its relevance over the past twenty years.[80] During the visit of James B. Miles, the secretary of the American Peace Society, in advance

76 Adolphe Quetelet, *Du système social et des lois qui le régissent* (Paris: Guillaumin 1848), 219–23, 340; *Concours institué par les sociétés anglo-américaines de la paix, au Congrès de Bruxelles, septembre 1848. Rapport des commissaires* (Bruxelles: Hayez 1849), 42; Christoph De Spiegeleer, *Een blauwe Progressist. Charles Potvin (1818–1902) en het liberaal-sociale Denken van zijn Generatie* (Brussel: ASP 2011), 132.

77 Nadine Lubelski-Bernard, 'BARA (Louis-Adrien)', in *Biographie nationale de Belgique*, vol. XLII (Bruxelles: Bruylant 1983), 33–42.

78 Bara, *Paix* 1872, XII.

79 HP (February 1873), 188.

80 Revue de Belgique (15 September 1871), 8.

of the Brussels international law conference of 1873, Bara again figured. At a meeting of the *Société d'économie politique* in Paris, at which Passy and Visschers were also present, the latter remarked that the peace movement had 'perhaps too long neglected the legal question'.[81] Passy also admired the work, including it in the catalogue of his peace society.[82] Even radically republican peace advocates like Charles Lemonnier, one of the leaders of the *Ligue internationale de la paix et de la liberté,* endorsed it. He called it a fine work, 'much less sterile' than Quaker peace propaganda.[83]

Even outside of pacifist circles, Bara was known. In the 1870s, the *Larousse* encyclopaedia brought up his critique on arbitration in its corresponding lemma. The editors had not read Bara themselves, but had relied on a recent treatise on peace of the Belgian pacifist Emile de Laveleye (1822–1892).[84] Among international lawyers, Bara first got mentioned in the *Revue de droit international* in 1897, but only in a footnote. However, the Italian legal scholar Augusto Pierantoni (1840–1911) devoted three pages to the old Belgian essayist in his history of international law in the nineteenth century. Other law professors who brought up Bara included Leonid Kamarovsky (1846–1912), Alejandro Álvarez (1868–1960) and Ernest Nys (1851–1920). The latter, who is also sometimes described as the 'first' historian of international law, cited the 'important work' in a number of articles.[85]

In the twentieth century, the mid-nineteenth century text continued to charm people. In the 1950s, a Belgian author called Gabriel Devos published a summary of the book. Devos was a Europeanist, who emphasised the prescient aspects of what he called Bara's 'supranational' law. He

81 JE (March 1873), 502.

82 Bulletin de la société des amis de la paix (hereafter : BSAP) (March to July 1877), 94.

83 Charles Lemonnier, *Les États-Unis d'Europe* (Paris: Bibliothèque Démocratique 1872), 69.

84 'Arbitration', in Pierre Larousse (ed.), *Grand dictionnaire universel du XIXe siècle* (Paris: Administration du grand dictionnaire universel 1866–1877), 314–5; Émile de Laveleye, *Des causes actuelles de guerre en Europe et de l'arbitrage* (Bruxelles: Muquardt 1873), 7.

85 Revue de droit international et de législation comparée. 1st series XXIX (1898), 333–84, 334; Augusto Pierantoni, *Storia del diritto internatiozonale nel secolo XIX* (Napoli: Marghieri 1876), 104–7; Leonide Kamarowsky, *Le tribunal international* (Paris: Pedone-Lauriel 1887), 387–9; Alexandre Alvarez, *La codification du droit international. Ses tendances – Ses bases* (Paris: Pedone 1912), 227; Ernest Nys, *Le droit international, tome III* (Bruxelles: Castaigne 1906), 63; Ernest Nys, 'La Belgique et le droit international', in Émile Rossel (ed.), *La Patrie Belge* (Bruxelles: Rossel 1905), 871–900, 92; Ernest Nys, 'The Codification of International Law'. *American Journal of International Law* 5(4) (1911), 871–900, 884–5; Koskenniemi, 'Histories of International Law 2013, 220.

interpreted Bara as a precursor to the ideal of European unification.[86] Not everyone was impressed, however. In 1946, shortly after World War Two, Hans Morgenthau (1904–1980) wrote *Scientific Man vs. Power Politics.* In it, he severely criticised liberal-rationalist belief in 'scientific' solutions to what essentially remained political issues. He identified nineteenth century 'peace sciences' like Bara's as the origin of this folly.[87] Incidentally, the book inaugurated Morgenthau's post-war shift to the 'realist' school of international relations, which to Koskenniemi signalled part of the end of the 'heroic' period of international law.[88]

2.2 *Intellectual Germs of the International Law Societies*

More than just about anyone else connected to the international peace movement of the nineteenth century, Bara trusted in law as an autonomous reform factor. Other publicists by and large imagined that legal codification could only succeed through the medium of a congress or nations or a judicial tribunal. Political cooperation preceded codification. Bara had reversed that order. An 'enlightened' draft code was to inform political action. Politics had to follow the enlightened reason of specialist lawyers, rather than the other way around. Unlike nearly every other peace project of this era, Bara spent very little attention to the workings of a political congress of nations. He devoted only a few pages to the topic of federative peace. Although he too famously used the celebrated phrase 'united states of Europe', he did not dwell long on it. Legal science would first need to develop sufficiently within the confines of the existing balance of power, until confederal reform was viable. Sparing in details, he mainly suggested that scholars investigate precedents.[89] That might appear paradoxical, considering the essay was meant to outline a practical approach. However, the young lawyer's faith in scientific methodology was such that he could envision a form of legal development that did not rely on legislative work by an international political organisation.[90]

---

86 Gabriel Devos, *La science supranationale de Louis Bara* (Courtrai: Vermaut 1953), 6–7.

87 Hans Morgenthau, *Scientific Man vs. Power Politics* (London: Latimer 1946), 84; Peter Van den Dungen, 'Varieties of Peace Science: An Historical Note'. *Journal of Peace Science* 2(2) (1977), 244–5.

88 Koskenniemi, *Gentle Civilizer* 2001, 465–74; see also Oliver Jütersonke, *Morgenthau, Law and Realism* (Cambridge: CUP 2010), 138–41.

89 Bara, *Paix* 1872, 133–4, 197–8.

90 De Rycke, 'Legislating Utopia' 2020, 620–1.

Most contemporary peace friends did not consider this tactic, precisely because they did not believe in the effectiveness of legal doctrine as such. Even at the peace congresses, people like Burritt still dismissed it as mere 'argument' and 'opinion', written by people without actual political authority. It would take several decades for Burritt to shift towards a project not entirely dissimilar to Bara's. Other leaders, foremost the London Peace Society's Henry Richard, never warmed to the idea, and continued to prefer more direct parliamentary lobbying tactics.[91]

In the mid-century, likeminded authors could be counted on one hand. The only similar ones that could be found were a certain Jean-Baptiste Ferrer and a German law professor from Bonn, named Peter Kaufmann (1803–1872).[92] In Britain, an antiquarian called William Henry Black (1808–1872) suggested that a body of specialist jurists should prepare a *'corpus juris publici'*, similar to Justinian's, and encouraged specialised professorships. However, he was unable to get speaking time at London '51.[93]

The proposals of these various publicists constituted early precursors to the initiatives of the future peace through law movement. The parallels between their recommendations to the peace societies and the international law societies founded in 1873 were striking. Rolin-Jaequemyns's *Revue* always emphasised that international law was a science, in the sense that those who adhered to a scientific methodology stood the best chance of progressing it. Co-founders of the *Institut de droit international* like the aforementioned de Laveleye likewise stressed that science needed to develop autonomously if international law was to improve.[94] The American lawyer David Dudley Field entertained similar views, which led him to write his *Draft Outlines of an International Code,* published in 1872 – the same year as Bara's book. Although Field and Bara arrived at the same idea independently of each other, Field did eventually cooperate with the American

91 See chapter 7.

92 Ferrer, of whom little is known, pleaded for the dual combination of an international code and a 'tribunal arbitral'. The congress that had to develop these institutions was to be composed of jurisconsults, sent out in equal number by every state. These experts voted by majority on an international code. Jean-Baptiste Ferrer, *L'ère nouvelle. Nécessité d'un code international et d'un tribunal arbitral des nations* (Paris: Plon 1863), 5–19; Peter Kaufmann, *Die Idee und der praktische Nutzen einer Weltakademie des Völkerrechts* (Bonn: Habidt 1855), 9.

93 HP (September 1851), 194–5.

94 *Annuaire* 1877, 22–3.

peace movement in establishing the Association for the Reform and Codification of the Laws of Nations.[95]

However, in the late 1840s, these developments were still far away. The Peace Congress Committee was adamant that the international meetings should first and foremost recommend arbitration and disarmament to the governments of the 'civilised world'. Like they had done after their convention in London in 1843, the organising committee tried to present their official resolutions to important men of state. In the wake of the Paris congress, for instance, a delegation met with the newly elected president of the French Republic, Louis-Napoléon Bonaparte. As had typically been the case when adherents of the peace movement with a high-profile politician, they were received cordially by the latter, but simultaneously politely brushed off. With the French president, Hugo, Girardin, and the others mostly stressed the need for mutual European disarmament. The budding dictator, who was to engage in several wars during his time in office, agreed with the views of the peace congress, but said it was not the right time.[96]

Two years later, his coup d'état indirectly contributed to the end of the international peace congress cycle. The rise of a new Napoleonic empire triggered another invasion panic in Britain. The upsurge of militarism back home made the London Peace Society cancel its plans for another international congress. The eruption of the Crimean War another two years later definitively killed any plans in that direction. For the next thirty years, people would occasionally suggest to revive the congresses. Henry Richard was especially keen to do so, but every attempt to do so was thwarted by the hostile international political climate.[97] Only in 1889 would the international peace movement resume its practice of holding regular large-scale 'universal' peace congresses.[98]

During the short interval of the original peace congresses, the Anglo-American peace societies were able to consolidate their political programme. Internally, the congresses allowed the London Peace Society succeeded in forwarding arbitration and disarmament as the chief goals of the international peace movement to the outside world. They achieved in attracting an up until then unprecedented amount of public attention to proposals that had already been fermenting for some time. The peace

95 See chapter 7.

96 *Proceedings Paris* 1849, 119–20.

97 HP (January 1864), 6–11.

98 These were held until 1913. Another series ran from 1921 to 1939. Lambert, 'Dynamics' 2016, 126.

congresses of the 1840s in many ways represented the culmination point of an exceptionally fruitful era for the peace societies. Over the span of some twenty years, they had transformed from obscure religious clubs to political pressure groups able to get the international press to write about a more or less coherent programme. Every aspect of this programme would be reiterated in some form or another for decades, if not centuries, to come.

Although the British peace movement would remain loyal to arbitration as conceived by Cobden and Sturge, the legal arguments that had at first glance failed on the European congress floor would not go away either. The 'dissident' opinions of Burritt, Bara and others would powerfully resurface several years later, rivalling in importance those of the 'moderates' of the 1840s. Essentially, almost every subsequent normative argument delivered by a member of the institutional peace movement could be traced back directly or indirectly to one already made in the middle of the century. With their name made and their practical programme consolidated, the crucial task for peace friends was from then on to set about actually realising it all. To do so, they would need political allies. The era of the 1850s to the early 1870s would be marked by both unexpected political successes, as well as a number of sobering confrontations with the limits of pacifism.

CHAPTER 6

Trials of the Anglo-American Movement (1848–1873)

> 'The day is fast coming, when this cause, in its influence on ourselves as a conservator of the Union, will be found to have an importance of which few, if any, now dream.
>
> The Advocate of Peace (1853)

1 The Antebellum American Peace Movement

Can pacifism survive the onslaught of war? After the success of the international peace congresses, the Anglo-American peace movement was thrown into a prolonged era of turbulence. The Crimean War silenced the London Peace Society during the 1850s, but the end of the conflict directly led to one of the first – albeit non-binding and vague – arbitration clauses agreed upon by Western powers in a multilateral treaty. An ensuing Declaration similarly offered an original model for a multilateral law-making treaty agreed upon by a 'congress of nations'. The Anglo-American peace societies had high hopes that the legal programme they had agreed upon during the peace congresses was finally beginning to be applied into state practice. The first major great power war in over forty years had not destroyed the organised peace movement. Their resolve had been tested and proven resilient. At least this was how the Anglo-American peace friends themselves liked to frame it; especially the British, who had been the most personally affected by the recent war with Russia.[1]

The American peace movement also initially surfed on the high of their success. The Mexican War had buoyed the peace societies up into a larger anti-war coalition, which had been especially strong in their native New England. In the early 1850s, American peace friends further capitalised on their increasing respectability when the upcoming Charles Sumner

1 See the final part of chapter 2.

 | DOI:10.1163/9789004733688_008

associated his rising political star with their movement. Sumner's erudition and eloquence translated themselves into two seminal pacifist classics of the nineteenth century. They combined an understanding of the intellectual predecessors of peace thought with the legal agenda of the modern-day peace movement. Around the same time, the American Peace Society began its own arbitration campaign on the federal level. Astonishingly, most of all for the peace friends themselves, the Senate Committee on Foreign Relations endorsed their legal project – not once, but twice: in 1851 and again in 1853.

As the years progressed, however, clouds began to gather over the Anglo-American peace societies. This time, the cause of their distress lay in the west, and it was up to the American peace advocates to test their mettle. The rebellions in Europe and India made the American Peace Society reaffirm its loyalty to law and order in the domestic sphere. This had ever been the concern of its secretary, the cautious George Beckwith. He had finally been able to undermine the position of the reformists in 'his' society. Unlike them, Beckwith believed that pacifism only stood a chance if it stayed aloof from other social issues, and focussed exclusively on the abolition of interstate war. Unfortunately, the problem of slavery at home would not go away, leading to a crisis that affected the entire Anglo-American peace movement. In 1848, however, the pacifists were still characteristically optimistic.

1.1 *The Erudition of Charles Sumner*

The first public speech of Charles Sumner (1811–1874) had an impact like no peace society lecture ever had. A lawyer of some local prominence already in his native Massachusetts, Sumner had been asked to deliver one of the orations at the ceremony of Boston's Fourth of July festivities. Then as now, the day was a celebration of the already deeply mythologised American Revolution. A military parade had been one of the main attractions of the day. In the harbour, the U.S.S. Ohio was decked out from top to bottom in American flags. Under escort of a ceremonial guard, the town's notables went to the great hall of Tremont Temple. A hundred schoolgirls – all clad in white – sang patriotic anthems, many of them heroizing past battles. Close to the mayor, in the front rows, sat a hundred military officers in full dress. Men like them thought very little of peace friends, typically dismissing them as unpatriotic cowards. Their prejudices were proven wrong when the young speaker stepped to the lectern and showed to all present that advocates of peace could indeed – to put it colloquially – have some serious guts.

Sumner elaborately defended what he called the 'true grandeur of nations' before his 2,000 audience members that day in 1845.[2] True grandeur, he lectured, was not found in war. True national honour and glory were won through 'works of justice and beneficence'. What would the United States gain by a war with Mexico over Texas, or with Britain over Oregon? No 'honest heart' should endorse the vaunted adage of 'our country, be she right or wrong'. Should their young republic follow the negative example of the European powers, and spend exorbitant sums on military establishments in time of peace? Sumner referred to statistics that emphasised the immense war debt of Britain, and the enormous military budgets in Europe.[3] Their country had a much smaller army and navy, Sumner admitted, but it was still grossly out of proportion compared with the total federal budget. In one of the speech's most remembered passages, he compared the salary of the captain of the Ohio with that of the president of Harvard. Sumner asserted that the former, even when on leave, still earned more than the latter, who was never 'off-duty'. Taking it further still, in front of quite a few of its officers, Sumner calculated that a single naval gun of the U.S.S Ohio down in the harbour cost more than the entire Massachusetts Supreme Court and the governor combined. The actual 'glory' of the United States lay in the 'judicial labours of Marshall' and the 'immortal judgments of Story'.[4]

Reactions to the speech were mixed. To no one's surprise, tension was palpable during the banquet afterwards. The naval officers present reluctantly attended, feeling insulted. One state senator gave a very coarse retort, full of personal attacks against Sumner, for which the senator was not rebuked, but loudly applauded, especially by the military men. A succession of other speakers delivered toasts in a similar vein, ridiculing the impudent attorney. One of them toasted on 'the Millennium', when 'the principles of the orator of the day will be susceptible of practical application'. Eventually, one of his sympathisers brightened the mood with a couple of jokes, helped by Sumner's stoicism, who wisely decided not to engage. In spite of the tense atmosphere at the event itself, the controversial Fourth of July oration soon earned some approving comments. While many objected to it, among them Joseph Story, who felt 'compelled to dissent', Sumner could count on

---

2 Edward Pierce, *Memoirs and Letters of Charles Sumner. Vol. II. 1838–1845* (Boston: Roberts Brothers 1877), 344–5.

3 Charles Sumner, *The True Grandeur of Nations: an Oration delivered before the Authorities of the City of Boston, July 4, 1845* (Boston: American Peace Society 1870), 7–9, 61–71, 73–80.

4 Ibid., 82–8; Pierce, *Memoirs II* 1877, 344–5.

the praise of the editor of the popular *North American Review,* as well as several religious periodicals. When it was published in August, the religious and anti-slavery press reprinted significant parts of it.[5]

Having himself extensively drawn from its propaganda, Sumner was naturally also embraced by the Massachusetts and the American Peace Societies, both of them located in Boston, the city in which he had delivered his speech. Upham and May each sent their compliments. The reformist president of the Society, Coues, praised Sumner's 'strength and eloquence'.[6] Burritt in turn wrote to Sumner that he had launched his very own 'Young America' movement.[7] Beckwith agreed with May that the newspapers had misrepresented Sumner's message.[8] The American Peace Society published its own edition, and disseminated thousands of copies. The speech quickly spread across the Atlantic to the London Peace Society, where it proved equally popular. The speech was eventually reprinted for decades as part of the canon of the Anglo-American peace literature, growing into a nineteenth century pacifist classic.[9]

Sumner himself became a member of some prominence of the American Peace Society, serving as a member of the American Peace Congress Committee in 1849, a vice-president between 1853 and 1865, and also assuming positions in the board of directors and the executive committee.[10] Having declined to attend the European peace congresses of Paris and Frankfurt, Sumner ceased to be an active member from 1849 onwards. Other radical causes, most notably anti-slavery, took over his political ambitions once he was elected a senator in 1851, even if he remained a nominal member.[11] Before he did so, however, the politician gave the American Peace Society's annual address in 1849, called *The War-System of the Commonwealth of Nations.*[12] Like *The True Grandeur*, it evolved into one of the society's most

5 Ibid., 355–7, 359–64, 368–9.
6 Ibid., 361–2, 364.
7 Tolis, *Burritt* 1968, 134–5.
8 Pierce, *Memoirs II* 1877, 361.
9 Phelps, *Anglo-American Peace Movement,* 1930, 70–2.
10 Lawson, *Plowshares* 1975, 548, 550, 551; Charles Sumner, 'Stipulated Arbitration, or a Congress of Nations, with Disarmament', in *His Complete Works. Vol. III* (Boston: Lee and Shepard 1900), 117–21.
11 Edward Pierce, *Memoirs and Letters of Charles Sumner. Vol. III. 1845–1860* (Boston: Roberts Brothers 1894), 39–40.
12 Charles Sumner, *War-System of the Commonwealth of Nations: an Address before the American Peace Society, at its Anniversary in Boston, May 28, 1849* (Boston: American Peace Society 1870).

widely circulated annual addresses.[13] Together, the two speeches articulated the distinctly legalist approach to peace, as favoured by Sumner and the American Peace Society.

Much of Sumner's analysis ran parallel to the earlier analyses by Upham and Ladd, as also espoused in the peace journals. While Sumner's pacifism was also partly rooted in religion, as it did for most every peace friend in the antebellum era, his publications devoted far more space to economic and legal cases against war. The latter especially took centre stage in his speeches. The central problem of the peace and war question, Sumner argued, was that 'international law expressly establishes the arbitrament of war for the determination of controversies between nations'.[14] Like pacifist authors before him, the lawyer took umbrage with the conventional definition of war as a 'trial of right', as he found it defined in the works of Lord Bacon, Kent, Vattel, Bynkershoek, Whewell and Lieber.[15] Like judicial combat in municipal law, war in international law was a pernicious custom that had to be abolished by progressing civilisation.[16] In terms of sources, states could draw from both positive and natural law, but Sumner too underlined that states were not exempt from acknowledging 'one and the same Law of Right', in the form of the 'supreme moral law'. Those Christian states bound within their 'commonwealth of nations', with the law of nations as its 'supreme law', had to discover a way through which their 'custom' or 'institute' of war could be abolished, in keeping with the law of God, which trumped everything.[17]

In terms of the legal programme of the American peace movement, Sumner was acceptable to both conservatives and reformists. He stuck to the compromise of the London peace congress of 1843. In his *War-System* speech before the American Peace Society in 1849, Sumner invited every member of the movement to unite 'in the effort now making, at home and abroad, to establish arbitration treaties'. Like Sturge and Cobden in Britain, and Beckwith in the United States, Sumner believed that Jay's arbitration project was 'rational, humane, and cheap', and 'not open even to the superficial objections launched against a Congress of Nations'.[18] In 1872, just

13 Lawson, *Plowshares* 1975, 13.
14 Sumner, *True Grandeur* 1870, 14–5; Sumner, *War-System* 1870, 8, 24–33.
15 Sumner, *True Grandeur* 1870, 15–7.
16 Ibid., 38–43; see also Charles Sumner, 'The Law of Human Progress', in *His Complete Works. Vol. II* (Boston: Lee and Shepard 1900), 241–90.
17 Sumner, *True Grandeur* 1870, 45–7; Sumner, *War-System* 1870, 14–7, 19.
18 Ibid., 95, 100–1.

before the *Alabama claims* was awarded in Geneva, Sumner introduced an arbitration motion in the U.S. Senate.[19] Nonetheless, Sumner took the ultimate goal of an international legal institution more seriously than Beckwith or Cobden. Only a legislative diplomatic congress and a judicial court offered 'the most complete and permanent substitute for war'. These institutions should erect a 'Magna Charta of international law, by which the crime of war shall be forever abolished'.[20]

Sumner's knowledge of historical pacification plans was impressive to contemporary standards. In fact, it remains impressive today. From history, he drew on a by then familiar canon, including the Amphyctionic Council and Achaean league from antiquity, the Hanseatic league from the Middle Ages, and the Swiss and German Confederations, the League of Armed Neutrality from 1780, and the United States from modern times. He also passingly mentioned the assemblies of the European Concert, that had at the very least 'professed' to secure peace.[21] It was in his overview of individual intellectual efforts, however, that Sumner's erudition shone through.

Within the canon of great thinkers on the topic he placed not only household names like Henri IV, Grotius, William Penn, Rousseau, and the *abbé* de Saint-Pierre, but also authors little known within contemporary peace propaganda. The latter included seventeenth century authors like the Jansenist theologian Pierre Nicole (1625–1695), the little-known writer of the *Traité sur les moyens de conserver la paix avec les hommes,* the French political author Émeric Crucé (1590–1648), who published the *Nouveau Cynée,* and an incredibly obscure peace plan by count Ernest of Hesse-Rheinfels (1623–1693), which Sumner learned about through Leibnitz.[22] As far as could be ascertained, these three were seldom or never mentioned by nineteenth century adherents of the peace movement. Most remain obscure today.[23] Sumner seemed especially well-versed in German writings. As mentioned earlier, Sumner was one of the first to introduce Immanuel Kant to the American peace movement, arguing that his essay on a 'special league' on the basis of a true 'Treaty of Peace' may yet preserve the once-famed

19 Charles Sumner, 'Arbitration as a Substitute for War', in *His Complete Works. Vol. XX* (Boston: Lee and Shepard 1900), 80–2.

20 Sumner, *War-System* 1870, 93–5, 101.

21 Ibid., 49, 56–9, 101–2.

22 Ibid., 62–65.

23 Arcidiacono's textbook, for example, mentions Crucé, but omits many of the names mentioned by Sumner.

philosopher from Konigsberg from threatening obscurity.[24] Sumner's remarkably greater knowledge of European intellectual pacification traditions, as compared to most Americans, may have been attributable to his European travels from the late 1830s, which included Germany.[25]

In doing so, Sumner had arguably written one of the most comprehensive historical overviews of the nineteenth century. He was responsible for introducing the legacy of European peace thought into American pacifism, combining intellectual sophistication with political acumen.

1.2 *The American Arbitration Campaign*

By the early 1850s, at around the same time when Beckwith was consolidating his power, arbitration clauses were beginning to surpass a congress of nations in relative importance. While the *Advocate* still occasionally brought it up, it was on nowhere near the same level as in the 1830s. The petitions themselves were almost exclusively devoted to stipulated arbitration. Their phrasing was relatively standard. Typically, the petitioners tried to frame it as a harmless proposition, compatible with the national honour, leaving the recourse to force ultimately intact. A petition from 1851, for example, merely asked that any arbitration clause should provide that hostilities could only begin six months after formal notice has been given. That way, the peace society hoped, war could at least be delayed, if nothing else.[26] Compared to the sweeping reforms demanded by the reformists, this was a limited ambition. Beckwith was careful to proceed with caution, to ward off any imputation of utopianism.

Comparatively little is known about the specifics of the parliamentary arbitration petitions launched in the 1850s. The societies themselves generally did not include comprehensive lists of the amount of signatures each

---

24 Ibid., 70–2. Sumner mentioned *Zum Ewigen Frieden, Idee zu einer allgemeinen Geschichte in Weltbürgerlich Absicht,* and the *Metaphysische Anfangsgrunde der Rechtslehre.* Philip Berry was the only other author to reference Kant. Livermore, *Mexico* 1850, 57.

25 Other German writers included the 1763 work by Totze, based on Henri IV, and the 1767 treatise by Jakob Heinrich von Lilienfeld (1716–1785). Early nineteenth century German philosophers included Johann Gottlieb Fichte (1762–1814) and Carl Heinrich Schwab (1781–1847). Edward Pierce, *Memoirs and Letters of Charles Sumner. Vol. I. 1811–1838* (Boston: Roberts Brothers 1877), 196–341; Pierce, *Memoirs II* 1877, 36–147. Sumner, *War-System* 1870, 69–89.

26 AP (September & October 1850), 276–7; AP (January & February 1850), 171–4; AP (March & April 1850), 183–4; AP (May & June 1850), 208–9; AP (July & August 1850), 249–50; AP (April 1856), 49–52; AP (June 1860), 92–4; AP (January 1852), 14–6.

individual petition had obtained. The scholarly literature likewise does not offer exact numbers. Nonetheless, it is generally accepted that the American Peace Society achieved its most successful Congressional lobbying in the early 1850s. In February 1851, and again in February 1853, the Senate voted on the recommendations contained in reports of the Senate Committee on Foreign Relations to adopt arbitration in U.S. foreign policy.

In both instances, its support was restrained, merely advising the president 'to secure, whenever it may be practicable, a stipulation in all treaties hereafter entered (…) providing for the adjustment of any misunderstanding (…) by referring the same to the decision of disinterested and impartial arbitrators, to be mutually chosen'.[27] No action was subsequently taken by the Senate. The peace friends, in their characteristic optimism, professed it had been due to a lack of time, but historians have hypothesised that partisan politics offered a more plausible explanation. After all, they were supported most predominantly by Northern Whigs and Free Soilers, men who also endorsed free trade and anti-slavery, and several of whom co-founded the Republican Party.[28] Similar resolutions before state legislatures where such opinions predominated, like those of Vermont, Massachusetts, Maine, Rhode Island, and Connecticut – all in New England – passed without problems. Unlike in Britain, the U.S. arbitration campaign was not accompanied by public demonstrations, not even in New England. In fact, the whole campaign went largely ignored by the popular press.[29]

The 1851 report was remarkably positive about the American Peace Society's juridical propositions. Beckwith himself confessed that he had been taken by surprise by the unexpectedly warm reception of the petitions and memorials. The American Peace Society's leader recounted that when he went to Washington to meet with the chairman of the Senate Committee, he did not expect much. After all, Henry Foote was not only a man who had aimed a gun at his opponent in Congress during the debates on the Compromise of 1850, but he also hailed from Mississippi. A decade later, he would sit in the Confederate Congress.[30] Expecting to be brushed off after a

---

27 Quotation from the 1853 resolution. The peace societies were disappointed that their petitions had not been brought before a dedicated committee. The Congressional Globe (February 5, 1851), 437; The Congressional Globe (February 22, 1853), 761; AP (January & February 1851), 29–32.

28 Curti, *Crusade* 1929, 179, 195–7; AP (May & June 1849), 70.

29 Curti, *Crusade* 1929, 197; AP (January & February 1851), 29–32.

30 Michael Perman, 'Foote, Henry Stuart, in *American National Biography Online*. 2000, available at: doi.org/10.1093/anb/9780198606697.article.0400386.

twenty minute conversation, Beckwith was interrupted ten minutes in by his host, who fully agreed: 'That's right, sir; that's right. I like the principle, it has so much practical common sense. Indeed, it is the very principle we have so long adopted for the peaceful adjustment of difficulties between the thirty-one states of our own Confederacy'.[31]

The report of 1853 was similarly favourable, even though the Senate Committee was again chaired by a Southerner, the Kentucky judge Joseph Underwood. It went into some considerable detail on the financial and economic expenses of Western militaries, citing similar statistics to those found in the pages of the *Advocate*. Like senator Foote before it, it referred to the precedent of the United States itself. However, the committee did not recognise the short-term possibility of any high court of nations, instead recommending arbitration clauses. Whether a board or a single individual, it was held that the arbitrators must be 'eminent jurists having little or no connection with political affairs'. However, the committee members took care to provide sufficient political leeway. If the award was rejected, the parties could still resort to arms. One reason for rejection might be that the award was 'palpably unjust', analogous to the domestic legal maxim of *fraus omnia corrumpit.*[32] Obviously, this could completely undermine the system, since parties could unilaterally invoke that exception. The report was aware of that issue, claiming that an unmotivated rejection would 'bring general odium', that arbitrators would take care to avoid unreasonable awards, and that the progress of civilisation would increasingly dispose Christians to settle their differences peacefully.[33]

The American Peace Society clung very strongly to these reports, despite indications that the Senate was less agreed on this topic than might be inferred from pacifist propaganda. The reports featured very prominently in the *Advocate* in the ensuing years, forming the latest additions to a list that also included the successful resolutions of New England state legislatures, beginning with the previously mentioned 1838 Legaré report from Massachusetts.[34] Similar to their selective reading of the 1838 report, the *Advocate* wrote that the Senate Committee had been 'unanimous and cordial' in adopting it, even though in reality the minority in the Committee had 'utterly dissented from the conclusion as well as the reasoning'.[35] As already

31 AP (June & July 1853), 308–9.

32 AP (April 1853), 257–65.

33 Ibid., 264–7.

34 See chapter 1. E.g. AP (November 1855), 353–7.

35 AP (June & July 1853), 312; The Congressional Globe (February 22, 1853), 761.

mentioned, nothing came of the resolutions afterwards. The peace societies again overemphasised the positive aspects, grasping at every straw in the face of the overall indifference or hostility that met the campaign in larger society and in other political spheres.

If Congress stood moderately receptive to the pacifist message, the executive remained largely non-committal. Several U.S. presidents had at one time or another met with representatives of the peace societies. In the 1820s, Worcester already received written responses from former presidents John Adams and Thomas Jefferson. In the late 1830s, Ladd met with Van Buren and his cabinet, who received him 'respectfully', but the peace leader left it with the conviction that he 'the million must speak before their rulers will hear', feeling brushed off.[36] Beckwith, during his long term of office, met with several U.S. presidents in person. President Tyler, who received from Beckwith the paper containing the resolutions of the 1843 London peace conference, duly acknowledged the potential of arbitration, but overall kept himself to polite platitudes and the implication that the voting public would have to be persuaded more before Washington would act.[37] About ten years later, Beckwith met with president Fillmore and a few cabinet members with a copy of the 1853 Committee report. The secretary of the treasury could hardly believe that the Senate Committee on Foreign Relations had unanimously consented with such a report – which it had not – but confided that he supported it. Unfortunately, key members such as the secretary of state and the president himself were less enthusiastic.[38] Still, it was not as bad as president Taylor's hostility. In Britain, Richard Cobden had recently managed to elicit from Lord John Russell the declaration that he would consider a general arbitration treaty with the United States. The president, however, a famous general, replied that he was the 'greatest peace man in the country', and dismissed international peace as a futile project.[39]

In the spring of 1854, Elihu Burritt dined with two other guests at the White House with president Franklin Pierce. Burritt told the president that he had previously spoken warmly about the concept of arbitration. When he then asked whether this meant that the president would therefore support the resolutions of the peace conferences, Pierce proved more reluctant. He answered his guest that the United States would likely never find an

36 AP (June 1839), 11.
37 AP (April 1844), 192.
38 AP (June & July 1853), 309.
39 Decades later, Bismarck would say something similar. Curti, *Crusade* 1929, 195.

'impartial arbitrator' among the European powers, and also that the Monroe doctrine precluded him from involving the United States in such a campaign.[40]

Overall, no president could fundamentally agree with the worldview of the peace movement. While notable enough to at times meet and engage with the highest political level, the peace societies were not influential enough to draw from such interviews more than an exchange of polite pleasantries, if not outright commonplaces, similar to the lot befalling those delegations meeting with European statesmen and monarchs. Like had already been charged by Worcester and Dodge, even the most cynical statesman would publicly claim to be a peace-loving man. As much as the presidents of the United States may have possessed a genuine concern for international peace, their high office and experience with politics did not allow them to share the peace movement's terrific optimism about their more pacific international legal solutions. All shared Pierce's sentiment that 'the people of all countries' were still too prone to 'war and warlike manifestations'.[41]

Two relative successes of arbitration in the 1850s were therefore, similar to article 21 of the Treaty of Guadalupe Hidalgo before, only dubiously creditable to the efforts of the arbitration campaign. The first 'success' was to be found in the two fisheries treaties concluded between the United States and Britain in 1853 and 1854. The first treaty dealt with outstanding claims provoked by unresolved questions in previous treaties on North-American fishing grounds. The second treaty was the larger 'Reciprocity' treaty, granting among other things fishing and navigation rights to the U.S. in British-Canadian waters.[42] Beckwith saw his chance and lobbied with president Fillmore and secretary of state Everett for the upcoming claims agreement to include an article that arranged for arbitration of 'all future disputes' that could not be resolved through negotiation. Fillmore and Marcy admitted that they had not thought of writing this principle into a treaty, preferring to decide it on an ad hoc basis. Still, in a second interview, they told Beckwith that they might agree on it if the British would concur as well. Beckwith promptly asked a friendly senator to sound out the British minister, who likewise responded well to the idea.[43] Sensing a great opportunity in

40 BB (May 1854), 150–1.

41 BB (May 1854), 151.

42 Frederick Haynes, 'The Reciprocity Treaty With Canada of 1854'. *Publications of the American Economic Association* 7(6) (1892), 7–70.

43 AP (June & July 1853), 310.

the fisheries negotiations, the peace leader intensified his campaign. Several ecclesiastical bodies resolved to support the society's efforts, more tracts were printed, the circulation of the *Advocate* was doubled, and new agents toured the states circulating petitions, Beckwith himself travelling over three thousand miles.[44] In Britain, the leading British peace friends, including Henry Richard and Richard Cobden, joined in the effort, similarly interviewing the foreign secretary, Lord Clarendon. They had learned from Beckwith that the United States was not unwilling to consider an arbitration clause. The secretary was sceptical, and therefore surprised to hear from the British delegation of the 1853 Underwood Senate report. Clarendon asked for a copy, which Cobden promised to deliver.[45]

Whether the peace societies of the U.S. and Britain were responsible for the inclusion of a modest arbitration clause in the two treaties, remains debateable. Beckwith, though taking solace in the fact that it was included at all, admitted that neither treaty article covered 'all misunderstandings relative to any and every treaty between us and England'.[46] True enough, both merely installed binational commissions, dealing exclusively with disputes related to treaty provisions, and which only resorted to a third-party umpire in case of disagreement, similar to the Jay Treaty and the Treaty of Ghent.[47] Judging from the usual political response to peace petitions and memorials, the societies most likely did not exercise much, if any, diplomatic influence on these treaty negotiations, in spite of the grand ambitions of the peace advocates themselves. At best, they may have nudged Lord Clarendon a bit in the right direction, as he a few years later introduced a 'good offices' clause into the peace treaty ending the Crimean War.[48]

The second 'success' of the peace movement, the 23rd Protocol of the Paris Peace Treaty, similarly boosted the morale of the American peace movement. Their isolation from the Crimean War had not shielded American peace friends from many of the same feelings of anxiety as the British. For decades, they had sung the praises of the period of relative peace among the world's great powers. Suddenly, these same great powers were engaging in a vicious struggle. Even worse, the war enjoyed considerable

44 Curti, *Crusade* 1929, 199; AP (August 1853), 325–9; AP, November 1853, 369–70, 383–4.

45 HP (June 1853), 227, 233–4.

46 HP (June 1853), 233; AP (July & August 1854), 127; AP (November 1859), 359.

47 See chapter 1. *Treaties and other International Acts of the United States of America. Vol. 6. Documents 152–172: 1852–1855* (Washington: Government Printing Office 1942), 112–3, 668–9.

48 AP (June 1854), 84–6; AP (July & August 1854), 126–7. See the end of chapter 2.

popular support among British and Russian citizens. The American Peace Society's report of 1855 lamented that 'the work of the past thirty years' had been put to naught.[49] As such, news of the 'arbitration' clause in the peace treaty met with exhilaration also on the western shore of the Atlantic. The American Peace Society admitted it was 'still in a very imperfect form', due to its non-binding character, but nevertheless, the Protocol would serve as the 'vantage-ground' from which to 'push forward the claims of justice and humanity'.[50] From that point onwards, the Treaty of Paris became a fixture in the growing list of political precedents used by the American societies to prove that their work had 'not been in vain'.[51]

By 1859, the Americans could therefore look back not only on the Paris protocol, but also on the British arbitration motion of 1849, the supportive resolutions adopted by several state legislatures, promising conversations with a number of presidents, as well as two more or less approving Senate reports.[52] These latter reports also offered the societies an unexpected ray of hope concerning the domestic cause of peace. For a long time, the society had 'done next to nothing at the South', hardly any propaganda penetrating much beyond the Mason-Dixon line. Few imagined that the Southern planters would be receptive to pacifist ideologies. The society could not hide its astonishment over the unexpected support of 'Senators *from the South*'. The Senate Committee of Underwood had after all mostly consisted of senators of Southern and Western states. Perhaps, some fancied, the 'most enlightened statesmen of the South' could unite with 'the people' of the North? They mused: 'The day is fast coming, when this cause, in its influence on ourselves as a conservator of the Union, will be found to have an importance of which few, if any, now dream.'[53]

1.3 *Defining War Out of Existence*

On the afternoon of 22 May 1856, senator Sumner was quietly working at his desk in the Senate chamber, unaware of two Southern colleagues who were advancing towards him. A couple of days before, he had attacked the legislation that had repealed the Missouri Compromise.[54] The Kansas-Nebraska

---

49 AP (June 1854), 81–7; AP (June 1855), 289–90; Ziegler, Antebellum 1992, 119–25.

50 AP (August and September), 120–3.

51 AP (June and July 1856), 110; AP (October 1859), 350; BB (October 1856), 45–7.

52 AP (November 1859), 359–60.

53 AP (October 1853), 366–7.

54 Charles Sumner, 'The Crime against Kansas: the Apologies for the Crime; the True Remedy', in *His Complete Works. Vol. V* (Boston: Lee and Shepard 1900), 125–342.

Act of 1854 had created two new U.S. territories. The act had provided that the legality of slavery there would be decided through the electoral voice of its inhabitants, rather than through Congress. Predictably, over the past two years, these frontier regions had degenerated into a lawless Wild West battleground between anti-slavery settlers from the North and pro-slavery settlers from the South. Violent raids, electoral fraud and political murder caught the attention of the rest of the country. In the middle 1850s, so-called 'Bleeding Kansas' became the focal point of the great divide running through the United States on the juridical status of slavery. Brutality was not limited to the frontier, however, as Sumner would soon found out when one of the two senators interrupted his train of thought in a soft, yet stern voice. He claimed that Sumner had insulted South Carolina in his last speech, as well as his friend. Before the representative from Massachusetts could respond, he was struck by the gold-topped wooden cane of his assailant. An unusually tall man, Sumner got stuck between his chair and his desk, and, blinded by the first strike, was helpless against the many blows that followed. The other Southerner kept bystanders at bay with a gun.[55]

FIGURE 6.1 Charles Sumner finding out whether the pen is mightier than the sword.

55 William James Hull Hoffer, *The Caning of Charles Sumner: Honor, Idealism, and the Origins of the Civil War* (Baltimore: Johns Hopkins University 2010), 7–36.

When order was eventually restored, reactions were mixed. The Northern press was outraged. The 'caning of Sumner' was yet another example of Southern 'chivalry' and the manners to be expected from slaveholders. In the South, on the other hand, many could hardly contain their glee. Hundreds sent new canes to replace the one that had been broken during the attack, carrying such disturbing inscriptions as 'Hit him again'.[56] Sumner himself was unable to participate in politics for a number of years, suffering from a debilitating head trauma which transformed into chronic pain for the rest of his life. The American Peace Society too lost any services the senator, who was still a valuable, if no longer active member, may have been able to provide.[57]

More fundamentally, the affair was symbolic of the latent philosophical problem characterising all pacifism. Like other peace organisations, the American Peace Society was reaching the moment in its existence where it had to decide whether 'peace' and 'justice' were mutually reconcilable. Should peace friends insist that peace had to be maintained 'at any price', or, conversely, that certain moral principles trumped others and that a just war was sometimes legitimate? To some degree, this was a continuation of their long-standing internal debates on the legitimacy of defensive war. However, the events of the late 1840s and 1850s made these issues much more salient, to the point of critically endangering the raison d'être of the peace movement itself. Could you remain a peace friend when millions lived in cruel servitude? Could you criticise those who took up arms to free the oppressed? During the 1850s, in the run-up to the Civil War, the American Peace Society crystallised its stance on the right of revolution, non-intervention and the juridical nature of defensive war. All of these positions would be severely put to the test in the great national crisis of the 1860s, when the slavery question finally caught up with American pacifism – and the nation itself.

Practically every member of the peace movement was opposed to slavery. Although the American Peace Society proper was not part of the abolitionist movement, many members stood sympathetic to the anti-slavery cause, or were also members of abolitionist societies.[58] In the 1820s, Worcester described American slavery as 'plague spots on the body politic'. Like many other contemporaries, the founder of the Massachusetts Peace Society remarked on the 'inconsistency' in the way in which fellow-citizens celebrated

56 Hoffer, *Caning* 2010, 66–96.

57 Lawson, *Plowshares* 1975, 468, 548.

58 Ibid., 130.

their own Revolution, while keeping up 'a system of tyranny and flagrant injustice, that violated every principle for which we contended in the Revolution'.[59] Although this peace leader was opposed to any kind of violent solution, he argued that, if defensive war was legal, Southern slaves had every right to fight for their freedom.[60] Commenting on a recent insurrection, Worcester deplored the loss of life on both sides, but added that 'him who is without fault cast the first stone at the poor slaves that on this occasion gained a victory'.[61] His successor, William Ladd, saw his cotton plantation fail because he had attempted to replace slave labour with the free labour of European immigrants.[62] Other peace friends, like Samuel J. May or Charles Sumner were more famous for their abolitionism.[63] William Lloyd Garrison, the radical non-resistant, also personified the radical branch of immediate abolitionism, castigating moderates for their timidity in the pages of one of the most influential anti-slavery papers, *The Liberator*.[64] Garrison was particularly opposed to the rivalling American Colonization Society, which judge Jay also denounced.[65] While the anti-slavery movement had split into a series of different organisations along the ideological spectrum, the far smaller peace movement possessed only one viable national society.

Beckwith was keen on keeping the delicate topic of slavery out of the scope of his society, although it always remained a somewhat schizophrenic position. On the one hand, most members could not fail to see the intricate connections between slavery and peace. Little had changed since Worcester's case that slavery entailed an eternal risk of slave uprisings, necessitated standing armies, promoted an overall mentality that desensitised citizens to human suffering and stimulated the so-called 'war-spirit' of society. Slavery also undermined constitutional liberties and it gave rise to 'new and bitter conflicts' between the North and South.[66] As the society's essays anxiously sought to prove, slavery had also been one of the root causes of the recent

59 FP (1827, n° VI), 177–9.

60 FP (1816, n° V), 28–9.

61 FP (1827, n° X), 317–8.

62 Ladd's biographer claimed that he regretted his use of slaves later in life. Hemmenway, *Memoir Ladd* 1872, 31–3.

63 Lawson, *Plowshares* 1975, 130.

64 Kraditor, *Abolitionism* 1967, 11–32.

65 Ibid.

66 E.g. FP (1827, n° V), 149–52; AP (March 1843), 27–8, AP (April 1844), 184–6; AP (December 1856), 189–92.

war with Mexico.[67] On the other hand, Beckwith himself, along with his supporters, believed that, in order to keep the peace movement a distinct movement, it should prioritize peace over abolitionism. In response to the increasing radicalisation of anti-slavery and the fierce conflict unfolding in Kansas, the leading man of the national society cautioned that 'the grand and only appropriate object of peace as a distinct department of reform' was the abolition of interstate war. As painful as it might sound, peace work was 'not to cure all evils; not to avert or settle all disputes; not to keep husbands and wives (…) or different sections of a country, at peace with each other'. To the extent the society should concern itself with domestic issues, it was to encourage the same principles it espoused in foreign relations: 'law, reason and moral influence'.[68]

The leadership's determination to focus exclusively on interstate war produced a more distinct shift in both the religious and the legal argument. On the religious level, the Sermon on the Mount was increasingly subordinated to the scriptural admonition in Romans that citizens ought to respect the legitimate authority of the state to enforce law and order.[69] The shift was likely caused by domestic concerns on 'Bleeding Kansas', although the American peace friends were also paying attention to foreign events, such as the 1857 Indian Rebellion. Even if some saw it as divine retribution for the immoral way in which the British had conquered India, the society equally condemned the Indians for turning to violence.[70] These deeply disturbing domestic and international events, coupled with the experience of two decades of political action and factional infighting, made the American Peace Society prioritise the rather more mundane objective of law and order over the Millennium.[71] Most conservatives, foremost Beckwith, could no longer support any pacifism that undermined the state. Governments had to prevent internal anarchy at all costs, through armed force if need be.

On the legal level, this translated itself into a number of relatively surprising positions. Rather than merely branding civil war as a subspecies of offensive war, which had been Worcester's tactic, the society effectively defined it out of existence.[72] The insistence that only official governments could wage 'war' properly speaking, was taken quite far. In the *Advocate,* the

67 E.g. AP (October & November 1848), 282–5. See chapter 1.

68 AP (October & November 1856), 147–50.

69 Ziegler, *Antebellum* 1992, 117–48.

70 Ibid., 127; AP (January & February 1858), 14–24; AP (March & April 1858), 37–8.

71 Ziegler, *Antebellum* 1992, 131.

72 As already noticed by Ziegler. Ibid., 132.

incident of 'Shays's Rebellion' was dusted off as an illustration. Suppose that it had been more than an unsuccessful local uprising, but the catalyst for a succession of bloody battles in which thousands of men were involved.[73] As the writer rhetorically asked: 'Would this have been war? Certainly not, as we understand it. It was, though on a more extended scale, what the sheriff does (…).'[74]

From the point of view of international legal doctrine, that standpoint was quaintly old-fashioned, and out of touch with nineteenth century innovations. To deny equal legal status to insurrectionists, if only within the scope of the hostilities, was to reason like medieval and early modern theologians and lawyers up to and including Grotius. Since subjects did not possess the required *auctoritas,* they could not be seen as lawful combatants according to the laws of war. Because they remained under the authority of their sovereign, they could be punished according to the laws of the land, and, for instance, be summarily tried and executed if caught. While that legal solution functioned with small-scale uprisings and banditry, scholars increasingly realised that this approach was inoperable in the context of larger revolts. Hobbes's social contract theory implied that the people could shed their loyalty when their sovereign turned from a protector into an oppressor. Mainstream literature built on Hobbes's innovations, with Vattel eventually introducing a three-fold distinction. Separate from both 'rebellion' and 'insurrection', a 'true' civil war was legitimate if the rebels claimed a just cause and sought to rid themselves of their government's authority altogether, and replace it with a new one. In that case, the war should be treated as the legal equivalent of an interstate war.[75] The 1863 Lieber Code largely agreed with Vattel.[76] If seen as participants in an interstate conflict, the older government had to turn to its belligerent powers under international law and should not criminally prosecute prisoners of war.[77]

To be sure, this view still left plenty of grey areas, so that whether or not a government decided to recognise an insurgency depended on a complex array of factors.[78] The most important factor was arguably pragmatism. To

73 Shays's Rebellion was a short-lived uprising in Massachusetts in the summer of 1786.

74 AP (May 1859), 263–4.

75 Neff, *War* 2005, 251–5; Vattel, *Droit Des Gens. Tome second* 1758, 238 (§ 287) – 248 (§ 296).

76 *Instructions for the Government of the Armies of the United States in the Field, Prepared by Francis Lieber, LL.D. and Revised by a Board of Officers,* arts. 149–51, (New York: Nostrand 1863).

77 Neff, *War* 2005, 255–7.

78 Ibid. 268–73.

treat any rebel government, and the thousands of more or less uniformed soldiers it might deploy, as ordinary criminals, was legally possible, but that decision would expose captured governmental soldiers to reprisals, if the actual power configuration on the field was equal enough.[79]

As in other instances, the American peace friends had the example of the American Revolutionary War to contend with. Following the internal logic of the society, the British government had every right to suppress the colonial rebellions of 1775.[80] Of course, to openly deny or even question the justice of the American Revolution was political suicide. The society was well-aware of the backlash it or its auxiliaries had endured whenever it had dared to engage with the 'moral evils' of the struggle that had gained the independence of their country.[81] Furthermore, besides being deeply venerated at home, the Revolutionary War was one of the first instances of state practice where a government had de facto recognised the belligerent legal status of its treasonous subjects, through parliamentary legislation that safeguarded captured rebels from criminal prosecution.[82] The society sidestepped the issue by declaring the Revolutionary War a 'perilous experiment (...) a solitary case amid almost numberless others of utter failure and ruin'.[83] Distancing himself from an inconvenient precedent, Beckwith and his supporters doubled down on their insistence that law and order reigned supreme.

Taking this line of thought to its other extreme, the American Peace Society at this point theorised that an invading army should be treated exactly like domestic criminals. Some members solved the decades-old debate on defensive war with the same fell stroke with which they tried to shut down the debate on civil war. Armed defence against a foreign invader, the *Advocate* asserted, was not war but merely 'upholding the supremacy of law'. Why should invading troops expect to be treated any differently than murderers and robbers? No government should tolerate the traditional exemptions to its laws. Rather than paroling captured officers on their word of honour, as was customary under the existing laws of war, the

79 Neff, *Blue and Gray* 2010, 21.

80 From the British perspective, the so-called 'Patriots' had of course been anything but patriotic.

81 Thomas Grimké, *Address on the Truth, Dignity, Power and Beauty of the Principles of Peace, and the on the Unchristian Character and Influence of War and the Warrior* (Hartford: Olmsted 1832), 41–8; Curti, *Crusade* 1929, 52–3.

82 Neff, *War* 2005, 255–6.

83 AP (October & November 1856), 149.

defenders should 'hang some dozen or twenty of the principal officers' in order to set an example to the lower ranks, who could be pardoned, 'unless known to have been wantonly guilty of murder'. As long as the government which resorted to these retributive measures was steadfast in its own refusal to engage in aggressive war, this course was but the normal exercise of sovereignty. That the invader might retaliate with its own executions, was no objection: 'so might a band of robbers'.[84]

As lightly as members of the society may have dismissed that severe objection, their suggestion was completely unviable either in politics or in law. Apart from the cultural norms associated with war, prosecuting invading troops as common criminals would effectively abolish the distinction between a state of war and a state of peace. As before, peace friends were again unwittingly following in the footsteps of medieval just war theory. The underlying thought did not substantially differ from the reasonings of theologians who approached every armed conflict as an unequal contest between right and wrong. If war did not suspend the laws of civil government, only 'acts of war' could exist, which might be lawful or unlawful.[85] To peace friends like Beckwith, a defensive action under this theory did not even qualify as an 'act of war', but as a 'deed of state sovereignty'.[86]

State practice and doctrine obviously did not share that analysis. Beckwith knew perfectly well that the law of nations had long recognised 'war in due form', which put each side on equal legal footing, citing from Vattel in illustration. However, if that doctrine did not comport with the law of nations, 'we claim that the law of nations should comport with this doctrine'.[87] All this appeared remarkably doctrinarian, especially coming from the leading conservative member of the society. However, it should not be forgotten that the conservatives also believed in natural justice and a monistic moral-juridical order. They supported government by calling it 'sanctioned by the God of Peace and Love for the benefit of mankind'.[88] Beckwith shocked no one by declaring that 'one law should be alike for all'.[89] This conviction also aligned well with the state-centricity supported in the peace society's political arbitration campaign. Even Ladd had emphasised the importance of state sovereignty.

84 AP (January 1854), 6; AP (May 1859), 264–6; AP (January & February 1861), 165–7.

85 Neff, *War* 2005, 57–8.

86 AP (January 1854), 6.

87 Ibid.

88 AP, March 1858, 36.

89 AP, January 1854, 6.

The American Peace Society's fundamental respect for state sovereignty was preserved throughout the antebellum era through its staunch support for non-interventionism. Peace friends in both the U.S. and Britain insisted that no state had a right to interfere in the internal affairs of another state, either through arms or by imposing certain policies and laws. Within the context of the congress of nations envisioned by Ladd and many reformists, non-intervention was promoted not only to obtain governmental approval, ever keen to avoid limitations on sovereignty, but also to allay fears that the 'free institutions' of the U.S. would be endangered by membership of an institution which would include the meddlesome European great powers.[90] Disapproval of the interventions of the Concert of Europe and the Holy Alliance – a distinction many did not make – was prevalent across the U.S. peace movement, and contributed also to the success of stipulated arbitration, because it entailed even less ties with such authoritarianism. The only time when the American Peace Society wavered in its commitment to the principle was in the wake of the revolutionary wave of 1848.[91]

The visit of the exiled Hungarian nationalist Kossuth to the United States in 1851–1852 occasioned the American Peace Society's most elaborate analysis of non-intervention. Kossuth was welcomed upon his arrival as a true revolutionary hero on par with the likes of the marquis de Lafayette. Feted in the press and hosted by both the president and Congress, Kossuth attempted to garner support for the Hungarian cause, like he had earlier done in Britain.[92] Warned by the London Peace Society of the 'seductive influence' of the celebrity, judge Jay issued a lengthy public letter on the so-called 'Kossuth excitement'.[93] Elsewhere, the *Advocate* had already described non-intervention as a law of nature, if not yet a positive international law. The peace society imagined that all states had a vested interest in non-intervention. In the long run, emperors would themselves insist upon it 'as a barrier against the whirlwind of democratic revolutions sweeping with resistless force over all Europe'.[94]

Jay agreed that Kossuth was deeply mistaken in pretending that a natural 'law of humanity' existed by which a third power ought to intervene against

---

90 AP (January 1839), 186.

91 AP (May & June 1848), 193–200; AP (October & November 1848), 265–8.

92 Ronald Michael Zarychta, *Louis Kossuth and the United States, 1848–1852* (Carnegie Mellon University: unpublished doctoral thesis 1976), 42–113.

93 AP (February 1852), 17–22; William Jay, *The Kossuth Excitement: a Letter* (Boston: American Peace Society 1852).

94 AP (March 1852), 36–7.

another intervening third power. The president of the society found no such principle in the divine laws of scripture, nor any of its corollaries. It was absurd to combat Russia for its assistance to Austria, but not Austria itself. The United States would also be hypocritical if it fought for the right of 'a distant nation' to establish shaky political institutions, when it did not care at all about the three million slaves at home.[95] The *Advocate* in the same issue added that the 1851 London Peace Congress had written non-intervention into 'one of its strongest resolutions'.[96] Doubling down on that rebuttal, the peace society wondered why their state should ever intervene to enforce international law: 'Why? What is this code but a selection of precedents from the combined action of civil and ecclesiastical despotism handed down to us from dark and barbarous ages?'. The law of nations was 'beautiful without', but 'within full of rottenness'. To forcibly punish an illegal intervention was but to give further credence to a 'law of *corrupt* nature in its most malignant form'. A 'radical change of the international law' was needed, but this could only be achieved through 'moral power'.[97]

By their wholesale condemnation of any form of armed intervention, the U.S. peace movement set itself at odds withs part of contemporary state practice and doctrine. Along with most of the British, the American pacifists rejected political intervention for its close ties with authoritarian great power politics in Europe. They also rejected most forms of humanitarian intervention, at least those with an armed component to them. Although the members of the peace societies were deeply concerned with human suffering, they could only allow 'moral' interventions, such as diplomatic pressure and material relief, for instance food shipments to areas afflicted by famine.[98] This would have angered a number of nineteenth century lawyers, who argued in the later nineteenth century that the refusal to assist peoples fighting for liberty was 'an egoistic policy'. Jurists like Pasquale Mancini, Pasquale Fiore, Augusto Pierantoni, Henry Wheaton, or James Lorimer held that a positive duty to intervene existed under natural law.[99] Although peace friends were likewise deeply influenced by natural law reasonings, their priorities laid far more with 'peace' than they laid with

95 AP (February 1852), 17–20.

96 Ibid., 23

97 AP (May 1852), 66–7.

98 As suggested, for instance, in Upham, *Manual* 1836, 359.

99 Wheaton simply wrote that the positive law of nations made no distinction between a just and an unjust war. Fiore cited by Neff, *War* 2005, 224; Wheaton, *Elements* 1836, 71 (§ 16); Mura, 'Construction' 2020, 109–225.

'justice', because the means suggested by many to acquire the latter were ideologically unacceptable for most pacifists.

Unlike most adherents of the peace movement in Europe, virtually all Anglo-American pacifists – moderates and radicals – did not allow international law to be enforced through arms.[100] This partly stemmed from their religious axioms, which were never taken that far by European sympathisers. Continental adherents occasionally espoused similar views to those of Mancini and others.[101] Anglo-American religious peculiarities were undoubtedly also reinforced by these countries' advantageous geographical and political situation. The United States was securely removed from the turmoil of the European continent, which few of America's pacifist moralists were keen to embroil themselves in.[102] Basically, American pacifists had never had much skin in the game. For most New Englanders, war remained an abstract and distant phenomenon.

2 The Crisis of the American Civil War

As the 1850s came to an end, however, the American peace friends approached their own hour of trial. Having defined revolution and defensive war out of existence, and having discredited the right of intervention, the American Peace Society under Beckwith's leadership seemed to have resolved the dilemma of 'peace' and 'justice' firmly in favour of the former. However, as much as its leaders wished to avoid topics unrelated to the abolition of interstate war, these kept coming up in domestic events most members could not ignore. In October 1859, an abolitionist named John Brown led an attack upon a weapons arsenal at Harpers Ferry in Virginia. Brown's failed attempt to instigate a general slave revolt caused a sensation in the press. First branded as a fanatic, he was soon turned into an abolitionist martyr. Beckwith stressed that the laws of civil government, however unjust, had to be obeyed. However, in the society's 1860 annual address, the reformist May praised Brown as 'the hero of Harpers Ferry'.[103] While the domestic crisis escalated, the society became increasingly despondent. The *Advocate* despaired that, apart from the peace societies and the Quakers, very

100 E.g. AP (April 1854), 60–2.

101 See for instance Louis Bara or Francisque Bouvet in chapter 5.

102 See also Ceadel, *War and Peace* 1987, 188.

103 AP (April 1860, 64); AP (August 1860), 85.

few people still believed in peace principles.[104] The following year, they were horrified to learn that state after state in the South was seceding from the Union, giving rise to a 'republic of slaveholders'.[105]

Any hope the society initially still fostered for a peaceful solution was shattered when news reached the North that the secessionists had attacked the federal troops garrisoned at Fort Sumter, in South Carolina. President Lincoln officially called the crisis a rebellion, convened Congress together in an emergency session and ordered an initial mobilisation of 75,000 troops. The Civil War had begun.

2.1 *Civil War as a Police Action*

The American Peace Society led by Beckwith stuck to its guns. In the *Advocate's* first wartime issue, the society proclaimed that they fully supported, 'as loyal citizens', the president's 'legitimate effort' to enforce the nation's laws.[106] The annual report of that year stressed that the conflict at hand did not fall under the strict purview of the peace societies: 'Ours is a work of prevention'. Peace friends only tried to inculcate a general pacific mindset in society, it was said. However, if their good advice was to be so utterly disregarded by the South, 'the result is perfectly legitimate'. The official position of the American Peace Society was therefore that it 'has had no voice or agency in the case, and of course cannot be held to any responsibility in saying what shall be done'. To decide on a course of action was the government's responsibility. The peace society was not coy about what that implied: 'they must be expected to do so in the usual way of violence and blood'. Going further still, friends of peace were not only expected to 'acquiesce in the result', but even to lend their moral and active support 'to the government over them'.[107]

At no point in the course of the war did the American Peace Society and its auxiliaries budge from this hard-headed view on the armed conflict in their country. Even as the battles added up and the number of fatalities increased into the hundreds of thousands, the American peace movement kept maintaining that the entire war was just a succession of acts of domestic law enforcement. In 1861, the society had taken care to emphasise that this was not 'a new position' of the peace society. They claimed that they

---

104 AP (February 1860), 194.
105 AP (March 1861), 197–9.
106 AP (June 1861), 258–9
107 AP (July 1861), 268–9.

had only ever opposed interstate war.[108] That was very much debateable. If viewed from the perspective of Beckwith and the policy he had managed to push through during the 1850s, this argument had some validity. From his perspective, the American Peace Society had indeed not substantially changed its views.

Considered from the more long-term perspective, on the other hand, it did not at all represent the original position of the American Peace Society. To say that the peace movement had not changed its politics since its origins in 1828 was stretching it very far. Back in the early 1830s, members like Thomas Grimké – a Southerner, no less – still commanded much influence in the society. Grimké had infamously claimed that in the event of a piratical attack on Charleston, he would simply meet the invaders unarmed with Sunday-school children.[109] Things had evidently changed. In 1863, the *Advocate* rhetorically asked whether the people of Philadelphia had a moral or legal right to resist a 'gang of desperadoes' bent on plundering and burning their city. That was self-evident. Just so, the U.S. federal government possessed a sovereign right to quash rebellions. The means deemed fit to do so were strictly speaking irrelevant. The use of 'all the usual enginery of war' did nothing to alter this legal fact.[110] While the peace friends admitted that they themselves also tended to describe the ongoing conflict as 'war', they hastened to add that they never did so in the 'ordinary' sense of 'an *international* war'. The 'war' could only be called as such 'in loose parlance', but definitely not in any legal sense. This distinction, obtuse for many, mattered a great deal to people wanting to 'stand on the side of law and order'.[111]

In characterising the Civil War this way, the American Peace Society was more adamant than even the federal government itself. Like most citizens in the North, Lincoln's administration consistently refused to recognise the Confederacy as a legitimate sovereign state. From 1861 to 1865, the Union insisted that it was only engaging in law enforcement, albeit on a massive scale. The U.S. Congress never issued a formal declaration of war, instead enacting in 1861 several pieces of legislation which made it criminal to engage in various acts of rebellion. On the other hand, the Northern leadership simultaneously conducted the war according to the international laws of war. Confederate prisoners of war were not tried for treason, but instead temporarily locked up in special prison camps, as one would do with

108 Ibid., 269.

109 See chapter 1 for the first mention of Grimké.

110 AP (March 1863), 237–46.

111 AP (September & October 1861), 295–6

captured men in a conventional interstate war. The reasons were obvious. As noted earlier, it was simply impossible to hold individual trials on such an enormous scale in this situation. Furthermore, the Confederacy would be sure to retaliate in kind. In spite of all theoretical debates, the Civil War could therefore reasonably be described as a de facto, if not a de jure, interstate war.[112]

The peace friends led by Beckwith could not accept any concessions whatsoever. At the beginning of the war, the *Advocate* launched into another series of attacks on 'war in due form' doctrine. Vattel, one article complained, held that 'war in form, as to its effects, is to be accounted just on *both sides*'. Prisoners of war could not be punished, because soldiers only executed the will of their sovereign. However, as the peace society had already asserted before the Civil War, interstate war was not an exercise of state sovereignty 'in its legitimate sphere'. To the extent international law still endorsed it, the law would have to change.[113] A fortiori, the society bitterly regretted that the 'the rebel party are using every exertion to dignify the present strife with the character of international war, in order to secure for it the sanction of international law, with rights equal on both sides (...). If the federal government were to treat the rebellion as the illegal act that it was, the *Advocate* had 'no doubt' that the conflict would have 'long ere this been brought to an end'.[114] After four years of war, the peace society became, if anything, only more hardened in its resolve. If a war was to be fought, one article fumed in 1865, then let it be a real one. If the rebels mistreated U.S. soldiers, then the Union should pay the insurgents back in kind, through strict retaliation. As one peace friend wrote it: 'A mongrel, fitful policy, half-peace and half-war, we can regard with little respect'.[115]

Articles such as this were not one-off misses by disgruntled, but otherwise isolated members. They represented mainstream opinion within the American peace movement. Less vindictive approaches to the conflict were few and far between. At the beginning, a few voices suggested peaceful means to end the conflict. Some suggested to revise the old status quo antebellum, by turning slavery into a purely state competence. Others said to simply let the Southern states go their own way, believing that their Confederacy would eventually collapse by itself, or that a long war was simply not worth the effort. However, they were a clear minority. By far most members

112 Neff, *Blue and Gray* 2010, 6–21.

113 AP (March 1861), 204–5.

114 AP (December 1861), 344.

115 AP (March 1865), 241.

agreed with Beckwith that the North was fighting for a just cause: the preservation of the Union and the abolition of slavery. The Southerners had pushed the North around for too long and needed to be taught a lesson they would never forget, through fire and blood. God and the Millennium stood on the side of justice.[116]

The American Peace Society became consumed with the passions that engulf a nation at war. Every suspicion that New Englanders had long harboured towards the South quickly turned into outright demonising. The *Advocate* began to portray Southerners as merciless criminals, whose slave-holding culture had robbed them of their humanity. The peace society's propaganda focussed especially on instances, real or imagined, of rebel maltreatment of prisoners of war. Northern peace friends were appalled by the atrocities committed by Confederate guerrilla's, like the infamous sack of a Kansas town by Quantrill's raiders.[117] By comparison, they gave considerably less thought to how their side conducted the war. If the *Advocate* was to be believed, Northern soldiers behaved themselves overall relatively well. The pacifist journal barely reported on the deplorable conditions in Union prisoner of war camps, or on how general Sherman marched to the sea in Georgia in 1864. The general had resorted to scorched earth tactics which had ensured that his name would be reviled for generations to come in the South.[118]

The *Advocate* did at times express conflicted feelings about the war. It featured the occasional report on Union misdeeds, like the looting of captured plantations. The peace society could likewise not bring itself to joining in the praise of Sherman's successful campaign in Mississippi, that had caused so much civilian destruction: 'Such is war, and such is its *commendable* deeds!'[119] Generally, however, the society's coverage was grossly skewed in favour of the Northern cause. The miseries caused by their side's bluecoats were the unfortunate, but inevitable side-effects of a legitimate 'police action'.

Its devotion to the Union war effort did not spare the American Peace Society from the same sort of abuse that the London Peace Society already had to go through during the Crimean War. In July 1861, just a few months into the conflict, Beckwith lamented in the *Advocate* that 'our patience has of late been tried in this respect beyond measure by the misstatements

116 Ziegler, *Antebellum* 1992, 157–9, 161; AP (July 1864), 104–5; AP (December 1868), 174.
117 AP (October 1864), 152–6.
118 Ziegler, *Antebellum* 1992, 159.
119 AP (April 1864), 64; AP (June 1864), 74.

respecting us, set afloat alike from the press and the platform'. It was complained that if peace friends were to formally disclaim every 'libel' or 'caricature' about their society, 'we shall have little time left for anything else'.[120] The likes of Beckwith were especially upset about the fact that so many were confusing the 'peace party', which wanted to end the war through concessions to the South, with the 'peace society', which was resolutely in favour of the fight.[121] Such misunderstandings brought with them other repercussions. By the middle of the war, the society felt forced to confess that 'in this darkest hour', their funding was beginning to dry up. They could only count on the financial support of 'a small circle' of their most devoted backers. The next year, the society's books actually went in the red, for the first time in seventeen years. In December of that year, the month when charitable societies usually received most of their donations, the Americans had to humiliatingly ask British sympathisers for additional financial relief.[122]

Most Americans never could or wanted to grasp the fine-grained distinction in the American Peace Society's policy between interstate war and a domestic police action. All the casual observer noticed was a 'peace society' supporting a conflict that had every external characteristic of a traditional war. Beckwith never managed to successfully convey his seemingly self-contradictory views to the larger public. This was painfully evident from the number of articles in the *Advocate* that basically repeated the same thing, namely that the conflict was not a war in the legal sense, but only a case of domestic law enforcement. Almost every other issue during the entire Civil War defended this view, meaning that the message obviously did not sink in.[123]

2.2 *British Appeals for Intervention*

Perhaps more painful still was the reaction of the London Peace Society. The oldest and staunchest allies of the American Peace Society could hardly believe what they were reading in the journal of their sister society. From the beginning, the British interpretation of the conflict could not be more different. The Americans unsuccessfully tried to convince their colleagues across the pond to their point of view. Amasa Walker, who had met most of

---

120 AP (August 1861), 290–1.

121 AP (November 1861), 327–8.

122 AP (October 1863), 356; AP (May 1864), 56; AP (December 1864), 196.

123 E.g. in AP (March 1863), 237–46; AP (September 1864), 133–5; AP (January 1865), 202–3; AP (July 1866), 293–6; AP (August 1866), 316.

the British leadership in person at the congress in Paris in 1849, sent a letter to Henry Richard asking how he would feel if rebels should rise up in England and threaten London itself. Did this not justify a legitimate police action? Had the British themselves not already done the same during the Indian Rebellion? Unfortunately, the secretary of the London Peace Society was not convinced. In a long letter of reply, he did not pretend to imagine what he would do under similar circumstances. He only attempted to advise what he believed peace friends '*ought* to do'. The British pacifist felt that the American peace friends had 'invented a theory', which they had 'persuaded themselves' would be able to reconcile pacific principles with patriotism. While this theory might satisfy the conscience of many in the United States, Richard sharply noted, it 'would not satisfy *my* conscience'. It was full of 'inconsistencies' and 'self-contradictions'. At best, Romans 13 allowed for just punishment following due process of law. Richard conceded that there indeed existed a grey area between police action and civil war. However, surely the Americans could understand that when over a million armed men were confronting each other in gargantuan battles, 'the line has been a long way passed'.[124]

Both American and British peace friends felt like they were talking past each other. In a sense, the Civil War also became somewhat of an internecine fight for the Anglo-American peace movement. At no other point in their long mutual history was the relationship between their peace societies so fraught with tension. The British refused to accept the American legal conceptualisation of the war, which deeply hurt the Americans. Like many other contemporary Britons, British peace friends did not necessarily support the Union. Not everyone believed that the North was fighting to eradicate slavery. Rather, it was merely to force the secessionists back into the Union. Although the abolition of slavery was indeed not an explicit war goal at the very beginning, most modern historians concur that the Civil War was caused by slavery. Especially after the Emancipation Proclamation, it became identified with abolition.[125] Henry Richard, writing a few months before the Proclamation, thought that the gospel trumped even the British and American constitutions. He believed that up until the shelling of Fort Sumter, the Confederacy had intended to secede peacefully. Perhaps the

124 HP (May 1862), 57–60.

125 Michael Vorenberg, *Final Freedom. The Civil War, the Abolition of Slavery, and the Thirteenth Amendment* (Cambridge: CUP 2001), 8–22, 36–53.

Northern states should have let them.[126] Needless to say, such remarks were like a red rag to a bull in America.

For a long time, neither the British cabinet nor the British peace friends thought that the war would end in a complete Northern military victory. In 1864, the *Advocate* quoted one of the many articles in the *Herald* that condemned the conflict, along with all Americans who believed that 'out of the evil good may come'. The American pacifist journal disapproved that the British still refused to call the conflict 'a *rebellion*', or that the London Peace Society condemned the U.S. government as much as the rebels, while only the latter were breaking the law 'wholesale'.[127] The American pacifists were especially furious that the London Peace Society around the beginning of the conflict had suggested that Britain should diplomatically intervene through some kind of mediation or arbitration. Richard had done as much in his controversial public letter to Walker.[128] Although the British peace friends only ever suggested that 'a friendly power' should offer its good offices at the invitation of the U.S. government, the British cabinet was actually considering at the time to impose European mediation on the warring parties. Palmerston only gave up this plan when it became clear that Northern public opinion stayed firmly in favour of continuing the fight, despite the toll of battles like Antietam.[129]

Their vastly different understandings of the conflict made the American and British peace societies exchange the kind of passive-aggressive innuendo's that were not conducive to a good relationship. Believing that battles were only delaying the inevitable, the *Herald* was dismayed that their American sister society should frame a European diplomatic intervention as 'on behalf of the South'.[130] Even worse, some Americans had outright implied that they sided 'with rebellion and slavery'. The British felt that they were trying their utmost to resist 'all provocations' launched against them by American peace friends. In turn, the Americans tried to make it clear that the British barely realised just 'how disrespectfully they treat us'.[131] When the Irish again plotted to revolt in the United Kingdom right after the end of the war, the American Peace Society was vindictive enough to rub it in.

126 HP (May 1862), 59–60.

127 AP (July 1864), 112–3.

128 HP (May 1862), 60.

129 Kinley J. Brauer, 'British Mediation and the American Civil War: a Reconsideration'. *The Journal of Southern History* 38(1) (1972), 49–64.

130 HP (September 1863), 242–3.

131 Ibid.; see also AP (April 1866), 54–7; AP (May 1866), 77–80.

They noted 'with satisfaction' the course of the London Peace Society towards the threatened Fenian Rising in a resolution at the annual meeting of 1866. The British had not condemned their government's use of force to combat the separatists.[132] Evidently, the Americans had enough of the holier-than-thou attitude of people both geographically and emotionally far removed from the scene of the conflict. One can only wonder if the Americans realised just how similar their hostile reaction to the British sounded to how the average European must have felt when lectured on the sins of just war by the peace societies around 1848.

2.3 *Defects of Neutrality Law Exposed*

As acrimonious as the relationship may have been because of their disagreement on the legal nature of the conflict, the Anglo-American peace societies did find more common ground with respect to the questions that it raised about maritime neutrality law. To an extent, this might seem paradoxical, considering the hugely different legal consequences that followed from whether or not the conflict was branded a civil war or an interstate war. Especially the American societies were hypersensitive about this. They were severely frustrated that in 1861 both Britain and France had decided to grant rights of belligerency to the Confederacy. Their example was followed by a handful of other states. Although this did not equate to a recognition of the South as an independent sovereign state, it did have important implications on how the war was to be fought at sea. While the federal government may have treated the rebels according to the laws of war *on land,* they were reluctant to do the same *at sea,* where the Union navy was indisputably stronger. If vessels sailing under the Confederate flag were branded as mere pirates, their navy would be subject to far fewer restrictions than if the same ships were part of the fleet of a legitimate belligerent.[133] The *Advocate* extensively complained about the British and French proclamations of neutrality that had granted belligerent right to the rebels.[134]

It again provoked a series of American attacks on the current state of international law. In a lengthy article from 1863, the peace friends vented their old critique that it was 'not a real code, but simply a treatise'. However, this time they explicitly complained that 'either Mr. Bull or Mr. Bonaparte' set the rules – 'the public law of Europe is whatever France and England

---

132 AP (June 1866), 92. Repeated in AP (May 1866), 77.

133 Neff, *Blue and Gray* 2010, 167–9.

134 AP (November 1863), 363–4; AP (April 1863), 252–3; AP (January 1865), 203–6; AP (February 1865), 228.

may agree to consider it (...), and the law of nations will be enforced upon all who have not the courage and strength to resist'.[135] Although the London Peace Society understandably did not join into the attack on the dominance of their country in international law-making, they could agree with the American Peace Society that the many contemporary unclarities in international maritime law needed to be addressed.

The recognition of belligerency of the Confederacy raised a host of hitherto unanswered legal issues on the rights of neutrals. Several incidents increased Anglo-American tensions during the war. One of the most festering issues was the Union blockade on Confederate ports. Over the course of the war, the effectiveness of this blockade was consistently tested by smugglers. Although blockade-runners often sold British goods, legal fights about the right of blockade mostly annoyed the South. The Confederacy hated that Britain took an 'effective blockade' to mean any naval investment that significantly increased the risk of capture. The besieged Southerners, meanwhile, of course wanted it to mean *total* prevention of ingress and egress. On the Union side, the American Peace Society was relatively satisfied with the British interpretation of this right, which aligned with the Union's interests.[136] The *Advocate* thus observed: 'the blockade-running business, we see not how she could restrain'.[137]

The British peace movement was more outspoken. The Northern blockade and the *Trent* affair had caused insurance premiums of British-flagged ships to spike, leading to a competitive disadvantage. In March 1862, Liberal politicians saw their chance and introduced a motion, seconded by Bright, to reopen the debate on the Marcy amendment. Back in 1856, this had been the American proposal to get Britain to accept the protection of *all* private property at sea, regardless of flag. Perhaps unsurprisingly, Cobden became involved as well. The free trader went even further, by demanding that the right of blockade should also entail a simultaneous land investment. He also wanted neutral ships to be immune to searches.[138] The London Peace Society fully agreed with this more extensive view. The *Herald* reported extensively on the Parliamentary debate and related efforts. The journal heavily protested the suggestion of Conservatives to disregard the Declaration of Paris in case of a naval war with the United States or France. The British

135 AP (November 1863), 357–60.

136 Neff, *Blue and Gray* 2010, 175; Lemnitzer, *Privateering* 2014, 139–43.

137 AP (April 1865), 257.

138 Richard Cobden (ed. Anthony Howe), *The Letters of Richard Cobden. Volume 4. 1860–1865* (Oxford: OUP, 2015), xxxix-liv; Lemnitzer, *Privateering* 2014, 150–3.

peace friends invoked passages from Kent, Wheaton and Phillimore on the sanctity of treaties.[139] Palmerston's chief case against adopting the Marcy Amendment – and a fortiori Cobden's additions – held that this would undermine Britain's naval supremacy. Blockades would have little impact this way, depriving Britain of its most effective weapon. While this argument was powerful enough to leave British policy ultimately unchanged, it was unacceptable for the domestic peace movement. They hoped that a British politician would be able to transcend narrow national self-interest and act on broader Christian grounds.[140]

The second issue of maritime law resonated strongly across both sides of the Atlantic and beyond. A few months after the Commons debate on maritime neutrality law, in July 1862, the Birkenhead shipyard launched a new steamer. Simply called 'No. 290', it was manned by a fully British crew as it navigated its way out of British waters. Elsewhere, two others similarly departed with armaments. Near the Azores, in international waters, the three ships met. As the steamer was outfitted with an array of British-made armaments, its captain mounted a gun-carriage to read his commission from Jefferson Davis, the president of the Confederacy. Steamer No. 209 was to be baptised the *C.S.S. Alabama*, meant to support the fight for Southern independence. Most of the sailors present agreed to join its crew, despite having the British nationality. Thus equipped, the new warship hoisted the battle ensigns of the Confederacy and sailed off into the horizon.[141]

Over the next two years, the *Alabama* proved itself exceptionally successful in preying on Northern merchant shipping. No other Confederate warship managed to capture as many ships as this vessel. Over the course of her career, she burned more than sixty Union merchantmen. While impressive, those losses barely dented the flow of Northern trade, let alone the greater war effort. Nonetheless, commerce raiders like the *Alabama* provoked panic and outrage. More significantly still, they caused an enormous transfer of Union cargo shipping to foreign companies. Since the Paris Declaration, neutral flags protected private property. It would take the U.S. merchant marine decades to recover from this effect.[142] In the political realm too, there was clamour in the Union to authorise letters of marque to help hunt the *Alabama* and other such raiders. The House even passed a bill

139 HP (April 1862), 38–9.

140 Lemnitzer, *Privateering* 2014, 151–2; HP (April 1862), 38–40.

141 Arthur Sinclair, *Two Years on the Alabama* (Boston: Lee and Shepard 1896), 10–8; Neff, *Blue and Gray* 2010, 177–8.

142 Neff, *Blue and Gray* 2010, 178–9.

authorising the president to do so. However, the cabinet ultimately decided against it. Among those who helped dissuade Lincoln sat Charles Sumner, a close advisor of the president during the war. Conformable to the long-held positions of the American Peace Society, he advised against it because privateering was immoral. More pragmatically, he added that this violation of the Declaration, even if the United States was not a party to it, would cause needless tensions with those European powers that had.[143] Unbeknownst to the crew of the *Alabama,* their ship was to play a large part in the development of both international law and the international peace movement in the years to come.

3 The *Alabama Claims* Era

In the early summer of 1864, less than a year before the end of the Civil War, the *Alabama* left port for the last time. The raider had been finally tracked down by a Union warship, the *U.S.S. Kearsarge.* Rather than staying cooped up in France for the rest of the war, its captain decided to try and fight his way out. Hundreds of onlookers began lining the shore, very excited by the prospect of a daring battle on Sunday morning. An English gentleman on holiday in France even shadowed the *Alabama* in his yacht. He had reportedly given his children a choice between attending church and witnessing a naval battle. His boat was joined by a French frigate, ready to lay it into whichever warship dared to carry their war into French territorial waters. Soon enough, the crowd gathered on the coastline could hear the distant booms of cannon fire. This continued for an hour. The *Alabama* was able to get two shots into the hull of the *Kearsarge,* but they had glanced off the latter's improvised armour. The *Kearsarge's* gunnery proved more accurate, so that the rebel began to make water. Realising that all hope was lost, the rebel captain struck his colours. Rather than offering his sword to the enemy captain – considered the honourable course of action at the time – he threw his sword into the sea and got picked up by the English vacationer, who whisked the fallen officer away to England. The *Alabama's* captain eventually made it back home, mere weeks before the Confederacy capitulated.[144]

143 Lemnitzer, *Privateering* 2014, 135–8.

144 Tom Bingham, 'The Alabama Claims Arbitration'. *International Law and Comparative Law Quarterly* 54(1) (2005), 6–7; Adrian Cook, *The Alabama Claims. American Politics and Anglo-American Relations, 1865–1872* (Ithaca: Cornell University Press 1975), 15–6.

The *Advocate* at the time reported, with some satisfaction, that 'the pirate Alabama' had at long last been sunk. However, they were disconcerted by the different reactions it caused in Britain and their own country. The American pacifists copied a number of passages in American newspapers which stressed that 'England is in truth at the bottom of all these outrages upon our commerce'.[145] Indeed, already before the *Alabama* first left its British drydock had the U.S. government been aware of the fact that an ostensibly neutral state had been used as a launching platform for attacks on the Union. Back in 1862, Northern spies had unsuccessfully attempted to gather the evidence needed to allow the authorities to prevent the new steamer from leaving. Although the British government actually cooperated, it was hindered by the British courts. As such, a number of Southern raiders managed to slip through the nets, among them the *Alabama*. After the war, neither the American public nor its government had forgotten the damage caused by what they perceived to have been a violation of the duties of neutrals and of international law.[146]

The Civil War had made longstanding antipathies between Americans and Britons flare up to levels unseen since the boundary crises and the Revolutionary War. Hotheads on both sides openly spoke of a possible war. Fortunately, their respective governments were keen on a diplomatic settlement. The arbitration of the *Alabama claims* in 1872 concluded a long era of popular mistrust between the two powers, and in the long run heralded the beginning of their relative rapprochement in the final years of the century.[147] In the legal realm, its relevance to international law was not lost to historians, and neither was it to contemporaries. Disillusioned by war, but inspired by its aftermath, the Anglo-American peace societies renewed their efforts for an improved international code and a permanent institution of adjudication. Increasingly aided and joined by sympathetic professional international lawyers, the peace societies shed their exclusively moralist skin of yore. Henceforth, juridical reform would be carried into their platform to hitherto unseen levels. The American Peace Society founded an unofficial international law society in 1873, with the help of many of the most important lawyers of the time. The London Peace Society decided to renew their parliamentary campaign. Succeeding where they had failed in 1849, their arbitration motion of 1873 inspired similar initiatives elsewhere. From 1873

145 AP (August 1864), 127–8.

146 Neff, *Blue and Gray* 2010, 177–9.

147 Cook, *Alabama Claims* 1975, 243–6.

onwards, their movement definitively oriented itself to the path of 'peace through law'.

3.1 *Geneva as 'Pacifist' State Practice*

Any arbitration plan produced after the Civil War was unescapably influenced by the *Alabama claims* tribunal. After the war, the United States was determined to make Britain pay for the damage caused by British-built Confederate raiders. The *Alabama Claims* quickly became the centre of a prolonged and heated debate in the two countries. This should not surprise, given that the U.S. was demanding a truly exorbitant sum – multiple times the annual British budget.[148] However, the administrations of Andrew Johnson and Ulysses S. Grant were adamant. Despite the ridiculous size of American demands, the British cabinet eventually agreed to settle via arbitration. The Treaty of Washington, signed in May 1871, was the result of years of negotiations, involving also other bilateral disputes.[149] The peace societies on both sides of the Atlantic kept a close eye on every development, and made much of the eventual success of the arbitral tribunal convened in Geneva in 1872. Before entering into pacifist interpretations, the legal history of the case itself warrants some attention.

Its first article singled out the claims caused by Southern warships, named after the most notorious of them, and stipulated that they be referred to a tribunal of five arbitrators. The tribunal consisted of one arbiter appointed by Britain and the U.S. respectively, the three others to be selected by the king of Italy, the emperor of Brazil, and the president of the Swiss Confederation. This was novel. An earlier convention, agreed upon in 1869, had not been ratified by the U.S. Senate. Its arbitration clause had still been more in the vein of earlier Anglo-American agreements, such as Jay or Ghent. The document of 1869 had provided for a binational commission, only resorting to a third umpire in case of disagreement within the former body. It had been heavily denunciated by Sumner in one of his customary invective speeches. Other articles in the Washington Treaty arranged procedural questions, like the exchange of cases and counter-cases.[150] The most substantially important article was unquestionably article VI. This one set

148 Roy Jenkins, *Gladstone* (London: MacMillan 1995), 259; cited by Bingham 'Alabama Claims' 2005, 1.

149 John Bassett Moore, *History and Digest of the International Arbitrations to which the United States has been a Party. Volume 1* (Washington: Government Printing Office 1898), 391–682; Bingham 'Alabama Claims' 2005, 12.

150 Bingham 'Alabama Claims' 2005, 12–5.

out the rules of international law that the arbiters were to apply. The first rule held that a neutral state had to use 'due diligence' to prevent either the fitting out or leaving of any ship expected to carry on war against a third state with which the neutral state was at peace. The second rule prohibited a neutral state from allowing its ports to be used as a base of operation against third states. The last one again emphasised due diligence to prevent violations of these duties by any person within its jurisdiction. These three rules were subsequently known as the 'Washington rules'. The U.S. and Britain not only agreed to obey these norms in the future, but also to invite other states to accede to them.[151]

Once the British and Americans had been able to exchange their respective arguments, the tribunal formally convened in June 1872. The award formally proclaimed at the Genevan town hall by the end of summer was not in Britain's favour. The British state was held liable for the damage caused by three warships, including the eponymous *Alabama.* As compensation, the tribunal agreed on the sum of fifteen and a half million dollars, including interest. That was a staggering amount of money. To put it into perspective: in relation to the British budget, it was equivalent to 150 billion pounds today.[152] The British arbiter, who had consistently dissented, was unable to hide his disappointment. He reportedly arrived an hour late, refused to sign the official document and – amid the raising of the flags and the bangs of an artillery salute– unceremoniously left early.[153]

The *Alabama claims* arbitration eventually achieved a canonical status in international law. The case remains a fixture in obligatory historical introduction chapters in handbooks on public international law today, where it is often characterised as heralding the beginning of international adjudication.[154] Part of what made the *Alabama* arbitration so celebrated was that Britain actually paid the damages it was ordered to. At first, however, the precedent did not appear as such to most contemporaries.

Indeed, it was remarkable that Britain had consented to it in the first place. Even without knowing the merits of the case, the Washington rules

151 Ibid., 16; Treaty between the United States and Great Britain, 8 May 1871, 143 CTS 145, art. VI.

152 Jenkins, *Gladstone* 1995, 359; Bingham 'Alabama Claims' 2005, 1.

153 Bingham 'Alabama Claims' 2005, 23–24.

154 Janis offers a too optimistic reading, ignoring much of the larger legal and political context. Janis, *American Tradition* 2004, 134–7; Martti Koskenniemi, 'The Legacy of the Nineteenth Century', in David Armstrong (ed.), *Routledge Handbook of International Law* (Oxon: Routledge 2009), 141, 149; Malcolm Shaw, *International Law* (Cambridge: CUP 2003), 104–5.

appeared tailored for the United States. Why did British diplomacy abandon the domestic legal argument so quickly? Their own courts had blocked several attempts to seize vessels. Even if this argument was not a very strong one – Parliament could have simply changed the law – Gladstone's decision to accept the award had a tinge of idealism to it. He was after all known for being a devout Christian. Nonetheless, the case should not be exaggerated into something it was almost certainly not. The most plausible explanation offered as to why Britain acquiesced was rooted – as usual – in power politics. In the long-run, the precedent of the *Alabama claims* imposed a heavier burden on neutrals than it did on belligerents. The British empire was the only state in the world that possessed a global network of refuelling stations as well as a shipbuilding industry. The award was the price to pay for shoring up its naval might. Perceptive American jurists noted this as well.[155] It went not unchallenged in British politics either. Gladstone was punished for it at the next general election, which he lost.[156] The negative decision, combined with the domestic backlash, ensured that the Washington rules never transformed into general norms of international law. Britain felt, like many international lawyers, that the tribunal had interpreted due diligence too strictly. The Second Hague Peace Conference of 1907 confirmed that neutrals only had to enforce their existing national laws.[157]

In the seven years that the *Alabama claims* was arousing public interest, the American Peace Society kept up support for a peaceful solution through arbitration. The pages of the *Advocate* printed every bit of news the society could find. Their understanding of the concept of arbitration was becoming more sophisticated too. In 1868, the *Advocate* published a detailed account of the Anglo-American mixed claims commissions of the early nineteenth century. The society had commissioned it from a lawyer, another indication that peace through law was on the rise in the U.S. peace movement.[158] At the annual meeting of 1869, the society adopted a resolution supporting arbitration through 'an authorized body of commissioners'. This solution should be provided for by treaty beforehand, in order to eliminate preliminary negotiations 'in times of passion'.[159] This alluded without question to

155 Neff, *Blue and Gray* 2010, 184; Richard Brent, 'The Alabama Claims Tribunal: the British Perspective'. *The International History Review* 44(1) (2021), 26–7; Bingham 'Alabama Claims' 2005, 24.

156 Brent, 'Alabama Claims' 2021, 26.

157 Neff, *Blue and Gray* 2010, 185.

158 AP (May 1868), 63–8.

159 AP (July 1869), 101–2.

the negotiations that would two years later result in the Treaty of Washington. They commended this bilateral agreement especially for its 'formal establishment of great and important principles of international law'.[160]

Once new arrived that the tribunal in Geneva had produced its award, the Americans could not be more elated. The American Peace Society alternately called it 'one of the most important diplomatic acts of the age', 'a new and glorious epoch in the history of nations', and a 'grand victory of peace'.[161] The award was almost immediately embedded in a greater teleological historical narrative. Quoting from Emory Washburn, a Harvard law professor, the *Advocate* made much of 'agencies in operation, whose power is stronger than even nations themselves', who worked out a 'moral revolution' which was 'laying deeper and firmer the foundations of a sound and humane system of international law'. The peace friends fully agreed. The Genevan award had indisputably proven that arbitration was a practical substitute for war. Although the dispute had been settled between states with kindred legal systems, its precedent would nonetheless 'enormously' increase the difficulty of resorting to hostile actions in the future, even among third states. The American Peace Society had never believed, just like most politicians on both sides of the Atlantic, that the claims controversy would lead to war.[162] Still, it was 'the most important step (…) ever taken' towards 'a tribunal of reason' rather than one of arms.[163] The Treaty of Washington, including its three rules of maritime neutrality, was regarded as building on the Paris Declaration of 1856.[164]

3.2 *Renewed American Interest in Codification*

The American response to the Washington Treaty and the Geneva arbitration could not be viewed separately from ongoing changes in the institutional composition of the U.S. peace movement. The American Peace Society's rigid behaviour during the Civil War came back to bite it in the post-war years. The American peace movement had long been characterised by its schizophrenic attitude on the issue of just cause. Back in the 1840s, the radical wing of American pacifism had separated itself from the national society. Though the anarchical non-resistant society proved unable to overcome its own doctrinism, absolutist pacifism had not died with it. In the

160 AP (June 1871), 69.
161 AP (October 1872), 221–2; AP (November 1872), 228–9; AP (June 1873), 47.
162 AP (October 1872), 221–2; Brent, 'Alabama Claims' 2021, 25–7.
163 AP (November 1872), 228.
164 AP (April 1873), 25; AP (June 1873), 45–6.

late 1860s, they reorganised into another organisation. Beset by another rival, the American Peace Society itself underwent changes too. The decades-long reign of its pragmatic secretary, the ageing Beckwith, was drawing to a close. In his place arrived a new generation of peace advocates, one that was more willing to try out new ideas, inspired by older rejected projects. While Burritt too was reaching a ripe old age, he came to live long enough to see his project for a code become partly realised in the winter of his life.

Initially, everything was again business as usual at the first post-war annual meeting of the American Peace Society. It was held barely a month after the surrender of Robert E. Lee at the Appomattox court house. The western-most Confederate forces had laid down their arms just a few days before. The meeting's main resolutions confirmed that the American peace friends had been right all along. Law and order had been upheld in the United States. Civil government was a legitimate instrument to order human society, as ordained by God. The society concluded that it was now more important than ever to further promote 'a peaceful policy at home as well as abroad'. Somewhat like the ashes left behind after a forest fire, the American Peace Society resolved to use the opportunities opened up in the wake of a long, bloody and personal conflict to renew and expand its operations.[165]

To some extent, the American peace movement realised this ambition. A number of signs indicated that interest again began to grow as the dust of the war settled. In 1868, the society announced new stereotyped versions of the Sumner speeches, along with a 'revised and enlarged edition' of Ladd's essay. It also set up a 'Western department' in Kansas, staffed by a paid agent.[166] Up until then, the society had been all but non-existent in the West. There had even been an independently organised peace convention in Iowa that had established a peace society in that state.[167] The American peace movement was slowly recovering – and becoming more diverse in the process.

One of the most conspicuous features of this emerging new wave of American peace agitation was the prominence of women in it. While women had been involved in the peace movement since the beginning, they had never been able to integrate themselves into leadership positions,

165 AP (June 1865), 278–9.
166 AP (November 1868), 150–5; AP (January 1873), 14; AP (March 1873), 18–9.
167 AP (August 1870), 272–3.

leaving little official record of their activities. From the 1870s onwards, however, female leaders gradually began to emerge.

The most important one to mention in this story – which ends right at the cusp of this shift – was Julia Ward Howe (1819–1910). Howe remains best known for her stirring song the *Battle Hymn of the Republic,* the unofficial anthem of the Union. After the war, however, she launched an *Appeal to Womanhood Throughout the World.* The pamphlet was a scathing response the horrors of the Civil War and the ongoing Franco-German War. Howe exclaimed: 'Thus man have done. Thus men will do. (…) Let women now leave all that may be left of home for a great and earnest day of council.' It is said to have inspired the modern annual mother's day celebration. In 1872, she managed to inspire a short-lived 'Women's International Peace Society' in Manchester.[168]

Very little could as yet be discovered about the legal argumentation, if any, espoused by early female pacifist figureheads like Howe. Like male peace friends, they were concerned with a range of issues. For women especially, the suffrage question understandably loomed larger than international peace. Howe nonetheless paid some attention to international law. In 1871, she set up a meeting in New York that drew responses from the larger peace movement. Doyens of the American Peace Society like Upham, Walker, and Burritt encouraged her attempt to set up a female society. At the meeting, the lawyer David Dudley Field lectured on his project for a permanent court of arbitration he was working on with the American Peace Society. Very little could be discovered about what her society did afterwards, as was so often the case. Judging from rare reports, Howe's organisation appeared to have adopted a similar project to that of the American Peace Society.[169]

Much more is known about the break-away peace society, featuring women and men, that had split from the American Peace Society to represent the voice of radical American pacifism: the Universal Peace Union. It filled the ideological gap that had existed since the collapse of the Non-Resistance Society and the and the marginalisation of reformists in the national society. Many of the members of the new club were veterans from both factions, including Wright, Ballou, Blanchard and others. Its leader,

168 AP (February 1910), 26–8; AP (July 1873), 50–1, 56; Voice of Peace (hereafter: VP) (January 1873), 13–4; VP (March 1873), 7; Ceadel, *Idealists* 2000, 29–30, 99.

169 *Proceedings of a Peace Meeting held at Union League Hall, New York, December 23rd, 1870, for the Purpose of Free Consultation on the Subject of a Woman's Peace Congress for the World* (Philadelphia: Gillam, 1871), 12–3, 22–5; VP (January 1873), 13–4.

however, was relatively new to organised pacifism. This was a woollens merchant by the name of Alfred H. Love (1830–1913). Reputedly, he first showed his pacifism when he was drafted in 1863. Standing in front of a glaring recruitment officer, who was visibly recovering from wounds suffered in combat, he asked for the penalty for conscientious objection. The soldier promptly said: 'Obey the laws or be shot'. Love replied equally fast: 'I am ready in five minutes in yonder lot'.[170]

Whether true or not, the peace society he led was equally unambiguous about where it stood in the peace question. At its foundational meeting in Boston, one participant asserted that the American Peace Society did not go far enough by refusing to condemn defensive war. He demanded 'a more uncompromising stand against all resorts to deadly force'. Another speaker, the non-resistant Adin Ballou, said that '*die rather than kill,* is the watchword of our movement'. Their sole guide was to be the 'one moral and divine law', meaning 'love to God and love thy neighbour as thyself'.[171] Beckwith tried in vain to persuade the assembly to more moderate views. His plea to only focus on interstate war was mocked by Wright, the old non-resistant. The proceedings emphasised that the assembly was 'fervently devoted to pure and radical peace principles'. Another meeting spoke of 'a general desire to avoid the mistakes which have made enterprises of this kind comparative failures in this country'.[172]

Love's Universal Peace Union was moderately successful in offering an alternative to the American Peace Society. Unlike the latter society, Love and his supporters were Christian perfectionists, who placed peace within a larger Millennialist framework, similar to the religious sensibilities of the first peace societies. Like other millenarian societies, or the old Non-Resistance Society, it resembled a sect. Although Love credited his Peace Union with various peace initiatives, it seldom played much of a part in any. In its obituary, the American Peace Society noted that it had been very difficult to work with Love, because of his bad habit to bring into the peace campaign issues not considered to be 'germane or judicious'.[173] During his

170 Thomas Curran, *Soldiers of Peace. Civil War Pacifism and the Postwar Radical Peace Movement* (New York: Fordham University Press 2003), 1.

171 *Proceedings of the Peace Conventions, held in Boston, March 14 & 15, 1866; and in Providence, May 16th, 1866* (unknown location: Universal Peace Union 1866), 6, 8–9.

172 Ibid., 23.

173 Alfred Love, *A Brief Synopsis of Work Proposed, Aided, and Accomplished by the Universal Peace Union during the Last 31 Years* (unknown location: unknown publisher 1897), 2–16; AP (November 1913), 222–3; Curran, *Soldiers of Peace* 2003, 195–7.

career, the *Advocate* only rarely reported on the Universal Peace Union. Scholars have assessed that the society's most tangible legacy was to have introduced non-resistance pacifism into the twentieth century, through correspondence with Leo Tolstoy.[174]

The Universal Peace Union was unclear about the institution and doctrines it wanted to see realised on the political level. Its constitution referred to a 'congress of nations', without adding specifics.[175] Its journal regularly referred to 'arbitration', but it took a considerable time before the Peace Union developed this concept further. Only in 1879 did a delegation of the Union present a blueprint for an international court to the president. An 'international tribunal of arbitration' would hold yearly sessions in the capital cities of its member states. Similar to so many other projects before it, it was to be made up of two representatives of each member. Unlike Ladd's court of nations, every vote was to be weighed in proportion to the number of citizens in the representative's home country. The Peace Union did not discuss the legal criteria on which a decision was to be based. Presumably, representatives could rely on more than legal norms. The codification of international law was fully absent from the proposal. Unlike the old Non-Resistance Society, the Peace Union was not actively opposed to those who did pursue this objective. Overall, however, it shared with its anarchistic predecessor a deep-rooted conviction that secular law was subordinate to God's law. Its members were more comfortable critiquing human-made laws for falling short of 'the Gospel standard' than they were at offering constructive alternatives. Individuals and states merely had to obey the basic moral principles espoused by Jesus. The rest would sort itself out.[176]

In the American Peace Society, meanwhile, the balance again shifted in favour of the codification scheme when Beckwith finally died in 1870. His pragmatic views made him limit the peace society's ambitions to what seemed practical. In international law, that meant bilateral arbitration. Beckwith's death, combined with the *Alabama claims* and the synergy between Burritt and Field, finally opened up new possibilities. Burritt, who had outlived his old rival, persuaded Beckwith's successor to alter the programmatic course of the national society. Less than two months after the end of the tribunal in Geneva, the *Advocate* announced that it would seize on this 'golden opportunity' to hold another international peace congress. Its ambition was to build on Burritt's proposals from the 1840s, and lay the

174 Curran, *Soldiers of Peace* 2003, 198.

175 *Proceedings* 1866, 20.

176 Curran, *Soldiers of Peace* 2003, 126–7.

groundwork for an international legal code.[177] Because that project also heavily involved the newly-emerging European peace societies, this story concludes our final chapter.

3.3 *Renewed British Interest in Codification*

The London Peace Society had been as inspired by the *Alabama claims* as the Americans. The *Herald* reported extensively on every facet of the dispute between 1866 and 1872. It reproduced many articles of the *Advocate,* like the open letter from Lieber or the long piece on arbitration published in the *North American Review*.[178] Likewise, it recorded the efforts undertaken by the society itself to support a peaceful resolution. Unlike the Americans, the British already sent petitions to Parliament in 1866. Richard's circular contained a model form that brought up the 23rd Protocol of the Paris Peace Treaty. It did not purport to assert anything on 'the nice points of international law', other than that it should be settled by an 'impartial arbitration'. In 1868, the peace society accompanied a deputation to the foreign secretary, again asking to resolve things through arbitration. They again stressed that Britain had a special duty to honour the Protocol, as it had been originally proposed by their state in 1856.[179] The London Committee likewise lobbied with Clarendon, who was again foreign secretary in 1869, asking for an arbitration clause in any upcoming treaty with the U.S.[180]

When new reached them from Geneva of the award, the London Peace Society was not as unhappy with it as other Britons. The pacifists disregarded the 'rowdies and blusterers' on either side – 'these worthies effectually neutralise each other'. Overall, if an award appeared to be 'violently denounced' on both sides of the Atlantic, then the decision 'may be taken to be on the whole substantially fair and just'.[181] The society's commentary in the *Herald* even revealed itself to be glad that the tribunal had ruled against Britain, because it offered their state the opportunity to prove its deference to the rule of international law. They observed approvingly that the principle of arbitration itself had not been attacked in the ensuing parliamentary debate. At the same time, they venerated the president of the

177 AP (November 1872), 228–9.

178 HP (January 1866), 9–11; HP (October 1866), 109–114; HP (November 1866), 121–126; HP (December 1866), 133–137; HP (November 1871), 286–9.

179 HP (April 1868), 44–7.

180 HP February 1869), 165–7.

181 HP (October 1872), 130–1.

tribunal, the Italian count Federico Sclopis, as somewhat of a lawyerly hero.[182]

As was typical, the pacifist reading was far too rosy. The British arbiter, Lord Alexander Cockburn, had a very dim view of the Italian president, and could barely disguise his contempt for his foreign colleagues. Cockburn had openly quarrelled with the president. He was not alone in this. A foreign office diplomat had privately described Sclopis as 'a pasty faced, burly, fat, pompous, obstinate old man'. This could not be reduced to any British superiority complex, or whether or not they regarded any specific arbiter as disfavouring British interests. A major factor were the different legal cultures. The British were accustomed to reason according to precedent, whereas the foreign panellists were more versed in civil law traditions. As such, one of the members of the British council complained that the Italian and Swiss had been 'more disposed to push their own theories of what international law ought to be than to consider accurately what it is'.[183] Cockburn's dissenting opinion underlined that 'the question does not depend on the lucubrations of learned professors or speculative jurists', but on the 'common assent' of states. He objected that his fellow arbiters had given more credence to the opinion of 'savants', than to 'existing positive law'.[184]

Although this important dissent went unnoticed in the *Herald,* it was paralleled in the peace society's own internal legal discussions. Over the past few years, the British peace movement had itself been interacting more closely with people who had been attempting to do precisely that which Cockburn was accusing his fellow arbiters of. It should be recalled that in the same year as the Geneva award, Louis Bara's controversial peace congress essay was finally published. This Belgian lawyer had been extremely critical about the society's focus on arbitration because of his own emphasis on a code.[185] After the death of Beckwith, the American peace friends were similarly again pushing more towards codification than arbitration. Even inside the London Peace Society, people held divergent views. Should the society continue its policy of promoting immediate methods of dispute

182 HP (August 1872), 104–5; HP (November 1872), 154; HP (May 1873), 230–1; HP (September 1873), 316.

183 Quoted in Brent, 'Alabama Claims' 2021, 9.

184 Moore pointed out that Cockburn's dissenting opinion was three times as long as the opinions of all of the other arbitrators put together. *Moore, History vol. 1* 1898, 659–661; *Papers Relating to the Treaty of Washington. Volume IV. Geneva Arbitration* (Washington: Government Printing Office 1872), 230–544.

185 See chapter 5.

settlement, like arbitration and mediation? Or, alternatively, should the British peace friends join the ongoing effort towards a more direct material change of international law through some method of codification?

Several voices were urging the national peace society to adopt the latter course. In his lecture before the society in 1871, the historian John Robert Seeley recommended a European federation, with an executive power and a 'law-court'. This court was to be distinct from the legislative congress, as 'an ambassador cannot possibly be at the same time a judge'. While it sounded eerily similar to how Ladd had already conceived it, the professor had arrived at his scheme independently. Richard felt it necessary to inform his guest speaker that he had somewhat misunderstood the character of the peace movement. It did not cherish 'extreme views' against 'all war', as had apparently been Seeley's impression. The movement had been promoting 'various schemes of arbitration' already since the 1830s, and was only opposed to the armed enforcement of international law. This, he claimed, was his main objection to an otherwise fine lecture. However, the secretary was probably being polite. He also made an off-hand remark that Seeley's European federation seemed similar to the ideal of the *Ligue internationale de la paix et de la liberté.* This was not a compliment, as Richard was anxious to distance his own society from this league, which in his eyes mixed up the peace question with 'other extreme and irrelevant opinions'. The Welshman considered a European union totally utopian.[186]

The society had similarly mixed opinions about several other recent writers who had published on federative peace solutions. The first was James Lorimer, a professor at the university of Edinburgh. Lorimer was a renowned specialist of international law and an upcoming co-founder of the *Institut de droit international.*[187] This man agreed with the peace movement that international law in its current condition was defective. In 1867, he published his vision on international organisation.[188] The peace society did not oppose it as such. The *Herald* duly copied an outline of his proposed confederation, which was in itself just another variant of a congress of nations, based on the domestic example.[189]

186 HP (April 1871), 197–9.

187 Koskenniemi, *Gentle Civilizer* 2004, 33.

188 HP (August 1867), 233. *Transactions of the Royal Society of Edinburgh. Vol. XXIV* (Edinburgh: Robert Grant & Son 1867), 557–668.

189 Bruno Arcidiacono, 'La paix par le droit international, dans la vision de deux juristes du XIXe Siècle: Le débat Lorimer-Bluntschli'. *Relations internationales* 149 (2012), 13–26; HP (August 1867), 234; Van der Linden, *Peace Movement* 1987, 912.

Rather, British peace friends took offence at the Scottish professor's misrepresentation of previous peace plans. Lorimer had claimed that previous publicists had invariably gone astray by attempting to redraw the European map. While this critique definitely applied to many such plans, from Henri IV all the way down to many contemporary examples, it was nonetheless too sweeping. The society had itself on this basis always rejected such proposals. Their commentary pointed out that Cobden had 'shrunk from large schemes of European federation', precisely because the European political system was in constant flux.[190] The peace society sent a copy to the American Peace Society because of the book's support for an international court, but otherwise did little with Lorimer's scheme.[191]

Comparatively more deference was given to the work of Frederic Seebohm (1833–1912). Seebohm was the son of a Quaker merchant and became himself a renowned historian of medieval English history. Simultaneously, however, Seebohm was a trained jurist and a well-respected barrister.[192] In 1871, he published *On International Reform*. He claimed to have written it in reaction to the European arms race and recent calls to abandon the policy of non-intervention.[193] His book contained much that could appeal to the peace societies. Seebohm dissected the failings of 'international lynch law', a term which he may have borrowed from Sumner's *True Grandeur* speech.[194] In its stead, he wanted to see '*positive international law* and *an essentially judicial system* between nations'. With the exception of documents like the 1856 Paris Declaration, this lawyer believed most of international law consisted of 'rules of morality', rather than of binding positive rules. He dismissed arbitration as an effective substitute for war. Similar to Bara, only 'just laws, well defined, and clearly recognised beforehand', could *prevent* many conflict from escalating into open hostilities. The 'simple justice' by an 'honest' arbiter did not allow the same level of predictability and 'impartial' justice as a code. To realise this code, Seebohm suggested 'similar declarations' to the one from 1856.[195]

The British responded relatively well to Seebohm's book, despite its criticism of arbitration. Their review in the *Herald* praised the well-crafted

190 HP (August 1867), 133.
191 AP (June 1871), 61.
192 Van der Linden, *Peace Movement* 1987, 912.
193 Frederic Seebohm, *On International Reform* (London: Longmans, Green, and Co. 1871), unnumbered preface.
194 Ibid., 91–4.
195 Seebohm, *Reform* 1871, 94, 100, 105, 108.

argument it made for an international judicial tribunal. Seebohm did not propose a federative congress of nations, which likely helped. The London Peace Society was not opposed to a permanent tribunal in the strictly judicial sense, akin to the Supreme Court of the United States. The philosopher John Stuart Mill had proposed much the same. The society's main objection to it was similar to the qualms they had about Lorimer and Seeley's plans. Like them, Seebohm had allowed for international law to be enforced through international police actions. The British peace friends were quick to add that the 'chief and final power' of any tribunal was '*moral* force'. Nonetheless, the society decided to recommend the book to persons interested in the peace question, 'at home and abroad'.[196] Perhaps it was through the British peace friends that Seebohm's proposal made its way into European pacifist circles. A French translation appeared in 1873, with a foreword by Frédéric Passy.[197] It was also analysed by one of the prize essayists of his organisation, the Belgian jurist Eugène Goblet d'Alviella, in the *Revue de Belgique.* The Belgian lawyer was impressed by the great similarities to Bara's critique.[198] Auguste Visschers referred to both Bara and Seebohm in the run-up to the international law conference held in Brussels in 1873.[199]

The last publicist of note to have become enmeshed in the London Peace Society's internal debate on the respective merits of codification and arbitration was Leone Levi (1821–1888). Like Seebohm and Lorimer, Levi was a trained lawyer with a special interest in international law. Unlike the others, he was an emigrated Italian Jew who had only arrived in Britain in the 1840s. Levi was also the only one who was a member of the London Peace Society itself. His chief interest lay in the codification of international commercial law. He had already in the early 1850s tried to interest the peace society in his plans, initially to no avail.[200] Like many others, Levi coupled economic interdependence with peace.[201] The Italian-born lawyer only gradually managed to increase his influence in the society. In 1861, he got

196 HP (May 1871), 218; Seebohm, *Reform* 1871, 124.

197 Frederick Seebohm, *De la réforme du droit des gens. Introduction par Frédéric Passy* (Paris: Franklin 1873).

198 See also chapter 7. Revue de Belgique (15 November 1872), 233.

199 JE (March 1873), 502.

200 Leone Levi, *The Law of Nature and Nations as affected by Divine Law* (London: Cash 1855); Ceadel, *Origins* 1996, 466; HP (August 1855), 241; HP (November 1856), 132; G.R. Rubin, 'Levi, Leone (1821–1888)', in *Oxford Dictionary of National Biography*. 2004, available at: doi.org/10.1093/ref:odnb/16551.

201 Annamaria Monti, 'Leone Levi (1821–1888) and the History of Comparative Commercial Law', in William Eves, John Hudson, Ingrid Ivarsen, Sarah B. White (eds.), *Common*

himself elected into the Committee. However, it took him another ten years to become a voice to be truly reckoned with.[202] Part of what contributed to Levi's rise was his involvement in another organisation: the National Association for the Promotion of Social Science.

Founded in 1857 to stimulate research into newly emerging social sciences, this organisation quickly developed itself into a centre of progressive and academic thinking on a wide range of issues, peace among them.[203] It held yearly congresses in various British cities. These meetings actually provided a forum for the respective ambitions of the peace movement on both sides of the Atlantic. In 1866, at Manchester, the American jurist David Dudley Field delivered an address on the codification of international law. The association appointed a committee to frame such a code, but it was delayed numerous times, and Field only managed to publish his *Draft Outlines* in 1872. His project attracted the interest of the American Peace Society, which led to the 1873 Brussels peace conference.[204] The British peace movement equally tried to push its reform agenda at the social science congresses. In 1868, Richard read a paper on disarmament before the economy department, which agreed to look further into the matter.[205] However, Levi was a much more prominent member of this association. At the 1870 Newcastle congress, he read a paper on the 'Defective state of international law'. This text was also published elsewhere, including as a separate tract of the London Peace Society.[206] He read a paper before a meeting of the international law section the next year, in which he proposed a more specific 'plan of arbitration and mediation'. Levi supposed that his ideas could be discussed at the European diplomatic congress that was generally expected to follow at the end of the Franco-German War.[207] The association appointed a committee to discuss it, similar to the committee that had been

Law, Civil Law, and Colonial Law. Essays in Comparative Legal History from the Twelfth to the Twentieth Centuries (Cambridge: CUP 2021), 249, 254.

202 Ceadel, *Idealists* 2000, 93.

203 Ibid. 78–9.

204 Lawrence Goldman, 'The Social Science Association, 1857–1886: A Context for Mid-Victorian Liberalism'. *The English Historical Review* 101(398) (1986), 95–134; Van der Linden, *Peace Movement* 1987, 635–636. See chapter 7.

205 HP (June 1868), 65.

206 Leone Levi, *Defective State of International Law* (London: unknown publisher 1870); Edwin Pears (ed.), *Transactions of the National Association for the Promotion of Social Science. Newcastle-Upon-Tyne Meeting* (London: Longmans, Green, Reader, & Dyer 1871), 173–5; HP (July 1871), 242–3.

207 Edwin Pears (ed.), *Transactions of the National Association for the Promotion of Social Science. Leeds Meeting* (London: Longmans, Green, Reader, & Dyer 1872), 237–9.

inspired by Field. At their congress of 1871, Levi reported this committee's conclusions.[208]

Levi's basis critique of international law and the international political system was widely shared in the association. In his paper for Newcastle, the lawyer was clear: 'The root weakness in international law is that is not a law.' Relying on John Austin's popular contemporary 'command theory' of law, Levi understood law to be 'a command or precept', which 'an inferior is obliged to obey'.[209] Under such a definition, norms regulating the relations of sovereign entities in a horizontal order could of course not qualify. Like so many others, Levi concluded that it consisted mostly of moral guidelines, rather than of norms that could actually constrain foreign policy. At previous congresses, speakers had said much the same. In 1866, a short paper was read on 'an international high court'. The paper then read claimed that 'any system of international law under which such incessant breaches of the peace of nations are possible, is hardly worthy of the name of (…) law'. There had to be a 'judicial interpretation of the law of nations'.[210] In 1868, another paper on international law literally referred to Austin. However, this time it did not go so far as to deny the legal character of international law itself. Even domestic law was not necessarily invalidated by breaches, and it would furthermore be 'a political mistake' to no longer call the rules governing interstate relations 'law'. Shedding it of the general respect connotated to the term 'law' might render it a self-fulfilling prophecy. It agreed with previous statements that the European arms race was dangerous, and that the ultimate purpose of international law was peace. Some remedy had to be found, so that the balance of power would no longer determine how international law was to be interpreted. The events of the Civil War had only once again illustrated the ancient insight of Thucydides: 'Belligerents have always exercised and will always exercise such rights as they dare, and neutrals will endure such restrictions as they must'.[211]

While easy agreement might be found on the many faults of international law, the committee found it much harder to agree on a solution. Levi

---

208 Ibid., 239–44.

209 The 'Austinian challenge' holds that law needs credible enforcement mechanisms to be considered 'law'. *Defective State* 1870, 3; David Lefkowitz, *Philosophy and International Law. A Critical Introduction* (Cambridge: CUP 2020), 8–19.

210 Edwin Pears (ed.), *Transactions of the National Association for the Promotion of Social Science. Belfast Meeting* (London: Longmans, Green, Reader, & Dyer 1868), 168.

211 Edwin Pears (ed.), *Transactions of the National Association for the Promotion of Social Science. Birmingham Meeting* (London: Longmans, Green, Reader, & Dyer 1869), 137–58.

himself eschewed any sort of political federation. Rather, he advised a mixed system. A permanent international council, composed of the diplomatic agents of each member state, should act as a 'high court of reference and advice' for all interstate disputes. In all cases that touched strictly upon matters of law, the council should resort to arbitration. Levi sketched out all possible compositions for this tribunal, including Lieber's idea of a law faculty, but settled on a commission similar to the *Alabama* tribunal in Geneva. On the other hand, cases which touched upon national security or the balance of power – in other words, the so-called vital interests – would have to be handled through mediation. That would have to be done by the council, which could offer good offices or even – in the gravest matters – impose its judgment through a majority vote.[212] In its broad contours, the committee of the association agreed with Levi's plans, under the condition that state sovereignty would be safeguarded. While the technical details could be debated endlessly, the most fundamental point of disagreement was the question of enforcement. Returning to Austin's famed challenge, opinions differed on whether the backing of physical force would give the tribunal the credibility it needed, or, conversely, whether it would not just 'tenfold' worsen the evils of war by dragging third states into a conflict that might otherwise have stayed more limited.[213]

Levi afterwards continued to devote himself to international codification. However, the Committee of the London Peace Society ultimately decided to continue their longstanding focus on more direct methods of dispute settlement. The most influential member of the Committee, secretary Richard, decided to pick up where Richard Cobden, who had meanwhile died in 1865, had left off in 1849.

3.4 *Success of the British Arbitration Campaign*

While the London Peace Society could only applaud all of these initiatives, evidence of the growing interest of professional lawyers into their cause, the leadership was not convinced that they should drastically change course themselves. Disturbed by the recent surge in appeals to have international law enforced through arms, the society repeated its old position that international law could not be enforced violently.[214] Furthermore,

212 Leone Levi, *Proposals for a Plan of Arbitration and Mediation for the Settlement of International Disputes, to be submitted to any European Conference which may be held at the Conclusion of the Present War* (unknown location: unknown publisher 1871), 1–14.

213 *Leeds Meeting* 1872, 239–44.

214 Van der Linden, *Peace Movement* 1987, 912.

these remained works published by comparative outsiders, with the exception of Levi. The news of the Washington Treaty in 1871 struck someone like Richard as much more important than the latest crop of purely theoretical peace proposals. At the end of the year, the Committee announced its intention to have Richard propose another arbitration motion. Buoyed by the *Alabama claims* arbitration, the society believed that this time it could succeed where it had failed in its first arbitration campaign of the 1840s.[215]

Like it had been for Cobden, the political campaign of Richard proved more arduous than originally anticipated. The society was forced to delay it numerous times, as it was dependent on the progress of the tribunal in Geneva. They had set up hundreds of meetings and lectures in 1872 alone, and were naturally embarrassed that the whole thing had to be postponed again and again.[216]

Other than that, however, these public gatherings generally went well. Perhaps because they usually attracted an already sympathetic audience, acts of dissent were rare. Richard was present at many of them in person, and reported that the most typical question raised about his proposal was how awards would be enforced. The pacifist invariably answered that public opinion sufficed.[217] It was only once the success of the award seemed secured by its British acceptance that the campaign could definitively go ahead. As one report phrased it, few would dare 'pooh pooh' arbitration as an abstract theory now that two great powers had successfully used it to settle an important dispute.[218] In all, some 1,163 petitions had been sent in preparation, totalling some 200,000 signatures. Often, only the president of the meeting had signed the document, making the society claim that the actual number of citizens they represented was much higher, numbering in the millions. Even taking into account that the society liked to inflate its importance, these were numbers to be reckoned with.[219]

It was a sweltering July evening in 1873 when the secretary of the London Peace Society was finally able to address the Commons on the issue to which he had given most of his adult life. In spite of the late hour and the oppressive heat, the public gallery was 'filled to overflowing'. Some

215 HP (December 1871), 299.

216 HP (December 1871), 304; HP (January 1872), 1–6, 10–1; HP (February 1872), 13–7, 25–6; HP (March 1872), 30–4; HP (August 1872), 102; HP (October 1872), 124–7; HP (December 1872), 157–9.

217 HP (October 1872), 125.

218 HP (January 1873), 170.

219 HP (August 1873), 298–9; HP (September 1873), 312.

250 M.P.'s had also decided to show up, which, although not a very large number, could be worse for a 9 P.M. sitting. Richard's motion advised her Majesty's government to contact 'foreign powers with a view to the further improvement of international law, and the establishment of a general and permanent system of international arbitration'.[220]

It was an ambitious proposal. The M.P. had in the meetings of 1872 and early 1873 suggested that the governments should in a first step appoint 'the most eminent jurists' of their countries to draw up a code of international law. In a second step, they should establish a permanent 'great court of nations'.[221] It was influenced by a combination of the social science conferences and contemporary American plans to codify international law. Miles, the secretary of the American Peace Society, had visited Richard in person for this purpose. However, the British secretary was opposed to unofficial meetings of lawyers, preferring to rely on the 'natural and legitimate organs of national sentiment'. He had little trust in men without a political mandate, however well-qualified they may be. Such an unofficial international law society could at best be an 'auxiliary means', but it was better to directly go to the source of all political power: Parliament.[222] The British secretary was anxious to have his motion passed, which explained why he kept it vague in the official text.

In his speech, Richard relied on the full scale of legal argumentation as had been honed by pacifists since their gradual politicisation in the 1830s. Anxious to avoid the stigma of utopianism, he listed all the instances in nineteenth century state practice in which Britain herself had resorted to peaceful arbitration. He brought up the bilateral commissions of the Treaty of Ghent, several private claims commissions, as well as various arbitrations conducted in the Vattelian sense by another sovereign. Aware that people like Palmerston often dismissed arbitration as only applicable to trivial matters, Richard reminded the assembly that the bloody Crimean War had allegedly been caused by a quarrel over religious rights in the Holy Land. Another major legal precedent was the 23rd Protocol of the Paris Peace Treaty. Although this idealistic clause had 'hitherto remained inoperative', it

220 HP (August 1873), 273–281; *International Arbitration and the Improvement of International Law. The Debate in the House of Commons, on Tuesday, July 8th, 1873, the Motion of Mr. Henry Richard for an Address to the Crown* (London: Hodder & Stoughton 1873), 5; *Hansard's Parliamentary Debates: Third Series. Vol. CCXVII.* (London: Cornelius Buck 1873), 52–90.

221 HP (January 1872), 2; HP (January 1873), 171.

222 See chapter 7. HP (May 1873), 230; HP (May 1873), 236–7.

retained a distinct value as a declaration of intent. Had the condemnations of the slave trade at the Congresses of Vienna and Verona not similarly boosted the fight against the slave trade?[223] Naturally, he made much of the successful conclusion of the *Alabama claims*. Britain had proven her honour by showing 'respect for law' and her readiness to 'submit to a judicial decision' even if against her interests.[224]

Richard had likewise not forgotten his desire to have international law codified. Omitted from the actual motion, he highlighted it in his oral defence. The 'three rules' of the Washington treaty were a modest attempt in the right direction already. True, these were phrased very vaguely, and perhaps interpreted too widely by the Genevan tribunal. However, did there ever exist a norm which 'clever and practiced lawyers' could not interpret in two or three different ways if it suited them? Once the laughter had died down, the M.P. proceeded to suggest an 'international commission' to investigate international law, and 'reduce it into something like a clear and coherent system'. This was 'a great necessity of civilization'. If 'law' was to be used in the 'rigid sense', there 'hardly exists such a thing at present'. The many customs, treaties, admiralty court decisions, and opinions of jurists may have had some effect on the frequency of war, but few would claim that it amounted to law as commonly understood. It lacked an authority to 'give it force', and a tribunal to 'administer it'.[225]

Richard pointed to several precedents, most of which have already been discussed. The only novel one was still ongoing. Richard said there was 'a remarkable experiment now in progress in Egypt'. An international commission in Constantinople was busy drafting a code and a constitution of an international court to administer justice in Egypt between natives and foreigners. Could the same not be done for the whole civilised world?[226] Richard was referring to the mixed court system that would be active from 1876 to 1949. Like they had done in the past, peace friends were relying on an unfortunate example because of their limited knowledge of contemporary political events. While the Egyptian mixed courts would indeed become popularly known as 'international courts', they exercised their extensive jurisdiction under a veneer of Egyptian sovereignty. They were dominated by Western jurists, appointed by their own governments, and very resistant to attempts of the local government to regulate them. Most of the code

223 *Debate* 1873, 17–30.
224 Ibid., 27.
225 Ibid., 30–4.
226 Ibid., 32–3.

was based on French law. This extraterritoriality was thus mostly an expression of colonial domination.[227] Given that British pacifism was opposed to colonialism, as seen previously, Richard's referral to the code of 1873 was probably done in good faith, even if it was marked by the era's prevailing Eurocentrism.

As during the Cobden debate of 1849, Richard's most formidable opponent was the prime minister himself. In this case, the peace movement's champion did not face Russell or an unapologetic hawk like Palmerston, but Gladstone, who generally preferred to focus on domestic issues while keeping the peace abroad.[228] While even he might not have been very sympathetic to the peace societies, at least he did not personally despise them as much as Palmerston had during his career. Nonetheless, the leading man of British politics could not support the motion. In spite of Richard's precautions, Gladstone felt that the peace party was asking too much. Cobden had proposed bilateral talks, but Richard wanted a general system. The prime minister agreed in principle, but estimated that present European politics did not allow such an initiative. For him, the massive and ongoing arms race was not a reason to launch ambitious arbitration schemes, but rather a reason to avoid it.[229]

Like any good rhetorician, Gladstone tried to use his opponent's own arguments against them. In what must have come as an unexpected move for Richard, the prime minister waved about a copy of Émile de Laveleye's (1822–1892) *On the causes of war*. De Laveleye was a respected member of the Belgian peace movement. An edited version of his booklet was published in English by the London Peace Society. Like all European pacifists, this Belgian did not care about non-resistance, believing instead in credible means of self-defence. The pacifist had therefore ended his book with an appeal for compulsory military service. Gladstone naturally seized on the

227 David Todd, 'Beneath Sovereignty: Extraterritoriality and Imperial Internationalism in Nineteenth Century Egypt'. *Law and History Review* 36(1) (2018), 108; Will Hanley, 'International Lawyers without Public International Law: the Case of Late Ottoman Egypt'. *Journal of the History of International Law* 18(1) (2016), 100; Hoyle's assessment that it was not act of colonial domination must be disagreed with here. Mark Hoyle, 'The Structure and Laws of the Mixed Courts of Egypt'. *Arab Law Quarterly* 1(3) (1986), 343–4.

228 Ceadel opposed Gladstone's 'moderate interventionism' to 'Palmerston's meddling'. Martin Ceadel, 'Gladstone and a Liberal Theory of International Relations', in Peter Ghosh and Lawrence Goldman (eds.), *Politics and Culture in Victorian Britain. Essays in memory of Colin Matthew* (Oxford: OUP 2006), 78.

229 *Debate* 1873, 40–1.

opportunity it offered. It seemed that the geopolitical situation was so dire that even Richard's European bystanders were forced to come to conclusions 'that must be so painful' to them.[230]

A fortiori, an international court relying only on moral force, as proposed by both De Laveleye and Richard, was unrealistic in light of the international context. Again, Gladstone professed to endorse the project *in theory*. However, not unlike Palmerston had done in 1849, the prime minister objected to the peace movement's examples selected from state practice. The *Alabama claims* was not a good precedent. This arbitration had been achieved between insular states, far removed from each other, with a shared language, shared values and a shared legal culture. The continental-European powers, on the other hand, were too consumed by their mutual rivalries, caused by their close proximity to one another. He found proof of this in the recent Franco-German war, popularly believed to have been caused by Napoleon III feeling insulted. The British cabinet had offered mediation, but was rejected, 'even though it would be impossible to conceive questions better qualified to be disposed by arbitration'. Gladstone claimed the cabinet had made its offer in accordance to the 23rd Protocol, which was unlikely given that it had in every other instance refused to accept its applicability itself. It might be recalled how the peace society had invoked it in vain during the *Trent* affair in 1861.[231]

Gladstone implicitly admitted to the real reason why 'altruistic' British overtures towards mediation or arbitration were looked at with suspicion on the Continent. The 'three rules' of the Washington Treaty had originally been intended to become a general standard. However, efforts to get the rest of Europe to accede had all been suspended. According to the prime minister, 'there was even now more or less of an opinion afloat among the various countries of Europe that the Three Rules were meant to give selfish expression to that which was for the interest of Great Britain and America'.[232] Like we have seen, this was not without merit. The Washington rules imposed a heavier burden on neutrals and states with little naval power than on the British empire with its enormous fleet. Given the self-interested motives of British diplomacy across most of the nineteenth century, people like Richard were indeed probably being too idealistic. Britain possessed

---

230 Émile de Laveleye, *On the Causes of War, and the Means of Reducing their Number* (London: Peace Society 1872); Lubelski-Bernard, *Mouvements pacifistes en Belgique* 1977, 466–99; *Debate* 1873, 41.

231 *Debate* 1873, 35–8.

232 Ibid. 44–5.

little credibility in this area and was unlikely to achieve much success even if it would somehow adopt the peace society's platform into its foreign policy.

Of course, Gladstone had no intention whatsoever of giving in to pacifist demands. He wanted to continue his policy of non-intervention in Europe's many wars, and nothing more. Only continued adherence to this would every year 'add more and more weight to the abstract doctrines' preached by the peace societies. In his reply, Richard emphasised that he did not want to propose anything 'sudden, violent, and extreme'. He merely wanted the government to continue its tentative steps to improve international law. The society's M.P. framed it as a gentle nudge – an 'instruction'. This might have contributed to the curious result of the debate. One sympathetic M.P. had called it up until then 'almost a repetition' of the one from 1849. Indeed, just like Palmerston, Gladstone tried to 'move the previous question', in order to end the debate without a vote on the merits. However, as several papers wrote, the result took everyone, 'and most of all Mr. Richard', by surprise. Close to midnight, the Commons divided. A majority of ten M.P.'s voted against dismissal. The motion itself was therefore accepted without the need for another division.[233]

The London Peace Society was exhilarated. Most of the August edition of the *Herald* was spent on covering every aspect of the vote and its subsequent reception. The British pacifists again analysed it from a quantitative and qualitative perspective. Quantitatively, they again calculated that the votes in favour represented some ten million citizens, which was one third of the country. Qualitatively, most of the 'ayes' had come from large population centres, confirming the society's belief that their strongest base of support came from the 'intelligence and mercantile and commercial power of the country'. Significantly, while most supporters had been Liberals, eight Conservatives had also voted in support of Richard, suggesting it had not been entirely on partisan grounds. While encouraging, cross-partisan support should not be exaggerated, as the 48 other Conservatives present had voted against it.[234]

Assessments in the popular press were more divided. The non-conformist press and certain outlets, like the *Illustrated London News*, reported positively, agreeing that Britain should take steps towards a permanent system of arbitration or increased codification. Other papers were less kind. The

233 Ibid., 46, 48–51 46; HP (August 1873), 281, 283, 290.

234 HP (August 1873), 285–6; Ceadel, *Idealists* 2000, 97–8.

Times remained, as always, sceptical. How much nearer stood Europe today at realising the dream of St. Pierre as opposed to a century ago? At any rate, for it to succeed, Europe would need a much more pronounced sense of unity. Any international court should also have 'force at its command'. While the proposal was not 'wholly removed from the sphere of reason', it was still ahead of its time. The 23rd Protocol had 'utterly failed' to prevent the Franco-German war, and thus would fail every other international law that idealistically tried to run ahead of the march of progress. This was not per se an unsatisfactory analysis for the peace advocates. Even if they still remained relegated to the fringe, it must still have been satisfying to observe their old adversary agreeing that the 'future supremacy of international law' would someday materialise.[235]

The motion's immediate political impact was likewise modest and ambiguous. The queen's official reply corresponded to Gladstone's objections. It affirmed that Britain would continue her standing policy, which was already supportive of arbitration and the rule of international law.[236] No concrete action was taken afterwards, as was of course to be expected. Interestingly, it made a much stronger impression outside British politics. In the autumn of 1873, Richard toured the European continent to encourage similar motions elsewhere. Over the course of his long journey, the pacifist met with sympathetic voices in Belgium, the Netherlands, Germany, Italy, Austria, Hungary and France. His travels were not without success. In the wake of the British motion, the legislatures of Belgium, the Netherlands, Italy and even Sweden – untouched by the international peace movement – adopted similar resolutions.[237]

From this point onwards, it was clear that the arbitration campaign was no longer the sole domain of the London Peace Society. The 1870s have been described as the decade of an 'arbitration craze'. British civil society spawned a host of bodies which campaigned for arbitration independently from the old peace society and its auxiliaries. Like the latter, these were responding to ongoing insecurity on the international scene, as well as the financial costs of the European arms race. However, they were reluctant to call themselves 'peace societies' because their members had little affinity with the absolutist Quaker views dominant in the London Peace Society.

235 HP (August 1873), 287–96.
236 HP (August 1873), 283.
237 Van der Linden, *Peace Movement* 1987, 915; Ceadel, *Idealists* 2000, 97–8.

FIGURE 6.2 Henry Richard's caricature by Spy in Vanity Fair in the 1880s indicated that the British peace movement had become a small, yet established fixture of British political life.

This society had never abandoned its two-tiered membership system, requiring the upper echelons to condemn *all* war.[238]

In a sense, the mushrooming of rival arbitration societies, based on less absolutist grounds, was the conclusion of a gradual development that had begun ever since Cobden's dalliances with the peace movement in the 1840s. Although not yet clear for Richard at the time, the motion of 1873 marked the end of a long hegemonic reign of the London Peace Society in the British peace movement. It would continue to lose ground to other

238 Ceadel, *Idealists* 2000, 87.

organisations over the remainder of the nineteenth century. These included the working-class organisations of William Randal Cremer, mentioned during the introduction of the London Peace Society in a previous chapter. The journal of his first society, the *Arbitrator,* copied the London Peace Society's views during the 1870s. Arbitration was a concept relatively well-known to working men, because of its increasing use in domestic labour disputes in this decade.[239] Mixed-gender bodies like the International Arbitration and Peace Association or the International Arbitration League increasingly outcompeted their grandfather organisation.[240] By the outbreak of World War One, the Quaker-dominated society had lost most of its vigour. The peace society ceased to exist entirely in 1939, thus concluding an era that began with Napoleon and ended with Hitler.[241]

During its most active years, roughly the period between 1843 and 1873, the London Peace Society had through processes of trial and error been able to deploy the language of law and legal argument into the realm of political discussion. Realising that the dogma's of their Quaker faith were unsuited for mass appeal, they advanced an international legal instrument which they believed to be devoid of ulterior political motives. However, no legal argument can be divorced from the politics behind it. The precedents they selected from state practice, be it the mediation of the Sulphur War of 1840 or the *Alabama claims* award, were not as altruistic as peace friends optimistically tended to assume. Like the mixed courts that would be set up in Egypt, they failed to fully appreciate the self-serving motives behind seemingly noble intentions.

If Western state practice widely adopted arbitration in the ending decades of the nineteenth century, it was not necessarily part of some millenarian journey toward the inevitable rise of the international rule of law. Historians have long since problematised the surge of arbitration clauses in the decades leading up to 1914. Anglo-American support for it had never been entirely idealistic. Admittedly, a sense of idealism certainly animated many of its proponents. However, the concept of arbitration espoused by British and American diplomats was one dominated by the common law, and was also considered a means to consolidate similar strategic interests. People like Cremer and Burritt shared with politicians an underlying assumption that the Anglo-American 'race' had a duty to 'civilise' the world

239 The Arbitrator (special edition, no. 18), 2–14.

240 Cooper, *Patriotic Pacifism* 1991, 213; Ceadel, *Idealists* 2000, 132–6, 151–86.

241 Ceadel, *Idealists* 2000, 193–5.

according to the Protestant model.[242] It was rather striking, for instance, that even during the revival of interest in arbitration following the *Alabama claims,* the English-speaking peace societies had still not come across the by then longstanding South-American practice of inscribing a *'clause compromissoire'* into regional treaties. Virtually no mention of it could be found in either the *Advocate,* the *Herald,* or any other journal. While this was perhaps excusable in the 1840s, when accurate news on international affairs was still relatively hard to find, especially about the more 'peripheral' areas, this neglect had a half-life. By the 1870s, South American states had been using modes of arbitration for almost fifty years; almost every arbitration clause up to 1868 involved a South American state.[243] The total ignorance of the Anglo-American peace movement of this wealth of state practice by as late as 1873 could only be ascribed to a form of ingrained cultural myopia in which Britain and the United States stood as the centre of the 'civilised world'.

As limited in geographical or cultural scope as the institutional peace movement had long been, the late 1860s and early 1870s nonetheless featured a remarkable expansion in one area: the European continent. From 1867 onwards, the Anglo-American peace societies were, for the first time, joined by a viable and fully autonomous institutionalised peace movement in Europe itself.

---

242 Justina Uriburu, 'Imperialism through Adjudication in Latin America'. *Leiden Journal of International Law* 36(1) (2023), 212–3.

243 Steven Harris, 'The Global Construction of International Law in the Nineteenth Century: The Case of Arbitration'. *Journal of World History* 27(2) (2016), 309–11.

CHAPTER 7

Rise of a European Movement (1867–1873)

> 'Your work is the culmination of all the American Peace Society has tried to do for thirty years.'
>
> ELIHU BURRITT (1873)

1 The Luxembourg Crisis

In the spring of 1867, citizens in France, Germany and the Netherlands found themselves involved in a grave diplomatic crisis. Many feared that they were standing on the brink of war. Its immediate cause was the conflict between Napoleon III and the Prussian chancellor Otto von Bismarck. The latter had been successfully carrying his policy of *Blut und Eisen* to neighbouring states. In 1864, he had avenged the Prussian defeat against the Danes of the 1850s, by annexing the prized provinces of Schleswig and Holstein. Two years later, in 1866, the combination of superior manoeuvring and bolt-action rifles – the first of their kind to be employed en masse – had crushed Austria's army in the decisive battle of Königgrätz. Few observers had expected the Austrian empire to be defeated so easily. In France, meanwhile, there was great frustration about the Mexican intervention, which had recently ended in a humiliating failure. The European balance of power seemed to be shifting.[1]

Buoyed partly by public opinion, and partly by his own ambitions, the French emperor aspired to buy the Grand Duchy of Luxembourg from the Dutch king. The Duchy had been allocated to William III's grandfather at the Congress of Vienna. However, the territory had come with a price. Luxembourg, although held in personal union with the Dutch, was formally a

1 Jörg Ulbert, 'France and German Dualism, 1756–1871', in Carine Germond & Henning Türk (eds.), *A History of Franco-German Relations in Europe. From "Hereditary Enemies" to Partners* (Basingstoke: Palgrave Macmillan 2008), 43–5; Edward Shawcross, *France, Mexico and Informal Empire in Latin America, 1820–1867. Equilibrium in the New World* (Basingstoke: Palgrave Macmillan 2018), 197–236.

 | DOI:10.1163/9789004733688_009

part of the German Confederation. This put a heavy burden on the Netherlands, which was thus forced play some part in the Confederation's politics. The Dutch citizenry, however, preferred that their state stayed aloof from power politics after 1839. Their king was therefore more than happy to consider Napoleon's offer to take the controversial territory off his hands for a hefty sum. At first, Prussia seemed willing to play along. The German Confederation was dissolved after the Austrian war and Luxembourg was not incorporated into the new North German Confederation. Bismarck indicated that he could tolerate it, if it was presented as a *fait accompli* for the public, before the Prussian *Landtag* convened.

Unfortunately, the plan was leaked. Mere days before the treaty was to be signed, the German states were in uproar. The outburst of German nationalism was so strong that Bismarck probably would not have been able to oppose it, even if he had wanted to. After all, Luxembourg city was one giant fortress city, perched on a strategic position between France and Germany. It frustrated a potential attack on France through Belgium, but facilitated French offensives on Germany. At the time, the fortress was manned by a Prussian garrison. In both France and the German states, parts of public opinion vocally cried for war. The Prussian minister in the Hague let it be known in the beginning of April that signing the sale of Luxembourg meant signing a declaration of war.[2]

The diplomatic solution that was eventually achieved attained some brief notoriety in international law. Like they had done during some previous crises, the European great powers convened together in a multilateral diplomatic assembly. The London conference of 1867 led to the Treaty of London of 11 May 1867, which neutralised the disputed territory. From a legal point of view, the document was not uncontroversial. The first article spoke of a 'collective guarantee', rather than an individual one. Back in 1839, Palmerston had legally committed Britain to defend Belgium against any threats to the country's sovereignty. However, in 1867, both the prime minister and the foreign secretary claimed that the provision's phrasing only triggered an obligation to defend Luxembourg upon the concert of *all* signatory states. This interpretation effectively rendered it, in the foreign secretary's words, more of a 'moral guarantee' than a legal one. In congruence with the desire of many Britons, including not least the London Peace Society, the British

2 Van der Linden, *Peace Movement* 1987, 639; Amry Vandenbosch, *Dutch Foreign Policy since 1815. A Study in Small Power Politics* (The Hague: Nijhoff 1959), 57–62; Geoffrey Hicks, '"Appeasement" or consistent Conservatism? British Foreign Policy, Party Politics, and the Guarantees of 1867 and 1939'. *Historical Research* 84(225) (2011), 520.

cabinet was unwilling to incur more legal obligations on the Continent that might inadvertently drag the country into an armed intervention.[3]

The London Peace Society did not report on this disputable, and somewhat cynical, interpretation of the treaty. Rather, the society praised that the powers had convened the conference before, instead of after any war, which the peace friends had always been pressing for. At the eve of the conference, the Committee presented a memorial to the foreign secretary. Their secretary, Henry Richard, was especially pleased that Britain had invoked the 23rd Protocol of the Treaty of Paris in the run-up to the meeting. Nonetheless, he used the opportunity to press upon the only means that could address the causes, rather than the symptoms of the 'deep-rooted and deadly malady' that afflicted Europe. What was needed most of all, was disarmament and the establishment of a 'system of international law'. Europe needed an 'international tribunal' to combat the 'anarchy' triggered by the absence of international law worthy of the name. The language already resembled that of his motion of 1873.[4]

While upsetting the peace friends of Britain, the Luxembourg Crisis exercised a much more longer-lasting impact on the other side of the Channel. For decades, the British peace advocates had been disappointed in the lack of European involvement in their cause. The Genevan and Parisian peace societies had both proven unviable and were little noticed outside of their immediate environment. The same had rang true for the short-lived societies set up by their agent in Belgium, or the German peace society that had existed for a few months after the 1850 Frankfurt peace congress.[5] The only organisation worthy of the name was the *Ligue* of Edmond Potonié-Pierre, but this league also was mostly a fringe affair.[6] However, during his next visit to Paris that same year, Richard marvelled at the amount of pacifist literature he could find in bookshops. These works were not just translations of Anglo-American texts, as had up until then often been the

3 Hicks, 'Guarantees of 1867 and 1939' 2011, 517–21; Mowat, R.B. (ed.), *Select Treaties and Documents to Illustrate the Development of the Modern European States System. 1815–1916* (Oxford: Clarendon 1916), 41–4.

4 HP (June 1867), 208, 210–1; HP (August 1867), 241.

5 Lubelski-Bernard. *Mouvements pacifistes en Belgique* 1977, 325–34; The *Königsberger Friedensverein* was shut down by the Prussian police within the year. Its organ was a small annex to a local newspaper. The society endorsed the resolutions of the peace congresses. Van der Linden, *Peace Movement* 1987, 345–8; Carl Ludwig Siemering, *Von der ersten deutschen Friedensgesellschaft zu Königsberg i. Pr., 1850–1851* (Frankfurt: Knauer, 1909).

6 See chapter 4.

NURSE AND BABY.

NURSE HOLLAND (*dandling* BABY LUXEMBURG). "It's no use, Jentlemans: she vill not go to no vone." (*See Telegrams.*)

FIGURE 7.1 An American cartoon mocking Franco-German haggling over little Luxembourg.

case, but published by domestic peace societies. Perhaps the French were not the incorrigible warmongers that Anglo-American prejudice had long popularly portrayed them as.[7]

7 HP (July 1867), 226–8.

Three such societies saw the light of day in the second half of 1867. The first two were based within France proper. One of them suffered the same fate as the German one of the 1850s. The *Union de la paix,* established by masonic lodges in the Norman town of Le Havre, was a little too outspoken, and quickly caught the attention of the imperial police. It was harassed and subjected to numerous restrictions. The organisation barely lasted two years. The other peace society proved itself more skilful at evading the restrictions on speech and assembly imposed by the Second Empire. Although its final years were known as the 'liberal' empire, the experiment in Le Havre showed that pacifists still had to tread carefully if they wanted to steer clear of trouble. This peace society was established in Paris, and counted among its members well-respected economists, lawyers, bankers and pastors. Their leader was Frédéric Passy (1822–1912), whose stature as a pacifist leader eventually surpassed that of even Henry Richard. In 1901, Passy would win the first Nobel Peace Prize, along with Henri Dunant of the Red Cross movement. His first organisation was initially called the *Ligue internationale et permanente de la paix.* After the Franco-German War, it renamed itself to the *Société française des amis de la paix* – translated as the French Peace Society later on in this chapter.[8]

The name-change of Passy's society was directly provoked by the third organisation to emerge out of the Luxembourg Crisis. This was the notorious *Ligue internationale de la paix et de la liberté.* Although its name was incredibly similar to Passy's league – many even at the time could not keep them apart – its ideology and composition was in many ways significantly different. This peace league was not located in France, despite many of its founders having the French nationality. More than any other peace society of the mid-nineteenth century, the 'league of peace and liberty' was truly international in its aspirations and membership. In its early years, it consisted of a highly diverse blend of exiled European republicans, liberals, nationalists, moderate socialists, anarchists, and even some women. It was led by French republican *proscrits,* who hated Napoleon III with a passion, and by extension every other crowned head of Europe. Unlike Passy or Richard, but similar to many of the European pacifists previously discussed, like Francisque Bouvet or Louis Bara, the Genevan-based league did not unconditionally believe in *si vis pacem, para pacem.* Their creed was *si vis pacem,*

8 Cooper, *Patriotic Pacifism* 1991, 33–36, 213–214; Van der Linden, *Peace Movement* 1987, 633–673.

para libertatem. For them, peace was inseparably intertwined with domestic political and socio-economic questions.[9]

In spite of their different ideological underpinnings and different memberships, all three European peace societies almost immediately adopted the course of 'peace through law'. All three shared the longstanding European distrust of arbitrations conducted without a positive code. This had already been the chief critique levelled by continental delegates during the peace congresses of the 1840s.[10] While no organisation rejected arbitration as conceptualised by the London Peace Society outright, they were far more enthusiastic about the proposal launched by the American Peace Society in the summer of 1873 to organise an international law conference in Brussels later that year. Both Passy and Lemonnier shared the American belief that public opinion would be increasingly able to evolve international law into a more just and pacific direction. The main point of contention between the two organisations was not that international law as it stood was rather ineffective in preventing war or upholding the sanctity of treaties. On the contrary, they took this observation as their premise.

Rather, all three organisations differed on whether the contemporary international political system could accommodate their campaign. Passy held that existing governments, whether democratic or not, would be receptive to his 'scientific' peace campaign, based on law and political economy. This represented the longstanding views of the Anglo-American peace societies, with whom Passy easily cooperated. The other two organisations were more sceptical. The *Union de la paix* preferred some unofficial 'tribunal' of international jurisconsults, which would devise a draft code and act as a kind of shadow international court. A committee of jurists had to issue unofficial judgments on political crises. This 'tribunal' was to be the organ of international public opinion. The Genevan League did not seek an unofficial course. Their recommendations had to be implemented by governments, but not the ones currently existing. Drawing heavily from Immanuel Kant's *Zum Ewigen Frieden* and the Jacobin legacy of the original French Revolution, Lemonnier was convinced that only a European federation of republican states, domestically guaranteeing a catalogue of natural rights, had a chance of revolutionising international law and inaugurating pacific

9 At the time of writing, the Wikipedia entry for the *Ligue de la paix et de la liberté* claimed it was founded by Frédéric Passy. Amusingly, it thus shared in the same confusion as that of the nineteenth century. Cooper, *Patriotic Pacifism* 1991, 36–43; Van der Linden, *Peace Movement* 1987, 675–816.

10 See chapter 4.

international relations. This viewpoint stood at the centre of the League's 1873 conference, wholly devoted to the reform of international law through the great dream of *les États-unis d'Europe.*

These new initiatives were not by themselves revolutionary, but merely built on the legalist project that had been debated and practiced, to various degrees of sophistication, by the international peace movement throughout most of its nineteenth century history.

1.1 The *Union de la paix*

The most short-lived French peace society to emerge out of the Luxembourg Crisis was the *Union de la Paix.* It had been founded by the masonic lodges of the provincial port town of Le Havre, on the Channel's coastline. The Peace Union's leading man was Félix Santallier (1830–1885). Santallier at the time edited the *Journal du Havre,* a local democratic newspaper. A year before the Luxembourg Crisis, he wrote an essay on peace which he read before his lodge.[11] Up until then, freemasonry had not been expressly involved in the peace movement. However, continental-European freemasonry, which was much more anticlerical and rationalistic than contemporary British freemasonry, shared many of the same ideals as the peace movement. So-called 'Latin' freemasonry, as it was practiced in France and Belgium, had a decidedly cosmopolitan tinge to it. Its adherents believed in universal brotherhood, irrespective of nationality or religion. While not a formal part of the peace movement, peace societies and masonic lodges recruited largely from the same pool of liberally inclined urban upper-middle-classes. Several of the European peace friends discussed up until now belonged to a lodge, including inter alia Louis Bara, Charles Potvin and Edmond Potonié.[12]

During the two years in which the Peace Union was allowed to exist by the authorities, albeit under constant surveillance and with numerous restrictions, it managed to recruit some 1,500 supporters. Most came from masonic lodges.[13] Contrary to what has been written by the peace historian

11 Van der Linden, *Peace Movement* 1987, 631–2.

12 Ibid., 632; Lubelski-Bernard, Nadine. 'Freemasonry and Peace in Europe, 1867–1914', in Charles Chatfield and Peter van den Dungen (eds.), *Peace Movements and Political Cultures* (Knoxville: University of Tennessee Press 1988), 82–3; Van der Linden, *Peace Movement* 1987, 632. See chapters 4 and 5.

13 Cooper, *Patriotic Pacifism* 1991, 33; Van der Linden, *Peace Movement* 1987, 634; *Union de la paix entre tous les peuples civilisés. Premier bulletin.* (Le Havre: Cazavan 1867), 7; *Union de la paix entre tous les peuples civilisés. Deuxième bulletin* (Le Havre: Leclerc

Sandi Cooper, Santallier's society was not isolated from the rest of the peace movement, neither in France nor elsewhere.[14] Its honorary members included nearly all leading peace friends of the day, such as Chevalier, Garnier, Potonié, Visschers, Richard and Sumner. Alfred Love's Universal Peace Union from the distant United States was abundantly represented. Santallier was on equally friendly terms with Passy's league in Paris. The Peace Union even received a 'generous donation' from the London Peace Society. Unfortunately, it was not to be. Santallier and his adherents had been too outspoken about French foreign policy. Somewhere in 1869 or early 1870, the authorities ordered him to cease all propaganda. The freemason grudgingly complied.[15]

1.1.1 Early French Support for Non-Governmental Codification

The legal reform scheme defended by Santallier's Peace Union was sketched out in a small number of pamphlets and bulletins. Further details could be found in the pages of the British *Herald,* which, as always, dutifully reported on every piece of pacifist activity it could discover. From these sources, it appeared that Santallier's project took a similar direction as Bara, Kaufmann, Ferrer and Burritt. Inspired by an article from an English newspaper, reprinted in a recent issue of the *Herald,* Santallier got enamoured by the idea of a 'European scientific authority' that would codify international law. In his eyes, this was the only feasible route towards international justice. Because international law was not formally set by an international legislator, nor by international courts of law, it had to find its guarantees in 'moral influence'. Masonic lodge were to gather adhesions for the Peace Union by circulating its pamphlets to other lodges and sympathetic individuals of influence. Once this Union was sufficiently established, a central committee was to invite the cooperation of the most morally upright and skilled international lawyers in the world. These lawyers had to codify 'the most useful customs favourable to the peaceful development of universal progress'. This

1868), 1; *Union de la paix entre tous les peuples civilisés. Troisième bulletin* (Le Havre: Santallier 1869), 14.

14 Cooper, *Patriotic Pacifism* 1991, 33.

15 Van der Linden, *Peace Movement* 1987, 638; *Union de la paix. Troisième bulletin* 1869, 2; Lévy-Guénot, 'Autour de Félix Santallier. Une croisade pacifiste à la veille de 1870'. *La révolution de 1848 et les révolutions du XIXe siècle* 19(93) (1922), 206.

'international tribunal' was also to formulate legal opinions about any ongoing international disputes and armed conflicts.[16]

Santallier's naturalistic conception of legal 'science' strongly informed his assessment of the viability of what otherwise appeared an ambitious project. He laid it out in the open in his 'appeal' to jurists. According to the Peace Union, social laws were similar to the laws of physics, in the sense that they were not created, but 'discovered'. Any 'true law' inherently contained its value, and only had to be formulated well enough to convince any reasonable person. Therefore, 'all useful and advantageous legislation' had been deducted from pre-existing customs which had proven to foster 'harmonious' social relations. Santallier pointed to the medieval trade customs that had sprung from bottom-up and had inspired subsequent domestic codifications.[17] Evidently, this reasoning was much more in the vein of the older pragmatic naturalism espoused by late eighteenth century and early nineteenth century lawyers, rather than the radical positivism that was slowly emerging in the latter decades of the century. While Santallier was positivistic to the extent that his international law was to be gotten from empirical observation, it was becoming increasingly disputed that there existed some eternally valid norms that transcended political subjectivity.[18] Inside the peace movement, of course, people were generally not inclined to accept the amorality that the premisses of a strict positivism logically implied. Essentially, Santallier operated in the same framework as Louis Bara twenty years earlier.

Proceeding in a similar vein as the Belgian author and the upcoming international law societies, the Peace Union did not seek to set up an official government body. The international tribunal had to function as a focal point for public opinion. It was to provide the 'concentration of moral forces' necessary to force governments to act otherwise. This had been the crucial mistake of all previous pacification schemes. The application of 'the judiciary principle to political conflicts' had invariably ended in failure across history. The Amphyctionic League had collapsed in on itself. The medieval papacy had lost its authority on account of religious dogmatism. The plans of Henri IV and Saint-Pierre had been based on the 'concert of governments'. However, this was all counter-productive. Santallier was convinced

16 *Union de la paix. Premier bulletin* 1867, 1, 10–1; Félix Santallier, *L'union de la paix entre tous les peuples civilisés. Proposition adressée à la loge l'Aménité, au Havre* (Le Havre: unknown publisher 1867); HP (August 1867), 237–8; HP (September 1867), 248–9, 251–4.

17 *Union de la paix. Premier bulletin* 1867, 8.

18 Santallier, *Proposition* 1867, 12–3; Neff, *Justice* 2014, 217–9; 225.

that any intergovernmental effort could only lead to 'transitory and fragile' political constructions, which would either quickly disintegrate or turn into an empire of their most powerful member.[19] His pessimism was understandable, considering he was being overtly hindered by the Bonapartist repression apparatus and had experienced the war scares produced by *Realpolitik*.

The London Peace Society was not convinced, despite their overall sympathy for the peace society in Le Havre. The French freemason had urged the British peace societies to adopt his strategy. He also heavily implied that the organised peace movement had accomplished little because of its focus on governments.[20] Santallier did not appear to have been particularly well-informed about the peace movement, as anyone reasonably acquainted with the Anglo-American peace societies would have known that this was simply untrue. Henry Richard corrected him that the peace societies had from the very beginning addressed themselves first and foremost to the people. Only after public opinion had shifted in the right direction would *'laws* and *institutions'* change, the British pacifist wrote back. He added that the peace society often addressed governments for purely strategic reasons. In many cases, 'a memorial to the sovereign or a minister' was the only way to get the society into the press. Richard argued that the British constitution was better suited for 'double action' than elsewhere in Europe, but that political agitation should nonetheless always be directed *'towards'* the government, rather than 'apart from it'.[21] The answer was fully in line with Richard's longstanding concern about the respectability of the peace movement. Already during the congresses of the 1840s had he been anxious to give a pragmatic and inoffensive colouring to these meetings. Pacifists needed to operate in existing institutional environments and keep a safe distance away from revolutionary politics.[22]

Ultimately, the most interesting aspect of Santallier's Peace Union, from a legal point of view, rested in its resemblance to other projects. Here was yet another scheme to introduce a 'legal conscience' to the world, to borrow the celebrated phrase from the *Institut de droit international*. Like the schemes that had preceded it, the freemasons of Le Havre sought to recruit legal specialists into their cause, in order to bolster the legitimacy of their arguments. The main difference with the projects of Bara, Kaufmann, Black, or Ferrer rested in the fact that for the first time it had been given an

19 Santallier, *Proposition* 1867, 8–9; HP (September 1867), 251–2.
20 HP (September 1867), 252–4.
21 HP (October 1867), 262–3.
22 See chapter 5.

institutional implementation. While these men had written in the capacity of mere individuals, the Peace Union was a moderately sized and relatively well-connected organisation. Unfortunately, it operated under hostile domestic political conditions. The project would only be successfully realised six years later, by the 1873 international law conference held in neutral and liberal Belgium. Even then, it required the cooperation of multiple peace societies. The one in Le Havre was never reconstituted after the fall of Napoleon III. Its members, including Santallier, had instead joined the one that did manage to survive its infancy: the *Ligue internationale et permanente de la paix,* headed by Frédéric Passy.

1.2 The *Ligue internationale et permanente de la paix*

In April 1867, as France and Prussia seemed to be tethering on the brink of war, a handful of voices in France cautioned against the sabre-rattling they were hearing all around them. They printed their views in *Le Temps,* one of the country's most influential liberal newspapers. The paper published a series of articles criticising the government for its handling of the Luxembourg affair. They included a public letter written by the noted political economist Frédéric Passy, who invited readers to help found a permanent peace league. Passy directed his call to 'forward-looking politicians' who knew 'not to play with fire', economists and industrialists, and every other pacifically inclined Christian.[23] Somewhat to the surprise even of the paper's own editor, Passy's call proved very successful. Those who signed up included industrialists like Jean Dollfus and Émile Peugeot, a financier like François Arlès-Dufour, and well-known clergymen from various denominations. Catholics were represented by Alphonse Gratry, a theologian holding the seat of Voltaire in the *Académie française,* and Charles Loyson, better known as *Père Hyacinthe,* who had made a name for himself as a charismatic preacher at the Notre Dame cathedral. They were joined by the Protestant pastor Joseph-Martin Paschoud, and even the grand rabbi of Paris. From abroad came support by people like Gustave de Molinari, Émile de Laveleye, Auguste Visschers, and – naturally – Richard and the London Peace Society.[24]

The League's most important founder was Frédéric Passy, one of the most famous pacifists of the nineteenth century. In terms of stature, Passy belonged into the same category as Noah Worcester, William Ladd, Elihu

23 *Le Temps* (11 April 1867), 1; *Le Temps* (25 April 1867), 1–2; *Le Temps* (26 April 1867), 1–2: *Le Temps* (27 April 1867), 1–2.

24 Cooper, *Patriotic Pacifism* 1991, 33–4.

Burritt, Richard Cobden and Henry Richard. It is telling of the contemporary obscurity of the first international peace movement that Passy has not remained a household name outside of specialist circles.[25]

The life story of Frédéric Passy paints a portrait of a pragmatic and moderate liberal, who believed that pacifism only stood a chance if it worked together with established governments. This required pacifists to frame their arguments in a language that was understandable to politicians and everyone else sceptical of grand utopianism: law and political economy. He was born into a well-to-do family of public servants. His father had served under Napoleon in Waterloo. Many of his family members had likewise been officers in the First Empire. Passy himself mused in old age that he might easily have become ensnared by militarism himself, if it were not for the grimly realistic war stories relayed in his extended family. His granduncle kept a portrait of the Haitian revolutionary leader Toussaint Louverture in his house, despite having fought against him. In his twenties, the French invasion of Algeria scandalised Passy. He began to wonder who was right: 'the supposedly inferior races, who only wanted to live in peace in their own land, or we, who wished to bring them civilisation along with their servitude'. It all undoubtedly informed the League's anticolonialism, discussed later on.[26]

Despite having studied law, Passy quickly grew more interested in political economy. He published profusely, eventually being elected into the *Académie des sciences morales et politiques*. He was influenced in particular by the ideas of Frédéric Bastiat. As we have seen in a previous chapter, Bastiat favoured absolute economic freedom. Free trade stimulated commercial expansion, brought prosperity, and stimulated international understanding. Passy agreed to such an extent with his idol that, very often, his arguments could be traced back directly to Bastiat.[27] Passy was not foolish enough to think that economic inequality was unrelated to the peace question. Rather, he simply reversed the order: first point on the agenda should be the

---

25 Michael Clinton, 'Frédéric Passy: Patriotic Pacifist'. *Journal of Historical Biography* 2 (autumn 2007) (2007), 35–9, 55; Alain Alcouffe and Fanny Coulomb, 'Pacifism of the French Liberals in the late 19th and early 20th Centuries. Frédéric Passy and Léon Walras, Candidates for the Nobel Peace Prize', in *18th ESHET Conference – Liberalisms: perspectives and debates in the history of economic thought, The European Society for the History of Economic Thought (ESHET), May 2014, Lausanne, Switzerland,* available at: hal.archives-ouvertes.fr/hal-02051636.

26 See more infra. Frédéric Passy, *Pour la paix. Notes et documents* (Paris: Charpentier 1909), 1–6.

27 Alcouffe & Coulomb, 'Passy' 2014, 15–6; Passy, *Paix* 1909, 3–9.

reduction of military expenditure. This paved the way to further liberalisations of the economy, which would eventually raise the standard of living to such an extent that the social question would automatically resolve itself. Of course not everyone agreed, especially the later socialist factions of the peace movement. The early twentieth-century French socialist Jean Jaurès – a monumental pacifist in his own right – criticised Passy's liberal-economic orthodoxies.[28]

Passy's interpretation of pacifism aligned well with the positions of the London Peace Society. He did not actively participate in any of the peace congresses. His first involvement was with Edmond Potonié in the 1850s, when they established a bilingual Anglo-French journal. The experiment was a failure, not least due to disagreements with the far more socially-feeling Potonié.[29] Although Passy was himself a republican who welcomed the rise of the Third Republic, he was perfectly willing to work with more authoritarian governments. Like the Anglo-American peace societies, Passy heavily disapproved of the Genevan League of peace and liberty. The Parisian and Genevan peace friends only slowly started to see more eye to eye after the new republic had been founded, and the League of Geneva had begun to moderate its tone. By contrast, Passy and Richard immediately got along extremely well with each other. The secretary of the London Peace Society was present at the first annual assembly of the Parisian League.[30] Both men shared the same legalistic sensibilities, believing that the only path to success was through government, and more specifically parliament.

After the war, there was a brief risk for a potential rift, when the visit of Miles, the secretary of the American Peace Society, forced the League to choose which plan to support: codification, as asked by Miles, or arbitration, as brought to Parliament by Richard. While the League's members inclined towards Miles's international law project, arbitration as such was not rejected. Indeed, when Passy's society changed names for a third time, in 1891, it renamed itself to the *Société française pour l'arbitrage entre nations*. The peace society founded by Passy ultimately lasted until 1948.[31] The most

28 Alcouffe & Coulomb, 'Passy' 2014, 18; Cooper, Sandi. 'Pacifism in France, 1889–1914: International Peace as a Human Right'. *French Historical Studies* 17(2) (1991), 359–86.

29 Clinton, 'Passy' 2007, 39.

30 *Première assemblée générale. 8 juin 1868* (Paris: Guillaumin 1868), 77–7; *Deuxième assemblée générale. 21 juin 1869* (Paris: Guillaumin 1869), 56.

31 It merged with the *Association de la paix par le droit* in 1889, one of the many French peace societies established after 1873. Clinton, 'Passy' 2007, 48; Cooper, *Patriotic Pacifism* 1991, 214.

important achievement of Passy in the peace cause was his role, along with William Randal Cremer, in setting up the Interparliamentary Union in 1889, an organisation associated with eight Nobel Peace Prize laureates. The Interparliamentary Union, which originally intended to promote arbitration and the rule of international law, has played a significant part in the establishment of the Permanent Court of Arbitration ten years later, in 1899.[32]

Despite Passy's support for parliamentary means towards international legal reform, the *Ligue* could hardly be regarded as a mass organisation. While Passy ideologically strove towards a society with a relatively broad basis of moderate liberals, it remained a small club. By 1869, the Parisian League reported it had about six hundred members, a figure that in all likelihood dropped after the Franco-German War. This was in the first place a conscious decision of its founders. It was clearly intended for philanthropists. Founders had to pay one hundred francs, and associate members five francs.[33] As was the case for most peace societies, this was much too steep for the lower-middle-classes and the working classes, who made up the bulk of European society.

Apart from his own elitism, the potential for expansion of Passy's league was hindered by domestic realities. Legally, freedom of speech and of assembly were very restricted under the Second Empire. When Henry Richard attempted to hold another peace conference in Paris in 1867, on the occasion of the *Exposition universelle,* similar to the 1851 conference held during the Great Exhibition, he was denied permission. Likewise, Passy's League was forbidden to deliver public lectures. Petitions were confiscated. In the spring of 1868, the law got somewhat liberalised, but public assemblies remained barred from discussing any political and religious issues. The League even had to communicate the programme and list of speakers for its first conference, held in June 1868, to the police in advance.[34] All of these restrictions disappeared with the coming of the Third Republic, but legal barriers were not the only ones afflicting French pacifism.

Socially, organised pacifism faced the same issues in France like elsewhere. Many early subscribers left because of political disagreements with other members. Outside of the organisation, followers of Joseph de Maistre considered pacifism unnatural. Although de Maistre's conservatism was not

32 Cooper, *Patriotic Pacifism* 1991, 85–7; Zlatko Šabič, 'Building Democratic and Responsible Global Governance: The Role of International Parliamentary Institutions'. *Parliamentary Affairs* 61(2) (2008), 259, 263.

33 Cooper, *Patriotic Pacifism* 1991, 34.

34 Van der Linden, *Peace Movement* 1987, 656.

mainstream either in French society, pacifism and its overall connotations with progressist thought were certainly not uncontroversial in many circles. *Père* Hyacinthe got into trouble with his bishop because of his involvement in the League. He had made the mistake of preaching for oecumenism, while every proper Catholic should know, his superior lectured him, that there existed no salvation outside of the Church. Hyacinthe ended up leaving his order after a public letter attacking Catholic dogma's, which got him excommunicated.[35] Abroad, the Genevan League's militant republicanism did not help either to make pacifism come across as respectable, especially as the two peace leagues had almost indistinguishable names.

Once the Franco-German War erupted in the summer of 1870, the League faced a similar backlash as the London Peace Society had endured during the Crimean War, or the American Peace Society during the Civil War. Like the Americans just a few years earlier, the League was supportive of the war effort, albeit only after Napoleon III had been captured at the battle of Sedan, thus ending the Second Empire. Passy was not in Paris during the famous siege and the Commune, and the League did little beyond sending ineffectual statements to Wilhelm I and his consort.[36] After the armistice, resentment over the lost provinces of Alsace and Lorraine sore high, meaning that pacifism risked being associated with defeatism. To violent revanchism, Passy opposed so-called 'legal revanchism'. Friends of peace were no less patriotic than any other Frenchman, Passy and his bystanders argued, and would restore the prestige of *la patrie* by having it propose great reforms of international law.[37]

Despite these obstacles, the League managed to support a more or less continuous peace campaign from 1867 onwards. The peace movement had finally found firm footing in France. Its legalist bent was discernible from the very beginning. Initially, the League had no official programme in the way that the Peace Union of Le Havre had. Rather, it expressed a diversity of legal reform ideas through its various publications. The League produced two types of propaganda.

First came the literature published by the organisation itself. From the beginning of 1868 onwards, a so-called *'Bibliothèque de la paix'* saw the light of day. Unlike the propaganda of the Anglo-American peace societies, which had become more variegated by then, it consisted of a series of tracts written exclusively for an educated audience. Its contents were diverse.

---

35 Van der Linden, *Peace Movement* 1987, 651–3.

36 BSAP (January 1872), 22–28; Passy, *Paix* 1909, 39–60.

37 See infra.

One was a compilation of anti-war quotes from various historical authorities, called *Guerre à la guerre*.[38] Another was penned by a doctor and elaborated on the many diseases caused by military campaigns.[39] One of the most popular texts was the first in the series: *Guerres contemporaines*, a statistical overview of the size of Europe's armies and the annual expenses they engendered. It was extensively commented on by the London Peace Society, and translated into English.[40] Others contained, among other things, speeches by members of the League, including the proceedings of its two pre-war conferences. The series ended in 1872. After the war, it was replaced by a regular *bulletin* and an *almanach*.[41]

Another source of legal argument was unleashed through – yet again – an essay concours. In 1869, the League offered up the substantial sum of 5,000 francs for the best essay on *Le crime de la guerre*. It had been the brainchild of the aforementioned Émile Peugeot, who donated the first 500 francs out of his own deep pockets. The jury consisted of Passy, joined by Édouard de Laboulaye (1811–1883), and Jules Simon (1814–1896). Originally intended for January 1870, the war naturally delayed the whole plan. The jury report was only published in 1872. By then, Simon has also been replaced by Denis-Dominique Farjasse (1801–1890). This act made the entire jury consist of trained jurists. De Laboulaye was a professor of comparative law at the *Collège de France*, with longstanding pacifist sympathies. Fascinated by the United States, he had translated the works of Channing, one of the founders of the Massachusetts Peace Society. This same man had also proposed the idea of gifting a monument to the American republic, eventually realised as the Statue of Liberty. The third jury member, Farjasse, was another member of the League. In 1873, he translated the book of Seebohm, discussed in the previous chapter, into French, with a foreword by Passy.[42] All in all, forty *mémoires* were sent in from across Europe. One even came in from Sweden. The essay by Alfred Love from the faraway Universal Peace Union arrived too late, and has thus far remained untraceable.[43]

---

38 A. Larrieu, *Guerre à la guerre* (Paris: Guillaumin 1868).

39 F. Guilhaumon, *La guerre et les épidémies. D'après les mémoires de la société des sciences médicales de Metz* (Paris: Guillaumin 1868).

40 Paul Leroy-Beaulieu, *Recherches économiques, historiques et statistiques sur les guerres contemporaines (1853–1866)* (Paris: Lacroix, Verboeckhoven, et compagnie 1869); Paul Leroy-Beaulieu, *Contemporary Wars (1853–1866). Statistical Researches respecting the Loss of Men and Money involved in Them* (London: London Peace Society 1869).

41 Van der Linden, *Peace Movement* 1987, 657.

42 Seebohm, *Réforme* 1873.

43 BSAP (February 1872), 1–46.

The laureates selected by this jury reflected the League's legalist sensibilities. Three authors received first prize, worth a 1,000 francs. All were published around 1872, accompanied by a short foreword by Passy. The first was Léon Henry, his book entitled *Le crime international.* The second was Eugène Goblèt d'Alviella (1846–1925), author of *Désarmer ou déchoir.* Both were trained jurists. Henry served as a judge in Niort, a provincial town in the east of the country. Goblet d'Alviella was Belgian, and was still in university. He reportedly wrote his essay between two exams. The printed edition of his work was greatly expanded, and influenced by the Franco-German War and the books by Seebohm and Bara, which had appeared in the meantime.[44] The third winning book, *Le crime de la guerre dénoncé à l'humanité,* came from Henri Dupasquier (1815–1875), a Swiss manufacturer and an early member of the League. Only Dupasquier did not have a law degree. His book was the only one not to focus on legal issues.[45] Three other works did not receive a prize, but were published nonetheless, several of them equally with forewords by Passy.[46] This appeared to have been a chosen tactic of the leader of the Parisian League, as he wrote such forewords for many other books on the peace question in the early 1870s, otherwise unconnected to the essay contest. Some of these also engaged with issues of international law.

Taken all together, these publications explored many of the legal issues which had been interesting the international peace movement for decades. The first viable French peace society did not operate in a vacuum, but built on the models handed down to them from elsewhere and from France's pre-existing investigations into the peace question. Like the Anglo-American peace societies, the peace League of Paris debated how the moral perfection of natural law could be translated into a positive code. What institutions would be able to achieve this? Such debates were vitally important, because their answers would determine not only the internal cohesion of the international peace movement, but also the success of the

44 Léon Henry, *Le crime international* (Paris: Larose 1872); Eugène Goblet d'Alviella, *Désarmer ou déchoir. Essai sur les relations internationales* (Paris: Guillaumin 1872); Fernand Vanlangenhove, 'GOBLET D'ALVIELLA (Eugène-Félicien-Albert, comte)', in *Biographie nationale de Belgique*, vol. XLI, Supplément, Tome III (Bruxelles: Bruylant 1979), 359–62; Van der Linden, *Peace Movement* 1987, 567–8.

45 Henri Dupasquier, *Le crime de la guerre dénoncé à l'humanité* (Paris: Guillaumin 1873); Van der Linden, *Peace Movement* 1987, 658.

46 Michel-Édouard Laporte, *L'Alscace reconquise* (Paris: Franklin 1873); Henri Dumesnil, *La guerre. Étude philosophique* (Paris: Guillaumin 1872); M.L. Mézières, *De la polémanie, ou folie de la guerre dans l'Europe actuelle* (Paris: Bellaire 1872).

larger political campaign. Would the new wave of French pacifists prove able to produce pragmatic solutions in the eyes of the outside world, or would they lose themselves in hopeless utopianism? Specifically for the French political context, its litmus test revolved around whether the society's vaunted legal project would be able to restore Alsace and Lorraine to France.

1.2.1 Codification versus Arbitration

Codification almost immediately assumed a relatively prominent position in the literature produced by the French peace League. Its most fervent proponent in the essay contest was Goblet d'Alviella, who ranked it above every other measure in terms of its importance. His was also the most legalistic one of all the published essays. In a lengthy postface written after the Franco-German War, almost as long as the original text, the young lawyer elaborated on the impact the war had had on his views on international legal reform. Despite his young age, the lawyer had little illusion that public opinion alone sufficed to abolish war. Had the events of the late 1860s and early 1870s not seen the masses support the ambitions of their governments? Had they not even themselves pressured cabinets into wars?[47] The Italian lawyer Pasquale Fiore was evidently too optimistic, Goblet d'Alviella assessed.[48] He did not dismiss it entirely, however. Opinion could certainly contribute to peaceful international relations, through mass education, economic liberalisations, and political emancipation. Even then, however, an 'international juridical organisation' remained a necessity. States needed to have access to the same legal remedies as individuals. This was the 'essential objective' that the peace movement needed to pursue.[49]

Goblet d'Alviella's interpretation of the international rule of law was in the same tradition as Louis Bara and other continental-European peace friends before him.[50] He also shared certain traits with more ambitious Anglo-American peace friends like William Ladd and Elihu Burritt. Relying on the domestic analogy, like most Western liberals, the Belgian lawyer thought any functional legal order depended on the *trias politica* of, to begin with, 'a common code of positive law', secondly, 'tribunals to apply

47 Goblet d'Alviella, *Désarmer* 1872, 159.

48 Ibid., 169. He likely referred to the preliminary observations in Pasquale Fiore (transl. Paul Pradier-Fodéré), *Nouveau droit international public suivant les besoins de la civilisation moderne. Tome premier* (Paris: Durand et Pedone-Lauriel 1868), cxiv, 28–29.

49 Goblet d'Alviella, *Désarmer* 1872, 161–3.

50 See chapters 3, 4 and 5.

these laws', and, lastly, 'a public force powerful enough to guarantee the execution of every judgment rendered by these tribunals'. As such, he was opposed to arbitration as conceived by the likes of William Jay, Richard Cobden, and Henry Richard. Goblet d'Alviella did not deny the value of the 23rd Protocol of the Paris Peace Treaty, or the *Alabama claims*. Arbitrations could buy time, sure, and resolve certain disputes which the parties were already intent on settling without violence. Nonetheless, 'arbitration can never replace *la loi*'.[51]

His critique largely coincided with those typically made against ad hoc arbitrations. Such 'juries' did not produce a consistent body of case law, limited as the arbiters were by the confines of their case. Any award was therefore of only limited value to third parties. Those tasked with settling disputes on a normative basis needed predetermined principles. Anterior codification remained a necessary condition. Goblet d'Alviella referred to the troubled prehistory of the *Alabama claims* and the 1871 Washington Treaty when he assessed that the lack of predetermined agreement on a minimum of substantive and procedural ground rules were a cause in itself of diplomatic tensions.[52] He certainly wished Henry Richard best of luck with his motion, but otherwise he preferred peace societies that strove towards an international code and a high court of nations.[53]

Anxious to avoid the stigma of utopianism, Goblet d'Alviella only wished to work through official channels. Peace societies should lobby their governments to further expand on existing precedents. What kind of positive law already existed? Which rules had been *'formally'* accepted by the majority of European states, and could therefore be considered the 'rudimentary beginnings' of international legislation? Like other peace friends since 1856, Goblet d'Alviella was impressed by the success of the Declaration of Paris. Writing from the 1870s, he was able to add several other such instruments, such as the 1868 Declaration of St. Petersburg and the 1864 Geneva Convention. In both instances, a large number of states had in one fell stroke agreed to codify certain international norms.[54] Law-making treaties such as this needed to be repeated, far beyond maritime law or the *ius in bello*. Every area of international law was in need of similar codifications. This was very much in the same spirit as Seebohm, whom the Belgian jurist had

51 Goblet d'Alviella, *Désarmer* 1872, 163–9.

52 Ibid., 163–5; see also Neff, *Justice* 2014, 329.

53 Goblet d'Alviella. *Désarmer* 1872, 167; see also chapter 6.

54 Ibid., 176–9; Neff, *War* 2005, 186.

positively reviewed in the *Revue de Belgique*.[55] He had also reviewed the old essay by his compatriot Louis Bara, which had likewise been recently published.[56] However, despite acknowledging the congruence between his own ideas and those of the two other essayists, Goblet d'Alviella confessed to prefer Seebohm over Bara. It was better to prioritise law-making treaties covering specific topics, rather than some hazy declaration of general principles.[57]

The Belgian lawyer equally disliked any reform plan that sought to undermine state sovereignty. In his review of Bara's book, this had been a major point of critique. Goblet d'Alviella reproached his predecessor for essentially discarding the entire concept of international law. It ought to be recalled that the winner of the 1849 essay contest had proposed a legal code modelled after the *code civil*, to be eventually enforced through a federation of European states. For Goblet d'Alviella, that meant skipping more than a few steps. International law implied the existence of a horizontal legal order, in the sense that states remained formally independent. He was of course writing as positivism was on the rise, heavily emphasising this aspect of international law.[58] The Belgian prize essayist from 1872 did not disagree with his colleague from 1849 that an alliance of European states, called the 'United States of Europe' perhaps, might in some distant future see the light of day. However, this had to take the form of a loose confederation. Its otherwise sovereign member states should only divest those powers necessary to enforce communal laws. In other respects, to preserve individual liberties, it had to maintain a large degree of administrative decentralisation. Most of this was mere conjecture. All that could be hoped for in the near future was a permanent diplomatic conference, tasked with establishing some sort of diplomatic code.[59]

By 1872, many peace friends associated a federative peace solution with the repressions of the Holy Alliance. For Goblet d'Alviella, the old alliance served as a warning for overly idealistic peace plans. He was relatively well-informed about their intellectual history, mentioning inter alia Poděbrady, Henri IV, and Saint-Pierre. The problem had been that their plans tended to

55 Revue de Belgique (1872, vol. XIII), 241–254.

56 Revue de Belgique (15 November 1872), 223–233. See chapter 5 for Bara.

57 Goblet d'Alviella, *Désarmer* 1872, 182–4. Like Bara and Seebohm, the *Revue de droit international et législation comparée* cited Goblet d'Alviella as an opponent of arbitration. RDIL (1898, vol. XXIX), 333–84; De Rycke, 'Legislating Utopia' 2020, 611.

58 Ibid., 231–2; De Rycke, 'Legislating Utopia' 2020, 610, 613–4, 616–7.

59 Goblet d'Alviella, *Désarmer* 1872, 117–118, 209–12.

overcomplicate things, while simultaneously – and paradoxically – preserving a certain status quo. Saint-Simon had wanted a European king, whereas Saint-Pierre's scheme had been somewhat materialised, but in the form of the Holy Alliance – *'on peut la juger par ses œuvres!'*[60] Only a few parts of Kant's peace plan appealed to him. Unlike the Genevan League, Goblet d'Alviella did not centre his attention on the German philosopher's republican peace theory. Rather, he focussed on the former's call for the legalisation and institutionalisation of international relations.[61] The lawyer dismissed Lemonnier and his ilk as 'intolerant' fanatics, who denied the existence of parliamentary monarchies and the need for gradual reforms. Kant's main contribution to pacifist thought rested on his appeal that states had to live in a 'legal condition'. Kant was among the first to develop 'the true principles of natural law', thereby laying the foundations for the future international code.[62]

As could be surmised from the above, Goblet d'Alviella too was influenced by natural law thought, despite his positivistic inclinations. Although codification remained the preserve of politicians and the lawyers who assisted them, they would have to model their codes on certain 'natural' principles. Like all other peace friends, this lawyer was moved by a terrific sense of optimism about progress. He was convinced that universal peace was the 'natural and inevitable crowning achievement of all our civilisation'. The man traced the birth of natural law back to Roman law, to a phase from Ulpian asserting that all men were born free and equal under natural law – 'all of modern law derives from this phrase'. According to such axioms, it followed that war was unnatural. Like other peace friends, Goblet d'Alviella dismissed just cause doctrine, and its accompanying 'war in due form' legal fiction as it had been popularised by inter alia Vattel. If one only listened to 'reason and conscience', there could be neither a legitimate *ius ad bellum,* nor even a *ius in bello.* However, like most other European pacifists, he was pragmatic enough to acknowledge that both dimensions of the laws of war allowed for exceptions. In the *ius ad bellum,* legitimate self-defence was perfectly lawful. During war, lawyers had been able to humanise customary law since the seventeenth century. Now, they had been joined by philanthropists like Henri Dunant. If this laudable trend continued, Goblet d'Alviella

60 Ibid., 49, 170–1.

61 Hendrik, 'Myth' 2018, 118.

62 Goblet d'Alviella, *Désarmer* 1872, 46, 58–9, 171–2.

reasoned, there would eventually come a point that the only humanisation left would be the abolition of war itself.[63]

Conclusions like those above illustrated both the strengths and weaknesses of reasoning according to natural law. As we have seen previously, Anglo-American pacifists like Ladd and Burritt similarly aspired for the codification of international law based on naturalism.[64] They interpreted this source of law through a religious lens, more specifically that of an evangelical Christian. A European such as Goblet d'Alviella similarly wanted a code, but argued it from a vastly different cultural and legal perspective. Goblet d'Alviella was not the only associate of the Paris League to endorse a code. At its first public conference, Auguste Visschers, by then the doyen of the European peace movement, reminded the new generation that the peace congresses of the 1840s had already endorsed a project for codification. He compared its significance with that of the *Code Napoléon.*[65] One of the rejected essays, published in 1873 under the name *L'Alsace reconquise,* likewise demanded a code.[66] Its author, a mathematics and history professor called Michel-Édouard Laporte, specified at the 1873 meeting of the Genevan peace League that an international code should only incorporate norms that could be traced back to natural law. He claimed to have been inspired by *'l'école allemande'* that used history to distillate universally applicable principles out of older institutions – a clear reference to Pandect jurisprudence. However, like Louis Bara before him, whom Laporte may or may not have read, he appeared to belong more to the ensuing 'Romanist' school, that stuck closer to the Enlightenment rationalist tradition.[67] Religion took a far less prominent place in such thinking than it did overseas, yet it was clear that a codification project could be supported from both religious and secular points of view.

63 Ibid., 7–8, 25, 84–5, 100–9.

64 See chapters 1 and 5.

65 *Première assemblée* 1868, 63–9.

66 Laporte, *Alsace* 1873, 165.

67 Friedrich Carl von Savigny (1779–1861) founded the 'historical school' of jurisprudence, which held that law was the product of the specific historical development of a people. The successors of Savigny fell apart in Romanists – or 'Pandectists', after one of the most consulted handbooks of Roman law – and Germanists. The latter were generally more opposed to codification, as that might obstruct the natural development of the *Volksgeist.* David Rabban, *Law's History. American Legal Thought and the Transatlantic Turn to History* (Cambridge: CUP 2012), 92–102; see also *Bulletin officiel des assemblées tenues à Genève les 7, 8 & 9 septembre 1873* (Genève: Imprimerie coopérative 1873), 84–5.

In their own way, European pacifists believed, like the Anglo-American pacifists, in universally and eternally valid legal principles. Substantively, these differing bases for naturalistic reasoning elicited hugely different norms *de lege ferenda,* as could be inferred from the European support for defensive war and international humanitarian law – both of them taboo subjects among evangelical pacifists. However, on the formal level, there seemed to be a fertile area for cooperation between European and Anglo-American peace friends. Could both sides agree on a common international codification project?

The question of whether or not to support codification only became pressing for the Paris League after the war, which had by then renamed itself in the *Société française des amis de la paix.* A first small attempt to get the newly styled French Peace Society to incorporate international codification into its platform came from the erstwhile leader of the Peace Union from Le Havre. The society knew and respected Santallier, and organised a special meeting to hear his proposal. In line with his plan from before the war, he suggested that the peace movement should set up an international meeting of 'eminent jurisconsults' in a neutral city, forming a kind of international 'Areopagus'. The meeting should result in a declaration of the *'droits des nations',* similar to the one made in 1789 for individuals. He ended with a call for the French Peace Society to work together with its 'sister societies' on this grand project. According to the society's journal, Santallier aroused 'great interest'. Over the course of the discussion, some participants mentioned its resemblance to the plans of Burritt in the United States, of Rolin-Jaequemyns in Belgium, and even of Richard and Seebohm in Britain. A code was part of a permanent jurisdiction, whereas arbitration could only act as a mere short-term palliative.[68]

Codification only definitively cemented itself in the French Peace Society's policy in the beginning of 1873. In February of that year, Passy presided over yet another extraordinary meeting. This time, the guest of honour had come from all the way across the Atlantic. The secretary of the American Peace Society, James B. Miles, who had succeeded Beckwith three years earlier, presented the plan he, Burritt, and Field had been preparing in the United States. France was the first stop on Miles's continental-European tour. He had first landed in Britain, and had consulted with Henry Richard.[69]

68 BSAP (July-August 1872), 7–16.

69 See chapter 6.

The London Peace Society, as the French found out through the *Herald,* had sympathised with his project to organise an unofficial conference on the codification of international law. However, they had declined to give an official endorsement, believing that any serious discussion on codification could only be had via official state diplomacy.[70] Miles was requesting much from the French society. Not only did he ask of them to officially cooperate with the American Peace Society, he also wanted Richard to abandon his own campaign. A French show of support could pressure him to drop his arbitration motion, and close ranks with the rest of the international peace movement.[71]

Miles's proposal was taken very seriously by the French Peace Society. This was by no means to be taken for granted, as few really knew either him or the American Peace Society very well yet. Most contacts with the U.S. since 1867 had been with the Universal Peace Union.[72] Many French pacifists likewise knew Richard, in some cases already since the peace congresses of the 1840s. The unknown American, on the other hand, barely spoke French. Garnier and Passy had to act as translators. The entire meeting had even been set up last-minute, as he had arrived in Paris almost unannounced.[73] Still, Miles brought with him letters of adhesion not only from the Universal Peace Union, but also from Burritt – another known quantity – as well as a host of American eminencies. These included state governors, mayors, businessmen, and specialists of international law like David Dudley Field, Francis Lieber, Emory Washburn, and Theodore Woolsey. The latter two were academics working at Harvard and Yale respectively. This certainly impressed the French peace friends.[74] Clearly, they were not dealing with just another isolated idealist, who had conjured up some grand yet completely impracticable scheme for world peace, as the peace societies and their concours tended to attract.

Like it had been for those Anglo-Americans who preferred Ladd's project for a congress of nations – i.e. codification through diplomatic means – over Jay's plan for arbitration in the 1840s and 1850s, the French Peace Society's

70 BSAP (February 1873), 2–14.

71 Ibid., 4–9.

72 The first *bulletins* of the League contained correspondence with Alfred Love, but did not even mention the American Peace Society. *Ligue internationale et permanente de la paix. Deuxième bulletin* (Paris: unknown publisher 1867), 5, 14–7, 24.

73 BSAP (February 1873), 4.

74 The report adds '(*mouvement*)' after Miles read his list of adhesions and showed his proof. Ibid., 5, 7.

preference for codification did not necessarily mean that it was therefore opposed to arbitration. There was a large basis of support for some type of institutionalised method of arbitration among its members. Léon Henry, another laureate of the contest, theorised a *'tribunal suprême'* that would adjudicate all interstate disputes.[75] Goblet d'Alviella proposed something alike, although he called it an *'Haute-Cour générale'*.[76] Passy likewise tended to agree. He disliked that many still considered arbitration a joke. He also hated that in France, people like himself, who propagated pacific ideas 'based on international laws fixated by the common accord of nations' were treated as *'ideologues* and *utopians'*.[77]

Similar to the English-speaking peace societies, whose journals the French Peace Society received and read, the *bulletin* turned to state practice to counter such charges. French peace friends appeared to be about as informed about it as their peers. Their list included not only the 23rd Protocol of the Paris Peace Treaty or the *Alabama claims,* but also the bilateral Anglo-American arbitrations of the middle nineteenth century, as well as more recent examples. They referenced the arbitration clauses that John Bowring, the Benthamite erstwhile member of the London Peace Society, had inserted in several treaties during his diplomatic career .[78] They cited the 1867 London conference, that had supposedly been held in pursuance of the 1856 Paris Peace Treaty. Like Richard would do in 1873 during the debate on his arbitration motion, some people even brought up the mixed court system about to be introduced in Egypt, which they interpreted as a high court of nations 'in miniature'.[79]

---

75 Henry, *Crime* 1872, 157–8.

76 Goblet d'Alviella. *Désarmer* 1872, 185–6.

77 *Les maux de la guerre et les bienfaits de la paix. Première réunion publique tenue à Paris le 10 février 1869 par les amis de la paix. Discours de MM. Ed. Laboulaye, président. Frédéric Passy. Suivis d'une conférence faite à Metz sur le respect mutuel par M.B. Faivre* (Paris : Pichon-Lamy et Dewez, 1869), 67; BSAP (July-August 1872), 41.

78 Late in his career, John Bowring was contracted by the governments of Siam and Hawaii to negotiate commercial treaties with several European States. According to the London Peace Society, he inserted arbitration clauses in seven such treaties. Bowring's relationship with the London Peace Society was seriously damaged by the Second Opium War, which he had directly provoked. Upon his death in 1872, the *Herald* remarked that 'the sad episode' of his governorship of Hong Kong 'should not be allowed (…) wholly to overshadow the valuable services' he rendered to the peace cause. See also chapter 1. BSAP (July-August 1872), 38; HP (November 1872), 141–3; HP (December 1872), 160; Bowring, 'Bowring' 2011, 427–9.

79 BSAP (July-August 1872), 38; The Egyptian mixed courts were also mentioned positively in Goblet d'Alviella. *Désarmer* 1872, 210–1.

As this last example illustrated, the French Peace Society's knowledge about state practice and the finer points of international law had its limitations. Not a word was said about the colonial aspects of some of these instruments, nor that these entailed widely different legal mechanisms or had even been just about entirely political – as in the case of the 1867 London conference. Like all the other peace societies, the French were fully oblivious of the South-American treaty practice in that regard. The broader principle was considered more important than any legal technicalities, as it had almost always been for the peace movement. The important thing, for Passy, was that non-violent dispute settlement mechanisms like arbitration would come to be recognised for their 'practical value'.[80]

The French peace friends shared the assessment of Goblet d'Alviella or Bara that arbitration could only transform from a laughingstock into a sound instrument of statecraft if it was based on a clear code. Institutional forms of interstate dispute settlement, like an arbitral court in the broadest sense, could only function in the context of a *'droit nouveau'*. This entailed a 'better defined law of nations', as well as a less bellicose diplomacy, and a more confident and enlightened public opinion.[81] Passy repeated it in his long preface to Henry's book in 1872. The growth of arbitration clauses over the past couple of decades had been laudable, but insufficient. Quoting explicitly from Seebohm, Passy compared stipulated arbitration to a wooden board floating in the sea: it might save someone from drowning on occasion, but it was hardly a real ship. The real measure was a 'jurisdiction', consisting of a code and an institutionalised court system.[82] The leading man of the French Peace Society had been equally influenced by Santallier, whose presentation before the society that year he described as 'full of good sense'. Arbitration was only an *'expedient'*, not a *'system'*. Already at the first assembly of the League in public, in 1868, the proceedings called the Peace Union's objective of a legal code 'analogous' to their own. In the same vein, it cited the efforts of Leone Levi, a Committee member of the London Peace Society, to codify international commercial law.[83] All of this language strongly mirrored Louis Bara's critique of arbitration from 1849, whose published book was now being sold by the French Peace Society as part of its propaganda library.[84]

80 BSAP (July-August 1872), 46.
81 Ibid., 47–8.
82 Henry, *Crime* 1872, lv–lvii.
83 Ibid., lvii–lviii; *Première assemblée* 1868, 69–70; see chapter 6.
84 BSAP (March-July 1877), 94.

Miles therefore met with a positive reception in Paris. The peace society almost immediately agreed with their guest that the non-official path seemed best. The secretary of the American Peace Society had argued that any official diplomatic attempt to lay the groundworks of a new international code would likely be torpedoed by self-interest and national rivalries. Only 'international opinion' could represent 'universal interests' and 'universal conscience'. In light of the recent war between France and Germany, and the ever-escalating European arms race, it should not surprise that many found this to be a persuasive alternative. That being said, however, the society was not about to frontally attack their faithful friend and ally Henry Richard by undermining his own efforts. Considering any non-official draft code still needed governmental approval to become positive law, the French did not see any actual contradiction between the projects of Miles and Richard. Upon Miles's return to Paris one month later, having in the meanwhile gathered letters of adhesion from many European international lawyers, the society definitively granted its official approval. In a carefully formulated resolution, the French Peace Society vowed to give its support to some *'haut aréopage'* preparing an unofficial international legal code. It was to do for the entirety of international law what the Treaty of Washington had achieved for maritime law. At the end of 1873, Passy dutifully took part in the Brussels international law conference, discussed at the end of this chapter.[85]

1.2.2 Legal Revanchism and Self-determination

Despite their universalist aspirations, the French Peace Society's support for the American project was not entirely devoid of ulterior motives. As mentioned earlier, the Franco-German War had not done the reputation of pacifism any good. The Treaty of Frankfurt of 1871 had legally transferred sovereign control over Alsace and Lorraine to Germany. According to the law of nations then in existence, this peace treaty had been perfectly valid. It was of course obvious to everyone that the Third Republic, as the defeated party, had been coerced in signing a treaty manifestly favouring the newly proclaimed German empire, the victorious party. However, in the nineteenth century, such circumstances were legally irrelevant according to mainstream politics and legal scholarship, as war did not carry any particular mark of legal reprobation. The only realistic limitation to the victorious

85 BSAP (February 1873), 9–14; BSAP (March-April 1873), 17–30.

party's terms was its own – political – assessment of how far it should or could push it, taking into account a wide variety of extra-legal factors.[86]

It goes without saying that most patriotic Frenchmen, including its small peace movement, did not see this quite the same way. The desire to return these lost territories to France immediately turned into a national obsession. For many, the most straightforward means to do so was to quickly rebuild the army and take them back the same way they were lost: through conquest. The chronic tensions caused in Franco-German relations by this revanchism were a major contributing factor to the First World War.[87]

Knowing better than to swim against the prevailing current, and likely just as outraged as any other countryman, Passy and his colleagues tried to give a peaceful colouring to the general sense of indignation. Their answer was 'legal revanchism'. It was neatly summarised in the society's *bulletin*. France would have its vengeance by taking the initiative in introducing an international legal code enshrining the principle of national self-determination. To enforce this legal code, an international tribunal should see the light of day. It would have to be competent to pronounce judgment on 'the special case' of Alsace and Lorraine.[88] The Frankfurt Peace Treaty had only taken into consideration the European balance of power, which had long been the enemy of the peace movement. Authors like the aforementioned Laporte, who wrote *L'Alsace reconquise*, a heavily remodelled version of his essay, were of a similar vein.[89] Léon briefly contemplated the neutralisation of the provinces, like Luxembourg in 1867.[90] Overall, however, French pacifists expected self-determination to lead to an overwhelming vote by the inhabitants to return to the French bosom – conveniently

86 Today, article 52 of the 1969 Vienna Convention on the Law of Treaties declares a treaty void if it has been procured by the threat or use of force in violation of the relevant rules in the U.N. Charter. As discussed in the introduction, the present study does not accept the thesis that nineteenth century use of force law was much more stringent than traditionally believed. Christian Tomuschat, 'The 1871 Peace Treaty and the 1919 Versailles Treaty', in Randall Lesaffer (ed.), *Peace Treaties and International Law in European History. From the Late Middle Ages to World War One*, ed. (Cambridge: CUP 2004), 383–7.

87 Ibid., 389, 395–6.

88 BSAP (August 1873), 147.

89 Laporte, *Alsace* 1873, 1–20, 163, 191–220.

90 Henry, *Crime* 1872, i–xiv, liii–lv.

ignoring the sizeable German-speaking portion of its population. Dupasquier called this *'une revanche morale'*.[91]

To their credit, some within the French Peace Society were not afraid to take their support for the concept of self-determination to its logical consequences vis-à-vis the non-European world. France was infuriated that territory had been 'stolen' from it, yet failed to realise just how hypocritical this must have sounded to the peoples France had itself been subjecting to colonialism. Imperial troops had invaded Vietnam in 1858. In the same year as the Luxembourg Crisis, France had still annexed additional provinces from the indigenous polities, and it did not appear after the war that the Third Republic had any ambitions of letting go of any of the possessions it had inherited in Asia. Before the Indochina wars, France had also participated in the Second Opium War against China.[92]

The most outspoken attack on French colonialism was written by an army officer called Paul Émile Marie Réveillère, who wrote several publications, some of them prefaced by Passy. He did so under the pen name 'Paul Brandat', as it was unbecoming for a military man to be a member of the French Peace Society.[93] In a public letter to Passy, 'Brandat' explicitly compared the recent European war to the ones France had been waging in Asia. China had fought a defensive war against an aggressor, who had tried to disguise his materialistic motives behind the shallow pretext of a *'mission civilisatrice'*. As the soldier, who may have seen some of it first-hand, acerbically put it: 'To the applause of every bigot of France, we have stolen, violated, and massacred for the glory of an infallible Pope'. Going even further, he added: 'If we had had even a quarter of Vietnamese bravery, not a single German would have seen his country again.' Brandat, for whom international law stretched beyond Europe, claimed that France had only reaped what it had sown. He reasoned that if European states violated with impunity the principle of self-determination abroad, one should not be surprised if a powerful state suddenly decided to do the same to a weaker state in Europe itself. Its admission into the law of nations – i.e. in positive

91 Dupasquier, *Crime* 1873, 251; see also Frédéric Passy, *Revanche et relèvement. Exposé de la situation aux membres de la Ligue internationale et permanente de la paix* (Paris: unknown publisher 1872), 1–28.

92 Pascal Blanchard and Nicolas Bancel, 'La fondation du républicanisme colonial. Retour sur une généalogie politique'. *Mouvements* 2(38) (2005), 26–33.

93 Van der Linden, *Peace Movement* 1987, 874.

law – would be 'an immense progress towards greater European stability and the final abolition of war'.[94]

Brandat's reasoning followed a larger and older European sensibility. Already in the 1840s, citizens living in the smaller European states of pre-unified Germany and Italy observed with apprehension the aggressive conduct of the great powers towards non-Western polities. Fearing that a similar lot might befall them, colonialism indirectly encouraged nationalism, as a more unified political entity was felt to grant more security in European politics. Believing in a more Hobbesian world than the peace movement, many thought these unified states should possess colonies of their own.[95] While starting from the same premisses, more idealistically inclined people such as Brandat moved in the opposite direction. Any thoughts of reclaiming Alsace and Lorraine through force were 'unjust and criminal'. France should spare no effort to give the inhabitants themselves, and only them, the right to decide to which country they would rather belong. The same rang true for the peoples of Asia.[96]

The right of self-determination would still need a considerable amount of time to develop further, both in international law and in the French peace movement. In international law, the right of self-determination was by no means an accepted principle in the nineteenth century. Even after World War One, it was still little more than a political guideline. Self-determination only became a leading principle of international law after 1945.[97] In the peace movement, the concept's history has stayed relatively obscure. The early propaganda of the French Peace Society did not yet extensively critique colonialism, beyond relatively individual writers like Brandat. The country was still reeling from its defeat. France drastically increased its colonial expansion after the Berlin Conference of 1884. This made the colonial question slowly enter into the French peace movement's campaign. In his preface to a pamphlet from 1908 entitled *Pacifisme et colonisation,* Frédéric Passy denounced *'cette fausse politique colonial'*. The

94 Paul Émile Marie Réveillère [pseud. Brandat], *Mers de Chine* (Paris: Pichon 1872), 1–12.

95 Šedivý, *Para Bellum* 2021, 274–93.

96 Réveillère, *Mers* 1872, 13–4.

97 Tomuschat, '1871 Peace Treaty' 2004, 385; Neff, *Justice* 2014, 435–8; Arnulf Becker Lorca, *Mestizo International Law. A Global Intellectual History* 1842–1933 (Cambridge: CUP 2014), 225–304.

booklet itself did not object to colonialism as such, but only to the inequal and unjust treatment of subaltern peoples.[98]

The French Peace Society's legalist critique of the feelings of revanchism permeating French society was likely as dissident as the adherents of Passy were willing to go in the early 1870s. The society's chief concern had always been to work with government, rather than against it. However, although many of its individual members occupied prestigious positions in French society, their organisation itself remained a marginal force in the short term. The Frankfurt Peace Treaty was simply too bitter a pill to swallow in France. When most broadsheets and journals were weekly crying for vengeance, Passy's legal alternatives must have struck people as somewhat naïve. Adding insult to injury, Passy and his colleagues saw their old rivals, whom they not too long ago had dismissed as marginal and ineffectual, rise into positions of power in the Third Republic. The exiled radical republicans of the *Ligue internationale de la paix et de la liberté* had returned to France. Many of them now holding political office, these men had come a long way since their first chaotic conference held in the late summer of 1867, in Geneva.[99]

1.3 The *Ligue internationale de la paix et de la liberté*

No peace society of the nineteenth century was launched with even remotely as much noise as the *Ligue internationale de la paix et de la liberté*. The operative word in its title, distinguishing it from every other peace society that came before it, was 'freedom'. As the preface to its proceedings described it, the international peace meeting of Geneva '67 might not have been the first of its kind in Europe, but it was the first one that sought for '*la paix par la liberté*. The organisers were not coy about what that implied. Its honorary president was the world-renowned Italian revolutionary republican leader Giuseppe Garibaldi, the man who, with the help of his famous Redshirts, had violently overthrown the Neapolitan king in 1860. In his opening speech, Garibaldi proposed that their meeting should adopt a congress of nations, composed of the democratic representatives of the European peoples, as its platform. While this was not particularly unusual within the peace movement, Garibaldi added that it should also declare the papacy abolished as an institution. On the morning of the third day, the congress discovered that its president had quietly left the city again, ahead

98 François Nicole, *Pacifisme et colonisation. Précédé d'une lettre-préface de M. Frédéric Passy* (Paris: Comité d'action républicaine aux colonies françaises 1908), 5–6, 29–30.

99 Cooper, *Patriotic Pacifism* 1991, 44.

of its official ending. He had gone to do exactly what he had called for out on the tribune: lead an army on Rome to try and overthrow the pope.[100]

The atmosphere Garibaldi had plunged otherwise tranquil Geneva in was opposite to the one when he first arrived. Whereas a mere forty-eight hours ago just about the entire city and its surrounding countryside had seemingly showed up to cheer their hero, the atmosphere was now decidedly grim. During the night, placards had popped up in many streets denouncing the activities of the congress. Geneva's Catholic populace, spurred on by the local bishop and the aristocracy, threatened to shut down the whole affair, by force if need be.[101]

To be sure, Garibaldi did not carry sole blame. The whole meeting was bound to attract controversy either way. Its uniquely international composition ensured that some historians have described the congress of 1867 as not just an international meeting of 'peace friends' – taken in its broadest sense – but also as an accidental 'congress' of Europe's secret police. After all, the congress had received well over 6,000 adhesions. Unlike the congresses organised by the Anglo-American peace societies, these came from all across Europe. Some 2,000 came from Switzerland, another 1,000 from France, and several hundred were Belgian, Italian, Russian, British and Polish citizens.[102] Some 6,000 men and women managed to squeeze their way into the actual congress hall. Most of the speeches were not for the faint of heart. Italians joined Garibaldi in his attack on the Papal States. Germans took stabs at the conservative powers that had crushed the dreams of the 1848 revolutions. Socialists of various nationalities blithely ignored the entire programme and questioned the right of property.[103] As one might surmise, the Genevan congress attracted an eclectic ensemble of critics of

100 Most Italian peace friends, who emerged from the early 1870s onwards, had grown up during the *Risorgimento* and considered 'just war' perfectly natural. Cooper, Sandi. 'The Reinvention of Just War among European Pacifists before the First World War', in Harvey L. Dyck (ed.), *The Pacifist Impulse in Historical Perspective* (Toronto: Toronto University Press 1996), 307–11; *Annales du congrès de Genève. 9–12 septembre 1867* (Genève: Vérésoff & Garriques 1868), 136–40, 203–5.

101 *Annales de Genève* 1868, 203–4; Charles Lemonnier, *La vérité sur le congrès de Genève* (Genève: Vérésoff & Garrigues 1867), 1–2, 22–3; Hippler, 'Nationalist Peace' 2015, 182–3.

102 The League itself claimed to have collected over 20,000 written adhesions. *Annales de Genève* 1868, viii, 1–7; Cooper, *Patriotic Pacifism* 1991, 36.

103 One can imagine Gustave de Molinari, the libertarian Belgian political economist, nearly bursting a vein having to suffer through such speeches. *Annales de Genève* 1868, 157–9.

FIGURE 7.2 Garibaldi welcomed by cheering throngs for the opening congress of the *Ligue internationale de la paix et de la liberté.*

the status quo, from moderate liberals and social-democrats to unapologetic libertarians and communists.[104]

Under the circumstances, it was a small miracle that the congress managed to vote on any resolution at all. Angry mobs of Catholic or conservative locals, armed with clubs, began roaming the streets. By the third day, they tried to force their way into the meeting hall, already filled well above capacity. The distinction between actual delegates and audience members completely disappeared, as people broke the wooden banisters and sat wherever they could, including the stairs and the tables reserved for the press, which was widely present. Judging from the proceedings, such as they are, there must have been an enormous amount of shouting. Interruptions of whoever was speaking in front were the norm, rather than the exception. Its organisers complained afterwards that 'the enemies of the congress' had attempted to create their own majority to sabotage it from the inside. When that did not work, they had instead simply tried to create enough chaos. Not every speaker was intimidated. One Italian, seeing the hostile reactions his attack on the pope provoked in one half of the audience – *'À bas les*

104 Cooper, *Patriotic Pacifism* 1991, 36–7.

révolutionnaires!' – patiently waited with folded arms until the noise had died down, upon which he calmly repeated why the papacy should be abolished. He did so with 'a sardonic grin'.[105]

Undeterred, the congress did eventually get several resolutions passed. It did so close to midnight, after hours of heated back-and-forth debate. By then, the congress was up to its third president, as the second one's voice had faltered. James Fazy, the leader of the local Radical Party, who had been appalled by the degree of extremism displayed during the congress, had made a last-ditch effort to block every single resolution. Like other Genevans, he had become upset that these foreigners may have abused Swiss neutrality. They threatened Switzerland's security with their reckless campaign.[106] One Swiss remarked they had hosted not a peace congress, but a congress for war. 'Everything has been attacked: religion, all things worshipped, and even God itself!' Another suggested they should simply throw the whole sorry lot into the lake.[107]

The main achievement of the congress of 1867 was the founding of a permanent League, based in Geneva, to pursue 'peace through democracy and freedom'. It welcomed members from all across Europe. Unlike the Parisian League, set up in the same year, it was a much more accessible society. Members only had to pay 1,20 francs per year – considerably less than in Paris. The League quickly set up so-called 'sections' in various places, including France, Belgium, Germany, Italy and Britain. It simultaneously started a tradition to hold an annual congress, held in various Swiss cities, until it settled exclusively on Geneva after 1873.[108] Although not nearly as turbulent as the first one, these congresses continued to attract a far more truly international membership than the ones which had been organised by the Anglo-American peace societies in the 1840s. The second one included not

105 *Annales de Genève* 1868, 24, 233; Lemonnier, *Vérité* 1867, 22–4.

106 Ibid., 23–4.

107 *Annales de Genève* 1868, 259–60, 267; Lemonnier, *Vérité* 1867, 23–4.

108 The congresses between 1868 and 1868 were respectively held in Bern, Lausanne, Basel, Lausanne, Lugano, and Geneva. There are no proceedings of the one in Basel, as it had been de facto cancelled by the Franco-German War. *Bulletin sténographique du deuxième congrès de la paix et de la liberté* (unknown location: unknown publisher 1868); *Bulletin officiel du congrès de la paix et de la liberté* (Lausanne: Association Typographique 1869); *Bulletin officiel du congrès de la paix et de la liberté* (Lausanne: Association typographique 1871); *Bulletin officiel du sixième congrès* (Genève: Imprimerie coopérative 1872); *Bulletin Genève 1873*; all resolutions were also reprinted in *Résolutions votées par les vingt-un premiers congrès. Recueil officiel* (Genève: Bureau des États-Unis d'Europe 1888), 17.

only Swiss, but also French, Germans, Italians, Poles and English, as well as a handful of delegates from smaller nationalities, including Sweden, Serbia, Spain and Romania. That being said, France and Switzerland always heavily outnumbered the rest.[109] Precise estimates of the membership totals of the League do not seem to exist in the literature, but it was likely a significantly larger body than its quasi-namesake in Paris, without it being a mass organisation either. Professionally, people active in the League came from a wide variety of backgrounds. Most in the leadership were teachers or university professors. Many had law degrees.[110]

Women were accepted into the League already in 1868, in yet another act scandalising polite society. The organisation added the emancipation of women to its program and incorporated a number of them into leadership positions. In the early years treated in this chapter, the most significant female figures were Marie Goegg (1826–1899) and Elisa Lemonnier (1805–1865). Goegg had been the one to ask the founders of the League why they had excluded women in 1867. Although she played an important organisational role within the League, she quickly became more interested in other issues than peace alone. Specifically, she founded the *Association internationale des femmes* in 1868, a feminist organisation, which she insisted was to be run entirely by women. Although it was originally viewed as an affiliate to the League, it had by 1870 turned into an autonomous organisation, predominantly concerned with women's education.[111] Like other early female pacifists, she did not appear to have written anything specifically about international law. Both Goegg and Lemonnier were married to important leaders of the League: Amand Goegg (1820–1897) and Charles Lemonnier (1806–1891). The latter was the most relevant early leader responsible for the League's rapid shift towards 'peace through law'.

Lemonnier had launched the original call for an unofficial international peace congress in the wake of the Luxembourg Crisis. As a young man, he

109 *Bulletin* 1869, 4; Donatella Cherubini, 'Si Vis Pacem, Para Libertatem et Justitiam. Les États-Unis d'Europe, 1867–1914', in Marta Petricioli, Donatella Cherubini & Alessandra Anteghini (eds.), *Les États-Unis d'Europe. Un projet pacifiste* (Bern: Peter Lang 2004), 11.

110 Cherubini, 'Para Libertatem' 2004, 11–2.

111 The proceedings in the Genevan university library were all donated by Marie Goegg. Cooper, *Patriotic Pacifism* 1991, 39, 41–42; Cherubini, 'Para Libertatem' 2004, 19; Jo Vellacot, '"Transnationalism" in the Early Women's International League for Peace and Freedom', in Harvey L. Dyck (ed.), *The Pacifist Impulse in Historical Perspective* (Toronto: Toronto University Press 1996), 362–78; Regula Luda (transl. Pierre-G. Martin), 'Marie Goegg-Pouchoulin', in *Dictionnaire historique de la Suisse*. 2006, available at: hls-dhs-dss.ch/fr/articles/009305/2006-12-28/.

had become interested in Saint-Simonianism during his legal studies. In particular, he adopted the French philosopher's notions about universal peace. However, in adulthood, during the long years of the Second Empire, Lemonnier drifted away from Saint-Simon in favour of Immanuel Kant. A part of the republican opposition against the emperor, the man was professionally active as a journalist for the *Phare de la Loire*. This daily paper, described as one of the 'rare democratic journals' active in the country at the time, printed a series of articles condemning the war scare. It did not refer to the simultaneous efforts in *Le Temps*. Considering the other differences, both peace leagues were likely set up fully independently from each other.[112] The call for action did not go unheeded. Soon afterwards, Lemonnier attended a small meeting of public intellectuals, in the house of Émile Acollas (1826–1891), another republican lawyer. Upon deciding on Switzerland as the best location for their congress and expected league, these men received news from Jules Barni (1818–1878), an exiled French republican, that Geneva could be a suitable location. Barni had taught history and philosophy at the *Académie*. He was specialised in Kant, having created a major French translation of the German thinker's oeuvre, including *Zum Ewigen Frieden*.[113] Joined by a sympathetic group of local Swiss, these men devised the League's programmatic ambitions.

Once established, the Genevan peace League, like most other peace societies before it, had to deal with significant internal issues concerning its ideological course. Its first two peace congresses were still attended by numerous socialists, in various shades of radicalism. The closest adherents of Karl Marx were absent from the beginning. Marx, by then a prominent socialist figurehead, had tried to prohibit members from the First International from attending the 1867 peace congress, which was deliberately held a day after the Lausanne meeting of the First International. Marx was not a

---

112 *Phare de la Loire* (29 April 1867), 1; *Phare de la Loire* (9 May 1867), 1; Van der Linden, *Peace Movement* 1987, 675–7; Alessandra Anteghini, 'Charles Lemonnier (1806–1891), précurseur de l'européisme fédéraliste', in Marta Petricioli, Donatella Cherubini & Alessandra Anteghini (eds.), *Les États-Unis d'Europe. Un projet pacifiste* (Bern: Peter Lang 2004), 180–1.

113 Immanuel Kant (transl. Jules Barni), *Éléments métaphysiques de la doctrine du droit, suivis d'un essai philosophique sur la paix perpétuelle et d'autres petits écrits relatifs au droit naturel* (Paris: Durand 1853); Immanuel Kant (transl. Jules Barni revue par A. Lagarde), *Projet de paix perpétuelle* (Paris: Hatier, 1988); Van der Linden, *Peace Movement* 1987, 678–81; Sudhir Hazareesingh, 'An Intellectual Founder of the Third Republic: the Neo-Kantian Republicanism of Jules Barni (1818–78)'. *History of Political Thought* 22(1) (2001), 131–65.

pacifist himself, and was suspicious of people who did not subordinate the peace question to the underlying conflict between labour and capital, like he did.[114] The flirtation between the League and the First International, tiny as it was, proved short-lived. In 1868, the latter adopted a resolution denying the former's *raison d'être*, advising it to dissolve itself and join the First International. In turn, the second congress of the peace League rejected the Russian anarchist Mikhail Bakunin's proposed resolution urging a collectivist restructuring of the economic system. The centre-left economic sensibilities of the French republicans represented a sound majority. Bakunin and his clique drew their conclusions and immediately left the League in disgust, leaving Lemonnier, Acollas, Barni and other 'moderates' in a position to begin work on a more cohesive political programme.[115]

The single overarching ambition of the Genevan peace League was caught in the title of its journal: *Les états-unis d'Europe.* It was a bilingual French-German periodical – quite the statement in itself – begun in January 1868. Plagued by chronic financial difficulties initially, like every other beginning peace society, its frequency alternated between weekly and monthly issues. The journal was banned by the Second Empire, meaning issues had to be smuggled in, and it did not appear during the war. In spite of all these obstacles, the historian Sandi Cooper called the League's journal a 'well-written, critical publication', commenting on European political affairs. It lasted into the twentieth century. One of its chief editors was Lemonnier himself.[116] The journal explained that the states of Europe, great and small, could only achieve lasting stability if they all united themselves into a larger political entity, governed by the rule of international law. While the League opposed colonial wars, its focus was mostly on the European continent. In this way, the League of peace and liberty inscribed itself into the larger history of Europeanism.

The organisation extensively engaged with Kant's peace project, and the examples to be had from existing federal states like Switzerland and the United States. While these things had already been done, to a certain extent, by other peace organisations, it distinguished itself on one crucial point: international peace depended on domestic justice. Unlike Passy in France, Richard in Britain, or Beckwith in the United States, the republicans of the League dismissed any system that included autocratic states. Building on the Jacobin legacies of the 1789 and 1848 revolutions, the members of this

114 Cooper, *Patriotic Pacifism* 1991, 36.

115 Ibid., 40; Van der Linden, *Peace Movement* 1987, 698–715; *Bulletin* 1868, 214–56.

116 Cooper, *Patriotic Pacifism* 1991, 38; Cherubini, 'Para Libertatem' 2004, 15–6.

league only accepted democratic states, ensuring a variety of political and civil rights to its citizens, into the European federation.[117]

Although the League considered itself a part of the international peace movement from the onset, its sister organisations did not see it quite the same way initially. The American Peace Society called its 1869 Lausanne congress 'infidel in spirit and tendency'. The *Advocate* claimed it was 'not strictly nor properly a *Peace* congress', as the League's 'grand aim' was *'a political reconstruction of all Europe'*.[118] The British were just as harsh. The *Herald* branded the Genevan peace congress a total failure. The British journal assessed that the organisers should have produced 'a more definite programme', and not given 'unconditional license of speech' to 'all the wild spirits of Europe'. They had declined the invitation to participate, and with good reason, it seemed to them. The founders of the new League had been 'studiously bent upon alienating the sympathies and affronting the prejudices of as many as they could'.[119]

For his own part, Lemonnier thought the Anglo-Americans hopelessly misguided. In a speech for the students of the *Université libre de Bruxelles* – the one at which Bara had studied – he reproached Passy for following the British position that peace could be achieved through peace, 'without ever touching on the political'. The preface to the proceedings of the 1867 congress had been dismissive about the peace conferences of the 1840s. They had been animated by 'Christianity or some vague philanthropy', which made 'abstraction' of the political conditions necessary for peace.[120] It did not appear that the members of the League were particularly well-informed about the peace movement. In 1872, Lemonnier's short history of the movement made no mention of the Cobden motion, the 23rd Protocol, or the writings of Upham, Ladd, or Jay. On the contrary, he dismissed the campaign of the Anglo-Americans as 'sterile' and excessively religious. He thought the London Peace Society had only become political with Richard's

117 An early forerunner was the republican schoolteacher Pierre Malardier (1818–1894), an old *quarante-huitard,* who appeared on the earliest membership lists. Already during the reign of Bonaparte III, he published several pamphlets advocating a federative republican peace very similar to that of the League. Pierre Malardier, *Confédération européenne. Réalisation du droit international* (Bruxelles: Lacroix, Verboeckhoven & Compagnie 1861); Van der Linden, *Peace Movement* 1987, 778.

118 AP (December 1869), 180; *Résolutions vingt-un premiers congrès* 1888, 4.

119 HP (October 1867), 257–8.

120 Les États-Unis d'Europe (hereafter: EUE) (7 March 1869), 1; *Annales de Genève* 1868, viii.

motion, which was rather mistaken.[121] Ironically enough, his own League's bad early reputation stuck too. Lemonnier complained that both the London and the American societies silenced the League. The only peace society with which the Genevan League maintained friendly relations was the society led by Passy. Sharing similar secular sensibilities, apart from the emphasis on domestic justice, the relationship between the League and the French Peace Society began to markedly improve after the Franco-German war.[122] Lemonnier regretted that they did not all structurally coordinate their efforts. After all, Lemonnier remarked, everyone seemed to pursue similar goals around 1873, most notably a general codification of public international law.[123]

Contrary to the contemporary opinions of many of its peers, the Genevan League was a legitimate part of the international peace movement. To a certain degree, Lemonnier should have known that its stances would provoke potential allies. Especially the Anglo-American peace societies, who were made up mostly of evangelical Christians, were easily triggered by positions that contradicted their religious sensibilities. It did not help that the Genevan League, just as the Parisian League, accepted defensive war as self-evident. That being said, the Anglo-Americans did not represent the League's programme in good faith. Although it might have seemed counterintuitive considering its radically republican political demands, or its support for martial characters like Garibaldi, the League never officially endorsed anything but non-violent means. Again and again, its literature emphasised that it relied exclusively on *'la persuasion par la parole et par la presse'*, albeit both *'en toute liberté'*. The League affirmed its focus on non-violent legal means of reform by adding *'et justitiam'* to its motto of *'si vis pacem, para libertatem'* in 1884.[124]

In fact, the League eventually even came up with the very word 'pacifism' itself. The French lawyer Émile Arnaud (1864–1921), who succeeded Lemonnier as its president, coined it in 1901 to replace the old phrase 'friend of

121 Lemonnier remarked that he did not know all the details about the American peace societies. This was indicative of a growing need for a general history by the 1860s. Charles Lemonnier, *Les États-Unis d'Europe* (Paris: Bibliothèque démocratique 1872), 67–76.

122 EUE (6 November 1873), 4; Richard did send the HP with admirable punctuality. Miles only ever sent one copy of the AP, despite receiving all of the literature of the Genevan League

123 EUE (6 November 1873), 3–4

124 Ibid., 4; see also *Résolutions vingt-un premiers congrès* 1888, 10–1; Cherubini, 'Para Libertatem' 2004, 6, 28.

peace'. He wanted it to designate the new consensus that had emerged in the international peace movement by the turn of the twentieth century. By then, sympathisers took it for granted that international peace and domestic justice, in the form of a series of human rights, were inextricably intertwined. He wanted to distinguish 'pacifists' – i.e. those who supported a very specific political-ideological agenda in line with that of the League – from those who opposed war on other grounds, like religion or socialism.[125]

Pacifism, as understood by the first generation of the League of peace and liberty and its successors, essentially entailed a type of liberal internationalism that was not dissimilar to that campaigned for elsewhere in the international peace movement. Over the span of six years, the League transformed itself from a raucous assembly of 'wild men' to a more or less typical peace society. The organisation sought to establish a rules-based international order, composed of a set of international institutions, and promoting liberal democracy. None of the other peace societies, despite their unwillingness to exclude autocratic governments, denied that constitutional states with a separation of powers, and a certain democratic representation – to the standards of a nineteenth century moderate – were the ideal state actors to work with. The League merely took this more seriously than the others; it was not just a facilitating condition, but a necessary condition for international legal reform to succeed.

The League's position might be best compared to that of other radicals in the peace movement. In the Anglo-American world, the religious roots of peace activism led some, like the non-resistants, to quietism and the total condemnation of just cause doctrine. In Europe, where pacifist ideologies had always been more politically outspoken, radicalism instead led to the other end of the spectrum. The use of force was perfectly legitimate, the League believed, if applied by liberal institutions and a reformed system of international law. Specifically, it had to be implemented by the 'United States of Europe', a variant of the congress of nations formulae which peace friends in Europe had been sporadically bringing up for decades by then. Its key difference with its antecedents was that this European unity had to be modelled on republican forms of government. The League was also the first to draw its inspiration explicitly from Immanuel Kant, who had up until then been surprisingly obscure within the international peace

125 Cooper, 'Pacifism in France' 1991, 364; Cooper, *Patriotic Pacifism* 1991, 60; Cherubini, 'Para Libertatem' 2004, 41; Grossi, *Pacifisme européen* 1994, 31–2.

movement, despite the congruences between the ambitions of nineteenth century peace friends and those of the eighteenth century philosopher.

Although the League never dropped its uniquely republican character, it did gradually alter its tone. By the Geneva congress of 1873, its interpretation of 'peace through law' was not vey dissimilar to that of other bodies elsewhere. Unlike their first Genevan meeting of 1867, the assembly was closed to people not specifically invited. The congress itself was completely devoted to the two legal topics that were animating the peace movement at

UN NUMÉRO: 20 CENT.

3me SÉRIE. — QUATRIÈME ANNÉE. *Si vis pacem, para libertatem.* No 3. — JEUDI 25 AVRIL 1872

LES ÉTATS-UNIS D'EUROPE

DIE VEREINIGTEN STAATEN VON EUROPA -- GLI STATI UNITI D'EUROPA

THE UNITED STATES OF EUROPA

JOURNAL DE LA LIGUE INTERNATIONALE DE LA PAIX ET DE LA LIBERTÉ

PARAISSANT LE JEUDI

FIGURE 7.3 The masthead of an 1872 issue of the *États-Unis d'Europe.*

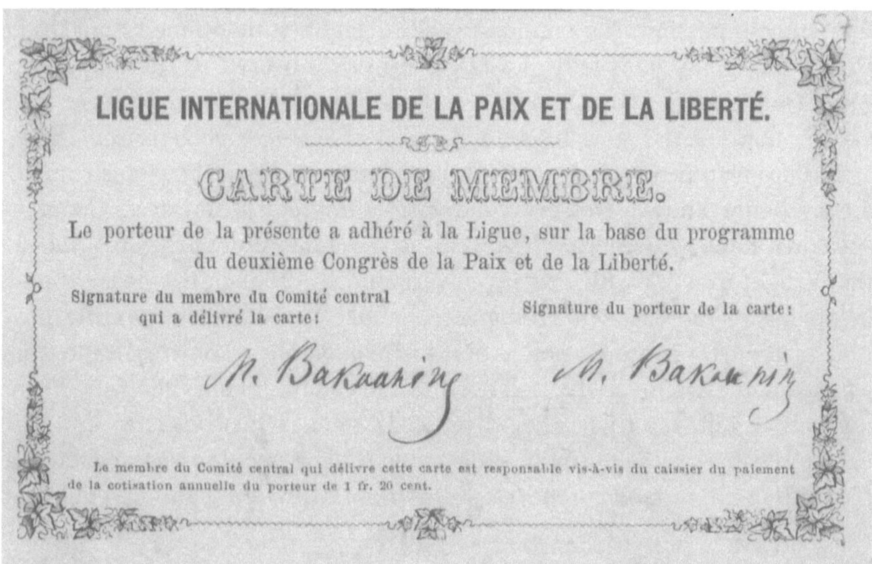
LIGUE INTERNATIONALE DE LA PAIX ET DE LA LIBERTÉ.

CARTE DE MEMBRE.

Le porteur de la présente a adhéré à la Ligue, sur la base du programme du deuxième Congrès de la Paix et de la Liberté.

Signature du membre du Comité central qui a délivré la carte: M. Bakounine

Signature du porteur de la carte: M. Bakounine

Le membre du Comité central qui délivre cette carte est responsable vis-à-vis du caissier du paiement de la cotisation annuelle du porteur de 1 fr. 20 cent.

FIGURE 7.4 Membership card of the Russian anarchist Mikhail Bakunin of the *Ligue internationale de la paix et de la liberté.*

the time in both the United States, Britain, and France: codification and arbitration. The extent to which the League was concerned with similar topics was evident from the fact that many international lawyers had to decline the invitation. They had already agreed to attend the specialist meeting convened by Rolin-Jaequemyns, held in the same week. The 1873 Geneva congress of the League might safely be described as the third important international law congress held in what turned out to be the fateful year 1873. Like the other initiatives, the ways in which the League too ended up centring international legal reform deserves a closer examination.

1.3.1 Republican Peace, or the 'United States of Europe'

Immanuel Kant, despite his fame today, had been remarkably absent in the campaigns of the peace movement up until 1867. As we have seen, members of the peace movement drew inspiration from a small canon of so-called 'classical' pacification schemes, inherited from previous centuries. Time and again, publicists referred back to Henri IV, Saint-Pierre and Rousseau. Sometimes, they added political theorists like Bentham or Saint-Simon to their list, although these were less of a given than the first three. Modern observers might be startled by the glaring omission of the one who arguably produced the most enduringly appealing peace scheme of them all: *Zum Ewigen Frieden*. It was cited only once or twice in the more than seven hundred pages comprising the American Peace Society's *Prize Essays,* and even then only in passing. The London Peace Society first mentioned Kant in the *Herald* in the 1850s, as part of a larger historical overview. The first Anglo-American to have given him any serious attention seemed to have been Charles Sumner, in his well-disseminated *War-System* speech from 1849.

In European peace circles, the philosopher from Konigsberg was comparatively better known. Not everyone was as impressed, however. Generally speaking, Kant was received less well the more one veered towards policies that sought to work with existing governments. Although the peace friends belonging to the *Société d'économie politique* represented a minority position in French economic policy due to their emphasis on free trade, they were nonetheless men who belonged to the establishment. Believing in the natural laws of free trade, they dismissed Kant's pacifist ideas as impractical, as 'old hat', or as outright undesirable.[126] The people most attracted to the notion of republican peace were those with left-leaning republican

126 Sartorius, the winner of Sellon's concours, was also influenced by Kant through Fichte. See chapters 3, 4 and 5.

sympathies, like Constantin Pecqueur, Francisque Bouvet, Pierre Malardier, or Louis Bara. The latter even literally compared himself to his illustrious predecessor.[127] Until the late 1860s, however, no organised peace society had been modelled after the provocative proposals forwarded in *Zum Ewigen Frieden.*

By contrast, the founders of the Genevan League of peace and liberty were all intimately acquainted with Kant's philosophy. Jules Barni, the first president of the League, was a specialist. Between the 1840s and the 1860s, he translated numerous works from Kant, including the peace plan.[128] Already back in 1853, Barni extensively commented on it, in the long introductory analysis to his translation of the *Metaphysical Elements of Justice,* part of the *Metaphysics of Morals.* He did so against the backdrop of the coup d'état, when the former school teacher – he lost his job for refusing to swear the oath of allegiance – was hardening in his republicanism.[129]

From this analysis, it was apparent that he understood Kant's ideas very well. He faithfully showed his appreciation for the preliminary and the definitive articles of the scheme – which was structured as a treaty – as well as the supplements and the secret article at the end.[130] Barni completely agreed that permanent and universal peace was the ultimate *telos* of international law. It did not matter that this might appear unattainable, because people should behave *as if* this were possible. Avoiding war was a duty mandated by reason – as a type of categorical imperative. He concurred that a federation of republican states was a necessity. Barni thought little of the legal justifications in war declarations. These had nearly always been insincere. He affirmed Kant's conviction that, in the absence of some political alliance actually enforcing international law, no state would ever desist from its claims 'on legal grounds alone'.[131]

In at least two ways, the French translator of Kant, despite sharing the latter's moral idealism, was even more radical than his example. He detailed these dissenting views in some of his later writings. Firstly, Barni was aware that the Prussian philosopher had been more conservative than people like himself, as Kant had understood a 'republican' state to be one that merely separated the legislative power from the executive power. True democracy,

127 De Rycke, 'Legislating Utopia' 2020, 620–1.
128 Hazareesingh, 'Barni' 2001, 132.
129 Ibid., 135–6.
130 Kant (transl. Barni'), *Doctrine du droit* 1853, cxv–cxxii.
131 Ibid., xciii, cxx; see the famous phrase 'tiresome comforters' in Kant (ed. Kleingeld), *Writings* 2006, 79.

Kant had argued, would lead to despotism. The future founder of the League of peace and freedom strongly disagreed. He reproached Kant's focus on the excesses of the French Revolution, forgetting that sovereignty in a republic ultimately rested on the people, as the aggregate of each individual's fundamental human rights.[132]

Secondly, Barni was more open to the right of intervention than his guide, or, for that matter, most of the contemporary peace movement. He agreed with his peers and with Kant that a state should in principle abstain from interfering in the internal affairs of another. Unlike Kant and the Anglo-American peace societies, however, Barni denounced an unqualified adherence to this principle. A too rigid application was nothing less than 'international egoism'. Barni specifically had in mind the idea of a 'holy alliance' intervening in instances of blatant injustice, such as the eighteenth century partitions of Poland.[133] Although taboo in much of the peace movement, Barni's understanding of armed intervention as a moral duty under the right circumstances was not in itself controversial in the nineteenth century. Many, if not most, international lawyers deemed it perfectly permissible. It was especially popular among naturalist lawyers – ever the moralists among jurists – but even more positivistic leaning lawyers did not completely condemn it. As always, the precise requirements for intervention differed depending on which treatise one opened.[134] Barni also stayed vague about it.

The rest of the League largely agreed with Barni's assessments and his neo-Kantian sensibilities. At the next four peace congresses following Geneva, the League detailed what a 'republican' state truly entailed. The assembly voted inter alia for the abolition of standing armies, the abolition of capital punishment, mandatory and state-funded primary education for both sexes, legal equality between the sexes, universal suffrage, separation of church and state, and the right of self-determination, in particular for the inhabitants of Alsace-Lorraine.[135] The right of intervention, by contrast, was never adopted in an official resolution, at least not any intervention by a state actor. The League did swear to intervene itself in the event of any war,

132 Kant (transl. Barni), *Doctrine du droit* 1853, cxviii; Revue de Paris (15 March 1856), 499–501; Hazareesingh, 'Barni' 2001, 151.

133 This critiqued the fifth preliminary article. Kant (transl. Barni), *Doctrine du droit* 1853, xcv; Barni, Jules. *La morale dans la démocratie* (Paris: Germer Baillière 1868), 227–8; Hazareesingh, 'Barni' 2001, 152.

134 Neff, *War* 2005, 217–25.

135 *Résolutions vingt-un premiers congrès* 1888, vii–ix.

through public propaganda efforts. However, the Franco-German War divided the organisation. Its French adherents rallied behind the Third Republic after Sedan, increasing tensions with their German colleagues. Barely anyone showed up to the planned 1870 congress and the handful who did dejectedly declared: '*la parole est au canon*'.[136] In 1873, a short paper advised that, since a state's sovereignty was derived from the fundamental rights of its people, intervention was warranted if these fundamental rights were threatened by a local government. The League did not adopt this suggestion in the eventual resolution. However, the League did pay lavish attention to the paper's final conclusion. According to its author, the development of international law would eventually lead to 'the *Völkerstaat* dreamed of by Kant'.[137]

The possible outlines of a republican 'federation' had by then already been painstakingly discussed by the League of peace and liberty. The organisation never agreed on a definite blueprint of how it envisioned the 'United States of Europe'. Like the American Peace Society's plan for a congress of nations in the time of Ladd, the adherents of the League preferred to propagate the larger principle, rather than lose themselves in technical details that would not be necessary in the foreseeable future anyway. For starters, the theorists of the League did not really clarify whether they thought of it as a federation or a confederation. The first implies a closer connection between its constituent parts, all of them essentially constituting a single sovereign entity. A confederation, on the other hand, is a much looser political construct. It consists of states who remain fully sovereign, apart from those competences that they chose to delegate to the – usually weak – central authority. The difference between the two, however, is often vague, and semantic, depending on how one wishes to interpret the underlying foundational legal instruments. Kant himself was ambiguous on whether he wanted a *Völkerstaat,* i.e. some kind of unified world state, or only a *Völkerbund,* i.e. some kind of permanent league of otherwise sovereign states. Scholarship remains divided, with some even positing that the *Völkerbund* constituted but an intermediate step towards the more long-term goal of a *Völkerstaat*.[138]

136 Ibid., viii, 34–5.

137 *Bulletin* 1873, 89–92.

138 Chris Melenovsky, 'International Right and Kant's World Federation'. 2018, working paper (uploaded by the author), available at PhilArchive: philarchive.org/archive/MELIRA-2, 1–4; Georg Cavallar, *Kant and the Theory and Practice of International Right* (Cardiff: University of Wales Press 2020), 113–5.

Judging from its propaganda, the League seemed to have favoured a decentralised union, in which member states retained a large degree of legislative autonomy. Like just about everyone else in the nineteenth century peace movement, it talked of 'federation' and 'confederation' interchangeably.[139] Adherents consistently advised 'decentralisation', which in nineteenth century parlance was loosely synonymous to federalism.[140] They believed that centralisation was a tool of monarchs, who wished to cement their power and build up their military capabilities. The Central Committee of the League advanced instead that 'the European confederation' was 'the natural consequence of the application of the federative principle' to the European states. Many Italian and French members concurred.[141]

Nonetheless, nationalist sympathies prevented the League from endorsing the complete erasure of the concept of the nation-state. According to Lemonnier, 'the idea of federation excludes the idea of fusion'. The peoples of Europe should be able to keep their existing state-structure – as long as it was republican – and should join the European federation on a contractual basis. Diversity stood at the very core of the League's Europeanist project: 'the concept of a federation encompasses and presupposes a plurality of nations (...)'.[142] Member states were to delegate only those competences to the federation that related to international peace and security.[143]

Like peace friends had since the very beginning, Lemonnier and his colleagues turned to domestic examples for more specific guidelines. They singled out two specific federative states, which should be very familiar by now: Switzerland and the United States. The German Confederation, which had disappeared by the early 1870s, was seldom if ever mentioned. Lemonnier dismissed it as a failure. Rather, he thought the United States of Europe needed a more 'solid' constitution, like the one of the United States of America. He especially admired the separation of power in the country, as well as the way in which it managed to combine extensive residuary powers

139 *Bulletin* 1868, 196; Lemonnier, *États-Unis* 1872, 131; one of the few authors to actually make the proper distinction was Goblet d'Alviella. *Désarmer* 1872, 207.

140 'Decentralisation' was used more often than 'federalism' in France. Anteghini, 'Lemonnier' 2004, 191.

141 E.g. *Bulletin* 1868, 76, 236; *Bulletin* 1869, 30–1, 70, 76, 80.

142 Anteghini, 'Lemonnier' 2004, 193; EUE (22 May 1873), 3–4; Lemonnier, *États-Unis* 1872, 183–4.

143 Anteghini, 'Lemonnier' 2004, 9–10.

for its states with a powerful central government.[144] In the Swiss case, proponents were not dealing with the same documents as count de Sellon had in the 1830s. In 1848, Switzerland had received a new constitution and become a federal state. One speaker in particular, at the 1868 Bern congress, detailed the relevant articles.

This was Élie Ducommun (1833–1906), who would win the second Nobel Peace Prize in 1902.[145] He singled out the provisions that restricted cantonal law in favour of the national level, as well as the ones that precluded the cantons from maintaining standing armies of their own. They were instead defended through a collective security mechanism.[146] The League endorsed these recommendations in a resolution through which the League officially endorsed the Swiss and American examples for any future European union.[147] In later meetings, the League similarly concurred with calls to replace national standing armies with militia forces. Only the federation itself should keep a small standing army.[148]

Although the process towards the United States of Europe was to be a gradual one, beginning with perhaps only three or four states, the League wanted an international legal order fulfilling all three aspects of the *trias politica*. In this way, the pacifists again went further than Kant, who did not speak of a central executive authority to enforce the federation's international law. The *foedus pacificum* of which the philosopher spoke in his second article did not explicitly advocate for an institutionalised world government.[149] The League however, did advise a three-fold constitutional structure for the European federation. Already at the third congress, the organisation declared that 'the fundamental and permanent cause' of the latent state of war in which Europe found itself, was the total absence of an 'international legal institution'. This legal institution had to take the form of

144 Lemonnier, *États-Unis* 1872, 136–7; see also EUE (31 October 1872), 4; *Bulletin* 1868, 196; *Résolutions vingt-un premiers congrès* 1888, 26.

145 Sara Lorenzini, 'Les États-Unis d'Europe and the First Nobel Peace Prizes. An Outline', in Marta Petricioli, Donatella Cherubini & Alessandra Anteghini (eds.), *Les États-Unis d'Europe. Un projet pacifiste* (Bern: Peter Lang 2004), 143, 145–9.

146 This was similar to how Sellon had invoked the Swiss Federal Pact of the 1830s. See chapter 3. *Bulletin* 1868, 206–11.

147 *Résolutions vingt-un premiers congrès* 1888, 24–6.

148 Ibid., 9, 20, 33.

149 One specialist described it as a 'mutual nonaggression pact'. Michael W. Doyle, 'Kant and Liberal Internationalism', in Pauline Kleingeld (ed.), *Toward Perpetual Peace' and other Writings on Politics, Peace, and History* (New Haven: Yale University Press 2006), 206.

a 'tribunal' that replaced the caprices of war and diplomacy, mostly based on force and deception respectively, with decisions based on law. The tribunal had to work with an international legal code, and its judgments had to be enforceable through an international 'coercive force'. Every part of this triangle had to be ultimately legitimated by the people. The only way this could be done was if every member state was a democratic republican state itself prior to joining.[150]

As such, the League's neo-Kantian conception of the 'United States of Europe' did not immediately rule out all cooperation with the larger 'peace through law' campaign of the rest of the international peace movement. Although the League put more emphasis on domestic justice than the others, its conception of the international rule of law depended on an international code and juridical methods of interstate dispute settlement. These had been the subject of pacifist discussion for decades, even if most people in the League itself were not aware of this. However, as previously seen, international legal reform received a massive amount of new attention in the wake of the *Alabama claims* and the Franco-German War. In the early 1870s, the Genevan League too cemented its concern with legal reform. Crucially, they became more aware of the efforts of peace friends elsewhere. Like Passy in France, Lemonnier and the rest of the leadership would have to decide whether to support Miles's plan for non-governmental codification, or instead co-opt the mostly British arbitration campaign.

1.3.2 Codification versus Arbitration

Contrary to what one might have expected, given the animosity between the Genevan League and the London Peace Society, the former's members were not totally opposed to arbitration. Certainly, at first, Lemonnier thought rather little of this legal instrument, so cherished by the British. He first gave it some thought after the *Alabama Claims* had been successfully concluded. The vice-president of the League at the time, Lemonnier did not want to overexaggerate its importance. He observed that the proceedings of the arbiters Geneva had been hindered by the lack of codified international law. There was no assurance that the next arbitration would be similarly successful. The only system that could structurally guarantee success was a republican federation, with a code, a tribunal, and a collective enforcement mechanism. Richard's arbitration motion was honourable, sure enough, but it did not address these fundamental underlying issues of

150 *Bulletin* 1869, 177–8.

international law. Even if Richard's effort somehow actually resulted in a series of arbitration clauses, would these clauses then be respected? Would Bismarck not simply answer: *'Dieu et le canon Krupp!'*?[151] The French republican was not that far off the mark. Bismarck's response, when he learned of the pacifist demands for arbitration, was deeply condescending.[152] Nonetheless, despite his scepticism, Lemonnier was prepared to accept it as a means to an end. Arbitration could perhaps help pave the way to the United States of Europe, the only construct by which to realise a written and enforceable system of international law.[153]

At the League's Lugano congress of 1872, arbitration clauses became an official topic of discussion for the first time. A long introductory paper introduced the concept to the assembly. It was written by one Paul Lacombe, a French lawyer and historian, at the request of the Central Committee. The man had acquitted himself of his task a bit too well. Lemonnier wrote that his conclusions seemed to contradict *'la pensée-mère'* of the League, and did not represent the League's official views. It was easy to see why Lemonnier was offended. Lacombe had singled out the peace plans of Saint-Pierre, Kant, and Saint-Simon, and identified their joint mistake. They had all required European political cooperation prior to the establishment of a dispute settlement procedure. This was the root of their 'irredeemable utopia'. Lacombe contrasted this with the good sense contained in Richard's motion. France needed to copy this initiative, but be 'more precise'. Rather than a multilateral treaty between several states, the country needed to conclude a bilateral arbitration treaty with Britain. The United States of Europe would not be realised anytime soon. Lacombe thought this were original ideas.[154] In reality, he had unwittingly repeated essentially the same arguments as William Jay had formulated against Ladd's plan for a congress of nations thirty years earlier. The League was only catching up.

Like people tend to do, Lemonnier at first refused to budge from his views when confronted with opposing perspectives. He made it clear that the League belonged to the radically republican school of Mazzini, Hugo

151 EUE (11 July 1872), 4.

152 According to a member of the Geneva League, when Richard and Passy travelled to the 1878 Congress of Berlin, the German chancellor answered: 'Arbitration? But that is what we are doing here right now!' Cited from Bergami, 'Quelle démocratie' 2014, 28–9. One of Bismarck's successors said that treaties 'burn like tinder' if they had to. Cooper, *Patriotic Pacifism* 1991, 114; Zollman, 'Mediation and Arbitration' 2020, 173–4.

153 EUE (11 July 1872), 4; EUE (13 November 1873), 3–4.

154 He even cited the 23rd Protocol as a useful precedent, unaware of the role the London Peace Society had played in it its creation. *Bulletin* 1872, 95, 97–106.

and Garibaldi. Peace did not just entail the absence of war, but the end of human suffering. Both the oppressed and the oppressor wanted 'peace', but this meant revolt for the one, and status quo for the other. Only the republic, he lectured Lacombe, guaranteed respect for human autonomy, and brought natural morality into government. Nonetheless, the League might support arbitration, as long as one did not have exaggerated expectation about it. It might be able to resolve *'les petites questions'*, but anything more than that was wishful thinking. Lemonnier rightfully guessed that Britain would not let the *Alabama Claims* judgment, which had settled an issue of international law in a way that was mostly against British interests, turn into a binding precedent. Alsace-Lorraine would likewise not be settled through arbitration.[155] At the Geneva congress of 1873 the next year, he continued in the same vein. France and Prussia had gone to war three years ago *'sans aucun souci'* about the 23rd Protocol of the 1856 Paris Peace Treaty. The 'three rules' of the Washington Treaty had not been extended to other states, and had failed to become general rules of international law. If the British government somehow decided to pay heed to Richard's motion, and started to make diplomatic overtures to establish some permanent system of arbitration, it would be viewed 'by the great majority of governments as a pure utopia, as a threat, or even as a trap'.[156]

Nonetheless, the League as a whole was beginning to gradually shift its strategy as it was becoming more moderate and legalist in tone. In both 1872 and 1873, its annual congress adopted resolutions in favour of arbitration. The one from 1872 declared that it not only had to support every effort to promote arbitration clauses, but had to undertake initiatives of its own, whenever it was opportune. The resolution still added, however, that the United States of Europe remained the ultimate object. Twelve months later, in 1873, the arbitration resolution was present once again, but made no more mention of the United States of Europe at the larger goal. In 1874, the peace congress even adopted a draft arbitration treaty.[157] In its own way, the League had underwent a similar development as the Anglo-American peace societies. The 1872 resolution eerily paralleled the compromise of the 1843 London peace conference between the American and British peace societies.[158]

155 *Bulletin* 1872, 118–9.

156 *Bulletin* 1873, 58–60.

157 *Résolutions vingt-un premiers congrès* 1888, 48–64.

158 See chapter 2 for the 1843 London peace conference.

It is difficult to single out specific reasons for this remarkable volte-face. Several factors were most likely at play. Firstly, it was apparent that Lacombe's scepticism on seeing the European federation realised anytime soon were more broadly shared in the organisation than Lemonnier was prepared to publicly admit. One must also consider that the League in these years suffered major blood loss, as many of its French subscribers – next to the Swiss the dominant nationality – were entering into government positions in the Third Republic. This likely rendered those remaining more welcoming to governmental solutions than before. Lastly, even Lemonnier himself was not as opposed to this strategy as he let on. Despite his perspicacity about the flaws of arbitration, which was much greater than with someone like Richard, he ultimately came to recommend it himself. In 1873, he confessed that 'international morality' was not yet sufficiently developed. His arguments were the same as the Anglo-Americans, starting with judge Jay, had brought to bear against the congress of nations plan. Essentially, it did not touch upon state sovereignty, and required *'aucune réforme'*.[159] It would still be at least ten to fifteen more years until the League lost all of its reservations against this instrument, but the origins of its turn to legal 'pragmatism', such as it was, began in the early 1870s.[160]

Due to its outsider status at the time, the League did not participate in either of the two codification conferences organised in 1873 in Belgium. It did not stop its adherents from discussing the subject themselves at their own congress that same year. Its second day was wholly devoted to 'determining the fundamental principles of modern international law'. Two papers were read. One of them was from Laporte, who had written a peace essay for Passy's League before the war. The other one was written by one Frédéric Collard, of whom little is known.

The accepted resolution itself simply declared that 'positive law had to be conformable to morality', and that morality was founded on individual rights. From there, it logically followed that the League endorsed the legal equality of states and the right of self-determination for the peoples. The League likewise underlined that the use of force was only legitimate within the context of international law thus circumscribed.[161] The League afterwards never engaged in detail with codification, at least not during its peace congresses. After 1873, most dealt with arbitration, an international court,

159 *Bulletin* 1873, 57–9.

160 Bergami, 'Quelle démocratie' 2014, 27–30.

161 Ibid., 91–2.

and the neutralisation of disputed territories.[162] This might be explained by what has already been said about its own slow moderation, which led the League to eventually shift towards less dramatic solutions.

1.3.3 Excluded from the First International Law Societies

Due to its comparatively much larger emphasis on morality and natural justice, the Genevan League did not have good relations with the *Institut de droit international* that was founded in September 1873. Its journal paid only little attention to it. It copied a report from the *Phare de la Loire* on its inaugural Ghent meeting. The article's tone was condescending. According to the French paper, the congress had passed 'completely unnoticed'. The number of absentees surpassed the number of participants. It had taken umbrage at the conspicuous absence of French jurists, and the ambiguous position of Rolin-Jaequemyns about Alsace-Lorraine. The French republicans, along with the Genevan League, assessed there was 'little serious or practical' to be expected from the Institute's '*soi-disant* scientific' programme.[163]

Conversely, the men of the Institute thought the same way about the men and women of Geneva. Although Rolin-Jaequemyns's *Revue de droit international et de législation comparée* was not hostile to the idea of a 'European union' as such, the periodical did believe that the Genevan pacifists exaggerated the significance of this 'panacea' – as if there was no 'salvation' or 'law' outside of a confederation. These people, like all the other peace societies, were well-meaning 'amateurs', but international law was a 'science' advanced by professional lawyers adhering to a scientific methodology. International law did not depend on the 'political dogmas' of the League.[164] Though the Institute's own 'scientific' approach was itself riddled with subjective political biases and resorts to natural law, its ambitions were much less grandiose. Unlike members of the League, Institute members often served as legal councils for their governments, and therefore preferred to stick to small-scale recommendations and definitions in their

162 *Résolutions vingt-un premiers congrès* 1888, 53–151.

163 EUE (25 September 1873), 3–4; EUE (6 November 1873), 3; Genin, *Laboratoire belge* 2018, 109–14.

164 Albéric Rolin, Gustave's brother and also a law professor connected to the Institute, wrote as late as 1923 that its very name already 'evoked derision in those composed enough to read their debate reports'. By contrast, Rolin described the peace congresses of the 1840s as 'brilliant and generous'. RDIL (1875, vol. VII), 510–2, 516; Albéric Rolin, *Les origines de l'institut de droit international, 1873–1923* (unknown location: Vromant 1923), 14–5.

academic studies. It should not surprise that many of the lawyers invited by the League for its 1873 meeting declined. They included men like Augusto Pierantoni, Carlos Calvo, Gustave Moynier, Count Sclopis, and even Rolin-Jaequemyns himself.[165]

At least some of their excuses were probably white lies, considering the vast ideological differences between the two organisations. As to be deduced from their respective composition and ambitions, they understood the 'science' of law differently. In the nineteenth century, the idea of 'science' was not necessarily commonly understood in the same strictly positivistic sense as today – i.e. as a series of methodologies based on the observation of empirically verifiable facts, reproducible via repeated experiments. Modern legal scholars, who are frequently reluctant to call themselves 'scientists', are often startled by the ease with which their nineteenth century forebears called their work 'scientific'. This was of course because the intellectual life of the latter was still determined by rationalistic and naturalistic modes of thought, which – as we have already abundantly seen – were highly subjective, and largely determined by all of the conscious and subconscious biases of whomever relying on it. Applied to the case of the League and the Institute, their fundamental philosophical difference was about which interpretative actor was capable of 'discovering' the set of international laws that could guarantee peace and stability in international relations. The men of the Institute felt that they most of all were fit for such a lofty calling. It was in themselves that the organic and historical 'conscience' of law evolved and manifested itself. This was a decidedly elitist – and pretentiously self-serving – way of looking at things.[166]

The League, whose members had much greater democratic sensibilities, did not agree. They shared an underlying assumption that functioning positive international laws had to be derived from some kind of rational and moral system discoverable by human reason. However, people like Lemonnier and Barni did not believe that a handful of isolated lawyers were fit for the job. Only the decision-making mechanisms of self-confidently 'republican' states, configured in a permanent multilateral political system, fulfilled the conditions required for rationalist international law-making. Put in the

165 Koskenniemi, *Gentle Civilizer* 2001, 40–1; Lisa Bartolomei, 'The Impact of Civil Society on International Relations: the Ligue internationale de la paix et de la liberté', in Marta Petricioli, Donatella Cherubini & Alessandra Anteghini (eds.), *Les États-Unis d'Europe. Un projet pacifiste* (Bern: Peter Lang 2004), 125; *Bulletin* 1873, 125; *Bulletin* 1873, 70–4.

166 Koskenniemi, *Gentle Civilizer* 2001, 47–51.

League's own terms: only the 'peoples', through their democratically elected representatives, could create norms that would actually work in practice. Governments would not care what some *lawyers*, of all people, had to say if their opinions contradicted important policy ambitions. Like Kant had written, lawyers were only 'tiresome comforters'. If, by contrast, these lawyers merely affirmed the 'immoral' actions of governments, they violated the categorial imperative. Because of such different 'sensibilities', for want of a better word, the Genevan League and the Institute paradoxically both ended up accusing each other of being 'unscientific', even though neither's perspective would be considered 'scientific' by today's mainstream positivist standards.

By contrast, the Genevan League had a much more intuitive sympathy with the other international law congress organised in 1873, in Brussels, which at least partly agreed with its own vision of what constituted 'scientific' law-making. At the Geneva congress of that year, Laporte explicitly gave his support what he called 'the American project' to have an assembly of jurisconsults and 'publicists' elaborate a draft code of public international law. He considered involvement of the latter category essential, precisely because they were not professional lawyers. Unlike the latter, who were by virtue of their profession technical and cautious, non-specialist 'publicists' – such as himself – were better able to grasp the bigger picture and suggest novel norms.[167]

The League as a whole did not adopt specific resolutions about the event in Brussels, but its journal did pay attention to it. It noted the preliminary travels of Miles through Europe already with some interest. Once the actual conference had concluded, Lemonnier observed in the *États-unis d'Europe* that 'two schools of thought' had been present. One of them, as defended by people like the lawyer Farjasse of the French Peace Society, realised that international law, 'like any other branch of law', derived from the same – naturalistic – source: the autonomy of the individual. The second school, endorsed by some of the 'most considerable' participants, used a less idealistic source: sovereignty. Lemonnier reproached specialists like Bluntschli, Holtzendorf, and Rolin-Jaequemyns for reducing public international law to 'an empirically established fact', deductible from state actions alone. The French pacifist underestimated, as we have just seen, the extent to which the jurists who pretended to embody the 'enlightened conscience of the civilised world' still resorted to subjective naturalistic reasoning. None of

167 *Bulletin* 1873, 84–5.

these men were unadulterated positivists *à la* Oppenheim – far from it.[168] Even so, it was still obvious that the 'men of 1873' from Ghent were not eager to have their 'conscience' dictate overly strict limitations on the right of states to use force that blatantly contradicted all state practice. The League, by way of its mouthpiece Lemonnier, could only support the former faction, i.e. the 'publicists' identified by Laporte. They were the only ones able to condemn any and all use of force excepting defensive war. The League all took umbrage at the fact that most professional jurists, such as those of the Institute, had not unanimously and severely condemned the annexation of Alsace and Lorraine as illegal. Otherwise, however, it supported the ambitions of Brussels '73.[169]

The League of peace and liberty remained on the side-lines of the codification movement, because of its strong fixation on popular sovereignty. Once it did began to gradually loosen its programme, from the early 1870s onwards, its newfound 'pragmatism' – relatively speaking – led it to arbitration as their key practical solution. While admitting the value of a code, the League itself never produced a draft code of any kind, unlike several other peace friends and contemporary professional lawyers. Codification had been a subject of debate for a long time by the time the Genevan League entered into the picture. It first became salient during the steady politicisation of the Anglo-American peace societies during the 1830s and 1840s. The topic was a fixture at the peace congresses of the 1840s, but due to its ambitious and very political nature, it had been gradually cast aside. Three decades later, however, the combined influence of the *Alabama Claims,* the Franco-German War, and some internal changes in the American peace movement – most notably the death of the American Peace Society's conservative secretary – made it resurface again. In 1873, it led to the birth of a dedicated international law society. This organisation, which eventually came to be known as the *International Law Association,* symbolised the convergence of interests between pacifists and progressive lawyers, which had been latent for decades. From that point onwards, until the Great War and beyond, the international peace movement definitively pushed legal methods to the foreground of its platform.

---

168 EUE (13 February 1873), 2; EUE (27 February 1873), 3; EUE (8 May 1873), 4; Koskenniemi, *Gentle Civilizer* 2001, 51–4.

169 EUE (6 November 1873), 3–4.

2 The *Association for the Reform and the Codification of the Law of Nations*

On the morning of Friday, the 10th of October 1873, Elihu Burritt saw one of his great ambitions realised as he walked into the stately town hall of Brussels. He had become rather advanced in years by then, at the age of sixty-three. Long gone were the days of working the forge in his New England village. His life's journey had brought him to places far and wide. He had lectured before an untold number of audiences. Many of his lectures had been ill-attended. Sometimes, he had spoken before thousands. He had travelled up and down between America and Europe. He had been mocked and ridiculed beyond count, but he had also dined with senators and presidents. He had made lifelong critics, as well as lifelong friends. He had experienced a prolonged era of peace, but had at the same time seen war scares come and go, actual wars erupt, and the amount of weaponry in the 'civilised' world grow ever greater and ever deadlier. People, both inside and outside the peace societies, had called his idealism naïve or utopian. Still he persevered, driven forward by an austere religious zeal.

Outliving many of both his enemies and his old friends, Burritt now sat in the resplendent fifteenth century town hall of the Belgian capital. Sitting alongside him were other leading men of the peace movement, like Auguste Visschers from Belgium, Frédéric Passy from France, Henry Richard from Britain, and James B. Miles from the United States. These pacifists were joined by the type of men whom the peace societies had for many decades both supported and criticised. They were specialist lawyers, well-versed in the law of nations, and included such names as Mountague Bernard, Carlos Calvo, Johann Caspar Bluntschli, Gustave Rolin-Jaequemyns, and Augusto Pierantoni. As a whole, they could 'complete the chain of law and order', as Burritt himself had termed it during the peace congresses of the 1840s. In more way than one, Burritt's life was representative of the development the international peace movement had gone through up until then. It was only fitting that the story of the peace movement's evolving understanding of 'peace through law' should end with the event co-instigated by one of the movement's oldest, poorest, yet most dedicated adherents.

2.1 *The American Code Committee*

The interest of Burritt in the codification of international law has already been extensively discussed in previous chapters.[170] In keeping with his stubbornly optimistic character, the now elderly Burritt had still not abandoned the ambition that he had inherited from his old mentor William Ladd, the good-humoured founder of the American Peace Society. However, Ladd had been succeeded by George Beckwith, who lacked his predecessor's sense of diplomacy and clashed hard with reformist members like Burritt. Having won the war after years of internal battles, Beckwith led the American Peace Society with a firm hand. He did not want to devote the limited resources of 'his' society on a project that in his eyes seemed indelibly connected to Ladd's wildly ambitious dream of a congress of nations. Disillusioned, Burritt dialled down his pacifist efforts in the next two decades, especially after his League of Universal Brotherhood had collapsed in the 1850s. However, by 1871, he had returned to the United States after a long sojourn in Britain. He also reconnected with the American Peace Society around this time. By this time, the society was no longer led by Beckwith, with whom Burritt never got along. He had been finally replaced by James Browning Miles (1822–1875). Miles had been a long-time member of the society. In 1848, he had sat on the American Peace Congress Committee. Nonetheless, his rise was somewhat meteoric, as he really did not appear in any of the society's public activities until his election as corresponding secretary in 1871. Like Beckwith, Miles was a Congregationalist clergyman prior to assuming the most important leadership position in the society. Unlike his predecessor, Miles and Burritt instantly liked one another. Together, they set up nearly forty public meetings celebrating the Washington Treaty in 1871.[171]

Already in April of 1871, a month before the actual treaty was to be signed, the former blacksmith published his embryonic ideas in the *Advocate*, in an article entitled 'A Preliminary Congress of Juris-Consuls and Publicists'. In it, he recalled the peace congresses of twenty years earlier. Considering the success of those meetings, what more could not be done now, when the peace movement had grown even more established? Against the backdrop of the Washington Treaty and the late Franco-German War, which had given so many Western Europeans first-hand experience of war,

170 See chapters 1 and 5 in particular.

171 Van der Linden, *Peace Movement* 1987, 914.

the peace society should 'convene a congress of the first and ablest jurists in Christendom', in Amsterdam or London perhaps.

The proposal oozed with confidence, and Burritt's characteristic positivity: 'We have connections enough, influence enough, and money enough to do this thing; to convene the most august and influential assembly that ever met on earth'. He did not think many specialists would refuse their call. From the United States, the peace society could enlist Sumner or Field, both of whom were known to be sympathetic to pacifism. If men like them accepted, the professors of Oxford and Cambridge would certainly join as well. The entire thing was unprecedented according to Burritt. 'So far as we know, never did two great writers on international law meet and sit down together to consult and compare notes'. Not unlike Rolin-Jaequemyns's reasoning around the same time, the American peace friend strongly believed in the moral authority exercised by 'all the living Vattels, Puffendorfs, Stowells, Wheatons, Kents, and Storys of Christendom'. Not unlike European peace friends, this American envisioned a code as a necessary preliminary to grander ambitions. In the long run, this code would 'pave the way for that periodical Congress and permanent High Court of Nations'. Having worked himself in a lyrical mood, he dubbed these institutions 'the Parliament of Man, the Federation of the World'.[172] Burritt's inspiration was the plan devised by William Ladd, way back in the 1830s, whose 'practical plan' thirty-three years later 'stands before the world'.[173]

Miles and most of the American Peace Society had warmed up to Burritt's proposal by 1872. At its annual meeting, the peace society adopted a resolution that the 'misunderstanding' surrounding the Washington Treaty necessitated 'an international peace congress' to draft an international code, which could be recommended to governments. The 'present lull of war among the nations' offered an excellent opportunity.[174] As it happened, no congress materialised that year. It was only after the successful conclusion of the *Alabama claims* arbitration that the peace society definitively seized on 'the golden opportunity'. Barely a month after the award, the leadership, as headed by Miles, issued its call for 'bringing the leading minds of nations together in an international congress'. It appeared that Burritt's assessment of the society's relative clout had not been unwarranted. By January 1873,

---

172 AP (April 1871), 40.

173 Around this time, the American Peace Society was publishing biographies of some of its early leaders: Worcester, Ladd, and Beckwith. AP (May 1872), 177; AP (June 1871), 66; AP (October 1872), 222–224; Hemmenway, *Memoir Ladd* 1872, 13–5.

174 AP (July 1872), 196.

the peace friends had already collected a respectable list of adherents, including ten state governors. The most distinguished jurist on the list was David Dudley Field (1805–1894).[175]

Unlike most supporters, Field took an active part in the preparations of the upcoming conference. He represented the juridical side of the organisation. A New York lawyer, he had made a name for himself with his work on several state codifications in the 1850s and 1860s.[176] As seen in a previous chapter, Field had already been independently entertaining the project of an unofficial, but general codification of public international law. According to the peace historian Irwin Abrams, Field may have been inspired by the German-American lawyer Francis Lieber, who had a similar idea in mind, and had intimated this vision to his colleague. As we have also seen previously, Rolin-Jaequemyns, Gustave Moynier, and possibly also Burritt, reading about it in the *Advocate,* were likewise inspired by Lieber's pet project.[177] Unlike the others, Field made his first moves already back in 1866, at the Manchester conference of the British social science association, five years before Burritt and Rolin-Jaequemyns were to launch their own schemes. Of course, it was just as likely that Field – and also Burritt – had thought of their respective projects independently from the German-American jurist.

Be that as it may, the difficulty of cooperating remotely prevented the committee appointed by the association failed to make much progress. Field decided to take on the gargantuan task by himself, resulting in the *Draft Outlines of an International Code* to be published in 1872, right when the American Peace Society was preparing its work on the codification congress.[178] His draft code included a part on 'the preservation of peace'. Its provisions put limits on the armed forces of states, and sketched out the contours of a 'high tribunal of arbitration' with a binding jurisdiction and a complementary annual diplomatic congress. Needless to say, the American Peace Society reviewed it favourably.[179]

The *Advocate* duly expressed its appreciation for Field's labours, and connected it to its own project. The American peace friends did not pretend it

---

175 AP (January 1873), 1–2; Van der Linden, *Peace Movement* 1987, 915–6.

176 Stephen Subrin, 'David Dudley Field and the Field Code: a Historical Analysis of an Earlier Procedural Vision'. *Law and History Review* 6(2) (1988), 313–9.

177 Irwin Abrams, 'The Emergence of the International Law Societies'. *The Review of Politics* 19 (3) (1957), 367–8.

178 Field, David Dudley. *Draft Outlines of an International Code* (New York: Diossy, 1872).

179 Ibid., 367–73; AP (February 1873), 12–3.

was a 'complete and perfect code', which even they sensed was unrealistic, but they nonetheless called it a 'very successful beginning' and 'an effort in the right direction'. The rising popularity of arbitration increased demand for an international code. The society's original idea was to convene 'a parliament composed of two bodies'. The first was to be the most restrained one. Provisionally dubbed a 'senate of publicists', it was to have only about 'thirty or fifty' members, each of them 'such men as their respective governments would choose if they themselves should inaugurate a Joint High Commission'. As this phrasing already implied, the Treaty of Washington provided the example of how to proceed. Miles, being an ordained minister, likened the procedure to how Bible translations were revised by committees of 'eminent scholars'. The other body was open to people without specific expert credentials on matters of international law. Instead, it was to be 'a great popular assembly (...) embracing men of all professions (...) who shall discuss the economic, moral, and religious aspects of the subject'.[180] The 'two distinct bodies' were not expected to work too closely together. They were to meet at separate dates and at separate locales.[181]

By the time contemporary subscribers to the *Advocate* would have read about this, Miles was already on a ship sailing towards Europe, to sound out the opinions of the peace societies and international lawyers of the Old World. He should have been accompanied by Burritt for this task, but his friend had been injured in a train accident and had to recover at home. It fell upon Miles alone to convince sceptical Europeans. Like Burritt had done before him, the American reverend came to European shores without really knowing anybody, or speaking any other language than English. Nonetheless, thanks to the letters of introduction from the project's eminent American supporters, Miles quickly managed to access the appropriate networks. His meetings with the London Peace Society and the French Peace Society have already been detailed earlier in this chapter and in the previous one.[182]

Having secured tentative support in Paris and London, Miles continued to places where the Anglo-American peace societies traditionally rarely ventured. Specifically, he made a tour of Italy, Austria, Germany and Belgium, before he returned home by way of Paris and London. During his trip, he acquired the written opinions of an impressive number of specialists. They

180 Ibid.

181 Ibid., 13; AP (January 1873), 6; AP (February 1873), 10–1; AP (July 1873), 49; 204–8; Curti, *Burritt Letters* 1937, 204–8.

182 Ibid., 13; AP (April 1873), 29; Curti, *Burritt Letters* 1937, 204, 208–9.

included count Sclopis, who had presided over the *Alabama claims* tribunal, Baron Itajubá, another member of the Genevan arbitration commission, Édouard Drouyn de Lhuys, a diplomat and a former minister of Napoleon III, Félix de Parieu, another former minister, and Vernon Harcourt, a Liberal British politician. He even spoke with prime minister Gladstone about it. The others included scholars and practitioners like Carlos Calvo, Pasquale Mancini, Augusto Pierantoni, Mountague Bernard, John Westlake, and Gustave Rolin-Jaequemyns. Other men of note whom Miles reached out to were Auguste Visschers and, importantly, Gustave Moynier. Moynier was not only one of the leading men in the Red Cross movement – distinct from the peace movement – but also a lawyer who had, like Lieber, Field, and Burritt, proposed a similar codification project. In 1871, he had even contacted Rolin-Jaequemyns in Ghent for this purpose.[183] Most of the abovementioned jurists became involved in both projects. They attended both the Ghent and Brussels conferences.

The division that would emerge between the 'popular' and the 'expert' factions during the congress in Brussels was immediately discernible. In principle, at least, everyone concurred that the voice of public opinion needed to be heard in international law-making. However, the legal specialists nearly all pushed against the second part of Miles's plan. Count Sclopis's letter was illustrative. He agreed that modern public opinion could be seen as the *'esprit général'* identified by Montesquieu. However, public opinion needed to be expressed through the appropriate official channels: 'The very idea of a great unofficial gathering of 1,800 or 2,000 persons frightens me.' Sclopis most likely had in mind the chaotic early congresses of the Genevan League of peace and liberty. Instead, he recommended Miles to pursue the parliamentary route. If the combined national legislatures of the United States, Britain, and France all pushed for an international congress, the 'voluntary deafness' of the cabinets would be overcome. If that proved too difficult, the Italian jurist suggested that the meeting should be limited to 'a certain number of distinguished jurists'.[184] Similar advice came for Drouyn de Lhuys, Parieu, Itajubá, Mancini, Heffter, Holtzendorff and Westlake. The latter could not endorse Miles's project at all, unless it was completely in

183 AP (March 1873), 20–2; AP (April 1873), 28–9, 31; AP (May 1873), 33, 36–40; AP (June 1873), 41–2; see also Abrams, 'International Law Societies' 1957, 364–7; Van der Linden, *Peace Movement* 1987, 920.

184 AP (August 1873), 57; Céline Spector, 'Esprit général'. 2013, working paper (uploaded by the author), available at Dictionnaire Montesquieu: dictionnaire-montesquieu.ens-lyon.fr/fr/article/1376474276/fr/.

the vein of the one being contemplated by Gustave Rolin-Jaequemyns in Belgium. It should also forgo the usual, overly absolute, condemnations of *all* war.[185]

Until his European trip, the secretary of the American Peace Society appeared to have been totally oblivious of the similar project undertaken by the editor-in-chief of the first dedicated international law review. Around the same time, Rolin-Jaequemyns had been contemplating a similar plan, albeit focussed exclusively on a small number of jurists who would work together in a dedicated academy, dealing with general principles and smaller topics. His letter to Miles, dated March 1873, contained all of the elements of his project as they are known today in legal history.[186]

Despite the similarities between the ambitions of Miles and Rolin-Jaequemyns, the rivalry between the two projects was evident from the start. The Belgian was very adamant about keeping his own Institute distinct from the peace movement. In fact, his *Revue* wrote very dismissively of the peace societies, as we have already seen, and its founder refused to take a seat in the organising committee of the Brussels conference. Although he took part in the event itself, he did so most of all to keep a close eye on it. Several years later, he quietly cancelled his membership of the law society founded in Brussels.[187] For their own part, the peace friends quickly realised that Rolin-Jaequemyns was not their friend. Visschers privately accused him of bad faith, and intensely disliked how his compatriot publicly belittled the peace friends. Burritt never forgave 'the Ghent schemer'. Believing the peace movement had been first, he bitterly wrote of 'stolen thunder' by 'that invidious Ghent movement that is cutting in ahead of us'. He warned Miles that he would have 'more to meet with self-seeking friends like him in Ghent than from open enemies of the cause'.[188] Burritt's distrust was not entirely unjustified. Rolin-Jaequemyns had admittedly already been considering his own project well before Miles's visit, but he might nonetheless have been encouraged to proceed upon hearing of the many adhesions collected by the American pacifist. In the history of international law too, only the

185 AP (August 1873), 57–59, 64; AP (September 1873), 65–7, 70–2

186 Abrams, 'International Law Societies' 1957, 369–70; AP (August 1873), 64.

187 *List of Members* [Institute of Advanced Legal Studies Archives, International Law Association files], ILA 01/02/01.

188 Curti, *Burritt Letters* 1937, 215–6, 224–5; Abrams, 'International Law Societies' 1957, 370–1.

Ghent initiative has been identified as ushering in a 'heroic' period, whereas the Brussels meeting has been relegated to a mere footnote.[189]

Once the secretary of the American Peace Society was back on American soil, in May 1873, he and Field set up the so-called 'International Code Committee'. Its first meeting was in the private home of the latter in New York. Interestingly, Alfred Love of the Universal Peace Union was also present, along with Charles Sumner. Judging from offhand remarks in Miles's correspondence, it appeared that the American Peace Society was not wholly on board with this new direction. Burritt told him he should give up his post in the society if 'the malcontents' continued to oppose him, and instead become 'Secretary of the International Code Committee of America'. These anonymous opponents may have been leftover adherents of Beckwith's view favouring stipulated arbitration.[190] However, it was never pushed that far. Far to the contrary, after the success of his arbitration motion in July, even Richard felt magnanimous enough to cooperate with the Americans. The peace societies being thus more or less united – with the noted exception of the Genevan League – the final assignment was to find enough willing and able lawyers. This is where Field's networks must have entered into the equation, along with the one built by Miles. Eventually, the Committee spanned approximately thirty men. Not everyone of them was a lawyer. The invitation for the congress was signed by five: Miles, Field, Woolsey, Washburn and William Beach Lawrence. The last one had been a colleague of Field in the code committee of the British social science association. Lawrence joined the Ghent Institute later on, like most other lawyers involved in the American project.[191]

Everything was almost set for the actual conference. The Americans had originally wanted to hold it in New York. Burritt felt the British should not again 'foot all the bills', like they had done during the mid-century European peace congresses. Equally importantly, however, he believed the United States to be 'the most *neutral* in Christendom', due to its lack of 'entangling alliances' with European powers. The country had also adopted 'the *first* and *only* rules of international law ever adopted and acted upon by governmental authority'. Burritt, oddly forgetting about the 1856 Paris Declaration, called the United States 'the very *birth-place* of international law' because of

189 Koskenniemi, *Gentle Civilizer* 2001, 41.

190 Curti, *Burritt Letters* 1937, 212–3.

191 AP (September 1873), 72; Van der Linden, *Peace Movement* 1987, 923–4; James B. Miles, *Association for the Reform and Codification of the Law of Nations. A brief Sketch of its Formation* (Paris: Brière 1875), 7–11.

the three rules contained in the Washington Treaty that had guided the Geneva arbitration.[192] However, the Europeans had demurred, reluctant to travel all the way to America. Therefore, they requested Auguste Visschers, the former president of the 1848 Brussels congress, to make the proper arrangements. Despite his age – he would die the next year – the Belgian peace friend ensured the meeting had the appropriate amount of pomp and circumstance. Burritt had sold it to him as continuing in the vein of the peace congresses of the 1848 congress. This was not entirely correct, as only Louis Bara's much-maligned essay had proposed a project approximately similar to the one of 1873. Burritt had stood relatively isolated in his prioritising of codification back in the 1840s. Nonetheless, there was certainly some truth and sincerity in Burritt's feeling that the upcoming codification congress was 'the culmination of all the American Peace Society has tried to do for 30 years'.[193]

2.2 *A Shared Pacifist-Legalist Sensibility*

Like the mid-century peace conferences before it, the Brussels international law conference held in October 1873 had to find some way to bridge the divergent legal approaches and sensibilities each participant brought to the table. Compared to past events, the Brussels meeting was a much smaller affair. It was to be *'à huis clos',* i.e. on invitation only. In all, thirty-four people attended. There were slightly more professional jurists present than members of peace societies. Present on behalf of the peace movement were, apart from Visschers, Miles and Burritt themselves, Passy, Richard, Goblet d'Alviella, and de Laveleye. Other men of note were Arturo de Marcoartu (1829–1904) and Charles Rogier. The latter had back in 1848 given permission for the Brussels congress as the leader of the liberal cabinet at the time. The former was a rare – and perhaps the only – Spanish adherent of the international peace movement. He made most of his pacifist achievements after 1873.[194] The jurists present were of a similar stature in their, at the time, still small professional and academic discipline. The most noteworthy were Travers Twiss, the British scholar who would help legitimise the Congo

192 Curti, *Burritt Letters* 1937, 204–6.

193 Ibid., 217; Van der Linden, *Peace Movement* 1987, 924.

194 Cooper, *Patriotic Pacifism* 1991, 49–50; Beales, *History* 1931, 126; Edwin Pears (ed.), *Transactions of the National Association for the Promotion of Social Science. Bristol Meeting* (London: Longmans, Green, Reader, & Dyer 1870), 188–92; Arturo Marcoartu, *Internationalism* (London: Stevens and Sons 1876); HP (November 1871), 281; HP (October 1872), 139; AP (November 1872), 229; AP (December 1873), 94.

Free State, as well as Field, Rolin-Jaequemyns, Calvo, Bernard and Bluntschli. The latter had agreed because he feared that otherwise no German would be present, just like the French had been absent in Ghent a month earlier. Like Field, Bluntschli had already published a draft code of his own.[195]

The Brussels meeting had a simple, yet extremely ambitious programme. The imprint of the peace societies was very visible. The first point on the agenda was a discussion on the best ways to achieve a codification. The second dealt with international arbitration. Participants were to discuss not only the contours of an arbitral institution, but also its procedure and possible enforcement mechanisms. Lastly, the conference had to determine how it could institutionalise its future activities.[196] This was a lot of ground to cover in only three days. Just a month before, many of the conference's members had spent three days trying to set up the Institute of International Law. Now, the organisers seemed to expect them to give a technical colouring to the entire legal programme of the peace movement? As to be expected, the conference did not substantially address any of its grander ambitions. Most of the event was spent debating how the new association was to position itself vis-à-vis the existing Institute, founded just a few weeks earlier. Everyone was keen to avoid double work, but the larger issue revolved around the barely hidden tensions between the pacifists and the professional lawyers.

The opening debate on codification was almost instantly derailed this way. The opening speech of Miles the day before had still been drenched in the rhetoric of the peace societies. The secretary of the American Peace Society had called for a dethroning of 'the lynch law' currently existing, and its replacement by 'righteous beneficent law' written by 'the best minds in all the world'. He compared the inevitability of this international code to the all-permeating and unchanging laws of physics and biology, as was typical

195 *Reports of the First Conference held at Brussels, 1873, and of the Second Conference held at Geneva, 1874* (London: West, Newman, & Co. 1903), 5–7; Van der Linden, *Peace Movement* 1987, 924; Fitzmaurice mistakenly wrote that personal problems prevented Twiss from attending – his wife had been unmasked as a former prostitute. However, all reports affirm he was there. Andrew Fitzmaurice, *King Leopold's Ghostwriter. The Creation of Persons and States in the Nineteenth Century* (Princeton: Princeton University Press 2021), 397; Johann Caspar Bluntschli, *Das moderne Völkerrecht der zivilisierten Staaten, als Rechtsbuch dargestellt* (Nördlingen, Beck 1868); Betsy Röben, *Johann Caspar Bluntschli, Francis Lieber und das moderne Völkerrecht 1861–1881* (Baden-Baden: Nomos 2003), 241–58.

196 *Reports Brussels 1873* 1903, 5–6.

for nineteenth century natural lawyers. A deeply religious person, he spoke: 'Law, which is only another name for the will of God, reigns throughout this universe'.[197] The next day, however, when the actual business of codification was to be discussed, Miles was in for a cold shower. The lawyers, despite whatever naturalistic sensibilities they may have had, agreed with Field that any international code would essentially be a treaty. If the idea was to have states actually adopt their suggestions into such a legally binding document, they could only proceed in very small steps. Bluntschli wanted to begin with 'special treaties' covering specialist subjects. In fact, the Swiss-born professor wanted the meeting to discard public international law entirely from its programme, and replace it by private international law, which was less politically sensitive. Barely thirty minutes into the discussion on codification, the conference already moved to the third point of its agenda. After all, in what way would the Brussels initiative still be different from the Ghent Institute if it pursued Bluntschli's suggestions?[198]

Bluntschli steered the debate in the direction Rolin-Jaequemyns had been hoping for. As the leader of the delegation of the Institute, he clarified that his own project was 'a purely scientific institution'. It sought to 'express as far as possible the juridical conscience of the civilized world', albeit only as 'a learned body'. In this capacity, its Ghent conference had appointed committees on procedure in arbitration, the Washington rules, and private international law. It was evident that he did not want a rival on these matters. Rolin-Jaequemyns suggested that the association to be founded in Brussels should limit itself to the popularisation and vulgarisation of the work of the Institute. Other lawyers were of a similar opinion. The most outspoken among them, apart from Rolin-Jaequemyns himself, was Mountague Bernard, the Oxford professor. A year earlier, Bernard had already interpreted the *Alabama claims* in a much more sober way than the peace societies. In a memorandum to the foreign secretary, he underlined that the adverse award only concerned this particular bilateral dispute, and in no way set a precedent for a larger international norm.[199] In keeping with his distaste for excessive idealism, this British scholar – who had actually helped negotiate the Washington Treaty – opposed any talk of a general codification. Parliament would never sanction such a detailed treaty, especially not one initially devised by 'a body of private individuals'. Bernard would show himself the greatest sceptic of the conference, constantly dissenting and even

197 Ibid., 13–4.
198 *Reports Brussels 1873* 1903, 17–8.
199 Brent, 'Alabama Claims' 2021, 2–3.

outright voting against several resolutions. Afterwards, he wrote to the *Times* that he had reluctantly agreed to attend, but thought of the whole project as 'little better than a chimera'. He was one of those 'friends' Burritt had warned Miles of.[200]

Against such opposition, the representatives of the peace societies found themselves outnumbered. Goblet d'Alviella identified three possible outcomes. The first one was to go extremely broad, and add all other possible aspects of international relations to the programme, apart from codification. The second one was to simply disband, and join the Institute. The third route, finally, was the one the Belgian pacifist lawyer supported himself. This was to have the Ghent Institute and the Brussels project stand as distinct, but closely connected organisations. Goblet d'Alviella recognised that he, despite his law degree, was not a match for the world-renowned specialists of the Institute – 'a law degree is not a proof of science'. It was best to leave the technical elaboration of legal standards to the experts. However, this was not how politics worked. There was still a need for men who could influence larger public opinion, specifically the national legislatures of states. There needed to be a separate organisation for this, as suggested by Rolin-Jaequemyns and Bluntschli. Miles agreed with his Belgian colleague, and concurred that this organisation should be distinct from the Institute.[201]

The eventual compromise was an uneasy one, if its vagueness was anything to go by. A committee of seven had drafted two resolutions, which were both ultimately accepted. The first one underlined that the Association was to be a broad one, consisting of 'jurists, economists, legislators, politicians, and others'. It conceded that the Institute would 'cope with the scientific parts', but took great care to add that the Association had been conceived independently from the Ghent project. The second resolution was read by Rolin-Jaequemyns, on behalf of the Institute. It emphasised that the majority of the members of the Brussels Association were already members of the Institute. The Association would take care of the 'practical application' of international law, and advance it in public opinion. It reserved for it the right of examine every issue 'from all points of view, and particularly from the political, economical, and social point of view (...), while avoiding *double emploi*'.[202] It seems unlikely that this 'compromise' settled the matter. As we have seen, Rolin-Jaequemyns continued to dismiss

200 *Reports Brussels 1873* 1903, 19–20; Abrams, 'International Law Societies' 1957, 376–7.

201 *Reports Brussels 1873* 1903, 20–2.

202 Ibid., 44–7

the peace societies, and leading peace men like Burritt afterwards complained that the Association only got 'what comes through the crumbs that fall from the Ghent man's table', since both bodies tried to recruit from the same small pool of specialists.[203]

One of the main points of contention between the pacifists and the lawyers was the importance of arbitration in international legal reform. Both organisations were devoted to arbitration. As already remarked by Rolin-Jaequemyns in Brussels, the Ghent Institute had set up a dedicated committee, and the *Revue* likewise gave space to arbitration schemes in its pages for the first twenty or so years. In 1904, the Institute even won the Nobel Peace Prize for it, along with William Randal Cremer.[204]

However, the differences between the lawyers and pacifists were glaringly obvious. The discussion in Brussels could be easily summarised. The latter wanted stronger and more immediate legal norms than the former. Bluntschli was another case in point. A more cautious man than the peace friends, he wanted the resolution to make explicit allowances for the 'vital interests' of states. As previously noticed, this vague phrase was the bane of the nineteenth century arbitration movement. European and American diplomats were, unlike their South-American colleagues, typically not keen on having their state's foreign policy options constrained in advance by an overly specific arbitration clause. Most of the lawyers supported Bluntschli. The most vocal ones were, as to be expected, Mountague Bernard and Rolin-Jaequemyns.[205]

Unlike during the codification debate, the opposition of the representatives of the peace movement this time was much more open and intense. They may have been forced to admit that lawyers were, in principle, better suited to discuss the technicalities of a code. Arbitration, on the other hand, was a specific subject to which their societies had been giving attention for close to half a century. Their whole interest in a code derived from its use in interstate dispute settlement and conflict prevention. There was no question that they would allow the most important resolution regarding their ultimate objective be thus hollowed out. Both Passy and Richard were clear. The leader of the French Peace Society understood perfectly well that the principle of binding arbitration stood no chance at all of becoming political reality anytime in the near future. The reforms desired by the conference would take decades to materialise. Nonetheless, there was value in setting a

203 Curti, *Burritt Letters* 1937, 225.

204 Koskenniemi, *Gentle Civilizer* 2001, 18; Genin, *Laboratoire belge* 2018, 128–136.

205 *Reports Brussels 1873* 1903, 24–36.

firm principle from the outset. What message would it send if even the publicists already added: *'Seront exceptées telles et telles matières'?*

The leader of the London Peace Society agreed. Not without reason, as state practice would show, he argued: 'It may be true in grammar that the exception proves the rule, but in morals and politics I am afraid the exception destroys the rule.' This had been the fault of the 23rd Protocol of the 1856 Treaty of Paris, the evergreen precedent for the peace societies. Richard drew from experience. He recalled that, having been instrumental in its adoption back in 1856, the society had pleaded for its application during the *Trent* affair five years later. However, Richard had been directly rebuffed by the foreign secretary, who could easily claim that the issue did not fall under the scope or intention of the Protocol, 'falling back on the reservations made in the Paris Protocol'. Richard did not want to repeat the same mistake. The resolution ought to be 'as explicit and unambiguous as possible'.[206]

For the sake of completeness, it must be added that the division was not completely clean. A peace friend like Auguste Visschers felt that 'vital interests' could benefit small powers also. The neutrality of Belgium was not open for arbitration. From the lawyerly side, Twiss agreed that any international law must be framed for the benefit of weaker states. The exception for 'vital questions' was a sword that cut both ways. Conversely, the Italian scholar Pierantoni, one of the youngest members of the conference, conversely found himself more in the middle. He did not object to a qualified support for arbitration, but thought 'vital interests' gave 'too much liberty to certain governments to evade the duty of arbitration'. As possible alternatives, the jurist suggested 'natural rights', 'independence', or even 'honour'. However, these middle-of-the-road suggestions were not really picked up by the others, who leaned either towards one or the other end. They certainly could not interest the peace friends, who had long opposed overly gratuitous invocations of 'honour' in diplomacy.[207] Mancini, another Italian lawyer, in turn emphasised that the resolution should contain the word 'obligatory'. This should not surprise that much. One of the originators of the budding Italian peace movement, Mancini would propose his own successful arbitration motion in the Italian parliament a few weeks later. As an ardent nationalist, he was overall more radical in his politics than a moderate like Rolin-Jaequemyns.[208]

206 Ibid., 27–30, 40–2.

207 Ibid., 25–6.

208 Beales, *History* 1931, 121, 146.

The eventual resolution adopted on arbitration was an overwrought piece of diplomacy itself. Like the one on codification, it had been debated *en petit comité*, leaving no paper trace of any discussions. The text tried to please everyone. One the one hand, it called arbitration the most 'just, reasonable, and even obligatory' means to settle disputes. On the other hand, however, it admitted that certain exceptions could apply, but that these exceptions were 'rare'. Whether it succeeded in pacifying the conference's internal differences was questionable. Not relenting, Bluntschli wanted it added in the minutes that some consented to the word 'obligatory' only in the sense of 'moral obligation'.[209]

In the long term, the Association for the Reform and Codification of the Law of Nations, founded at the Brussels conference of 1873, would stray away from its roots. Although the peace movement had played a crucial part in its founding, its foundational meeting already suggested that the division between the utopianism of the peace friends and the tendency towards pragmatism of professional lawyers would not be easily overcome. The Association did fulfil some of its initial promises. As it matured, the organisation did indeed manage to attract a relatively broad membership. The pacifists and lawyers were joined by an array of businessmen. However, as one might expect, these men did not always have the same high-minded aspirations as the peace movement. True, major shipowners had an obvious interest in international stability, but mostly such people were more concerned with mundane legal issues more directly affecting their business interests. It was revealing that, reflecting on the achievements of the Association of the past thirty years in 1903, the Association thought its 'greatest triumph' to have been the unification of the rules of General Average.[210] However valuable that may have been, it was hardly stuff warming the cockles of one's heart, especially not the cockles of people who dreamt of world peace. Nonetheless, adherents of peace societies faithfully attended the congresses of the Association, making sure that resolutions on codification and arbitration were passed. As time went on, however, their role was increasingly diminished. From 1889 onwards, the peace movement resumed its old practice of organising large international annual conferences, and their interest in the Association, in which they were outnumbered, faded. In 1895, the Association symbolically completed its shift to the pragmatism

209 *Reports Brussels 1873* 1903, 43–4.

210 Ibid., ix.

already advised by some of its founding lawyers. That year, it changed its name into the International Law Association, which it still holds today.[211]

The Association and the Institute mostly differed about what organ was best positioned to persuade governments to alter their foreign policy. Men like Rolin-Jaequemyns were more cautious, and felt that only small-scale restatements by specialists could achieve anything. By contrast, several of his peers thought this far too modest. Several Institute members, such as Mancini, de Laveleye and Pierantoni, had more pronounced convictions. They found a lot of common ground with pacifists like Passy and Richard, who thought that jurists needed to work closely together with other societal elites. The executive's hand could be forced if enough pressure was applied to it, but this had to be achieved through a combination of expert consensus and parliamentary lobbying. Only this strategy was, as the International Law Association still phrased it at the turn of the twentieth century, 'likely to have practical effect'.[212]

The developments of the late 1860s and early 1870s, both outside and inside the international peace movement, did not constitute a turning point as such for the way in which peace friends interpreted 'peace through law'. As we have seen previously, and as Burritt stated it himself, there was a certain degree of continuity between the first international law societies and the political-legal programme of the mid-century peace movement. Both codification and arbitration had been advocated already since the 1830s and 1840s. Of course, it was glaringly obvious at the Brussels conference that peace friends continued to have more 'radical' visions, relatively speaking, than many jurists. Nonetheless, the birth of the Association was unique in one major aspect. For the first time in the history of the international peace movement, international lawyers openly worked together with the peace friends towards a shared objective. The professionalisation of international law as a discipline in the 1870s overlapped with the efforts of the international peace movement to professionalise itself. Although not every specialist lawyer stood sympathetic to pacifism, it seemed evident to enough of them that there was potential for a mutually beneficial alliance. Here were people who shared the same goals, and possessed the organisational structure to translate their shared sensibility into an actual political campaign.

211 The Institute likewise quickly abandoned its initial pretentions. It quietly dropped the title 'organ of the civilised world' when it revised its statutes in 1880. Ibid., viii–xi.

212 *Reports Brussels 1873* 1903, vi.

Between 1873 and 1914, the close connection between the international peace movement and elite circles of international jurists became only more pronounced. The biographies became increasingly intermingled. Many famous international lawyers at this time were also members of a peace society, and nearly all leading pacifists were, vice versa, interested in the development of public international law. The peace movement itself grew exponentially in the last twenty years before the Great War. On the eve of the conflict, it was estimated that there were some 190 active peace societies, spread all over Europe and North America. They published journals in at least ten languages. This outburst of peace activity was centrally coordinated by the International Peace Bureau, established in 1892.[213]

To a certain extent, the international peace movement even became part of the establishment. The interest of men like Passy and Richard in the parliamentary route resulted in the Interparliamentary Union in 1889. Within a decade, it had become a well-respected organisation, made up of hundreds of M.P.'s, ministers, professors of international law, and even diplomats who would be involved in the Hague Peace Conference of 1899. Although delegates of civil society were never granted official status during such events, many diplomatic delegations openly mingled with the pacifists that came to lobby. These pacifists, men and women, brought with them model arbitration treaties and select restatements of international law. It was a far cry from the lonely wanderings of Richard and Sturge in Paris in 1856. While not a mass movement, the international peace movement had overcome its initial isolation. Especially in the oldest strongholds of the peace movement, in places like Britain, the United States and France, it was not unusual for a lawyer interested in international law to join a pacifist society. Several high-profile politicians lent members of the peace societies a sympathetic ear that went beyond the usual polite pleasantries.[214]

None of this would have been possible without the efforts of the earliest supporters of the ideal of 'peace through law' in the international peace movement. They often spent their entire lives without seeing any tangible results for their labours. Elihu Burritt too did not live to see most of the above developments. He did not witness the international legal institutions inspired by them that are today associated with the *ius contra bellum*. He passed away in 1879, back in his hometown in Connecticut. During his intense life, he played a seminal role in the transformation of the peace

213 Cooper, *Patriotic Pacifism* 1991, 60, 87.

214 Ibid., 57, 60–115, 213–4.

movement from a loosely connected patchwork of purely philanthropical societies to an internationally coordinated network of civil society actors, whose membership encompassed influential businessmen, political economists and professional lawyers. The death of Burritt on his small New England farm marked the end of one era and the beginning of another.

Conclusion

> 'Si mon siècle me repousse, j'espérerai en l'avenir.'
> LOUIS BARA (UNKNOWN YEAR)

By the mid-1870s, almost every subject of the emerging 'peace through law' movement had already been covered by the international peace movement. Over the course of half a century, the societies for 'permanent and universal peace' had become enmeshed in an international civil society network that could truly call itself an international movement. The original peace societies had gone through sometimes very harsh ordeals, and had seen their relative popularity rise and decline through time. The Crimean War and the Civil War had wrecked the Anglo-American peace societies as much as the 1840s had initially uplifted them. Even the most recent organisations in France and Switzerland had not escaped the Franco-German War unscathed. Their congress in Brussels with professional international lawyers had not been to the liking of everyone, although it established links with those lawyers who proved sympathetic to pacifism. These encounters with the 'outside world', as well as the societies' own internal intrigues, had continuously challenged the movement's juridical analyses and solutions. Like all legal argument, this vernacular discourse was constructed through interactive and dialectic processes over time. The campaign of the peace movement was not undertaken in an intellectual vacuum, as some lonely reverie, but was part of a much larger conversation, held within peace societies, between peace societies, with ordinary citizens, with politicians, with lawyers, with rivalling ideologies, and with philosophers who had theorised on peace sometimes centuries before.

Contrary to longstanding prejudices against pacifism, those dialogues clearly involved persons who were far from blind to the many accusations of utopianism levelled against them. Like anyone else involved in international law, friends of peace sought to advance their ideological positions in ways pragmatic enough to be agreeable to others in the political arena, without compromising their core values. Much like ordinary international lawyers, early pacifists had to balance their legal argument. They needed to

 | DOI:10.1163/9789004733688_010

find ways to transform their grand ambitions into functioning black letter law.

Although it is impossible to give justice to every shade of grey, it is nonetheless useful to return to some of the questions raised in the beginning. The most basic, yet challenging one was simply: *why?* Why did these people, whom throughout history have often been dismissed as unworldly utopians, blind to all practicalities, choose to frame some of their most important arguments in the language of *law?* As seen throughout, law was unavoidable. Anyone thinking deeply enough about the issue of peace and war inevitably ended up having to fit their analysis into a normative framework. These frameworks did not always correspond to those laid out in the doctrinal textbooks. Vernacular legal discourse often critiqued theory and practice in harsh terms. Not wanting to stay armchair generals, the international peace movement engaged in various acts of legal imagination to construct peaceful alternatives. In doing so, the peace societies inserted their own politics into their campaign for a *ius contra bellum*. Even though many of these politics have since become subjected to new insights, they have created a legacy within international law powerful enough to reverberate well into the present.

1 The Vernacular Critique of Law

Legal history has undeservedly dismissed the early and mid-century peace societies as unconcerned with 'hard' legal questions. In every geographical area, the same general pattern returned. Although every peace society attracted people for whom the law of nations was far removed from their daily concerns or activities, each society invariably found itself engaging with it sooner or later. Many of these texts have been forgotten by lawyers, or were never included into the 'canon' of international legal history to begin with. Even for those countries that modern legal historians have traditionally associated with the peace movement, the picture has thus far been incomplete. In the United States, for instance, pacifist journals abounded with articles dealing with legalistic questions. Several of the most significant self-standing tracts and books, like those of Thomas Upham, discussed the law of nations at length. They did so in the years when the peace societies have been considered to be still in their 'sentimental' or 'naïve' religious phase. The same applied to the British peace societies. The *Herald of Peace* or the works of someone like the Quaker moralist Jonathan Dymond do not feature in any legal history, despite the importance these works have had for contemporary peace friends.

This also rang true for the legal discourse produced by actors who did not speak English. In France too, various publicists discussed how the law of nations could be reformed in a peaceful direction. Even in small states like Switzerland or Belgium, early friends of peace paid significant attention to the notion that 'law' could facilitate peace. Count de Sellon did not let his Calvinism get in the way of a remarkably legalist sensibility. At the peace congresses, legal resolutions stood at the top of the programme. That legal programme was already debated both on the conference floor, as well as in the prize essay by Louis Bara. Although Bara was exceptionally devoted to the legal point of view, virtually every essay concours, be it organised by the Americans, the British, the French, the Swiss, or the Belgians, touched upon issues of international law. An entire vernacular 'ecosystem' existed outside of the traditional boundaries of diplomacy and academic doctrine. Many of these 'forgotten' pacifist texts have never been studied by legal historians – or by hardly anyone at all, in some cases.

The international peace movement came to address the law of nations for much the same reasons as anyone else: *ubi societas, ibi ius.* Law exists wherever society exists. Even the most 'anarchic' system of horizontally coexisting political entities has at the very least an implicit set of rules constraining the behaviour of its members. This is still valid, even if those rules might appear immoral to external observers, are set by the most powerful members, do not apply equally, or do not conform to those rules as they are said to exist in theory. As law-abiding citizens, the members of the peace societies were not about to question the rule of law. On the contrary, they took it for granted that everyone had to adhere to law. However, it appeared to them that the law binding states lacked most aspects that in their eyes rendered law both legitimate and effective. For friends of peace, as well as others, *law* in the true sense of the word had a strong moral dimension. Not just any system of international normativity was worthy of being dignified with the name 'international law'.

It is from this perspective that the extremely harsh critiques of nineteenth century international law by peace friends should be understood. These people were not 'realists' in the sense that they could not believe in the possibility that rules were able to steer international relations. They were 'realists' in the sense that many of them were highly sceptical about the validity of the law of nations as they perceived it to exist in their days. Elihu Burritt was far from alone in claiming that the law of nations that he read about in books was 'not law, but argument'. Burritt's personal hero,

William Ladd, said much the same when he described international law as 'a nose of wax' that great powers could twist and turn as they pleased. In Britain, Jonathan Dymond was just as appalled by how 'incoherent and inconsistent' this branch of the law seemed. Even an M.P. like John Bright felt little shame, during the height of the Crimean War, in writing confidently that 'the law of nations is not my law, and at best it is a code full of confusion and contradictions'. It was the same in Belgium, where Louis Bara posited that doctrines were contaminated with *'de l'à peu près'*; for this lawyer it was hardly a science, but merely a self-contradictory mess of apologies for power politics. Bara's compatriot Gustave de Molinari would not entrust his country's security to international law as it stood. In that, he echoed Count de Sellon, who thirty years before already desired more credible legal guarantees against the encroachments of Switzerland's ambitious neighbours. Even in France, the state at the root of the fears of many Swiss and Belgians, many expressed a desire for legal reform. Michel Chevalier could only answer the question whether international law existed at all with an unconvinced: *'Oui et non'*.

Importantly, as we have seen, the peace movement was not alone in its denunciation of the law of nations. Sellon cited the French lawyer Isambert. Bara quoted the Italian politician Pellegrino Rossi verbatim. The Belgian Royal Academy, despite its wariness of utopianism, did not object to any of Bara's scathing critiques. Rather, its report merely remarked, casually, that its laureate might just as well have cited their own fellow *académicien,* Adolphe Quetelet. This statistician had recently written a book in which he too had reproached international law for masking the 'crimes that states commit between themselves'.[1] Going further still, such assessments were really nothing new. They probably long predated even the French Revolution of 1789. Many peace friends cited from documents that were written in the eighteenth century, like the works of Jeremy Bentham or the *Déclaration des droits des gens* by *abbé* Grégoire. For a movement that was at one time described by a sympathetic observer as 'the best abused movement in Europe', it almost seemed as if tearing into the law of nations was one of the least controversial things that a friend of peace could do. They were more likely to meet with heads nodding in quiet agreement than anything else. This was the case at least on the level of diagnosis, although not necessarily also on the level of how the failings of law should be remedied.

1 De Rycke, 'Legislating Utopia' 2020, 601; Quetelet, *Du système social* 1848, 221.

Lack of faith in the security guarantees offered by contemporary international law partly accounted for the peace movement's relatively small size throughout most of the nineteenth century. Like we have observed throughout, widespread 'defencist' attitudes in civil and political society ensured that 'the military spirit' so lamented by peace friends stayed alive and well. Most people, even in Britain and the United States, preferred a credible military deterrent for their security. If the peace societies struggled to establish a foothold in Germany or Italy, or any other place for that matter, it was not just because of governmental repression. The legalistic and internationalist solutions offered by the peace movement simply did not appeal enough. Many Europeans, especially those living in smaller states, observed with apprehension how great powers could violate international law with impunity, or, worse, how those powers claimed with a straight face that their actions had been in accordance with international law, even if those justifications contradicted ordinary understandings of justice.[2]

Pacifism tends to do well in that odd twilight zone between peace and war. The threat of war must be palpable enough to make people anxious, while still latent enough to offer hope that something can be done about it. It was not a coincidence that the first peace societies were set up immediately after the Napoleonic Wars, that Sellon founded his following the crisis of 1830, that the first French societies were initiated after the crises of 1840 and 1848, and that the next major wave of European societies coincided with the war scare of 1867. As no society is monolithic, it sufficed for a handful of people to get it going each time. The majority likely only hardened in its 'defencism', with another minority doubling down on its 'militarism'. Once war actually erupted, pacifism tended to go dark, especially if the war effort was intensely supported at home.[3] In that sense, pacifism suffered much the same fate as international law, if the popular adage *inter arma silent leges* may be believed to carry a grain of truth in it. The peace societies knew better than to lecture about arbitration when many hundreds or even thousands of soldiers and civilians alike were fighting and dying each day.[4]

Contrary to popular stereotypes, peace friends were not optimistically blind to the possible ways in which international law could be 'misused' by

---

2 This conforms to the insecurity thesis of Miroslav Šedivý, cited throughout.

3 It should be kept in mind that Britain not only possessed peace societies, but also pro-imperial societies.

4 See chapters 2 and 6 in particular for the inactivity of the peace societies during the Crimean War and the Civil War.

politics. Their assessments of 'just cause' doctrine in particular were decidedly unsentimental. The Anglo-Americans had no illusions. They rejected any notion that something like a 'just cause' could supersede the divine prohibition on war. Even Noah Worcester, writing already in the 1820s, felt that no political leader bent on war would be prevented from doing so, because they would not be able to justify their actions as 'defensive'. The American Peace Society was torn apart over the question whether or not such exceptions would not invalidate the rule. The British had always been clear. For most of the members of the London Peace Society, 'just cause' doctrine was simply 'the cloak for crimes', a position from which the Quaker-dominated society never really budged, to the mild frustration of some of its more pragmatic sympathisers.[5]

Europeans were more tolerant in this regard, as we have seen, but even they generally did not want to preserve existing doctrines on this topic. To the extent they tolerated the use of force, European peace friends agreed with their Anglo-American colleagues that state behaviour in the international sphere had to regulated by law. This could not just be any law, but law that was codified, adjudicated by institutions, and that was therefore more clearly enforceable. In short, it was law that had ceased to be 'a nose of wax', but law that had become 'objective'. It had to be law able to resist the caprices of traditional aristocratic diplomacy, or, put more largely, the subjectivity of politics in general.

Despite vast and substantive internal disagreements on all of the above and more, the international peace movement could be said to have one great opponent: the indeterminacy of international law. Even today, the notion that international law is inherently indeterminate, allowing for two opposing positions to be argued at the same time, strikes many as deeply counterintuitive, and is ignored and opposed at least as often as it is enthusiastically endorsed. Who today, lawyer and layman, does not still scratch their head in bemusement when reading that a textbook like that of Vattel was popular, precisely *because* it was full of internal contradictions?[6] Such

5 See chapters 1, 2, and 6.

6 See the introduction. Several scholars have critiqued the postmodern critique of international law and have even compared postmodern lawyers with the early Realists of international relations. Mary Ellen O'Connell, *The Power & Purpose of International Law. Insights from the Theory & Practice of Enforcement* (Oxford: OUP 2008), 93–5. Outside of law too, there is never a shortage of gleeful stabs at postmodernism, from Calvin & Hobbes cartoons to the Sokal hoax. The historian's case against the 'theorists' was made in Richard Evans, *In Defence of History* (London: Granta 2018).

a reaction would be little different from that of William Ladd in the 1830s, when he drew up a list of legal issues that needed to be addressed, because every textbook had a different view on it. Unlike modern observers, people like Ladd were naturally born long before either legal realism or poststructuralism were introduced into intellectual life. However, like every other kind of legal discourse, pacifist vernacular legal discourse that aspired to bring 'objectivity' into the law of nations was animated by various political agendas. These ranged from the very explicit to ones so implicit that they were hardly noticed even by the peace societies themselves.

2 The Politics of Legal Pacifism

These underlying political agendas caused many of the conflicts about international law within the peace movement. Although it would be impossible to reiterate every proposal, it is a useful exercise to summarise the most prominent political fissures that ran through this ideologically highly diverse movement, and which impacted its legal discourse sometimes very profoundly. In total, eight broad themes consistently returned across every chapter. These were the main determinants of the debate.

2.1 *Religion*

The first fault line was very glaring for all to see, and revolved around religion. It was obvious that the Anglo-Americans were much more religiously driven than the Europeans. If a random Belgian at the Brussels or Paris congresses was hypothetically asked to describe a 'friend of peace', he would have probably conjured up a black-clad, Bible-thumping Englishman with a funny hat.[7] However, as we have seen, the Anglo-American peace societies did not consist solely of Quakers. There were hardly any in the American Peace Society, which more than likely contributed to the disagreements in this organisation on the legal course to be pursued. However, the impact of religious differences on whether or not one supported arbitration clauses or the more dramatic course of a congress of nations should not be exaggerated. The London Peace Society was relatively more radical than the American Peace society, but never wavered from its commitment for arbitration clauses once they settled for it in 1843. The American Peace Society, on the

7 A running gag has been how every foreigner who came into contact with the British Quakers made some comment on their curious appearance.

other hand, never truly made up its mind, even though its leadership inclined towards the same course as the British national society until the decease in 1870 of its somewhat Machiavellian leader, the pragmatic George Beckwith.

Religion arguably made it biggest legal impact on the fringes of the movement. Pessimistic pacifists left the American Peace Society in 1838. The New England Non-Resistance Society pressured the other peace friends to abandon the legalistic path altogether, because they equated law with politics, which was irredeemably sinful. Only God's law mattered for these people, and the only way to stay faithful to divine law was on the individual level, to safeguard one's soul. Moderate American peace friends therefore always had to consider a vocal minority whose distrust towards the law of nations could not be overcome. As the rise of the Universal Peace Union showed after the Civil War, such radical pacifism was a force to be reckoned with in religious American pacifist circles, even if non-resistants represented a tiny minority within larger U.S. society. It was eccentric enough to provide fodder for stereotypes, and saddle the wider peace movement with the stigma of being doctrinarian.

That was a far cry from the sensibilities of most Europeans. There, the 'danger', if we can even call it that, came from the other end of the spectrum. From the very beginning, European sympathisers had been more concerned with related secular causes, like democratic representation, social justice, and nationalism. Early French peace advocates such as Constantin Pecqueur or Francisque Bouvet were of course also Christians, but ones who had not or barely been exposed to Millennialism. The *Société de la morale chrétienne* already remarked early on that religion was taken much further overseas.

There were fewer taboos in Europe. That showed itself best when these two 'pacifist cultures' met during the international peace congresses. While the mid-century congresses cemented transatlantic ties, it came at the cost of exposing latent divisions. Louis Bara's essay was the perfect case in point. Despite winning a contest that had been funded by the British, it was never published during Bara's short lifetime. Bara had seen both defensive war and the armed enforcement of law as self-evident, while the Anglo-American societies had always favoured absolute non-intervention. Once the essay did appear in print thirty years after it was written, published by a European, the British reproached it for totally ignoring 'the Gospel of Christ'. The Genevan *Ligue internationale de la paix et de la liberté* shared many of Bara's sensibilities and more. One of its leaders, Charles Lemonnier, thought little of the 'sterile' propaganda of the Quakers, which lost itself in endless abstractions about Jesus and in doing so sidestepped nearly every political hot potato that really mattered in his eyes. What peace could there be within a system of rivalling monarchies, or with a pope holding secular powers? On their part, the British Quakers thumbed their noses at those blasphemous 'wild men' of the League.

2.2 *Legal Culture*

Next to religion, the other major fault line between peace friends was legal education. Like religion, it must be approached with nuance. On the one hand, it was obvious that varying legal backgrounds had the potential to cause frictions. European jurists were trained in civil law systems, whereas the Anglo-Americans were used to the common law. Someone like Bara, a young law school graduate, venerated the *code civil,* whereas an American lawyer like William Jay had during his career as a judge always been much less reliant on codified norms. Dymond represented a popular Anglo-American viewpoint when he praised the flexibility of 'equity', a typical concept from the common law. Equity accommodated lapses into religious morality, which was much harder to do when operating within the strict letter of a code. Conversely, that flexibility was what abhorred Europeans. Bara let it slip that 'arbitration and arbitrariness' shared a common etymology. European critics like Suringar and Goblet d'Alviella agreed. In that sense, it was interesting how pacifist legal conflicts mirrored those between professional lawyers. During the celebrated *Alabama claims* arbitration, applauded by peace friends of all stripes, the British arbiter had been just as frustrated about his continental colleagues' modes of legal reasoning, as Bara had thirty years earlier been about those of the British Quakers.

However, just like religion, the obstacles caused by clashing legal cultures were not insurmountable. Several mitigating factors ensured that the international peace movement still agreed on a more or less coherent juridical programme during their international meetings. The perhaps most significant one touched upon the most basic characteristic of vernacular legal discourse: it was rarely technical.

As almost every writer of a prize essay remarked, the point of their intellectual effort had not been to propose some ready-made blueprint that diplomats could immediately copy-paste into a treaty. Even in those instances when a peace plan included a draft treaty, its author usually indicated that they had merely sketched out the broad outlines. Authors like Upham or Ladd did not write detailed alternative doctrines, but mostly contented themselves with mapping out the big issues that needed to be addressed in law and pointing out the right way forward. At the European peace congresses of the 1840s too, the organisers took care to limit their event to a very general platform that avoided technicalities. This general sentiment returned, and featured most prominently, at the 1873 Brussels international law congress. The peace friends present agreed to a separate association of 'publicists' because this was the role they were already familiar and comfortable with, even if Rolin-Jaequemyns might have pushed for it because he did not want a 'dilettante' competitor to his own *Institut de droit international*.

In doing so, the peace movement was not particularly unique. Societal pressure groups have always been about political ambitions and not about rules for the sake of rules. Somewhat ironically, peace friends were in that sense more aligned with the views of the governments they otherwise distrusted than with some of their allies in the professional legal community. Like diplomats, most advocates of peace by and large considered codification to be a political activity. In almost every peace project, political cooperation preceded codification. Be it Ladd, Burritt, Pecqueur, Bouvet, or most others, each time the author proposed a congress of nations first, which would allow formal representatives to begin work on enacting new international rules. Lawyers entered into the picture in a subsidiary role, to iron out the finer points of what had been decided by others, not unlike how modern M.P.'s or ministers do not need to have a law degree themselves to set policy directions.

Of course, such a view does not exactly flatter the self-image of the legal profession. Consequently, the more one considered law an autonomous 'science', the more one resisted this course of action. Lawyers like Rolin-Jaequemyns believed they represented the 'conscience of the civilised world'. It was unsurprising that the handful of peace friends who entertained similar beliefs arrived at similar proposals as the founder of the *Institut.* Yet again, Louis Bara's conception of the law of nations as a 'science of peace' was the perfect example. Later pacifist lawyers like Walther Shücking concurred that codification was a technical work best left to the experts.[8] This belief was heavily criticised by Hans Morgenthau, who famously – or infamously, depending on one's opinions – abandoned his career as an international lawyer to instead help set up the 'realist' school of international relations.[9]

8 Neff, *Justice* 2014, 362–3.

9 See chapter 5; see also De Rycke, 'Legislating Utopia' 2020, 612, 615, 623.

Related to the discussion on the 'scientific' character of law, terminological unclarities were a boon as much they might have also been a handicap. It was not difficult to see why the peace movement was hindered by its problems to clearly delineate its object. One of the strongest arguments of Lord Palmerston during his parliamentary battle with Cobden in the summer of 1849 derived from that. Politically savvy as he was, the foreign secretary intuitively understood that it would not sit well to outright oppose arbitration. Outside of a minority of militarists, who could be against the peaceful settlement of disputes? Still, the man who only six months later would personally command a naval squadron to blockade the Greek coastline, because of a private dispute of a shady British merchant, was not about give in to a bunch of Quakers and free traders. He undermined the peace movement by pointing out that every 'precedent' in state practice cited by Cobden had really been 'mediation', and had therefore been a 'political' affair. As observed, Palmerston had been mostly correct. The argument proved to be an evergreen. Thirty years later, the German chancellor Bismarck similarly sent the delegates of the peace societies away with the cynical message that 'arbitration' was exactly what he and his colleagues had always been doing. Indeed, peace friends, just like lawyers, liked to cherry-pick from doctrine, even if this sometimes came back to haunt them when an opponent like Palmerston smugly pointed out those parts they had conveniently left out.

On the whole, however, it is arguable that vagueness about 'arbitration' and 'federalism' were more of an advantage than a disadvantage. Men like Palmerston and Bismarck would never be convinced, regardless of how careful the peace societies articulated their legal positions. Like Richard observed, even the Anglo-American peace societies had always directed most of their attention to convincing the broader public. That statement was not fully correct, considering publications like the American *Prize Essays* had been distributed to every ambassador, parliamentarian and monarch the American Peace Society could reach. Nonetheless, there was truth to it overall. The *Prize Essays* were directed just as well, if not more, to an educated middle-class public. The same might be said about all other propaganda with an ostensibly 'dual purpose'. That public did not consist solely of lawyers. Rather, it consisted of people of all professional backgrounds with a shared interest in the larger underlying values represented by 'arbitration' or a 'congress of nations'. Legalistic details did not interest them.

2.3 *Constitutionalism*

The peace movement wanted most of all to introduce the rule of law into the international domain. Even if peace friends might have quarrelled sometimes intensely about whether a bilateral solution or a multilateral one was most 'practical', they never disagreed on that underlying fundamental. Of course, sometimes a friend of peace might not have realised the full extent of the animosity between rivalling projects. Much of it went on behind the scenes, as was the case with how the congress of nations proposal was treated after Ladd's death in the 1840s. Few delegates to the peace congresses probably realised the trouble Burritt had to go through in keeping his congress of nations resolution on the agenda. Nonetheless, this did not obstruct the larger 'peace through law' aspect of the peace campaign. Even Auguste Visschers, who never lost interest in a European confederation, managed to work together well with the Anglo-Americans. Many peace friends were able to compromise on their own preferences because a legal concept like 'arbitration' did not just denote a specific dispute resolution mechanism, but because it was a placeholder term. They supported 'arbitration' not just for the sake of having a *clause compromissoire* in the next fisheries treaty. Rather, they signed a petition or voted for a resolution because they believed that there had to be an alternative to power politics.

For nearly all of them, the litmus test for any alternative was the extent to which it approached the platonic ideal of the rule law within a constitutional state. There had to exist a separation of powers that would allow the formation of 'just' rules. Rules were considered 'just' when they corresponded to certain moral values or 'scientific' truths, or had been accepted by a representative majority after public deliberation. The purpose of those rules was to help objectify the settlement of international disputes. Even in the absence of codified law, mechanisms should be in place to render third-party adjudication as impartial as possible. Finally, any and all law should be enforceable. Depending on the individual peace friend, this could range from armed enforcement by an international executive to loosely coordinated non-violent sanctions. In all cases, however, the combination of a legislative and a judicial authority would facilitate the task of public opinion to cry havoc about any violations of the rule of international law. Like the states themselves, the community of states had to become 'constitutional' in the broad sense.

Peace friends turned to specific constitutional examples on two levels. One was practical, the other was more rhetorical. On the practical level, they needed specific existing examples to emulate. Only a handful of states reached the high standards that the peace friends set for the law of nations.

The ones that invariably returned were the United States and Switzerland, as well as Britain and France. Despite their internationalism, many peace friends were obviously not fully immune to chauvinism. Nonetheless, these were indeed some of the most constitutionalist states at the time. Even French peace friends often referred glowingly to the institutions of the United States, like their compatriot Alexis de Tocqueville had done in the late 1830s. Of these four, the United States and post-1848 Switzerland were cited most often by peace friends favouring some sort of federative world order. Even before the major constitutional overhaul of 1848, count de Sellon already described his alpine home as an 'architect's model' with the potential to inform future European political cooperation.

Rhetorically, nineteenth century friends of peace invoked international law for the same reasons as civil society continues to invoke 'law' today. When a newspaper op-ed, an N.G.O., or an intellectual complains about how international law has been 'violated', they seldom refer to a specific ruling or treaty. It might be doubted to what extent most laymen have ever heard of article 2(4) of the U.N. Charter, or can tell the differences between the I.C.J. and the I.C.C. That should not be expected. Rather, they use the general phrase 'international law' as a kind of catch-all phrase that allows them to judge the conduct of powerful state actors to alternative standards. Koskenniemi has called this a 'constitutionalist mindset'. Law has not only a technical, but also a *cultural* and *political* significance. It is less programme, and more methodology. According to modern legal philosophers, this entails a kind of 'secular faith' in the universality of law, now that religion has lost its intellectual validity.[10]

2.4 *Colonialism*

Of course, while the idea of international law as an application of critical reasoning goes some way toward explaining the persistently recurring use of legal vocabularies already in the mid-nineteenth century, the relevant cultural and political contexts were different back then. Nowadays, the notion of 'universality' is suspect. In the 1800s, this was much less the case. The most glaring example was undoubtedly the glaring Eurocentrism displayed by most peace friends. The majority of proposals for a congress of nations, for arbitration treaties, or for some codification of international law, only talked about how it affected Western European and North

10 Martti Koskenniemi, 'Miserable Comforters: International Relations as New Natural Law'. *European Journal of International Relations* 15(3) (2009), 415–6; Crawford and Roman, 'Continued Relevance' 2015, 103.

American states. A typical project would assume Britain, France and the United States to take the organisational lead. Regionalism could be taken quite far. More than one European, especially the French, would sometimes not even include the United States, which they mistrusted as an emerging rival power threatening European interests.

To the very limited extent non-Europeans were mentioned at all, they featured as an afterthought. They were rarely attributed any agency of their own. On the contrary, legal reforms would in many visions allow the member states of the proposed international organisation to redirect their efforts to a shared civilising project, rather than on 'internecine' European warfare. Such was the case with Bara, Marchand, and even Victor Hugo, to name just a few. Friends of peace were not immune to the prejudices of the social environments they grew up in, and took it for granted that Christianity, and Western culture in general, represented the highest standard of human 'civilisation'. To achieve universal peace was to export Western cultural models, including its laws, to the rest of the world.

Such paternalism did not leave every peace friend blind to the dark side of colonialism. The peace movement also produced some of the most stringent critiques of colonialism. The Anglo-American peace societies were on the whole very critical of how this ostensibly noble endeavour was put into practice. In a way, their scepticism and outright indignation mirrored that about just cause doctrine. The London Peace Society in particular, operating from the heart of the British empire, dismissed some of the most common legal justifications in no uncertain terms. Dymond wondered 'what we should say to a canoe-full of Indians who should *discover* England'? Later publicists agreed that the standard of civilisation 'opened a wide field for oppression, injustice and inhumanity'. In the U.S., some voiced similar concerns about how the Native Americans were treated. The American Peace Society accused its fellow citizens of hypocrisy. Why praise the resistance of Greeks and Poles, but condemn those resisting aggression closer to home? The tribal warriors appeared to have only been 'guilty of a skin not colored like our own', as one compassionate peace friend put it. In Europe too, both Passy and the Genevan League opposed the bloodshed that accompanied colonialism.

Nonetheless, it would probably go too far to regard the mid-century peace movement on the whole as an 'anti-colonial' movement. Most societies only reported intermittently on colonial warfare and often did not oppose colonialism as such. The closest thing to an exception was the London Peace Society, whose *Herald of Peace* consistently denounced every new armed conflict that erupted in their country's vast and ever-expanding empire. However, being committed religious absolute 'pacifists', the society tended to reproach the natives just as much for turning to violence, as their own country for provoking them through misgovernance or imperial encroachment. French peace friends were little different. The political economists of France shared many sensibilities with their British peers, who opposed imperial expansion primarily on financial grounds. Colonies required many subsidies to stay afloat, as well as large militaries to protect them. Furthermore, the metropolis often imposed monopolies, contrary to principles of free trade. However, even those peace friends who opposed it out of humanitarian considerations often did not single out colonial wars as a particularly horrible moral evil. The Anglo-American peace societies in particular preferred to fight 'war' in the abstract. At any rate, it was hard for both Anglo-Americans and Europeans to discredit the civilising mission, if only because they often tended agree with it in principle. Arguing against the idea that Europeans had a duty to 'help' non-Christians was as difficult to do for peace friends, as it was for Palmerston to admit that he could not care less about arbitration when a gunboat could do the job just as well.

A last possible reason as to why the peace societies did not gave more attention to colonial violence revolved around information. Most peace friends relied on the popular press to understand current events. To the extent they could, their journals reported on abuses, in the same way that their other propaganda tried to counter the sanitised popular imagery of war with exposés of its brutal realities. During the Mexican War, for instance, the *Advocate* not only portrayed the American expeditionary force as a band of ill-disciplined adventurers terrorising innocent civilians – an image which modern historians have largely confirmed – but it even tried to give the Mexican perspective to an American audience. However, that strategy had its limitations. Not everything reached them, and any news that did was inevitably looked at through a contemporary cultural prism.

A glaring example in the legal realm was discovered in the Anglo-American campaign for stipulated arbitration. It nearly exclusively relied on 'precedents' from Anglo-American bilateral state practice. Most peace friends did not speak Spanish, or hold the South American republics in any particularly high regard. This led them to completely omit the long-running Latin-American tradition to include arbitration clauses. The arbitration clause in the Treaty of Guadalupe Hidalgo, ending the war with Mexico, so celebrated and oft-cited by the American peace societies, had not been proposed by the American plenipotentiary, but by the Mexican one. The United States only agreed to it after it had been made non-binding, and therefore politically harmless. The incident did not spur the American peace societies to dig deeper into what was happening further down south on their own continent.

Ladd seemed to have been the only American with a deeper interest into his neighbours. He spent several days in Washington D.C. studying the state papers on the Congress of Panama, which was often described as an 'Amphyctionic council' at the time. However, even Ladd, who was very open-minded by contemporary standards, could not shake popular stereotypes. He concluded that a law-making international congress would only succeed when convened *'by a respectable state'*, meaning of course his own country or a European one.

2.5 *Reception of Peace Theory*

Rather, the Americans focussed more on the intellectual inspirations that they shared with Europe. It almost immediately became customary in peace propaganda to include a list of preceding authors who had written on the practical means to achieve peace. This list was included in just about every prize essay, and endlessly repeated in lectures, speeches, and journal articles dealing with 'practical' solutions. This list was nearly always the same. The most frequently quoted 'classical' peace projects were those of Henri IV and Saint-Pierre, written in the late sixteenth and early eighteenth centuries respectively. Rousseau's commentary on Saint-Pierre usually also made it on to the list. Other plans were much rarer. In European peace circles, Saint-Simon was most often included, especially in the first half of the century, when Saint-Simonianism was most popular. Apart from the ones brought up just now, it really depended on the individual peace friend's personal erudition. Some men, like the American lawyer and senator Charles Sumner, were extraordinarily well-read and cited authors whom even modern experts probably still need to look up should they encounter their name. Most peace friends, however, limited themselves to just a handful of familiar names that they had simply copied from other propaganda texts. In that sense, peace propaganda could be very self-referential.

Overall, it was startling just how obscure some publicists were in nineteenth century pacifist circles, who are today considered canonical. The most important ones were the British philosopher Jeremy Bentham and the German philosopher Immanuel Kant. In spite of what one might think, Bentham really did not feature all that much in the propaganda of the London Peace Society. As a utilitarian, he was not the first frame of reference for the evangelical Christian leadership of the peace society. To the extent Bentham was occasionally brought up early on, either in Britain or elsewhere, it was in reference to his works on constitutionalism or codification. His ideas on peace, although written already in the 1700s, were only published in 1843. Even then, it took decades for Bentham to grow into a more familiar name for the peace societies. Kant fared little better. He was barely mentioned by the Anglo-American peace societies. Until Sumner, it appeared as if they had either never heard of *Zum Ewigen Frieden,* or did not consider it particularly noteworthy. Kant was comparatively better known in Europe, but even there he was far from unanimously endorsed. Surprisingly, perhaps, he was most popular among radical pacifists. Republicans like Bara, Malardier and Lemonnier latched onto the German philosopher's notion of a 'republican' peace.

Peace friends co-opted this intellectual pedigree in various ways. Like law, it served both a rhetorical and a practical function. Rhetorically, the existence of a long tradition of thinking about peace and war helped them expel the popular prejudice that their proposals were utopian. If a king like Henri IV or a philosopher like Rousseau already considered it feasible, then surely the 'modern' era should be able to realise it? Practically, peace friends approached the old peace plans just as instrumentally. No nineteenth century author copied any project wholesale. Rather, like with doctrine, they cherry- picked those aspects that appealed to them, and modified them to suit their needs. Count de Sellon, for instance, was uninterested in a geographical reordering of the European map, even though this was a substantial part of the plan of Henri IV, whom he idolised. Rather, he singled out the idea of a *tribunal arbitral,* because he viewed it as an application of the 'legislative principle' in international law, something which Sellon was also pleading for in domestic Genevan politics at the time. The Genevan League similarly 'decontextualised' Kant. Its leadership left Kant's rather cautious notion of a 'republican' separation between the legislative and the executive branch behind it, and gave it a much more democratic colouring. Others were not always explicit about whose book exactly they took a page out of. Ladd claimed originality only for a high court of nations. However, as we have seen, the founder of the American Peace Society likely got the idea from Bentham or Mill. At any rate, it was not that original anyways. Other authors had imagined similar courts both before and independently from Ladd – or Bentham, for that matter.

2.6 *Internationalism*

Nationalism was a key reason why many peace plans of the nineteenth century international peace movement preferred to focus on institutional and procedural mechanisms, rather than a redrawing of the political map. They were 'patriotic pacifists', as Sandi Cooper has titled her seminal history.[11] Part of their fixation on national boundaries was simple logistics. As we have seen throughout, the early peace societies were limited to their immediate environs. The American Peace Society did not even manage to extend its sphere of activities beyond New England for almost fifty years, let alone the entirety of North America or the world. The peace societies only very slowly managed to found international fora for transnational cooperation, the first of them being the peace congresses of the 1840s. On a more fundamental level, the 'nation' was long seen as an emancipatory movement that could transcend particularism. Europe was populated by a wide variety of small states, most notably in Italy and Germany. Other nationalities were incorporated into militaristic empires like Russia or Austria. Of course, the 'nation' too is a highly subjective concept, which can itself incorporate many ethnicities that might prefer more political autonomy themselves within an ostensible 'nation-state', which not every peace friend realised at the time.

On this topic, much like many others, the international peace movement had been deeply conflicted from the very start. Some peace friends, like Edmond Potonié, had always been true cosmopolitans. Even during the years when the ideals of Mazzinian democratic nationalism were still strong, during the 1840s, not all peace friends were blind to the dark sides of nationalism. Agents from the London Peace Society travelling through Germany complained that Prussian children played with real guns, albeit unloaded ones. The peace society described the country at one time as 'one vast army camp'.[12] Nonetheless, especially in continental Europe, nationalism had many positive connotations. Bouvet in France or Bara in Belgium agreed with Cobden in Britain that the Hungarians were fighting with a just cause against the Austrian and Russian authorities. Even someone like Constantin Pecqueur, another cosmopolitan, believed that a world state could only be realised after emancipation on the national level. Most did not want to discard the state as the primary actor within international law. Their cosmopolitan ambitions were 'inter-nationalist' in a strict sense, even if for some only out of pragmatism.

11 Cooper, *Patriotic Pacifism* 1991, 208.

12 Burritt wrote about one encounter with a German that 'he seemed like most of the Germans that we have met, to have no faith in anything except brute force'. Curti, *Burritt Letters* 1937, 62.

Pacifist internationalism only gradually shifted towards its modern connotations as antonymous to nationalism. The first successful peace society with a truly international composition was the *Ligue internationale de la paix et de la liberté,* founded a few years before the Franco-German War. However, even then their platform included the self-determination of the peoples as one of the most desirable concepts to incorporate as a principle of international law. Its more moderate French counterpart, the French Peace Society, led by Frédéric Passy, similarly did not fundamentally reject nationalism. To do so would have been political suicide. Rather than opposing the torrent of revanchism, Passy and his allies tried to give the indignation of their countrymen a legalistic colouring. If the Germans had showed their 'barbarism' by conquering Alsace and Lorraine through brute force, then France would prove its 'enlightened' nature by winning the lost provinces back through magnanimous and 'selfless' proposals for international law reform. The connections with nationalism faded over time, more or less in tune with how the rest of the peace movement came to co-opt the Genevan league's linkage of world peace with domestic justice. Universal republican values superseded particularism.

2.7 *Natural Law*

Not all of these various political agendas were necessarily understood as such by the peace friends themselves. Oftentimes, they would have seen them as axiomatic. These were not simply proposals for good policy, but proposals that conformed to certain timeless and universal 'truths'. As we have seen again and again, the notion of natural law featured prominently in the legal imagination of the nineteenth century international peace movement. Most were pragmatic enough to realise that their naturalistic precepts had to be adopted into some kind of positive legal instrument, such as a treaty or a judicial ruling. Nonetheless, these only gave expression to underlying natural norms, or served to facilitate their realisation. They did not substitute them. Positive law flying in the face of natural law was seen as doomed to fail.

This was most obvious with the religiously inspired legal discourse of the Anglo-American friends of peace. They did not have a doubt in their mind that their interpretation of scripture was the only correct one, at least with regards to what Christ had lectured about war. If humanity wanted to get rid of war once and for all, and introduce the Millennium into this world, governments would need to enact positive legislation that respected divine commandments. However, subjectivity disguising itself as universalism was not limited to religious circles. In the field of political economy too, peace friends usually did not frame their preferences as political choices. Far from it, their opinions were all 'scientific', and therefore elevated above ordinary political discourse. Free trade was 'proven' to foster peace. The boundaries between science and religion could be blurred. For someone to whom it was self-evident that God not only existed, but also corresponded to their Christian conceptions of divinity, it was simply inconceivable for 'scientific' laws to conflict with the laws of God. Cobden summarised it aptly when he exclaimed that 'Free trade is the international law of the Almighty'.

However, similar manifestations of self-evident objectivity returned also in the more secular pacifist circles of continental-Europe. Political economists like Chevalier or de Molinari were little different from their British peers in framing their economic positions as 'scientific'. Free trade was sacrosanct and not open for serious discussion. Those who opposed it were either of bad faith, or did not yet properly understand it. The Genevan League likewise claimed its republican values were grounded in 'science'. As observed, the most illustrative example of this was the 'science of peace' of Louis Bara. His 'science' beautifully encapsuled the peace movement's broader attempts to construct an international legal order suffused with a catalogue of timeless and universal political values, many of which might today be described as broadly 'liberal'. An uncompromising rationalist, Bara was convinced that his model would eventually be universally accepted. He took it so far that he ignored the political path altogether in his essay, one of the only early peace advocates to do so. Bara wrote almost nothing about confederations. Rather, his predictions about the autonomous development of international law closely resembled the motivations of Rolin-Jaequemyns and the illustrious 'men of 1873'.

2.8 *A Pacifist Legal Conscience*

In many ways, the *'conscience juridique'* that made jurists professionalise and autonomise international law in the last few decades of the nineteenth century was not unique to the international law society founded in Ghent in 1873. Something like it had already existed for years in many different places. The international peace movement had been shooting some of its arrows on international law since the very beginning. Although many vernacular legal proposals did not assume the exact institutional forms of the international law societies, they all shared many similar concerns as Rolin-Jacquemyns would have in the late 1860s and early 1870s. Both peace friends and 'professional' lawyers yearned for objectivity and universalism. They envisioned a similar future for international law: a future that was predicated on the legal equality of states, of international legal institutions, of relatively greater democratic legitimacy of diplomacy, and of stronger legal obstacles against the use of force. These progressist or even 'liberal' values were not presented as subjective political choices. No, they were presented as unavoidable. Much of the discourse was quasi-teleological.[13]

A latent convergence of interests between certain lawyers and parts of civil society had been ever present. Progressist lawyers and peace friends both drew from much deeper intellectual wells. Many of the most fundamental critiques has already been formulated in the eighteenth century, by people like the French *philosophes*, by Bentham, or by Kant. Given how international legal reform remained a salient issue in nineteenth century intellectual and political society, it should perhaps not surprise that the long search of the peace movement for practical means towards the reform of international law resulted in a few early proposals to eerily resemble later initiatives. At least four or five authors advocated for some kind of concerted activity of expert lawyers and publicists to remedy the faults of the law of nations. The most detailed and prominent of these was the 1849 essay by Louis Bara.

One of the first practical implementations occurred in Brussels, in 1873. The momentum generated by the *Alabama claims* and a recent European war allowed peace friends interested in that course to make their move. Some of it was also just dumb luck. If Beckwith had not died in 1870, or had not lost much of his credibility during the Civil War, Burritt would perhaps not have been able to gain access to the resources of the American Peace Society. Even if the predecessor of the International Law Association had not been founded in 1873, similar motivations animated some of the founders of the *Institut.* Several of its early members, like Field and de Laveleye, had connections to the peace movement. Even those who did not were intellectually connected to several of the peace societies. Some of the Anglo-American participants in particular were driven by a Protestant-Christian desire for perfectionism that would not have been out of place in the American Peace Society. Their main difference with religious peace friends was their much greater technical knowledge.

The politics of both the 'men of 1873' and of the peace movement were varied and heterogenous, but nonetheless conspired to form a peculiar legalistic sensibility. They were convinced not only of the righteousness of their views, but also of their inevitability. A hundred and fifty years later, many of their utopian ideas have indeed come to fruition. The *ius contra*

13 Koskenniemi, 'Politics of International Law' 1990, 4–32.

bellum has gone from a laughing-stock to the reigning paradigm of public international law, whether one agrees with it or not. What part did the early nineteenth century peace friends play in this tremendous long-term development?

3 Legacies of 'Peace through Law'

Much like its politics, the actual influence of the nineteenth century international peace movement has been diffuse, and therefore difficult to pinpoint exactly. Depending on how one looks at it, the impact of the early peace movement can range from anything between pitifully small to ridiculously substantial. As nearly always in history, the most accurate assessments are somewhere in the middle. The movement's immediate impact was indeed hardly noticeable, but its ideals have since captured the world's legal imagination and have developed into nearly unassailable foundational principles.

The track record of what the peace friends objectively achieved in the years between 1815 and 1873 was modest by any standard. In international law, their biggest feat was undoubtedly Henry Richard and Joseph Sturge managing to get a non-binding arbitration clause inserted into the treaty ending the Crimean War in 1856. A close second would be the role of the peace societies in setting up one of the first dedicated international law societies. The International Law Association still exists, even though it lost its connections to organised pacifism by 1914. Other tangible accomplishments were few and far between. As we have seen, the American Peace Society was uninvolved in the Mexican effort for an arbitration clause in the peace treaty with the United States in 1848. All peace friends had considerable difficulties being taken seriously and few of their juridical recommendations were translated into foreign policy during the mid-century.

While perhaps disappointing for some, not all was bleak. To an extent, the greatest achievement of the international peace movement was to have survived at all. The nineteenth century saw countless philanthropical societies come and go. Even today, one would not want to pay money for every ill-conceived attempt at improving the world. Early friends of peace faced enormous obstacles. They were separated from each other by sometimes gigantic geographical distances. Their societies were in perennial need of funding. They saw themselves mocked and ridiculed and those living in more conservative states even had to face governmental repression. In times of war, they were inevitably accused of cowardice or even treason.

Under those circumstances, it was a small miracle that these people not only managed to keep their societies running, but also made them grow and sometimes even thrive. They convinced some of the foremost legal minds of their countries to adjudicate their essay competitions. They were granted audiences with various heads of state and leading ministers. They even set up a series of international congresses in Europe, hundreds of kilometres from home. In a strictly organisational sense, they were far from unsuccessful, considering their size and means.

The most enduring achievements of the earliest peace friends proved to be on the theoretical level. By the time the international peace movement achieved the zenith of its popularity, somewhere in the years before World War One, nearly every major idea had already been thoroughly explored. If the founding generations were indeed utopians, they were utopians who well-understood the many angles of their ideals. If the first peace societies had not been founded around 1815, it was certainly possible for similar societies to have emerged later or elsewhere. Nonetheless, these other societies would have probably had to go through similar intellectual debates and organisational struggles. As it happened, however, the generations from Passy and Lemonnier onwards had the benefit of being able to draw from more than half a century of organised pacifist experience. The popular campaign for international arbitration of the late nineteenth and early nineteenth century essentially revolved around plans first developed in the 1830s and 1840s. Proponents of federalist peace solutions could likewise not ignore the great speech of Victor Hugo on the 'United States of Europe', or the many paper plans which had given substance to that grand ambition. Just like the first peace friends read the works of Saint-Pierre and Kant, so would future pacifists be inexorably influenced by the works of their nineteenth century predecessors. It is impossible to read the books of someone like count Coudenhove-Kalergi (1894–1972), one of the founding fathers of the European Union, and not be startled by the similarities of his pacifist ideals to those of the nineteenth century peace movement.[14] The same applies for other projects, from the International Court of Justice to the United Nations.

Within the confines of this study, it is impossible to tell to what extent the role of the peace friends was causational, rather than correlational. To a large extent, undoubtedly, the peace movement was just an expression of

14 Martyn Bond, *Hitler's Cosmopolitan Bastard. Count Richard Coudenhove-Kalergi and his Vision of Europe* (Montreal: McGill-Queen's University Press 2021), 78–89.

much more profound shifts, moving at a glacial pace. Peace friends would be the first to recognise that, despite their own self-aggrandising boasts. Like their journals wrote again and again, numerous factors were slowly turning the public sentiment against war, with or without the involvement of the peace societies. To name just a few: increased international travel, improved education, foreign news, and other sorts of globalisation. These have all contributed to instil a sense of shared values, or have at least rendered it more difficult to dehumanise adversaries. It was not a coincidence that more than one advocate of peace focussed as much on those goals, as they did on the reform of international law. Burritt was not only the leader behind the Brussels international law conference of 1873, but also the man who campaigned for 'ocean penny postage'. Many events that briefly uplifted the peace friends had been out of their control, like war scares and international crises. Applied to the 'peace through law' movement in the *longue durée*, the mass experience of two world wars probably did more to popularise pacifism and the need for legal reform than all pacifists and lawyers combined. The peace movement was the keeper of a little flame, little heeded by most. Under the right conditions, however, that weak light had the potential to ignite into a fiery blaze.[15]

Most great political reforms have been preceded by an avant-garde. Like every other vanguard, the international peace movement between 1815 and 1873 operated on the fringes of political and legal society. Once its ideologies began to slowly drip into the mainstream, from the final decades of the century onwards, the laurels understandably went to those pacifists and jurists whose achievements were plain for all to see. However, it would be severely mistaken to discredit the role played by the ones who had carried the torch during long periods of adversity. As much as the peace movement may have been a product of much broader developments, it was nonetheless still a factor in its own right. It were the founding generations who had ensured that, when the circumstances turned more favourable, the alternative visions were in place. With their critiques of the status quo, early pacifists echoed the roles of the philosophers they admired. Their relevance was not limited to philosophical speculation. As members of a social movement emerging out of civil society, friends of peace spoke directly to the public opinion from which they sprang and which they sought to further mould. In their own lifetimes already, the peace societies subverted the dominant political and legal ideologies.

15 Ceadel, *Origins* 1996, 19.

Revue de la Paix

Organe de la Société française pour l'Arbitrage entre Nations

JUSTITIA

PAX

SOMMAIRE

CH. RICHET, *professeur à la Faculté de médecine.* — L'Arbitrage et le conflit vénézuélien.

ANDRÉ WEISS, *professeur à la Faculté de droit.* — Le Droit de la Paix.

FÉLICIEN CHALLAYE, *agrégé de philosophie.* — A propos de notre Indo-Chine.

FRÉDÉRIC PASSY, *de l'Institut.* — Cinquante millions.

Chronique : I. *Notre Société :* Frédéric Passy. — II. *Le Mouvement pacifique :* à l'École des Hautes Études sociales ; la Délégation des sociétés françaises ; à la Chambre des Députés, etc. — III. *Les Puissances, la Guerre et la Paix armée ;* l'armée allemande ; les suites de la guerre anglo-boer, etc. — IV. *Progrès de l'idée d'Arbitrage et de solidarité internationale :* Nouvelle cause soumise à la Cour Permanente ; Commission franco-anglaise, etc.

Bibliographie. — *Hirondelle ou vautour ; Un apôtre de grand chemin ; Pour la Paix, pour la Liberté ; Tableau synoptique pour servir à l'étude du compte rendu officiel de la Conférence de La Haye.*

10, Rue Pasquier, Paris

Dépôt général : SCHLEICHER frères, 15, rue des Saints-Pères

E. Sonrel.

FIGURE 8.1 Art nouveau cover of the journal of Frédéric Passy's peace organisation in 1903. Notice the importance of law in both the illustration and the table of contents.

In a century when international law was mostly used as an apology for aggression and imperialism, rather than as a bulwark against it, the friends of peace were among those to raise their voice against it, in spite of overwhelming odds, convinced as they were of the righteousness of their cause.

Although the *ius contra bellum* has become a reality by the twenty-first century, many of the problems that the old peace friends faced still feel very modern. As anyone will readily admit, realist or idealist, the reign of 'permanent and universal' peace has not yet begun. The Millennium has not descended upon the earth. Eerily similar questions continue to vex jurists, politicians and citizens. How could an objective and universal world order look like? Is it even at all possible? Postmodernity does not afford the same level of intellectual certainty as the men and women of the nineteenth century had. Law is neither faith nor science, but politics; and all law might be politics, but not all politics is law. To be persuasive in politics requires mastering multiple languages. The pacifists always understood this and drew from a wide range of vocabularies. They turned to religion, science, economics and simple humanitarianism. None of these, however, could function without law. It is in norms where the rubber meets the road. It is in rules where utopia confronts reality and vice versa. Only history can cast judgment over the relative merits and failings of old discourses, legal or otherwise.

Most friends of peace have been long forgotten. Only a few traces remain of their campaign. Bertha von Suttner's bust graces the entrance of the Peace Palace library. In Wales, Henry Richard stands in the market square of his small hometown as 'the apostle of peace'. A similar honour befell Elihu Burritt in the erstwhile village where he was born and died. An allegorical representation of 'peace' commemorates the person 'to whose love for humanity the world owes the first international peace congress'. Burritt's hero, William Ladd, only ever got a small bronze plaque. It ends with the simple message: 'Blessed are the peace makers, for they shall be called the children of God'. Passy's name can be read on just a couple of unassuming street signs. Most passers-by undoubtedly ignore these inconspicuous memorials. None are as grandiose as the countless monuments towering over stately boulevards, honouring military leaders. Most friends of peace are not remembered at all. The only evidence that they have ever existed lies in yellowed pages hidden away on some shelf. Any personal memory of them died with their loved ones as the 1800s receded into the past.

Maybe most would have preferred it this way. None of these men and women worked to become popular. They worked to make the world a slightly less violent place for the next generation, one conversion at a time.

Today, the ambitions of the friends of peace live on in the mundane day-to-day activities of an impressive number of institutions. Their old ideals are still breathed into life not only by U.N. commissions, law professors, or judges, but also by parliaments, N.G.O.s, news desks, classrooms and many more unexpected places. When international lawyers struggle to realise the promises contained in the idea of *ius contra bellum,* the history of the peace movement reminds them that they have never stood alone in this endeavour. The rule of law begins and ends with ordinary people and their sense of justice. To continue in this timeless ambition is the only monument that matters.

Bibliography

Archives & Libraries

Archives d'état de Genève
Archives de l'Académie royale de Belgique
Bibliothèque de Genève
Bibliothèque Marguerite Durand
Bibliothèque nationale de France
Bibliothèque Sainte-Geneviève
British Library
Erfgoedbibliotheek Hendrik Conscience
Institute of Advanced Legal Studies Archives
Internationaal Instituut voor Sociale Geschiedenis
La Courneuve – Centre des Archives diplomatiques
Library of Congress
Maine Historical Society
Max Planck Institute for Legal History and Legal Theory
Peace Palace Library
Royal Library of Belgium
Vlaams Vredesinstituut
Zentralbibliothek Zürich

University libraries and archives:
- Goethe Universität Frankfurt
- Institut catholique de Paris
- Katholieke Universiteit Leuven
- Université catholique de Louvain
- Université de Mons
- Université libre de Bruxelles
- Universiteit Gent
- Vrije Universiteit Brussel

Databases

Archive.org
Bayerische Staatsbibliothek

Belgicapress
BnF Gallica
Cairn.info
EBSCOhost – American Antiquarian Society (AAS) Historical Periodicals Collection
Europeana
Google Books
JSTOR

Source Collections

Bowring, John (ed.). *The Works of Jeremy Bentham* (Edinburgh: Simpkin, Marshall & Co., 1843).

Chesson, F.W. (ed.) *The Political Writings of Richard Cobden* (London: Cassel, 1886).

Curti, Merle (ed). *The Learned Blacksmith. The Letters and Journals of Elihu Burritt* (New York: Wilson-Erickson, 1937).

Horowitz, Valerie (ed). *The Unsigned Essays of Supreme Court Justice Joseph Story. Early American Views of Law* (New Jersey: Lawbook Exchange, 2015).

Howe, Anthony (ed.). *The Letters of Richard Cobden. Four Volumes* (Oxford: Oxford University Press, 2007–2015).

Kleingeld, Pauline (ed). *'Toward Perpetual Peace' and other Writings on Politics, Peace, and History* (New Haven: Yale University Press, 2006).

Meier-Smith, Matson (ed.). *Memorial of Mr. David Low Dodge, consisting of an Autobiography, prepared at the Request and for the Use of his Children; with a few Selections from his Writings* (Boston: Whipple, 1854).

Mowat, R.B. (ed.). *Select Treaties and Documents to Illustrate the Development of the Modern European States System. 1815–1916* (Oxford: Clarendon, 1916).

Pierce, Edward (ed.). *Memoirs and Letters of Charles Sumner. Four Volumes* (Boston: Roberts Brothers, 1877).

Unknown editor. *Charles Sumner. His Complete Works. With Introduction by Hon. George Frisbie Hoar. Twenty volumes* (Boston: Lee and Shepard, 1900).

Van den Dungen, Peter (ed.). *From Erasmus to Tolstoy. The Peace Literature of Four Centuries; Jacob ter Meulen's Bibliographies of the Peace Movement before 1899* (New York: Greenwood Press, 1990).

Legal Documents

Charter of the United Nations, 24 October 1945, 1 UNTS XVI.

Covenant of the League of Nations, 28 June 1919, The Avalon Project, Yale Law School, available at avalon.law.yale.edu/20th_century/leagcov.asp.
Declaration respecting Maritime Law between Austria, France, Great Britain, Prussia, Russia, Sardinia, and Turkey, 16 April 1856, 15 CTS 1.
General Treaty for the Re-Establishment of Peace between Austria, France, Great Britain, Prussia, Sardinia and Turkey, and Russia, 30 March 1856, 114 CTS 409.
Geneva, Constitution pour la ville et république de Genève, 24 August 1814.
Holy Alliance between Austria, Prussia and Russia, 8 February 1815, 65 CTS 199.
Tratado de Union, Liga y Confederación perpetua entre las Repúblicas de Colombia, Centro América, Perú y Estados Unidos Mexicanos, 15 de julio de 1826, Dipublico.org, available at www.dipublico.org/12355/tratado-de-union-liga-y-confederacion-perpetua-entre-las-republicas-de-colombia-centro-america-peru-y-estados-unidos-mexicanos-15-de-julio-de-1826-congreso-de-panama-1826/.
Treaty between the United States and Great Britain, 8 May 1871, 143 CTS 145.
Treaty of Amity and Commerce Between His Majesty the King of Prussia, and the United States of America, 10 September 1785, the Avalon Project, Yale Law School, available at: avalon.law.yale.edu/18th_century/prus1785.asp.
Treaty of Peace and Amity between his Britannic Majesty and the United States of America, *American State Papers. I. Foreign Relations* (Washington: Gales and Seaton, 1833).
United Nations, Secretariat, 'Outline of the Codification of International Law in the Inter-American System with Special Reference to the Methods of Codification' (6 May 1947), UN Doc A/AC.10/8.
United Nations, International Law Commission, 'Report of the Commission to the General Assembly on the Work of its Fifty-Third Session' (23 April–1 June and 2 July–10 August 2001), UN Doc A/56/10, 85, 112.
United States, Articles of Confederation, 15 November 1777, Library of Congress, available at: www.loc.gov/resource/llsalvol.llsal_001/?sp=127&r=-0.547,-0.008,2.094,1.768,0.

Pre–1901 journals and newspapers

Advocate of Peace
Advocate of Peace and Universal Brotherhood
Archives de la société de la paix de Genève
Bond of Brotherhood
Bulletin de la société des amis de la paix
Correspondance cosmopolite

Die Friedens-Warte
Friend of Peace
Hansard's Parliamentary Debates
Harbinger of Peace
Herald of Peace
Journal de l'Ain
Journal de la société de la morale Chrétienne
Journal des débats
Journal des économistes
Journals of the House of Commons
L'économiste belge
L'indépendance belge
La paix des deux mondes
La presse
Le constitutionnel
Le moniteur universel
Le rameau d'olivier
Le temps
Les États-Unis d'Europe
Monthly Magazine
Phare de la Loire
Revue de Belgique
Revue de droit international et de législation comparée
Revue des deux mondes
The Calumet
The Congressional Globe
The Non-Resistant
The Spectator
The Times
Transactions of the National Association for the Promotion of Social Science
Voice of Peace

Pre–1901 Books, Pamphlets, and Articles

A Circular Letter from the Massachusetts Peace Society, respectfully addressed to the Various Associations, Presbyteries, Assemblies and Meetings of the Ministers of Religion in the United States (Cambridge: Hilliard and Metcalf, 1816).

A.G. *Peace (Permanent and Universal). The Law of Christ* (London: Ward & Co., 1847).

All War Anti-Christian; or the Principles of Peace, as contained in the Holy Scriptures, explained and proved by the Tracts of the Society for the Promotion of Permanent and Universal Peace (London: Thomas Ward, 1840).

Ancillon, Friedrich. *Tableau des révolutions du système politique de l'Europe depuis la fin du quinzième siècle. Première partie. Tome premier* (Berlin: Quien, 1803).

Annales du congrès de Genève. 9–12 septembre 1867 (Genève: Vérésoff & Garriques, 1868).

Annuaire de l'institut de droit international. 1877 (Gand: Van Doosselaere, 1877).

'Arbitration', *Grand dictionnaire universel du XIXe siècle*, ed. Pierre Larousse (Paris: Administration du grand dictionnaire universel, 1866–1877).

Bacheler, Origen. *Dissertation on a Congress of Nations, for the Adjustment of International Disputes without Recourse to Arms* (New York: Collier, 1837).

Bara, Louis. *La science de la paix. Programme. Mémoire couronné, à Paris, en 1849, par le congrès des sociétés anglo-américaines des amis de la paix*, ed. Charles Potvin (Bruxelles: Muquardt, 1872).

Bazan, Patrice. *D'une paix universelle et permanente* (Paris: Baudouin, 1842).

Beckwith, George. *The Peace Manual: or, War and its Remedies* (Boston: American Peace Society, 1847).

Berry, Philip. *A Review of the Mexican War on Christian Principles: and an Essay on the Means of Preventing War* (Columbia: Johnston, 1849).

Blakslee, Solomon. *An Address delivered before the Members of the East-Haddam Branch of the Massachusetts Peace Society* (Middletown: Clark & Lyman, 1820).

Bluntschli, Johann Caspar. *Das moderne Völkerrecht der zivilisierten Staaten, als Rechtsbuch dargestellt* (Nördlingen, Beck, 1868).

Bogue, David. *On Universal Peace; being Extracts from a Discourse delivered in October 1813* (London: Clay, 1826).

Bogue, David (eds. Jean-Jacques de Sellon and Susanne Guers). *Paix universelle Durant le millénium. Discours prononcé à Gosport par David Bogue, accompagné de notes, et suivi du traité de la Sainte Alliance* (Genève: Guers, 1829).

Bolles, John. *Essay on a Congress of Nations for the Pacific Adjustment of International Disputes* (Boston: Whipple & Damrell, 1839).

Bonaparte, Louis-Napoléon. *Des idées napoléoniennes* (Paris: Paulin, 1839).

Bonaparte, Louis-Napoléon. *Œuvres de Napoléon III. Tome troisième* (Paris: Plon, Amyot, 1869).

Bouvet, Francisque. *République ou monarchie, ou principes d'ordre social* (Paris: Mie, 1832).

Bouvet, Francisque. *Du rôle de la France dans la question d'Orient. Congrès universel et perpétuel à Constantinople* (Nantua: Arène, 1840).

Bouvet, Francisque. *Lettre adressée à citoyen Proudhon* (Bourg: Milliet-Bottier, 1849).

Bouvet, Francisque. *La Turquie et les cabinets de l'Europe depuis le XVe siècle. La question de l'Orient* (Paris: Giraud, 1853).

Bouvet, Francisque. *La guerre et la civilisation* (Paris: Dentu, 1855).

Bouvet, Francisque. *Introduction à l'établissement d'un droit public européen* (Paris: Dentu, 1856).

Bouvet, Francisque. *Le problème européen* (Paris: Renou et Maulde, 1866).

Bowring, John. *Autobiographical Recollections of Sir John Bowring. With a brief Memoir by Lewin B. Bowring* (London: Henry S. King, 1877).

Bright, John. *The Letter of John Bright, Esq., M.P., on the War, Verified and Illustrated by Extracts from the Parliamentary Documents, &c.* (London: Cash, 1854).

Bulletin sténographique du deuxième congrès de la paix et de la liberté (unknown location: unknown publisher, 1868).

Bulletin officiel du congrès de la paix et de la liberté (Lausanne: Association Typographique, 1869).

Bulletin officiel du congrès de la paix et de la liberté (Lausanne: Association typographique, 1871).

Bulletin officiel du sixième congrès (Genève: Imprimerie coopérative, 1872).

Bulletin officiel des assemblées tenues à Genève les 7, 8 & 9 septembre 1873 (Genève: Imprimerie coopérative, 1873).

Burritt, Elihu. *Ten-Minute Talks on All Sorts of Topics* (Boston: Lee and Shepard, 1874).

Burritt, Elihu. *Walks in the Black Country and its Green Borderland* (London: Sampson, Law, Son, and Marston, 1869).

Burritt, Elihu. *Elihu Burritt; a Memorial Volume containing a Sketch of his Life and Labors, with Selections from his Writings and Lectures, and Extracts from his Private Journals in Europe and America*, ed. Chas. Northend (New York: Appleton, 1879).

Channing, William. *A Sermon, preached in Boston, July 23, 1812, the Day of the Publick Fast, appointed by the Executive of the Commonwealth of Massachusetts, in Consequence of the Declaration of War against Great Britain* (Boston: Greenough and Stebbins, 1812).

Cheever, George. *A Discourse on the Virtues and Public Services of the late Judge Jay* (Boston: American Peace Society, 1860).

Chevalier, Michel. *Politique européenne* (Paris: Bureau du Globe, 1832).

Chevalier, Michel. *Politique industrielle et système de la méditerranée* (Paris: unknown publisher, 1832).

Chevalier, Michel. *Du progrès. Discours à l'ouverture de son cours au collége de France* (Paris: Guillaumin, 1852).

Clarkson, Thomas. *Thomas Clarkson's Interview with the Emperor Alexander I of Russia, as Aix-la-Chapelle, as told by Himself* (London: Poyser, 1930).

Clarkson, Thomas. *An Essay on the Doctrines and Practice of the Early Christians as they Relate to War. Addressed to those who Profess to have Regard for the Christian Name* (London: Bensley, 1840).

Cleveland, Aaron. *Life of Man Inviolable by the Laws of Christ, shown in Two Sermons…* (Colchester: Skinner, 1815).

Cobden, Richard. *The Three Panics. An Historical Episode* (London: Ward & Co., 1862).

Concours institué par les sociétés anglo-américaines de la paix, au Congrès de Bruxelles, septembre 1848. Rapport des commissaires (Bruxelles: Hayez, 1849).

Condorcet, Nicolas de. *Réflexions sur ce qui a été fait et sur ce qui reste à faire, lues dans une Société d'Amis de la paix* (Paris: imprimerie de l'Assemblée Nationale, 1789).

Congrès des amis de la paix universelle réuni à Paris en 1849 (Paris: Guillaumin, 1850).

Coquerel, Athanase. *Sermons de A.L.C. Coquerel* (Amsterdam: Delachaux, 1819).

Coquerel, Athanase. *Sermons par Athanase Coquerel* (Paris: Cherbuliez, 1843).

de Las Cases, Emmanuel. *Mémorial de Sainte-Hélène. 8 volumes* (Bruxelles: Remy, 1822–1823).

De la Sagra, Ramon. *Utopie de la paix. Extraits des doctrines émises au congrès de la paix réuni à Bruxelles au mois de septembre 1848* (Paris: Capelle, 1849).

de Pradt, Dominique Dufour. *Congrès de Panama* (Paris: Béchet ainé, 1825).

Deuxième assemblée générale. 21 juin 1869 (Paris: Guillaumin, 1869).

Dodge, David Low, *The Mediator's Kingdom not of this World; but Spiritual, Heavenly, and Divine…* (New York: Williams & Whiting, 1809).

Dodge, David Low. *War Inconsistent with the Religion of Jesus Christ, by David Low Dodge. With an Introduction by Edwin D. Mead* (Boston: Ginn, 1905).

Dumesnil, Henri. *La guerre. Étude philosophique* (Paris: Guillaumin, 1872).

Dunant, David. *Aux mânes de Jean-Jacques comte de Sellon, citoyen de Genève, philanthrope par excellence* (Genève: Gruaz, 1839).

Dupasquier, Henri. *Le crime de la guerre dénoncé à l'humanité* (Paris: Guillaumin, 1873).

Durand, Ferdinand. *Des tendances pacifiques de la société européenne, et du rôle des armées dans l'avenir. Deuxième édition* (Paris: Dumaine, 1844).

Dymond, Jonathan. *Essays on the Principles of Morality, and on the Private and Political Rights and Obligations of Mankind* (London: Hamilton, Adams & Co., 1836).

Dymond, Jonathan. *Observations on the Applicability of the Pacific Principles of the New Testament to the Conduct of States; and on the Limitations which those Principles Impose on the Rights of Self-Defence* (London: Clay, 1840).

Ferrer, Jean-Baptiste. *L'ère nouvelle. Nécessité d'un code international et d'un tribunal arbitral des nations* (Paris: Plon, 1863).

Field, David Dudley. *Draft Outlines of an International Code* (New York: Diossy, 1872).

Gabourd, Amédée. *Histoire contemporaine comprenant les principaux événements qui se sont accomplis depuis la révolution de 1830 jusqu'à nos jours et résumant, durant la même période, le mouvement social, artistique et littéraire. Tome deuxième* (Paris: Didot, 1864).

Gallison, John. *A Proposed Memorial to the Congress of the United States* (Boston, 1819).

Gardes, Jean-Jacques. *Notice sur le comte de Sellon, suivie d'une élégie chrétienne à sa famille* (Nismes: Durand-Belle, 1839).

Gasc. Ferdinand E. A., *Lettres à M. Ramon de la Sagra sur l'utopie de la paix* (Paris: Ledoyen, 1851).

Gibbes, George. *A Letter to the American Peace Society* (Paris: Brière, 1842).

Girardin, Émile de. *Les 52. VII–VIII. La politique de la paix* (Paris: Lévy Frères, 1849).

Girardin, Émile de. *La paix* (Paris: Libraire Nouvelle, 1855).

Girardin, Émile de. *La politique universelle. Décrets de l'avenir* (Paris: Librairie Nouvelle, 1855).

Girardin, Émile de. *Questions de mon temps, 1836 à 1856. Questions politiques. Tome neuvième* (Paris: Serriere, 1858).

Girardin, Émile de. *L'Empereur Napoléon III et l'Europe* (Bruxelles: Librairie de l'Office de Publicité, 1859).

Girardin, Émile de. *L'équilibre européen* (Paris: Lévy Frères, 1859).

Goblet d'Alviella, Eugène. *Désarmer ou déchoir. Essai sur les relations internationales* (Paris: Guillaumin, 1872).

Gondon, J.J.B. *Du droit public et du droit des gens, ou principes d'association civile et politique; suivis d'un projet de paix générale et perpétuelle. Tome III* (Paris: Brasseur, 1807).

Grimké, Thomas. *An Oration on the Absolute Necessity of Union, and the Folly and Madness of Disunion* (Charleston: Riley, 1829).

Grimké, Thomas. *Address on the Truth, Dignity, Power and Beauty of the Principles of Peace, and the on the Unchristian Character and Influence of War and the Warrior* (Hartford: Olmsted, 1832).

Grimké, Thomas. *To the People of the State of South-Carolina* (Charleston, 1832).

Guilhaumon, F. *La guerre et les épidémies. D'après les mémoires de la société des sciences médicales de Metz* (Paris: Guillaumin, 1868).

Gurney, Joseph. *Observations on the Religious Peculiarities of the Society of Friends* (London: Arch, 1824).

Gurney, Joseph. *An Essay on War, and on its Lawfulness under the Christian Dispensation* (London: Clay, 1840).

Hancock, Thomas. *The Principles of Peace exemplified in the Conduct of the Society of Friends in Ireland, during the Rebellion of the Year 1798 with some Preliminary and Concluding observations. In Three Parts* (London: Clay, 1840).

Haynes, Frederick. 'The Reciprocity Treaty With Canada of 1854'. *Publications of the American Economic Association* 7(6) (1892).

Heaton, Adna. *War and Christianity contrasted; with a Comparative View of their Nature and Effects…* (New York: Wood & Sons, 1816).

Hemmenway, John. *The Apostle of Peace. Memoir of William Ladd, with an Introduction by Elihu Burritt* (Boston: American Peace Society, 1872).

Henry, Léon. *Le crime international* (Paris: Larose, 1872).

Howitt, William. *Colonization and Christianity. A Popular History of the Treatment of the Natives by the Europeans in All their Colonies* (London: Longman, Orme, Brown, Green & Longman, 1838).

Instructions for the Government of the Armies of the United States in the Field, Prepared by Francis Lieber, L.L.D. and Revised by a Board of Officers (New York: Nostrand, 1863).

International Arbitration and the Improvement of International Law. The Debate in the House of Commons, on Tuesday, July 8th, 1873, the Motion of Mr. Henry Richard for an Address to the Crown (London: Hodder & Stoughton, 1873).

Jay, William. *The Life of John Jay: with Selections from the Correspondence and Miscellaneous Papers, vol. 1* (New York: Harper, 1833).

Jay, William. *An Inquiry into the Character and Tendency of the American Colonization, and American Anti-Slavery Societies* (New York: Leavitt, Lord & Co., 1835).

Jay, William. *War and Peace: the Evils of the First, and a Plan for preserving the Last* (London: Ward, 1842).

Jay, William. *A Review of the Causes and Consequences of the Mexican War* (Boston: Mussey & Co., 1849).

Jay, William. *The Kossuth Excitement: a Letter* (Boston: American Peace Society, 1852).

Jay, William. *War and Peace: the Evils of the First, and a Plan for preserving the Last. Reprinted from the Original Edition of 1842 with an Introductory Note by James Brown Scott* (New York: Oxford University Press, 1919).

Jouer aux soldats: histoire véritable (Londres: Société de la paix, 1847).

Kamarowsky, Leonide. *Le tribunal international* (Paris: Pedone-Lauriel, 1887).

Kant, Immanuel (transl. Jules Barni). *Éléments métaphysiques de la doctrine du droit, suivis d'un essai philosophique sur la paix perpétuelle et d'autres petits écrits relatifs au droit naturel* (Paris: Durand, 1853).

Kaufmann, Peter. *Die Idee und der praktische Nutzen einer Weltakademie des Völkerrechts* (Bonn: Habidt, 1855).

Ladd, William. *The Essays of Philanthropos on Peace & War* (Portland: Shirley & Edwards, 1825).

Ladd, William. *Essays on Peace & War. New Series* (Portland: Shirley, 1827).

Ladd, William. *Dissertation on a Congress of Nations* (Unknown location: Loring, 1832).

Ladd, William. *The Hero of Macedon, or History of Alexander the Great viewed in the Light of the Gospel* (Boston: Loring, 1832).

Ladd, William [pseud. Philanthropos]. *On the Duty of Females to promote the Cause of Peace* (Boston: Ford, 1836).

Ladd, William. 'History of the Peace Societies', in *Scientific Tracts for the Diffusion of Useful Knowledge*, eds. Samuel Fish et. al. (Boston: Light & Stearns, 1836).

Ladd, William. *Obstacles and Objections to the Cause of Permanent and Universal Peace considered by a Layman* (Boston: Hitchcock, 1837).

Ladd, William. *Obstacles and Objections to the Cause of Permanent and Universal Peace, considered* (London: Thomas Ward, 1840).

Ladd, William. *An Essay on a Congress of Nations, for the Adjustment of International Disputes without Resort to Arms. Containing the Substance of the Rejected Essays on that Subject with Original Thoughts and a Copious Appendix* (Boston: Whipple and Damrell, 1840).

Ladd, William. *An Essay on a Congress of Nations for the Adjustment of International Disputes without Resort to Arms, by William Ladd. Reprinted from the Original Edition of 1840 with an Introduction by James Brown Scott. With a New Introduction by Mark Weston Janis* (New Jersey: Lawbook Exchange, 2007).

Laporte, Michel-Édouard. *L'Alscace reconquise* (Paris: Franklin, 1873).

Larrieu, A. *Guerre à la guerre* (Paris: Guillaumin, 1868).

Laveleye, Émile de. *On the Causes of War, and the Means of Reducing their Number* (London: Peace Society, 1872).

Laveleye, Émile de. *Des causes actuelles de guerre en Europe et de l'arbitrage* (Bruxelles: Muquardt, 1873).

Les maux de la guerre et les bienfaits de la paix. Première réunion publique tenue à Paris le 10 février 1869 par les amis de la paix. Discours de MM. Ed. Laboulaye, président. Frédéric Passy. Suivis d'une conférence faite à Metz sur le respect mutuel par M.B. Faivre (Paris: Pichon-Lamy et Dewez, 1869).

Lemonnier, Charles. *La vérité sur le congrès de Genève* (Genève: Vérésoff & Garrigues, 1867).

Lemonnier, Charles. *Les États-Unis d'Europe* (Paris: Bibliothèque Démocratique, 1872).

Leroy-Beaulieu, Paul. *Contemporary Wars (1853–1866). Statistical Researches respecting the Loss of Men and Money involved in Them* (London: London Peace Society, 1869).

Leroy-Beaulieu, Paul. *Recherches économiques, historiques et statistiques sur les guerres contemporaines (1853–1866)* (Paris: Lacroix, Verboeckhoven, et compagnie, 1869).

Levi, Leone. *The Law of Nature and Nations as affected by Divine Law* (London: Cash, 1855).

Levi, Leone. *Proposals for a Plan of Arbitration and Mediation for the Settlement of International Disputes, to be submitted to any European Conference which may be held at the Conclusion of the Present War* (unknown location: unknown publisher, 1871).

Ligue internationale et permanente de la paix. Deuxième bulletin (Paris: unknown publisher, 1867).

List of Donors and Subscribers to the Society for the Promotion of Permanent and Universal Peace (unknown location: unknown publisher, 1836).

Livermore, Abiel. *The War with Mexico Reviewed* (Boston: Forbes, 1850).

Lord, Eleazar. *Thoughts on the Practical Advantages of Those who hold the Doctrines of Peace over Those who vindicate War* (New York: Seymour, 1816).

Love, Alfred. *A Brief Synopsis of Work Proposed, Aided, and Accomplished by the Universal Peace Union during the Last 31 Years* (unknown location: unknown publisher, 1897).

Lucas, Charles. *Du système pénal et du système répressif en général, de la peine de mort en particulier* (Paris: Béchet, 1827).

MacNamara, Henry. *Peace, Permanent and Universal: its Practicability, Value, and Consistency with Divine Revelation. A Prize Essay* (London: Saunders and Otley, 1841).

Malardier, Pierre. *Confédération européenne. Réalisation du droit international* (Bruxelles: Lacroix, Verboeckhoven & Compagnie, 1861).

Marchand, Philippe-René. *Nouveau projet de traité de paix perpétuelle* (Paris: Renouard, 1842).

Mézières, M.L. *De la polémanie, ou folie de la guerre dans l'Europe actuelle* (Paris: Bellaire, 1872).

Miles, James B. *Association for the Reform and Codification of the Law of Nations. A brief Sketch of its Formation* (Paris: Brière, 1875).

Mill, James. 'Law of Nations', in *Essays on Government, Jurisprudence, Liberty of the Press, and Law of Nations* (London: Innes, 1829).

Molinari, Gustave de. *Les soirées de la rue de Saint-Lazare. Entretiens sur les lois économiques et défense de la propriété* (Paris: Guillaumin, 1849).

Molinari, Gustave de. 'Paix – Guerre', in *Dictionnaire de l'économie politique. Tome second*, eds. Charles Coquelin and Gilbert Guillaumin (Paris: Guillaumin, 1853).

Molinari, Gustave de. *La question d'Orient envisagée au point de vue de l'économie politique et du droit public* (Paris: Hennuyer, 1854).

Molinari, Gustave de. *L'abbé de Saint-Pierre. Membre exclu de l'académie française. Sa vie et ses œuvres* (Paris: Guillaumin, 1857).

Molinari, Gustave de. *Napoléon III, publiciste* (Bruxelles: Lacroix, Van Meenen & Compagnie, 1861).

Molinari, Gustave de. *Questions d'économie politique et de droit public. Tome II* (Paris: Guillaumin, 1861).

Molinari, Gustave de. *Le congrès européen* (Bruxelles: Lacroix, Verboeckhoven, et Compagnie, 1864).

Molinari, Gustave de. *Notice sur M. Joseph Garnier* (Nice: Cauvin, 1876).

Molinari, Gustave de. *L'évolution politique et la révolution* (Paris: Guillaumin, 1884).

Molinari, Gustave de. *Le droit de la paix et le droit de la guerre* (Paris: Guillaumin, 1887).

Morley, John. *The Life of Richard Cobden. Volume 1* (Cambridge: Cambridge University Press, 2010).

Nicole, François. *Pacifisme et colonisation. Précédé d'une lettre-préface de M. Frédéric Passy* (Paris: Comité d'action républicaine aux colonies françaises, 1908).

Paley, William. *The Principles of Moral and Political Philosophy* (London: Baldwyn, 1821).

Papers Relating to the Treaty of Washington. Volume IV. Geneva Arbitration (Washington: Government Printing Office, 1872).

Passy, Frédéric. *Revanche et relèvement. Exposé de la situation aux membres de la Ligue internationale et permanente de la paix* (Paris: unknown publisher, 1872).

Passy, Frédéric. *Pour la paix. Notes et documents* (Paris: Charpentier, 1909).

Pecqueur, Constantin. *Économie sociale des intérêts du commerce de l'industrie et de l'agriculture, et de la civilisation en général* (Paris: Desessart, 1839).

Pecqueur, Constantin. *De la paix. De son principe et de sa réalisation* (Paris: Capelle, 1842).

Pierantoni, Augusto. *Storia del diritto internatiozonale nel secolo XIX* (Napoli: Marghieri, 1876).

Portalis, Joseph-Marie. 'Rapport sur les mémoires adressés au concours pour le prix sur la question du droit des gens', in *Mémoires de l'Académie royale des sciences morales et politiques de l'Institut de France* (Paris: Firmin Didot Frères, 1841).

Porter, Charles. *Review of the Mexican War, embracing the Causes of the War, the Responsibility of its Commencement, the Purposes of the American Government in its Prosecution, its Benefits and its Evils* (Auburn: Alden & Parsons, 1849).

Potonié-Pierre, Edmond. *Historique du mouvement pacifique* (Berne: Steiger & Cie, 1899).

Première assemblée générale. 8 juin 1868 (Paris: Guillaumin, 1868).

Prize Essays on a Congress of Nations (Boston: Whipple and Damrell, 1840).

Proceedings of the Peace Convention, held in Boston, in the Marlboro Chapel, September 18, 19, & 20, 1838 (Boston: Knapp, 1838).

Proceedings of the Peace Conventions, held in Boston, March 14 & 15, 1866; and in Providence, May 16th, 1866 (unknown location: Universal Peace Union, 1866).

Proceedings of a Peace Meeting held at Union League Hall, New York, December 23rd, 1870, for the Purpose of Free Consultation on the Subject of a Woman's Peace Congress for the World (Philadelphia: Gillam, 1871).

Proudhon, Pierre-Joseph. *La guerre et la paix. Recherches sur le principe et la constitution du droit des gens* (Paris: Lévy Frères, 1861).

Proudhon, Pierre-Joseph. *Du principe fédératif et de la nécessité de reconstituer le parti de la révolution* (Paris: Dentu, 1863).

Quérard, Jean-Marie. *La France littéraire, ou dictionnaire bibliographique. Tome dixième* (Paris: Didot frères, 1839).

Quetelet, Adolphe. *Du système social et des lois qui le régissent* (Paris: Guillaumin, 1848).

Quincy, Josiah. *Address, delivered at the Fifth Anniversary of the Massachusetts Peace Society, December 25th, 1820* (Cambridge: Hilliard and Metcalf, 1821).

Rees, Evan (ed.) *Extracts from the Writings of Erasmus, on the Subject of War* (London: Clay, 1840).

Rees, Evan. *Sketches of the Horrors of War, chiefly selected from Labaume's Narrative of the Campaign in Russia, in 1812. Translated from the French, with some Observations* (London: Clay, 1840).

Reports of the First Conference held at Brussels, 1873, and of the Second Conference held at Geneva, 1874 (London: West, Newman, & Co., 1903).

Report of the Proceedings of the Third General Peace Congress, held in Frankfort, on the 22nd, 23rd, and 24th August, 1850 (London: Gilpin, 1851).

Report of the Proceedings of the Fourth General Peace Congress, held in Exeter Hall, London, on the 22nd, 23rd, and 24th July, 1851 (London: Gilpin, 1851).

Report of the Proceedings of the Peace Conference at Edinburgh, October 12th and 13th, 1853 (Edinburgh: Thomas Nelson, 1853).

Résolutions votées par les vingt-un premiers congrès. Recueil officiel (Genève: Bureau des États-Unis d'Europe, 1888).

Réveillère, Paul Émile Marie [pseud. Brandat]. *Mers de Chine* (Paris: Pichon, 1872).

Richard, Henry. *Memoirs of Joseph Sturge* (London: Partridge, 1865).

Roberts, Mary [pseud. A Lady]. *An Examination of the Principles which are considered to support the Practice of War* (London: Clay, 1840).

Roberts, Mary [pseud. A Lady]. *Historical Illustrations of the Origin and Consequences of War* (London: Clay, 1840).

Rousseau, Jean-Jacques. *Collection complète des œuvres de J.J. Rousseau. Tome vingt-troisième* (Genève: unknown publisher, 1782).

Santallier, Félix. *L'union de la paix entre tous les peuples civilisés. Proposition adressée à la loge l'Aménité, au Havre* (Le Havre: unknown publisher, 1867).

Sartorius, Johann Baptist. *Organon des Vollkommenen Friedens. Gekrönte Preisschrift* (Zürich, Höhr, 1837).

Scott, John. *War Inconsistent with the Doctrine and Example of Jesus Christ. In a Letter to a Friend* (London: Clay, 1840).

Second Annual Report of the Committee of Inquiry of the Massachusetts Peace Society (Cambridge: Hilliard and Metcalf, unknown year).

Seebohm, Frederic. *On International Reform* (London: Longmans, Green, and Co., 1871).

Seebohm, Frederick. *De la réforme du droit des gens. Introduction par Frédéric Passy* (Paris: Franklin, 1873).

Sellon, Jean-Jacques de. *Un mot sur la proposition de M. J.-J. de Sellon, pour la suppression de la peine de mort, suivi des point principaux qui doivent être traités dans le concours, et de quelques fragmens sur ce sujet* (Genève: Le Double, 1826).

Sellon, Jean-Jacques de. *Lettre de l'auteur du concours ouvert à Genève en 1816, en faveur de l'abolition de la peine de mort, à l'un de ses honorables collègues du Conseil souverain* (Genève: Lador, 1827).

Sellon, Jean-Jacques de. *Extraits tirés d'un journal allemand, destiné à rendre compte de la législation et du droit dans toutes les contrées civilises. Dirigés par MM. Zacharie et Mittermaier, accompagnés d'annotations et de réflexions de M. J. J. de Sellon* (Genève: Barbezat, 1829).

Sellon, Jean-Jacques de. *Fragmens extraits des mémoires de Commines et de l'histoire des ducs de Bourgogne, suivis des scènes dramatiques* (Genève: Barbezat, 1829).

Sellon, Jean-Jacques de. *Mes Réflexions. Tome II* (Genève: Lador, 1829).

Sellon, Jean-Jacques de. *Lettre sur la guerre, adressée à M. de ***, suivi de la 2e édition d'un article sur l'Afrique, publié en 1829* (Genève: Vignier, 1830).

Sellon, Jean-Jacques de. *Vœux adressés au futur congrès* (Genève: Vignier, 1830).

Sellon, Jean-Jacques de. *À qui appartiennent le titre et les droits de la souveraineté dans la République et Canton de Genève?* (Genève: unknown publisher, 1831).

Sellon, Jean-Jacques de. *Considérations sur l'initiative* (Genève: Lador, 1831).

Sellon, Jean-Jacques de. *Fragmens des ouvrages de Jérémie Bentham, accompagnés de réflexions de M. de Sellon, membre du conseil souverain de Genève. Dédiées aux amis du gouvernements représentatif* (Genève: Vignier, 1831).

Sellon, Jean-Jacques de. *Traduction littérale du préambule du code de Léopold, grand-duc de Toscane, en Vertu duquel il a aboli la peine de mort dans ses états, accompagnée de quelques notes de M. de Sellon* (Genève: Gruaz, 1831).

Sellon, Jean-Jacques de. *Quelques observations de M. de Sellon sur l'ouvrage intitulé 'Nécessité du maintien de la peine de mort, tant pour les crimes politiques que pour les crimes privés'* (Genève: Gruaz, 1831).

Sellon, Jean-Jacques de. *Lettre de M. de Sellon, président de la société de la paix de Genève, à l'éditeur des Archives de cette société* (Genève: Schmiedt, 1832).

Sellon, Jean-Jacques de. *Lettre de M. de Sellon, président de la société de la paix de Genève, à M. ***, sur le Pacte Fédéral et sur les travaux des sociétés de la paix de l'Amérique septentrionale, de l'Angleterre et celle de Genève* (Genève: Gruaz, 1832).

Sellon, Jean-Jacques de. *Recueil des lettres adressées aux archives de la société de la paix par son président* (Genève: Gruaz, 1832).

Sellon, *Recueil des lettres à l'éditeur* (Genève: Gruaz, 1832).

Sellon, Jean-Jacques de. *Cahier de lithographies relatives à la Société de la Paix de Genève* (Genève: Bonnant, 1833).

Sellon, Jean-Jacques de. *Fragmens de l'Émile de Rousseau, et des lettres de Lord Chesterfield sur l'éducation, publiés par M. de Sellon, président de la Société de la Paix de Genève; avec ses notes et ses réflexions. Dédiés par lui à ses neveux et petits-neveux de Cavour* (Genève: Gruaz, 1833).

Sellon, Jean-Jacques de. *Fragmens de l'ouvrage intitule: de l'influences des mœurs sur les lois, et de l'influence des lois sur les mœurs, auquel l'Académie française a décerné un prix extraordinaire de 10,000 francs; par M. Matter…* (Genève: Vignier: 1833).

Sellon, Jean-Jacques de. *La guerre est-elle une œuvre chrétienne?* (Genève: Jarrys, 1833).

Sellon, Jean-Jacques de. *Lettre du fondateur de la société de la paix de Genève, à l'un de ses honorables collègues, sur la séance anniversaire du premier décembre 1833* (Genève: Vignier, 1833).

Sellon, Jean-Jacques de. *Notice historique sur la Société de la paix, fondé à Genève en 1830, par M. le comte de Sellon* (Genève, Bonnant, 1833).

Sellon, Jean-Jacques de. *Réflexions sur la révision du pacte fédéral de 1815* (Genève: Vignier, 1833).

Sellon, Jean-Jacques de. *Seconde lettre du fondateur de la société de la paix de Genève, aux journaux de tous les pays, sur les effets du discours du président des États-Unis contre la France* (Genève: unknown publisher, 1833).

Sellon, Jean-Jacques de. *Adresse du fondateur de la société de la paix de Genève, aux chrétiens de toutes les communions et de tous les pays* (Genève: Gruaz, 1834).

Sellon, Jean-Jacques de. *Courtes réflexions de M. de Sellon sur l'événement du 1er février 1834* (Genève: unknown publisher, 1834).

Sellon, Jean-Jacques de. *Dialogue sur la peine de mort, sur le système pénitentiaire et sur la guerre* (Genève: Jarrys, 1834).

Sellon, Jean-Jacques de, *Nouveaux fragmens de M. de Sellon, président de la Société de la paix de Genève, commencés au mois de juin 1833, et faisant suite à ceux publiés par lui au mois de janvier de la même année, dédiés aux mères de famille, présentes et à venir* (Genève: Gruaz, 1834).

Sellon, Jean-Jacques de. *Appendice des fragmens de M. de Sellon, publiés en 1834* (Genève: Gruaz, 1835).

Sellon, Jean-Jacques de, *Qu'est-ce que la société de la paix* (Genève: Fick, 1835).

Sellon, Jean-Jacques de. *Kurzer Inbegriff der Arbeiten des Grafen von Sellon. Stifter und Präsident der Friedensgesellschaft zu Genf* (Genf: Gruaz, 1836).

Sellon, Jean-Jacques de. *Lettre du fondateur de la société de la paix de Genève aux sociétés de la paix de l'Angleterre et des États-Unis d'Amérique, sur le différend qui s'est élevé entre la France et la Suisse* (Genève: Oursel, 1836).

Sellon, Jean-Jacques de. *Programme d'un concours ouvert par le fondateur de la société de la paix de Genève, et faisant suite à celui qui indiquait: les meilleurs moyens de procurer une paix générale et permanente* (Genève: unknown publisher, 1836).

Sellon, Jean-Jacques de. *Résumé des efforts tentés par le comte de Sellon, fondateur de la société de la paix de Genève, pour introduire dans les codes nationaux et dans les lois internationales le principe de l'inviolabilité de la vie de l'homme; suivi de deux programmes destinés à servir cette cause (en lui procurant des défenseurs habiles parmi les concurrents qui aspirant aux prix promis par ces deux programmes) et de quelques réflexions sur le progrès journaliers qu'elle fait dans le monde civilisé* (Genève: Gruaz, 1836).

Sellon, Jean-Jacques de. *Nouveaux mélanges politiques, moraux et littéraires n°1* (Genève: Gruaz, 1837).

Sellon, Jean-Jacques de. *À MM. les journalistes de tous les pays* (Genève: unknown publisher, 1838).

Sellon, Jean-Jacques de. *Lettre écrite par le comte de Sellon à M. ***, étudiant en droit à l'Académie de Genève, en réponse à celle qu'il lui avait adressée, le 13 janvier 1838 en son nom et au nom de ses collègues, pour le remercier de l'envoi d'un opuscule intitule Quelques questions…* (Genève: Gruaz, 1838).

Sellon, Jean-Jacques de. *Nouveaux mélanges politiques, moraux et littéraires n° 3* (Genève: Gruaz, 1838).

Sellon, Jean-Jacques de. *Nouveaux mélanges politiques, moraux et littéraires n° 4* (Genève: Gruaz, 1838).

Sellon, Jean-Jacques. *Quelques questions de droit pénal, constitutionnel et international, soumises à messieurs les étudiants de la faculté de droit de l'académie de Genève, pour leurs exercices* (Genève: Pelletier, 1838).

Sellon, Valentine de. *Discours prononcé par la comtesse Valentine de Sellon au banquet d'honneur du congrès international de la paix offert par le comité français au comité étrangers le 4 octobre 1878* (Paris: Hennuyer, 1878).

Sellon, Valentine de. *La peine de mort au vingtième siècle* (Paris: Guillaumin, 1877).

Sellon, Valentine de. *Feuilles éparses* (Paris: Guillaumin, 1878).

Sellon, Valentine de. *Comptes-rendus de la presse sur les écrits de Valentine de Sellon. Lettres tirées de sa correspondance* (Paris: Dentu, 1882).

Seventh Annual Report of the Committee of the Society for the Promotion of Permanent and Universal Peace (London: Bensley, 1823).

Sinclair, Arthur. *Two Years on the Alabama* (Boston: Lee and Shepard, 1896).

Société de la morale chrétienne, *XXIVe séance générale annuelle* (Paris: Bureau de la société de la morale chrétienne, 1845).

Stokes, William. *A Permanent Congress of Nations as a Substitute for War in the Settlement of International Disputes* (Manchester: Brimner, 1860).

Story, Joseph. *A Discourse pronounced upon the Inauguration of the Author as Dane Professor of Law in Harvard University, on the Twenty-Fifth Day of August, 1829* (Boston: Hilliard, Gray, Little, and Wilkins, 1829).

Sturge, Joseph. *A Visit to the United States in 1841* (London: Hamilton, Adams, and Co., 1842).

Sumner, Charles. *The War-System of the Commonwealth of Nations: an Address before the American Peace Society* (Boston: Ticknor, Reed, and Fields, 1849).

Sumner, Charles. *The True Grandeur of Nations: an Oration delivered before the Authorities of the City of Boston, July 4, 1845* (Boston: American Peace Society, 1870).

Sumner, Charles. *War-System of the Commonwealth of Nations: an Address before the American Peace Society, at its Anniversary in Boston, May 28, 1849* (Boston: American Peace Society, 1870).

Suringar, Willem Hendrik. *Discours prononcé par M. Suringar, d'Amsterdam, vice-président au congrès de la paix, dans la deuxième séance, tenue à Paris le 23 aout 1849* (Paris: Ducloux, 1849).

The Peace Congress at Brussels, on the 20th, 21st, and 22nd of September 1848 (London: Thomas Ward, 1848).

The Proceedings of the First General Peace Convention: held in London, June 22, 1843, and the Two Following Days: with the Papers laid before the Convention, the Letters read, &c. &c. (London: Peace Society's Office, 1843).

The Question of Arbitration in the House of Commons. Being the Substance of the Debate on Mr. Cobden's Motion in Favour of Arbitration Treaties instead of War, for the Settlement of International Disputes. With an Appendix. (London: Gilpin, 1849), 20; HP (July 1849).

Transactions of the Royal Society of Edinburgh. Vol. XXIV (Edinburgh: Robert Grant & Son, 1867).

Treaties and other International Acts of the United States of America. Vol. 6. Documents 152–172: 1852–1855 (Washington: Government Printing Office, 1942).

Tuckerman, Bayard. *William Jay and the Constitutional Movement for the Abolition of Slavery* (New York: Dodd, Mead & Company, 1893).

Union de la paix entre tous les peuples civilisés. Premier bulletin. (Le Havre: Cazavan, 1867).

Union de la paix entre tous les peuples civilisés. Deuxième bulletin (Le Havre: Leclerc, 1868).

Union de la paix entre tous les peuples civilisés. Troisième bulletin (Le Havre: Santallier, 1869).

Upham, Thomas. *The Manual of Peace; exhibiting the Evils and Remedies of War* (Boston: American Peace Society, 1842).

Ware, Henry. *Memoirs of the Rev. Noah Worcester, D.D.* (Boston: Munroe, 1844).

Whelpley, Samuel [pseud. Philadelphus]. *Letters addressed to Caleb Strong, Esq. Late Governor of Massachusetts, showing that Retaliation, Capital Punishment, and War, are prohibited by the Gospel; justified by no good Principle; not Necessary to the Safety of Individuals or Nations: but Incompatible with their Welfare; Inconsistent with the Christian Character; and Contrary to the Laws of Christ. Third Edition* (Providence: Miller & Hutchens, 1818).

Worcester, Noah. *A Solemn Review of the Custom of War; showing that War is the Effect of a Popular Delusion, and proposing a Remedy* (Stockport: Stanhope Press, 1816).

Worcester, Noah. *The Substance of a Pamphlet, entitled a Solemn Review of the Custom of War: Showing, that War is the Effect of Popular Delusion, and Proposing a Remedy* (London: Lomax, 1816).

Wright, Henry Clarke. *Defensive War proved to be a Denial of Christianity and of the Government of God: with Illustrative Facts and Anecdotes* (London: Gilpin, 1846).

Pre–1901 Anonymous Publications

La paix universelle. Idée napoléonienne devant l'histoire (Paris: Dentu, 1864).

Life of William Allen, with Selections from his Correspondence (London: Gilpin, 1846).

Nouveau projet de paix perpétuelle entre tous les peuples de la chrétienté (Paris: Delaunay, 1826).

The Duty of a Christian in a Trying Situation: a Letter to the Author of a Pamphlet, entitled "The Mediator's Kingdom..." (New York: M'Dermut, 1810).

The Question of War Reviewed (New York: New York Peace Society, 1818).

Pre–1901 Legal Scholarship

Blackstone, William. *Commentaries on the Laws of England. Volume II* (New York: William E. Dean, 1853).

Fiore, Pasquale (transl. Paul Pradier-Fodéré). *Nouveau droit international public suivant les besoins de la civilisation moderne. Tome premier* (Paris: Durand et Pedone-Lauriel, 1868).

Grotius, Hugo (transl. Francis Kelsey). *De Jure Belli ac Pacis Libri Tres. Volume 2. Book 1.* (eds. Arthur, E. R. Boak, Henry A. Sanders, Jesse S. Reeves and Herbert F. Right (Oxford: Clarendon Press, 1925).

Isambert, François-André. *Annales politiques et diplomatiques, ou manuel du publiciste et de l'homme d'état* (Paris: Constantin, 1823).

Kent, James. *Commentaries on American Law, vol. I* (New York: Halsted, 1826).

Klüber, Jean-Louis. *Droit des gens moderne de l'Europe. Tome premier* (Stuttgart: Cotta, 1819).

Klüber, Jean-Louis. *Droit des gens moderne de l'Europe. Tome second* (Stuttgart: Cotta, 1819).

Klüber, Jean-Louis. *Droit des gens moderne de l'Europe. Tome premier* (Paris: Aillaud, 1831).

Klüber, Jean-Louis. *Droit des gens moderne de l'Europe. Tome second* (Paris: Aillaud, 1831).

Martens, Fyodor. *Traité de droit international. Tome 1* (Paris, Chevalier Maresq., 1883).

Martens, George Fréderic de. *Précis du droit des gens moderne de l'Europe fondé sur les traités et l'usage. Pour servir d'introduction à un cours politique et diplomatique* (Gottingue: Dieterich, 1801).

Martens, George Fréderic de. *Précis du droit des gens moderne de l'Europe* (Gottingue: Dieterich, 1821).

Martens, George Fréderic de. *Précis du droit des gens moderne de l'Europe. Tome premier* (Paris: Guillaumin, 1856).

Martens, George Fréderic de. *Précis du droit des gens moderne de l'Europe. Tome second* (Paris: Guillaumin, 1856).

Moore, John Bassett. *History and Digest of the International Arbitrations to which the United States has been a Party. Volume 1* (Washington: Government Printing Office, 1898).

Oppenheim, Lassa. *International Law. A Treatise. Vol II. War and Neutrality* (London: Longmans, Green, and Co., 1906).

Phillimore, Robert. *Commentaries on International Law. Volume 1* (Philadelphia: Johnson, 1854).

Vattel, Emer de. *Le droit des gens ou principes de la loi naturelle, appliqués à la conduite & aux affaires des nations & des souverains. Tome II* (Londres, 1758).

Vattel, Emer de. *Droit des gens, ou principes de la loi naturelle, appliquée à la conduite et aux affaires des nations et des souverains. Nouvelle édition. Tome premier* (Paris: Aillaud, 1830).

Vattel, Emer de. *Droit des gens, ou principes de la loi naturelle, appliquée à la conduite et aux affaires des nations et des souverains Nouvelle édition. Tome second* (Paris: Aillaud, 1830).

Wheaton, *Elements of International Law: with a Sketch of the History of the Science* (Philadelphia: Carey, Lea & Blanchard, 1836).

Wheaton, Henry. *History of the Law of Nations in Europe and America; from the Earliest Times to the Treaty of Washington, 1842* (New York: Gould, Banks, 1845).

Books

Abbenhuis, Maartje. *The Hague Conferences and International Politics, 1898–1915* (London: Bloomsbury, 2019).

Abbenhuis, Maartje. 'Peace, Security, and Deterrence: "The greatest work of civilization". The Hague Peace Conferences of 1899, 1907, and 1915', in *A Cultural History of Peace in the Age of Empire*, ed. Ingrid Sharp (London: Bloomsbury Academic, 2020).

Alvarez, Alexandre. *La codification du droit international. Ses tendances – Ses bases* (Paris: Pedone, 1912).

Anghie, Antony. *Imperialism, Sovereignty and the Making of International Law* (Cambridge: Cambridge University Press, 2004).

Anteghini, Alessandra. 'Charles Lemonnier (1806–1891), précurseur de l'européisme fédéraliste', in *Les États-Unis d'Europe. Un projet pacifiste*, eds. Marta Petricioli, Donatella Cherubini & Alessandra Anteghini (Bern: Peter Lang, 2004).

Antonetti, Guy. *Louis-Philippe* (Paris: Fayard, 1994).

Arcidiacono, Bruno. *Cinq types de paix. Une histoire des plans de pacification perpétuelle (XVIIe–XXe siècles)* (Paris: Presses Universitaires de France, 2011).

Aspremont, Jean. *After Meaning. The Sovereignty of Forms in International Law* (Cheltenham: Elgar, 2021).

Audren, Frédéric and Halpérin, Jean-Louis. *La culture juridique française. Entry mythes et réalités. XIXe–XXe siècles* (Paris: CNRS éditions, 2013).

Badem, Candan. *The Ottoman Crimean War (1853–1856)* (Leiden: Brill, 2010).

Bainville, Jacques. *Les dictateurs* (Paris: Perrin, 2019).

Baker, John Hamilton. *An Introduction to Legal History* (Oxford: Oxford University Press, 2019).

Ballou, Adin. *Christian Non-Resistance in all its Important Bearings* (Philadelphia: Universal Peace Union, 1910).

Banner, Stuart. *The Decline of Natural Law. How American Lawyers once used Natural Law and Why they Stopped* (Oxford: Oxford University Press, 2021).

Bartolomei, Lisa. 'The Impact of Civil Society on International Relations: the Ligue internationale de la paix et de la liberté', in *Les États-Unis d'Europe. Un projet pacifiste*, eds. Marta Petricioli, Donatella Cherubini & Alessandra Anteghini (Bern: Peter Lang, 2004).

Basabe, Nere. 'L'Europe au-delà de ses frontières: l'élargissement de l'espace européen dans les projets de 1830–1848', in *Europe de papier. Projets européens au XIXe siècle*, eds. Sylvie Aprile, Christina Cassina, Philippe Darriulat and René Leboutte (Villeneuve d'Ascq: Presses universitaires du Septentrion, 2015).

Bayly, Christopher. *The Birth of the Modern World 1780–1914* (Oxford: Blackwell, 2004).

Beales, A.C.F. *The History of Peace. A Short Account of the Organised Movements for International Peace* (London: Bell & Sons, 1931).

Beaud, Olivier. *Théorie de la fédération* (Paris: Presses Universitaires de France, 2009).

Beaulac, Stéphane. *The Power of Language in the Making of International Law* (Leiden: Martinus Nijhoff, 2004).

Bederman, David. *International Law in Antiquity* (Cambridge: Cambridge University Press, 2001).

Belchem, John. *Popular Radicalism in Nineteenth Century Britain* (Basingstoke, Palgrave Macmillan, 1996).

Bélissa, Marc. *Fraternité universelle et intérêt national (1713–1795). Les cosmopolitiques du droit des gens* (Paris: Kimé, 1998).

Benton, Lauren and Ford, Lisa. *Rage for Order. The British Empire and the Origins of International Law. 1800–1850* (Cambridge: Harvard University Press, 2016).

Bergami. Carol. 'Entre tradition de 1848 et souvenir napoléonien. Un européisme politique rallié au Second Empire', in *Europe de papier. Projets européens au XIXe siècle*, eds. Sylvie Aprile, Christina Cassina, Philippe Darriulat and René Leboutte (Villeneuve d'Ascq: Presses universitaires du Septentrion, 2015).

Bianchi, Andreas. *International Law Theories. An Inquiry into Different Ways of Thinking* (Oxford: Oxford University Press, 2016).

Biaudet, Jean Charles. *La Suisse et la monarchie de juillet, 1830–1838* (Lausanne: Roth, 1941).

Bicknell, Edward John. *A Theological Introduction to the Thirty-Nine Articles of the Church of England* (Eugene: Wipf and Stock, 2007).

Blamires, Cyprian. *The French Revolution and the Creation of Benthamism* (Basingstoke: Palgrave Macmillan, 2008).

Bluche, Frédéric. *Le bonapartisme* (Paris: Presses Universitaires de France, 1981).

Bond, Martyn. *Hitler's Cosmopolitan Bastard. Count Richard Coudenhove-Kalergi and his Vision of Europe* (Montreal: McGill-Queen's University Press, 2021).

Borgeaud, Charles, *Histoire de l'université de Genève. L'Académie et l'université de au XIXe siècle, 1814–1900* (Genève: Georg, 1934).

Brock, Peter. *Pacifism in the United States. From the Colonial Era to the First World War* (Princeton: Princeton University Press, 1968).

Brock, Peter. *The Quaker Peace Testimony 1660 to 1914* (York: Sessions Book Trust, 1990).

Broglie, Gabriel de. *La monarchie de Juillet 1830–1848* (Paris: Fayard, 2011).

Brunnée, Jutta and Toope, Stephen. *Legitimacy and Legality in International Law. An Interactional Account* (Cambridge: Cambridge University Press, 2010).

Cahen, Raphaël. 'Le projet européen de Krause', in (Krausisme juridique et politique en Europe, ed. Oscar Ferreira (Paris: Classiques Garnier, 2021).

Caron, Jean-Claude and Vernus, Michel, *L'Europe au 19e siècle. Des nations aux nationalismes (1815–1914)* (Malakoff: Armand Colin, 2019).

Carwardine, Richard. *Evangelicals and Politics in Antebellum America* (Knoxville: University of Tennessee Press, 1997).

Cavallar, Georg. *Kant and the Theory and Practice of International Right* (Cardiff: University of Wales Press, 2020).

Cazals, Géraldine. 'Le grand dessein d'Emeric Crucé: une paix générale et la liberté de commerce par tout le monde', in *Les échanges maritimes et commerciaux de l'Antiquité à nos jours, vol. 1*, ed. Philippe Sturmel (Paris, L'Harmattan, 2014).

Ceadel, Martin. *Thinking about Peace and War* (Oxford: Oxford University Press, 1989).

Ceadel, Martin. *The Origins of War Prevention. The British Peace Movement and International Relations, 1730–1854* (Oxford: Clarendon, 1996).

Ceadel, Martin. *Semi-Detached Idealists. The British Peace Movement and International Relations, 1854–1945* (Oxford: Oxford University Press, 2000).

Ceadel, Martin. 'Gladstone and a Liberal Theory of International Relations', in *Politics and Culture in Victorian Britain. Essays in memory of Colin Matthew*, eds. Peter Ghosh and Lawrence Goldman (Oxford: Oxford University Press, 2006).

Chaline, Nadine-Josette. *Empêcher la guerre. Le pacifisme du début du XIXe siècle à la veille de la Seconde Guerre mondiale* (Amiens: Encrage, 2015).

Charle, Christophe (transl. Miriam Kochan). *A Social History of France in the Nineteenth Century* (Oxford: Berg, 1994).

Cherubini, Donatella. 'Si Vis Pacem, Para Libertatem et Justitiam. Les États-Unis d'Europe, 1867–1914', in *Les États-Unis d'Europe. Un projet pacifiste*, eds. Marta Petricioli, Donatella Cherubini & Alessandra Anteghini (Bern: Peter Lang, 2004).

Church, Clive and Head, Randolph, *A Concise History of Switzerland* (Cambridge: Cambridge University Press, 2013).

Cohen, Lauren. 'Representations of Peace. Bertha von Suttner, Activist and Visionary on Dreams, Peace, and Justice', in *A Cultural History of Peace in the Age of Empire*, ed. Ingrid Sharp (London: Bloomsbury Academic, 2020).

Cook, Adrian. *The Alabama Claims. American Politics and Anglo-American Relations, 1865–1872* (Ithaca: Cornell University Press, 1975).

Cooper, Sandi. *Patriotic Pacifism. Waging War on War in Europe, 1815–1914* (Oxford: Oxford University Press, 1991).

Cooper, Sandi. 'The Reinvention of Just War among European Pacifists before the First World War', in *The Pacifist Impulse in Historical Perspective*, ed. Harvey L. Dyck (Toronto: Toronto University Press, 1996).

Cooper, Sandi. 'Peace, War, and Gender: the Evolution of Women's Voices', in *A Cultural History of Peace in the Age of Empire*, ed. Ingrid Sharp (London: Bloomsbury Academic, 2020).

Corten, Olivier. *Le droit contre la guerre* (Paris: Pedone, 2014).

Cortright, David. *Peace. A history of Movements and Ideas* (Cambridge: Cambridge University Press, 2008).

Coste, Clément, Frobert, Ludovic, and Lauricella, Marie (eds.). *De la république de Constantin Pecqueur (1801–1887)* (Besançon: Presses universitaires de Franche-Comté, 2017).

Crawford, James and Nicholson, Rowan. 'The Continued Relevance of Established Rules and Institutions relating to the Use of Force', in *The Oxford Handbook of the Use of Force in International Law*, ed. Marc Weller (Oxford: Oxford University Press, 2015).

Crossland, James. *War, Law and Humanity. The Campaign to control Warfare, 1853–1914* (London: Bloomsbury, 2018).

Curran, Thomas. *Soldiers of Peace. Civil War Pacifism and the Postwar Radical Peace Movement* (New York: Fordham University Press, 2003).

Curti, Merle. *The American Peace Crusade 1815–1860* (Durham: Duke University Press, 1929).

De Graaf, Beatrice. *Fighting Terror after Napoleon. How Europe became Secure after 1815* (Cambridge: Cambridge University Press, 2020).

de la Rasilla, Ignacio. *International Law and History* (Cambridge: Cambridge University Press, 2021).

De Spiegeleer, Christoph. *Een blauwe Progressist. Charles Potvin (1818–1902) en het liberaal-sociale Denken van zijn Generatie* (Brussel: ASP, 2011).

d'Amat, Roman. 'BOUVET (François-Joseph-Francisque)'. In *Dictionnaire de biographie française. Tome septième*, eds. M. Prevost and Roman d'Amat (Paris: Letouzey, 1956).

DeBenedetti, Charles. *The Peace Reform in American History* (Bloomington: Indiana University Press, 1980).

Denfeld, Claudia. *Hans Wehberg (1885–1962). Die Organisation der Staatengemeinschaft* (Baden-Baden: Nomos, 2007).

Deonna, Henry. 'SELLON, de SELLON', in *Dictionnaire historique et biographique de la Suisse*, vol. VI (Neuchâtel: Administration du dictionnaire historique et biographique de la Suisse, 1932).

Devos, Gabriel. *La science supranationale de Louis Bara* (Courtrai: Vermaut, 1953).

Dhondt, Frederik. *Balance of Power and Norm Hierarchy: Franco-British Diplomacy after the Peace of Utrecht* (Leiden: Brill, 2015).

Dhondt, Frederik. 'Bij uitsluiting aan den souverein, zonder eenige de minste ruggenspraak?' Soevereiniteit, grondwet en volkenrecht, van Verenigd Koninkrijk der Nederlanden tot Koninkrijk België', in *De Grondwet van het Verenigd Koninkrijk der Nederlanden van 1815: staatkundige en historische beschouwingen uit België en Nederland*, eds. A. Alen, A.W. Heringa, D. Heirbaut, and C. Rotteveel-Mansveld (Brugge: Die Keure, 2016).

Dhondt, Frederik, 'Permanent Neutrality or Permanent Insecurity? Obligation and Self-Interest in the Defence of Belgian Neutrality, 1830–1870', in *International Law in the Long Nineteenth Century (1776–1914). From the Public Law of Europe to Global International Law?*, eds. Inge Van Hulle & Randall Lesaffer (Leiden: Brill, 2019).

Dhondt, Frederik. 'Portalis le jeune et le droit des gens', in *Joseph-Marie Portalis. Diplomate, magistrat et législateur*, eds. Raphaël Cahen and Nicolas Laurent-Bonne (Aix-en-Provence: Presses universitaires Aix-Marseille, 2020).

Dhondt, Frederik, 'Édouard Descamps (1847–1933): from 'negative neutrality' to 'positive pacigerate', in Sean Morris (ed.), *The league of nations and the development of international law: a new intellectual history of the advisory committee of jurists* (London, Routledge, 2021).

Doyle, Michael W. 'Kant and Liberal Internationalism', in *Toward Perpetual Peace' and other Writings on Politics, Peace, and History*, ed. Pauline Kleingeld (New Haven: Yale University Press, 2006).

Drescher, Seymour. *Capitalism and Antislavery. British Mobilisation in Comparative Perspective* (London: Macmillan, 1986).

Eley, Geoff. 'Nations, Publics, and Political Cultures: Placing Habermas in the Nineteenth Century', in *Habermas and the Public Sphere*, ed. Craig Calhoun (Cambridge: MIT, 1992).

Evans, Richard. *In Defence of History* (London: Granta, 2018).

Fakkar, Rouchdi. *L'influence internationale de Saint-Simon et ses disciples* (Genève: Chevalier, 1967).

Fatio, Olivier. 'L'enseignement de la théologie à l'Académie de Genève en 1831'. In *Genève protestante*, ed. Olivier Fatio (Genève: Labor et Fides, 1983).

Figes, Orlando. *Crimea* (London: Penguin, 2010).

Fitzmaurice, Andrew. *King Leopold's Ghostwriter. The Creation of Persons and States in the Nineteenth Century* (Princeton: Princeton University Press, 2021).

Fried, Alfred. *Handbuch der Friedensbewegung* (Berlin: Verlag der Friedens-Warte, 1911).

Gallavresi, Giuseppe. 'Le *centenaire d'un précurseur: Jean-*Jacques de Sellon'. In *Revue internationale de la croix rouge* 149 (1931).

Garvey, Gregory. *Creating the Culture of Reform in Antebellum America* (Athens: University of Georgia Press, 2006).

Gaurier, Dominique. 'Cosmopolis and Utopia', in *The Oxford Handbook of the History of International Law*, eds. Bardo Fassbender and Anne Peters (Oxford: Oxford University Press, 2012).

Gaurier, Dominique. *Histoire du droit international. De l'Antiquité à la création de l'O.N.U.* (Rennes: Presses universitaires de Rennes, 2014).

Genin, Vincent. *Le laboratoire belge du droit international: Une communauté épistémique et internationale de juristes (1869–1914)* (Bruxelles: Académie Royale, 2018).

Ghervas, Stella. 'La Sainte-Alliance: un pacte pacifique européen comme antidote à l'Empire', in *Europe de papier. Projets européens au XIXe siècle*, eds. Sylvie Aprile, Christina Cassina, Philippe Darriulat and René Leboutte (Villeneuve d'Ascq: Presses universitaires du Septentrion, 2015).

Ghervas, Stella. 'Definitions of Peace', in *A Cultural History of Peace in the Age of Empire*, ed. Ingrid Sharp (London: Bloomsbury Academic, 2020).

Ghervas, Stella. *Conquering Peace from the Enlightenment to the European Union* (Cambridge: HUP, 2021).

Glennon, Michael. *Limits of Law, Prerogatives of Power. Interventionism after Kosovo* (Houndmills, Basingstoke: Palgrave, 2001).

Glennon, Michael. *The Fog of Law. Pragmatism, Security, and International Law* (Stanford: Stanford University Press, 2010).

Goldfrank, David. *The Origins of the Crimean War* (London: Routledge, 1994).

Grossi, Verdiana. *Le pacifisme européen, 1889–1914* (Bruxelles: Bruylant, 1994).

Grossi, Verdiana. 'Victor Hugo et sa perception des États-Unis d'Europe', in *Les États-Unis d'Europe. Un projet pacifiste*, eds. Marta Petricioli, Donatella Cherubini, and Alessandra Anteghini (Bern: Peter Lang, 2004).

Haidt, Jonathan. *The Righteous Mind. Why Good People are divided by Politics and Religion* (New York, Penguin, 2012).

Halpérin, Jean-Louis. *Five Legal Revolutions since the 17th Century. An Analysis of Global Legal History* (Dordrecht: Springer, 2014).

Hamilton, Charles Iain. *Anglo-French Naval Rivalry, 1840–1870* (Cambridge: Clarendon Press, 1993).

Hartwig, Matthias. 'Colour Books', in *Encyclopedia of Public International Law. Vol. 9, ed. Rudolf Bernhardt* (Amsterdam: North Holland, 1986).

Hathaway, Oona A and Shapiro, Scott. *The Internationalists: How a Radical Plan to Outlaw War Remade the World* (New York: Simon & Schuster, 2017).

Hazareesingh, Sudhir. *La légende de Napoléon* (Paris: Tallandier, 2005).

Henkin, Louis. *How Nations behave. Law and Foreign Policy* (London: Pall Mall, 1968).

Hermann, Irène. *Genève entre république et canton. Les vicissitudes d'une intégration nationale (1814–1846)* (Genève: Passé Présent, 2003).

Hippler, Thomas. 'From nationalist Peace to democratic War. The Peace Congresses in Paris (1849) and Geneva (1867)', in *Paradoxes of Peace in Nineteenth Century Europe*, eds. Thomas Hippler and Miloš Vec (Oxford: Oxford University Press, 2015).

Hoffer, William James Hull. *The Caning of Charles Sumner: Honor, Idealism, and the Origins of the Civil War* (Baltimore: Johns Hopkins University, 2010).

Janis, Mark. *The American Tradition of International Law. Great Expectations, 1789–1914* (Oxford: Oxford University Press, 2004).

Janis, Mark. *America and the Law of Nations, 1776–1939* (Oxford: Oxford University Press, 2010).

Janis, Mark. 'North America: American Exceptionalism in International Law', in *The Oxford Handbook of the History of International Law*, eds. Bardo Fassbender and Anne Peters (Oxford: Oxford University Press, 2012).

Jarret, Mark. *The Congress of Vienna and its Legacy. War and Great Power Diplomacy after Napoleon* (Tauris: London, 2013).

Jennings, Lawrence Charles. *French Anti-Slavery. The Movement for the Abolition of Slavery in France, 1802–1848* (Cambridge, Cambridge University Press, 2000).

Jouannet, Emmanuel. 'Les dualismes du Droit des gens', in *Vattel's International Law in a XXIst Century Perspective*, eds. Vincent Chetail and Peter Haggenmacher (Leiden: Nijhoff, 2011).

Jouannet. Emmanuelle Tourme. *Le droit international, le capitalisme et la terre* (Bruxelles: Bruylant, 2021).

Jütersonke, Oliver. *Morgenthau, Law and Realism* (Cambridge: Cambridge University Press, 2010).

Kant, Immanuel (transl. Jules Barni revue par A. Lagarde). *Projet de paix perpétuelle* (Paris: Hatier, 1988).

Kessler-Mata, Kouslaa. *American Indians and the Trouble with Sovereignty. A Turn toward Structural Self-Determination* (Cambridge: Cambridge University Press, 2017).

Kohl, Clayton. *Claims as a Cause of the Mexican War* (New York: Graduate School New York University, 1914).

Kolb, Robert. *Ius Contra Bellum. Le droit international relative au maintien de la paix. Précis* (Basel: Helbing Lichtenhahn, 2009).

Kolla, Edward James. *Sovereignty, International Law, and the French Revolution* (Cambridge: Cambridge University Press, 2017).

Kölz, Alfred. *Histoire constitutionnelle de la Suisse moderne. Ses fondements idéologiques et son évolution institutionnelle dans le contexte européen, de la fin de l'Ancien Régime à 1848* (Berne: Stämpfli, 2006).

Koskenniemi, Martti. *The Gentle Civilizer of Nations. The Rise and Fall of International Law 1870–1960* (Cambridge: Cambridge University Press, 2001).

Koskenniemi, Martti. *From Apology to Utopia. The Structure of International Legal Argument* (Cambridge: Cambridge University Press, 2006).

Koskenniemi, Martti. 'The Legacy of the Nineteenth Century', in *Routledge Handbook of International Law*, ed. David Armstrong (Oxon: Routledge, 2009).

Koskenniemi, Martti. 'Ruling the World by Law(s): The View from around 1850', in *Europe 1815–1914: Creating Community and Ordering the World*, eds. Martti Koskenniemi and Bo Stråth (Helsinki: Helsinki University Press, 2014).

Koskenniemi, Martti. *To the Uttermost Parts of the Earth. Legal Imagination and International Power, 1300–1870* (Cambridge: Cambridge University Press, 2021).

Korman, Sharon. *The Right of Conquest: the Acquisition of Territory by Force in International Law and Practice* (Oxford: Clarendon Press, 2003).

Kraditor, Aileen. *Means and Ends in American Abolitionism. Garrison and his Critics on Strategy and Tactics, 1834–1850* (New York: Random House, 1967).

Lachs, Manfred. *The Teacher in International Law: Teachings and Teaching* (Dordrecht: Martinus Nijhoff, 1987).

Laity, Paul. *The British Peace Movement 1870–1914* (Oxford: Oxford University Press, 2001).

Lange, Christian. *Histoire de l'internationalisme. Tome I. Jusqu'à la paix de Westphalie (1648)* (La Haye: Martinus Nijhoff, 1919).

Lange, Christian. 'Histoire de la doctrine pacifique et de son influence sur le développement du droit international', in *Recueil des cours de l'Académie de droit international de La Haye* (1926, vol. XIII).

Lange, Christian and Schou, August. *Histoire de l'internationalisme. Tome II. De la paix de Westphalie jusqu'au congrès de Vienne (1815)* (Oslo: Aschehoug, 1954).

Le Mahieu, Dan Lloyd. *The Mind of William Paley: A Philosopher and His Age* (Lincoln: University of Nebraska Press, 1976).

Lefkowitz, David. *Philosophy and International Law. A Critical Introduction* (Cambridge: Cambridge University Press, 2020).

Lemnitzer, Jan. *Power, Law and the End of Privateering* (Basingstoke: Palgrave Macmillan, 2014).

Leonards, Chris and Randeraad, Nico. 'Building a Transnational Network of Social Reform in the Nineteenth Century', in *Shaping the Transnational Sphere Experts, Networks and Issues from the 1840s to the 1930s*, eds. Davide Rodogno, Bernhard Struck and Jakob Vogel (New York: Berghahn, 2015).

Lesaffer, Randall. 'International Law and its History: the Story of an Unrequited Love Affair', in *Time, History, and International Law*, eds. Matthew Craven, Malgosia Fitzmaurice, and Maria Vogiatzi (Den Haag: Martinus Nijhoff, 2007).

Lesaffer, Randall. 'Too Much History: From War as Sanction to the Sanctioning of War', in *The Oxford Handbook of the Use of Force in International Law*, ed. Marc Weller (Oxford: Oxford University Press, 2015).

Lesaffer, Randall. 'Peace through Law: The Hague Peace Conferences and the Rise of the Ius Contra Bellum', in *War, Peace and International Order? The Legacies of the Hague Peace Conferences of 1899 and 1907*, eds. Maartje Abbenhuis, Christopher E. Barber and Annalise Higgins (Abingdon: Routledge, 2017).

Lincoln Lambert, Vanessa. 'Between Global Governance and European Union: the Writings of Constantin Pecqueur', in *Europe de papier. Projets européens au XIXe siècle*, eds. Sylvie Aprile, Christina Cassina, Philippe Darriulat and René Leboutte (Villeneuve d'Ascq: Presses universitaires du Septentrion, 2015).

Liu, Lydia. 'Henry Wheaton (1785–1848)'. In *The Oxford Handbook of the History of International Law*, eds. Bardo Fassbender and Anne Peters (Oxford: Oxford University Press, 2012).

Lorca, Arnulf Becker. *Mestizo International Law. A Global Intellectual History* 1842–1933 (Cambridge: Cambridge University Press, 2014).

Lorenzini, Sara. 'Les États-Unis d'Europe and the First Nobel Peace Prizes. An Outline', in *Les États-Unis d'Europe. Un projet pacifiste*, eds. Marta Petricioli, Donatella Cherubini & Alessandra Anteghini (Bern: Peter Lang, 2004).

Lubelski-Bernard, Nadine. 'BARA (Louis-Adrien)', in *Biographie nationale de Belgique*, vol. XLII (Bruxelles: Bruylant 1983).

Lubelski-Bernard, Nadine. 'VISSCHERS (Auguste)', in *Biographie nationale de Belgique*, vol. XLIV (Bruxelles: Bruylant 1985).

Lubelski-Bernard, Nadine. 'Freemasonry and Peace in Europe, 1867–1914', in *Peace Movements and Political Cultures*, eds. Charles Chatfield and Peter van den Dungen (Knoxville: University of Tennessee Press, 1988).

Lubelski-Bernard, Nadine. 'de MOLNARII, Gustave'. In *Nouvelle biographie nationale*, vol. 6 (Bruxelles: Académie royale des sciences, des lettres, et des beaux-arts de Belgique, 2001).

Luginbühl, Beatrice. *Im Kampf gegen die Todesstrafe: Jean-Jacques Comte de Sellon (1782–1839). Ein Plädoyer für die Unantastbarkeit des menschlichen Lebens* (Zürich: Schulthess Juristische Medien, 2000).

Lustig, Doreen. 'The Peace Movement and Grassroots International Law'. *Yearbook of International Humanitarian Law* 24 (2021).

Lynch, Cecelia. 'Peace Movements, Civil Society, and the Development of International Law', in *The Oxford Handbook of the History of International Law*, eds. Bardo Fassbender and Anne Peters (Oxford: Oxford University Press, 2012).

Marauhn, Thilo. 'How many Deaths can Article 2(4) UN Charter die?', in *The Justification of War and International Order, eds.* Hendrik Simon & Lothar Brock (Cambridge: Cambridge University Press, 2021).

Marcoartu, Arturo. *Internationalism* (London: Stevens and Sons, 1876).

Martin, William. *Histoire de la Suisse* (Lausanne: Payot, 1963).

Mattelart, Armand. *Histoire de l'utopie planétaire. De la cité prophétique à la société globale* (Paris: La Découverte, 2009).

Monti, Annamaria. 'Leone Levi (1821–1888) and the History of Comparative Commercial Law', in *Common Law, Civil Law, and Colonial Law. Essays in Comparative Legal History from the Twelfth to the Twentieth Centuries*, eds. William Eves, John Hudson, Ingrid Ivarsen, Sarah B. White (Cambridge: Cambridge University Press, 2021).

Morgan, Simon. 'From Warehouse Clerk to Corn Law Celebrity', in *Rethinking Nineteenth Century Liberalism. Richard Cobden Bicentenary Essays* (London: Routledge, 2017).

Morgenthau, Hans. *Scientific Man vs. Power Politics* (London: Latimer, 1946).

Morison, Samuel Eliot. 'Dissent in the War of 1812', in *Dissent in Three American Wars*, eds. Samuel Eliot Morison, Frederik Merk, and Frank Freidel (Cambridge: HUP, 1970).

Moyn, Samuel. *Humane. How the United States abandoned Peace and reinvented War* (New York: Farrar, Straus and Giroux, 2021).

Müller, Thomas Christian. 'Switzerland 1847/49. A Provisional, Successful End of a 'Democratic Revolution'?', in *Europe in 1848: Revolution and Reform*, eds. Dieter Dowe et al. (New York: Berghahn, 2001).

Neff, Stephen. *The Rights and Duties of Neutrals. A General History* (Manchester: Manchester University Press, 2000).

Neff, Stephen. *War and the Law of Nations* (Cambridge: Cambridge University Press, 2005).

Neff, Stephen. *Justice in Blue and Gray. A Legal History of the Civil War* (Cambridge: Harvard University Press, 2010).

Neff, Stephen. *Justice among Nations. A History of International Law* (Cambridge: Harvard University Press, 2014).

Nitz, Stephan. *Theorien des Friedens und des Krieges. Kommentierte Bibliographie zur Theoriegeschichte. Band 1: Altertum bis 1830* (Baden-Baden: Nomos, 2010).

Nys, Ernest. 'La Belgique et le droit international', in *La Patrie Belge*, ed. Émile Rossel (Bruxelles: Rossel, 1905).

Nys, Ernest. *Le droit international, tome III* (Bruxelles: Castaigne, 1906).

O'Connell, Mary Ellen. *The Power & Purpose of International Law. Insights from the Theory & Practice of Enforcement* (Oxford: Oxford University Press, 2008).

O'Flaherty, Niall. *Utilitarianism in the Age of Enlightenment. The Moral and Political Thought of William Paley* (Cambridge: Cambridge University Press, 2019).

Orford, Anne and Hoffman, Florian (eds.). *The Oxford Handbook on the Sources of International Law* (Oxford: Oxford University Press, 2016).

Ozouf, Mona. 'Le légicentrisme républicain'. In *Le siècle de l'avènement républicain*, eds. Mona Ozouf and François Furet (Paris: Gallimard, 1993).

Pellissier, Pierre. *Émile de Girardin. Prince de la presse* (Paris: Denoël, 1985).

Perreau-Saussine, Amanda. 'Lauterpacht and Vattel on the Sources of International Law: the Place of Private Law Analogies and General Principles', in *Vattel's International Law in a XXIst Century Perspective*, eds. Vincent Chetail and Peter Haggenmacher (Leiden: Nijhoff, 2011).

Phelps, Christina. *The Anglo-American Peace Movement in the Mid-Nineteenth Century* (New York: Columbia University Press, 1930).

Pitts, Jennifer. *Boundaries of the International. Law and Empire* (Cambridge: Harvard University Press, 2018).

Pletcher, David. *The Diplomacy of Annexation. Texas, Oregon, and the Mexican War* (Columbia: University of Missouri Press, 1973).

Primi, Alice. *Femmes de progrès. Françaises et allemandes engagées dans leur siècle, 1844–1870* (Rennes: Presses universitaires de Rennes, 2010).

Porter, Andrew (ed.). *The Oxford History of the British Empire. Volume III. The Nineteenth Century* (Oxford: Oxford University Press, 1999).

Rabban, David. *Law's History. American Legal Thought and the Transatlantic Turn to History* (Cambridge: Cambridge University Press, 2012).

Richard, Carl. *The Golden Age of the Classics in the United States. Greece, Rome, and the Antebellum United States* (Cambridge: Harvard University Press, 2009).

Riot-Sarcy, Michèle. *Histoire du féminisme* (Paris: La Découverte, 2015).

Röben, Betsy. *Johann Caspar Bluntschli, Francis Lieber und das moderne Völkerrecht 1861–1881* (Baden-Baden: Nomos, 2003).

Rolin, Albéric. *Les origines de l'institut de droit international, 1873–1923* (unknown location: Vromant, 1923).

Rosanvallon, Pierre. *La démocratie inachevée* (Paris: Gallimard, 2000).

Rosenfeld, Friedrich. *Die humanitäre Besatzung: Ein Dilemma des ius post bellum* (Nomos: Baden-Baden, 2009).

Roth-Isigkeit, David. 'Niccolò Machiavelli's International Legal Thought: Culture, Contingency, and Construction' in *System, Order, and International Law. The Early History of International Legal Thought from Machiavelli to Hegel*, eds. Stefan Kadelbach, Thomas Kleinlein, and David Roth-Isigkeit (Oxford: Oxford University Press, 2017).

Royle, Edward and Lockyer, Roger. *Chartism* (London: Routledge, 2014).

Saint-Pierre, Charles Irénée Castel de. *Projet pour rendre la paix perpétuelle en Europe. Tome premier* (unknown publisher, 1712).

Schaffner, Tobias. 'Francisco Suárez S.J. on the End of Peaceful Order among States and Systematic Doctrinal Scholarship', in *System, Order, and International Law. The Early History of International Legal Thought from Machiavelli to Hegel*, eds. Stefan Kadelbach, Thomas Kleinlein, and David Roth-Isigkeit (Oxford: Oxford University Press, 2017).

Shaw, Malcolm. *International Law* (Cambridge: Cambridge University Press, 2003).

Shawcross, Edward. *France, Mexico and Informal Empire in Latin America, 1820–1867. Equilibrium in the New World* (Basingstoke: Palgrave Macmillan, 2018).

Schnakenbourg, Éric. *Entre la guerre et la paix. Neutralité et relations internationales, XVIIe–XVIIIe siècles* (Rennes: Presses Universitaires de Rennes, 2013).

Schulz, Matthias. *Normen und Praxis. Das Europäische Konzert der Großmächte als Sicherheitsrat, 1815–186* (München: Oldenbourg, 2009).

Scott, James Brown. *Peace through Justice. Three Papers on International Justice and the Means of Attaining It* (Oxford: Oxford University Press, 1917).

Scott, Richenda. *Quakers in Russia* (London: MW Books, 1964).

Šedivý, Miroslav. *Crisis among the Great Powers. The Concert of Europe and the Eastern Question* (London: Bloomsbury, 2016).

Šedivý, Miroslav. *The Decline of the Congress System. Metternich, Italy and European Diplomacy* (London: Tauris, 2018).

Šedivý, Miroslav. *Si vis Pacem, para Bellum. The Italian Response to International Insecurity, 1830–1848* (Vienna: Austrian Academy of Sciences, 2021).

Šedivý, Miroslav. *The Victory of Realism. The German Quest for International Security 1839–1853* (Paderborn: Brill Schöningh, 2024).

Schrijver, Nico. 'The Ban on the Use of Force in the U.N. Charter', in *The Oxford Handbook of the Use of Force in International Law*, ed. Marc Weller (Oxford: Oxford University Press, 2015).

Sinha, Manisha. *The counterrevolution of Slavery. Politics and Ideology in Antebellum South Carolina* (Chapel Hill: University of North Carolina Press, 2000).

Simon, Hendrik. 'Anarchy over Law? Towards a Genealogy of Modern War Justifications (1789–1918)', in *The Justification of War and International Order, eds.* Hendrik Simon & Lothar Brock (Cambridge: Cambridge University Press, 2021).

Steiner, Bernard. *Life of Henry Barnard. The first United States Commissioner of Education, 1867–1870* (Washington: Government Printing Office, 1919).

Stewart, James Brewer. *Holy Warriors. The Abolitionists and American Slavery* (New York: Hill and Wang, 1976).

Taylor, Alan. *American Colonies. The Settling of North America* (New York: Penguin, 2002).

Taylor, Alan. *The Civil War of 1812. American Citizens, British Subjects, Irish Rebels, & Indian Allies* (New York: Random House, 2010).

ter Meulen, Jacob. *Der Gedanke der Internationalen Organisation in seiner Entwicklung, zwei Banden* (The Hague: Martinus Nijhoff, 1929).

Thompson, F. M. L. 'Cobden, Free Trade in Land and the Road to the Abbey National', in *Rethinking Nineteenth Century Liberalism. Richard Cobden Bicentenary Essays* (London: Routledge, 2017).

Tolis, Peter. *Elihu Burritt. Crusader for Brotherhood* (Hamden: Archon Books, 1968).

Tombs, Robert and Tombs, Isabelle. *That Sweet Enemy: Britain and France. The French and the British from the Sun King to the Present* (London: William Heinemann, 2006).

Tomuschat, Christian. 'The 1871 Peace Treaty and the 1919 Versailles Treaty', in *Peace Treaties and International Law in European History. From the Late Middle Ages to World War One*, ed. Randall Lesaffer (Cambridge: Cambridge University Press, 2004).

Traz, Robert de. *L'esprit de Genève. Préface d'Alfred Dufour* (Lausanne: Éditions l'Age d'Homme, 1995).

Ulbert, Jörg. 'France and German Dualism, 1756–1871', in *A History of Franco-German Relations in Europe. From "Hereditary Enemies" to Partners*, eds. Carine Germond & Henning Türk (Basingstoke: Palgrave Macmillan, 2008).

van der Linden, Wilhelmus H. *The International Peace Movement 1815–1874* (Amsterdam: Tilleul, 1987).

Vandenbosch, Amry. *Dutch Foreign Policy since 1815. A Study in Small Power Politics* (The Hague: Nijhoff, 1959).

Vanderkindere, Léon, *L'Université de Bruxelles, 1834–1884. Notice historique faite à la demande du Conseil d'Administration* (Bruxelles: Weissenbruch, 1884).

Vanlangenhove, Fernand. 'GOBLET D'ALVIELLA (Eugène-Félicien-Albert, comte)', in *Biographie nationale de Belgique*, vol. XLI, Supplément, Tome III (Bruxelles: Bruylant 1979).

Vec, Miloš. 'Sources of International Law in the Nineteenth-Century European Tradition. The Myth of Positivism', in *The Oxford Handbook on the Sources of International Law*, eds. Anne Orford and Florian Hoffman (Oxford: Oxford University Press, 2016).

Vellacot, Jo. '"Transnationalism" in the Early Women's International League for Peace and Freedom', in *The Pacifist Impulse in Historical Perspective*, ed. Harvey L. Dyck (Toronto: Toronto University Press, 1996).

Verdebout, Agatha. *Rewriting Histories of the Use of Force. The Narrative of 'Indifference'* (Cambridge: Cambridge University Press, 2021).

von Suttner, Bertha. *De Wapens Neer!* (Amsterdam: Bibliotheek van het Vredespaleis, 2019).

Vorenberg, Michael. *Final Freedom. The Civil War, the Abolition of Slavery, and the Thirteenth Amendment* (Cambridge: Cambridge University Press, 2001).

Waresquiel, Emmanuel de. *Penser la Restauration, 1814–1830* (Paris: Tallandier, 2020).

Wetter, J. Gillis, *The International Arbitral Process: Public and Private, vol. 1* (Dobs Ferry: Oceana Publications, 1979).

Wilkins, David. *American Indian Sovereignty and the U.S. Supreme Court. The Masking of Justice* (Austin: University of Texas Press, 1997).

Witte, Els. *De constructie van België* (Leuven: Lannoo, 2006).

Whitney, Edson. *The American Peace Society. A Centennial History* (Washington: American Peace Society, 1928).

Woodcock, George. *Anarchism: a History of Libertarian Ideas and Movements* (Toronto: Broadview Encore Editions, 2004).

Ziegler, Valarie. *The Advocates of Peace in Antebellum America* (Indianapolis, Indiana University Press, 1992).

Zollmann, Jakob. 'Interstate Mediation and Arbitration. Concepts, Cases and Actors of Third Party Dispute Resolution (Seventeenth to Nineteenth Century)', in Karl Härter (ed.), *On Mediation. Historical, Legal, Anthropological and International Perspectives* (New York: Berghahn, 2020).

Articles

Abrams, Irwin. 'The Emergence of the International Law Societies'. *The Review of Politics* 19 (3) (1957).

Alford, Roger. 'The Nobel Effect: Nobel Peace Prize Laureates as International Norm Entrepreneurs'. *Virginia Journal of International Law* 49(1) (2008).

Aprile, Sylvie. 'L'accueil des réfugiés en Europe au XIXe siècle. Des lois pour assister ou pour renvoyer'. *Monde(s)* 1 (2019).

Arcidiacono, Bruno. 'La paix par le droit international, dans la vision de deux juristes du XIXe Siècle: Le débat Lorimer-Bluntschli'. *Relations internationales* 149 (2012).

Aspremont, Jean. 'Martti Koskenniemi, the Mainstream, and Self-Reflexivity.' *Leiden Journal of International Law* 29(3) (2016).

Bergami, Carol. 'Européisme et cosmopolitisme. D'une spécificité européenne dans le pacifisme français des années 1840'. *La Contemporaine* 2012/4(108) (2012).

Bergami, Carol. 'Quelle démocratie pour quelle organisation internationale? Le pacifisme français et la naissance d'un constitutionnalisme républicain, 1840–1889'. *Les cahiers Irice* 2(12) (2014).

Bernard-Lubelski, Nicole. 'Les débuts du pacifisme féminin'. *Les Cahiers du GRIF* 14–15 (1976).

Bingham, Tom. 'The Alabama Claims Arbitration'. *International Law and Comparative Law Quarterly* 54(1) (2005).

Blanchard, Pascal and Bancel, Nicolas. 'La fondation du républicanisme colonial. Retour sur une généalogie politique'. *Mouvements* 2(38) (2005).

Bowring, Philip. 'Sir John Bowring: the Imperial Role of a Lifelong Liberal'. *Asian Affairs* 42(3) (2011).

Brauer, Kinley J. 'British Mediation and the American Civil War: a Reconsideration'. *The Journal of Southern History* 38(1) (1972).

Brent, Richard. 'The Alabama Claims Tribunal: the British Perspective'. *The International History Review* 44(1) (2021).

Butler, William. 'Congress of Nations: a Nineteenth Century View'. *World Affairs* 128 (2) (1965).

Campanelli, Alessandro. 'Le Règlement du 2 octobre 1820 et la création de la faculté de droit de Genève. *Commentationes Historiae Iuris Helveticae* 17 (2020).

Carroll, Francis. 'Kings and Crises: Arbitrating the Canadian-American Boundary Dispute and the Belgian Crisis of 1830–1831'. *The New England Quarterly* 73 (2) (2000).

Claeys, Gregory. 'Mazzini, Kossuth and British Radicalism, 1848–1854'. *Journal of British Studies* 28(3) (1989).

Clayton, Andrew. 'The Debate over the Panama Congress and the Origins of the Second American Party System'. *The Historian* 47(2) (1985).

Clinton, Michael. 'Frédéric Passy: Patriotic Pacifist'. *Journal of Historical Biography* 2 (autumn 2007) (2007).

Cole, Graham. 'William Paley's Natural Theology: An Anglican Classic?'. *Journal of Anglican Studies* 5(2) (2007).

Conway, Stephen. 'Bentham on Peace and War'. *Utilitas* 1(1) (1989).

Conway, Stephen. 'Bentham, the Benthamites, and the Nineteenth-Century British Peace Movement'. *Utilitas* 2(2) (1990).

Conway, Stephen. 'John Bowring and the Nineteenth-Century Peace Movement'. *Historical Research* 64(155) (1991).

Conway, Stephen. 'The Politicization of the Nineteenth-Century Peace Society'. *Historical Research* 66(3) (1993).

Cooper, Sandi. 'The Work of Women in Nineteenth Century Continental European Peace Movements'. *Peace and Change* 9(4) (1984).

Cooper, Sandi. 'Review of *The International Peace Movement*'. *The American Historical Review* 95(3) (1990).

Cooper, Sandi. 'Pacifism in France, 1889–1914: International Peace as a Human Right'. *French Historical Studies* 17(2) (1991).

Curti, Merle. 'Pacifist Propaganda and the Treaty of Guadalupe Hidalgo'. *The American Historical Review* 33(3) (1928).

Davis, John. 'Palmerston and the Sicilian Sulphur Crisis of 1840: an Episode in the Imperialism of Free Trade'. *Risorgimento* 1(2) (1982).

de Blois, Matthijs. 'Blessed [Are] the Peacemakers... Grotius on the Just War and Christian Pacifism'. *Grotiana* 32 (2011).

De la Reza, Germán. 'The Formative Platform of the Congress of Panama (1810–1826): the Pan-American Conjecture revisited'. *Revista Brasileira de Política Internacional* 56(1) (2013).

De Rycke, Wouter. 'Recensie van *Le laboratoire belge du droit international*'. *Pro Memorie. Bijdragen tot de Rechtsgeschiedenis van de Lage Landen* 22(1) (2020).

De Rycke, Wouter. 'Legislating Utopia. Louis Bara (1821–1857) and the Liberal-Scientific Restatement of International Law in the Nineteenth Century Peace Movement'. *Journal of the History of International Law* 23(4) (2020).

Dealy, Ross. 'The Dynamics of Erasmus' Thought on War'. *Erasmus Studies* 4 (1) (1984).

Debrune, Jérôme. 'Le système de la méditerranée de Michel Chevalier'. *Confluences Méditerranée* 36(1) (2001).

Dhondt, Frederik. 'The Law of Nations and Declarations of War after the Peace of Utrecht'. *History of European Ideas* 42(3) (2016).

Drolet, Michael. 'Industry, Class and Society: A Historiographic Reinterpretation of Michel Chevalier'. *English Historical Review* CXXIII(504) (2008).

Dunbabin, John. 'The 1831 Dutch Arbitration of the Canadian-American Boundary Dispute: another View'. *The New England Quarterly* 75(4) (2002).

Ellenbogen, G. 'English Arbitration Practice'. *Law and Contemporary Problems* 17(4) (1952).

Finnis, John. 'Blackstone's Theoretical Intentions'. *The American Journal of Jurisprudence* 12(1) (1967).

Fitzmaurice, Andrew. 'The Genealogy of *Terra Nullius*'. *Australian Historical Studies* 38(129) (2007).

Franck, Thomas. 'Who killed Article 2(4)? Or: changing Norms governing the Use of Force by States'. *The American Journal of International Law* 64(5) (1970).

Frick, Stephen. 'Henry Richard and the Treaty of Paris of 1856'. *National Library of Wales Journal* XVII (1972).

García-Salmones, Mónica. 'Walther Schücking and the Pacifist Traditions of International Law'. *The European Journal of International Law* 22(3) (2011).

Genequand, Christiane. 'Un philanthrope de choc: J.-J. de Sellon en prison pour injures et coups'. *Revue du vieux Genève* 15 (1985).

Goldman, Lawrence. 'The Social Science Association, 1857–1886: A Context for Mid-Victorian Liberalism'. *The English Historical Review* 101(398) (1986).

Guymer, Laurence. 'The Wedding Planners: Lord Aberdeen, Henry Bulwer, and the Spanish Marriages, 1841–1846'. *Diplomacy and Statecraft* 21(4) (2010).

Hanley, Will. 'International Lawyers without Public International Law: the Case of Late Ottoman Egypt'. *Journal of the History of International Law* 18(1) (2016).

Harris, Steven. 'The Global Construction of International Law in the Nineteenth Century: The Case of Arbitration'. *Journal of World History* 27(2) (2016).

Haskell, John. 'Divine Immanence: the Evangelical Foundations of Modern Anglo-American Approaches to International Law', in *Chinese Journal of International Law* 11(3) (2012).

Hazareesingh, Sudhir. 'An Intellectual Founder of the Third Republic: the Neo-Kantian Republicanism of Jules Barni (1818–78)'. *History of Political Thought* 22(1) (2001).

Hicks, Geoffrey. '"Appeasement" or consistent Conservatism? British Foreign Policy, Party Politics, and the Guarantees of 1867 and 1939'. *Historical Research* 84 (225) (2011).

Holton, Sandra. 'John Bright, Radical Politics, and the Ethos of Quakerism'. *Albion: a Quarterly Journal concerned with British Studies* 34(4) (2002).

Hoyle, Mark. 'The Structure and Laws of the Mixed Courts of Egypt'. *Arab Law Quarterly* 1(3) (1986).

Irwin, Douglas and Chepeliev, Maksym. 'The Economic Consequences of Sir Robert Peel: a Quantitative Assessment of the Repeal of the Corn Laws'. *The Economic Journal* 161(640) (2020).

King, Henry and Graham, James. 'Origins of Modern International Law'. *Dispute Resolution Journal* 51(1) (1995).

Koskenniemi, Martti. 'The Politics of International Law'. *European Journal of International Law* 1(1) (1990).

Koskenniemi, Martti. 'Into Positivism: Georg Friedrich von Martens (1756–1821) and Modern International Law'. *Constellations. An International Journal of Critical and Democratic Theory* 15(2) (2008).

Koskenniemi, Martti. 'Miserable Comforters: International Relations as New Natural Law'. *European Journal of International Relations* 15(3) (2009).

Koskenniemi, Martti. 'Histories of International Law: Significance and Problems for a Critical View'. *Temple International and Comparative Law Journal* 27(2) (2013).

Lada, Zsuzsanna. 'The Invention of a Hero: Lajos Kossuth in England (1851)'. *European History Quarterly* 43(1) (2013).

Lambert, Vanessa. 'The Dynamics of Transnational Activism: the International Peace Congresses, 1843–51'. *The International History Review* 38(1) (2016).

Laurin, M.T., 'Un précurseur de la Société des Nations. Francisque Bouvet, représentant de l'Ain en 1848'. *La révolution de 1848 et les révolutions du XIXe siècle* 21 (105) (1924).

Lawson, David and Kuehl, Warren. 'Journals of the American Peace Society'. *World Affairs* 141(2) (1978).

Lesaffer, Randall. 'Aggression before Versailles'. *European Journal of International Law* 29(3) (2018).

Lévy-Guénot. 'Autour de Félix Santallier. Une croisade pacifiste à la veille de 1870'. *La révolution de 1848 et les révolutions du XIXe siècle* 19(93) (1922).

Love, Ronald. 'The Symbiosis of Religion and Politics: Reassessing the Final Conversion of Henri IV'. *Historical Reflections* 21(1) (1995).

Malanson, Jeffrey J. 'The Congressional Debate over U.S. Participation in the Congress of Panama, 1825–1826: Washington's Farewell Address, Monroe's Doctrine, and the Fundamental Principles of U.S. Foreign Policy'. *Diplomatic History* 30 (5) (2006).

Markovits, Stefanie. 'Rushing into Print: "Participatory Journalism" during the Crimean War'. *Victorian Studies* 50(4) (2008).

Maynard, Douglas. 'The World's Anti-Slavery Convention of 1840'. *The Mississippi Valley Historical Review* 47(3) (1960).

Morgan-Owen, David. 'Scares, Panics, and Strategy: the Politics of Security and British Invasion Scares before 1914'. *Diplomacy and Statecraft* 33(3) (2022).

Mura, Eloisa. 'The Construction of the International Law Discipline in Italy between the Mancinian and Positive Schools', in *A History of International Law in Italy*, ed. Giulio Bartolini (Oxford: Oxford University Press, 2020).

Mützenberg, Gabriel. 'David Dunant, oncle et précurseur du fondateur de la Croix-Rouge'. *Revue suisse d'histoire* 30(3) (1980).

Mützenberg, Gabriël. 'Jean-Jacques de Sellon. Une société de la paix en 1830'. *Librarium. Revue de la société suisse des bibliophiles* 35(2) (1992).

Myers, Denys. 'Law and the Peace Society'. *World Affairs* 127(4).

Nehring, Holger. 'Peace Movements and Internationalism'. *Moving the Social* 55 (2016).

Nys, Ernest. 'The Codification of International Law'. *American Journal of International Law* 5(4) (1911).

Ostdiek, Bennett and Witt, John Fabian. 'The Czar and the Slaves: Two Puzzles in the History of International Arbitration'. *The American Journal of International Law* 113(3) (2019).

Paige, Tamsin Philippa. 'Mission Impossible? Reforming the UN Charter to Limit the Veto'. *Journal of International Peacekeeping* 25(2) (2022).

Petch, Simon. 'Law, Equity, and Conscience in Victorian England'. *Victorian Literature and Culture* 25(1) (1997).

Phillips, Andrew. 'Saving Civilization from Empire: Belligerency, Pacifism and the Two Faces of Civilization during the Second Opium War'. *European Journal of International Relations* 18(1) (2011).

Philips, Peter. 'Ancient and Comely Order: The Use and Disuse of Arbitration by New York Quakers'. *Journal of Dispute Resolution* 2016 (1).

Pound, Roscoe. 'Law in Books and Law in Action'. *American Law Review* 44 (1) (1910).

Reimann, Matthias. 'The Historical School against Codification: Savigny, Carter, and the Defeat of the New York Civil Code'. *The American Journal of Comparative Law* 37(1) (1989).

Rens, Ivo and Giesen, Klaus-Gerd. 'Jean-Jacques de Sellon, pacifiste et précurseur de 'l'esprit de Genève'. *Revue suisse d'histoire* 35(3) (1985).

Riot-Sarcey, Michèle. 'Histoire et autobiographie. "Le vrai livre des femmes" d'Eugénie Niboyet'. *Romantisme* 56(1) (1987).

Ruys, Tom. 'From *passé simple* to *futur imparfait?* A Response to Verdebout'. *Journal on the Use of Force and International Law* 2(1) (2015).

Šabič, Zlatko. 'Building Democratic and Responsible Global Governance: The Role of International Parliamentary Institutions'. *Parliamentary Affairs* 61(2) (2008).

Sager, Eric. 'The Social Origins of Victorian Pacifism'. *Victorian Studies* 23(2) (1980).

Šedivý, Miroslav. 'Honour as a Political-Legal Argument: the French July Monarchy, National Dignity, and Europe, 1830–1840'. *The Czech Historical Review* 116 (1) (2018).

Scott, Matthew and Megoran, Nick. 'The Newcastle Upon Tyne Peace Society (1815–50)'. *Northern History* XX(XX) (2017).

Simon, Hendrik. 'The Myth of Liberum Ius ad Bellum: Justifying War in 19th-Century Legal Theory and Political Practice'. *European Journal of International Law* 29(1) (2018).

Schachter, Oscar. 'The Invisible College of International Lawyers'. *Northwesthern University Law Review* 72(2) (1977).

Schazmann, Paul-Émile. 'Le comte Jean-Jacques de Sellon, philanthrope suisse'. *Larousse mensuel* 365 (1937).

Searle, Alfred. 'Friends (Quakers) and Arbitration'. *Arbitration: The International Journal of Arbitration, Mediation, and Dispute Management* 16(3) (1950).

Siemering, Carl Ludwig. *Von der ersten deutschen Friedensgesellschaft zu Königsberg i. Pr., 1850–1851* (Frankfurt: Knauer, 1909).

Subrin, Stephen. 'David Dudley Field and the Field Code: a Historical Analysis of an Earlier Procedural Vision'. *Law and History Review* 6(2) (1988).

Swaisland, Charles. 'The Aborigines Protection Society, 1837–1909'. *Slavery & Abolition: a Journal of Slave and Post-Slave Studies* 21(2) (2000).

Todd, David. 'Beneath Sovereignty: Extraterritoriality and Imperial Internationalism in Nineteenth Century Egypt'. *Law and History Review* 36(1) (2018).

Tyrrell, Alexander. 'Making the Millennium: the Mid-Nineteenth Century Peace Movement'. *The Historical Journal* 21(1) (1978).

Uriburu, Justina. 'Imperialism through Adjudication in Latin America'. *Leiden Journal of International Law* 36(1) (2023).

Van den Dungen, Peter. 'Varieties of Peace Science: An Historical Note'. *Journal of Peace Science* 2(2) (1977).

Van den Dungen, Peter. 'Peace History: an Introduction'. *Journal of Peace Research* 40(4) (2003).

Vagts, Alfred and Vagts, Detlev. 'The Balance of Power in International Law: a History of an Idea'. *The American Journal of International Law* 73(4) (1979).

Verdebout, Agatha. 'The Contemporary Discourse on the Use of Force in the Nineteenth Century: a Diachronic and Critical Analysis'. *Journal on the Use of Force and International Law* 1(2) (2014).

Whitten, Dolphus Jr. 'The Don Pacifico Affair'. *The Historian* 48(2) (1986).

Unpublished Doctoral Theses

D'Haeninck, Thomas. *Sociale hervormers op zoek naar een moreel reveil. Een sociaal-historische en transnationale studie naar de aanwezigheid van Belgen op internationale hervormingscongressen, 1850–1914* (Ghent: unpublished doctoral thesis, 2018).

Lawson, David. *Swords into Plowshares, Spears into Pruninghooks: The Intellectual Foundations of the First American Peace Movement, 1815–1865* (University of New Mexico: unpublished doctoral thesis, 1975).

Lincoln, Vanessa. *Organizing International Society: The French Peace Movement and the Origins of Reformist Internationalism, 1821–1853* (Berkeley: unpublished doctoral thesis, 2013).

Lubelski-Bernard, Nadine. *Les mouvements et les idéologies pacifistes en belgique 1830–1914* (Bruxelles: unpublished doctoral thesis, 1977).

Spahr, Thomas. *Occupying for Peace, the U.S. Army in Mexico, 1846–1848* (Ohio State University: unpublished doctoral thesis, 2011).

Volkmer, Andreas. *Kriegsverhütung und Friedenssicherung durch Internationale Organisation: Deutsche Ideen und Pläne 1815–1871* (Marburg: unpublished doctoral thesis, 2012).

Zarychta, Ronald Michael. *Louis Kossuth and the United States, 1848–1852* (Carnegie Mellon University: unpublished doctoral thesis, 1976).

Website Articles

Alcouffe, Alain and Coulumb, Fanny. 'Pacifism of the French Liberals in the late 19th and early 20th Centuries. Frédéric Passy and Léon Walras, Candidates for the Nobel Peace Prize', in *18th ESHET Conference – Liberalisms: perspectives and debates in the history of economic thought, The European Society for the History of Economic Thought (ESHET), May 2014, Lausanne, Switzerland*, available at: hal.archives-ouvertes.fr/hal-02051636.

Aynes, Richard. 'McLean, John', in American National Biography Online. 2000, available at: doi.org/10.1093/anb/9780198606697.article.1100580.

Baxter, Maurice. 'Webster, Daniel', in American National Biography Online. 2000, available at: doi.org/10.1093/anb/9780198606697.article.0300525.

Bélissa, Marc. 'La déclaration du droit des gens de l'abbé Grégoire (juin 1793, 4 floréal an III)'. 2010, available at: revolution-francaise.net/2010/10/06/399-declaration-droit-des-gens-abbe-gregoire-juin-1793.

Boussonas, Lucien. 'Sellon, Jean-Jacques de', in *Dictionnaire historique de la Suisse*. 2010, available at: hls-dhs-dss.ch/fr/articles/026552/2010-05-03/.

Brogan, Hugh. 'Clarkson, Thomas (1760–1846)', in *Oxford Dictionary of National Biography*. 2004, available at: doi.org/10.1093/ref:odnb/5545.

Finkelman, Paul. 'Story, Joseph', in *American National Biography Online*. 2000, available at: doi.org/10.1093/anb/9780198606697.article.1100821.

Fuchs, Alfred. 'Upham, Thomas Cogswell', in *American National Biography Online*. 2000, available at: doi.org/10.1093/anb/9780198606697.article.1601684.

Genoud, François. 'Conclusum sur la presse et les étrangers', in *Dictionnaire historique de la Suisse*. 2005, available at: hls-dhs-dss.ch/fr/articles/017228/2005-08-10/.

Gern, Philippe. 'France. Les relations politiques', in *Dictionnaire historique de la Suisse*. 2018, available at: hls-dhs-dss.ch/fr/articles/003354/2018-01-22.

Glennon, Michael. 'How not to end War'. 18 October 2017, available at: www.lawfaremedia.org/article/how-not-end-war.

Hargreaves, Mary. 'Adams, John Quincy', in American National Biography Online. 2000, available at: doi.org/10.1093/anb/9780198606697.article.0300002.

Howe, Daniel. 'Channing, William Ellery', in *American National Biography Online*. 2000, available at: https://doi.org/10.1093/anb/9780198606697.article.0800251.

Huzzy, Richard. 'Chamerovzow, Louis Alexis (1816–1875', in *Oxford Dictionary of National Biography*. 2010, available at: doi.org/10.1093/ref:odnb/101107.

Langum, David. 'Greenleaf, Simon', in *American National Biography Online*. 2000, available at: doi.org/10.1093/anb/9780198606697.article.1100354.

Luda, Regula (transl. Pierre-G. Martin). 'Marie Goegg-Pouchoulin', in *Dictionnaire historique de la Suisse*. 2006, available at: hls-dhs-dss.ch/fr/articles/009305/2006-12-28/.

Magee, Karl. 'Hancock, Thomas (1783–1849)', in *Oxford Dictionary of National Biography*. 2004, available at: doi.org/10.1093/ref:odnb/12187.

Mandler, Peter. 'Howitt, William (1792–1879)', in *Oxford Dictionary of National Biography*. 2004, available at: doi.org/10.1093/ref:odnb/13998.

Melenovsky, Chris. 'International Right and Kant's World Federation'. 2018, working paper (uploaded by the author), available at PhilArchive: philarchive.org/archive/MELIRA-2,

Milligan, Edward. 'Gurney, Joseph John (1788–1847)', in *Oxford Dictionary of National Biography*. 2004, available at: doi.org/10.1093/ref:odnb/11771.

Oberg, Michael. 'Wirt, William', in *American National Biography Online*. 2000, available at: doi.org/10.1093/anb/9780198606697.article.0300543.

Osborne, Peter. 'Roberts, Mary (1788–1864)', in *Oxford Dictionary of National Biography*. 2004, available at: doi.org/10.1093/ref:odnb/23767.

Perman, Michael. 'Foote, Henry Stuart, in *American National Biography Online*. 2000, available at: doi.org/10.1093/anb/9780198606697.article.0400386.

Perry, Lewis. 'Wright, Henry Clarke', in *American National Biography Online*. 2000, available at: doi.org/10.1093/anb/9780198606697.article.1500862.

Price, Watkin William. 'Price, Joseph Tregelles (1784–1854)', in *Dictionary of Welsh Biography*. 1959, available at: biography.wales/article/s-PRIC-TRE-1784

Read, Donald. 'John Bright', in *Encyclopaedia Britannica*. 2022, available at: www.britannica.com/biography/John-Bright.

Roper, Donald. 'Kent, James', in *American National Biography Online*. 2000, available at: doi.org/10.1093/anb/9780198606697.article.1100488.

Rubin, G.R.. 'Levi, Leone (1821–1888)', in *Oxford Dictionary of National Biography*. 2004, available at: doi.org/10.1093/ref:odnb/16551.

Skouteris, Thomas. 'The Turn to History in International Law', in *Oxford Bibliographies*. 2017, available at doi.org/10.1093/obo/9780199796953-0154.

Spector, Céline. 'Esprit général'. 2013, working paper (uploaded by the author), available at Dictionnaire Montesquieu: http://dictionnaire-montesquieu.ens-lyon.fr/fr/article/1376474276/fr/.

Sterling, David. 'Caleb, Strong', in *American National Biography Online*. 2000, available at: doi.org/10.1093/anb/9780198606697.article.0300472.

Taylor, Miles. 'Bright, John (1811–1889)', in *Oxford Dictionary of National Biography*. 2004, available at: doi.org/10.1093/ref:odnb/3421.

Waxman, Matthew. 'The Mexican-American War and Constitutional War Powers'. 2020, available at www.lawfaremedia.org/article/mexican-american-war-and-constitutional-war-powers.

Subject Index

Name and Author Index

www.ingramcontent.com/pod-product-compliance
Lightning Source LLC
LaVergne TN
LVHW102229300926
849160LV00006B/75